The Meaning of
the Renaissance and
Reformation

EDITED BY RICHARD L. DeMOLEN

Essays by

Richard L. DeMolen

Lauro R. Martines

Margaret E. Aston

John M. Headley

Arthur J. Slavin

John C. Olin

Richard B. Reed

De Lamar Jensen

The Meaning of
the Renaissance and
Reformation

Houghton Mifflin Company • Boston

Atlanta • Dallas • Geneva, Illinois • Hopewell, New Jersey

Palo Alto • London

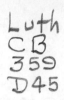
To the Folger, Huntington and Newberry Libraries, whose facilities
and holdings offer the specialist
in Early Modern Europe both inspiration and instruction.

Cover: *View of Paris*, print by Israel Silvestre, 1658. Gabinetto
Nazionale Delle Stampe, Rome.

Printed in the U.S.A.

Library of Congress Catalog Card Number: 73-9186

ISBN: 0-395-12632-0

Contents

Preface

Occasionally the historian attempts to assign unique qualities to a period of history in an effort to define the indefinable, to capture an elusive spirit, or to find unity and continuity where there may be none. Here are eight essays in the history of the Renaissance and Reformation, which were written specially for this volume, and with the exception of the first, they make no claims to synthesis. Although the Age of Renaissance and Reformation is given certain time limits, along with geographical and topical restrictions, the volume as a whole emphasizes the variegated religious, political, economic, intellectual, and cultural history of Western Europe during the fourteenth, fifteenth, and sixteenth centuries. Indeed, the purpose of the essays is to provide the reader with an interpretation and analysis of the spectrum of the age. If in the end the reader recognizes the Renaissance and Reformation as an Age of Intellectual Revolution, as a time when man applied his rational and creative powers to art, literature, science, and technology and applied the concept of human dignity to religion and politics, something of the diffusive and indomitable spirit of that era will have been rekindled.

The introductory essay tries to integrate the subjects of the other essays and to interpret the age in terms of a central theme. The editor argues that the Age of Renaissance and Reformation was an intellectual revolution; that the transition from the Middle Ages to modern times was evolutionary in its development but revolutionary in its effects. In the second essay, Lauro R. Martines perceives the Italian Renaissance as a changing whole but concentrates his focus on urban development and the influence of the city. It was as early as the twelfth century that the cities of Italy acquired a new way of looking at society and politics, and by encouraging individuality and self-expression, they contributed to art, scholarship, and science in succeeding generations. Margaret E. Aston turns to the Northern Renaissance in the third essay and centers her discussion on Erasmus of Rotterdam and his unique influence on northern humanism. Although many men recognized the genius of Erasmus, most of them rejected his philosophy of Christ: they preferred freedom and self-expression to reason and cooperation. The fourth, fifth, and sixth essays examine the nature of reformation in the Renaissance. John M. Headley characterizes the Continental Reformation as a religious movement which perceived a new reality. Immobilized by wealth and immersed in bureaucracy, the medieval church, after 1300, failed to satisfy the needs of a changing society, and in failing to comprehend its responsibilities it invited insurrection. The Reformation which followed constituted a search for authority, and under Martin Luther's direction, protesters of the sixteenth century acknowledged scripture as the supreme authority. Extending this discussion, Arthur J. Slavin sees the English Reformation from two perspectives: as a conscious effort to restore the past and as a revolutionary force in sixteenth-century society. Slavin devotes most of his essay to the development of these two forces in the reign of Henry VIII, and argues that beginning in the 1520s, England became irrevocably Protestant. John C. Olin concludes the section on reform by examining the reformation and renewal within the Catholic Church of the sixteenth century. His approach is positive: it emphasizes Catholic action rather than the Church's inadequacies or its program of anti-Protestant repression. In this way, he explains the survival of Catholicism in an age of violent opposition. The last two essays enlarge Olin's thematic approach. Richard B. Reed believes that the Renaissance provided the political, religious, social, and technological incentives that made the Age of Discovery possible. Expansion was a reflection of growing nationalism and the centralization of government, but its enduring success depended upon the printed word. Without it, the discoveries of the Renaissance would have gone unnoticed. De Lamar Jensen ends the volume with a study of international relations. He traces the development of power politics and diplomacy in the sixteenth and seventeenth centuries, and concludes that the recognition of retaliatory sanctions in the seventeenth century secured acceptance for the concept of a community of autonomous but interdependent states.

These collected essays owe their conception to Houghton Mifflin Company. At their invitation I selected the contributors and arranged the topics of the essays. Throughout the period of preparation, the contributors and the house editors gave generously of their counsel, encouragement, and expertise, all of which are gratefully acknowledged.

R.L.D.

The Meaning of
the Renaissance and
Reformation

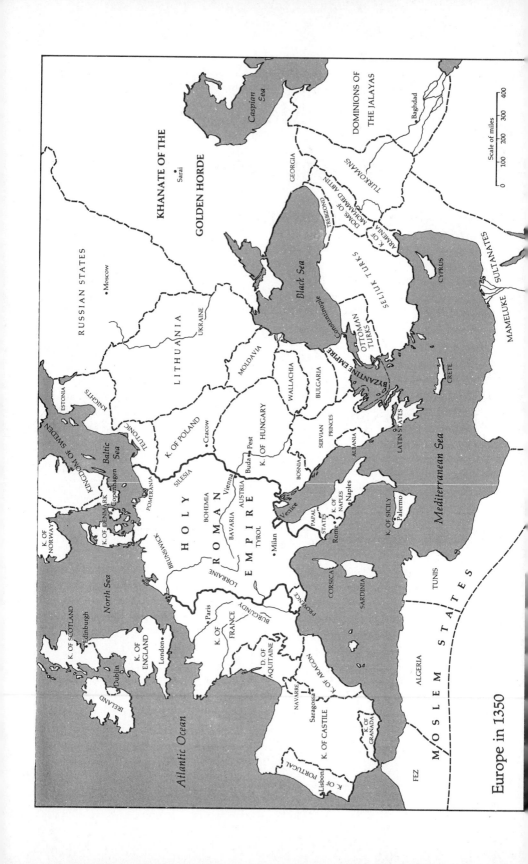

Europe in 1350

RUSSIAN STATES

•Moscow

KHANATE OF THE

GOLDEN HORDE

Sarai•

Caspian Sea

DOMINIONS OF

THE JALAYAS

Baghdad•

Scale of miles

0   100   200   300   400

TURKOMANS

GEORGIA

DOMS OF
MOHAMMED ABTIN

K. OF
ARMENIA

TREBIZOND

MAMELUKE
SULTANATES

CYPRUS

SELJUK TURKS

Black Sea

LITHUANIA

UKRAINE

MOLDAVIA

WALLACHIA

BULGARIA

Constantinople

OTTOMAN
TURKS

BYZANTINE EMPIRE

CRETE

Mediterranean Sea

KINGDOM OF SWEDEN

ESTONIA

KNIGHTS

TEUTONIC

Baltic Sea

POMERANIA

K. OF POLAND

Cracow•

SILESIA

Buda•   •Pest

K. OF HUNGARY

BOSNIA

SERVIAN
PRINCES

ALBANIA

LATIN STATES

K. OF
NORWAY

K. OF DENMARK

Copenhagen•

BRUNSWICK

H O L Y

Vienna

BOHEMIA

AUSTRIA

BAVARIA

TYROL

Venice•

PAPAL
STATES

Rome•

K. OF
NAPLES

Naples•

K. OF SICILY

Palermo•

North Sea

R O M A N

E M P I R E

LORRAINE

•Milan

TUNIS

CORSICA

SARDINIA

K. OF SCOTLAND

Edinburgh•

Dublin•

K. OF
ENGLAND

London•

•Paris

K. OF
FRANCE

BURGUNDY

PROVENCE

Atlantic Ocean

IRELAND

D. OF
AQUITAINE

NAVARRE

K. OF ARAGON

Saragossa•

K. OF CASTILE

K. OF
GRANADA

K. OF
PORTUGAL

Lisbon•

ALGERIA

FEZ

M O S L E M   S T A T E S

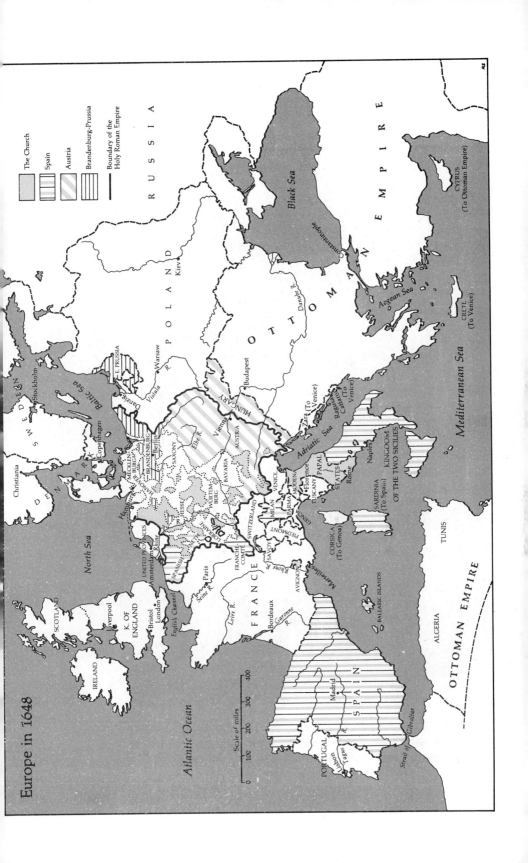

Europe in 1648

An engraved title page designed by Peter Paul Rubens—Downfall of the Ancient
World and Recovery of Its Antiquities. *The page appears in Hubert Goltz,*
Romanae et Graecae Antiquitatis Monumenta *(Antwerp, 1645). Courtesy of the
Folger Shakespeare Library, Washington, D.C.*

I.

The Age of Renaissance
and Reformation

RICHARD L. DE MOLEN

*In the wide ocean upon which we venture, the possible ways and directions are
many; and the same studies which have served for this work might easily, in other
hands, not only receive a wholly different treatment and application, but lead also
to essentially different conclusions.*

JACOB BURCKHARDT, The Civilization of the Renaissance in Italy (1860).

THE AGE OF RENAISSANCE and Reformation (circa 1300–1650)
may be characterized as an intellectual revolution of immeasurable internal and external dimensions—a movement which was evolutionary in
its origins but revolutionary in its effects. The revolution was so shattering
that it transformed the neatly labeled microcosm that was medieval Europe
into the dynamic and divergent macrocosm of the Renaissance. By invoking
the phrase intellectual revolution, we mean to characterize a period in which
man's mind was freed from a metaphysical position of dependency on God to
a transcendental vision—that it was stretched, enriched, and deepened. Moreover, we mean that man realized in this period that his perception of the world
was no longer valid and had to change, and that with his changing perception
the world changed. Where once man had been positioned securely at the
center of the universe, in a hierarchical order, there were now limitless
horizons. Man was confronted by no known boundaries, no permanent
definitions, no certain knowledge. Man was at a loss for where he was and
had to make a new place for himself.

Economics, politics, geography, the natural sciences, the fine arts, all de-

1

veloped specific responses to man's growing quest for individual expression in this world. We may take as examples: the development of France and England into national monarchies; the tenuously balanced politics of Italy's "Big Five" powers; the advent of typography and engraving; the geographical discoveries which doubled the known surface of the earth; new geometrical techniques of art and empirical methods of science; the sun's replacement of the earth as the center of the universe; the telescope's revealing of bigger and better heavens and the microscope's discovery of worlds within a world.

The Renaissance Seen as Initially an Economic Phenomenon

The obvious question to be asked is what triggered the revolution and why? There are many possible answers, but the long-range cause was economic. The High Middle Ages (1000–1300) had ushered in an age of economic revival and prosperity. The appearance of a fluid money economy enabled the Italian city-states to use their wealth to bolster their authority against feudal lords. Feudalism's complex network of personal relations between suzerain and vassals, its agricultural economy and limited need or use for money, its lack of city life and commercial exchange—all tended to decentralize government and to limit central authority.

In contrast to the self-sufficiency of feudalism, the eleventh and twelfth centuries saw the steady growth of interregional trade, the revival of old cities and the establishment of new ones, the appearance in urban centers of merchants and craftsmen who provided and exchanged goods with the rural countryside. All these developments stimulated the circulation of money and the introduction of wages as a method of payment in place of feudal services. Gradually, the new money economy permanently weakened the feudal system and strengthened urban oligarchies, as merchants played pope against emperor, and emperor against lord, in order to expand the scope of their government.

The revival of trade in these centuries also transformed the nations of Western Europe. The French and English monarchs learned to tax their subjects and to use that source of income to secure their authority. The effort to regain central authority enlarged the monarch's role in the administration of justice, in organizing new military units, and in regulating trade. Increased governmental responsibilities and a reorganized military system, which provided well-equipped and disciplined forces with regular pay and new, expensive weaponry, not only decreased the status and power of the feudal nobility but required additional royal revenues for their maintenance. The need for taxes prompted kings to tax their subjects directly, thus reducing their dependency on vassals, and to introduce royal agents into every fief. At the same time, the citizens of the realm demanded a share in government that forced their kings to establish such representative bodies as the English Parliament and the French Estates General. Winning control over taxes was the most important factor in establishing a centralized government in France and England, but it also legitimized representative demands.

Although French kings continued to levy taxes directly, the Estates General became inoperative by the fifteenth century because of divisions of interest among the French nobles, clergy, and bourgeoisie. The English Parliament, however, contributed to an effective central government; and because it represented the affluent, it could never be wholly ignored by the king. As the royal state expanded its functions and laws, local town autonomy was necessarily encroached upon until eventually the monarchy regulated all commerce and industry and developed an economic policy of mercantilism. The state's assumption of legal and economic control, in which taxation played so large a part, marked a victory over local authorities and the beginning of the modern nation-state.

In Italy, on the other hand, a national state was impossible because of the conflict between the emperor and the pope. The ensuing paralysis subsided when the three territorial states of Florence, Venice, and Milan were able for more than forty years to maintain what Wallace Ferguson believes to be "the first consciously-calculated balance of power politics in the history of modern Europe," this they were able to do largely on the basis of the economic monopoly which they enjoyed. Italy's commercial wealth grew out of the exchange of goods between the eastern Mediterranean and western Europe. During the tenth and eleventh centuries, this trade gave rise to rich, populous cities which determined the political life of central and northern Italy. Prosperity brought an early decline to Italy's weak feudal structure, and, at the start of the fourteenth century, the cities, by playing the papacy against the empire, broke the imperial power and became self-governing, republican communes. While the republican form of government was short-lived, Florence, Venice, and Milan emerged as the triumphant rulers of Italy and maintained a prosperous economy. A glance at the magnitude of Venice's control of seaport commerce and at Florence's rich opportunities afforded by its commerce, banking, and large export industries confirms Ferguson's economic theory of the evolution of government. It seems evident that the money economy provided by the initiation and dynamic growth of Italian trade and finance was the primary source of strength in the development and balance of Italy's territorial powers.

Italy became the heart of the medieval commercial revolution which flourished and penetrated the rest of Europe. Parallel with the economic growth was a revival of science and law, the dawning of a new era of literature and art, a tentative growth of religious and political individualism, and the spread of education and social consciousness. This upward mobility, however, was marred by natural and man-made disasters. In the mid-fourteenth century, plague, famine, war, birth control, and other factors led to a population decrease which was especially reflected in the cities. Demographic statistics of Florence reveal a decline from about 100,000 to 70,000 from the time of Dante to Boccaccio. Other areas of Europe also experienced decline: for instance, England's population of approximately 3,700,000 in 1350 fell to about 2,100,000 in the early fifteenth century. Similar statistics could be cited for most European cities and states.

Significantly, the population of Europe in the mid-fourteenth century stagnated at a level below that of the High Middle Ages. The result was a shrinking market which, in turn, contributed largely to an economic recession. The organization of international trade was obstructed by the collapse of the Mongolian Empire in the Far and Middle East by Turkish conquest in the Near East. Incipient nationalism within European states also raised economic barriers which served to reinforce the economic depression.

Although the Middle Ages saw moderate inflation and the growth of credit money, the various wars of the Renaissance, such as western Europe's Hundred Years' War, the Angevin-Aragonese contest between southern Italy and Sicily, Turkish battles with southeastern and east-central Europe, Germany's local conflicts, and the war between the Habsburgs and France, led to a steepening inflation which could not support the burden of war. War, moreover, introduced disease and famine.

Since inflation could not pay the price of warfare, new taxes were developed, outstripping those levied earlier during the peak of the commercial revolution. Consequently, France and England saw the end of town autonomy, while Italy's independent towns acquiesced to despotism. During this same period, peasants and artisans from England to the Balkans, and from Tuscany to Flanders, rose in scattered revolts. Similar uprisings occurred in Hungary, Germany, northeastern Italy, Switzerland, and northern France in the early sixteenth century.

There were other ominous signs of stagnation during the Renaissance. Land prices and landlords' profits were at their lowest ebb; land reclamation and colonization were arrested; the demand for wool diminished as evidenced by the weavers' strike in Florence in 1378; Italy's 5 to 8 per cent interest rate was lower than the previous rate of the High Middle Ages; and, in 1458, the banking capital of the Medicis was only 30,000 florins as compared with the Peruzzi capital of 100,000 florins in the early fourteenth century. Significantly, while the High Middle Ages had absorbed a growing quantity of foodstuffs, raw industrial materials, and available manpower from all levels of society, opportunities in the Renaissance were limited to the townspeople. And even then, town and artists' guilds were becoming rigid, exclusive hierarchies. The gap between rich and poor, exploiters and exploited, is reflected by the purchases and investments of the rich in the armament and luxury industries. Technological progress continued, but there were few new inventions except for the printing press and advances in metallurgy. Insurance was the new business of the age, but it was little more than glorified gambling. Similarly, though the humanist school offered a superior education for the elite, the Renaissance failed to bring meaningful changes in technical education or literacy to the masses. It fostered the worst forms of disparity. Within an initial context of disruptive financial and social conditions, the Renaissance saw an eventual stabilizing of the economy, wherein Italy preserved her commercial position and helped promote solvency in other countries.

The Italian Renaissance

In short, the Italian Renaissance was no phenomenon conceived miraculously in the late fourteenth and early fifteenth centuries. The High Middle Ages had bequeathed a dynamic Florentine capitalism; a growing European population which fostered crafts and industries; a pragmatic Venice already exploiting her link between the North and East by trading slaves with Alexandria and salt with the Lombard plain and by purchasing luxuries with the coins of exchange; spreading monasteries and churches which represented great wealth and greater expenses; new-born cities created by prosperity and steeped in Roman ideas of law, order, and government; a reverence for ancient traditions and learning as suggested by the return to classical studies; a conflict between the aristocracy and rising merchant class; an image of the ideal man in politics and culture; ideas in art, science, technology, and philosophy which had traveled through trade routes from Byzantium, Islam, France, Burgundy, and Flemish towns; and a see-saw struggle between popes and emperors for land, money, and power which left Italy without a state system of national law or secular jurisdiction.

In spite of the disparities and differences that prevailed in Italy, the social and economic organization of the Italian cities supported the cultural and artistic phenomenon of the Renaissance. It is also evident that political violence, diplomatic intrigue, class jealousies, land-hungry city-states, endless wars, and a lack of national law necessitated and encouraged the emergence of Florence, Rome, Milan, and Venice as political powers. Nevertheless the unique characteristics of the Renaissance directly evolved from the ideas which shaped the thinking of the age. The Italian Renaissance was preeminently an expression of ideas and a search for the ideal.

The Florentine Renaissance received its initial impetus from the quest into the Graeco-Roman past for a political ideal. Once Florence had identified with antiquity, it encouraged classical education which dictated the requisites for *l'uomo universale* or complete man. Since Florence represented the vanguard of humanism and Venice was the most affluent and enduring outpost of the Italian Renaissance, this essay will deal primarily with these two city-states in characterizing both the creative and the chaotic conditions of that era.

The Renaissance in Florence

In the course of the Renaissance, all Italy echoed with the fury of war. Florence, economically and strategically vulnerable to Milan, to the Papal Patrimony, to Siena and to Pisa, was able to survive the political holocaust through resourcefulness, diplomacy, war and, most of all, money provided by merchant and craft guilds. Power alternated for generations between the oligarchs and the bourgeoisie who fought to gain control of the Signory, the government body which ruled the city, made war or peace, and collected taxes. Florence's intellectual leaders, Salutati, Bruni, and Poggio, were concerned with this troublesome dilemma and turned to the historical precepts of the past for a solution to their problems and some insight into the destiny of man. Having discovered Cicero's ancient philosophy, they wove its threads into a political pattern of their own. By 1343, after failing to dominate Tuscany, Florence initiated a diplomatic policy whereby it allied itself with neighboring city-states rather than subsume them. This was the first outward expression of the Ciceronian idea that "men must dedicate their lives to civic virtues in order to lead the good life, and it lies at the heart of humanism." The attempt at alliance tended to convince Florence that it was the real heir of republican Rome. Furthermore, the leaders of government who believed they had found their solution to Florence's political problems in the past did not hesitate to share this idea with the artists whom they patronized, such as Ghiberti, Donatello, and Brunelleschi.

When in 1402 Florence narrowly missed being overwhelmed by Milan's Gian Galeazzo Visconti, it believed that deliverance from Milan was due to its civic virtues and republican constitution. The fact that during the heat of the conflict Florence appointed Chrysoloras, the city's first and most influential teacher of Greek, as a public lecturer, underscores the city's belief in the worth of classical learning as the molder of a citizen's character, and this conviction became deeply entrenched in the Florentine tradition. Thus faith in its classic, Roman values sharpened Florence's identity with the past and largely accounts for the accelerated interest in philosophy, history, art, and classical education. Its classical education, as defined by Vittorino da Feltre, posed a double-edged image of the complete man. Man was a fusion of intellect and body with obligations to self and society. His education was more than the mastery of the classics; it also included gentlemanly breeding. Such training necessitated a cultivation of modesty, the desire for beautiful things and a repugnance for all that were not. Gentility became a principal goal of Renaissance man and through the mastery of the *studia humanitatis* (grammar, rhetoric, moral philosophy, poetry, and history) he could achieve recognition as a gentleman. Florence's escape from Milan's control was significant in that it infused the city with a sense of triumphant liberation and acted as a positive impetus, encouraging receptivity to and enthusiasm for both the classical and the new.

In 1417, the death of the ruling oligarch, Maso degli Albizzi, once more unleashed the hatred between the old ruling class and the guilds. After cunningly exploiting class jealousies, Giovanni de Medici and his son, Cosimo, established themselves behind the façade of a republican constitution. During the half century of Medicean rule, Florence dominated the intellectual and artistic life of Italy. The Medici, responding to an oligarchic tradition, returned a tithe of its usurer's profits to the city in the spirit of civic consciousness. This belief in civic consciousness and in identification with the past was maintained and exemplified by the architecture, sculpture, and paintings commissioned by the Medici. As Athenian statues taught citizens the lessons of public life, so did Donatello and Michelangelo's David teach Florence that she was a "giant-killer". Brunelleschi, recreating the ancient and austere architectural harmonies, provided a proper atmosphere for the display of public virtuousness. Paintings of Fra Angelico, Filippo Lippi, and Benozzo Gozzoli reveal a sense of the "power of human destiny and weight of human character." Lorenzo de Medici encouraged philosophers, such as Pico della Mirandola, and promoted Ficino's Florentine Academy for the purpose of intensifying the humanist view toward life which Florence thought she alone held.

Florentine Thought

Italian humanism soon provided a model of literary elegance and historical criticism which contained within it the idea that classical antiquity offered an ideal of perfection and that it was the destiny of humanists to accomplish a renaissance of the learning, arts, and sciences of antiquity. Furthermore, in providing classical source materials, humanism revived numerous ancient ideas and philosophies, reinterpreted or combined with other doctrines. And although humanism did not express a philosophical system as such, it contributed enormously to a belief in the importance of man. The label "studia humanitatis" implied that these studies contributed to the education and cultural refinement of a desirable human being and hence were of utmost concern for man qua man. Among the notable humanists who specifically set forth this attitude toward man that emphasized individualism and the importance of personal experience and feelings were Petrarch, with his highly personal work the *Secretum,* and Giannozzo Manetti, with his mid-fifteenth century treatise on man's dignity and excellence. As Paul O. Kristeller has noted, Machiavelli, a later humanist, expressed most clearly the connection between the concern for man and the admiration of antiquity when he wrote that "since man's nature is always the same, study of the ancients was most valuable because they offered human models of excellence."

After humanism the greatest intellectual current of the Italian Renaissance was Platonism. Albeit humanism enjoyed a broader range of influence and Aristotelianism possessed stronger institutional and professional support, nonetheless, Platonism's philosophical origin had a significant and deep impact upon Renaissance literature. Indeed, in Kristeller's words, Platonism's influence may be traced to "the personal appeal of its ideas to the experiences and inclinations of individual thinkers and writers." One concept that especially appealed to poets and literary critics was the doctrine of divine madness as expressed in Plato's *Ion* and *Phaedrus*. Another aesthetic notion then current was the analogy drawn by Cicero, Seneca, Plotinus and other Neo-Platonic authors between the conceptions of the artist and the ideas in the mind of the divine creator—a concept which was adopted by Albrecht Dürer and others. Moreover, it has been partly established that the iconography of Botticelli, Raphael and Michelangelo express philosophical ideas of Platonic origin. The culmination of Platonism in the Italian Renaissance, however, resides in the work of Marsilio Ficino, leader of the Florentine Academy, and his pupil Pico della Mirandola. By keeping it in mind that both Ficino and Pico were imbued with the education and stylistic and classical standards of the humanist, one could easily conclude that Florentine Platonism was in many respects an off-shoot of the humanistic movement. But Ficino's attempt to translate and explicate Platonic and Neo-Platonic works and to revive Platonistic teaching was merely a reflection of the overall trend in Renaissance Italy to restore the arts, ideas, and institutions of classical Greece.

In recognizing the humanistic contributions to Platonism, it must also be remembered that both Ficino and Pico studied scholastic philosophy so that they could advance beyond the vague aspirations of earlier humanists to a systematic philosophy. The *Platonic Theology* of Ficino, for example, emphasizes man's superiority over other creatures in the variety of his arts and skills, and accords man's soul a central position in the universal hierarchy, thus making the soul the "center of nature, the middle term of all things." Pico's famous *Oration* takes up the same theme of man's central importance but detaches him from his fixed, central place in the universal hierarchy and stresses man as a world unto himself, free to choose his way of life.

In assessing the relative importance of scholastic training in the development of Ficino's and Pico's metaphysical systems, it must be noted that Aristotelianism was a third major intellectual current in the stream of Renaissance thought. Because of their systematic and encyclopaedic character, Aristotle's writings, which encompassed logic, rhetoric, poetics, ethics and metaphysics, as well as physics, natural history, Arabic medicine, and mathematics, enjoyed particular dominance in philosophical thought. By the middle of the thirteenth century, his treatises had become the basis of philosophical instruction at the universities and provided a frame of reference for all trained philosophical thinkers. Thus Aristotelianism in the late Middle Ages, and down through the Renaissance, bequeathed to all professional philosophers a common source of material, a common terminology, a common set of definitions and problems, and a common method of discussing those problems.

It is also obvious that the humanism of Florence, which reflected ancient Rome's governmental structure, brought stability to the city-state. Furthermore, the city's efforts to develop a civically conscious and responsible citizenry, coupled with the genius of its artists, bequeathed to the modern world an artistic brilliance yet to be equalled. Before the end of the 1400s, however, humanistic learning had become the cult of the privileged, and the growing esotericism of art, literature, and philosophy narrowed its social appeal. Self-indulgent leaders lost their social identity with the city, having shown little concern for its future and having dangerously withdrawn from the active world of trade and defense. Thus, with the contraction of trade, failure of the London branch of the Medici bank, expensive wars, plagues, revolting *piagnoni* (followers of Savonarola), and oligarchic intransigence, Florence could no longer appeal to the bourgeois tradition of civic virtue since it had been exchanged for the aristocratic accomplishments of Vittorino's genteel pupils.

The Renaissance in Venice

This was the Florentine Renaissance that Venice inherited. By 1400 Venice was unrivalled in trade and had a stable and powerful government under the firm control of the patricians. Unlike Florence, Venice during the High Middle Ages had followed a policy of isolation and exclusion from the rest of Italy. That is, rather than seeking safety in alliance with other city-states, it survived by maintaining an aristocratic state ruled and regimented by its Senate and Council of Ten, commercially exploiting its favorable geographic location and avoiding Italian affairs.

Despite fear of involvement in matters concerning other city-states, Venice's concern for its northern European trade market and awareness of the necessity of its acquiring more territory in order to be heard in the councils of Italy induced a change in political strategy. Once involved in the vortex of politics and war, Venice was forced to push westward and southward against Milan and Rome. Ultimately, Venetian territory stretched from Lake Como in the west to Trieste in the east; from the high Alpine valleys in the north to Ferrara in the south. Of the numerous economic plums thus gathered, the most enticing attraction was the land.

Guidecca and Murano, Venice's spacious suburbia, were soon encroached upon by the tenements and warehouses of an expanding glass works company.

Hence the valley of the Brenta and the hills of Cadore drew Venetian aristocrats to the life of the countryside. In contrast to an earlier Venice, patrician living became an indulgent, Arcadian existence, the delights of which sapped the strength of the merchants and diverted them from their business pursuits. Villas built by Palladio dotted the landscape: their interiors were painted by Veronese and Tiepolo, and Titian and Tintoretto painted portraits of their owners.

That this atmosphere of leisured self-indulgence permeated urban Venice can be seen by the failure of its galleys to probe the New World or to seek African gold. Nevertheless, Venice was still quick to adopt and exploit at great profits such technical improvements as the Flemish discovery of oil painting or Germany's printing press. By 1530 there were over 200 printing presses in Venice and some of them were pouring out Castiglione's *Book of the Courtier,* that marvelous handbook of gentility which could teach even. crude, boorish, and inordinately rich men all the finer points of aristocratic elegance and etiquette. A wealthy Venice grew wealthier as the nouveau riche of Europe frantically pursued the ideal of true noblesse. Castiglione's requirements for gentlemanly training demanded that a man have a classical education, be graceful in deportment, proper in his style of dress, and a connoisseur of music, painting, and the literary arts. And no price was too high for entry into society's "ingroup". Even the Signory, determined to impress its power upon the populace, commissioned hundreds of artists, such as Bellini, Giorgione, Carpaccio, Veronese, Tintoretto, and Titian, to immortalize their glorious and heroic deeds in frescoes for the Doge's palace and the Piazza San Marco. Merchant guilds and patricians followed suit and adorned churches, hospitals, schools, and monasteries.

Beneath the overweening magnificence, Venice experienced the slow depletion of that special aggressive vitality which made her the dominant maritime power of Europe. Indeed, its plush exterior and jaded aristocracy, having a complete humanist education, served as a model for an otherwise unsophisticated Western society, and still haunts the world today.

Why Did the Renaissance Happen?

In view of the preceding evidence, the important questions remain: Why the Renaissance? Why did it happen? The answer, for Robert Lopez, lies in tracing the "indirect repercussion of economic facts on the development of ideas." He hypothesizes an inverse relationship between economic conditions and the development of culture: The economic depression indirectly resulted in a cultural expansion. Or, in other words, as the men of the Renaissance experienced and witnessed the adverse effects of financial failure, there was a corresponding development of a cultural ideal. Furthermore, Lopez contends that the cast of the Renaissance was largely shaped by those economic and social changes of the High Middle Ages which crumbled feudalism, weakened the religious structure, and created a new wealthy elite.

Keeping in mind the economic pattern of recession and stabilization in the Renaissance, Lopez points to a contemporary, dualistic attitude of both extreme pessimism and extreme optimism which could be seen as a reflection of the financial conditions. Despite appearances, the pessimist and the optimist were essentially similar in that they both despaired of the cycle of history, sought escape from reality in literary, philosophical, or mathematical diversions, and looked to an ideal of perfection in the past. The major difference was that the optimist took classical antiquity as his ideal, and, feeling a close affinity to it, related to and expanded its characteristics in his own life. The result was an impatience with self-discovery and fulfillment. And in the fulfillment process, the optimist might be individually aggressive or politically ruthless.

As has been pointed out, Renaissance man lacked the idea of social progress which, according to Lopez, was "germane to economic expansion." Nor had the idea of religious progress survived the end of the commercial revolution and the failures of the social revolts in the fourteenth century. Furthermore, the existence of a fundamentally inflexible aristocracy and the lack of a recognized hierarchy of states and nations allowed little social mobility and provided no leadership.

In the absence of an aristocracy of "blood and money," which had first been undermined by the medieval commercial revolution and secondly by the ensuing regression, humanist culture became increasingly significant and came to serve as a symbol of nobility, power, prestige, and wealth. Indeed, Lopez contends that this new culture-symbol was already being cultivated by the thirteenth-century noblemen and merchants who wrote lyric poems on love and courtship, and that, in fact, their emphasis on the ideal of a "gentle heart", which was "unconnected with birth or riches and attainable by cultivating one's soul," anticipated the Renaissance notion that "humanistic culture is true noblesse."

To demonstrate his hypothesis that culture is inversely related to economics, Lopez singles out Italy, where businessmen were also statesmen. During the medieval period, investment in culture was basically a nonbusiness proposition. Good management obviously did not mobilize too many resources in something which had a limited function. Thus Genoa, extremely businesslike with well-educated inhabitants, had only a small cathedral and no universities, while northern France, though economically depressed, had the largest cathedrals, and Paris had the largest faculty of theology. Practical investments seemed to prohibit investment in culture for culture's sake. In the Renaissance, however, as the value of land dropped and interest rates declined, statesmen and businessmen, through patronage, vied with one another for power and prestige, thus turning culture into an economic venture. Hence, Lopez views the depression and stagnation of the Renaissance as playing a decisive and necessary role in the evolution of the "state as a business to the state as a work of art." Furthermore, he suggests that the close of the Renaissance may have been brought about by one cultural investment too many, namely, the building of St. Peter's for which Pope Leo X proclaimed a special jubilee indulgence, thereby igniting the Reformation.

That the Renaissance optimist looked to the classical past, and, taking it as his ideal, related it to his own time and life, suggests that not only were classical ideas reinfused into the culture but that classical form and structure were adopted, expanded upon, and introduced into the contemporary European world. Drawing upon classical traditions, Italy's literati invested plays, epics, pastoral ecologues and prose with specific classical structure. Beyond that, two new literary forms were introduced: the pastoral romance and the romantic epic.These forms may be found in Boccaccio's *Ameto* and Sannazaro's *Arcadia* and traced to Montemayor's Spanish *Diana* and Sir Philip Sidney's English *Arcadia*. Petrarchan sonnets also served as a vehicle for the spread of Neo-Platonism throughout Europe; Italian comedies provided form and structure for Shakespeare's and Lope de Vega's romantic comedies, which best expressed the new concept of love in the Renaissance; and Ariosto's and Petrarch's national epics influenced Spenser's *The Faerie Queen,* generally thought to be "the most complete fusion of Renaissance literature outside of Italy." Thus the creative spirit of Italy generated that same spirit throughout Europe.

Renaissance Religious Ideas

Despite the influx of classical ideas into Renaissance thought, the assumption that totally new religious concepts emerged would be misleading. Renaissance thinkers found in the life of the ancient Greeks a fundamental belief in the ability of man's natural reason to propose sound solutions. They also found that in classical Greece the terms *demiourgous* and *poetes,* usually applied to God alone, were applied to man. Affirming faith in natural reason and ascribing a creative principle to man seem to be the governing factors behind the conscious strivings of man toward complete self-realization and self-determination. The Renaissance gave creativity back to man, and, hence, lessened his concern for immortality through Christ and increased his concern for immortality through economic, literary, artistic, and political pre-eminence.

One noteworthy religious difference, however, between the Middle Ages and the Renaissance was the belief in immanentism, and this created a strikingly new image of God. In contrast to the transcendence of the Jewish God, immanentism brought God and Christ back into the world, thus permeating all reality. All of nature was seen as vitalistic, vibrant, and infused with the energy of God. This attitude indirectly encouraged the rise of such new sciences as botany, biology, zoology, and paleontology, because bringing God down into nature made it easier for man to find God without the necessity of revelation. Immanentism aroused man's interest in nature, which, in turn, led to the founding of new sciences.

The spiritualizing of everything external also formed the basis for a blending of all religions and a tolerance of all cults. That it was a major concern of the Renaissance to eliminate religious differences and to establish religious unity is apparent from the efforts of Ficino's Florentine Academy to achieve syncretism, of Erasmus' reduction of Christianity to simplest affirmation, and of the attempt of syncretists to divest Christianity of its historical core, thus negating its essential and unique character. Indeed, the Renaissance reveals a great effort to blend separated disciplines, to break down artificial barriers between compartmentalized science and art, art and the crafts, mathematics and engineering; or, in other words, between theory and practice, speculation and experiment, systematic bases and practical procedures.

Renaissance Motifs as Syntheses of a Classical Heritage and New Ideas

Erwin Panofsky has suggested that the backward looking posture of Renaissance man may have given a perspective to the classical world which allowed a total, integrated, interacting vision. Perhaps it was the whole and unified panorama of the past which then sparked the conscious effort of the Renaissance toward reintegration and interdisciplinary communication. Once begun, this integration opened up new and undreamt of worlds in which geometry became perspective, perspective created new art, art turned to science, and mathematics offered the only certain and evident knowledge.

The city-states of Italy were uniquely suited for the rebirth of interest in the ways of classical Greece and Rome. As the home of the largest empire the Western world had seen, ancient Rome had acquired a classical, cosmopolitan stamp, which persisted throughout Italy down through the centuries. Though the ancient temples might be torn down and used for building barns, the beauty which they had once possessed somehow was lodged in the memory of even the simplest peasant. Urbanization accomplished by the Romans was something Italy never lost; and trade with foreign and domestic neighbors continued, although wars and civil disorders seemed to decimate Italy. With the invention of movable type, the treasures of classical thought became widely known, thus greatly enhancing the influence of the classical notion that man was "the measure of all things," and this in turn seized the Italian mind and kindled a longing for knowledge.

A strong force was necessary to unite the divergent aspects of the Italian cities into a cogent rather than destructive whole. Because of the furious struggle between the papacy and the Holy Roman Emperor, however, the cities found themselves torn between two factions. Unable to find peace by allying themselves with either power, the members of the craft guilds set up their own government. But since they rarely agreed with one another, much less with rival factions, they were forced to ally with the family that had the most supporters and resources. The consequence was usually rule by one man or a small group of men. The prototype of the city-state ruler is described by Machiavelli in *The Prince*. To rule, one not only needed a stomach for the brutality requisite for eliminating one's opponents, but a strong business sense. Part of being a successful ruler consisted in knowing whom to be partners with, and when, as well as knowing how to dissolve a partnership. These early beginnings of diplomacy already evinced a great deal of sophistication. Complicated intelligence networks were accepted practice. Brutal though they may have been, most tyrants were usually endowed with a certain sense of esthetic delight. Patronage of the arts and display of finely wrought articles enhanced their image of power and provided a great contrast to the bloody political history of the age.

Prized though the objects of art were, the creators of exceptional pieces were prized even more. The Middle Ages had been the time of the anonymous artist who labored on the great Gothic cathedrals for the greater glory of God. In the Renaissance, artists created not only for their own glory, but also in rivalry with other artists who worked in the same medium. More specifically, there was a great deal of competition among individual artists as to who could more realistically depict the world. Still another unique aspect of Renaissance art was the willingness of the artists to "work out of any bag". Leonardo da Vinci, for example, designed costumes for an elaborate wedding while casting a bronze horse. But perhaps the most intriguing aspect of all Renaissance art is the brooding, mystical quality of eternal wisdom that seems to permeate it. There is a perceptible sense of man's dignity in objets d'art.

The Complementary Concepts of Humanism and the Devotio Moderna

Transalpine Europe's union of two apparently immiscible currents, humanism and the *Devotio Moderna,* began the development of Christian humanism, an intellectual movement which became the salient characteristic of the Northern Renaissance. Typified by Erasmus of Rotterdam, Christian humanists were literate, scholarly optimists who foresaw human perfection as man's ultimate earthly reward for following their simple set of recommendations. Beneath the aura of humanist optimism, however, lay pockets of pessimism. Religious unrest was widespread. It became increasingly intense in the second decade of the sixteenth century when, having found in Martin Luther its eloquent leader, it burst forth in full fury as the Reformation. Significantly, the cause of irritation was the same species of church corruption which had predicated the *Devotio Moderna.*

The *Devotio Moderna* was "spontaneously" generated by Christianity's predilection for self-purification. Beginning with the life's work of Gerard Groote, it grew into a multifaceted religious reform which sought to cast off the church's corruption through a return to primitive simplicity. Geographically centered on the River Yssel, the movement's influence spread throughout the Low Countries and Germany. Groote's "present day devotion" derived broad but simple principles from the Bible, early Christian manuscripts, and the teachings of selected medieval theologians. After Groote's death the work of the *Devotio Moderna* was continued by his protégé, Florentius Radewijns, and was embraced by three religious orders, the most notable of which was the Brethren of the Common Life.

The Brethren, a semimonastic brotherhood, strove to inspire clerical and church reform through the practice of virtue. Their "imitation of Christ" entailed a life of sacrifice, study, and labor. The Brothers lived primarily in the cities, where they supported themselves and simultaneously spread Christ's word by transcribing manuscripts, counseling, and teaching.

Humanism and the *Devotio Moderna* shared many ideas. Both emphasized simplicity and attempted to educate the young. The limited disdain with which the *Devotio Moderna* viewed the papal court and scholastic theologians was in keeping with humanist standards. Where they were not in full agreement, their divergent beliefs were often complementary. The humanist ideal of moral perfection was especially well-suited to adaptation by men who believed in free will.

The actual union of these two currents can be seen best in the work of Desiderius Erasmus, the foremost representative of Christian humanism. Erasmus was educated in the *Devotio Moderna* and early in life became a monk. He seemed destined for the cloistered cell. While pursuing his priestly studies, however, Erasmus read classical Latin texts which, through their tone and beautiful language, stimulated a life-long interest in the ancients. Ultimately, he exchanged the cowl for the laurel.

Christian humanism remained the demesne of the literate few. To the majority of Europeans, the ideal of human perfectibility must have sounded absurd. Nevertheless, the problems that humanism identified in the church were thought by many people to be signs of intrinsic corruption, requiring a fundamental change in church structure. When Martin Luther, who was in many ways thoroughly orthodox in outlook, began to articulate the feelings of dissatisfied people, a following developed. The protest movement that started with Luther would soon reach such intensity that it would fragment the church and destroy that hallowed concept of a one, holy, catholic, and apostolic church.

When humanism and the *Devotio Moderna* combined in northern Europe, they built a façade of optimism atop an unsound foundation of corrupt Christianity. The Christian humanism which grew out of the union of these two movements held forth perfection as a goal and simplicity as its panacea. Thus the Northern Renaissance, in a brief celebration of anticipated triumph, was played out in the shadow of the impending catastrophe of the Reformation. Indeed, the movement was so premature that a conservative reaction seemed inevitable. When the reaction came, it was passionate, violent, and tragic.

Anticipating the Protestant Reformation

The Protestant Reformation of the early sixteenth century was a reaction against the inconsistency in the ideals of Christianity and in the actual organization of the church and the practices of its members. Dissatisfaction with Catholicism was rooted in the court and the printing press. Political and economic conditions also facilitated the emergence of new Christian sects by predisposing countries to accepting religious change. The major reform movements—Lutheranism, Zwinglianism, Calvinism, and Anglicanism—enacted desired changes by revising the elements of Catholic doctrine that were subject to criticism. The Protestant movement, given direction by Martin Luther, was thus both a cause and an effect in the long chain of events which determined Europe's development during the sixteenth and seventeenth centuries, and the roots of that movement could be discerned in embryonic form long before the advent of Lutheranism.

The background of the Protestant Reformation involves religious, intellectual and political-economic trends which stimulated its development. For instance, there were many religious movements predating the Reformation spirit, including the Lollards, the Waldensians, and the Hussites—all heretical sects which preached "protestant" ideas. As early as the fourteenth century, the structure of the church was weakened by the Great Schism and the Babylonian Captivity. Without an effectively united papacy, abuses crept easily into church organization. Anti-clericalism derived from antagonism to the worldliness and immorality of the clergy, to their having lost contact with church members, and to the degrading educational status of rural priests. Two severely criticized abuses were the sale of spiritual offices (simony) and the sale of indulgences. Another source of dissatisfaction was the intervention of canon law in state issues: the church made a practice of selling religious dispensations for marriage or for the holding of benefices, and these dispensations exempted the buyer from certain civil laws. Heterodox feelings ultimately emerged from the specious practices of clergy and the questionable ethical and theological basis of papal prerogatives.

Many intellectual influences that incited religious discontent originated during the Renaissance. The critical spirit of humanism encouraged a return to first-century Christianity and to Christian idealism. Textual criticism was another facet of the critical spirit that anticipated Protestant thought. For instance, Lorenzo Valla, by uncovering as a forgery the Donation of Constantine, which sanctioned the Papal States of Italy with the pope as secular head, indirectly undermined papal supremacy. The techniques of the critical spirit provided an awareness of the need for reform by articulating inconsistencies within the church.

Advanced communications media, as by-products of the Renaissance spirit, were also instrumental in the development of the Reformation movements. Printing, implemented by engravings, had a profound importance as a vehicle of communication. By advertising their beliefs in the vernacular, religious movements made these beliefs accessible to both the aristocracy and the common people. Universities, often the centers of radical thought, became important catalysts, in that they furnished a sympathetic climate for the introduction of religious change.

The critical spirit of humanism, the development of printing techniques, and the university atmosphere provided a foundation for reform movements. Political and economic trends further precipitated the imminence of the Reformation. By encouraging national and secular loyalties, European monarchs were in effect exploiting reform movements as a way of diverting allegiances and of strengthening their own power. They were jealous of the income which was derived from papal taxation and naturally sought this revenue for their own purposes.

Discontent with a deteriorating church and a confused political-economic situation, operating within the framework of humanistic awareness, served as the breeding ground for vanguard reform movements: Lutheranism flourished in Germany and Scandinavia; Zwinglianism affected religious thought in Switzerland; Calvinism, more internationally appealing, was significant not only in Switzerland, but in France, Scotland, Poland, and Hungary as well; and Anglicanism developed its own brand of Protestantism in England. By 1520, Western Europe was ripe for reform, and a measure of its success, in succeeding decades, lay in the premature efforts of the past.

The Middle Ages and the Renaissance had bequeathed to the Age of Reformation such compelling influences as the Hussites in Bohemia and Moravia, the Lollards in England, and the Waldensians in Savoy and Piedmont; the mysticism of the *Devotio Moderna,* which culminated in Thomas à Kempis' *Imitation of Christ* and necessarily affected religious thinkers; France and England's anti-papal and Erastian reactions against the inordinate power and wealth wielded by churchmen; a divided Germany, politically helpless before the excessive clerical extortions levied upon the German peoples; a new biblical theology based on humanist scholarship which was replacing philosophical theology and supplying a new intellectual framework for the coming Reformation; Sigur de Brabant's double standard of truth that disputed philosophy's ability to confirm or deny the data of revealed religion and sharply divided reason from faith; a holy Roman See busily using church funds for its own self-aggrandizement and selling indulgences like a "salvation assurance company"; an increasingly impersonal ecclesiastical authority spiritually separated from the clergy and people; Erasmian rejection of the pomp and circumstance of the Catholic Church and Erasmus' desire to return to early Christianity and its simple affirmation of faith; new secular allegiances fostered by the economic and cultural vitality of growing towns and cities, the founding of new universities, and the rapid rise of book production. In view of this turbulent political, social, and intellectual background, the Reformation easily explains itself.

The Reformation: Luther versus Erasmus

The Reformation formally began in Germany when the Medici pope, Leo X, ostensibly seeking funds for the rebuilding of St. Peter's, promoted one indulgence sale too many. Its inception, however, as John Headley states, "cannot be understood or explained in terms of particular abuses but rather as a new apprehension of reality. A fundamentally religious movement, the Reformation raised the basic question of authority and thereby sprang the whole system of scholastic theology, papal government, and monastic piety." In view of the intense religiosity of the German spirit, the growing cultural identity which followed in the wake of such humanists as Celtis, Trithemius, and Wimpfeling, and the subsequent frustration occasioned by the absence of a political organization answering to the German sense of national purpose, it is not remarkable that Germany was the seat of the religious protest. Neither is it surprising that Martin Luther was the "Father" of the Reformation. Luther received his educational training in the Ockhamist "Via Moderna" school. He was a biblical theologian who believed that scripture was its own interpreter and he had mystic yearnings toward an "interior religion based on the communion of the soul with God." Following the Augustine-Pauline tradition, Luther propounded the doctrine of justification by faith alone, wherein the faithful believer appropriates the righteousness and unmerited imputation of forgiveness and victory simply through faith in Christ. Secondly, Luther adopted Augustine's doctrine of predestination but denied both the benefits of good works and the individual's ability to exercise free will in his efforts toward salvation. Thirdly, Luther expanded the doctrine of the Word, including within it the "preaching of the Word, the visible Word of the sacraments, and the written Word of the Scriptures interpreted as a whole." Part of the complexity of this doctrine rested on Luther's controversial theory of real presence, which stated that Christ's body was ubiquitous and actually present in the elements of bread and wine taken in the eucharist.

Among Luther's provocative religious concepts, his solifidianism—that faith alone assures salvation—had the most profound and practical repercussions, in that it renounced and rejected "pious observances, utterances and cash transactions; the purchase of pardons, prayers and tributes to saints; multiplication of requiem masses, monasticism and bodily mortification, and the host of endowments and institutions." It was the 1517 indulgence for St. Peter's that provoked Luther to write his famous *Ninety-Five Theses,* thus marking the beginning of the Age of Reformation. In 1520, after repudiating the authority of the pope and that of the general councils, Luther produced that provocative manifesto, *To the Christian Nobility of the German Nation.* Written in German, the manifesto reviewed the whole of the religious, ecclesiastical, and social problems; attacked the Roman court, the greed of the cardinals, papal officials, and pluralists; disputed clerical immunity from secular laws; and suggested that secular rulers should establish national churches. In two other treatises, Luther denied the pope's jurisdiction over any Christian, demanded a simplification of rites and ceremonies in the church, the abolition of pilgrimages, and equal education for girls as well as boys. Of the seven sacraments of the Catholic Church, he sanctioned only two, baptism and the eucharist. Aided by the printing press, Luther stormed all of Germany with his theological propaganda, converted thousands to Lutheranism, and persistently worked toward greater recognition of freedom of conscience.

On the surface Erasmus and Luther resembled one another. Both had been monks of the Augustinian order, had served the same cause of reform, and were spirited individualists. In the individuality of each, however, lay the fundamental differences which would ultimately bring them into direct confrontation with one another. Each viewed God and man from different perspectives: Erasmus saw man as a noble being, capable of attaining perfection, whereas Luther saw him as a culpable and depraved creature, totally dependent on God. The Erasmian God granted man a free will with which to attain perfection; Luther's God was a "benevolent dictator," a God of wrath and mercy. Erasmus, confident in his belief, trusted in the ability of the church to purge itself eventually of corruption; but Luther's beliefs precipitated the fragmentation of reform before the church initiated its own purification.

Erasmus' *Treatise on Free Will,* published seven years after the outbreak of the Reformation, amounted to a moderate philosophical refutation of Luther's doctrine. It seemed to satisfy no one but its author. Entirely in keeping with Erasmus' intellectual perspective, this carefully modulated restatement of the scholastic position on free will was an undisguised attempt to bring Luther around to the orthodox viewpoint. Unfortunately, it fell flat in an atmosphere charged with emotion. Contemporaries failed to see that in this work Erasmus gave expression to the essence of his beliefs. In a situation he deplored as tragic, one which was utterly destroying the intellectual, humanist world that he had sought to create, Erasmus managed to be everything that he had wanted others to be. His plea was one of the few examples of rational dissent.

Luther's efforts to repudiate the objectionable practices of the Catholic

Church gave a new direction to the restless, dissatisfied masses. Like the mystics, he advocated a religion based on the communion of the humble soul with God. Unlike the humanists, he viewed man as a being who without grace was powerless, thereby emphasizing the awesome perfection of God. For Luther, the sacrifice of Christ was the focal point of religious thought. He saw justification as an instantaneous act whereby the believer appropriates the righteousness of Christ.

The Reformation Continued: Other Figures in Other Places

The English Reformation, hovering mid-way between the declaration of the Ninety-Five Theses (1517) and the Council of Trent (1545–1563), which formalized Catholic reform, was sustained by acts of conscience: the heroic attempt by Catherine of Aragon to maintain her marriage to Henry VIII and the determined effort of the king to satisfy God by dissociating himself from his brother's wife. To be sure, Henry's eagerness for a male heir whetted his scrupulosity and moved him to annul his marriage to Catherine on the basis of scripture. The harsh judgment of Leviticus 20:21 hammers away: "If a man takes his brother's wife, it is impurity; ... they shall be childless." But Catherine played an equally decisive role in the English Reformation. In refusing to submit to the king's will, she forced Henry to defy the pope and to sever England from communion with Rome.

The ultimate success of English reform, however, depended upon popular support, nurtured by the feelings of rebellion that originated with the Lollards (ca. 1375–1430) and were beginning to resurface in the 1530s. Like the Germans of Saxony, the English had developed contempt for ecclesiastical bureaucracy and corruption. They desired a thorough-going reform of head and members and looked upon Henry, the defender of the faith, as the means to that noble end.

Just as England's centripetal government encouraged the English reform, so Switzerland's locally-controlled administrative, political, foreign, and religious functions allowed broad sections of the citizenry to participate in public affairs. Consequently, the development of Switzerland's religious concepts owed more to local attitudes and political structure than to any other factor.

When Huldreich Zwingli arrived in Zurich in 1518, he proceeded through political channels toward a methodical and carefully calculated religious reform. After gaining public notice and support by preaching to a lay magistracy, Zwingli proposed in 1523 sixty-seven articles of reform to Zurich's city council. The council adopted the proposals and proceeded to rescind papal and diocesan authority, decried religious iconography, dissolved monasteries and nunneries, and, with the endowments thus gained, initiated a welfare program and founded a theological college. By 1525, Zurich no longer held mass and Zwingli introduced a commemorative communion service, available to both laity and clergy; but, unlike the communion dictated by Luther's doctrine of real presence, Zwingli's service was considered only symbolically representative, since Christ's body had ascended to heaven and could not, therefore, be locally present in the sacramental bread and wine.

In keeping with Luther's solifidianism and predestination theories, Zwingli extended his theological concepts to include "double" predestination and applied his theology to the social and political level by casting the magistrate in the role of ecclesiastical reformer. Moreover he established a theocracy (composed of magistrates and pastors) which attempted to impress Christian discipline upon the community. Later, Zwingli disseminated his theology through traveling missionaries, such as John Hussgen, who was also known as Oecolampadius. Working through the guilds and lower orders of Berne's social hierarchy, Oecolampadius successfully converted Basel to Zwinglianism, and, in 1529, the city council gave official recognition to the Reformed Zwinglian Church. Thus, having turned western Switzerland toward the new religion, Oecolampadius set the stage for Guillaume Farel's conversion of Geneva, Calvin's fateful arrival, and the expansion of European Protestantism through the Genevan reform.

The birth of Calvinism in Geneva did not occur until 1541. Using Strasbourg as a model, Calvin established a theocratic government composed of a ministry of pastors, teachers, deacons, and a college of elders. He asserted the independence of the church and a self-governing status for it, and, at the same time, declared that the secular government ruled by divine right. He believed that church and state should mutually rule to protect the moral decrees of God, each keeping within the limits of ecclesiastical and secular jurisdiction. On purely theological issues, Calvin, indoctrinated by Martin Bucer, exalted God's supreme sovereignty and immutable will; but he also emphasized "the inner vision of the nature of God". Going beyond Luther, the Word for Calvin was an interaction between the scriptures and an inner light, under the power of God. Thus the sacraments were not necessary for salvation; nor was salvation absolutely assured. Man must perform good works and be sustained by an inward assurance achieved through an internal, active relationship with Christ. Accepting the Lord's Supper as a holy mystery, which he experienced as a spiritual partaking of God, Calvin believed in the simplification of cómmunion and the close adherence to scripture. Being less parochial than Luther, Calvin also advocated the essential brotherhood of mankind. This attitude, combined with his flexibility in the pursuit of an ecumenical dream, accounts largely for his success as a reformer. Despite some theological differences, Calvin and Heinrich Bullinger of Zurich were able to join forces through the "Consensus Tigurinus of 1549" and the "Second Helvetic Confession of 1566", thereby merging Calvinism and Zwinglianism into one reformed faith.

Several reasons made it easy for France, the Netherlands, Scotland, Germany, and Eastern Europe to adopt Calvin's Reformed Church. His teachings, clothed in a systematic language, were less subject to disputes than Luther's; his theology appealed equally to townsmen, landowners, tradesmen, and craftsmen. Geneva's bourgeois government, infused with a social discipline and ethical atmosphere, won ready acceptance in more conservative societies. Furthermore, Calvinism's early identification with city-states operating under republican virtues, with principal beliefs in committees, rule of law, and constitutional organizations, rapidly linked it with emerging nationalistic tendencies. It is significant, therefore, that the Reformed faith entered England during Henry VIII's turmoil with the Roman Church, regarding his marriage to Anne Boleyn. Without realizing the consequences, Henry opened the door to continental reform when he placed the vernacular Bible in the hands of the English people. Later, after Henry banished English Protestants, John Hooper, the Father of English Puritanism, gathered his Puritan views through the Swiss, and began propagating them in England as early as 1549. However, it was not until Elizabeth, pressured by the House of Commons, agreed to use Cranmer's Second Prayer Book and granted the Genevan Calvinists an office in a national church that Calvinism began to take real hold in England. The Church of England, weakened by internal dissension, found itself dominated by an active and integral Puritanism, which was rapidly spreading its reform principles. By the end of Elizabeth's reign the restive Anglicans began closing ranks again, inspired by a vision of a *via media* national church, and attracted by the liberal and latitudinarian tone of Erasmus, Bucer, and Melanchthon and the Catholic and Lutheran traits of the new Prayer Book. Consequently, by 1595–1596—a period significant for both the publication of Peter Baro's more humane doctrine of salvation for all men by means of the exercise of free will and Richard Bancroft's appointment as leader of the Anglican Church— Anglicanism, eagerly receptive to new ideas, began to flourish, and Puritanism began to decline. Thus, while the Tridentine Reform was forcefully being implemented under St. Ignatius Loyola's rule and Jacobus Arminius was preaching his antipredestinarian doctrine of 1598, Puritanism was struggling for survival until ultimately it crossed the Atlantic and created a New Jerusalem in Puritan New England.

In imitation of the spirit of the Brethren of the Common Life and the Roman Oratory of Divine Love, and in opposition to the doctrinal positions of Lutherans, Anglicans, and Calvinists, Roman Catholics responded to Protestantism with a reformation of their own. Almost on the heels of Luther's split with Rome, newly established orders of clerics and nuns swelled the ranks of Catholic reformers: the Theatines (1524) led the way as liturgists, the Capuchins (1525) as preachers, the Somaschi (1528) as social workers, the Barnabites (1530) as confessors, and the Jesuits (1534) and Ursulines (1535) as educators. These *milites ecclesiae* defended the faith and propagated the tenets of Roman Catholicism against a background of resentment and suspicion. Other forces were also at work: through enlightened popes, especially Paul III and Paul IV, the church in the mid-sixteenth century reasserted its authority and sanctified its apostolate. Finally, the church sought to preserve its achievements and to safeguard its integrity by codifying ecclesiastical doctrines and discipline. With the approval of the Council of Trent (1545–1563), Paul III reestablished orthodoxy in an age dedicated to innovation.

The Renaissance as Provoking Imperial Ambitions

The sixteenth century witnessed not only the richly diverse nature of reform in the Renaissance, but also the development of networks of overseas expansion. Motivated by "gold, glory, and the Gospel," the intrepid explorers opened up opportunities for world empire. The European nations that sent these romantic adventurers were far more practical. Ultimately, they saw their colonies as areas of great natural resources to be exploited according to the principles of mercantilism. America's gold and silver were to enrich European coffers and to strengthen nationalistic ambitions. As it was, the exploitation of colonies reinforced the position of the ambitious bourgeoisie throughout Europe. In cooperation with their monarchs, Europe's merchants became the architects of colonial policy. All Europe prospered. Moreover, the increased circulation of goods was accompanied by new and improved roads and bridges, fewer provincial tariffs, and reductions in banditry. But there are vicissitudes in any commercial revolution and Spain was the casualty here. Having drained the mines of South America, the Spanish empire was finally wrecked by inflation and greed. Charles V and Philip II were inept administrators; their expensive possessions and foreign policies embroiled Spain in nearly all of the wars of the Renaissance. Late in the sixteenth century, the Dutch revolt, the war with England, the financing of the Catholic Reformation, and the expense of Philip's Escorial Palace bankrupted Spain. Neither power nor diplomacy could extricate her from the morass of indebtedness. But Spain's loss was Europe's gain: and in the first half of the seventeenth century, France, England, and the Netherlands developed their own overseas empires.

Reformation, expansion, and politics were intertwined in the sixteenth and seventeenth centuries. The wealth of the New World transformed the Atlantic nations of Europe into greater powers than the city-states of Italy. Moreover, in the wake of Protestantism, political alignments in Europe were frequently conditioned by religious sympathies. Protestants were anxious to counteract the spread of Catholicism and Catholics wished to solidify their gains by extending their missions. An aggressive imperial policy was the result on all sides. In the end, Europe became dependent upon its vast overseas empires; and prosperity depended upon peace. To insure both, the European nations developed a system of international relations, grounded in power politics and sustained by diplomacy.

There have been few periods in the history of mankind in which the transition from the preceding to the following age makes so complete a metamorphosis that it may be regarded as a change in kind rather than in degree. The Age of Renaissance and Reformation marked the change from the medieval to the so-called modern age. As an era, it owes much of its character to the coexistence and synthesis of medieval, ancient, and modern elements; of decaying and obsolescent institutions and ideas, together with the new, still incomplete ones. The Renaissance and Reformation is at once a period of transition and a highly unique era. In contrast to the strictly regulated medieval way of life, dominated by Christian doctrine and limited by obligatory feudal relationships, the Renaissance and Reformation was an age of self-discovery. Intellectual activity was both admired and encouraged. Man became aware of his capabilities and asserted his independence as a creative, intelligent being. He felt his way beyond the Christian interpretation of nature toward a scientific explanation of the universe; expressed his hopes, fears, and observations in plays, novels, and epic poems; pondered the complexities of life within the framework of Neo-Platonism and mysticism. Confronted with a new conception of himself and his environment, Renaissance man tried to justify his existence in a world he could not fully understand.

Selected Bibliography

Renaissance historiography has been the subject of considerable debate. For the fullest discussion of its development, read Wallace K. Ferguson's *The Renaissance in Historical Thought: Five Centuries of Interpretation* (Boston, 1948) and *Renaissance Studies* (New York, 1970) together with Denys Hays' *The Italian Renaissance in Its Historical Background* (Cambridge, 1961). Johann Huizinga offers a provocative, but less favorable, view of Jacob Burckhardt's interpretation of the Italian Renaissance in "The Problem of the Renaissance," *Men and Ideas . . . ,* translated and edited by James S. Holmes and Hans van Marle (London, 1960), pp. 243–287. In defense of Burckhardt, read Hans Baron, "Burckhardt's Civilization of the Renaissance: A Century After Its Publication," *Renaissance News,* XIII (August 1960) : pp. 207–222. Four recent collections of re-interpretations may also be consulted with profit: Tinsley Helton, ed., *The Renaissance: A Reconsideration of the Theories and Interpretations of the Age* (Madison, Wisconsin, 1961) ; Wallace K. Ferguson, ed., *The Renaissance: Six Essays* (New York, 1962) ; Leona Gabel, ed., *The Renaissance Reconsidered: A Symposium* (Smith College Studies in History, XLIV [1964]) ; and Archibald Lewis, ed., *Aspects of the Renaissance: A Symposium* (Austin, Texas, 1967). Equally useful are the specialized studies by Erwin Panofsky, *Renaissance and Renascences in Western Art* (Uppsala, 1960) and Elizabeth L. Eisenstein, "The Advent of Printing and the Problems of the Renaissance," *Past & Present,* 45 (November 1969), pp. 19–89. Finally, for the best discussion of the Reformation in perspective, read Roland H. Bainton's essay "Interpretations of the Reformation," *The American Historical Review,* LXVI (October 1960), pp. 74–84, and *The Reformation Crisis,* edited by Joel Hurstfield (London, 1965).

Aeneas Sylvius Being Crowned Poet *by Bernardo Pinturicchio. Alinari.*

2

The Italian Renaissance

LAURO MARTINES

N O PERIOD HAS BEEN more challenged as a unit of historical time than that to which we give the French name *renaissance*, meaning rebirth. The debate has produced such a rich literature that when historians speak of "the problem of the Renaissance," they refer to a distinct and comprehensive field of inquiry.

Approaching the Renaissance

Guidelines for the prevailing conception of the period were drawn by the Swiss historian Jacob Burckhardt in his famous essay, *The Civilization of the Renaissance in Italy* (1860). He proposed to show that urban Italians of the period 1300 to 1530 were "the first-born among the sons of modern Europe." To demonstrate this he focused attention on their passion for politics and the building of states, their keen sense of individual consciousness, their revival —for worldly ends—of the body of classical literature, their attachment to the things of this world (e.g., art and the pleasures of travel), and their alleged scientific advances. Throughout the essay there is a marked emphasis on a mentality and spirit.

Burckhardt's interpretation received wide recognition and continues, with modifications, to govern our way of looking at the period. But it also aroused

27

much criticism and attempts at refutation. Denials and reassessments issued from every quarter. Even racism was brought into the dispute by H. S. Chamberlain and L. Woltmann, who argued that the outstanding Italians of the Renaissance period were overwhelmingly of Germanic and Nordic blood. More serious were the critics who concentrated their attacks on specific aspects of the Burckhardtian view: the alleged "discovery" by Italians of individualism, nature, the classics, and the physical world. After all, do we not hear individual cries of anguish from medieval men like Peter Abelard, the scholastic philosopher who loved one of his former pupils turned nun? Were not the builders of late twelfth-century cathedrals sharp observers of flora and fauna, as is attested by the sculpted capitals of Gothic architecture? Was not Aristotle scrupulously studied and Virgil lovingly read? Were not the scientific advances of the thirteenth and fourteenth centuries the achievement of scholastic thinkers associated with the medieval universities at Oxford, Paris, and Padua?

So it went. And here and there criticism persists. For Burckhardt's grasp of the Renaissance period was both comprehensive and somewhat irritating— particularly to specialists and to those with affection, professional or doctrinal, for the medieval "Age of Faith.'

But there is no need to make invidious comparisons. In addition to its innovative and exploratory currents, the Renaissance brought in or intensified profound human inadequacies: among them, new varieties of despotism, a readiness to believe in witchcraft, spasms of ideological terrorism, and a growing devotion to bettering the instruments of war. Nor is it clear that fifteenth-century sharecroppers (*mezzadri*) in central Italy were much better off than serfs on tenth-century manors. Progress is not inevitable and, in any case, does not follow a straight line.

The failure of Burckhardt's critics has been their exclusive concentration on fragments of his portrayal. They have seen only parts of a world which he saw as a whole. It may be foolish for the historian to think that he can see wholes if, thus disposed, he can in fact see only fantasies. But the specialist who insists that fragments alone are visible, and that each specialist has his own, is surely gazing at a fiction; for the piece which he has cut out for himself never had any existence as a distinct entity.

In keeping with the Burckhardtian approach, I shall try in this essay to perceive a changing whole, even when I seem to be looking at the parts; I shall do so by concentrating on the forefront of historical change—the city and the urban environment. Procedure of this sort is both standard and tricky: to focus on the vanguard of development is to rely upon a selective method for tracing the direction or path of change. I shall therefore be concerned with innovation and the ensemble of innovations. Something like this is what Burckhardt did. The idea of the Renaissance, like those, for example, of the Baroque or the Eighteenth-Century Enlightenment, depends upon such an approach.

City-states and Society

The urban environment will provide the continuing focus for this essay, but we must first see Italy in historical perspective.

The Alps divide Italy from the continent of Europe. To the south this pediment of mountains arches over a region of lakes and rivers—Italy's rich northern plain. Jutting out of the southwestern tip of the Alps and folding around under them is a chain of mountains, the Apennines, which snake down the length of the Italian peninsula for about 850 miles. The chain then curls around into Sicily, one coast of which lies less than 100 miles from Tunisia. The peninsula has great geographic and climatic variety, with extremes of cold and heat, rain and drought, fen and fertile plain, rocky plateaus and rich volcanic soils. Of men and local custom, crops and livestock, the variety is, or was, no less remarkable. Antiquity of culture and exposure to continual invasion made for a people of ingenuity, resignation, and tenacity—their response to what circumstance denied or power disrupted.

In the eleventh and early twelfth centuries, a time of revolutionary economic revival and mushrooming towns, much of Italy lay under the sovereign rule of the Holy Roman (or Western) Empire, whose boundaries reached from central Italy across the Alps and Germany to the shores of the North and Baltic seas. Southern Italy and Sicily were claimed by a line of Norman conquerors who overcame the ruling Byzantine Greeks and Arabs. The Church governed Rome and the adjoining countryside for a distance of more than 100 miles north and south. Venice was under the nominal rule of the Byzantine Empire, which stretched from the southern Adriatic across Greece to the mountains of Asia Minor (Anatolia). But all the rest of central and upper Italy, the so-called "Italic kingdom," belonged to the jurisdiction of the Western Empire and hence to the German emperors, who were also kings of Germany and Italy. Here government was greatly decentralized, being locally or regionally administered by appointees (often hereditary) of the emperor—counts, viscounts, margraves, and bishops with the temporal authority of counts.

The second half of the eleventh century was dominated by the acute struggle between pope and emperor for the control of major ecclesiastical office. Historians know the struggle as the Investiture Controversy. Defecting German princes, mistrustful of the emperor's potential powers and encouraged by the ardor and determination of the papacy, helped to enfeeble the imperial dignity, with the result in Italy that local government—easily drawn into local hands—greatly profited. Rendered stronger and bolder by their quickening economies, the cities reaped major advantages. The leading cities (e.g., Genoa, Milan, Vicenza, Bologna, Florence, Pisa, Perugia) came to be governed by sworn associations or communes, comprised mainly of local noblemen. By the middle of the twelfth century the communal movement had triumphed: throughout central and upper Italy, in most urban centers, the commune had taken over the government of the walled city and its rural outskirts. From this time on—with the empire increasingly reduced to the status of a legal fiction —all the most potent communes began to expand, reaching out deeply into the countryside to sweep under communal governance everything within their horizons. There ensued alliances and counteralliances among communes, as well as intercommunal and then interregional wars that lasted until the 1520s. The strong subjected the weak, and the political geography of the peninsula changed fundamentally.

Milan, Genoa, Venice, Florence, Pisa, and Siena (to mention only the preeminent) became prosperous, expansionist, and combative city-states. Each ran its own political and diplomatic affairs, thus claiming (despite the empire) a temporal sovereignty *de facto*. By the middle of the fifteenth century, the leading states in north and north-central Italy were the Duchy of Savoy, the Venetian Republic, the Duchy of Milan, and the Republic of Florence (which had swallowed Pisa in 1406). Situated between the last three of these were the lesser states of Mantua, Ferrara, and Modena, each under separate princely rule. Just south of Savoy, along the Ligurian coast, lay Genoa, whose political fortunes alternated between periods of self-rule and external domination. In Tuscany, Florence was hemmed in by two miniature but resolute city-republics, Siena and Lucca. The lands under papal rule occupied the middle of the peninsula, sprawling over the Apennines from one coast to the other, along a line that ran from Rome in the south to Bologna in the north. Meanwhile, southern Italy and Sicily passed from one dynasty to another—Norman, Hohenstaufen, Angevin, Hungarian, and Aragonese—by means of conquest, marriage, invitation, and trickery. Sicilian allegiance was transferred to the House of Aragon in the late thirteenth century, and Sicily remained divided from the mainland kingdom (Angevin, then Hungarian) until 1435, when Alfonso of Aragon succeeded in reuniting the kingdoms of Naples and Sicily.

I have presented these summary details to help convey a picture of the peninsula as a whole. Henceforth, my overriding concern will be with the cities of the central and northern plains and valleys which produced the Renaissance environment, first as republics and later, in some important instances, as urban concentrations under courtly one-man rule. The following pages deal with the direction of urban change.

From Orvieto to Milan, on both sides of the Apennine spine, the history of cities had four phases. 1) At the end of the eleventh century there occurred a spontaneous generation of communes, one in each city, governed by consuls from the feudal nobility and a small municipal aristocracy. 2) Late in the twelfth century, in response to a vigorous economy and the compelling rise of new men and of guilds, the commune began to widen its social base and to substitute for the collegiate rule of the consuls a modified collegiate government with a more impartial executive, the *podestà*. 3) The continuing tidal pressure of new men reached another and still more critical level in the second and third quarters of the thirteenth century, when a new commune with a more popular base, "the commune of the people (*popolo*)," challenged or overcame the established "podestaral" commune. 4) But social strain, class conflict, and the virulence of political faction persisted to such a degree that the commune of the *popolo* soon issued in one-man rule (e.g., Milan, Padua, Orvieto) or was drawn under the sway of oligarchy (Perugia, Florence, Siena).

This essay will concentrate on the fourth phase, the longest by far, which stretched from the later thirteenth to the early sixteenth centuries, taking in the classic Renaissance period.

The main differences between the thirteenth and fourteenth centuries involve changes in the economy and population. For more than two centuries the cities had benefited from amazing economic and demographic growth. Waves of immigrants surged from the countryside into the cities. All classes of men increased—merchants, artisans, and hired labor. Large numbers of new men amassed fortunes. Cities spilled beyond their walls two and three times, requiring new circumvallations. The year of Dante's exile from Florence (1301), that city had a population of about 110,000 souls; Milan, about 200,000; Venice and Genoa, 100,000 each; Bologna and Pavia, 50,000; Pisa, 40,000; Siena, Lucca, Padua and Perugia each between 30,000 and 40,000 souls.[1] But by the 1320s or 1330s the fast tempo of growth and expansion had been arrested. The demand on agricultural methods and resources around the cities may have been much too heavy—owing, perhaps, to population pressures. As a result, we now suspect that the catastrophic Black Plague of 1348 precipitated a cycle of ruin which had already been foreshadowed. The epidemic eliminated from one-half to two-thirds of the urban population. Recovery or return to the earlier, dynamic rate of expansion proved impossible. By the last quarter of the fourteenth century, the ascent of new men in numbers large enough to produce change had come to an end. Economic conditions were unfavorable: markets had shrunk, the times were uncertain, and commercial competition from abroad was keener. Overall production and profits in Italian cities had never been so low. The age which saw the facile amassing of fortunes was over. Exceptions had no effect upon the general picture.

From the end of the fourteenth century, political society no longer drew on new social elements, though this had been a major source of civic vitality. With few exceptions, the prominent urban families of the fifteenth century had already made a name for themselves by 1300 or 1325. Indeed, many rightly claimed a history stemming back to the twelfth century and before. Milan, Genoa, Venice, and Siena abounded in such houses. When the Duke of Milan was struck down in 1476, two of the three assassins turned out, unsurprisingly, to be noblemen from illustrious Milanese families (Lampugnano and Visconti). They alone had the boldness for such an audacious political adventure,

---

[1] Outside Italy, Paris alone had a population of more than 100,000.

just as in 1447 the short-lived but revolutionary establishment of a Milanese republic had been the work of Milanese noblemen and leading jurists. Similarly, at Florence in the 1480s, under the veiled signory, or lordship, of Lorenzo de' Medici, it was men from the old and influential families who felt most keenly the hand of the disguised prince, for they saw political office as theirs by right of birth. Their grandfathers and great-grandfathers had governed the city. Not for more than a century had new men entered important public office in any but the most negligible numbers.

In fifteenth-century Italy, politics was the business of princes, brilliant mercenaries (*condottieri*), and regional oligarchies; and the oligarchies rigidified, becoming closer and more exclusive, as the century ran its course. The distinct tendency was for the old ruling classes to become ruling castes, in the major city-states no less than in the lesser towns and subject territories.

We use the word *oligarchy* to mean rule by the rich and the few. Translated into actual numbers, this meant the political hegemony of from fifty to two hundred families in each of the major city-states. Realistically, however, the springs of effective power rested with the lesser number, as was sometimes dramatically demonstrated in emergency situations (*e.g.,* Florence in 1433–34; Milan in 1447; Lucca in 1522).

A devitalized economy and a narrowing of oligarchy could well make for a greater concentration of wealth and capital. There are indications that a consolidation of capital in fewer hands may have been a feature of the late fourteenth and fifteenth centuries. The evidence—partial and fragmentary—comes from Florence, Pistoia, San Gimignano, and Genoa. As new outlets for industrial and trade investment failed to develop, as war and the requirements of government intensified the demand for revenue, and as the fiscal machinery of the state was more effectively manipulated to favor the influential political families, the sum of monies and real property tended to devolve upon fewer men. In fifteenth-century Genoa even small industry was under the domination of the big merchants and financiers. The same was true in Venice.

For all the social tension and conflict at the height of the communal period (1180–1320), most cities then had energetic legislative councils and elastic, lively executive bodies. Organized along collegiate lines, the executive bodies (known as elders, wisemen, *signori*) functioned in unison with their legislatures. Large and small councils effectively interacted. There was more social flexibility, more substantial entry into the circuit of public office, and more salutary relations among the different organs of communal government. Then came the faltering rhythms which we have already described.

The new direction of economic and social change brought the need for stricter political controls. Oligarchies tightened their exclusive hold on the key offices of state and invested them with a greater concentration of authority. Nearly everywhere in fifteenth-century Italy there was a narrowing and focusing of the agencies of public authority, particularly those belonging to the executive sphere of government. In the Venetian republic the fortunes of the famous Council of Ten well illustrate this trend. At Milan, under the duchy, the Secret or Privy Council was more tightly organized and a large volume of judicial business passed over to the jurisdiction of the duke's secretaries and leading officials. In the Florentine republic, the oligarchy increased the powers of the principal magistracies (Priorate and Eight on Public Safety) ; there was also a greater use of plenipotentiary councils and of devious, more exclusive methods of election and appointment to public office.

As the executive arm of government grew more potent, the old legislative councils became more passive and in some cases lapsed into inactivity. Also undermined were the old communal courts, which surrendered many areas of traditional jurisdiction to the complex of executive offices.

The republican oligarchies in Venice, Florence, Lucca, and Genoa were able to realize a closer identity with the state by concentrating authority in certain magistracies, and by closing their ranks and thereby gaining greater prominence for the dominant families. Members of each oligarchy staffed the principal offices. Their sons began to appear in the public councils at the age of twenty-five or before and went on doing so, if they were so inclined, for the rest of their lives. By the time such men were forty or forty-five, their experience in government was so varied and intense that we may think of them as a class of professional public servants. Their professionalism was in their skills and experience more than in reliance upon the income from office, although members of this class sometimes came to depend upon salaries. All told, the professional ability of public officials was higher in the fifteenth century than at any previous time. This becomes strikingly clear when we study the manner and conduct of Italian diplomacy. Procedures and practices developed in the thirteenth and fourteenth centuries functioned most fully in the fifteenth century, and their possibilities were better exploited; and the appearance around 1450 of a new figure in relations between states, the resident or permanent ambassador, was no more than concrete exemplification of the degree of professionalism already attained. Yet this was his first appearance in the history of European diplomatic practice and we must credit the diplomacies of Milan, Florence, and Venice with this achievement.

Signories (e.g., Milan, Mantua, Ferrara) were city-states under one-man rule, and it is possible that they developed a higher degree of administrative professionalism. They were characterized by a more distinct reliance on stipends and favors; leading statesmen were at times experienced "foreigners" called in by the lord of the city to take on major political charges. At Milan a large number of men in government were career officials: treasurers, agents, fiscal auditors, judges, and ducal secretaries. Together with the notaries assigned to the different offices, they constituted a type of early bureaucracy. The place of notaries in the apparatus of government under signories had a close parallel in the oligarchical republics, particularly in Florence, where notaries were charged with maintaining the regulations governing each of the many public offices.

The fourteenth-century changes, first economic and then social, entailed political and constitutional transformations which made for a new kind of state. Whether we think of it as a regional or territorial state is immaterial. The point is that it disposed of a tougher and more invasive executive, a higher degree of centralization, broader and more demanding jurisdictions, and a bureaucratic or semiprofessional governmental apparatus. Everything was affected: from individuals and guilds to subject towns and territories, in such crucial areas as citizenship, taxes, and courts of justice. The emerging state—a new or Renaissance state—also encouraged the development of a concomitant legal–political theory. This body of thought based the new state's expanding claims on arguments from public utility, from sovereignty, from the security and necessity and even the majesty of the state. Hence, one of the modern conceptions of the state—the state seen very nearly as an end in itself—was already present in the legal–political thought of the fifteenth century.

Our attention is fixed on two interrelated topics, the state and the condition of political society, because they affected all aspects of life in the city-state. Moreover, with regard to the varieties of cultural expression, the political and civic dimension, being the most compelling, tended toward primacy, as we shall see in the next section of this essay.

In 1454–1455, the chief Italian states ratified the Peace of Lodi and entered into a mutual defense league (the *Lega Italica*). They seemed ready for an era of relative amity; the agreement promised more than a modicum of interregional harmony. In this fashion, they drew their foreign relations into line with the internal stability of the cities, where dangerous social tension, once so rampant, was now fleeting and repressible. Under the terms of the Italic League, the five major states—Venice, Milan, Florence, the Papal State, and the Kingdom of Naples—committed themselves to the defense of the status quo and the exclusion from Italy of foreign military intervention. More than six decades of continual warfare thus came to an end. Although geopolitical rivalries continued and some minor wars erupted, diplomacy and drawn-out negotiation now began, really for the first time, to replace the traditional readiness to obtain settlements or satisfaction by force of arms. But this era of diplomacy—we may so call it—was to last for only forty years.

In the autumn of 1494 Italian politics suddenly became European politics: the leading European powers—first France, then Spain and the empire—plunged into the tangle of Italian regional politics. Diplomatic details and the particulars of intrigue need not concern us. The material causes sprang from conflicting dynastic claims. Drawing on the old French Angevin title, Charles VIII of France suddenly decided, with unexpected determination, to claim the Kingdom of Naples, then under the rule of a branch of the Spanish Aragonese dynasty. In September 1494 he invaded Italy. Thus commenced the age of the Italian Wars. For the next two generations Lombardy, the Veneto, Rome,

Naples, and other parts of the peninsula became the battleground for French, Spanish, German, and Swiss armies. The Swiss entered the scene as hired mercenaries, the Germans as the instruments of both imperial and Spanish policy in Italy. Milan changed hands four or five times. Venice in 1509 was all but dismembered. Florence was compelled to pursue a ruinous Francophile policy. Genoa turned herself over to French suzerainty. Lodged between the larger states, tiny despotisms in central and north-central Italy were born and vanished within a few years. Although the ends of international struggle in Italy centered on Naples and Milan, Venice and Florence and the Papacy encouraged the diplomatic and military scrimmage or were inevitably sucked into it. And inevitably, too, they chose and changed sides, stalled or moved too precipitously, and were so completely bent on serving their most immediate interests that they did not hesitate to ally themselves with the French or Spanish against their own neighbors. The Italian sense of nation was as yet too feeble.

Italy's humiliation was keenly felt by watchful contemporaries, foremost among whom were Machiavelli, Castiglione, and Guicciardini. And it is here, at the level of political sensibility and self-awareness, that the Italian Wars took their greatest human toll. For the resulting physical injuries or economic losses were finite, but the moral and psychological wounds were endlessly profound. Political failure became the obvious and unequivocal lot of the Italian upper classes. Henceforth Milanese, Florentines, Pisans, Genoese, Neapolitans, and even Romans and Venetians had to look far beyond their frontiers for the sources of high policy, or for the causes and outcomes of their own wars.

The prospect was intolerable. Intellect blinked and imagination soared or dodged. There was a general loss of focus and firmness, political as well as moral. To be sure, the challenge also elicited sharp and brilliant perceptions, but these were often casually joined with distortions and startling exaggerations, as we can see in the political and historical writings of contemporaries. On the whole, however, loss of focus was dominant. Literature became dreamy and evasive, or bitterly satirical. There was a penchant for utopian writings (what else is Castiglione's *The Courtier?*). The painting of the vanguard broke with the cold, lapidary style of the fifteenth century and became idealized, dreamy, emotional, rich in gestures and compensatorily heroic, or individualistic and arbitrary in its treatment of space. As for religious reform, so necessary in early sixteenth-century Rome, this too was out of the question, at all events on the scale needed. For the power of reform within the Roman Church lay potentially with the Italian upper classes. Their political debacle, however, pointed up and surely deepened their inability to grapple with the most urgent problems of the day. This inability, or lack of purpose, had no necessary harmful effect on the continuing vitality of the arts (when men are lame and cannot run they can still write poems or songs about running) ; but it did mean a fundamental change of perception and a departure from the more focused, decisive, exploratory spirit of the early Renaissance.

The Public World

Thanks to recent studies of urban environments, we are coming to realize that people perceive space in different ways. My purpose here will be to show that space for the makers of the Italian Renaissance was somehow joined to a public morality, to a special regard for the civic or social or visible dimensions of experience.

Cities in fourteenth- and fifteenth-century Italy were not, of course, large in modern terms. A man could walk diagonally across Florence, one of the largest cities, in from thirty to forty minutes. The cities of medium size—*e.g.,* Padua, Siena, Perugia—could have been put into the space now occupied by one of our large state universities. If this observation comes as something of a shock, that is because we are accustomed, as Americans, to associate spectacular achievement with magnitudes of power, space, riches, and numbers. The distortion is ours. Athens was tiny.

The typical city was circumscribed by massive walls and usually had three or four principal gates. Streets were narrow and often long. Particular streets and quarters sometimes housed particular trades, such as tailoring or tanning. Much of daily life went on in those streaming public ways. Family dwellings were apt to include a workshop or working space, store, warehouse, or counter; and these gave directly onto the street, whether by way of open stalls, arches, loggias, or ample doorways. In traveling from one side of the city to another, citizens could not avoid the main thoroughfares. They became accustomed to the same faces. The funneling of human traffic onto a few bridges connecting major sections of the city, as in Venice or Florence, made daily encounters with citizens of all classes unavoidable. Living amidst great privilege and great disadvantage, they could not fail to pick out the faces, above all, of the well-born or the expensively-dressed and influential. In one way or another, citizens were always on show.

This was doubly true of men born into the illustrious and powerful old houses, such as the Doria, who captained the political life of a whole district in Genoa. In their heyday much the same was true of the Donati in Florence and the Salimbeni in Siena. Their battlemented towers overlooked large parts of the city; their rows of houses dominated entire streets; or they lived in bastion-like *palazzi* (huge town houses) which sometimes gave a name or character to particular neighborhoods. The chief patrons of their parish churches, they also had the dominant voices in the political councils.

We must imagine these men, on foot or on horseback, moving down the narrow streets, crossing the crowded bridges, approaching the circle or quadrangle of the main government palace, dressed in clothes which instantly revealed their individual or social identities. They knew each other on sight. In the streets they were always on display. Honor there was on trial.

And we must also imagine the streets swarming with more modest citizens—

craftsmen, artisans, or tradesmen—best known of course in their own parishes, and bound by bonds of loyalty to a neighborhood or parish, to a guild, or even to a leading family. They also lived much of their lives in a public and corporate space.

Citizens measured one another accordingly. There was no cleavage between the private and public aspects of experience. The world of the individual was invaded by the space and values of the neighborhood and the corporate grouping; and he welcomed this invasion, just as he also took part in it where others were concerned. For parish and guild, family clan and neighborhood association were the vessels, so to speak, from which he drew his security and identity.

We know too little about the values and family organization of the really poor—the jobless, the wage laborers, and the itinerant peddlers. History is always tightlipped about this level of society. But the record, such as it is, indicates that poor men sometimes drifted between town and country or moved from parish to parish in a quest for lower rents and higher wages. Not so the members of the tenacious and prosperous middle and upper classes, whose attachment to neighborhood, parish, and family seat was profound.

At least some of the implications are clear. We can begin to understand why exile from one's native city was an agonizing experience and why it was so readily used as a penalty in political conflict. The urban environment, affective and spatial, was such as to engage and bind the deepest passions of men. To be torn from home, driven into exile, was a kind of dismemberment. A leading Florentine thinker of Dante's period, Remigio Girolami (d. 1319), declared that a man severed from his native city is like an amputated hand, useless. The effects of such estrangement were most acutely felt, of course, by members of the political ruling class. They were the men best known in the city; they played for the highest stakes; together they disposed locally of the supreme temporal authority; they were born and bred to politics, until the triumph of one-man rule transformed such grooming into a preparation for service to a prince. They were known by their riches, their forebears, their *palazzi,* their political or artistic patronage, their administrative skills, and their shrewd marriage and business liaisons. They had their distinctive being in the public councils and in the streets and squares of the city: that is, in all those actions which in one fashion or another touched the affairs or attracted the attention of the entire community.

Not surprisingly, the Aristotelian stress on man as a political animal found an approving audience in the intelligentsia of the central and north Italian cities. Indeed, Remigio added an even more demanding note in his cold asseveration, "He who is not a citizen is not a man." Humanity thus seemed to have no reality outside a civil context.

This social and moral emphasis on citizenship persisted into the sixteenth century, if not quite so cuttingly. But there was no abatement in the profoundly affirmative attitude toward prestigious public office. In the early sixteenth century, the historian and lawyer Francesco Guicciardini (1483–1540) observed that, "in Florence you are hardly a man unless you have served in the Signoria [the city's chief executive body] at least once."

It follows that the effects and resonances of the public world were all-important. Within this larger contour, other activities such as art and worship took their place. In concrete terms the pervading impact of the public world is most effectively represented by the image of the city in painting: the city walls, towers, spires, arches, façades, and battlemented constructs which haunt so many Italian frescoes and paintings of the period from the fourteenth to the sixteenth centuries. Whether the city is seen in the distant background or is fragmentarily represented as architectural display in the near foreground, neither painters nor patrons seemed able to free themselves from the stamp of the city and its public ways. We shall see that the civic theme is to be found even at the heart of pastoral verse.

Humanism

The velocity and extent of change in the cities of late medieval Italy had a profound effect on consciousness. Especially susceptible were the dominant political and social groups who made the fundamental decisions. In the course of the thirteenth and fourteenth centuries, a new awareness gradually dawned upon them, an awareness or redirection most effectively articulated by their literary and educational spokesmen. In one of its manifestations this awareness was humanism. We may therefore look upon humanism as a phase in the history of consciousness—the consciousness of the men who fashioned the destinies of the Italian cities. Seen in this light, the true burden of the historian of humanism is to identify the link between humanism and the values, moral and ideological, of the dominant social groups within the cities. The point of the succeeding pages will be to do this.

Changes of consciousness gave rise to changes in the methods and scope of education. Between about 1250 and 1400, church schools lost their exclusive control over education for the laity. Florence and other cities saw the establishment of private schools run by and for laymen. The schoolmasters were often professional notaries, and their schools were designed to teach the elements of Latin and commercial arithmetic to the sons of tradesmen, urbanized noblemen, and merchants who trafficked on an international scale. Strictly utilitarian in its aims—for Latin was the language of contracts and formal diplomatic dispatches—this development was the first phase in a gradual but basic change in the aims of education.

At the level of university instruction, the late fourteenth century witnessed the beginning of a new current, with the lecturing in Florence of men like Giovanni Malpaghini (1346–1417), who taught rhetoric, poetry, and moral philosophy, and Manuel Chrysoloras (d. 1415), who taught Greek to an audience of adult enthusiasts. In the fifteenth century, the vanguard in course offerings at the universities was held by the humanistic subjects—rhetoric, poetry, history, and moral philosophy. But the next phase of far-reaching educational change at a more basic level really began around 1400, with the founding of small but select schools run by humanists: that of Roberto de' Rossi (1355?–1417) at Florence, of Gasparino Barzizza (1359?–1431) at Padua, of Guarino Guarini (1374–1460) at Venice, Verona, and Ferrara, and of Vittorino da Feltre (1373–1446) at Mantua. In these schools Christianity was taken so much for granted—indeed, Vittorino had his pupils attend daily Mass—that the major classical writers could occupy the heart of study. Henceforth the *studia humanitatis*—"the humanities"—provided the substance for the most innovative and vigorous wave in primary and secondary education.

Human, humane, the humanities: these words are no more than a remote echo of what the nouns *humanista* and *studia humanitatis* meant in fifteenth-century Italy. We must not confuse vague twentieth-century notions with their more precise Renaissance forebears.

Italian humanism put man where it was both most flattering and most dangerous to be: at the center of active inquiry. The first modern treatise on painting (*Della pittura,* 1435), composed by the humanist Leon Battista Alberti (1404–1472), directs painters to determine the sizes of objects in the picture space by the scale of the human figures there represented. Alberti's statement of this "law" conveyed an attitude of discovery. "Man is the measure." Protagoras had long since asserted the same thing, but after the achievements of Alberti and his circle neither painting nor sculpture was to recover from that perception.

In its most general and genuine sense Italian humanism was education for practical and worthy living; but it was education based on the study of the classical Roman and Greek writers. Florentine, Venetian, and other Italian humanists believed that classical literature held the rich and communicable remains of a momentous civilization, that it expressed a viewpoint centered on the value of man's activities in the world. This recognition was combined, as we shall see, with a keen appreciation of the secularity of time, the historical nature of time. There was no necessary conflict between these attitudes and Christianity, but the fact that the classical world was mainly pre-Christian was not entirely beside the point.

It is astonishing to note how many humanists were either members of the legal profession or career officials in government chancelleries, and just as many were born into professional or intensely political families. Three of the most celebrated—Petrarch (1304–1374), Lorenzo Valla (1407–1457), and Angelo Poliziano (1454–1494)—were sons of, respectively, a notary, a canon lawyer, and a civil lawyer. Four others of great preeminence—Coluccio Salutati (1336–1406), Poggio Bracciolini (1380–1459), Pier Candido Decembrio

(1392–1477), and Giovanni Pontano (1426?–1503)—were leading municipal, papal, and royal secretaries. In Venice nearly all of the most able humanists were drawn from the political partriciate.

These facts are mentioned in order to show that the humanist enterprise proceeded under the direction of, and in keeping with the values of, men brought up for practical activity in the urban community, whether in politics, the rough-and-tumble world of municipal administration, the law courts, the business of drawing up contracts (then the stock-in-trade of the notary), or the counting house. Immersed in practical affairs and oriented toward the accomplishment of everyday ends, such men had an urgent sense of time, a recognition of man's inescapable place in the world, and a sense of his achievements and possibilities. Thus the great appeal for them—or at least for the learned among them—of Aristotle's emphasis on action in his *Ethics;* and the even greater appeal of Cicero, with his emphasis not only on action and knowledge ("the true praise of virtue is in action") but also on eloquence, felicity, and force of verbal expression. Evidently, in the context of the evolved city-state, the orator easily came to represent the ideal fusion of action with wisdom, of will with contemplation.

Appropriately, in the history of modern Europe, the first great private libraries of classical works were built up by men of the sort described above: e.g., Niccolò Niccoli (1364–1437) and Antonio Corbinelli (1377?–1425), the sons of wealthy Florentine wool merchants; Giovanni Corvini (d. 1438?), political secretary to the last Visconti Duke of Milan; or rich citizens who stood at the forefront of public life, like the Florentines Palla Strozzi (1372–1462) and Cosimo de' Medici (1389–1464). No less than the most celebrated humanists, these men applauded the ardent search for the neglected manuscripts of ancient works, a pursuit first strikingly taken up in the first quarter of the fifteenth century.

Why did the break with medieval habits of thought not come sooner, in the thirteenth century, when Italian cities were at the peak of their economic and political vitality? The answer seems to be that the break was retarded by the very condition of urban experience: in this case the raw atmosphere of new cities populated by rustics, large numbers of illiterate noblemen, and tradesmen struggling to survive or to amass enormous fortunes. Since the traditional forms of orientation and feeling must often have seemed inappropriate, it must be that the experience of the urban populace—or whatever was novel in that experience—could not easily generate its own finished forms of expression over a short period of time, except perhaps in song. Particularly resistant in this regard was the fund of experience belonging to the new class of merchants and urban administrators, who eventually gave rise to humanism and provided the audience for it. In some respects their experience *had* to conflict with the prevailing modes of apprehension and cognition, which better suited a feudal society and an ecclesiastical intelligentsia. The intellectual tradition, after all, condemned all interest as usury. Temporal lordship was assigned heavenly essences. Government was often seen as punishment for sin. "Getting and spending" were regarded as inferior a priori to the gallant professions of arms, prayer, and contemplation.

Ideas of unity, hierarchy, and order; an overriding emphasis on authority, essences, and metaphysical reality—these provided the framework and foci for twelfth- and thirteenth-century thought. In a sense the entire fourteenth century, at all events in the world of the city-state, marks a decisive drift away from the more static and hierarchical assumptions of the late Middle Ages. But even Marsilius of Padua (c. 1275–1342), the most inquiring political thinker of the fourteenth century, was unread by his Italian contemporaries: his basic presuppositions were too much in conflict with established opinion concerning the temporal authority of the church. In the early fifteenth century, one of the most sophisticated conceptions of the unity of Christian society, that elaborated by the French thinker Jean Gerson (1363–1429), was still governed by a strict notion of the interlocking relationship between heavenly and earthly hierarchies. And within this scheme man had a fixed place.

Italian humanism worked a radical break with this tradition of thought. It put man at the center of intellectual and artistic inquiry but gave him no fixed nature, no metaphysical trappings or underpinnings. It focused on his humanity and his potential, and offered temporal glory rather than salvation.[2] It therefore emphasized the study of history, recognizing that man lives in a changing temporal continuum; and it laid great emphasis on the study of moral philosophy (hence, on the dilemma of choice), having stripped man of his fixed nature. Humanism assigned vast importance to rhetoric—the art of persuasion and eloquence—for the practice of this art (i.e., effective and graceful verbal expression) combined action and wisdom, taught a certain control over the emotions (of others and so of one's own), and underlined man's reliance upon the immediate social and civil community. Finally, humanism turned philology—the rigorous historical and grammatical study of language and literature—into its primary intellectual tool, thus opening the way to a better understanding of the literature of antiquity.

In short, it was by means of philology that the humanists approached the classical world, maintaining critical detachment from it, and at the same time sharpening their sense of identity and of their own creative role in the hammering out of a new age. Paradoxically, therefore, the intensive study of classical literature was a process of self-realization. The humanists looked to antiquity to affirm the vitality, value, and experience of the present. In this

---

[2] Hence the vision could issue in a dark pessimism, but this was rare. An example is the dialogue by Poggio Bracciolini, *On the Misery of the Human Condition* (1455), a work of profoundly somber accents.

way the old modes of thought were revolutionized: the impact of accumulated experience was finally able to determine the direction of intellectual and artistic development.

The syllabus of humanism had five interrelated disciplines: grammar, rhetoric, poetry, history, and moral philosophy. By cultivating these subjects, the fifteenth-century humanists altered the course of intellectual history.

1. *Grammar* meant, first, the study of Latin and then, ambitiously, Greek. It was a commonplace of Renaissance educational theory that all serious preparation for civil life began with the study of Latin grammar. In its highest form, grammar was indistinguishable from philology, for it entailed not only a mastery of the elements of grammar, of syntax, diction, usage, and orthography, but also a true understanding of their development: that is, a grasp of their precise place in the history of the language. This obviously meant a thoroughgoing familiarity with the history of literature. In this sense grammar was both a tool and a way of life; it opened all the doors of the intellect, but its mastery was the fruit of an austere schooling.

Lorenzo Valla was the outstanding philologist and in some ways the most brilliant humanist of the fifteenth century. Born in Rome in 1407, the son of a North Italian papal lawyer, Valla published his first work, *A Comparison of Cicero and Quintilian* (now lost), at twenty. He taught rhetoric at the University of Pavia in the early 1430s, thereafter drifting to Milan, Florence, and Genoa. In 1435 he settled in Naples, where he became secretary to King Alfonso of Aragon and Naples. In the 1430s and 1440s he brought out a variety of remarkably provocative works—philological, philosophical, and historical. Intellectually he was intensely combative: swift, arrogant, and courageous. Transferring himself to Rome in 1448, he served in a secretarial capacity under Popes Nicholas V and Calixtus III, and died there in 1457. His major philological work, *On the Graces of the Latin Language* (1435–1444) is a combined critical and historical grammar, as well as a handbook of rhetoric and style. It is marked by an astonishingly able grasp of the history of the Latin language. With Valla the possibilities of historical criticism receive a virtuoso demonstration, and in his perspicacity we have one of the first unmistakable examples of the modern historical sense. Nor did he hesitate to address his philology to Holy Scripture and church documents, as in his *Notes on the New Testament* (1449) and his learned harangue on *The Falsity of the Alleged Donation of Constantine* (1440).

2. *Rhetoric* or eloquence—the art of graceful but forceful persuasion— could obviously not be learned until the rules of grammar had been mastered. Cicero and Quintilian, the classical Roman rhetoricians, were taken to be the models in this realm, the princes of oratory. The choice of the word *oratory* is deliberate: it emphasizes that aspect of rhetoric pertaining to action, to a job of doing. For in their writings the humanists turned and returned to the practical and useful nature of eloquence, most especially in connection with its utility for civil or community service. In his humanistic treatise *Concerning*

Excellent Traits (ca. 1402), addressed to a son of the lord of Padua, Pier Paolo Vergerio (1370–1444) observes that "speaking and writing elegantly affords no little advantage in negotiation, be it in public or private affairs . . . but especially in the administration of the State." And in a short essay on literary education, *De studiis te litteris liber*, (ca. 1425), one of the most distinguished of all humanists, Leonardo Bruni (1372?–1444), holds—almost casually—that knowledge should have an application: "The high standard of education referred to earlier can only be achieved by one who has seen much and read much . . . but to make effective use of what we know we must add the power of expression to our knowledge."

These were views which found a ready audience in the intense social world of the city-state, particularly among the more alert and ambitious members of the governing classes.

3. *Poetry* helped to complete the individual; it enlarged his vision and added to his humanity. From it he could draw a fund of examples and enhance the force and variety of his own speech. The preferred poets were Virgil and Homer, then Seneca, Ovid, and Horace; but the vernacular poets, Dante and Petrarch, were by no means neglected. Carlo Marsuppini (1398–1453), first secretary of the Florentine republic from 1444 to 1453, translated the first book of the *Iliad* into Latin verse. He was followed in this effort by a major poet who was also the leading philologist of the second half of the century, Angelo Poliziano (1454–1494). At sixteen, Poliziano had translated books II-V of the *Iliad* into Latin verse, an accomplishment which brought him into Lorenzo de' Medici's entourage.

The most talented of all humanist poets, Francesco Petrarch (1304–1374), is sometimes called "the father of humanism" (as if such a designation made any historical sense). The son of a Florentine notary who suffered political disgrace and exile, Petrarch spent his life abroad, studied law for a time but soon rejected it for a life of writing and reflection. After taking minor religious vows, which gave him financial independence, he traveled widely and found patronage at Avignon, Rome, Milan, Padua, Venice, and elsewhere. Of particular interest for the fortunes of humanism—apart from his *De viris illustribus* (lives of famous Romans) and his stinging self-analysis in the *Secretum*—are Petrarch's Latin letters, known as the *Familiares*, which exhibit his boundless admiration for the world of antiquity, a longing to read Greek, a love of Cicero, familiarity with the history of ancient Rome, and an abandoned attachment to the elegance of classical Latin literature.

4. *History* was in some respects the unifying discipline of humanism. An affirmative view of the ancient world was, primarily, what the humanists had in common. When they united this view of the past with their study of the literature of antiquity, they invented philology and brought historical scholarship into being. Yet we must not think that their attitude toward history presupposed an abstract approach. They looked at the past in terms of specific men and events, and their impulse to study history had a limited ground: here

again they insisted on the element of utility, on the practical value for current affairs of the study of history, and not just ancient history. In *De viris illustribus*, Petrarch is frankly in search of the moral lessons to be drawn from historical biography. Another humanist, Vergerio, asserted in *Concerning Excellent Traits* that history holds the first place on the agenda of liberal studies because of "its attractiveness and utility, qualities which appeal equally to the scholar and to the statesman." The emphasis, then, was both moral and practical: scholars, statesmen, and leading citizens should all study history. Impelled by contemporary exigencies, humanists turned to history to find a vital link with their own times. So suggestive is the place of history in the program of humanism that we shall return to the topic later in this essay.

5. *Moral philosophy* was also at the core of the educational program of Italian humanism. At the university level, the subject was nearly always taught by professors of rhetoric, history, poetry, and Greek—such as the fiery and irascible Francesco Filelfo (1398–1481), who lectured on these subjects at the Universities of Bologna, Florence, Siena, and Pavia.

While always retaining their profound Christian indoctrination (though rather indifferently in some cases), the humanists managed to shift the focus of intellectual interest from religious concerns to the humanistic disciplines, from the realm of essences to more worldly considerations, and thus from God to man. Taking Christianity for granted, most leading humanists spent their intellectual energies talking and writing and thinking about the world of antiquity, man, and literature. In the process, man's mystical–Christian trappings were ignored or peeled away. The humanists paid tribute to man's dignity and potentialities—in Giannozzo Manetti (1396–1459) and Pico della Mirandola (1463–1494) the praise was rhapsodic—but at the same time they had to cast around for new moral and ideological accents. Their extraordinary penchant for moral philosophy and political history was the emblem of their de-emphasis of religion and theology. The subject-matter of moral philosophy was provided by the texts of Aristotle, Cicero, Plato, certain of the Church Fathers (as in the syllabus of so-called "Christian humanism"), and even the classical Roman historians, Livy and Suetonius. More popular still were the writings of the Greek biographer and moral philosopher Plutarch (ca. 46–ca. 120). His *Moralia* and *Lives* of illustrious Greeks and Romans were repositories of moral, historical, and biographical anecdotes.

In recent years, the most vital scholarship in this field has centered on the theme of civic virtue—i.e., the stress on social and political obligations—in the enterprise of Italian humanism. One way of dealing with this question has been to study the different values assigned to the ideals of the active and contemplative lives, for humanism accorded one type of worth to an active and useful life in the world (even riches were deemed to have a social and civic utility), whereas a life of contemplation (whether literary, monastic, or other) was granted a different sort of recognition. It is now clear that the early humanists, in Florence especially, sought to strike a fruitful balance between the two—

how else to explain their preoccupation with history, political and military, and with the biographies of worthies who had devoted their lives to worldly action? In the second half of the fifteenth century, however, emphasis on the active life suffered a setback and the *vita contemplativa* gained greater worth and importance. This shifting stress was a response to the tightening political and social situation in the Italian cities. The narrowing oligarchy made political discussion increasingly difficult, a situation which could not fail to blunt the probing quality of historical reflection. But the intellectual climate was suddenly changed again just before 1500, with the revitalization of the Florentine Republic and the military and political challenges from abroad which supremely tested the Republic of Venice, its ruling class, and its intelligentsia.[3]

The Literary Mainstream

The beginnings of a national literature are likely to be tentative and crude. In Italy the urban setting, rich in possibility, hastened the process of adaptation and refinement. The first noteworthy poets issued from Bologna, Florence, Lucca, Arezzo, Genoa, and Siena. Having no native vernacular precedents, they drew their inspiration from the courtly love verse of Provence and Sicily, and a few even composed in Provençal. But with Guittone of Arezzo (c. 1235–1294) and Cecco Angiolieri of Siena (c. 1260–c. 1312), the image of the city, a marked urban flavor, and a sharper, more flexible vernacular are already evident.

Dante Alighieri (1265–1321), possibly the greatest of all the peninsula's poets, sets an incredible standard for the beginnings of Italian poetry, for he is surpassing in his ease with language, the power of his imagery, his moral and intellectual passion, and the astonishing range of his imagination. Born into the lesser Florentine nobility, his education provided him with the flower of late medieval thought and Aristotelian scholasticism. Like most citizens of his class, he felt the need to plunge into civic and political affairs, and in 1300 he served a term in Florence's chief executive body. Late in 1301, his political faction overwhelmed by a sudden reversal, he was banished from the city and spent the rest of his days in exile, wandering through central and upper Italy but settling for a time in the Casentino, Forli, Verona, and Ravenna. The *Divine Comedy*—labeled "divine" by posterity—is the epic representation of his pilgrimage through hell, purgatory, and paradise. His major guides are Virgil and a young Florentine lady, Beatrice, the chaste and secret love of his youth. The poem lends itself to different critical approaches. At the literal level there is the action or pilgrimage. But at the symbolic and moral levels

---

[3] The outcome may be followed in W. J. Bouwsma, *Venice and the Defense of Republican Liberty* (Berkeley and Los Angeles: University of California Press, 1968).

the movement of the poem traces Dante's journey from confusion to clarity, darkness to light, sin to redemption, terror to beatitude. Memorable above all—above even the stupendous geography of the poem—are his brief conversations with the souls of the damned in hell, with those learning from their grief in purgatory, and with the saved in heaven. In the first two parts of the poem each sinner suffers a punishment which symbolically re-enacts, or is in close keeping with, the besetting sin. The movement and events in paradise bring out the range of the poet's theological learning.

Dante was not modest: he imagined himself in the company of Homer, Virgil, and Ovid (*Inferno*, IV, 35). He came as close as any poet has to "creating" a language, and produced the first sustained work of the Italian literary imagination. Much of the focus in the *Commedia* is intensely personal, which accords with the then-emerging interest in secular biography. But the finished poetic vision is impersonal. Dante works his experience into a distinct tradition of feeling and thought, an objective or social mode which satisfies his personal desire as well as a civic or social urge. In the commitment to poetry which enabled him to labor at the *Commedia* for years, we see a man who will have much in common with the artists of the High Renaissance. In this respect, as Burckhardt asserted, "Dante is the first artist in the full sense of the word."

No less addicted in this way was Dante's successor, Francesco Petrarch, whom we have briefly mentioned above. A professional writer, Petrarch is considered by many the first modern man of letters. His sonnets perfect the tradition of love poetry and may be deemed the fountainhead for the European lyric. Determined to win fame with his epic, *Africa,* and other Latin works, he pretended in later life to scoff at his 366 Italian lyrics; but he continued to polish them until his death and it is they, not the *Africa,* which secure his place in the front rank of European poets. Most of the poems concern the gentle Laura, a French lady first seen in a church. They spring from the tradition of chivalrous love, but its stylization has been shed: the lady is less unreal, the expressiveness and feeling more natural and mobile, the language more efficacious, and the confessional aspects very much more marked. Desire, hope, melancholy, loss, and frustration are sharply conveyed. It is the strong confessional strain in these poems and, indeed, in much of his literary output that reveals Petrarch as a Renaissance figure; this and his self-doubts, his self-torments, his constant need to scrutinize his motives, and his anxious determination to give his moods an articulated and polished form—that is to say, a "public" or publishable form. His longing for solitude, piety, and salvation was constantly at loggerheads with his urbanity and his hankering for the limelight and for fame and worldly pleasure.

The performances of Dante and Petrarch possessed a universal quality inherent in their vision—in their handling of the themes of sin and redemption, love, desire and loss. Their more prosaic contemporaries, the chroniclers and storywriters, were more bound to a particular time and place. This is true even of the best chroniclers, the Florentines Dino Compagni (c. 1255–1324) and Giovanni Villani (c. 1276–1348). But taken in the European context of fourteenth and fifteenth-century historical literature, they stand out in high relief. Their perception of secular causal relations is clear, and so their grasp of political and social events is firm. They have a sense of impersonal tensions and a lively awareness of change. Villani displays an interest in statistical data. They keep an eye not only on Florence but also on related events elsewhere in Italy and even abroad. Their diction and periods are accordingly sharp, varied, vigorous, and flexible. Compagni also achieves psychological nuance and color. And rarely absent is the practical eye of the astute burgher: a man riddled with pieties superficial and profound, but never in such a way that he loses sight of his material good. The language of Compagni and Villani reflects the nervous life of Florentine streets, the idiom of hustle and bustle, of shrewd negotiating, of canny giving and fast taking. It also displays the unction of a usage infused with moral and religious phraseology.

With Giovanni Boccaccio (1313–1375), the great storywriter of this period, we are of course on a different scale. Born in or near Florence, the illegitimate son of a rich and traveled merchant, Boccaccio was first apprenticed to a businessman in Naples and later made to study canon law. He then foiled all his father's designs and took up letters. His early works are romances in prose and poetry which draw upon myth and allegory. Boccaccio composed the hundred tales of the *Decameron,* his most celebrated work, sometime after the Black Plague of 1348. Narrated by the imaginary members of a gay company assembled near Florence, the stories are a composite of reality, fiction, and oral tradition, some drawn from such distant countries as Persia and China. We journey through the range of dramatic situations: comic and tragic, elegant and rustic, moving and utterly cynical. Love and lust, avarice and vanity, folly, tenacity and chicanery are much in evidence; so are the force, earthiness, clarity, and mobile stress of Boccaccio's language and style. Behind this romancer and raconteur there extends a tradition both oral and written, but his achievement would be inconceivable without the talent to seize upon the language, wit, and versatility of Florence and of the urban–courtly environment in Naples, where Boccaccio lived for at least ten years.

For nearly a century after Boccaccio's death militant humanism set the tone of the intellectual and literary life of Italy, with the result that the vernacular tradition suffered neglect, although three or four humanists produced a few works in Italian.

The later fifteenth century brought a triumphant return of the literary muse and Florence again dominated the opening phase. All eyes turned first to Lorenzo de' Medici "the Magnificent" (1449–1492), the veiled and unofficial lord of the city from about 1470 on. His youthful verse spans the range of feeling from austere spiritual hymns of praise to lubricious carnival songs. He is most effective in his satirical and pleasure-loving vein: in his pictures of Florentine tipplers (*I Beoni*) and hunting with falcons (*Caccia col Falcone*), his bantering view of love between rustics (*La Nencia*), and his emphasis on sexual delight (as in the carnival songs). His language is fresh and colorful, his vision capable of sharp modulation from gay to stern.

The humanist Angelo Poliziano, one of Lorenzo's circle, was perhaps the best lyric poet of his age. His masterpiece, *Stanzas for the Tournament,* shows a striking delicacy of touch, description, and mood. The unfinished poem—whose themes are youth, beauty, and love—was written in celebration of the jousting victory won by Lorenzo's brother in 1475. Poliziano may be considered (along with Pulci, discussed below) one of the first of the city's courtier-poets:

> *E tu, ben nato Laur, sotto il cui velo*
> *Fiorenza lieta in pace si riposa*
> (STANZE, *I, 4, 1–2*).

> *And you, well-born Lorenzo, under whose veil*
> *Gay Florence in peace reposes.*

He emerged, interestingly, at the very moment when the bourgeois republic was on the verge of being transformed into a Renaissance principality.

The other major poet of Lorenzo's circle, Luigi Pulci (1432–1484), was born into an ancient but impoverished Florentine family. Witty, gay, and skeptical, Pulci failed in commercial affairs and was forced to rely upon his literary talents and the patronage of the mighty. His gift for satire is well-exemplified in his mocking poem about rustic courtship, *Beca da Dicomano.* But his great celebrity depends upon the *Morgante,* a comic epic written to please Lorenzo's mother. Drawing on the popular traditions of the itinerant public singers (*cantastorie*), Pulci created a satirical version of the French romance about Roland. Morgante is a lovable giant with a great appetite for food and violence. Two other major characters are the comic Margutte, a blaspheming demi-giant, and the devil Astarotte, a kind of freethinker.

The poetry which issued from Lorenzo's circle was deeply bound up with Florentine life and particularly with the sentiments of the upper classes. These ties are reflected in its bold emphasis on physical pleasure, in an expressed fondness for rural life combined with a sardonic view of rustics, in the selective use of language which is ironically boorish, and in a gently derisive attitude towards knightly romance. Much of the circle's poetic output was pastoral in nature or has a pastoral patina. Countryfolk—the rural laboring class—are either idealized and rendered unreal or turned into coarse simpletons. Renaissance pastoral verse requires the dialectic of the city, but the relationship is one-sided: Tuscan sharecroppers wrote no verse in praise of cities.

In the late fifteenth century, southern Italy produced a pastoral poet of European rank, the learned Neapolitan nobleman Jacopo Sannazaro (1455–1530). His idyllic romance, *Arcadia,* with its wistful picture of rustic life, was immensely appealing to generations of sophisticated readers.

Poetry has a way of dominating the early phases of a literature, when its measured accents seem to draw on a greater vitality. We must take notice of three other epic poets before touching upon a few of the prose-writers.

Italy had long expressed an appetite for romantic tales about gallant and lovelorn knights. The *Song of Roland,* the rivalry between Saracen and Christian, and the Arthurian legends, borrowed from beyond the Alps, provided the stock characters and situations. In thirteenth-century cities much of the audience for these tales came from the feudal nobility in decline or the class of burghers on the ascent, those who had "made it" and who looked with admiration or longing at the proud and careless ways of the illustrious old houses. But as the tradition of knightly romance became popular, its nature and intent changed: Italian bourgeois and noblemen reared in cities pumped it full of satire, derision, and buffoonery. The majesty of Charlemagne and his paladins became plebeian roistering. We see this in Pulci's *Morgante,* and later in the *Orlando innamorato* (Roland in love) of Matteo Boiardo (1441–1494), count of Scandiano, the first memorable epic—though it is parody—to issue from the princely court of Ferrara. From Charlemagne on down, as one critic has put it, all the characters in this poem "speak and act like boors." In line, however, with the changing taste of the Italian princely courts, Boiardo already makes a distinct effort to introduce a more elevated note into his material. And this process of refinement or ennoblement will be carried on by the supreme poet of the high Renaissance, Ludovico Ariosto (1474–1533), also from the Ferrara court circle, in his *Orlando furioso* (mad Roland). Ariosto lived in a time of war, foreign invasion, and peninsular humiliation, accounting in part for the dreaminess and compensatory serenity of his epic (in which Roland's brains are whisked off to the moon). But it was also a time when nobility of blood and a strict aristocratic ideal were being taken more seriously than they had been for more than two hundred years, even in merchant cities like Florence and Lucca. With the last major poet in this line of development, the ill-starred Torquato Tasso (1544–1595), another Ferrarese courtier, the tradition reaches its noble completion. In his great epic, *Gerusalemme liberata* (Jerusalem delivered), pride and the grand gesture, decorum and high seriousness dominate. At the same time, in all the Italian cities, a courtly aristocracy had won the day both socially and politically. Only Genoa, Venice, and Lucca remained republics, but republics ruled by an inflexible and ancient patriciate.

For reasons of the sort which often elude historians, the moment was right for literary expression in the language of vernacular prose. For more than a generation after 1494, Italians suffered the shock of armed assault and humiliation, inflicted by the armies of France, Spain, and the empire. The debacle called forth a well-articulated cry of anguish (from, among others, Machiavelli and Guicciardini) and drew the Italians closer together as a linguistic nation. The definitive defense of the Tuscan tongue, Italian, came from a Venetian aristocrat and papal secretary, Pietro Bembo (1470–1547), later a cardinal, in his *Prose of the Vernacular Language* (1525). But he was only riding an irreversible wave. The most vigorous and interesting minds of the period were already committed to the vernacular. The searing and trenchant prose of the Florentine Niccolò Machiavelli (1469–1527) could have had no better medium than his own Italian. Indeed, the intellectual origins and powerful prose style of his *The Prince* (1513), a political primer of stunning insight and brilliant distortion, could only come from within the urban horizons of Italy at the beginning of the sixteenth century. The Mantuan nobleman Baldassare Castiglione's celebrated book *The Courtier* (begun in 1508), which set the social tone of the Italian ruling classes for the next two centuries, was composed in the vernacular and includes an able defense of it. And the most distinguished historian of the age, Francesco Guicciardini (1483–1540)— Florentine lawyer, aristocrat, and statesman—used Latin only for his judicial and legal opinions. The Italian of his political reflections, histories, and private diaries spans the range of stylistic requirement, from the aphorism to the sustained description and the long, ruminating period. The language of popular usage was now perfectly honed for the elegance of the courtier or the verve and scurrility of the first journalist, Pietro Aretino (1492–1556).

The Artistic Mainstream

The image of the city haunts Italian painting of the fourteenth and fifteenth centuries. Yet this is merely its superficial imprint. More profound were the effects of the city—the effects of particular urban values—on the nature and aims of art.

Looking back to the beginnings of their artistic period, fifteenth-century observers had already defined the decade right around 1300 as its starting point. Before that time Italian painting had been dominated by the so-called "Greek manner" (that is, the Byzantine style). This art was highly symbolic, hieratic, and stylized: an art in whose Italian expression the well-defined forms were stiff, the picture space flat rather than three-dimensional, and the human figure a spiritual presence more than a worldly embodiment.

The new art, that of Giotto (1266–1337) and his successors, marked a radical departure. And the adventure of Italian painting for the next two centuries was to be in the search for space and for "real" forms and atmosphere. It was to be a search for the objective, contrasting proportions among forms represented in the picture space; a search for the laws of perspective, for an understanding of human anatomy, for individual features (as in the portrait), and for action, gesture, and dramatic tension. All in all, it was a search for more realistic, earthly representations.

Why major cities like Milan and Venice lagged behind Florence and Siena in the development of a new artistic style is not at all clear. The obvious and standard explanation, which concentrates on the dominant artistic personalities, cannot throw light on this question, for what we want to know is why those personalities consistently appeared in some cities and not in others, and why the disparity persisted for about two hundred years.

It must suffice to point out that variations in values—moral, mercantile, and social—were marked enough among the cities of Italy to result in somewhat different artistic styles. These in due time had an effect upon artistic values. Up to about 1280 or 1290, generally speaking, Italian painting had a more or less uniform style in the Greek manner. Thereafter local and regional differences emerged sharply enough to disrupt the tradition and alter the direction of style. For example, political activity and high social position were much more accessible to new men in Florence than in Milan or Venice, and this had a direct bearing upon Florentine cultural values. Throughout the fourteenth and fifteenth centuries, Florentines consistently exhibited a greater inclination toward exploratory and innovative attitudes.

The first notable painter in the new style was the Florentine Giotto, who startled and delighted contemporaries with his ability to depict living forms. He worked in Rome, Florence, Assisi, Padua, and Naples. The cycle of frescoes in the Scrovegni chapel at Padua (1303–1305), illustrating scenes from the lives of Christ and the Virgin, show Giotto in the fullness of his powers. Well-rounded, firmly-planted, and usually caught in mid-action, his human forms, it was said at the time, lacked only the ability to speak. Contemporaries were accustomed, after all, to the more two-dimensional representations of the Italian Byzantine style. Giotto won immediate fame and a place in Dante's *Divine Comedy* (*Purg.* XI, 95). We may assume that Florentine and other burghers liked to see images and details of everyday life in the painting of the period, and no one reproduced these more effectively than Giotto.

At Siena the departure from the older manner was equally marked but different. There the new direction issued in a greater fluidity for the human form, a curvilinear style with its own resources for dramatic tension and a rich, symbolic use of color. Duccio (c. 1250–1319) and Simone Martini (1284–1344) are the finest practitioners of this art. We have outstanding samples of their work in Duccio's narrative of the *Life of Christ* (some forty-odd panels housed in Siena) and Simone's *Annunciation* in Florence. On the whole they did not, like Giotto and his most able successors, strive to reproduce the forms and space of the everyday world. Instead, they sought to express the essential meaning of Christian events by means of sheer visual lyricism. And this intention, with its persistent preference for linear elegance, lyrical color, and an undertone of preciosity, remained fundamental to Sienese painting down to the middle of the fifteenth century. Sienese taste was governed by values which were neither as utilitarian nor as rational and absorbed in the world as was the case in Florence.

Perhaps, as one art historian has suggested,[4] the undulant and more accessible forms of Sienese (and, indeed, of late Gothic) painting had a particular appeal for a certain kind of taste. I mean the taste which derived as much from the rather closed world of the Sienese shopkeeper, who could easily grasp

[4] F. Antal, *Florentine Painting and its Social Background* (London, 1948).

the pretty, ornamental forms of the style, as from that of the custom-bound Sienese nobleman, who was always attracted by the courtly aspects of the style. The latter looked to his farms, falconing and, in society, to his political bloc of noblemen. But neither small shopkeeper nor nobleman was likely to develop a bold or innovative view of the world. In Siena both these types enjoyed a political and social preeminence denied to their counterparts in Florence, where instead the big enterprising merchant prevailed over political and social affairs.

In response to Giotto and his successors, even Florence saw the emergence or reaffirmation of countervailing values which hindered the development of the new style. As an expression of historical thinking, it is defective (though routine) to say that the second half of the fourteenth century produced no artists the equal of Giotto. This is true, in a sense, but excessively literal-minded. More sophisticated analysis might have it that the second half of the century brought a conservative or regressive reassertion of taste and values. The result was that painters found it easier for a time to think of the picture space as a setting for stiffer, more hieratic forms. And outside Siena, this meant working in a manner whose resources had been so well used as to result in academic effects, at least until the new style had been more fully developed and could thus make possible additional alternatives.

In the third decade of the fifteenth century, a group of Florentines took the prevailing artistic style—now fused with the undulant elegance of International Gothic—and wrenched it from its retardant moorings. They set a new course. Four major artists and a theoretician brought about this redirection: Brunelleschi, Donatello, Masaccio, Ghiberti, and the humanist Alberti. In the preface to his revolutionary treatise *On Painting* (1435), Alberti pays tribute to the four artists.

Masaccio (1401–1428) may be thought of as the most daring and exciting painter of the fifteenth century. His frescoes in Florence, the famous *Tribute Money* (1427) in the Carmelite church and the *Trinity* (1426) in the church of Santa Maria Novella, provide the stupendous measure of his achievement. They display a mastery, laconic but absolute, of all the science that will go to complete the new art. This meant a system of focused perspective, a steady control over the distribution of masses in space, a keen attentiveness to the problems of light and radical foreshortening, an understanding of human anatomy, the ability to render individual human features (there is a self-portrait in the *Tribute Money*), a self-conscious use of classical Roman motifs, and a manifest grasp of naturalistic detail.

Painting was not the same after Masaccio: his audacity and perceptions brought the accomplished visual act into line with the vanguard of urban experience. One of the street scenes in his Carmelite cycle, depicting St. Peter and the cripple, shows us a fragment of Florence as it was in the 1420s, but it is a photographic image transformed by the lyricism and melancholy of the artist's slow *tempi*.

The history of Italian painting in the century after Masaccio does not lend itself to an easy summary or facile cataloguing. Cities and princely courts chose what they wanted from the new style and, of course, adapted the choice to local taste. But even outstanding "conservatives" like Fra Angelico (1387–1455) drew upon such innovations as foreshortening, although their subject matter might be entirely religious and their treatment rely heavily upon the symbolic use of color. At the same time a "radical" like Paolo Uccello (1397–1475), while addicted to the new system of focused perspective, remained attached to the linear graces of Gothic and to the pretty heads of the same style.

Perhaps we can say that in the century after Masaccio's death many painters of the first rank tended to narrow their scope, and thereby achieved a certain degree of specialization. With some, like Michelangelo, human anatomy and dramatic tension came to be the central preoccupation; with others, again, it was the play of light and shadow, foreshortening, the individual portrait, or (as with the chroniclers) the group portrait; and with still others it was the problem of atmospheric perspective. Most often, to be sure, two or three of these interests were fused, as in the art of Piero della Francesca and Leonardo da Vinci. On the whole, however, there was no way of ignoring the taste or needs of those who commissioned works of art—the class of patrons. Accordingly, as the principles of anatomy, foreshortening, and illumination were mastered, they were swiftly converted to use in portrait and group painting. Patrons wanted pictures of themselves, their families, and their worldly surroundings. Thus the great popularity of such painting in the period which saw the gradual perfection of the necessary techniques, a popularity characteristic not only of court circles but also of the rich and well-born of the republican oligarchies, Florence and Venice. Thus also, around 1500 and after, the taste for country scenes, for dreamy representations of rustic life (often in backgrounds)—for, in brief, the idealized opposite of the life-style indigenous to cities. And thus the passion for the nude, in painting as well as sculpture, which gave expression to the emphasis on earthly man: on the goods and pleasures of the civilized world of the city and court.

Three artists stand at the forefront of achievement in the century after Masaccio: Leonardo da Vinci (1452–1519), Michelangelo (1475–1564), and Raphael (1483–1520).

Born near Florence but trained in one of the city's best workshops, Leonardo established his mastery as a painter by about 1475. Later he moved on to the court of Milan and worked there for many years, then back to Florence, Milan again, Rome, and finally to Amboise in France (1516–19). He is justly as celebrated for his anatomical drawings, ruminations on nature, machine designs, and experiments (illustrated in his notebooks), as for his few surviving paintings. Driven by an overwhelming urge to understand the workings of nature, Leonardo concluded that the art of painting is the supreme expression of this knowledge: the art whereby men catch the multifarious effects of light, the nature of movement and of tensile action, and even—as in the portrait—"the motions of the mind." His fading *Adoration of the Kings*

(Florence), the *Virgin of the Rocks* (Paris), and two famous portraits attest conclusively to his conception of the painter's high office.

Michelangelo's lifelong preoccupation was exploration of the artistic possibilities of the human body. We know little about his apprenticeship, save that he was trained in Florence, for some years at least in the workshop of a quite competent artist of the second rank, Ghirlandaio. But his main inspiration derived from antiquity and from the sculptor Donatello. Michelangelo's talent was such that only princes and oligarchies could truly draw upon it, for his best work was done on a gigantic (and expensive) scale—the Sistine chapel, the tomb of Julius II, the Medici chapel. Only mammoth proportions satisfied his genius. No man ever feared size less. The frescoes of the Sistine ceiling, executed during his most productive years as a painter (1508–12), exhibit his grand manner in the glories and miseries of the human body. An unquiet spirit, he was tormented by his own artistic certitudes as well as by his vision of man's mixed destiny.

The genius of Raphael lay in his ability to learn from the major artists of his time and to make that learning an organic part of his vision. Born of a painter in the signorial town of Urbino and reared in the artistic ways of its illustrious court, he was invited to Rome at the age of twenty-five. There his new manner soon became synonymous with the classical style, which is to say that he achieved a magisterial blending of rational control and feeling. Balance, harmony, serenity and clarity are the stuff of his compositions. This is true not only of his smaller works, especially his gentle representations of the Virgin, but also of his major frescoes, for example his *School of Athens* (c. 1510) in the Vatican. Like Michelangelo, Raphael also produced his best work on commission from popes, princes, or bankers like his friend Agostino Chigi of Siena.

In the fifteenth and early sixteenth centuries, sculpture had considerable influence on painting. A number of leading artists, including Verrocchio and Michelangelo, did both with equal facility and brilliance. In a Renaissance workshop, apprentices might be trained to work as goldsmiths, decorators, sculptors, painters, and architects; and many of the best-known artists, from Giotto to Raphael and Michelangelo, were associated for years with major architectural undertakings.

One Florentine master dominates fifteenth-century sculpture by his power, expressiveness, and innovative eye—Donatello (1386–1466). His bronze *David* (Florence) was the first free-standing nude cast since classical times, and his equestrian statue of the soldier of fortune *Gattamelata* (Padua), modelled on the Marcus Aurelius in Rome, was the first monumental work of the period. In about 1415 he began to veer away from the undulant graces and pretty calligraphy of the International Gothic style. The next fifteen years saw him break through to a bolder, more austere manner in which the figure rests naturally on its own weight and draperies hang in accordance with gravity. His amazing series of narrative reliefs, located in Florence and Padua, show a startling grasp of perspective and of complex architectural masses and space (the city again!). There is a driving rationalism in his mature style, the style of hard-headed rather than sentimental Florence, but it is continually disrupted by the thrust of passion or immanent tensile values. Of affectation Donatello had none, neither in his work nor in his personal life. Like nearly all his contemporaries, he conceived of sculpture as public art, an art addressed to the viewer and embodying the social and public dimension of life. His creations were meant to be seen in public places—in squares, in outside niches, or in churches. No portrait busts are credited to him. He worked mainly for merchant guilds, churches, city governments, and rich citizens and statesmen.

The next sculptor to obsess and upset his contemporaries was, of course, Michelangelo, whose giants in marble enact the human drama through a display of tensile nerves, expression, gesture, and a kind of muscular explosiveness. The body was not given its due until Donatello and Michelangelo celebrated it as both man's attendant glory and his trap.

In the course of the fifteenth century, as sculpture was freed from its subordination to building masses such as churches and guild halls, architecture also took a new turn. Large townhouses and country villas began to lose their rough-and-tumble functionality: they received more thorough planning, and became more decorative and graceful (especially in Florence and Venice), developing into imposing testaments to authority and social position. Architects like Filippo Brunelleschi (1377–1446) and L. B. Alberti (1404–1472) made a scrupulous study of antique architecture. Much more fully and profoundly than others before them, they developed a view of architecture as an independent and noble pursuit, and so came to think in terms of fully-articulated structures. Brunelleschi, for example, not only solved the Renaissance problem of constructing huge domes but also sought effects which were calculated to the last detail. The architect was now gradually distinguishing himself from the master stonemason of the Middle Ages, and becoming a central planner and visionary, who could compose a whole city as well as a single building. A decisive rationalism—whose emblems were the circle, the cube, the easy-to-balance classical motif, a strict sense of ratio and proportion—became fundamental to architectural design. With such architects of the early and High Renaissance as Brunelleschi and Bramante (1444–1514), we see the end not of piecemeal building but of piecemeal planning, save where the architect was invited to finish an unfinished edifice. Particularly memorable as examples of rational central planning are Brunelleschi's Pazzi chapel in Florence (1429–46) and Bramante's *Tempietto* (little temple) in Rome (1502).

Science and Manual Labor

Science is not an absolute; like art and politics, it reflects the times, and changes with them. To claim that a twentieth-century method or a seventeenth-century attitude alone is or results in science may satisfy philosophical requirements; it cannot satisfy the historian, whose province is the broad path of change. When at last the method of science is all but completely computerized, we will not call the science of the first half of the twentieth century pre-scientific.

The old critics of Burckhardt's conception of the Renaissance found particular fault with his treatment of science in fifteenth-century Italy. What they really demanded was a survey of the names and accomplishments of individual scientists. We may reply that historians do not recognize or identify historical moments by counting noses alone. If it is true that before the seventeenth century there was no scientific method (that amalgam of logical procedure, experimentation, and mathematics), it is also undeniable that a specific sequence of changes prepared the way for the attitudes which issued in the scientific triumphs of the sixteenth and seventeenth centuries. From this viewpoint, the origins of modern science are seen to be inextricably bound up with the rise of cities from the twelfth century onwards.

To the medieval mind, the condition of manual labor was a sign of social inferiority. Imperial Rome with its widespread reliance upon slavery, played a part in creating this attitude. And Christianity, which had sought in Jesus to lend a certain dignity to labor, was sometimes used instead to cast a stain on it or, at any rate, to place it in a lowly light. Thus it was said that physical labor—the labor of the serf and lowly artisan—was no more than the mark of our fallen condition, the fruit of Adam's sin, the penance some must do, and so forth. It was associated with servitude.[5] The social structure of feudalism thereby benefitted.

The medieval workshop was assigned a lowly place in the hierarchy of social values. Even the rise of the city, with its multitudinous trades, did not easily change this ingrained prejudice. Something of the old feeling has persisted down to the twentieth century.

The medieval surgeon, who had no university education and was matriculated in the barbers' guild, cut bodies and amputated limbs, whereas the physician, turned out by the medical schools, would not deign to dirty his hands with such activity. How could this neat distinction between physical and intellectual labor fail to affect the status of experimentation and observation?

This question was to have a special bearing upon the medieval workshop. For, with the increasing laicization of society, in the period from the thirteenth to the fifteenth centuries, the artist was able, owing to the kinds of demands made upon him by the laity, to shed the stigma associated with manual labor, to rise socially, and to realize a new worth in the eyes of his social superiors. The struggle for the dignity of the artist was not finally won, however, until the early sixteenth century. Until then the old prejudices persisted. Brunelleschi, born into an old Florentine family, appalled his parents when he decided to enter an artist's workshop as an apprentice. Donatello refused to wear a

[5] Labor evidently took on a different face when done in monasteries by the rich or well-born for the good of their souls.

rich red cloak and mantle, a gift from Cosimo de' Medici, because they were "too fine" for him. In his treatise on architecture (post 1450), Alberti tries to establish the architect's intellectuality and thus his essential difference from the master stonemason.[6] And Leonardo da Vinci, in the early sixteenth century, still felt the need to argue that painting is nobler than sculpture because it is tidier, more intellectual, and therefore more suitable for gentlemen.

As a result of the secular demands of upper-class urban society, the excitement of artistic work and its new worldly renown, the social ascent of artists in the fifteenth century put them into constant personal touch with the class of patrons. This social proximity brought the nature and problems of the workshop to the sympathetic attention of princes, statesmen, noblemen, merchants, and humanist intellectuals. Gradually the workshop began to seem less ignoble, and a certain kind of manual labor, or dexterity, came to be closely associated with "the motions of the mind." There was give-and-take: the artist took from the humanist and from the experience of patrons, and could more easily draw upon a way of seeing which derived from the spreading fascination with antiquity; while the patron and intellectual developed a greater respect for the obstinate or challenging materials and problems to be found in the workshop. This traffic—particularly where leavened by an advanced urban economy—was fundamental to the origins of modern science: it presupposed an emphasis on the worth of operations involving manufactured or marketable goods. Emphasis also fell, accordingly, on the sources of productive power and on methods of transportation.

In the first stage of this intercourse, the artists of the vanguard became seriously interested in mathematics and optics, in an attempt to grasp the secrets of perspective and perspectival construction. Artists such as Brunelleschi, Ghiberti, Paolo Uccello, Paolo della Francesca, Francesco di Giorgio, and Leonardo frequented university men like L. B. Alberti and Paolo Toscanelli. In the second stage, gentlemen and theoreticians (e.g. Alberti, Toscanelli, Berengario da Carpi, Girolamo Fracastoro, Niccolò Tartaglia, Girolamo Cardano, and numerous lesser figures) passionately interested themselves in direct observation and in the problems associated with workshops, mechanics, navigational instruments, geography, medicine, anatomy, and botany. An aspect of this second stage was the founding of learned and scientific societies, as in Florence and Venice, which tended to draw their membership from the upper classes. The great shipyard in Venice, the old *arsenale*, became an object of scientific and technological interest for the first time.

The technological changes of the thirteenth and fourteenth centuries had already left their imprint on the imagination: changes involving mainly the harnessing of water power, the dramatic success of windmills, the invention of the crank, and the elaboration of great mechanical clocks. At the forefront of this line of change were the Italian, German, and Flemish cities, which

---

[6] Though in some circles during the medieval period the architect was highly ranked in theory, practice was another matter.

produced the decisive psychological and intellectual climate. They necessarily valued the physical operations involved in commerce, transportation, and manufacture. Men begin to tinker seriously with the idea of perpetual motion. In the third quarter of the fourteenth century, Nicholas Oresmus, mathematician and Bishop of Lisieux, already used a metaphor positing "the universe as a vast mechanical clock created and set running by God so that 'all the wheels move as harmoniously as possible.' "[7]

The difficult and gradual convergence of intellectual and manual activity, of trained reflection and direct observation, began to issue in a view of the physical universe as a system or construction which might be subject to mathematical regularities. The leading artists of the fifteenth century turned to mathematical perspective not only to produce accurate reflections of the world on flat surfaces but also to get at its proportions and harmonies. Some artists visualized the human body in terms of fixed proportions; others conceived of architectural design in terms of the symmetries of the body, which in some fashion, the dominant current of opinion had it, reflected the image of God. A strong interest in mathematics—and astrology—was also a feature of Italian Platonist thought during the later fifteenth century, especially, paradoxically enough, in its more mystic strain. Here the Hermetic writings on magic, religious cosmology, and astrology assume a prime importance. Influenced by those writings, the greatest of the Neoplatonists, Marsilio Ficino (1433–1499) and Pico della Mirandola (1463–1494), sought cosmic and worldly regularities and, indeed, came to believe in the possibility of man's harnessing the knowledge of these regularities for his own ends. A century later, "Kepler still saw his new astronomy in a context of harmonies, and he was well aware that the Pythagorean theory was also implicit in the Hermetic writings, of which he had made a careful study."[8]

We may sum up the preceding observations by noting that when the perspective and problems of the workshop were joined with the intellectual quest for mathematical regularity in the cosmos, the method of modern science was born. Toward the end of his *Discourse on Method* (1637), Descartes coolly expresses the attitude behind this merger: "By knowing the force and actions of fire, water, air, the stars, the heavens and all the other bodies around us— by knowing them as we know the various crafts of the artisans—we may be able to apply them, in the same manner, to every use befitting them, and thus make ourselves masters of nature and possessors of it."

But in Italy, long before the time of Descartes, a number of "gentlemen and theoreticians," as I have called them, had already set about trying to get things right. Their achievement was far from mean. The Paduan physician Giovanni Michele Savonarola, who flourished in the first half of the fifteenth century, published a general medical treatise which emphasizes the "description of cases," thereby opposing "the clinical spirit" to the practice of "ratio-

[7] Lynn White, Jr., *Medieval Technology and Social Change* (New York, 1966), p. 125.
[8] F. A. Yates, *Giordano Bruno and the Hermetic Tradition* (London, 1964), p. 151.

cinative medicine" (Sarton). Paolo Toscanelli (1397–1482)—a Florentine mathematician, cartographer, and physician—arrived at strikingly accurate computations for the comet of 1460 and left a famous letter and map (transcribed by Columbus), designating a sea route to the East by way of the West. In 1527 the renowned surgeon Berengario da Carpi (c. 1470–1550), abandoned the university chair he had held for twenty-five years to return to private practice. An extraordinarily able dissector, he published a classic treatise on skull fractures (*De fractura calvariae seu cranii*), successfully applied mercury to the cure of syphilis, and made important new discoveries concerning the heart, the brain, and the uterus. Girolamo Fracastoro of Verona (1478–1553), in a treatise on contagion (1546), seems to have been the first to hold that infection is caused by the transmission of tiny, self-multiplying bodies. A celebrated mathematician from the city of Brescia, Niccolò Tartaglia (d. 1557), was one of the four contemporaries—along with Cardano, L. Ferrari, and Dal Ferro—to make a critical contribution to the algebraic resolution of quadratic equations. His *Nova scientia* (1537) develops, *inter alia,* the fundamental theory of projectiles and is the first work to apply geometry to the science of projectile movement. Tartaglia's equally eminent contemporary, Girolamo Cardano (1501–1576), advanced a complete general theory and the basic formula for solving quadratic equations. Also a physician and natural philosopher, Cardano demonstrated the impossibility of perpetual motion.

So much, then, for the direction and a few of the highlights of scientific activity in the Italian cities of the fifteenth and early sixteenth centuries.

Political and Historical Thought

Just as the way we think about politics in the twentieth century has its origins in Renaissance Italy, so too does modern historical thought. And the two areas are discussed jointly here because, as we shall see, they developed together, very nearly as the result of a single process of the mind.

In 1420, Florentine ambassadors to the duke of Milan reported that one of his leading advisors had spurned their request for arbitration of Florentine–Milanese differences with the assertion that "Right is in the force of arms."[9] The ambassadors reacted with astonishment and dismay.

The episode raises an essential question: how is it that men are able to conduct politics on the basis of force or practical considerations and at the same time engage in formal political discussion predicated chiefly on strict moral views? For Florentines knew that the armies of Milan were uppermost in the scramble for influence. They knew that arms had shaped Italian regional politics for generations. In the 1370s, in illustration of this, Florence had gone

[9] Lauro Martines, *Lawyers and Statecraft in Renaissance Florence* (Princeton, 1968), p. 380.

to war with the papacy. In 1406, to secure their coastal flank, or so they said, Florentines had taken Pisa by force of arms. And they knew that for two hundred years and more the larger cities and communes had systematically subjected their lesser neighbors by pursing a policy of smash and grab.

Were the Florentine ambassadors honestly disturbed by the exchange? Yes, and there are two ways to explain their reaction. 1) The assertion of the Milanese statesman was an acknowledgement of the way men acted; it was not something they ever admitted in diplomacy. Common parlance itself could deal with political reality only by distorting it: that is, by putting it in the most brutal terms, as in the Milanese assertion that might makes right. Ordinary speech thus had failed here, for even at its worst politics is seldom so clear and simple. 2) The accepted language of political discourse did not admit of force as a useful or just or standard element in politics. The right of self-defense, or the armed claim to an established right, was not seen in terms of a vocabulary of force. Civil, natural, or divine law provided the rationale.

Until the end of the fifteenth century, the analysis of politics was couched in theological, moral, and legal terminology. On the whole it was theoretical. Reflections upon government or politics put the fundamental emphasis on notions of sovereignty, unity, essential hierarchies, or on abstractions drawn from divine, natural, and Roman law. In informal discussion about urban politics, factions, and political violence, men pointed to good and bad behavior, envy and pride, ambition and spite, virtue and vice. Marsilius of Padua, the only major thinker to introduce a revolutionary note into political reflection (by stressing the principles of consent and representation in his *Defensor Pacis,* 1324), was quite simply not read. From Dante in the fourteenth century to L. B. Alberti in the fifteenth, nearly all writers, when touching upon the nature of politics, used the occasion to launch into moral or philosophical speculation. The best legal mind of the fourteenth century, Bartolus (d. 1357), produced a brilliant analysis of tyranny—in the form, however, of a technical legal treatise intended for lawyers.

In political thinking, as in the understanding of what history is, the first notable changes—and then the first breakthrough—took place in Florence. The other leading center of intellectual activity in this sphere, Venice, made no substantial contributions until the sixteenth century, and then only in an atmosphere of crisis: under the impact of war, foreign invasion, and a prolonged and painful papal interdict. Significantly, no city-state under established princely rule (e.g., Milan, Rome, or Naples) produced a school of political or historical thought which redirected established ways of thinking. This achievement must be credited to the republican city-states of Florence and Venice.

Florence led the way, owing to her particular social and political conditions. Most other cities had long since buckled under the sway of princes and despots, and Venice had been under strict aristocratic rule ever since the opening years of the fourteenth century, but the situation in Florence, while also narrowing considerably, remained "open" enough to allow some of the lesser families and some new voices into its political–social establishment. Moreover, down to about 1475 or 1480 the power of the Medici family was far from absolute. Though increasingly dispersed or blunted, something of the active civic traditions of the upper classes persisted. Then, in 1494, with the expulsion of the Medici from Florence, the city was suddenly plunged into a ferment of intense republicanism. For the next eighteen years, and again in the late 1520s, the Florentine republican cause was confronted by two grave threats: those of strict oligarchy, favored by a group of leading aristocrats, and of absolute princely rule, guaranteed to follow in the wake of any restoration of the Medici.

In this context of conflicting ideologies and psychological strain, Florentines were driven to re-examine their political and historical premises. From this re-examination there arose a new mode of analysis.

The manner and content of Florentine political discussion began to change in the late fifteenth century, with a dim realization, soon to be made fully explicit, that politics occupies, or can be seen to occupy, an autonomous sphere. This insight—though it developed unobtrusively and men had often previously seemed to be on the verge of it—was swiftly turned into the finest cutting-edge in political discourse. Hitherto, as I have said, political reasoning had been weighted with a ballast of preconceptions derived from conventional morality, theology, and medieval ideas of natural law. Henceforth, leading thinkers would conduct the analysis of politics according to suppositions drawn more-or-less directly from practical political experience. Hitherto men had been unable to see the play of necessity and amorality in their political behavior. Henceforth, stepping closer to politics itself, they began to recognize judgments, passions and interests that had little or nothing to do with conventional moral norms.

The official record of consultations (the *Consulte e Pratiche*) held by the Florentine government charts the awakening sense of the autonomy of politics. In the period around 1500, the record comprises the minutes of many hundreds of individual speeches and shorter comments. Although only a minority of speakers bore witness to the new direction of thought, their way of looking at politics eventually prevailed. In addition to the preponderant traditional opinions, the record contains a vision of politics which emphasizes the instrumental uses of reason (i.e., calculation), the indispensability of experience, and the criterion of rational efficiency in the performance of political tasks. Two other factors are also given weight: *fortuna* and necessity, the former representing nonrational forces and their interference in human affairs, the latter designating circumstances that admit of no political alternative. Thus, the new elements that came to be stressed were calculation, experience, rational efficiency, *fortuna*, and necessity. To this range of values the second decade of the sixteenth century added yet another: the candid acknowledgment of force as a decisive factor in politics and history.

The new view of politics emerged piecemeal. In the years around 1500 no one man had more than a partial or fleeting vision of the new path. The act of drawing the fragmentary insights together into a new synthesis was to be the achievement of Niccolò Machiavelli (1469–1527).

Machiavelli was born to the most humble branch of an old Florentine family. His father was a learned and unsuccessful lawyer. Sent to private school-teachers as a boy, Machiavelli received the rudiments of a humanistic education. We know nothing about his intended career—possibly it was even business—save that he managed to secure a leading post in the Florentine chancellery, doubtless with the help of a highly-placed person, in the closing years of the century. For the next fourteen years, Machiavelli was able, as secretary to the republic's powerful magistracy in charge of war, to observe political behavior and high policy at very close quarters. Giving himself utterly to politics, he met many of the leading political personalities of the age and on a number of occasions was himself dispatched as a diplomatic envoy. His political career came to a sudden and brutal end in 1512 when, with the return of the Medici and defeat of the republicans, he was stripped of office, imprisoned, tortured, and banished to the country. Cast out of politics, his true passion, he took up the next-best activity—writing about it. But he would gladly have exchanged all his writings for the real thing. During this period of enforced retirement, he produced the most celebrated of his political and historical works: *The Prince,* the *Discourses,* the *Art of War,* and the *History of Florence.*

Machiavelli's sympathies were profoundly republican. In *The Prince,* however, and on that occasion only, he treated the nature of political power in a state under the rule of one man. There he laid down the recipe for successful government of this type—a measure of his fascination with the puzzles of political power, even in its despotic or monarchical forms. There too, as in his other major political work, the *Discourses,* the unifying theme was the pivotal importance of force in politics.

Machiavelli's political writings exhibit a characteristic approach and a recurrent cluster of ideas. He takes for granted that a whole field of experience is distinctively political, and claims this as his province. His procedure is boldly rationalistic: it treats the challenge of power in terms of means and ends. Taken in its particular context, the end determines the manner and timing of the means. Immediate and long-term ends are given their due, and long-term ends are clearly perceived. In his own analyses as well as in his recommendations, Machiavelli stresses the value of direct experience, observation, and learning from past example. Past example does not, however, mean past authority (e.g., Aristotle, Cicero); it means past action and successful achievement, above all that of republican Rome. He takes up specific questions—political health, republican failure, war, factionalism, leadership—only under the stimulus of immediate Florentine realities and failures; Machiavelli was not an abstract theorist and speculator. His writings are marked by a close interplay between experience and reflection, present and past, risk and reality. Although his ordinary procedure was aggressively rationalistic, he was also given—like many a leading thinker—to flashes of intuition and insight, which he then doubled back upon, considered in greater detail, and arranged into methodical steps.

Machiavelli's main preoccupation as a thinker was the challenge posed and the temptations offered by political power. For him political questions are finally decided by force. Politics has its own laws. To conduct it by any other code is to invite disaster, for power is what political men seek. Anything less than absolute commitment makes for error and defeat. Now, as politics has its own laws, the point is to look for the instructive regularities. Here Machiavelli's view of man is fundamental: men are acquisitive and self-centered, in politics supremely so. The strong body politic is one which relies astutely upon their acquisitive impulses, not for their sake but for the state's: that is to say, for the sake of those who run the state (there is some doubt here as to the state's impartiality). Rulers and ruled serve both different and the same ends, but the advantage is naturally with the rulers. Machiavelli ascribes much importance to necessity and *fortuna* in politics: these and the force of the opposition present the major obstacle to political undertakings. True leadership, however, can sometimes take advantage of necessity and *fortuna* by adapting to them in lightning-like fashion, thereby apparently turning them to its own ends. Hence the conditions of politics are not utterly hopeless even at their worst. The basis of all brilliant political leadership is *virtù,* which is also the foundation for the political health and civic spirit of dominant peoples. *Virtù* is a kind of inner force or driving energy. Often combined with a swift and penetrating intuition, it is the quality which best guarantees political success. It is, moreover, supple and keenly attuned to reality. What works today may not work tomorrow: times and circumstances change. Machiavelli's recipe for political success thus has an emphatic note of relativism. Power or force may be the supreme political factor (and prize), but the dynamic essence in his vision of politics is *virtù.*

History and historical writing were among Machiavelli's major intellectual interests. This is apparent on almost every page of his political writings. His perfect fusion of history and politics gave rise to a new genre, the *Discourses,* a combined political and historical commentary on the first ten books of Livy's history. But politics, Machiavelli's dominant passion, both produced and illuminated his great appetite for the study of history. Calling with astonishing ease and skill on the comparative method of study, he went to history for what it could tell him about political man and political problems, and about political Florence present and future. Indeed, students of Machiavelli have noted that he did not scruple to distort historical fact to strengthen arguments in support of his particular vision of politics.

At least one aspect of his achievement, however, drew upon an established tradition. The fifteenth-century humanists also studied the past for what it could tell them about the present. They looked upon history as example. For them, as for Cicero, it was "the guide of life" (*magistri vitae*). They studied the classical historians, focusing on Livy and Sallust, and they emphasized political and military matters. But they were drawn to such study by their intense attachment to their own times, as is plain from the historical works of the three major Florentine humanist historians of the fifteenth century: Leonardo Bruni, Poggio Bracciolini, and Bartolommeo Scala. The great public issues and achievements of Florence had spurred Florentines to reflect upon the city's history ever since the thirteenth century. This interest persisted vigorously and survived the destruction of the republic. In the fifteenth century, accordingly, when leading Florentine humanists, encouraged by the classics, turned their attention to history and historical writing, they had the stimulus not only of local history but also of a lively tradition of local historical writing in the form of chronicles, annals, diaries, and commentaries. Not surprisingly, they wrote histories of Florence.

But the influence of certain Roman historians on the actual writing of history remained paramount. Cicero's mark is also present. These influences are most clearly seen in the fifteenth-century historiographic practice of giving prominence to the speeches of leading public figures. In accordance with the procedure of classical historiography, these speeches were often invented, in the fashion suitable to the particular occasion, by the historian. If the aim of historical writing was to teach, to serve as a guide for the present, then the craft of the historian had a moral and rhetorical side as well, and it was no intellectual misdemeanor to concoct illustrative speeches for real historical occasions. On the contrary, historical narrative was thereby improved.

Yet to emphasize the rhetorical element in fifteenth-century humanist history is to get the focus wrong. Such emphasis reduces the achievement to a game of skill with words and noble sentiments. The fact is that the humanists revolutionized historical thinking. They imitated the classical Roman historians, but they also re-established history as a separate discipline requiring careful study and a minimum level of sophistication. They put composed speeches into the mouths of historical personages, but they also had an awakened sense of past time, of different historical periods, and of the centrality of politics and public institutions. They conceived of history moralistically, but they also rejected supernatural causation, so often adduced by medieval chroniclers. They gave a good deal of play, moreover, to material and psychological factors; they weighed their evidence and compared the relative worth of parallel chronicle and annalistic sources; Bruni and Scala even drew upon archival data. And they demonstrated that the work of the historian is not the casual stringing together of apparently important facts, as in the lucubrations of chroniclers, nor the whimsical recording of dramatic events, as in the pages of diarists, but rather the accomplished presentation of a narrative both descriptive and analytic. The rhetorical aspect was connected mainly with public orations and with some features of the representation of wars.

Meanwhile, Lorenzo Valla, whom I have already mentioned, made startling advances in the field of historical philology, and Flavio Biondo (1392–1463), a humanist based in Rome, founded the modern approach to archeology. With four books based upon a study of monuments and inscriptions and upon a critical reading of sources, Biondo made a spectacular contribution to our knowledge of the archeology and history of ancient Rome. But a searching attitude toward the problems of historical method was most evident in the city where the interplay between politics and history was most vital—Florence.

There, at the end of the fifteenth century, certain men began to feel that humanist historiography was deficient, and that there might well be more satisfactory methods of representation and analysis. The discussion came to a head with the rejection by Francesco Guicciardini (1483–1540) of Machiavelli's historical views. The prototype of the political scientist, Machiavelli was constantly in search of uniformities, of political and historical "laws." In his view, men were the same everywhere, acquisitive and violent; history repeated itself or abounded in close parallels; power and *virtù* were the central historical facts; one studied history to throw light on the present.

While accepting the centrality of power and part of Machiavelli's view of human psychology, Guicciardini held that history was too complex to be interpreted so geometrically. He had both more and less respect for men than did Machiavelli. He believed that no historical situation ever truly repeated itself. It was vain to seek laws, instructive patterns, parallels, or cyclic repetitions. Thus in his two histories of Florence and in his great *History of Italy*, Guicciardini shows a much greater care than Machiavelli for documentary sources, fine detail, and all the nuances and ramifications of a given event or situation. But even he could not rid himself of the conviction that history has much to tell us about the present. Deeply troubled by a Florence unstable in its political institutions and by an Italy prostrate before foreign armies, Guicciardini also turned to history, and especially to the history of his own times, in an extraordinary effort to make sense of the conflicting voices and disorder about him.

The Age as Vanguard

Cities and city-states provided the shaping environment for new developments from the thirteenth century onwards: first Florence, Padua, Bologna, and Siena; then Rome, Naples, Ferrara, Milan, Perugia, Mantua, and Venice. Some of the princely courts were already active as dispensers of patronage in the fourteenth century, but their achievement was not beyond question in this regard until the fifteenth century. Only then did their money and encouragement create broad avenues for influential initiatives, as in the fields of humanistic education, portrait painting and sculpture, Renaissance architecture, and military engineering.

But whether at Ferrara, Milan, or Mantua, the princely courts fell under the sway of urban ways and bourgeois values. In the thirteenth century, French notions of chivalrous love entered Italy through songs, verse, and stories. By the beginning of the fourteenth century, their primary audiences were the rich burghers (*popolani grassi*), municipal aristocrats, and urbanized noblemen, as well as lawyers, administrators, and citizen-favorites of the emerging princely courts. From about the time of Dante and Giotto (c. 1300), the "makers" of the Italian Renaissance were reared in urban centers or formed by their values; and the good life for most men of this type was unimaginable apart from residence in cities. Before 1300 there already stretched nearly two hundred years of intense civic development, the result of a booming commercial economy. Men had seen large-scale immigration into cities, the rise of international trade and banking, the emergence of sophisticated commercial and legal practices, and the elaboration of complex municipal codes. They witnessed political insurrection and pitched street battles, the making of a rich repertory of political skills and chicanery, the vigorous beginnings of urban planning; and they eventually revolutionized the content of education for the laity.

In the twelfth and thirteenth centuries the scale and fervor of city life in central and upper Italy made possible kinds of experience which would eventually conflict with the hierarchic views and ecclesiological emphases of the rural and feudal Middle Ages. To the traditional penchant for static categories and the ordering of ideal essences—so much in harmony with the outlook of men educated for or by the medieval Church—the cities brought a new way of looking at society and politics, and so a new way of looking at man and the things around him. Almost from the moment of their birth (c. 1100), the great urban communes were drawn into violent controversy with both church (in its temporal aspirations) and empire. The daily experience or developing practices of urban men came to be accorded a higher value. But this process—the gradual triumph of the everyday experience of cities—followed a very slow and uneven course. The hammering-out of new values has never been a swift process, at any rate not before the twentieth century.

The new path of experience received its first indefeasible expression in the middle of the twelfth century with the revival of the meticulous study of Roman jurisprudence, first cultivated at Bologna but swiftly taken up at Pavia and Padua, then at Perugia, Siena, Ferrara, and other cities. This fundamental reorientation of the approach to law came in response to the commercial revolution, a process summed up in the explosive rate of urban growth, the radical altering of property relations, and the ongoing transformation in the whole nature and compass of political authority.

The next step on the new path of development was the emergence of the Italian language. Not until the later thirteenth century did the vernacular, now wrenched from its Latin framework, attain a flexibility and richness fit for literature. By about 1360, with the conclusive performances of Dante, Petrarch, Boccaccio, and the early Florentine chroniclers, the job of refinement was near completion: Tuscan or, rather, Italian had been rendered a suitable vehicle for the conveyance of most feelings and subtleties.

The city had found its tongue but not yet its world-view. This was to be accomplished most tellingly by the fifteenth-century humanists, who found that their experience—of politics, pleasure, economic gain, and individual need—squared in many respects with values to be garnered from the literature of antiquity. Far from looking back, the humanists looked intently to the present. But to free themselves *for* the present they drew upon the past. By disengaging important segments of their experience from the gridwork of inherited preconception, and by reaching out for the culture of classical Rome and Greece, they updated their view of the fifteenth-century world and so their grasp of current reality. Ideology was brought more directly into line with experience.

It is also to the cities that we must look for the conditions which occasioned the rising expression and intensification of personal individuality. This new direction was forcefully expressed in the developing passion for biography, the collecting of familiar letters, the private diary, short lyric poem (in its confessional strain), portrait painting, portrait busts, and the development of more personal artistic styles. We may attribute this trend to the bracing stimuli of cities: the psychological effect of urban social mobility, vigorous and persistent from the twelfth to the early fourteenth century. Calling on the resourcefulness of individuals, this challenge to the personality drew on fresh sources in the fourteenth and fifteenth centuries, when the slow decay of the old corporate groups and habits—guilds, family clans, and hidebound adherence to the family trade—spelled the decay of group feeling and orientation in economic affairs. Henceforth the individual was somewhat less submerged in the close-knit group.

The new perception of reality was given its most effective representation in the work of artists of the vanguard. Florentines led the way. Donatello and subsequent sculptors sought a celebration of man in the dramatic possibilities of freestanding statuary, in the portrait bust, and in the living quality of crowds or individuals portrayed in bas-relief (*stiacciato*). The innovative thrust in painting, from Giotto to Leonardo da Vinci, was directed at rendering the picture plane as a window-like surface, thereby seeming to provide a new opening into the world. This end was served by the assiduous observation of men, spaces, and objects; and the discovery of focused perspective, virtuoso foreshortening, the use of oil paints (borrowed from the Flemish masters), the study of anatomy and light, and the apprehension of atmospheric perspective.

Changes in the whole manner of political and historical thinking were no less fundamental. Moving from a belief in the exacting nature of politics and a firm sense of periodicity, the fifteenth-century humanists (so much may be claimed for them) *invented* the tools of historical scholarship. With Machiavelli and some of his Florentine contemporaries, politics came to be regarded as an activity *sui generis,* with its own rules of conduct determined alone by affairs of state. Henceforth, historical exposition became much more than a partial exercise in the imitation of the best classical historians: it became a mode of analysis increasingly shaped by the exigent claims of political experience and by more stubborn forms of evidence. Once again, therefore, the burden (and leavening) of civic experience entered more fully into the evaluation of events and political relationships.

The place of science in Renaissance Italy, of all the grounds I have touched upon, has been least satisfactorily cultivated by scholarship. A great deal of work remains to be done, much of it with fourteenth- and fifteenth-century manuscripts. Clearly, however, the scientific realm of experience was not disregarded by the men who revolutionized political and historical thinking and who "worked out" the implications of a new way of *seeing* in the mastery of pictorial and architectural space and the crediting of power politics with a unique place in the affairs of men. In the leading current of the age, art and science were one: it was assumed that without the habit of keen and accurate measurement, one could not paint, sculpt, or build. The empirical traditions of the workshop and the practice of rigorous reflection were thus joined together. Artists and theoreticians (i.e., "natural philosophers") found a common meeting-ground, and from this congress there issued the beginnings of the modern scientific method.

Selected Bibliography

Jacob Burckhardt's classic essay, *The Civilization of the Renaissance in Italy,* can be found in many editions, usually in the S. Middlemore translation. Presented in a disarmingly simple fashion, the essay is remarkably complex in its method and implications. The standard work on changing views of the Renaissance is W. K. Ferguson, *The Renaissance in Historical Thought* (Boston, 1948). A stimulating discussion by a leading Italian historian, the late Federico Chabod, is *Machiavelli and the Renaissance,* translated by A. P. d'Entrèves (Cambridge, Mass., 1958).

General or comparative treatments in English of the Italian city-states are very scanty. An obvious point of departure is Gino Luzzatto, *An Economic History of Italy from the Fall of the Roman Republic to the Beginning of the Sixteenth Century,* translated by P. J. Jones (London, 1962). Most pertinent studies tend to concentrate on Venice, Florence, or Milan. But one may begin with M. V. Clarke, *The Medieval City State* (London, 1926) and D. Waley, *The Italian City-Republics* (New York, 1969). An essay by L. Martines, "Political Opposition in the Italian City-States," *Government and Opposition* III (Winter 1968) : pp. 69–91, offers a sketch of some of the principal developments. The best detailed narrative in Italian is by L. Simeoni, *Le Signorie,* 2 vols. (Milan: Francesco Vallardi, 1950). G. A. Brucker, *Renaissance Florence* (New York, 1969) ; D. Herlihy, *Mediaeval and Renaissance Pistoia* (New Haven, 1967) ; J. K. Hyde, *Padua in the Age of Dante* (New York, 1966) ; O. Logan, *Culture and Society in Venice 1470–1790* (New York, 1972) offer pictures of four Italian cities. A useful collection of readings has been edited by A. Molho, *Social and Economic Foundations of the Italian Renaissance* (New York, 1969).

Humanism has attracted a vast literature. The accents in this essay owe much to E. Garin, *Italian Humanism,* translated by P. Munz (New York, 1965); P. O. Kristeller, *Renaissance Thought,* 2 vols. (New York, 1964); H. Baron, *The Crisis of the Early Italian Renaissance,* 2nd ed. (Princeton, 1966); W. H. Woodward, *Vittorino da Feltre and other Humanist Educators,* 2nd ed. (New York, 1963); and L. Martines, *The Social World of the Florentine Humanists* (Princeton, 1963).

The literature of the period is best reviewed in two multi-volumed literary histories: the *Storia letteraria d'Italia* (Milan, 1933, 1938), especially the volumes by V. Rossi and N. Sapegno; and the *Storia della letteratura italiana* (Milan, 1965–69), edited by E. Cecchi and N. Sapegno. In English there is an interesting history by J. H. Whitfield, *A Short History of Italian Literature* (London, 1960).

Renaissance art has elicited a staggering number of histories, essays, monographs, and articles. Beginners may start with the appropriate chapters in H. W. and D. J. Janson, *The Picture History of Painting* (London, 1957) and go on to P. J. and L. Murray, *The Art of the Renaissance* (London, 1963). More advanced students will turn to A. Chastel, *Italian Art* (New York, 1963) and F. Antal, *Florentine Painting and its Social Background* (London, 1947). A broad historical and sociological view is presented by A. Hauser, *The Social History of Art* (New York, 1952). John Pope-Hennessy, *The Portrait in the Renaissance* (London: New York, 1966) is a major study by a leading art historian.

The history of science is served by the following short surveys, all of which shortchange the earlier Italian experience: M. Boas, *The Scientific Renaissance* (New York, 1962); A. R. Hall, *The Scientific Revolution: 1500–1800* (London, 1954); and A. R. and M. B. Hall, *A Brief History of Science* (New York, 1964). George Sarton has given us the major English reference work, *Introduction to the History of Science,* 3 vols. (Baltimore, 1927–1948). See especially volume III, ii. A good deal of material is also to be found in E. Garin, *Science and Civic Life in the Italian Renaissance,* translated by P. Munz (New York, 1969); L. White, Jr., *Medieval Technology and Social Change* (New York, 1966), chapter III; and M. Clagett, *Giovanni Marliani and Late Medieval Physics* (New York, 1941).

On the direction of political and historical thought the student should go directly to the works of Machiavelli and Guicciardini. Both recent and older translations are available. An important study is F. Gilbert, *Machiavelli and Guicciardini: Politics and History in Sixteenth Century Florence* (Princeton, 1965). J. R. Hale, *Machiavelli and Renaissance Italy* (London, 1961), is effectively concise and has much to recommend it. There are two noteworthy English studies on historical thinking in fifteenth-century Italy: B. L. Ullman, "Leonardo Bruni and Humanistic Historiography," *Medievalia et Humanistia* IV (1946): 45–61; and a recent book by D. Wilcox, *The Development of Florentine Humanist Historiography in the Fifteenth Century* (Cambridge, Mass., 1969).

Erasmus *by Quentin Masys, 1517. Courtesy of the Galleria Nazionale d'Arte Antica in the Palazzo Barberini, Rome.*

3.

The Northern Renaissance

MARGARET E. ASTON

Oh century! Oh letters! It is a joy to be alive!

ULRICH VON HUTTEN, Letter to Willibald Pirckheimer, 1518.

Immortal God, what a century do I see beginning! If only it were possible to be young again!

ERASMUS, Letter to Guillaume Budé, 21 February 1517.

HOW FORTUNATE IT IS for us, how unfortunate in many ways it was for him, that Erasmus lived nearly twenty years after the writing of these words! Had he died—as he himself, like others at the time, fully expected—in his fifties instead of his late sixties, at the outset of the Lutheran revolt, subsequent historians as well as contemporaries might have enjoyed the doubtful and no doubt endless pleasures of speculating on his position. How would the greatest exponent of northern humanism have acquitted himself in this dividing of ways?

Happily we have been spared that conundrum. Erasmus lived long enough to be appealed to by both sides and to respond with his own pen to Luther's stand. But he was already deeply misunderstood. It reflects both on the ambiguity of his own utterances and on the confusions of the moment that contemporaries were so ready to cast Erasmus for roles entirely alien to him. The heartfelt prayer in which Albrecht Dürer (in the privacy of his diary) apostrophized Erasmus as a "knight of Christ," the David who could take Luther's place in felling the Romish Goliath, was as misplaced as the hostile efforts of men such as Diego Lopez Zuñiga, who attempted to portray him as the prince of heretics, especially Lutherans. The very range of his utterances ensured such misreadings of Erasmus's position. And these misunderstandings show how, in the 1520s, the ground was shifting in ways which made Erasmus himself seem shifty. All he had accomplished was in a sense related to these changes, and yet they seemed to be taking the world away from, not toward, the objectives to which he had devoted his life. It is paradoxical that while Erasmus could only deplore the growth of religious dissension, and while the Reformation ended hopes of accomplishing much that he had worked for, knowledge of his writings was enlarged by these widening divisions.

It is natural that any account of what has come to be called, rather unhelpfully if not confusingly, the 'Northern Renaissance', should center upon Erasmus. In any period of history it is rare for one man to become the spokesman of a whole generation. Erasmus is the more remarkable in that he was the first European to do so. He demonstrated the very possibility of an individual addressing a continent. He created and, in doing so, assumed what has been called the "kingship of the pen." And by making himself into the literary arbiter of Europe, whose views were read and respected by popes, kings, bishops, men of learning, and a vast number of ordinary educated contemporaries, Erasmus contributed to and affirmed what by 1520 had become an undeniable fact—the intellectual initiative of the north. To understand how this came about we must consider the influences which shaped the northern humanists.

The Spread of Humanism: Greek Studies

The movement which we know as the Renaissance was a matter both of fresh skills and of fresh ways of thinking. Central to both was the revived study of Greek. Throughout this period Latin learning and scholarship continued greatly to predominate, but the vanguard of humanist educators was formed by the minority who possessed knowledge of Greek, the key to those founts of literature of which Cicero was thinking when he wrote about *humanitas*. Behind the excitement of the revived study of classical antiquity lay a passionate belief in the possibility of educating individuals—and societies—to higher levels of achievement. Many northern successors to Vittorino da Feltre and Guarino da Verona eagerly took to heart the teaching of Quintilian and Cicero, who had looked back to Greek models and Greek literature for the ideal of man discovering and shaping his whole self and learning to the full through a rounded education, the means of expressing it. "Distinguished men of letters have represented to us," ran a letter of Francis I appointing a king's printer for Greek in 1539, "that art, history, morals, philosophy, and almost all other branches of learning, flow from Greek writers, like rivers from their source."

John Colet, writing to Erasmus in 1516, bemoaned his lack of Greek, "without which skill we are nothing." After Petrarch's abortive efforts to read Homer in the original a great many individuals labored painfully to acquire this linguistic skill. If the lack of Greek was annihilating, the possession of it might seem everything. Was it not Greek letters and Greek literature which Raphael Hythloday took to and taught in Utopia? Latin, on the other hand, could there be left out of account since the Utopians in their wisdom would have found in Latin "nothing . . . they would greatly allow, besides historians and poets." The achievement of skill in Greek is therefore an obvious way of tracing the spread of humanist learning, and it demonstrates the generation gap—of more than one generation—that existed between the revivals of learning in the north and in Italy.

Enthusiasm for the Greek sources of learning was urgent enough, as Petrarch's example shows, to send men back to school when they had reached a time of life which to them—though not to us—was well past middle age. Alexander Hegius (1433–98), for example, who became headmaster of Deventer when Erasmus was a schoolboy there, was over forty when he learned Greek from Rudolph Agricola at Emmerich. Another man who humbled himself to learn from a younger, more gifted contemporary, was John Fisher (1459–1535), bishop of Rochester. Fisher had already played a large part in introducing both Greek teaching and Erasmus to Cambridge when in 1517 the celebrated humanist, leaving England for what proved to be the last time, stopped off at Rochester and gave some Greek instruction to his patron. Perhaps Erasmus had Fisher in mind when he wrote of the four men of his acquaintance, all famous for their works, none of whom had learned Greek before reaching forty.

It is clear that this enthusiasm, and the means of satisfying it, derived in the first instance from Italy. Early Renaissance patrons in the north—in England, Hungary or France—looked to Italy to satisfy their needs, whether for texts, teachers, or designers. So a succession of instructors carried the knowledge of Greek from Italy to other parts of Europe. Gregorio Tifernate of Città di Castello had lived in Greece and taught Greek in several Italian towns before he began eighteen months of lecturing at Paris in 1458. Among the enthusiastic listeners who benefited from his teaching were Robert Gaguin, Guillaume Fichet and Wessel Gansfort. In England the instruction given at Oxford in the 1460s by Stefano Surigone inspired the interest of William Sellyng, who was to make himself a Greek expert and one of the leading English humanists of the century. Others of his countrymen followed Surigone in both English universities. And Surigone himself, who also taught at Cologne, Strasbourg, and Louvain, was one of several Italians to be found in this period teaching rhetoric in German universities, where they may have helped to seed the taste for Greek learning.

Italy provided not only the stimuli, but also the means of learning—such as manuals and grammars from Italian presses, or the scholarship founded at Louvain by Raymond di Marliano to enable a student to pursue his studies in Italy. In some cases, however, Greek was brought north (as it had originally been taken to Italy) by Greeks themselves—some of whom came secondhand, as it were, from Italy. Several Greek refugees found their way to England in the later fifteenth century. The scribe Emanuel of Constantinople, one of several Greeks patronized by George Neville, archbishop of York, stayed some years in England and may have taught Greek to various people (perhaps including William Grocyn) besides his patron, to whom he presented a transcript of Demosthenes in 1468. And in the 1480s John Serbopoulos of Constantinople, who had links with Emanuel, was residing in England and transcribing Greek texts for academic patrons. In Paris, likewise, Greek studies were encouraged by the arrival of Greeks. After Tifernate's short-lived courses there, the teaching of Greek was resumed in 1476 by George Hermonymos of Sparta. He was not a very competent teacher, to judge from the later complaints of his pupils, but some of them were exceptionally able: Budé, Erasmus, Beatus Rhenanus. Reuchlin, at any rate, was satisfied with the opportunities which Hermonymos provided, and Lefèvre became his friend. Meanwhile in Spain in the early sixteenth century, the textual studies at Alcalá owed much to the Cretan Demetrios Doucas, who had had experience of Greek printing in the office of Aldus Manutius in Venice.

Jacques Lefèvre d'Etaples, the greatest French exponent of humanist learning in his day, for whom this linguistic enlightenment was of supreme importance, thought that its inception could be dated. In the preface to his *Commentaries on the Four Gospels* in 1521, he remarked that the increased knowledge of languages in his time, unmatched since the days of Constantine, "began to return about the time Constantinople was taken by the enemies of Christ, when a few Greeks, notably Bessarion, Theodore of Gaza, George of Trebizond, and Emanuel Chrysoloras, took refuge in Italy." This passage is interesting for two reasons. First, it shows the false premises on which, scarcely more than two generations after the event, the enrichment of western Greek learning was attributed to the fall of Constantinople in 1453. All the emigrants Lefèvre named—assuming that the Chrysoloras he referred to was the celebrated Emanuel who taught Greek in Florence at the end of the fourteenth century—were in Italy before 1453.[1] Second, this very misconception tells us something of great significance about contemporary attitudes toward Greek. For while it is undoubtedly true that individual Greeks contributed to the increased knowledge of their language

---

[1] John C. Olin, ed., *The Catholic Reformation: Savonarola to Ignatius Loyola: Reform in the Church 1495–1540* (New York, 1969), p. 114. Theodore of Gaza was in Italy, teaching Greek at Ferrara, in the 1440s; George of Trebizond, who came to Italy in the second decade of the fifteenth century, taught at Vicenza and Mantua in the 1420s and 1430s; Bessarion, having made a great impression as Greek envoy at the council of Ferrara–Florence, was appointed cardinal in 1439 and thereafter made his mark at the Roman curia.

and literature in the west, the erroneous conviction that this was a consequence of the fall of Constantinople was the result of an obsession, and one which (paradoxical as it might seem) was most powerful outside Italy. Faced with the spectacle of advancing Islam, Italy, it is true, produced some outstanding crusading enthusiasts. But from the days of Pierre Dubois and Roger Bacon and Ramon Lull, to Philippe de Mézières and up to Cardinal Ximenes and Guillaume Postel, it was transalpine Europe which germinated much of the most constructive thought on this tormenting issue.

Lefèvre's words draw attention to the intimate relationship between thoughts about Greek studies and the fate of the eastern church. For a great many people at the time, perhaps most, the context in which Greek learning was considered was not ancient but contemporary, not the Greek of Plato and Aristotle but rather that of the schismatic church in the east. This had, as we shall see, a profound effect upon the reception of humanist studies in the north. And it meant that the study of Greek in the fifteenth century (and later) still in part belonged, as it long had, to a missionary sphere. Such provision as was made to keep the study of Greek alive during the Middle Ages was largely related to hopes for reunion with the Greek church. This, for instance, was what inspired the foundation at Paris in the thirteenth century of a college to teach Oriental languages; and it was the need to be able to debate with Greek theologians and to keep open the lines of communication with Constantinople which accounted for Greek being taught at the papal court at Avignon in the first half of the fourteenth century.

Bearing this in mind, it seems likely that the negotiations between the eastern and western churches which took place at the Council of Ferrara–Florence in 1438–39, and the short-lived agreement which resulted, were of much greater significance in fostering Greek studies in the west than the long-fabled events of 1453. It might be taken as a reflection of the stimulus provided by the council that Piero da Monte, who was then far away in England serving as papal collector, was spurred (despite the unpropitious circumstances) to take up again the study of Greek which he had started in Ferrara; or that the university founded at Catania in Sicily in 1444 included the unusual provision for studies in Greek. Studies undertaken in such a setting might include, or lead to, any number of interests, but they were by no means necessarily in any degree humanist.

At the same time that humanist interests beyond the Alps grew, in certain places, with the help of Italians or native-speaking Greeks, many more individuals were finding their way to Italy. The earliest indigenous exponents of humanism in the north were those who—whether or not they had gone there expressly for this purpose—had experienced Italian culture firsthand. The mission which took Guillaume Fichet to Milan in 1469–70 played a part in the beginnings of the first Paris printing press which he and Jean Heynlin, prior to the Sorbonne, established in the college that year. Itself a humanist undertaking—its first book was the model letters of the Italian Gasparino Barzizza and in 1471 appeared Lorenzo Valla's *On the Elegances of the Latin Language*—the press marked the real arrival of humanism in Paris. Among those who rejoiced with Fichet (and urged him on to publish his own *Rhetoric*), was his friend Robert Gaguin—another who had direct experience of Italy.

Veteran students from German universities enlarged their capacities, and sometimes their vision, by pursuing their studies into Italy. Wessel Gansfort (c. 1419–89) had studied at Cologne, Heidelberg, and Louvain, and already begun to learn Greek and Hebrew, before his visit to Italy in 1470–71, where he met both Cardinal Bessarion and the future pope Sixtus IV. Gansfort's interest helped to promote linguistic studies, particularly through the stimulus he gave to two younger men, both of whose fame surpassed his: Agricola and Reuchlin.

Rudolph Agricola (1444–1485), a man of widely ranging interests and a versatility reminiscent of Castiglione's courtier (he illuminated manuscripts and built an organ, besides writing a life of Petrarch), was accepted as an equal by the Italians. He lived among them off and on for ten years (1468–79) and it was in Italy that he learned both Greek and Hebrew. Unlike Erasmus, who held him in great respect (treasuring the glimpse he had of him as a schoolboy at Deventer), Agricola was able to talk fluently to the Italians in their own vernacular; also unlike his great successor, he left few literary works. His influence, for all that, was great, partly for the very reason that he had so fully assimilated the best of what was to be learned in Italy, and was able to communicate his enthusiasm to others. Agricola, like Vittorino da Feltre before him and John Colet after him, was one of those gifted men who leave it to their pupils to enlarge the range of their virtues—and *virtù*. Erasmus, who could appreciate this quality (emphatically not one of his own), and who had through Deventer and Alexander Hegius a direct link with Agricola, was happy to commemorate this genealogy of scholars in which he was the third generation. Agricola, he wrote, forty years after this teacher's death, was "the first of all who brought to us from Italy some breath of better learning."

Johannes Reuchlin (1455–1522), whom Erasmus also celebrated in a very different connection, made several visits to Italy after his first journey in 1481 when he studied in Rome. It was in Florence later on that he was able to do most to advance his intellectual interests, thanks to the inspiration of that exceptional polymath, Pico della Mirandola. There Reuchlin became interested in the Hebrew studies to which he made so enormous a contribution, and there he found the teachers who enabled him to make his first strides forward with that language. Florence had a special magnetism during these last years of the fifteenth century, when the fame of Marsilio Ficino's Platonic academy added to the artistic radiance of Medici circles. Three great English humanists whose achievements—Greek as well as Latin—were extolled by Erasmus were all affected by the spell of Florence. Thomas Linacre (1460–1524), chiefly celebrated for his knowledge of medicine (which included translations of Galen) spent twelve years in the city; he was joined there by William Grocyn (c. 1446–1519), who took to student life in his forties to attend lectures and study Greek; John Colet (1466?–1519) spent four years away from Oxford, deepening in Italy his interest in Ficino's Platonism.

Not for nothing did Linacre, on his way home to England at the turn of the fifteenth century, erect an altar at the top of an Alpine pass which he dedicated to Italy as the "holy mother of studies." The debts owed to Italy are too numerous to count, and contemporaries were all too aware of them. On both sides of the Alps there was plenty of talk—defensive on one side, proud or arrogant on the other—about Italian superiority and transalpine barbarism. "The Italians," wrote Erasmus in England in 1509, "value themselves for learning and eloquence; and, like the Grecians of old, account all the world barbarians in respect of themselves; to which piece of vanity the inhabitants of Rome are more especially addicted, pretending themselves to be owners of all those heroic virtues, which their city so many ages since was deservedly famous for." At about this time Benvenuto Cellini, invited by Pietro Torrigiano to accompany him to London to work as an assistant on the royal tombs at Westminster, haughtily refused, placing an alleged insult to Michelangelo by Pietro above any desire to set eyes on "those brutes of Englishmen."

Yet, in fact, by about 1500 the balance of learning was significantly changing. The hope which Agricola had expressed thirty years earlier was already being realized: "that we shall one day wrest from proud Italy the reputation for classical expression which it has nearly monopolized . . . and free ourselves from the reproach of ignorance and being called unlearned and inarticulate barbarians." Jibes about barbarians might long continue, but the need to travel south for the civilizing influence of Italy became progressively less impelling.

When Erasmus first arrived in England, in the summer of 1499, he received a most pleasurable surprise. He found there a group of cultivated men, well acquainted with Italy and with humanist learning, who had reached that degree of intellectual sophistication he had seen and admired in Agricola. Colet, Grocyn, Linacre, and More—especially the first and last—recognized Erasmus's qualities and did something important for him: they showed him where he belonged. Many influences, necessarily, went to the making of so complex a personality as Erasmus. Clearly this visit meant much to him, particularly the meeting with Colet in Oxford, but there is no need to suppose that it caused some violent alteration in the course of his intentions for his life. Rather one might see it as a kind of homecoming, as he arrived for the first time (and Erasmus was now at least thirty) in a circle which shared his ideals and had already gone further than he had toward achieving them. Erasmus reached England with the reputation of a poet, but his training, his commitments, and his concerns involved much more than that. When he went back to Paris he was greatly fortified and stimulated by the examples of his new-made friends in England, and was in pursuit of objectives which had long been smoldering in his mind—to perfect his Greek for Biblical studies.

Erasmus did not need Italy for his humanist outlook or his humanist training. He had found in England, as he wrote soon after this visit, so much good learning, "exact and ancient, Latin and Greek, that now I hardly want to go to Italy, except for the sake of seeing it." And it was in Paris that he learned his Greek. Admittedly the going was not always easy. "My Greek studies," he wrote in March 1500 to his friend James Batt, "are almost exhausting my powers, while I have neither the time nor the means of procuring books or the help of a teacher." Yet despite repeated complaints about such deficiencies he stuck to his purpose, and by the time he at last reached Italy in 1506 it seemed to do little for him. "I knew more Greek and Latin when I went to Italy than I do now," he wrote with the confidence of retrospect in 1531. "My literary education owes nothing to Italy—I wish it owed a great deal. There were people there from whom I could have learnt, but so there were in England, in France, in Germany. In Italy there was really no opportunity, since I had gone there simply for the sake of seeing the place." This is not to say, of course, that Erasmus's scholarship, and perhaps his style—as opposed to his education— did not benefit considerably from what Italy had to offer. The greatly enlarged edition of the *Adages* brought out by Aldus in 1508 bears witness to the enrichment provided by manuscripts which the author was able to consult in Venice, while the Platonic influences evident in both the *Praise of Folly* and the *Enchiridion* show how Erasmus followed the studies of Italian humanists. But it remains true that he had found his humanist training and sense of values before he ever went to Italy.

A number of other famous humanists of the north who were contemporaries of Erasmus reflect this diminished dependence on Italy. Sir Thomas More, unlike Colet, Linacre, and Grocyn—all of whose achievements he surpassed— was educated entirely in England, and learned his Greek with Grocyn and Linacre, as well as with William Lily (who had acquired his in Rhodes). Lefèvre d'Etaples, though impressed by his Italian meetings with Pico della Mirandola and Ermolao Barbaro, does not seem to have learned Greek in Italy, but in Paris after his return. Meanwhile in Germany Conrad Celtis (1459–1508) was the first leading humanist of the empire to have received a humanist education at home before setting foot in Italy—and others of his generation distinguished themselves in humanist letters without ever going there at all.

Humanist learning can therefore be said to have arrived in northern Europe by the earlier years of the sixteenth century. If we judge it in this way, taking the continuous availability and fluency of Greek as an important criterion, it seems that the north took almost a century to catch up with Italy. How is one to explain this time-lag? It is not as if the north had not been in close contact with the best of Italian efforts since the days when Petrarch met Richard of

Bury in Avignon and there made discoveries which greatly helped his textual restoration of Livy. In the fifteenth century there were individuals who became polished stylists, with claims to genuine humanist distinction, in many parts of Europe. In France, Nicolas de Clémanges (c. 1360–1437) explored the resources of monastic libraries and found a complete text of Quintilian twenty years before Poggio Bracciolini, whose discovery of a copy of this work at St. Gallen in 1417 had much greater repercussions. Poggio himself, learning in 1451 of a dean of Utrecht who had collected several manuscripts of Cicero, was astonished to find a man so devoted to eloquence and good letters "so far from Italy." Yet currents of humanism flowed—almost underground—in places where the opportunities existed. Paris was one such place, where there seems to have been a trickle of humanist interests among officials of the royal administration: men such as Jean Lebègue (d. 1457), who followed his father in the king's service, and was the owner of a library which included both classical texts and works of Leonardo Bruni. The fashion for antiquity seeped steadily northward through the fifteenth century, sometimes emerging rather strikingly in the names which aspiring humanists bestowed upon their offspring. It was no accident, surely, that Humphrey, duke of Gloucester, the first significant patron of Italian humanists in England, named his daughter Antigone, or that Willibald Pirckheimer—whose father and grandfather had both studied in Italy—had sisters called Sabrina and Euphemia.

It takes more, however, than the enthusiasm of individuals to change long-established outlooks and institutions. It needs continuity of support—or revolutionary technology. Such promising humanist beginnings as there were in Parisian circles, or in England around Duke Humphrey, did not succeed in creating lasting new patterns of study in the north. To account for this failure it is not sufficient to point to the effects of the Hundred Years' War in France, or the Wars of the Roses in England. There was, after all, plenty of dislocation in the sixteenth century—and yet these studies survived. One obvious contrast between Italy and the rest of Europe in this formative period is the range of available patronage. In the fifteenth century the north could boast nothing to compare with the brilliant rivalry of Italian courtly society in Florence, Milan, Ferrara, Urbino, Rome, and Naples. Individuals such as the duke of Gloucester or John Tiptoft, earl of Worcester, or Matthias Corvinus of Hungary were exceptional and isolated, incapable of effecting a permanent change in the course of studies. In the "gothic" north, patrons themselves needed educating, and for fashions to change many people have to become aware of changes of fashion. From the end of the fifteenth century, royal actions did a great deal—if largely indirectly—to increase northern awareness of the exuberant world beyond the Alps. Between the Neapolitan venture of Charles VIII of France in 1494 and the sack of Rome by the troops of Charles V in 1527 (which damaged a number of Italian prospects), military affairs brought many different sorts of people into contact with the dazzle of Italy. Some of the plunders contributed directly to northern scholarship. John Lascaris, prised out of Medici Florence, was persuaded to settle in Paris, where he furthered the study of Greek. And the wholesale transfer to France of the Visconti–Sforza library from Milan enormously enriched the resources of the French royal library—which both Lascaris and Budé helped to reorganize when Francis I moved it to Fontainebleau.

When humanist learning finally became established in the north it had the advantage not only of royal patrons like Francis I and Henry VIII, but also of tools which made it possible to bypass or overtake established institutions and traditional modes of study. The arrival of printing made the teaching and learning of humanists—and others—less dependent upon formal institutional methods. What Aldus did for Greek grammar Reuchlin later did for Hebrew, and the strides forward which northerners were able to make in both languages in the early sixteenth century were closely linked with the availability of printed texts. Erasmus, deservedly famous as the first man of letters who earned his living by his pen, and who has left a vivid description of himself working against the clatter of Aldus's press, was only one of the increasing numbers whose living and learning revolved around printers' offices.

Northern and southern scholars shared many of the same desires and objectives. They wanted to recover the ancient world in order to recreate the new. For both, skill in Greek was an indispensable prerequisite. Yet there were age-old differences in the worlds north and south of the Alps, differences of outlook and education, which affected this transference of learning. In the north, where university teaching had always been more clerical than it was in Italy (with its tradition of secular learning), the study of theology held the place of honor which was given to law and rhetoric in the south. Theology, as we shall see, had its place in Italy, but the schools and scholars to which it owed its fame belonged elsewhere. These differences affected the transposition of humanist interests to the world beyond the Alps. The experiences of Poggio Bracciolini on his disappointing visit to England in 1418–22 might be taken as an indication of what was to happen later on a larger scale. Works of the Church Fathers at first seemed to Poggio second-best reading matter when he found himself, lacking materials to pursue his classical interests, taking to the study of St. Augustine, St. Jerome, St. John Chrysostom, but this gave him so great an appreciation of these authors that he regretted (at that time) the labors spent on other studies. Also indicative are the book tastes of Poggio's patron, Duke Humphrey, which reflect the concerns of the handful of other great English book-collectors of the fifteenth century. He pioneered in trying to form as complete a classical library as possible, but the translations which were made for him from the Greek were mainly works of theology or philosophy which would serve scholastic purposes. Not surprisingly, since learning is conditioned by upbringing and previous experience, what English humanists brought home from Italy was often chosen to fit, rather than reconstruct, the architecture of their domestic learning. The Greek manuscripts surviving from the collection of the accomplished humanist Robert Flemming (c. 1415–83) are religious works; and William Sellyng (d. 1494), the prior of Christ Church, Canterbury, whose proficiency in Greek was commemorated on his tombstone, turned his Italianate skill to translating a sermon of Chrysostom.

"Time was," wrote Roger Ascham in *The Schoolmaster* (published in 1570, two years after his death), "when Italy and Rome have been . . . the best breeders and bringers-up of the worthiest men . . . But now that time is gone." Doubtless many still disagreed with him, including those who, following in the steps of their forebears a century earlier, assumed that the paths of education should lead them to Italy. But however one judged the Italian scene in the later sixteenth century, its indispensability for the educational needs of northerners was surely a thing of the past. To recite the glories of the renaissance of letters, as John Leland had some years earlier, seeing how Greek and Latin and Hebrew were being studied and cultivated, meant recalling the achievements of Spain and France, Germany and England, alongside Italy.

Already there were towering figures to prove Leland's point. In Spain there was Elio Antonio de Nebrija (1444–1522), who used his ten years' experience of Italy to work for humanist studies at home, and whose publications included grammars in Greek and Hebrew as well as Latin. In France the work of Guillaume Budé (1468–1540) could be measured against that of Erasmus who was reportedly envious of the Frenchman's *De Asse* (1515), a pioneering work on Roman coinage which revealed the author's profound knowledge of antiquity. Budé was deeply concerned with the restoration of Greek. He helped to promote its study in various ways, including the publication in 1529 of his *Commentarii linguae graecae* and a few years later of a work in which— demonstrating the convictions he shared with other northern humanists—he defended Greek learning from the imputation of heresy, arguing its value for Christian studies.

The greatest contribution of all, of course, was that of Erasmus. Some of his most successful works were deliberately composed to fulfill the educational needs of "barbarous" northerners. The *Colloquies,* with their witty exchanges and pungent dialogue on contemporary affairs and failings, were written as models for schoolboy Latin and, though they provided pleasure for many other sorts of readers in their various editions after 1519, that remained their primary purpose. The same was true of the *Adages* (whose first appearance was in 1500), another work which Erasmus—who saw his books as children it was his duty to bring up and improve—lived with and enlarged through the course of his life. This growing collection of ancient proverbs, repeatedly supplemented by Erasmus's reading and annotative comment, was intended as a storehouse of the learning which the author had found so lacking in his youth. The *Colloquies* and the *Adages* were two of the great books of the Renaissance, and it is significant that they, like so many other influential works of the time—Castiglione's *Courtier,* for example—stemmed from that educational impulse which was the ruling humanist passion of the day. Erasmus, looking back on his work near the end of his life, could feel that he had served this need:

When I was a boy in my native Germany barbarous ignorance reigned supreme, to touch Greek was to be a heretic. And so for my part, small as it is, I have tried to stimulate the young to struggle out of the mire of ignorance towards purer studies. For I wrote these volumes not for the Italians but for the Dutch, for Flanders and Brabant. Nor have my attempts been entirely unsuccessful. So that learning might serve piety, I wrote the Enchiridion Militis Christiani; *I increased the* Adagia, *because I was ashamed of the scantiness of the first edition.*

Northern humanists produced works of rhetoric, poetry, history, and epigraphy comparable to those of their Italian predecessors and contemporaries. It was, however, the field of theology which gave northern studies their leading and most significant direction and which produced in the work of Erasmus the peak of their achievement. In him we can see the tools, methods, and wisdom of the *studia humanitatis* of the south grafted onto the Christian piety of the north to reach a new growth. It was a change of emphasis, not a break. Italian humanist learning, taken home and transplanted in the north, grew into a rather different tree. Or should one say that northerners cultivated a graft which Italians had tried but failed?

Northern Piety

The spiritual, as opposed to the intellectual, beginnings of the movement we are considering must take us back to the late fourteenth century. At this time when, after long years of papal absence from Rome, the contested election of 1378 opened a lengthy period of schism, the voices of northern Christians—admonitory, heretical, quietistic, or simply pious—seemed to take on an independent note of their own, as they called their spiritual leaders to task or sought for other means of religious regeneration. The same critical period that saw St. Catherine of Siena multiplying her appeals for reform, John Wycliffe moving towards a more extreme doctrinal position, and John Gerson formulating his views of conciliar authority, produced the beginnings of a movement which drew upon and replenished the springs of piety in northern Europe for many years to come. This is the movement already known in the fifteenth century as the *Devotio Moderna,* the most famous branch of which is the Brothers of the Common Life.

The two starting-points of the *Devotio Moderna* indicate the two directions in which, in the following century, it was to extend its influence. In 1374 Gerard Groote (1340–84), who had abandoned an academic career in Paris to take up a life of evangelical preaching, turned his house in Deventer into a hostel for a group of pious women. According to the constitution he drew up five years later, they were to live a communal life, sharing work and expenses, bound by no obligations of vows, and free to depart as they wished. After Groote's death, his friend and disciple Florence Radewijns (c. 1350–1400) brought to completion in 1387 the foundation at Windesheim of a monastery which Groote had inspired and which was, according to his wish, placed under the rule of the Augustinian canons.

From these simple but inspiring beginnings flowed two currents of vitalizing influence upon contemporary religion. One, more conventional but answering a widely-felt need of the time, was a response to the problem—which became more urgent as the fifteenth century proceeded—of how existing institutions could be made to answer the ancient Christian call to an ascetic monastic life. Groote and his followers were far from alone in recognizing this need, but the foundation at Windesheim proved particularly capable of meeting it, and grew into a congregation of houses, linked with the first in spiritual observance and a dedicated monastic life. Although there are signs that by the end of the fifteenth century the movement had lost some of the freshness of its first years and was succumbing to some of the less worthy aspects of contemporary monasticism, the Windesheim Congregation was still a regenerating source. In the 1490s, when French reformers were anxious to improve the houses of Château-Landon in the diocese of Sens and Saint Victor in Paris, it was to Windesheim that they looked for help. A prominent part in these moves was taken by Jean Standonck, whose dietetic stringencies were criticized as well as suffered by some of those (including Erasmus) who experienced the harshness of the reformed regime he had introduced at the Collège de Montaigu in Paris. Standonck was deeply affected by the spirit of the *Devotio Moderna*. It was he who went to Windesheim to seek help for Château-Landon, as the result of which a mission of six men was sent to France. They included Jean Mombaer (c. 1460–1501), whose *Rosary of Spiritual Exercises* influenced Ignatius Loyola.

The other, related part of Groote's movement, keeping to the pattern of his first house of sisters and the groups of his immediate followers at Deventer and Zwolle, remained unattached to any existing order. These Brothers and Sisters of the Common Life joined together in pursuit of a common devotional life which participated in the monastic ideal but imitated it without the formalities of vows or religious habits, and without any life-commitment to their profession. Like the first women who came together in Groote's house, they were at liberty to return to ordinary secular life. In these ways they were clearly distinguished from the established orders, with whom, however, they were linked through the Windesheim foundation, and to which they contributed members.

The Brothers of the Common Life also concentrated their activities toward specific ends, notably educational ones. Their common labor before the days

of printing was, in particular, the copying of books, and they were also—
though here their achievement has been exaggerated—closely associated with
the great expansion of education which took place in Germany and the Low
Countries in the fifteenth century. They became influential, and affected the
lives of many devout and perhaps disillusioned people, because they answered
a great need of the period. They helped to provide for the growing educational
demands—of laymen, as well as those who intended to enter the church—in
the greater urban centers. And, in times of religious uncertainty and ecclesiastical dislocation, they offered methods of spiritual consolation, islands of
contemplative security accessible to any reader who would take as his spiritual
weapon a book. The aims were not grandiose, but the results were very impressive. The achievement of the *Devotio Moderna* was not that of a network
of schools and teachers—as it has sometimes been made to appear—but that
of a less easily definable genealogy of spiritual inspiration, which was carried
by individuals and books as well as through continuing institutions.

It is necessary to make clear this distinction between the educational and
spiritual influence of the Brothers of the Common Life, since their work in the
former sphere seems to have been misunderstood. The Brothers were undoubtedly much concerned with the educational needs of their time, but it is a mistake to think of them as having had a revolutionary impact upon contemporary
education. The extent of their teaching was less far-reaching, and the methods
they employed less innovative, than has often been supposed. The Brothers
were not in the first instance, or ever primarily, schoolmasters, and several
of the more celebrated schools with which their name has been linked (such
as the chapter school at Deventer, or the city school at Zwolle) cannot be said
to have belonged to them or been under their direction. These schools existed
before the Brothers were founded, and though John Cele (1350–1417), the
famous rector of Zwolle, was in close communication with Groote, he was not
a member of the Brotherhood. The Brothers' calling was neither scholarship
nor teaching, and indeed both these activities might have been felt to conflict
with their pious preoccupations.

From the outset, however, members of the movement devoted themselves to
the needs, both material and spiritual, of the increasing numbers of boys who
came to be schooled in the towns and cities of the Low Countries. The hostels
which they founded to board these schoolboys were in some cases able to provide tuition or guidance for individual pupils, as for instance 's Hertogenbosch did for the youthful Erasmus, who by the time he got there had probably
completed all the classes of the school at Deventer. In general, however, what
the Brothers offered was spiritual guidance rather than teaching; they were
spiritual mentors and confessors more than they were ever schoolmasters. Only
in a relatively few and late cases do they seem themselves to have taken up
teaching, and founded or assumed the direction of schools. Among such exceptions was the small grammar school at Louvain which, after it came under
the control of the Brothers in 1433, they enlarged in 1470 into a regular board-

ing school which enjoyed a century's existence. And at Liège, where they had given instruction in their hostel, the Brothers started a school at the turn of the fifteenth century in which Greek and rhetoric were taught in the advanced classes. Such cases were exceptional. The work which the Brothers did in this sphere reflected their concerns as a whole; the objectives were devotional, not pedagogical, and focused upon the cities where pastoral needs were most pressing. "We have decided," wrote the Brothers in Zwolle in 1415, "to live in cities, in order that we may be able to give advice and instruction to clerics and other persons who wish to serve the Lord."

While recognizing this limitation, it would be a mistake to underestimate the influence of the *Devotio Moderna*. As spiritual directors, the Brothers were able to inspire many, not all of whom subsequently adopted a religious vocation, with the intensity of the inner religious life. Among those who respected the values of the movement, without ever formally belonging to it, were Wessel Gansfort and Erasmus's teacher Hegius. And Erasmus himself retained throughout his life the impressions of those early years he had spent in school at Deventer, at the Brothers' hostel in 's Hertogenbosch, and in the Augustinian house of Steyn where he was professed. He might in retrospect be critical —especially of unfair pressures to get him into a monastic order—but he took to heart and made his own the characteristics of the circles in which he received his education.

We should not, therefore, look to the Brothers of the Common Life for an enthusiasm for classical scholarship or humanist learning. If some of the schools with which they were associated did occasionally provide such teaching, they stand out from the traditional methods perpetuated by the others. And rarely did the Brothers produce, as opposed to influencing, men of learning. Gabriel Biel, who combined a professorship of theology at Tübingen (1484) with the office of prior of the Brothers at Urach, was unique in his double position. Such lack of intellectual leadership can scarcely be surprising given the constant tendency—which stemmed from the movement's founder— to turn aside from academic disputes and deadening scholastic controversy. "Why should we," asked Groote, "indulge in those endless disputes, such as are held at the universities, and that about subjects of no moral value whatsoever?" He had himself shown the way by his rejection of the University of Paris. It was a recipe for devotion more than a criticism. And the devout exercises which Groote and Radewijns bequeathed to their successors, and which influenced among others Thomas à Kempis, included the advice: "Resolve to avoid and abhor all public disputations which are but wranglings for success in argument, or the appearance thereof (such as the disputations of graduates in theology at Paris), and take no part therein."

This outlook, based upon the belief that there were higher truths to which scholastic argument rendered no useful service, was still a vital force in the *Devotio Moderna* in the later fifteenth century. It resembles an important strain of humanist thought—though Gansfort wrote, having witnessed the achievements of the humanists of Florence, that while the capacities of the Florentines exceeded those of the men of Zwolle, "Yet I prefer the incapacity of these to the subtlety of those." He found St. Paul's accomplishments in "barbarous" Thessaly and Corinth, as compared with learned Athens, to be a weighty argument against universities; "It goes to show that liberal studies are not very pleasing to God."[2] Through the *Imitation of Christ,* the mystical ideal of *docta ignorantia,* learned ignorance, about which Nicholas of Cusa had written, became familiar to the devotional exercises of many who were not bothered by the limitations and defects of university methods. "Of what value are lengthy controversies on deep and obscure matters, when it is not by our knowledge of such things that we shall at length be judged? . . . Truly, 'we have eyes and see not': for what concern to us are such things as *genera* and *species?*" Through Christ, "the teacher of teachers and lord of angels," the lowly mind could "understand more of the ways of the everlasting truth in a single moment than ten years of study in the schools." "Non alta sapere, sed bene agere," right acting rather than high learning, was the theme of the *Imitation.*

The Brothers of the Common Life did not belittle books or studies; they stressed that learning should be of the right sort. The mind of the reader must be devoutly, not inquisitively or acquisitively, directed; learning is the tool and servant of piety; intellectual subtlety has no independent value. From Groote's time onwards, their meditation focused upon the life of Christ and their learning upon the Gospel, the Scriptures, and the Church Fathers. The labor to which they were especially committed was the work of "holy writing" and, though the "good books" they copied were by no means limited to scriptural texts, it was the Bible which was the center of their daily readings and meditation. *Sacra scriptura* was their daily bread in more senses than one: both as the written labors which earned their living and as the day's learning in holy writ. The books which were copied for Groote (who was very well-read in the Scriptures, and who himself employed several scribes and added to his collection of books after he had taken up an evangelical career) were mostly Gospel commentaries and texts of the Fathers. And, as the four books which we know as the *Imitation of Christ* show, studded as they are with Biblical quotations, it was Bible-reading above all which enriched the mind of the Augustinian canon Thomas à Kempis.

The scriptural preoccupations of the *Devotio Moderna* took two directions which were significant as a foreshadowing of later developments. During the later fourteenth century, at a time when the Bible was being translated into various vernaculars, the Brothers participated in the effort to give the laity direct knowledge of Holy Writ. Their own Biblical studies—which differed

[2] E. F. Jacob, *Essays in the Conciliar Epoch,* 3rd ed. (Manchester, 1963), p. 131. Gansfort was not formally a member of the movement, as either a Brother or an Augustinian canon, but was closely associated with it, having lived in one of the Brothers' hostels, and having close links with St. Agnetenburg.

markedly from contemporary university practice in approaching the scriptural text without years of preparatory training—were open to laymen. At Zwolle, where an hour each day was devoted to the study of scripture, after services on Sundays and feast days the Brothers held a lecture or instruction intended for schoolboys, but open to interested comers, at which a Biblical passage was read in the vernacular and followed by a talk. Gerard Zerbolt (1367–98) defended the right of laymen to read the Bible in their own language, though he admitted that some of its books, such as Revelation, needed explanation. How much better, he thought, for them to read scripture than the frivolous romances that commonly held their interest.

It was a natural outcome of such beliefs for the Brothers to turn to Biblical translation. Some of the translations into Dutch which were made in the later fourteenth century can be attributed to Groote himself, including versions of the Psalms and other passages in his Dutch *Book of Hours*. This dates from 1383 and was later often printed, as well as being translated into Low German. Another Dutch Biblical translation which appeared before the end of the century, and which evidently stems from the same circles, includes more books of both testaments and prefaces arguing the case for vernacular scriptures. It seems clear that the followers of the *Devotio Moderna* acted on their belief that laymen should have Biblical texts in languages they understood; when, in the last decade of the fourteenth century, two lawyers put up a justificatory case for the Brothers of the Common Life (whose lawfulness had been called in question), they defended such vernacular scriptures, provided the translations were not distorted. One of them, Everard Foec, also argued the usefulness of schools equipped to teach Hebrew, Arabic, and Chaldean—a suggestion which was not new but which had to wait many years to become even remotely practicable.

In another instance as well the Biblical work of the *Devotio Moderna* was suggestive of future directions. This was not a work of translation but of textual scholarship. John Busch, the chronicler of Windesheim, relates how the Brothers "attempted to reduce all the original books of the Old and New Testaments to the text as translated by St. Jerome from Hebrew into Latin, using the best models obtainable." For this purpose they had to undertake manuscript research, collecting codices from different libraries in order to collate and correct textual variants. Both the objective and the work were remarkable, and to realize their aim of reconstituting Jerome's original text the Brothers gave the highest respect to the oldest texts and corrected a number of Hebrew expressions. They succeeded in producing an improved version of both books of the Vulgate, corrected throughout according to the oldest variants to which they had access, carefully punctuated and revised. It might seem that in this work we have a notable anticipation of sixteenth-century scholarship. There were, however, important differences which make it impossible to describe this labor as humanistic. First, although the Brothers had recourse to the oldest available texts, their aim was not to get back, with a fresh and truer grasp, to the textual context. Their concern was uniformity, not understanding. They wanted a single purified text for liturgical reasons, so that the different houses of their observance should not be using conflicting versions; the choir books in all their monasteries were to employ the one corrected Bible. Given the problems of manuscript diffusion, this was a remarkable enough aim. Also, unlike the humanists' textual studies, the Windesheimers' work on the Bible was static and finite; their investigation ended when they had arrived at their corrected version; it was not extended by the discovery and discussion of further variants. Once they had made their corrected Vulgate it was forbidden to make any textual alterations.

Like all reforming movements the *Devotio Moderna* had its limitations, but the inspiration of its first followers continued to feed subsequent spiritual streams. It was never simply or predominantly a spirituality of laymen, but there was a novelty about the way in which it answered the spiritual needs of seculars—men, women, and boys—in the growing urban centers of the later Middle Ages. It provided help, in ways which were more informal, less rigid, and more adaptable than the institutions of existing orders, for those who lived in the world of affairs while responding to an ancient ascetic summons— the most venerable of all Christian callings—the imitation of Christ. Perhaps the best way of approaching this far-reaching spiritual heritage, which influenced far more people than ever formally became members of the Brothers of the Common Life or the Windesheim Congregation, is through books.

Most celebrated of all the works produced in the circles of the *Devotio Moderna* is the *Imitation of Christ.* More properly described as four treatises joined together under the later title of "Admonitions useful for the spiritual life. Concerning the Imitation of Christ and the contempt of all the vanities of the world," this small work, long attributed to Jean Gerson, is now generally ascribed to Thomas Hemerken of Kempen, or à Kempis, who died in 1471 having spent most of his long and uneventful life as an Augustinian canon in the house of St. Agnetenburg near Zwolle, which was a member of the Windesheim chapter. À Kempis went to school at Deventer, and among his various writings left a testimonial to his awed respect for the "holy man" Florence Radewijns, of whom he wrote a biography. One of the most striking aspects of the enormous influence of the *Imitation* (of which there were many manuscript copies, as well as early translations and editions) is the way in which spiritual admonitions composed within and addressed to monastic circles could be welcomed and taken to heart by individuals of differing faith living in a variety of worldly circumstances. This reflects not only upon the author—and what he took for granted—but also upon that search for a pruned and simplified piety which characterized some of the strongest spirituality of the time. It turned away from outward ceremonial to concentrate upon exploring and strengthening inner spiritual resources through quiet reading and meditation. So the *Imitation,* which addresses its reader as a confessor might advise a penitent or speaks as a soul communing alone with God, says little about church ceremonies or saints, and nothing in recommendation of pil-

grimages, images, and relics. The emphasis throughout is upon the inner purification of the humble mind. "Some carry their devotion only in books,
pictures, and other visible signs and representations," but they are mistaken,
for while "Nature regards the outward characteristics of a man; grace con-
siders his inner disposition." "God walks with the simple, reveals himself to
the humble." It was an ancient message, but one of refreshing simplicity
amidst the multiplying ceremonies of the late medieval church.

Another book which belongs to this family was the *Rosetum,* or *Rosary of
Spiritual Exercises,* by Jean Mombaer. This work, first printed in full in 1494
and republished twice in the early sixteenth century, likewise has a spiritual
lineage of readers.[3] Mombaer—who, as we have seen, was sent to France on
one of Windesheim's reforming missions and died as abbot of Livry in 1501—
entered St. Agnetenburg about seven years after the death of à Kempis, in
1477–78. His work, like the *Imitation,* was written to aid that inner meditative
life which was the preoccupation of the Brothers (whose whole day, ideally,
was an unbroken sequence of spiritual exercises). Mombaer offered to this end
a veritable labyrinth of meditations covering all the subjects of piety and acts
of religious life, purposefully displayed for easy use and learning, accompanied
by a series of mnemonic verses. Great attention was paid to the method of
presentation and meditative order. The topics were grouped into "rosaries"
of a hundred and fifty points and into other clusters of seven for the days of
the week, ordered in a logical series to concentrate the mind on a determined
theme; the *Chiropsalterium,* which utilized the divisions of the hand, is a
visual example of these memory devices. Like Wessel Gansfort, part of whose
Scala Meditatoria was incorporated into the *Rosetum,* Mombaer treated meditation as a methodical ladder. Spiritual exercise of this kind could bring the
soul into communion with God at any time and place; without it, the reception of the sacraments was of little profit.

Finally, it is not out of place to consider here Erasmus's *Enchiridion Militis
Christiani.* This small book, written at St. Omer in 1501 at the request of a
friend, and first published two years later, holds an important place in Erasmus's *oeuvre* and points the course of his future work. The name *Enchiridion*
(already used by St. Augustine) indicates the character of the work: a pocketbook which should be ready to hand as a spiritual dagger. Erasmus, unlike
Mombaer and à Kempis, was specifically addressing a layman, but the two
weapons which he recommended for the soldiering Christian knight were not
unlike the tools of piety they had offered. "Two weapons should especially be
prepared for him who must fight . . . against the whole troop of vices, of
which the seven capital sins are numbered most powerful. These two weapons
are prayer and knowledge . . . prayer is indeed the more powerful, making it

---

[3] An earlier partial edition of the *Rosetum exercitiorum spiritualium et sacrarum
meditationum* appeared in 1491; editions were also published in 1504 (Basel) and
1510 (Paris). Pierre Debongnie, *Jean Mombaer de Bruxelles* (Louvain and Toulouse,
1927), pp. 305 ff.; Augustin Renaudet, *Humanisme et Renaissance* (Geneva, 1958),
p. 139.

possible to converse with God, yet knowledge is no less necessary." Erasmus
was here concerned with practical piety—the needs of an ordinary layman for
ordered procedures of devotion—and the rules he set down reflect some of
the emphases of the *Devotio Moderna.* The essential armoury for the layman's
mind was the Bible; he should be equipped by "an eager study of the Scriptures." "Bread is not as much the food of the body as the word of God is the
food of the soul." For one fortified with this nourishment, no assaults by inner
enemies need be feared. "Therefore if you will dedicate yourself wholly to the
study of the Scriptures, if you will meditate on the law of the Lord day and
night, you will not be afraid of the terror of the night or of the day." Erasmus,
true to his own beliefs, also carefully allowed for the role of secular learning,
classical poetry and philosophy, and brought Platonic theories of the spiritual
ascent of the soul to serve Christian thinking. He laid great stress on the need
to put invisible values above attendance to the visible ceremonies of worship.
To honor the bones of saints, to pilgrimage to the Holy Sepulcher, or to make
offerings before images were ritualistic acts involving many dangers to true
worship of Christ. Invisible piety was what was pleasing to God. The truly
Christian knight would "hear the word of God within." He had spiritual
wings with which to lift himself up, "from the body to the spirit, from the
visible world to the invisible, from letter to mystery . . . as if by the rungs of
Jacob's ladder." Erasmus, with his ample reading and amplifying aims, added
several rungs to the spiritual step-ladder of the *Devotio Moderna.*

Biblical and Patristic Studies

The religious works which were written and edited by the northern humanists were only one part of their literary output, but it is this part which gives
their work its distinguishing quality. To regard this as the special achievement
of the revival of studies in the north does not mean that we need either to
revert to the older view of Italian humanism as essentially pagan or to deny
that northern scholars found important precedents for their work in Italy. In
this field, as in others, there is no clear-cut line to be drawn between what
went on on either side of the Alps. Northerners can be seen as continuing, in
their own way, what had already been begun in Italy.

Since Burckhardt's day it has come to be seen that true paganizing was
exceptional in fifteenth-century Italy, even if the intense study of antiquity undeniably introduced "some intellectual detachment from older religious convictions."[4] That concern for stylistic improvement which led

---

[4] Denys Hay, *The Italian Renaissance in its Historical Background* (Cambridge, 1961),
p. 176. See also the recent remarks on the "mild tincture of paganism" which accompanied the study of antiquity in J. R. Hale, *Renaissance Europe, 1480–1520* (London, 1971), pp. 299–300.

Pietro Bembo to advise a correspondent against reading St. Paul (lest his style be spoiled) could lead toward Biblical studies as well as away from them. Yet the desire to imitate antiquity might do a great deal to obscure a writer's beliefs. Northern humanists, like their southern predecessors, sometimes used in the pursuit of literary elegance (or what seemed elegant) expressions which seem to belie their Christian vocation. The fact that Abbot Whethamstede of St. Albans (d. 1465) thought fit to lard a letter to his monks with pretentious allusions to pagan deities and to say, "we are erecting altars of incense to Neptune" should not delude us—any more than it would have worried his recipients—as to the true nature of his beliefs. Conrad Celtis's understanding of ancient learning went much deeper than this veneer of classical allusion but, though he combined Neoplatonic thinking with savage criticism of the church, he continued to revere the Virgin and the saints while referring to God the Father as Jupiter, and Mary as the Mother of the Thunderer. Erasmus himself is an example, apostrophizing the Virgin as "that true Diana."

Some important patristic work was done in Italy in the fifteenth century. The writings of the Fathers were part of the heritage of antiquity which humanists wanted to recover and restore, and the Italians managed to regain various previously unknown Greek patristic texts, and to translate into Latin a number of others. By the time that Humphrey, duke of Gloucester, commissioned his Italian secretary, Antonio Beccaria, to translate from Greek into Latin several treatises of St. Athanasius, various Greek Fathers had been rendered into Latin by Ambrogio Traversari. Appointed general of the Camaldolese order in 1431, Traversari was a skilled Greek scholar who played a large role in formulating the union between the Greek and Latin churches. He died shortly after, in 1439, leaving among the works he had completed in his relatively short life Latin translations of Chrysostom, St. Ephraem, the life and four orations of Gregory of Nazianzen, and treatises by St. Basil. George of Trebizond, whom we have already encountered through Lefèvre, translated, besides Plato and Aristotle, a number of patristic works from the Greek. Especially significant, in the light of later developments in the north, was the work done in this field by Giannozzo Manetti (1396–1459) and Lorenzo Valla (1407–57)—though only the latter had a direct influence on subsequent work. Both of these men were associated with Pope Nicholas V (who did much to encourage translators), and both found protection at the court of Naples, where Valla wrote his critical work on the Donation of Constantine, and where Manetti took refuge when his work was attacked.

Manetti's studies are particularly interesting for the way in which they anticipated later undertakings. As a humanist layman, whose ambition was to strengthen the foundations of theology by making a fresh translation of the Bible from the original sources, and who learned both Greek and Hebrew to carry out this work, it is remarkable that he was able to accomplish as much as he did. By taking into his service two Greeks, a Syrian and a Jew,

Manetti gained the necessary linguistic proficiency; he collected manuscripts and with the help of his teacher-servants read the entire Biblical text through twice. He had therefore thoroughly prepared himself by the time he embarked on his translation, of which only the New Testament and Psalter survive. The latter is outstanding in that it set out in three parallel columns the Septuagint, the Vulgate text, and Manetti's own text—apparently the first use of this method. Manetti—like Valla, whose work on the Donation was completed slightly earlier—was fully aware of the problems and possibilities of applying humanist linguistic skills to the sources of the faith. He was not afraid to direct his critical methods upon the most used portions of the Bible, and to re-write the text revered by long tradition—that of the Vulgate. In this he was a true precursor of Erasmus. And, like Erasmus, he encountered harsh crit-icism, though the opposition to Manetti was made even fiercer by the fact that he was a layman. The critics in both cases upheld the same point—the sanctity of the Vulgate text.

Valla's work has gained fuller recognition than Manetti's because it received the *imprimatur* of Erasmus. The *Annotations on the New Testament* which Valla wrote in the 1440s were found by Erasmus in the Premonstratensian library of Parc near Louvain in 1504 and published by him the following year. Valla's application of humanist criticism to the Vulgate text, his un-flinching readiness to point out the weakness of this version, and his scorn for the errors of translators and scribes and for those who stood by them in ignorance of Greek, are all abundantly clear. He used between three and seven Greek texts and three Latin translations to make his notes, and de-fended (in reply later to the charges of Poggio Bracciolini) alterations in Jerome's hallowed text. "If I correct something," he said, "I am not correct-ing Holy Scripture but its translation . . . In that work I was not speaking of the truth of the Gospels but of the elegance of the Latin language." He was not reprehending Jerome, but the textual degeneration of a thousand years. What, indeed, he asked, was Holy Scripture if not a faithful text?[5] Valla, in fact, true humanist that he was, could contemplate scriptural emendations on grounds of stylistic felicity as well as accuracy. Others might be shocked, but Erasmus had found an ally.

Erasmus's publication of Valla's *Annotations* is perhaps the best-known example of the kind of fertilization which could take place through the con-junction of two worlds. It was not alone. One may regard it rather as the most dramatic example of a gradual process of germination, in which earlier

---

[5] "Itaque, ne multus sim, si quid emendo, non scripturam sacram emendo, sed illius interpretationem: neque in eam contumeliosus sum, sed pius potius. . . . Ego autem in illo opere non de sententia Evangeliorum aiebam, sed de elegantia linguae Latinae." "Ubi quid dicas tu esse sacram scripturam? certe nullam, nisi veram interpretationem." *Laurentii Vallae Opera* (Basel, 1540), pp. 268–70; *cf.* Raymond Marcel, "Les Perspectives de l'Apologétique,' de Lorenzo Valla à Savonarole," *Courants Reli-gieux et Humanisme à la Fin du XVe et au Début du XVIe Siècle* (Paris, 1959), p. 86.

work of Italian scholars was put to use and published by northern humanists. Manuscripts of a number of the Italian translations of Greek Fathers
mentioned above had already found their way northward in the fifteenth
century. Several of Traversari's owe their presence in Oxford libraries to the
interest of two leading English humanist book-collectors, William Grey
(bishop of Ely from 1454 to 1478) and Robert Flemming. Another Oxford
man—unlike them no humanist—who owned Traversari's Chrysostom was
the crusty chancellor of the university, Thomas Gascoigne.[6] Some of these
texts reached more readers after northern presses had put them into print.
Thus Traversari's Latin version of the sermons of St. Ephraem appeared in a
French translation in Paris about 1500, and the 1480 Bruges edition of his
translation of the *Hierarchies* of Dionysius apparently served Colet as well
as Lefèvre (who republished this work). The same fortunes attended George
of Trebizond, whose Latin text of Cyril of Alexandria was printed by Josse
Clichtove. The list could be extended. It seems that northern humanists did
much to give their Italian predecessors the benefit of publication. Yet perhaps such editions tell more about associated chains of thought than they do
about direct lines of influence. As with Protestant reformers' editions of
earlier Hussite or Wycliffite writings, such publications might reflect the confirmation of existing or growing ideas, rather than the prompting of new
ones: the discovery and brandishing of allies, rather than the advertisement
of actual ancestry. Luther's remark about those who were Hussites without
knowing it has its parallel on the humanist plane. A humanist, by definition,
knew that he was one, but it was not until long after the invention of printing that he could meet and recognize all the thoughts and works of other
humanists. And so, while Erasmus and Hutten were confirmed in views they
already held by discovering such support in Lorenzo Valla, various other
northern humanists found their work assisted by what had already been done
in Italy.

It is surely significant, though, how much had to be done over again. The
great achievements in patristic and Biblical scholarship in this period were,
despite the Italian researches we have noted, mainly the outcome of indigenous
northern inspiration, and represented fresh approaches and new beginnings.
As at all times when great intellectual changes are in the air, the sources of
interaction and influence become too diffuse and vague to be properly trace-
able. Ideas become part of an individual's way of thinking without his
necessarily knowing exactly how he has come by them. Intellectual paternity
must always be partly putative. There were, however, some distinctive qualities about the northern ambience onto which humanist concerns were grafted,
and these helped to determine the direction of new studies. Northern human-

[6] R. Weiss, *Humanism in England during the Fifteenth Century*, 2nd ed. (Oxford,
1957), pp. 93, 103–104, 132; H. O. Coxe, *Catalogus codicum MSS, qui in collegiis
aulisque Oxoniensibus hodie adservantur,* part 1 (Oxford, 1852), pp. 22, 28, 31–
33, 48.

ism grew upon and out of the long traditions of transalpine piety and theology.

The study of the Bible should be considered in this setting. As has been seen in the work of the *Devotio Moderna,* it existed on two different levels—as it always had. On the one hand, there was the application of the highest learning to the scriptural text. On the other, there was popular knowledge and the processes by which ordinary unlettered or unlearned persons gained Biblical knowledge. In the developing schools of the north in the twelfth and thirteenth centuries, the Bible had been very intensively studied and commented upon, and its central role in the earlier part of that period is indicated by the very name *sacra pagina,* the sacred page, given to the subject in early faculties of theology. "Theology," however—and the name itself in our sense of the word only arrived in the twelfth century—became distinguished from Bible study as the term for those dialectical methods of exposition and organization which came into use at that time. Such techniques of study (we need perhaps to remind ourselves, after all the invective that has been heaped upon them) were refined tools in their day, extremely useful for reaching systematic formulations of Christian faith and for use in Biblical studies. It seems clear, though, that in the later Middle Ages a considerable part of such studies—and therefore of the work of theologians—had become dissociated from the direct study of the Biblical text. To some extent the study of theology became clogged by the sheer mass of work achieved; in combination with the perennial inertia of great educational establishments, this meant that very strong motivation was needed to make new beginnings. As Erasmus remarked, "a Faculty never dies," and its failure to do so may come to have a deadening effect. By the fifteenth century the direct study of the Bible had a relatively small place in university theology; many years of preliminary study of other texts, notably Peter Lombard's *Sentences* (c. 1150), were required before the scripture itself was reached. Many students (unlike, for instance, John Wycliffe, with his decades of study at Oxford) did not persevere long enough to reach this point. If we do not yet know enough about Biblical scholarship to draw a clear picture of the century-and-a-half after 1350, it seems evident enough that "the fifteenth century must have forgotten or disowned its ancestry: the dossier as a whole gives an impression of stunted growth. Biblical scholarship never achieved the standing of a separate discipline within the framework of sacred science. Students of theology got no preliminary training in language."[7]

Naturally enough, dissatisfaction at this state of affairs was expressed. Various efforts were also made to regenerate the study of the Bible. In Italy at the foundation of the *Collegium Gregorianum* at Perugia in 1362, Nicolas Capocci, cardinal bishop of Tusculum, provided that six of the forty scholars were to study theology. He explained this arrangement on the grounds that, "in these days few clerical scholars are to be found who are learned in holy Scrip-

---

[7] Beryl Smalley, "The Bible in the Medieval Schools," *The Cambridge History of the Bible,* vol. 2, ed. G. W. H. Lampe (Cambridge, 1969), p. 219.

ture [*sacra pagina*] and who know how to expound the word of God to the people."[8] John Gerson, regent in theology and chancellor of Paris, objected to the sterilities of formal theology and voiced the need to return from its subtleties to Scripture. The reforming movements associated with John Wycliffe in England and John Hus in Bohemia in the late fourteenth and early fifteenth centuries, which originated in the theology faculties of Oxford and Prague, both centered upon a return to Biblical sources. And both had the effect of turning attention toward fresh scriptural translation.

To cast even a cursory glance over the vernacular Bibles of this period is to gain some sense of the isolation of academic theology from lay piety. The later Middle Ages were extremely prolific in the production of vernacular Scriptures. By the end of the fourteenth century, the Bible had been translated into French, English, German, Czech, and Italian. The number of incunabula editions of these texts measures the extent of contemporary demand. In the year 1471, two complete Bibles were printed in Venice; the first German Bible to be printed, the Mentel Bible of 1466, was reissued in eleven new editions before 1500; before 1501, there had appeared more than thirty editions in six vernaculars.

The Brothers of the Common Life, whose movement, as we have seen, combined a rejection of academic disputes with a simpler scriptural piety, represented one effort to bridge the gap between Christian learning and Christian piety. The northern humanists were making another attempt to draw together these diverging strands—though their work was still maturing when it was overtaken by a fresh tide, in which the popular tended to outweigh the learned. At the heart of their studies lay the application of improved linguistic skills and critical methods to the Scriptures and to the Fathers—themselves revered as models for what the humanists were trying to do. This work was humanist not only in the sense that classical languages and classical learning were essential to it, but also in the continuous awareness of the wide purposes which textual studies served. They were to be the means of spiritual regeneration for individuals and for the whole of Christendom.

Having outlined the general setting, we may turn to the work of individual humanists. In France, Spain, England, and the Low Countries many assumptions were shared by Lefèvre, Ximenes, Colet, and Erasmus, but one may be as struck by their differences. All were concerned with Biblical renovation, but their methods embraced a wide range of criticism. All strove to renew the church; yet it was Erasmus, the only one of the four not to pursue this objective through an administrative office in the church (and who refused a cardinalate), who had far and away the greatest influence on the future—ecclesiastical and secular.

Jacques Lefèvre d'Etaples (c. 1455–1536), described by Pomponazzi as

[8] Hastings Rashdall, *The Universities of Europe in the Middle Ages,* vol. 2, ed. F. M. Powicke and A. B. Emden (Oxford, 1936), p. 41, n. 5.

"second to none in learning in this age," might seem in some ways to stand closer to the work of Italian humanists than Erasmus, yet in the end one may judge him to be less truly humanist. Sharing with Erasmus the desire "to join wisdom and piety with eloquence," to find harmony and enlightenment through a deeper knowledge of classical and Christian antiquity, he too devoted himself to years of textual labors. But in Lefèvre's case it is possible to discern more of a progression, from Aristotelian philosophy to mystical contemplation, while his evangelical piety threatened him more seriously with suspicions of sympathy with Protestant Reform. Whereas Erasmus removed himself from Basel after the outbreak of iconoclastic frenzy in 1529, Lefèvre, charged with Lutheran views in 1525, took refuge in Strasbourg, where the city authorities, steadily moving towards a full Reformation, had lately been removing ecclesiastical images.

Lefèvre made several visits to Italy, but he was a late beginner. His first journey took place in 1491–92, at which time he had published nothing, and his Greek learning (helped by the presence of George Hermonymos in Paris) was also taken up late. Direct knowledge of Italy impressed Lefèvre, like Colet, with Florentine Neoplatonism, but it was the pursuit of Aristotle, rather than Plato, which inspired his Greek learning. Insisting that a proper understanding of Aristotelian philosophy was indispensable to the study of the gospel, he embarked upon thirty years' labor of editing and commenting upon almost the entire corpus of Aristotle's works. Between 1494 and 1515 he produced editions of the *Physics, Nicomachean Ethics, Organon, Politics,* and *Metaphysics,* and also wrote paraphrases of most of Aristotle's works. Lefèvre's wide reading in the works of ancient historians, orators, and poets gave him a familiarity with the world of antiquity which enabled him to move about in it with the ease which distinguished the work of the best humanists. This intimacy and proximity, his union of learning with imaginative comprehension, make it possible to compare pages of his writings with those of Erasmus and Montaigne. Yet the comparison has to be made with reservations, for Lefèvre always wanted to penetrate through and beyond antiquity to mystical perceptions alien to these other essayists. Lefèvre, convinced that "the theology of the Aristotelians agrees and unites with Christian wisdom in a great harmony and concord," was thoroughly humanistic in his rejection of scholastic method and commentary, but Aristotle for him remained more of a "pious philosopher," moral and orthodox, than he was for secular Italian Aristotelians. Lefèvre's Aristotle was to be seen in the guise of priest and theologian, whose metaphysics and philosophy shone with the "immense light" of divine illumination, even though God had not yet appeared visibly in the world.

It is understandable that, with this outlook, Lefèvre was attracted by the work of Nicholas of Cusa, as well as Pico della Mirandola's cabalistic learning and Ficino's Platonism. These sympathies bore fruit in various editions, including the hermetic books attributed to Hermes Trismegistus and the *Celestial Hierarchy* of Dionysius the Areopagite. Such works reveal the way in which Lefèvre's humanism was fused with, transcended, and limited by his mysticism. His life reflects both the tension of conflicting traditions and the effort to fuse them. Drawn toward but rejecting the vocation of a monastic life, in a way reminiscent of Thomas More, he responded to the call of active reform by serving in the 1520s as vicar-general to Bishop Briçonnet in the diocese of Meaux. And Lefèvre's religious commitment got the better of his reasoning when he refused to accept such critical arguments as Grocyn put forward for doubting the Dionysian writings as authentic evidence of the early church.

The third and most important part of Lefèvre's work—his scriptural editions and commentaries—was truly evangelical. His search for illumination and Christian regeneration caused him to concentrate increasingly upon the study of Biblical texts and made him the most distinguished exponent of Christian humanism in France. He shared—with different emphases—the double concern expressed by Erasmus for purifying the sources of Christian doctrine and making them more widely available. Though unlike Erasmus in his critical inhibitions as well as his style (Lucian was as alien to Lefèvre as he was congenial to Erasmus), Lefèvre showed himself as a critic in his own right. The *Quincuplex Psalter,* which he brought out in 1509, was from this point of view a decisive achievement. It set out in parallel columns the different versions of Jerome's text which Lefèvre had discovered, interpolated with his own resumé and commentary. A contemporary called it a new form of exegesis, and though, as we have seen, Lefèvre was not the first to devise this method—nor indeed the first to put such an effort into print—his book marked an important step forward in Biblical scholarship. While remaining conservative in his elaborate allegorizing of the Psalms, Lefèvre ventured, despite the limitations of his Hebrew learning, timidly to suggest some textual corrections. Three years later came the Epistles of St. Paul, complete with grammatical notes and commentary. This also broke new ground. Beside the Vulgate text was printed (in modestly small type) a version which Lefèvre had made himself from the Greek, showing his concern to get back, behind the Vulgate if necessary, to the exact thought of the Apostle. That Lefèvre's grammatical corrections were often not very felicitous is less important than his readiness to make them—which he himself found it necessary to excuse on the grounds that the Vulgate could not be attributed to Jerome. Within his limits then, Lefèvre was prepared to reject ecclesiastical tradition in the cause of apostolic truth. This was demonstrated still more clearly in the *Discussion of Mary Magdalene* (1518), which argued, contrary to accepted views, that Mary the sister of Martha and Lazarus, Mary Magdalene who was delivered of seven devils, and the penitent who anointed Christ's feet were three different persons, not one. This work occasioned a considerable controversy, in which John Fisher defended the traditional interpretation while Josse Clichtove came to the support of Lefèvre.

For Lefèvre the power of the Gospel was transcendent. "The Word of God suffices. This alone is enough to effect life everlasting." He prefaced his *Commentaries on the Four Gospels* (1521) with a call to bishops and kings to devote themselves to intensifying true worship through the Word of God; " . . . and may this be the only striving, comfort, and desire of all, to know the Gospel, to follow the Gospel, everywhere to advance the Gospel." In the diocese of Meaux, Lefèvre had a bishop to answer this call, and there he was able to work for the cause of evangelical reform, especially through the publication of vernacular scriptures and liturgical translations.

Despite the conclusions of some of his contemporaries, Lefèvre was neither another Erasmus nor another Luther. He stood somewhere in between, sharing views with both, but in the end divided from both, distinct above all perhaps in the quality of mystical illumination without which he believed all humanist labors must leave the mind in some degree of darkness. But such distinctions did not inhibit the alarmist orthodox who were so distrustful of the activities of *humanistae theologizantes,* theologizing humanists. And Lefèvre, whose edition of St. Paul had been criticized for correcting the Vulgate, was in 1526 labelled, together with Erasmus, with this disparaging term by Noël Bédier, theologian of the Sorbonne. The grounds of this attack are interesting. Bédier found both Lefèvre's commentaries and Erasmus's *Paraphrases* of the New Testament objectionable in their claim to "drink from rivers which flow from the very source of divine wisdom, and not from distant rivulets which have degenerated through their great distance from that source; that is to say, they always have in their hands the writings of Origen, Tertullian, Cyprian, Basil, Hilary, Chrysostom, Ambrose, Jerome and others like them, instead of the scholastics, such as Peter Lombard, Alexander Hales, Thomas, Bonaventure, Richard, Ockham, and writers of this kind"—and for this they proclaimed themselves humanists.

In the history of Spanish humanism a dominant position is held by Cardinal Ximenes (or Jiménez) de Cisneros (1436–1517), whose Polyglot Bible was the outstanding humanist achievement of the peninsula in these years. Like most men of distinction in his time, Ximenes had his years of Italian experience— in his case six, spent practicing canon law in Rome. Later, he turned his exceptional influence and interests toward the concern common to contemporary Christian humanists: ecclesiastical reform, promoted by a program of studies. Ximenes was a Franciscan, an order he joined, significantly, years after having entered the priesthood and having occupied a diocesan office. In the 1490s, as confessor to Queen Isabella and archbishop of Toledo, he used his powerful position to direct various reforms, including (simultaneous with Standonck's work in France) the improvement of monastic observance. The two achievements for which he is deservedly famous are those which link him most closely with the ideas of the leading humanists of the north, whom he admired and tried to attract to his country. The foundation of Alcalá University, and the Complutensian Polyglot Bible produced there (*Complutum* being the Latin for Alcalá), belonged, however, to a rather different world from that of Erasmus. Behind the similarities of methods and intentions, lay a closer attachment to ecclesiastical horizons, as is attested by Ximenes' ten-year tenure of the rank of cardinal, which Erasmus refused.

The foundation at Alcalá, which finally opened, after years of preparation and building, in 1508, functioned within the context of ecclesiastical teaching and training. Ximenes was anxious to train an elite of educated clerics to serve his church, and theology—to which other arts and sciences were regarded as handmaidens—was to be the queen of his university. Hoping to renew theological studies by an infusion of the *via moderna* from the north, Ximenes made Alcalá innovative in the place it gave to nominalist teaching. The new school was, however, modernistic in other ways as well—and in ways more in tune with humanism. The cardinal was concerned with purifying the sources of learning, with the direct study of the Bible as the central task of theology. He also had a grandiose plan (only partially realized) for publishing the whole of Aristotle in both Greek and a new Latin translation.

Greek was for Ximenes the key to true theology, and the greatest novelty of his new university was the study of the Bible through the original languages of both testaments. Already in 1502 he seems to have begun to collect around him what has been described as a small Biblical academy of men—Jewish converts and hellenists—whose linguistic accomplishments could further his textual studies. Some of the specialists he attracted to his circle served both in the university and on the great Biblical edition. The converted Jew, Alfonso de Zamora, who inaugurated the teaching of Hebrew at Alcalá in 1512, and the Cretan Demetrios Doucas, who held the chair of Greek from 1513 to 1518, both played an important role in the preparation of the Polyglot. Alcalá, like the later foundation of Louvain in which Erasmus played a large part, was a center for multilingual studies, though the different languages did not have an exact parity. Forty chairs were planned, including one (abortively) for Arabic, but it was those in Greek, Hebrew and Aramaic in the trilingual college of St. Jerome whose achievements became famous. It is to be noted that Ximenes himself accorded precedence to Greek, the chair in which (unlike those in Hebrew and Arabic) was to continue to be filled providing anyone at all was present to benefit from its instruction.

If Ximenes' Biblical plans went back to 1502, it was from about 1510 that they began to take definite shape, and he intensified his search for manuscripts. Although he did not live to enjoy the success of the monumental work he had inspired, directed, and paid for, the bulk of it was completed by the time of his death. The New Testament was printed in 1514 and, three years later in the summer of 1517, the Old Testament was finished, four months before the Cardinal died. In the meantime was concluded an associated work, a triple lexicon for Greek, Hebrew, and Aramaic. The whole, finally presented to the world about 1522, represented an immense achievement of printing as well as learning, a genuine landmark in the history of Biblical scholarship. Yet one should not jump to the conclusion that Ximenes' aims were those of Manetti or Erasmus. Indeed, the way in which he himself referred to the Vulgate Latin flanked by Greek and Hebrew as resembling Christ between the two thieves tells us something about the limits of his work. It was essentially a matter of textual restoration, rather than the linguistic emendation dear to the minds of humanists. In some ways there is a closer parallel with the Biblical correction of the Windesheimers than with Erasmus's work. Cardinal Ximenes concentrated his batteries of scholarly skills not so much for comparative linguistic studies as to establish, through textual analysis of Latin, Greek, and Hebrew manuscripts, the correct words of tradition. The main objective of the undertaking was to end the multiplication of erroneous versions—multiplying through print even more seriously than they had in manuscript—by reconstructing through laborious comparison of texts the correct Vulgate. The whole operation was attended by a respect for authority alien to mature humanist thinking. To establish from variant manuscript sources the best and most ancient form of the text was a task of considerable magnitude, but the refusal to make corrections beyond the sanctions of such sources was also a considerable limitation. As his own words testify, Ximenes gave the place of honor to the Vulgate, to which the Greek and Hebrew were ancillary.

It would be wrong to disparage Ximenes' work for these reasons. The vital aim of his great labors was spiritual renewal. The verve of the edition lay in the urge to reach the inner pulse of the sacred text, to uncover the "hidden mysteries" of the divine spirit which lay beneath the shadow of the literal form. This itself can be related to humanistic intentions, and the cardinal expressed hopes of reviving the "hitherto moribund" study of Scripture. Yet the reactions of one of the humanist collaborators on the Polyglot reflect dissatisfaction with its methods. Elio Antonio de Nebrija entered the cardinal's service in 1513, and his Hebrew learning enabled him to do valuable work on the revision of the Bible in its final stages. He was as passionately concerned as was Ximenes for the restoration of the scriptural text, but was prepared to go much further than Ximenes in using linguistic knowledge to improve it. Nebrija would have liked a more rigorous comparative use of the triple linguistic sources; discrepancies in the Vulgate New Testament should be resolved by having recourse to the Greek; to understand differences in the Latin or Greek texts of the Old Testament it was necessary to ask questions about the Hebrew. The logical outcome would have been what Erasmus did, which was far from Ximenes' intention: to correct the Vulgate to the extent of making a new Latin translation. Nebrija himself claimed that his object was to reconstruct the original Vulgate, but he certainly conceived of this task differently from Cardinal Ximenes.

To turn to England and John Colet may seem, after Lefèvre and Alcalá, like moving into a sidestream—if not a backwater—of the humanist world. England in these years produced no great works of patristic or Biblical scholarship comparable to those of the continent. Leading English humanists long continued to look abroad for the publication, as well as the purchase, of texts. More's *Utopia* was first published at Louvain in 1516, and the first Greek

book was not printed in England until 1543. Yet if this tells us something
about the narrowness of the book market in England, as well as about the
internationalism of contemporary humanist pursuits, it leaves out of account
those currents of personal influence which could count for so much. Colet held
a respected place among the northern humanists, although he wrote little, and
has to be judged by report as well as by his work.

"When I listen to my friend Colet, I seem to be listening to Plato himself!"
wrote Erasmus. Thanks to the commendations of Colet's friends, it is still
possible to apprehend something of this outspoken, impetuous, self-denying
man, who was able to kindle the spirit of Erasmus and rebuke Henry VIII in
public without provoking his ire. As the only surviving child of a family of
twenty-two, he devoted much of the inheritance which came to him from his
father, a mayor of London, to the refoundation of the school of St. Paul's,
where he was appointed dean in 1504. He shared and exemplified the twin
dissatisfactions of the best contemporary humanists: with the aridities of traditional modes of learning, and the shortcomings of the institutions of the
church. What he learned at Oxford of scholastic Aristotelianism seems merely
to have made him aware of what his education lacked. He found "barren and
empty" those intellectual exercises which some called keenness of intellect in
the Scotists; "he said [reported Erasmus] that they seemed to him stupid and
dull, and anything but clever. For they argue about the opinions of others
and about words, gnawing now this and now that; and they dissect everything
minutely." And had his search—which he also confided to Erasmus—for a
spiritual community "really bound together for a Gospel life" been more successful, Colet might have made into the vocation of his maturity the life of
retreat which he prepared among the Carthusians for his old age. In those days
it was easier to find retreats for the mind than for the spirit. Yet the journey
which Colet made to Italy in the 1490s might be seen as a spiritual as well as
an intellectual pilgrimage—he went, as Erasmus put it, "like a merchant
seeking goodly wares."

What Colet had vainly sought in England, he found in Italy in the teaching
of the Florentine Platonists. Marsilio Ficino (whom Colet corresponded with,
but apparently never met) and Pico della Mirandola both profoundly influenced him. The different uses to which Colet and Erasmus put their Italian-
Greek experience might be taken as an indication of their differences of
upbringing and background, as well as temperament. Whereas Colet went to
Italy in his late twenties and returned after four years inspired by humanist
teaching and his increased knowledge of Italian Neoplatonism, he was nearly
fifty before he became fully alive to the need for profound Greek learning. His
continental learning was turned primarily not to literary or scholarly objectives, but to the evangelical work of preaching and lecturing on the text of the
Bible. Erasmus, on the other hand, who was not far off forty before he set foot
in Italy was by then, as we have seen, master of Greek; and for him the study
and restoration of antiquity were the united and preeminent tasks of reform.
Whereas Colet took as his forum the traditional organs of pulpit and school,

that of Erasmus, more modern and dynamic, was the scholar's study, opened to the world through the printer's office. Colet, though almost exactly the same age as Erasmus, belonged to a different generation. Perhaps this helps to explain his influence on his great contemporary, who was better placed to carry out the work which Colet, given different circumstances, might have liked to accomplish himself.

Colet's humanism, which took fruit in his new school and in his preaching, was essentially Biblical. Erasmus, referring to Colet's work at St. Paul's, describes how he adopted the unusual practice of preaching himself at every great feast in his own pulpit. "He did not take his topics piecemeal from the Gospels or Epistles, but he chose some connected argument and went through with it to the end in succeeding sermons, as for instance St. Matthew's Gospel, or the Creed, or the Lord's Prayer." The extent to which Colet had absorbed humanist learning became evident soon after his return from Italy in 1496, when he began to deliver a sequence of public lectures in Oxford (possibly to satisfy the requirements for the degree of B.D.) on the Epistles of St. Paul. He was concerned to make the apostle's words as alive to his hearers as they had been to the original audience. His exposition of Romans included a description of what Rome was like at the time St. Paul was writing, and Colet took pains to explain the historical circumstances in which the apostle admonished Christians not to oppose Roman rulers. It may seem an obvious enough approach now; it was novel and exciting at the time to be brought into direct contact with the circumstances of the Pauline world. The revolutionary way in which Colet had severed himself from accepted scholastic annotators and methods was evident in his Platonic interpretation, as well as in this concentration upon grammatical and historical exegesis of the scriptural text. He explicitly referred to Ficino "touching the excellency of love," and in his allegorical exposition of Genesis made use of Pico's commentary, the *Heptaplus*.

The statutes for St. Paul's school reflect the characteristic ingredients of Colet's humanist piety. His pupils were to unite pure style with pure doctrine. Schooled in the faith through vernacular learning of the catechism, creed and Ten Commandments, the children in his classes were expected to obey the rules of Latin prosody just as they were to kneel at the sound of the sacring bell. The authors they were to study were all such "as have the veray Romayne eliquence joyned withe wisdome specially Cristyn"—those who wrote with "clene and chast laten." The Fathers appeared as models alongside Sallust and Cicero.

All barbary, all corrupcion, all laten adulterate, which ignorant blynde folis brought into this worlde, and with the same hath distayned and poysenyd the old laten spech and the varay Romayne tong which in the tyme of Tully and Salust and Virgill and Terence was usid; whiche also seint Jerome and seint Ambrose and seint Austen and many hooly doctors lernyd in theyr tymes,—I say that fylthynesse and all such abusyon which the later blynde worlde

brought in, which more ratheyr may be callid blotterature thenne litterature, I
utterly abbanysh and exclude oute of this scole.

Yet Colet, with his desire for double purity, was not quite at home with his humanist Christian precepts. He was too conscious of the possible conflict between style and doctrine; his selection of authors safe for youthful study (Lactantius, Prudentius, Sedulius, St. Augustine, St. Jerome, and Baptista Mantuanus, and Erasmus) left outside the curriculum some of the best Latin literature. Humanist studies in England certainly owed Colet a great deal, but what he rejected was as much a part of his heritage as what he embraced.

So, once again, we are brought back to Erasmus. It is always hard to do justice to Erasmus, and never more so than in discussion of his Biblical and patristic writings, the center of his life's work. It takes greatness to appreciate the great, especially among contemporaries. It is a measure of Erasmus's uniqueness that he obtained recognition of a previously unparalleled kind among his contemporaries throughout Europe. When he arrived in England he was already known; when he left Basel he was given a ceremonial farewell. He received offers and invitations from Rome and Zurich, from the kings of France and England, from pope and emperor, and made more friends and enemies with his pen than anyone had ever done in the course of a lifetime. Had he chosen to, he could have enjoyed any number of secure positions, secular or ecclesiastical, instead of leading a roving uncomfortable existence which culminated in the horrors of becoming a householder in the antiquity of his sixties. But he preferred to remain as independent and unattached as possible, free to speak and write according to his own convictions. There was one overriding reason why he did so; he wished to be free to devote himself to his chosen work—the freeing of captive theology.

Having proceeded this far, it should now be easier for us to see this dedication in its proper setting. Erasmus's achievement was unique in its scale, its scope, and its quality, but it also belonged to a context, and among the influences which helped to forge it the *Devotio Moderna* and Colet's England must always be set alongside the critical *Annotations* and Greek studies of Valla's Italy. Erasmus's mind was cosmopolitan, unpledged to loyalties of nation or race; he took the whole of Europe for his library, study, audience—and home. Yet it was as Erasmus of Rotterdam that he made himself famous, as a Dutchman that he wrote, and in his own country that he would have liked to die as a last Dutch prayer escaped from his lips. "My dear Holland," whose fertility and manners he warmly defended, was "a country I must always praise and venerate, since to her I owe my life's beginning." His lifelong devotion to Biblical studies, and the belief that good learning and good life were intrinsically associated and had their deepest sources in the Christian gospel, went back to those Dutch beginnings and the nurturing influences of the Brothers of the Common Life.

England, too, through the perceptive Colet and the happy genius of Thomas More, helped to give Erasmus that assurance which is needed to undertake a vast work. What happened to Edward Gibbon on the Capitol on 15 October 1764 happened to Erasmus through various encounters over the years with the living and the dead. While Gibbon was inspired by ruins to write about decline and decay, Erasmus was inspired both by living decay and the examples of others, present and past, to undertake a work of rebirth, to renew the study of the Bible by restoring its text and the whole setting of scriptural knowledge. It was an aim which gained strength from the example of Colet's scriptural humanism. We do not have to suppose that Colet gave Erasmus anything which was not already present—perhaps more latent than active—in the latter's mind. Their meeting at Oxford in 1499 should be seen not as a dramatic turning-point, but rather in the light of one of the Proverbs of Solomon which Erasmus quoted in his *Adages,* "Iron sharpeneth iron; so a man sharpeneth the countenance of his friend." Erasmus was sharpened into delaying no further the inauguration of his *opus.* And the first step toward the fulfillment of that purpose was the acquisition of Greek.

Perhaps, like a questioner who is unaware that he has posed a critical question, Colet did not fully realize—at least until later—the importance of the spur he gave to Erasmus. Five years later the latter wrote to him in a tone of apology (or perhaps irritation) that "wandering in Greek gardens" was a means to gather "many things which will serve later even in the study of the Scriptures." Erasmus never lost his sense of purpose—even if others could not always see it. By March 1516, however, the world could be in no doubt. The appearance of Erasmus's New Testament was a historic moment for the world at large and for himself. It marked the achievement of an objective he had long been straining toward: the publication of the central document of the faith in its original apostolic language. At this point, clearly, he returned whatever debt he had incurred toward Colet; and Erasmus's book now spurred the dean to school himself in Greek, as he seems earlier to have spurred Erasmus.

There were, therefore, long years of resolute preparation and arduous study behind the achievement of 1516. Another milestone, already noted above, completes the triad of the most formative influences upon Erasmus. Erasmus's 1505 edition of Valla's *Annotations on the New Testament* was the outcome of a delighted recognition. In discovering this work (described by a recent authority as "probably the most crucial book he ever read")[9] Erasmus discovered his community of interest with one whom he already greatly admired as a master of Latinity. It became clear how humanist philological tools could be used for the highest religious purposes. Perhaps, in taking Valla so much to heart, Erasmus attributed to him some of his own features. But if he transformed what he gained, he was in no doubt as to the value of his debt, and the publication of the *Annotations* was almost like an advertisement for what was to follow. During the decade which intervened between its appearance and that of the *Novum Instrumentum,* Erasmus was furiously at work with his

---

[9] Louis Bouyer, "Erasmus in Relation to the Medieval Biblical Tradition," *Cambridge History of the Bible,* vol. 2, p. 494.

Greek, and with writings which prepared the way for his edition. By 1504 he had written four volumes (which no longer survive) on the Epistle to the Romans.[10] And when he left England in 1506 after his second visit, he left behind a manuscript containing a Latin translation of the New Testament which shows how far his project was already taking shape.

Erasmus's New Testament, containing the Greek text together with his Latin translation (first printed in full in 1519), received immediate recognition: applause and opposition. The delight of friends was matched by the criticism of opponents. This might seem surprising in view of the amount of Biblical studies and criticism already in progress. What was it that peculiarly distinguished the work of Erasmus? To answer that it was the fullness of his humanist learning is not entirely to beg the question; he had shown himself ready to go further than any of his contemporaries in applying the convictions of his scholarship to the scriptural text—even where it meant rejecting venerable, revered tradition. To his enemies this was nowhere more apparent than in the brazen daring of the title and the impudence of the new Latin translation, which did not merely correct the Vulgate but actually replaced it. To his friends, on the other hand, the greatness of the achievement lay in its very freshness: here they had the gospel readily available for the first time in its original tongue; here they could read (whether Greek scholars or not) the words of the New Testament with a directness and immediacy which endowed them with new life. They might feel they were reading it for the first time. Erasmus did for the New Testament, in his various editions, something comparable to what Aldus Manutius did for the Greek classics; he published the Greek text for the first time in readily accessible form, and in editions much larger, less cumbersome, and more "popular" than the Polyglot of Alcalá.

The alarm aroused by Erasmus's book was expressed to him before its appearance by the Louvain theologian Martin van Dorp. He wrote in terms which were friendly but highly critical. Having referred to the damages done by the *Praise of Folly*, he continued:

---

[10] Erasmus was long preoccupied by this work and keenly aware that it necessitated Greek learning. He stressed the value of St. Paul's Epistles in the *Enchiridion* ("Especially make yourself familiar with Paul. Him you ought to hold ever in your heart"), and this passage shows that he had already undertaken the work of interpretation although (as a letter to Colet of about December 1504 reveals) he felt hampered by his insufficient knowledge of Greek. We find him again in 1514 telling a correspondent about the commentaries he had undertaken on the Epistles. Though the four volumes Erasmus referred to have not survived, his paraphrase of Romans amounted, as the title makes clear, to a commentary; *In Epistolam Pauli ad Romanos Paraphrasis, Quae Commentarii vice possit esse* (Basel, 1518), and in the dedicatory epistle Erasmus speaks of the great labor involved in the task. M. Spinka, ed., *Advocates of Reform From Wyclif to Erasmus* (London, 1953), p. 379; *Cambridge History of the Bible,* vol. 2, p. 500; Margaret Mann Phillips, *Erasmus and the Northern Renaissance* (London, 1949), pp. 45, 54; T. A. Dorey, ed., *Erasmus* (London, 1970), p. 95; W. Schwarz, *Principles and Problems of Biblical Translation* (Cambridge, 1955), p. 131.

I also understand that you have corrected the New Testament, and written annotations on more than a thousand passages, not without profit to theologians. This again is a matter on which, in all friendship, I should like to give a warning to a friend. At the outset I pass over the sweat which Lorenzo Valla and Jacques Lefèvre have expended in this arena, whom you, undoubtedly, greatly surpass. But making corrections of any kind to holy letters, and emending the Latin manuscripts from the Greek at that, is a weighty matter. For if I were to show that the Latin translation had no trace of falsity or error, would you not agree that the labor of all those who try to correct it is supererogatory, unless the translators thereupon put us on notice that any passage whatsoever could be interpreted more significantly? But what I am now speaking of is truth and correctness, which I assert to be in our Vulgate edition. For is it likely that the whole universal church would have erred through so many centuries, who has always used, and still approves and uses this version? Is it probable that so many holy Fathers, so many consummate men, could have been mistaken, who relied on the Vulgate for the decisions on difficult matters in general councils, for their defence and elucidation of the faith, and for the framing of those canons to which kings have submitted their authority?[11]

Dorp expressed the horror which was felt by many theologians at the mere thought of correcting so hallowed a text as the Vulgate, venerated through the church's long usage. And here was Erasmus not merely making corrections and alterations, but offering an entire new Latin version, changing even the very title! This fundamental departure from tradition in the name of improved learning was indeed the crux, and the shock of conservatives was not to be dispelled by Erasmus's claim that his text was intended for private reading, not for formal ecclesiastical use. It is clear that Erasmus had taken a position very different from that of Ximenes, whose corrections were tempered with scrupulous reverence for the Vulgate text. This was carried even to the length of providing a Greek translation of the troublesome *Comma Johanneum* (the spurious addition on the Trinity in I John V, vv. 7 and 8), which Erasmus —also characteristically—omitted, though he restored it, after virulent opposition, in his third edition of 1522. Understandably, it was not Erasmus's New Testament, dedicated to Leo X in the confident hope of its welcome, which received the pope's licence in 1520, but the Polyglot of Cardinal Ximenes. But Erasmus, though his critical methods were very far from perfect, had done something unique for Biblical scholarship, and the scandal, as well as the praise, give the measure of his achievement.

[11] P. S. Allen and H. M. Allen, eds., *Opus Epistolarum Des. Erasmi Roterdami, denuo recognitum et auctum*, vol. 2, no. 304 (Oxford, 1906–58), p. 14. Dorp's letter was written about September 1514. There is a partial English translation, which I have found helpful, by F. M. Nichols, *The Epistles of Erasmus. From his earliest Letters to his fifty-first year*, vol. 2 (London, 1904), pp. 168–70. On this letter, see Phillips, *op. cit.*, pp. 73–75.

Closely linked with this Biblical work was the long series of patristic editions which occupied Erasmus through many years of his working life. Between 1516 and 1530 he brought out (in some cases supplementing his first edition with a later expanded version) editions of Jerome, Cyprian, Hilary, Irenaeus, Chrysostom, Ambrose, Athanasius, Augustine, and Basil. When he died he was working on Origen. It was a prodigious undertaking, enough in itself to make a lifetime's study for any ordinary man. Given Erasmus's other publications, it is an amazing accomplishment, even allowing for the assistants who helped him with the work. To the editor, these publications were indispensable to the task he had set himself. The Greek and Latin Fathers, classical authors of Christian antiquity, were essential to the true understanding of Christ and the Apostles, and must be read in their right shape. The words which Erasmus put into the mouth of a character in one of his *Colloquies* might well have been spoken by their author:

You see this book of the Gospels? In it one talks with me who long ago, as an eloquent companion of the two disciples on the road to Emmaus, caused them to forget the hardship of their journey but made their hearts burn most fervently in their wonder at his enchanting speech. In this book Paul speaks to me, in this Isaiah and the rest of the prophets. Here the honey-tongued Chrysostom converses with me, here Basil, here Augustine, here Jerome, here Cyprian, and other teachers as learned as they are eloquent. Do you know any other talkers so delightful that you would compare them with these? Or in such company, which never fails me, do you suppose solitude can become tedious?

One is reminded of Machiavelli's description of himself on his farm outside Florence, taking off his dirty workaday clothes to attire himself with courtly propriety for an evening's delightful converse with his favorites among the ancients. Erasmus's spokesman was certainly a very Erasmian sort of Carthusian—the kind which More or Colet or Lefèvre might have made—in defending the garb and calling of his order by appeal to such literary pursuits. And the diet of his learning was the Bible and the Fathers, teachers in whom true wisdom and true eloquence were combined.

Erasmus's patristic editions thus formed part of his whole majestic program. The Church Fathers, essential models for scriptural exegesis and for the eloquence of true philosophy, had to be restored to their correct form. As it was, they were hopelessly corrupt. "Jerome's works," wrote Erasmus, "especially those on the Bible, have been so corrupted that if Jerome himself were to come alive again he would neither know nor understand his own books." It was a fate with which their editor could heartily sympathize. Were not some of his own works issued during his lifetime in translations distorted by Protestant enthusiasm? One might, too, see a certain progression in the editions of these works corresponding to changes in Erasmus himself. He came to value the Greek Fathers above the Latin and to give the highest esteem of all to Origen, yet he remained faithful to the end to his early love for Jerome, whose letters he copied with his own hand near the beginning of his career. These two Fathers had a special significance in Erasmus's thought. Jerome, who had been entrusted by Pope Damasus I with the task of revising the Latin text of the gospels, who struggled despairingly with Hebrew, as Erasmus struggled with Greek, and who was accused, like Erasmus, of having dared to tamper with the accepted gospel text, was a fitting patron for the work which the great humanist assigned himself. Origen, to whose works Erasmus devoted the last year of his life, was likewise appropriate company for the stress of those later times. Having been among the Greek Fathers who attracted the attention of Nicholas V (under whose auspices a translation was made of one of his writings, printed at Rome in 1481), Origen's works were published more than once in the early sixteenth century. His views upon free will gave him particular interest for Luther's contemporaries, and Erasmus (who respected Origen to the point of saying that one of his pages was worth ten of Augustine's) had recourse to the Greek Father in his dispute with Luther over this issue. But Origen presented a problem, the very problem of authority which lay behind the contest and arguments of the contestants. His works had been condemned at the Council of Alexandria in 400. And so Luther chose to reject the authority to whom Erasmus had recourse.

Philosophia Christi: Friends and Enemies

If Erasmus stands at the very center of the movement we choose to call the Northern Renaissance, the kernel of Erasmus's thought is summed up in what he called *Philosophia Christi*. It is a term both straightforward and complex. To see it as an expression of avowed simplicity, carrying subtle undertones, is hardly unjust to the mind of its exponent. Erasmus did not invent the phrase. He was apparently making deliberate use of an archaism taken over—an adoption significant in itself—from the Greek Fathers. And before Erasmus, Rudolph Agricola had referred to the philosophy of Christ in a letter of 1484 which, discussing educational reform and the harmonizing of ancient wisdom and Christian faith, looks forward to Erasmus's meaning.

Philosophia Christi stood for everything that Erasmus loved best. It summarized that blending of ancient wisdom and Christian piety, the alliance of humanist learning and evangelical devotion, to which his writings gave the highest expression. This philosophy represents that world (to which a converted Utopia would have belonged) in which it was possible to exclaim, like a character in one of the *Colloquies,* "Saint Socrates, pray for us!" The two realms of reason and faith, antiquity and Christianity, so long conjoined and so long unsettled in their relationship, were to be fused into a new regenerative being. The writings of antiquity, published at last in their own proper eloquence, were to be the means of reaching contemporary Christian truth. The recovery of what was old would purify and renew. "For what else is the philosophy of Christ, which he himself calls a rebirth, but the restoration of an originally well formed nature?"

In Erasmus's usage the phrase *Philosophia Christi* brings together those two diverging strands of Biblical learning whose fortunes have been outlined above. If the "philosophy of Christ" summarized a program, it was a program with two united fronts: studies and evangelism. Yet it is unjust to make the distinction sound so categorical, when in its essence it never was. There is in fact no paradox in the circumstance that Erasmus, whose whole life belonged to the international world of those who were literate in Latin, who never published a word in any vernacular and preferred to avoid the bother of speaking one, should be found addressing himself to the interests of ploughmen and weavers. There is a sense in which, as his most heartfelt utterances reveal, they were never out of his mind, and for him it was one of the unspeakable tragedies of Luther's actions that he abused those evangelical obligations which, in their widest and deepest application, Erasmus had always respected. "The unlearned and rude multitude, which Christ died for, ought to be provided for also." "Christ would that the way should be plain and open to every man." In his *Enchiridion,* which was among the books Erasmus could claim he had written "as a plain man to plain men," appeared (without the name) a definition of Christ's philosophy. But to find the fullest explanations we have to wait for one of the new *Adages* published in 1515, the more famous *Paraclesis* prefacing the New Testament of 1516, and the fuller and more systematic *Ratio seu compendium verae theologiae* which was set before the second New Testament edition of 1519, "to kindle men's spirits to the study of theology."

In his *Sileni Alcibiadis,* which appeared in the *Adagiorum Chiliades* of 1515, Erasmus had a convenient topic for discoursing on a familiar theme: the contrast between contemptible outward appearances and inner spiritual wisdom. It may be read as an essay on the imitation of Christ. In his humble origins, his poverty, the trials of his life, and the mockery of his death, Christ was "the most extraordinary Silenus of all." He could have ruled the earth. "But this was the only pattern that pleased him, and which he set before the eyes of his disciples and friends—that is to say, Christians. He chose that philosophy in particular, which is utterly different from the rules of the philosophers and from the doctrine of the world; that philosophy which alone of all others really does bring what everyone is trying to get, in some way or another —happiness." The scriptures exemplified the same theme, the surprising veils concealing hidden truths. "The parables of the Gospel, if you take them at face value—who would not think that they came from a simple ignorant man? And yet if you crack the nut, you find inside that profound wisdom, truly divine, a touch of something which is clearly like Christ himself." The Apostles too were such Sileni, unschooled, unlettered, ridiculed, despised. Yet "what Aristotle would not seem stupid, ignorant, trivial, compared to them, who draw from the very spring that heavenly wisdom beside which all human wisdom is mere stupidity?" The world was stuffed with false appearances; most men were "like Sileni inside out," not least the men of the world of reputed learning. "In fact you may often find more true authentic wisdom in one obscure individual, generally thought simple-minded and half-crazy, whose mind has not been taught by a Scotus (the subtle as they say) but by the heavenly spirit of Christ, than in many strutting characters acting the theologian, three or four times Doctor So-and-so, blown up with their Aristotle and stuffed full of learned definitions, conclusions, and propositions." The philosophy of Christ, it is clear, had very little to do with theological schools.

In the *Paraclesis,* Erasmus contrasted the labors spent in pursuit of other philosophies—Platonic, Pythagorean, Stoic, Aristotelian—with those of Christ's. How easy, how simple, how attainable, in comparison, is the teaching of Christ, to be found in so few books, for which so little learning is necessary. Christ's philosophy was as open as the salvation that he preached. It was not limited to scholars learnedly annotating in their studies, or to professors with years of training in scholastic subtleties; it was the song and solace of ordinary working people. Only a few could be learned; but "all can be Christian, all can be devout, and—I shall boldly add—all can be theologians."

Only be teachable, and you will make great strides in this philosophy. Itself will supply you with a teacher, the Spirit, who imparts himself to none more readily than to the simple of heart.... This philosophy, unlike others, suits itself equally to all; it stoops to the small.... It is within reach of the lowest, just as it is the admiration of the greatest; and indeed, the further you progress in knowledge of its treasures, the more you will be moved by the sense of its majesty.... It rejects no one, of any age, sex, means or condition. The sun itself is not as common to all as the teaching of Christ.

It is not wrong to hear reverberations in these phrases of the *Imitation of Christ,* for Erasmus's thought belonged to that school. And, given such views, it was only logical to wish that the scriptures should be available in the vernacular. One passage in which Erasmus urges this has deservedly become famous, not only because it linked him with so many of his contemporaries—Protestant and Catholic—but also because these words are among the most urgent that he wrote. "I wish that all women might read the Gospel, and the Epistles of Paul. I wish that they might be translated into all tongues of all people, so that not only the Scots and the Irish, but also the Turk and the Saracen might read and understand. . . . I wish the countryman might sing them at his plough, the weaver chant them at his loom, the traveller beguile with them the weariness of his journey."

What *Philosophia Christi* amounted to, then, was a new theology. It stands contrasted, implicitly and explicitly (witness the passages quoted above), with those long corridors of medieval learning which, in the name of theology, led determined students through years of study toward the Biblical text. Erasmus's philosophy was not the philosophy of the schools. It embraced, as he was at pains to make plain, the concordant teachings of the best ancient philosophy; but it was centered upon direct religious experience through the scriptures, which was denied by the theology of scholastic argumentation.

The task which Erasmus had assigned himself—in common with other northern humanists, but more magnificently—was a work of renovation. He wanted to release theology from the chains which had fettered it since it began to neglect its original sources. The same fate had overtaken these as had befallen classical sources (to which he also attended through his editorial life); the originals had been abandoned and lost because summaries had been allowed to replace them. What Justinian had done for Roman Law, Peter Lombard had done for theology. To give the Fathers a freshly prominent position, therefore, was to make room for "guests of old days returning to claim their right of citizenship." Those who objected to this work as "new" had got things upside down, for they were calling " 'new' the things that are the oldest of all, and they call 'old' what is really new." It was ridiculous to call innovative the attempt to recover an earlier, more desirable, state of affairs. For, Erasmus continued, "among the doctors of the early Church the knowledge of the Scriptures was combined with skill in languages and in secular literature." What was new, on the contrary, was what was taught in the schools in the name of theology.

It is something new, when boys have to learn grammar, to stuff them with modus significandi, *and read them crazy lists of words which teach nothing but to speak faultily. It is something new to accept a youth as a student in Philosophy, Law, Medicine or Theology, who can understand nothing in the ancient authors owing to his ignorance of the language they speak. It is something new, to exclude from the Holy of Holies of Theology anyone who has not sweated for years over Averroes and Aristotle. It is something new to stuff young men, who are reading for a degree in Philosophy, with Sophistical nonsense and fabricated problems, mere brain-teasers. It is something new in the public teaching of the Schools, for the answers to differ according to the methods of Thomists or Scotists, Nominalists or Realists. It is something new to exclude any arguments which are brought from the sources of Holy Scripture, and only accept those which are taken from Aristotle, from the Decretals, from the determinations of the Schoolmen, from the glosses of the professors of papal law, or from precedents (inane for the most part) distorted from Roman law. If we are to be offended by what is new, these are the really new things. If we approve of what is old, the oldest things of all are what are being brought forward now. Unless, maybe, 'new' means coming from the century of Origen, and 'old' means what started up three hundred years ago and has gone from bad to worse ever since.*[12]

[12] Margaret Mann Phillips, *The "Adages" of Erasmus: A Study with Translations* (Cambridge, 1964), pp. 376–78.

The depth of Erasmus's concern spills out in the headlong rush of his examples: they read almost like a manifesto for humanist studies. One could fill more than a single book with the torrents of invective which flowed in the sixteenth-century tide of indignation against the scholastics. The story certainly does not begin with Erasmus. But he may be allowed to introduce us to an important phase of its development. It is clear from this passage that Erasmus thought learning had degenerated from the development of scholasticism through the three hundred years after 1200. This amounted to a rejection of medieval theology as such, from the time when the application of dialectical methods brought the study of *theologia* to overshadow *sacra pagina*. Erasmus's words also illustrate the humanists' objection to scholasticism on the double grounds of style and content—or its lack of both. Those who pursued "quantities, formalities, quiddities, haeccities" were building vacuous wordy structures destructive to good Latin. Worse still, this empty methodology was allowed to become an end in itself, so that abstruse cobwebs of syllogistic argument were spun endlessly around questions quite divorced from the true sources of Christian knowledge.

Such strictures were, of course, only the negative side of very positive theories, which had particularly clear results in the linguistic studies of the north. Transalpine humanists eagerly cultivated Italianate skills in Greek and built onto them, in a more systematic way than was done in Italy, plans for associated skills in Hebrew. There was certainly borrowing here too, for Hebrew studies belong to the history of the Italian, as well as the northern, Renaissance. After Manetti and Traversari (both of whom studied Hebrew), Pico della Mirandola made himself one of the most accomplished Hebraists of the day, and it was under his aegis, as we have seen, that Reuchlin took up Hebrew. In Italy, too, an important start was made in the publication of Hebrew works. A commentary on the Pentateuch by the eleventh-century Rabbi Rashi was printed at Reggio in 1475, and this was probably not the first Hebrew to come from an Italian press. A Hebrew press in Bologna produced the Psalter in 1477 and the Pentateuch in 1482, and the entire Old Testament was issued six years later by the Soncino office near Mantua. This last publication, reissued in two parts in 1492 and 1494 after the Soncino press had transferred to Brescia, was used by Luther for his German translation of the Old Testament. Meanwhile Aldus Manutius led the way in Hebrew, as he did in Greek, by publishing a primer; later a distinguished Italian Hebraist, Santes Pagninus, or Pagnini (1470–1541), wrote a Hebrew lexicon as well as making an influential Latin translation of the Hebrew Old Testament.

The fortunes of Pagnini—influenced as they were by politics and patronage —reflect the nature of the transfer of Hebrew skills from Italy. Leo X, a patron of Biblical learning who established a Hebrew printing press in Rome, appointed this scholar to teach Oriental languages, but after the pope's death in 1521 Pagnini moved to France, where he spent the last part of his life; it was at Lyons that his various works were printed. As Hebrew studies migrated north, they gained powerful momentum from the motives of northern humanists. This was evident not only in publications, but also in institutional foundations. The scriptural context in which humanists of the north took the study of ancient languages to heart is evident in the various educational foundations which, like the College of St. Jerome at Alcalá, were trilingual. Admittedly there was some variation in the interpretations given to this term. Bishop Fisher's lecturers in Latin, Greek, and Hebrew at St. John's College, Cambridge, corresponded to Ximenes' concern for Greek, Hebrew, and Aramaic, whereas the Belgian humanist Nicolas Clenardus (or Cleynaerts) spoke of his own trilingual studies in Hebrew, Chaldean, and Arabic. There can be no doubt, however, that the linguistic triad, whichever form it took, was fundamentally attached to theology, and the promotion of Christian scholarship through philological studies of scriptural languages was central to the purpose of these foundations. The most common and successful linguistic combination was that which was most directly Biblical: the Christ and thieves of the Complutensian Polyglot. These were the languages patronized by Francis I, whose royal readerships for Greek and Hebrew were planned in 1517, though not until 1530—thanks to the insistence of Guillaume Budé—did the foundation later known as the Collège de France come into being. In the early years of the sixteenth century, Vienna, Louvain, and Oxford likewise acquired colleges for studies in Latin, Greek, and Hebrew.

The words and deeds of Erasmus (who was no great Hebrew scholar himself) leave no doubt that trilingual knowledge was integral to the advancement of *Philosophia Christi*. To atempt the study of theology without such linguistic preparation was to Erasmus as reckless as it was impious. He used as an example of rash enterprises "an attempt to interpret Divine Scripture ... by one who was unschooled and ignorant of Greek, Latin, and Hebrew, and of the whole of antiquity—things without which it is not only stupid, but impious, to take on oneself to treat the mysteries of Theology. And yet— terrible to relate—this is done everywhere by numbers of people, who have learnt some trivial syllogisms and childish sophistries and then, heavens above, what will they not dare? What will they not teach?" At Louvain, Erasmus was able to participate directly in the creation of a trilingual foundation like that envisaged on a domestic level in his colloquy "The Godly Feast," in which the house of Eusebius greeted arriving guests with inscriptions in Latin, Greek, and Hebrew, while St. Peter was depicted on the door. From the beginning, Erasmus was the chief prop and advisor of the founder, Jerome Busleiden, and helped to shape his friend's design for the new college at Louvain toward the highest educational purposes. After Busleiden's death in 1517, Erasmus did a great deal to help the executors overcome various difficulties, and to set the college on its feet, so that the first classes could be held in 1518. The *Ratio verae theologiae,* which appeared at this time, giving a full account of Erasmus's views upon Biblical studies and the need for linguistic preparation in the three languages, amounted almost to a program for the incipient college. Louvain, "where men of vast learning will give free public instruction in the three languages" for the honor of studies and glory of Christ, of which Erasmus wrote so glowingly, stood for the highest of his hopes. The future might well have seemed full of promise in 1517—however later perspectives altered the significance of that year.

Trilingual studies must not, however, be considered only in a humanist setting. They derived also from an earlier ecclesiastical program, formulated at a time before learning in ancient languages had gained fifteenth-century humanist overtones. At the Council of Vienne in 1312, Clement V had issued a decree providing that two teachers respectively in Hebrew, Chaldean (Aramaic), Arabic, and Greek should be appointed at the Papal Curia, Paris, Oxford, Bologna, and Salamanca. This comprehensive plan for linguistic education does not seem to have had much success at the time, though funds at least were collected to pay teachers at Oxford and Paris, and some linguistic instruction was given at the papal court. But the scheme was not forgotten. The Council of Basel renewed the enactments of Vienne in 1434, and the Clementines which contained the decree (and became part of the *Corpus Iuris Canonici*) were printed several times in the fifteenth century. The men whose enthusiasm for trilingual studies took such definite shape in the sixteenth century were well aware of this precedent. They could regard themselves as fulfilling a long-planned project of the church—and they claimed to be doing so. Cardinal Ximenes' foundation at Alcalá and Bishop Fox's at Corpus Christi College, Oxford, were both officially based upon the Vienne decree; and Nebrija, Erasmus, and More all referred themselves to its authority. One might almost suppose, from the letter of educational advice which Pantagruel received from his father Gargantua, that the program of Vienne formed part of the utopian ideal of early sixteenth-century education: ". . . learn the languages perfectly; first of all, the Greek, as Quintilian will have it; secondly, the Latin; and then the Hebrew, for the Holy Scripture-sake; and then the Chaldee and Arabic likewise. . . ." Different individuals might choose different linguistic combinations, but all harked back to Vienne.

As soon as one starts to look into this ostensible continuity, however, there appear important differences of emphasis. The program of Vienne had an essentially missionary aim, in which Biblical learning and exegesis were entirely subordinate to conversion of the infidel. This missionary objective of the 1312 decree, which owed much to the ideas and actions of Ramon Lull (who himself learned Arabic for the missionary activities in which he died, and campaigned for language studies to help conversion), stands contrasted with the linguistic aims of sixteenth-century humanists. But it still profoundly moved some of Erasmus's contemporaries. Nicolas Cleynaerts, who added studies in Hebrew, Arabic, and Aramaic to his knowledge of Latin and Greek, shared ideas with Lull, some of whose works Lefèvre was inspired to edit. Another who came under Lull's influence was Guillaume Postel (1510–

81), an eccentric genius with grandiose missionary ideas who bears some resemblance to Pico della Mirandola in his extraordinary eclecticism and linguistic facility. Yet much of the linguistic study of northern humanists was undertaken with aims unlike those of Lull and Vienne. Differences of this kind seem discernible in the work of Erasmus and Ximenes. The latter, more closely attached to older ideals, entertained plans for a league to attack Islam and reconquer Jerusalem—a scheme which failed, though he did undertake a successful expedition to Oran in 1509. *Philosophia Christi* stood for a rather different world. For Erasmus, and others who shared his views, language teaching and textual studies were indispensable for the improvement not of unbelievers, but of the faithful. Other tasks were far more urgent than extending the bounds of Christendom. The first need was the renewal of Christianity itself. It was a work of conversion, but it looked inwards, not outwards: to the regeneration of individual belief and Christian institutions, the transformation of the Christian, rather than the non-Christian, world.

The campaign to make Greek and Hebrew an integral part of the study of theology, though it found defenders in existing institutions, as well as leading to the foundation of new ones, was accompanied by bitter attacks upon diehard conservatives of the old school who rigidly stuck to scholastic methods and rejected language studies. Erasmus and his allies constantly poked fun at their inveterate ignorance—and their defenses of ignorance. "Anything they don't understand they call Hebrew," remarked Ogygius in the famous Colloquy, "A Pilgrimage for Religion's Sake." Long after the "barbarous ignorance" of Erasmus's youth had been dispelled, he continued to lambaste those whose advice to the young was "Beware of the Greeks, you'll turn into a heretic! Keep away from Hebrew, you might get like the Jews!" Deep differences of outlook in the world of learning issued in several conflicts that show the ways in which the world was dividing before Luther began to make himself famous.

Two of these disputes involved the place of Greek study, and in both of them Thomas More came to its defense. He wrote answers both to Martin van Dorp's objections to Erasmus's New Testament and to the obstreperous opposition raised at about the same time by the "Trojans" at Oxford against the Corpus Christi College Greeks. These defenses are illuminating. In answer to the critics of the new learning at Oxford, More contended that a humanistic training in Greek and Latin, including the classical poetry, oratory, and history which were condemned as secular, did "train the soul in virtue" and lead toward theology, and that without such a foundation in the wisdom of the humanities no theologian could hope really to speak "to the people." Moreover, even were it granted that only theology should be studied, it was impossible to do so "without some skill in languages, whether Hebrew or Greek or Latin." Theology meant the study of scripture and the Fathers, Greek and Latin, and "anyone who boasts that he can understand the works of the Fathers without an uncommon knowledge of the languages of each and all of them will in his ignorance boast for a long time before the learned trust his judgment."[13] That More himself (so unlike Erasmus) was to spend much of the spiritual and intellectual energy of his later years in prolonged vernacular controversy with William Tyndale, may be taken both as his personal literary tragedy and as an indication of how the Protestant division cut into existing tensions in the northern humanist world.

More spoke as a convinced Christian humanist. Such beliefs are also embedded in his description of the non-Christian world of *Utopia*, a society based upon the ancient cardinal virtues, which accorded a paramount place to education, and which More contrasted implicitly and explicitly with the ills of contemporary Europe. Thomas More exemplified, in fact—in some ways even more than Erasmus, with whom he enjoyed so long and close a friendship—the breadth and diversity of interests which compounded northern humanism. Together they participated in the effort to regenerate Christian society through the restoration of good letters; they were drawn to each other by their common sense of humor and appreciation of satirical wit; the plea for peace which More included in *Utopia* was argued urgently by Erasmus in various writings, notably in his *Querela Pacis*. Yet More's later years and death show how their paths diverged, in ways indicative of their differing humanist allegiances as well as of the divisive effects of the Protestant revolt. Unlike Erasmus, More allowed himself to be drawn away from humanist Latin letters, to write his English controversial works. Also unlike his less committed friend, More's humanist sense of duty withdrew him from a Carthusian retreat to dedicated public service, which brought him under Henry VIII face-to-face with a terrible conflict of loyalties more acute than any which shook Erasmus.

The long defense which More wrote on behalf of Erasmus against Dorp shows how, in the controversies of this time, the humanists drew together to form a common front. His argument for the return to Biblical and patristic studies was accompanied by hard criticism, though he was careful to say that he did not attack all theologians or all their *quaestiones* for, kept in their place, these methods were good for sharpening wits. But they should not be lifelong studies, nor did the church's salvation depend on them. One of More's stories is worth quoting, since it illustrates so vividly what the humanists felt they were battling against. At a dinner party given by a rich and cultivated Italian merchant, there was present a theologian who had recently arrived in England and who hoped to increase his fame for disputation. In the course of dinner this monk repeatedly made a point of refuting whatever was said on any topic with a syllogism, and his contrariness continued when the merchant gradually steered the conversation to theology:

[13] Elizabeth Frances Rogers, ed., *The Correspondence of Sir Thomas More* (Princeton, 1947), pp. 115–16; *cf.* Myron P. Gilmore, *The World of Humanism*, 1453–1517 (New York, 1952), p. 214.

And as it began to leak out that the theologian was not as experienced in Scripture as he was in those subtle questionings [questiunculi], *he* [the host] *began to play him up, and to make his argument turn on appeals to authority. He invented on the spur of the moment certain quotations, which seemed to support his case, and which no one had ever heard of before—so freely had he made them up—yet he carefully gave to each an exact citation, attributing one to some epistle of St. Peter, another to St. Paul, another still he placed in the Gospel, never omitting to state the chapter—making a point, if the book had only sixteen chapters, to quote from the twentieth. And what did the good theologian do?*

He fought back hard, but he had to resort to some acrobatics.

For he had absolutely no idea of the contents of Holy Writ and never doubted that these quotations were to be found there; being under the obligation of yielding to the authority of Scripture, and at the same time not wanting to be shamed by giving way, he found himself in a tight corner from which he could only escape by Protean manoeuvres. As soon as any non-existent passage from Scripture was cited against him, he said 'well quoted, sir, but I understand the text in this way,' and then he would interpret it in two ways, one of which supported his opponent, the other of which provided his own means of escape. And if the merchant pressed the point more closely, and objected that the theologian's was not the true meaning, then this man swore so solemnly that anyone might have believed him, that Nicholas of Lyra interpreted it in this way.[14]

This account illustrates three aspects of contemporary theology which the humanists found objectionable: the delight in disputation, which set ability in the technicalities of debate above regard for the truth; the total, but concealed, ignorance of scripture; and (as a concomitant of both characteristics) the exaltation of scholastic commentary over the Bible itself. It is also interesting that More's playful contestant, whose Biblical learning was so profound, was a layman—a man such as Manetti or Dürer's friend Pirckheimer, who combined a life of public affairs in Nuremberg with editing some of the Greek Fathers.

The most outstanding controversy concerned not Greek but Hebrew. It centered upon the leading Hebraist of the time, Johannes Reuchlin. This confrontation is highly significant in that it shows, perhaps more clearly than any other event of the time, the position which had been reached by the northern humanists, presented as they were with a challenge to the very

---

[14] Rogers, *Correspondence of More,* p. 47; *cf.* W. E. Campbell, *Erasmus, Tyndale and More* (London, 1949), p. 72, and H. A. Mason, *Humanism and Poetry in the early Tudor Period* (London, 1959), p. 94. More's letter to Dorp was written on 21 October 1515.

principles of their teaching. Reuchlin, who was born at Pforzheim in Germany in 1455, can be called the first northern humanist whose linguistic crown was really triple, thereby excelling Erasmus, who praised him after his death as "that famous phoenix of learning."[15] By 1494 Reuchlin's knowledge of Hebrew was sufficiently advanced for him to bring out a work on the cabala, but the book in which he did most for Hebrew studies was the *De Rudimentis Linguae Hebraicae* of 1506, a Hebrew grammar which was a considerable improvement on all its predecessors, including that of Conrad Pellican produced three years earlier. The alphabet, dictionary and grammar in Reuchlin's book greatly helped the advancement of Hebrew learning; so did the pupils whom he taught and the patrons he persuaded to sponsor the study of the language. He could justifiably regard himself as opening new doors, and remarked of the dictionary in his grammar that, "before me among the Latins no one appears to have done this."

Most of the publicity which Reuchlin received for his achievement derived from his opposition. His career and the cause of Hebrew studies became a *cause célèbre,* thanks to the officious actions of a converted Jew called Johannes Pfefferkorn, who sparked an extremely acrimonious dispute. In 1509 Pfefferkorn, whose new-found zeal had already caused him to write at length against Jewish practices, succeeded in getting a warrant from the Emperor Maximilian for the destruction of all Hebrew books except the Old Testament. Among those who objected, Reuchlin, the leading expert, took a reasonable line, suggesting that while obviously blasphemous works should be destroyed, others should be allowed, since understanding of them would be beneficial to Christians. These differences issued in literary polemics; attacked by Pfefferkorn, Reuchlin fired back, including among his targets the theological faculty of Cologne, which from the outset had supported his opponent. Various exchanges took place, culminating in Reuchlin's being cited for heresy before the Cologne Inquisition by the inquisitor-general, Jacob von Hochstraten. The proceedings went on for years as the case was appealed to Rome and referred back to a papal commission. By the time Reuchlin's name was cleared in March 1514, the whole affair had become celebrated throughout Europe. Not that this was the end of it. Hochstraten appealed against the judgment and in 1520—by which time the case had become damagingly linked with Luther's—it went against Reuchlin, who submitted.

The book which made this controversy peculiarly celebrated was the *Epistolae Obscurorum Virorum,* published in 1515 or 1516. Appearing as an anonymous sequel to Reuchlin's own *Epistolae Clarorum Virorum,* and purporting to be an epistolary collection of Hochstraten, Ortwin Gratius,

---

[15] Craig R. Thompson, trans., *The Colloquies of Erasmus* (Chicago and London, 1965), p. 81; "That famous phoenix of learning, triple-tongued John Reuchlin, is dead," from "The Apotheosis of That Incomparable Worthy, John Reuchlin" (first printed in 1522). At the same time as he celebrated Reuchlin in this way, Erasmus was careful to keep his distance from the controversies surrounding the Hebraist.

and others associated with Reuchlin's opponents, the letters mercilessly lampooned the Cologne theologians and all obstinate obscurantists who were giving universities a bad name. The authors of this successful satirical work were Ulrich von Hutten and Crotus Rubeanus, both of whom had direct experience (at Cologne and elsewhere) of the academic world they ridiculed so wittily. The *Letters,* spiced with malice and a caustic sense of fun, open another window onto that polarizing world we have seen through the eyes of More and Erasmus.

Traditional theologians, disparaged as "theologers," are shown up as ridiculous in their defense of scholastics and scholastic methods, and in their absurd insistence on being addressed as "magister noster." They are represented as resolutely opposed to new learning in any form; to Greek and Hebrew, as tongues with no relevance to theology; to those who talked the "new-fangled Latin"; to "new-fangled theologians like Erasmus of Rotterdam" with his corrections of Jerome and the New Testament; to "Virgil and Pliny and the rest of the new-fangled authors"; and to poets at large—"the bane of the universities"—as unnecessary, dangerous, and threatening the faculties' existence because they lure away students. Old studies and new studies are made to seem irrevocably opposed, with the supporters of the former, fearful of being ousted by the latter, stubbornly maintaining that "it matters not much with which side [of a given question] a man holdeth, so long as he followeth the ancient ways."

Obviously the *Letters of Obscure Men* cannot be taken as a fair picture of the German university world. One has only to think of Conrad Celtis, the crowned laureate of Frederick III, taking up his lectureship in poetry at Vienna in 1497, or of Reuchlin himself, who, after all this controversy, ended his life as professor of Greek and Hebrew at Tübingen. The "new learning" and the universities were by no means as diametrically opposed as the *Letters* make them appear. Yet, greatly exaggerated though it was in this satire, a tension did exist between the old learning and the new—especially in theology—and there were genuine reasons why old arts faculty members might be afraid. Much humanist learning did have an extra-curricular character. It could be pursued outside institutional walls in newer ways: through printed books, by associations formed in printers' workshops, and in learned societies or literary sodalities like those in which Conrad Celtis brought together many German humanists of his day. Erasmus, who had made the whole of Europe his academy, did more than anyone else to open new academic doors. And whatever the winds which Luther set blowing through them, they were not to be shut.

Pfefferkorn's original challenge to Hebrew literature, and the ensuing opposition to Reuchlin, called into question the fundamentals of humanist study: the desire to revive good letters and Christian piety through a fuller understanding of the ancient past, using improved linguistic knowledge to this end. The controversy which resulted made explicit, in ways which were significant for the future, tendencies which had long formed part of humanists' thinking, but which had not before received such loud and clear expression. The revolt against scholasticism varied in time, place, depth, and motivation. While it may be seen as a feature of the work of earlier Italian humanists (and the most obvious way of distinguishing the attitudes of fifteenth-century humanists from those of the twelfth or any previous period of classical revival), it was the northern humanists of the sixteenth century who set the seal, as it were, upon this development. Once the opposition between "old" and "new" had gained the indelible force of polemical print, the rejection of scholastic methods became virtually a new orthodoxy. Like other forms of repression, it entailed loss rather than gain—a loss of understanding, as well as actual destruction of texts. But the recognition of conflicting orthodoxies had its place in the evolution of thought, scientific as well as literary and theological. "There are found," Bacon remarked in the *Novum Organum,* "some minds given to an extreme admiration of antiquity, others to an extreme love and appetite for novelty; but few so duly tempered that they can hold the mean, neither carping at what has been well laid down by the ancients, nor despising what is well introduced by the moderns." Reuchlin and his contestants were far removed from a world in which truth seemed to belong to "nature and experience" rather than the "felicity of any age."[16] But their words made a contribution to that dichotomy, itself venerable, between the wisdom of ancients and moderns.

Dividing Ways

Despite all the changes that had taken place, humanists and humanist patrons of the north in 1600, as in 1500, still looked to Italy for models of culture and civilization. In the days of Palladio, as in the days of Alberti and Brunelleschi, Italy provided patterns which the rest of Europe followed. From there Francis I fetched artists to embellish his palace at Fontainebleau, as Henry VIII seems to have employed Italians to decorate his extraordinary palace of Nonesuch. At the end of the century, when John Florio, the English translator of Montaigne, was helping his countrymen (including James I's queen) to gain mastery of Italian at home, many of Shakespeare's contemporaries were still, despite religious impediments, journeying to Italy to improve themselves linguistically and otherwise. There were still ways in which Italy led the world. And if humanist principles prevented Italian from becoming the *lingua franca* of Europe, Italian humanists did much to make Italian the second language of cultivated men for several generations.

The success of the humanists (if one regards it as such) can be measured

---

[16] Francis Bacon, *Novum Organum,* book 1, 1v, trans. and ed. R. Ellis and James Spedding (London, n.d.), p. 79. See Marie Boas, *The Scientific Renaissance, 1450–1630* (New York, 1962), pp. 27–28, for suggestive remarks about the effects upon science of humanist anti-scholasticism.

in the widespread acceptance of their linguistic views. The profound conviction that the best education is to be found in classical letters, that true eloquence and true wisdom must grow together, was fully taken to heart by northern Europe. Its results can be seen in the grinding round of "Tully" and Terence imposed upon boys in school, and in the huge amount of contemporary writing which poured from the presses in Latin. There were individuals who saw the case from the other side, such as Cornelius Aurelius (d. 1523), who wrote a history of the Low Countries in Dutch; Jean Lemaire de Belges (c. 1473–c. 1515), who reconciled the rival claims of French and Italian in his *Concorde des deux langages* (published in 1513) ; and Juan Luis Vives (1493–1540), who pointed out that the practice of ancient diction could never reach the same plane as that of contemporary usage and argued in favor of writing in the vernacular languages. But in general, so intent were the humanists upon the classicism of their formulas for eloquence and elegance, and so remote did the vernaculars seem from these ideals, that it was long before the stylistic criteria of Latin came to be applied to the vernaculars. The theories of the Pléiade and of Joachim du Bellay's *Deffence et illustration de la langue françoyse* (1549) took longer to reach England. Not until near the end of the sixteenth century was a studied effort made to apply to English the rhetorical rules and figures of speech (as opposed to the aureate neologisms) of Latin. And so northern humanists who wished to emulate the Italians (sometimes in a spirit of nationalistic rivalry) did so not in the vernacular but in the Ciceronian Latin they so earnestly cultivated. Robert Gaguin's history of France, Conrad Celtis's *Norimberga*—the prelude to his planned *Germania Illustrata* —and Polydore Vergil's *Anglica Historia* were all, in their differing ways, written to demonstrate the liveliness of the ancient heritage belonging to these nations.

Should it be taken to indicate the humanists' false sense of direction that the Latin to which they devoted themselves was eventually overtaken by the despised vernaculars, failing to prove permanently viable as the international language of the world of letters? Or that the works for which we value them are sometimes those of which they themselves made light? Both the *Praise of Folly* and *Utopia* were in the nature of holiday works for their authors, yet they are read by those who will never turn to the *Enchiridion* or the *History of Richard III*, let alone the theological writings of Erasmus and More. Undoubtedly there was a large amount of Latin literature written and printed in the Renaissance which remains unread and which, one may think, the world would not have been very different without. Yet that is only the negative side of the question. If More's contemporaries were juster to his intentions than we have been, in valuing his translations of Lucian above his *Utopia*, it cannot be left out of account that Lucian contributed to the making of *Gargantua* and *Pantagruel,* as well as to both *Utopia* and the *Praise of Folly.* It is surely no accident that those writers who speak to us most directly are those who succeeded most fully in steeping themselves in the literature and spirit of antiquity. Erasmus, as a perceptive friend told him in 1516, lived and wrote in a way that made him seem "present everywhere in Christendom," and part of the secret of his literary skill was his readiness to give himself away. "You are all generosity in communicating yourself to others." It was a generosity that Montaigne, essaying himself as the central topic of his study, sifting truth as "I roll about in myself," carried a whole philosophy further— but Montaigne had benefited from his reading of Erasmus. In both cases profound intimacy with the classics shaped a style which could mirror, as Erasmus felt it should, the writer's soul. "What pleases the reader best," he wrote, "is to feel as if he knows the feelings, character, intellect and outlook of the writer as well as if he had spent several years in his company." We have to wait to see the maturing vernaculars coming into their own, but it seems perverse to deny the enrichment which resulted from this period of fresh immersion in the classical past.

The whole "renaissance" process involved loss as well as gain. The humanist vision had its accompanying blindness. Whether or not one agrees that there was a "fatal flaw in humanism which draws a veil over Greek literature in the very act of discovering it"—fatal to the kindling of the poetic imagination[17]—it is undeniably true that the understanding of Greek remained smaller than that of Latin, and that even in the pursuit of Latin excellence there were hampering limitations. Most damaging was that tendency, already encountered in the case of Colet, to cultivate the style of antiquity at the expense of its content—a disjunction between Christian and humanist objectives which has its own ancient history. "We shall not let the earliest studies be infected with heathen errors," wrote Vives in his *De tradendis disciplinis* (1531). "Let the scholar begin the reading of the heathen, as though entering upon poisonous fields, armed with an antidote . . . he is to take from them only what is useful, and to throw aside the rest." Latin and Greek were the best languages, and those which dealt with the subjects most desirable for study. Yet to use them as they ought to be used, care was necessary, and this involved some of the best humanist educators in a kind of censorship. Colet's anxiety to guard his pupils from damaging thoughts determined his selection of authors at St. Paul's. Vives, declaring that "I have . . . sought to free the sciences from impious doubts, and to bring them out from their heathen darkness into the light of our faith," thought poetry should be expurgated for youthful study. The belief that it was possible to imitate the style of antiquity while avoiding the contaminating influence of some of its best thought contributed to the aridity of certain sixteenth-century studies. Yet the work of the northern humanists, at its best, through the animating spirit of *Philosophia Christi*, did much to ease the tensions between Christian and pagan values. Erasmus, whose avowed purpose had always been "to promote studies of good letters [*bonae literae*] and to bring these studies into harmony with theology," declared that "whatever is devout and contributes to good morals should not

[17] C. S. Lewis, *English Literature in the Sixteenth Century excluding Drama* (Oxford, 1954), p. 132; *cf.* p. 69.

be called profane." This was a view which opened books rather than closed them.

Transalpine humanists did a great deal more than simply continue the work of fifteenth-century Italy. They inherited linguistic skills and the hopes that went with them, but both were extended and transformed in their hands. The idea that the world should be renewed through the study of Latin, Greek, and Hebrew was an outgrowth of the sense of renovation which inspired the humanists of Italy and which, asserted with such triumphant affiirmation, has done so much to color our views of the period. But there was a difference. The humanists of the north, with their evangelical dedication, gave a fresh direction to these aims, and applied their critical labors more concentratedly toward the regeneration of Christian society. By about 1516–1518 much had been done, in books published or prepared and institutions planned or founded. It might well have seemed that the longed-for period of renewal was beginning.

The age which did arrive, however, appeared otherwise. In a sense, it is impossible to assess the achievement of the Northern Renaissance because it was overtaken at a critical moment by another more impetuous movement. The Protestants were also humanists, but they were humanists with a difference. Their sense of priorities, more urgent and decisive, pushed them forward in ways which more deliberate thinkers regretted. The delicate, easily-altered balance between the scholarly and the evangelical was pushed down hard on the evangelical side. "Luther," said Erasmus, who found much to lament in the spiritual impulsiveness of his younger contemporary, "Luther attributes very little importance to scholarship, and most of all to the spirit." The whole Lutheran affair appeared to him a tragedy which had "sprung from the hatred of good letters" and threatened the ruin of such studies.

Of course there was Protestant humanist work in abundance. Tyndale edited Isocrates, as Calvin did Seneca early in his career. Melanchthon edited many of the classics, and had already published Terence by the time he brought out his Greek grammar in 1518; he was a worthy successor to his great-uncle Reuchlin in his triple linguistic accomplishments. Between Wittenberg and Strasbourg and Cambridge, there were plenty of educational foundations which demonstrate the application of humanist procedures in Protestant education. But as Erasmus already recognized when, in the summer of 1523, he reluctantly and regretfully took up his pen to write his *Essay on Free Will*, which appeared the following year, Luther's challenge was a threat to his whole world. It seemed to him (and, as Luther himself admitted, Erasmus had put his finger on the heart of the matter) that Luther's view of free will and grace undermined the entire humanist position. It was as if dry land had become water on the map of spiritual certainties open to human reasoning. What to Luther felt like a boundless release of spiritual hope seemed to Erasmus a hopeless plunge into human negation. "One may object," he wrote against Luther, "to what does free choice avail if it accomplishes nothing? I reply to what does the whole man avail if God so works in him as a potter with clay and just as he could act on a pebble?" Their difference was a difference over human dignity, as well as over the means of divine salvation. Luther replied, "When God is not present and at work in us everything we do is evil and we necessarily do what is of no avail for salvation. For if it is not we, but only God, who works salvation in us, then before he works we can do nothing of saving significance, whether we wish to or not." Erasmus differed in his more hesitant manner and less categorical viewpoint: "to those who maintain that man can do nothing without the help of the grace of God, and conclude that therefore no works of men are good—to these we shall oppose a thesis to me much more probable, that there is nothing that man cannot do with the help of the grace of God, and that therefore all the works of man can be good."

The gulf between them was a matter of method as well as of ultimate spiritual conviction. To set divine grace and the promptings of the spirit so far above human reason seemed to Erasmus to unleash not only irrational spiritual assertiveness, but also uncontrollable conflict. "Now every Tom, Dick, and Harry claims credence who testifies that he has the spirit of the Gospel," which was hardly surprising if the deepest divine mysteries were prostituted before "common ears." The new generation seemed to have banished that spiritual liberty which might have served true piety, and to serve instead an unrestrained liberty of the flesh. Luther, less patient and temperamentally prepared for battle, was ready to justify both the assertiveness and the dissension. "Take away assertions and you take away Christianity"; "To wish to stop these tumults . . . is nothing else but to wish to suppress and prohibit the Word of God." Luther brushed aside as irrelevant and misconceived those hesitations which stemmed from Erasmus's basic differences of character and philosophy. To the man who lived by a revelation, intellectual reservations might seem to be "slippery writings"; the adherence to slow striving after human improvement makes "your thoughts about God . . . all too human." And no man could, in the end, be educated into spiritual vision—it was the learned who were often blind. The new evangelicals certainly built on the work of their predecessors, but they built so urgently that some things had to be left behind. Religious needs could not wait upon stylists and grammarians: where the fate of souls was at stake Utopias had to be set aside.

Yet it would be wrong to end on such a negative note. The Reformation's release of spiritual energy certainly unleashed considerable forces of destruction, giving grounds for some of the deep pessimism and dire fears of contemporary men of learning. It seemed as if the voices of reason and persuasion, the hopes of reform through peaceful educative processes and the enhancement of Christian piety, were being drowned in the clamor of aggressive disputation. Erasmus, Erasmianism, and the religious humanists appeared to have lost the day.

A great deal, however, remained of the movement which we have been considering. And, though it flowed into different channels and was transmuted in the process, the development of events in some ways enlarged rather than damped its influence. The impact of the "Northern Renaissance," as we have traced it, was inherently intellectual, scholarly, and artistic, and therefore confined to the limited though influential numbers of those who formed the most highly literate and cultivated circles of the day. The Christian humanists had indeed addressed themselves to the problems of society at large, and wanted to serve the interests of more than a cultured elite. But it was thanks in great part to their successors, often more Protestant than humanist, that essentials of humanist thinking passed into wider and more popular currency through the labors of school-founders and teachers, and a variety of translators and printers. Erasmus himself, as well as the classical authors on whom he had worked, came within the horizons of considerable numbers of vernacular readers.

The influence of the greatest northern humanist long outlived him. Although an "Erasmian" position became increasingly difficult to maintain during the polarization of thought which resulted from Luther's stand, Erasmus's ideas and works were not only attacked and condemned by Catholics and Protestants alike; they were also used and read by both sides. The essentials of Erasmus's thought, pushed aside from the realm of practical politics, long remained discernible among those individuals who valued toleration and reason as much as they disliked war and militancy, and who appreciated satire and irony as a way of drawing attention to contemporary ills. The range and force of his ideas can be traced in directions which diverge as sharply as Trent and the Jesuits from the Calvinists and Geneva. Like all great teachers, Erasmus taught far beyond the limit of his conscious intentions. From what he thought and wrote, from his marvelous ability to talk from his own peak in an individual, down-to-earth voice, there stemmed many misunderstandings, but also many trains of thought. Erasmus, belonging to two worlds while effectively fashioning a third, amply repaid his debt to man as well as God. He has had many posthumous debtors.

A Critical Bibliography

There are few outstanding studies devoted specifically to the northern Renaissance. Margaret Mann Phillips, *Erasmus and the Northern Renaissance* (London, 1949) is admirable, and my debts to it are obvious. A more recent summary account is that of Roberto Weiss, "Italian Humanism in Western Europe," in *Italian Renaissance Studies*, edited by E. F. Jacob (London, 1960), pp. 69–93. Helpful introductions will be found in various general works: *The New Cambridge Modern History*, vol. 1, ed. G. R. Potter (Cambridge, 1957), particularly the Introduction and Chapters 3, 5, and 6; vol. 2, ed. G. R. Elton (1962), Chapters 12 and 13; Myron P. Gilmore, *The World of Humanism, 1453–1517* (New York, 1952); Wallace K. Ferguson, *Europe in Transition, 1300–1520* (Boston, 1962); and J. R. Hale, *Renais-*

sance Europe, 1480–1520 (Fontana History of Europe, London, 1971), offers a fresh approach to the period.

The Northern Renaissance can only be approached through knowledge of Italian humanism. Two short surveys which provide useful introductions and bibliographical references are William J. Bouwsma, *The Interpretation of Renaissance Humanism*, 2nd ed. (American Historical Association, 1966) and Denys Hay, *The Renaissance* (London, 1963). Among fuller works which consider the extension of humanist values outside Italy are: Denys Hay, *The Italian Renaissance in its Historical Background* (Cambridge, 1961); Roberto Weiss, *The Spread of Italian Humanism* (London, 1964); R. R. Bolgar, *The Classical Heritage and its Beneficiaries* (Cambridge, 1954); W. H. Woodward, *Studies in Education during the Age of the Renaissance, 1400–1600* (Cambridge, 1906) has been reissued in paperback with a foreword by Lawrence Stone (New York, 1965). John Edwin Sandys, *A History of Classical Scholarship*, vol. 2, *From the revival of learning to the end of the eighteenth century* (Cambridge, 1908) still serves as a valuable comprehensive account. Wallace K. Ferguson, *The Renaissance in Historical Thought* (Boston, 1948) is the indispensable historiographical guide, and Werner Jaeger, *Humanism and Theology*, The Acquinas Lecture for 1943 (Milwaukee, 1943, gives revealing insight into the meaning of humanist studies. A comprehensive survey of the literature of the period is provided by a recent Penguin; A. J. Krailsheimer, ed. *The Continental Renaissance, 1500–1600* (Harmondsworth, 1971).

Franco Simone, *The French Renaissance: Medieval Tradition and Italian Influence in Shaping the Renaissance in France*, trans. H. Gaston Hall (London & New York, 1969), a translation of half of the author's *Il Rinascimento Francese* (1961), is helpful on the historiographical setting of the French Renaissance, and explores the role of Petrarch. On humanism in particular countries the following are leading works: Augustin Renaudet, *Préréforme et Humanisme à Paris pendant les premières guerres d'Italie (1494–1517)* 2nd edn. (Paris, 1953); a useful introduction to this major work is the same author's paper on "Paris from 1494 to 1517—Church and University; Religious Reforms; Culture and the Humanists' Critiques," originally published in *Courants Religieux et Humanisme á la Fin du XVe et au Début du XVIe Siècle*, Colloque de Strasbourg, 1957 (Paris, 1959), pp. 5–24, reprinted in translation in Werner L. Gundersheimer, ed. *French Humanism, 1470–1600* (London, 1969; New York, 1970), pp. 65–89; another volume which, like this last, forms a valuable collection of recent work by different authors on French humanism is A. H. T. Levi, ed. *Humanism in France at the end of the Middle Ages and in the early Renaissance* (Manchester, 1970). Arthur Tilley, *Studies in the French Renaissance* (Cambridge, 1922) has a chapter on "Humanism under Francis I." For German humanists, see Lewis W. Spitz, *The Religious Renaissance of the German Humanists* (Cambridge, Mass., 1963); Gerhard Ritter, "Die Geschichtliche Bedeutung des deutschen Humanismus," *Historische Zeitschrift* 127 (1923): 391–453;

Hans Baron, "Zur Frage des Ursprungs des deutschen Humanismus und seiner religiösen Reformbestrebungen," *Historische Zeitschrift* 132 (1925): 413–446. R. Weiss, *Humanism in England during the Fifteenth Century* (Oxford, 1957) is the authoritative work on English humanists; stimulating reading—which carries the subject further forward in time—will also be found in C. S. Lewis, *English Literature in the Sixteenth Century excluding Drama* (Oxford, 1954), and D. Bush, *The Renaissance and English Humanism* (Toronto, 1939). On Spain there is the great book of Marcel Bataillon, *Erasme et l'Espagne, Recherches sur l'Histoire Spirituelle du XVIe Siècle* (Paris, 1937); and for the Low Countries there are the studies of Alphonse Roersch, *L'Humanisme Belge à l'Epoque de la Renaissance, Etudes et Portraits* (Brussels, 1910; Louvain, 1933).

Among the many works on individual humanists the following may be singled out: J. Huizinga, *Erasmus of Rotterdam*, trans. F. Hopman (London, 1924 and 1952); Roland H. Bainton, *Erasmus of Christendom* (New York, 1969); Louis Bouyer, *Erasmus and the Humanist Experiment* (London, 1959); T. A. Dorey, ed., *Erasmus* (London, 1970), a valuable collection of papers by different authors on various aspects of Erasmus's work; R. L. DeMolen, ed., *Erasmus of Rotterdam* (New York, 1971) another symposium of assessments; P. O. Kristeller, "Erasmus from an Italian Perspective," *Renaissance Quarterly,* 23 (1970): 1–14; Eugene F. Rice, Jr., "Erasmus and the Religious Tradition, 1495–1499," *Journal of the History of Ideas,* 11 (1950): 387–411, reprinted in P. O. Kristeller and P. P. Wiener, eds., *Renaissance Essays From the Journal of the History of Ideas* (New York, 1968), pp. 162–186; Lewis W. Spitz, *Conrad Celtis, The German Arch-Humanist* (Cambridge, Mass., 1957); Hajo Holborn, *Ulrich von Hutten and the German Reformation* (New Haven, 1937); Charles G. Nauert, *Agrippa and the Crisis of Renaissance Thought* (Urbana, Ill., 1965); R. W. Chambers, *Thomas More* (London, 1935); J. H. Hexter, *More's Utopia: The Biography of an Idea* (Princeton, 1952; New York, 1965); Frederic Seebohm, *The Oxford Reformers,* 2nd ed. (London, 1869), for the work of Colet, Erasmus and More; J. H. Lupton, *A Life of John Colet, D.D.* (London, 1887, 1961); E. W. Hunt, *Dean Colet and his Theology* (London, 1956); Sears Jayne, *John Colet and Marsilio Ficino* (Oxford, 1963); Denys Hay, *Polydore Vergil; Renaissance Historian and Man of Letters* (Oxford, 1952); Eugene F. Rice, Jr., "The Humanist Idea of Christian Antiquity: Lefèvre d'Etaples and his Circle," *Studies in the Renaissance* 9 (1962): 126–60, reprinted in Gundersheimer, *French Humanism;* Augustin Renaudet, "Un Problème historique: la Pensée religieuse de J. Lefèvre d'Etaples," in his *Humanisme et Renaissance* (Geneva, 1958), a volume of papers on various aspects of the Renaissance, including a chapter on Jean Standonck and several on Erasmus; J. W. Brush, "Lefèvre d'Etaples; Three Phases of his Life and Work," in *Reformation Studies,* edited by F. H. Littell (Richmond, 1962), pp. 117–28; J. Dagen, "Humanisme et évangelisme chez Lefèvre d'Etaples," in *Courants Religieux,* pp. 121–34; L. Febvre, *Le Problème de l'incroyance au XVIe siècle. La religion de Rabelais,* rev. ed. (Paris, 1962) ; Louis Delaruelle, *Guillaume Budé. Les Origines, les Débuts, les Idées Maîtresses* (Paris, 1907) ; Donald M. Frame, *Montaigne: A Biography* (New York, 1965) ; William J. Bouwsma, *Concordia Mundi; the Career and Thought of Guillaume Postel (1510–1581)* (Cambridge, Mass., 1957) ; Robert Stupperich, *Melanchthon* (Philadelphia, 1965) ; F. Schalk, "Melanchthon et l'humanisme," in *Courants Religieux,* pp. 73–82; Quirinus Breen, *John Calvin: A Study in French Humanism,* 2nd ed. (Chicago, 1968).

On the Devotio Moderna the essays by E. F. Jacob on "The Brethren of the Common Life" and "The *De Imitatione Christi,*" reprinted in his *Essays in the Conciliar Epoch,* 2nd ed. (Manchester, 1953) provide good introductions. The 3rd, 1963, edition of these essays replaces the chapter on the *Imitation* by one on "Gerard Groote and the beginnings of the 'New Devotion' in the Low Countries." Albert Hyma, *The Christian Renaissance: A History of the "Devotio Moderna",* 2nd ed. (Hamden, Conn., 1965), and the same author's *The Brethren of the Common Life* (Grand Rapids, 1950) are sympathetic accounts but should now be read in conjunction with the much more ponderous work of R. R. Post, *The Modern Devotion: Confrontation with Reformation and Humanism* (Leiden, 1968), which modifies some earlier assumptions. A valuable compressed survey is that of Pierre Debongnie, "Devotion Moderne," in the *Dictionnaire de Spiritualité,* vol. 3 (Paris, 1957), cols. 727–47; *cf.* also 714–15 on "La devotio moderna." For wider discussions of the religious context, see P. Imbart de La Tour, *Les Origines de la Réforme,* 2nd ed., vol. 2 (Paris, 1946), and Francis Rapp, *L'Eglise et la Vie Religieuse en Occident à la Fin du Moyen Age* (Paris, 1971).

For Biblical studies, reference should be made to the relevant sections of *The Cambridge History of the Bible,* vol. 2, ed. G. W. H. Lampe (Cambridge, 1969), which includes discussions of vernacular scriptures in different parts of Europe before 1500, and L. Bouyer, "Erasmus in Relation to the Medieval Biblical Tradition," pp. 492–505; volume 3, edited by S. L. Greenslade (1963), has chapters by Roland H. Bainton, "The Bible in the Reformation," pp. 1–37, and Basil Hall, "Biblical Scholarship: Editions and Commentaries," pp. 38–93. W. Schwarz, *Principles and Problems of Biblical Translation* (Cambridge, 1955) is illuminating on the way in which the humanists transformed Biblical studies, and contains chapters on Reuchlin and Erasmus. Two helpful papers appear in *Courants Religieux,* referred to above: R. Marcel, "Les Perspectives de l' 'Apologétique', de Lorenzo Valla à Savonarole," pp. 83–100; D. P. Walker, "Origène en France au début du XVIe siècle," pp. 101–19. Also useful are Frank Rosenthal, "The Study of the Hebrew Bible in Sixteenth-Century Italy," *Studies in the Renaissance* 1 (1954) : 81–91; Robert Peters, "Erasmus and the Fathers: Their Practical Value," *Church History* 36 (1967) : 254–61. There is a chapter on "The Trilingual Colleges of the early sixteenth century" in P. S. Allen, *Erasmus: Lectures and Wayfaring Sketches* (Oxford, 1934).

On artistic developments, see the relevant pages of E. H. Gombrich's impressive survey, *The Story of Art* (New York, 1972) ; Otto Benesch, *The Art of the Renaissance in Northern Europe: Its Relation to the Contemporary Spiritual and Intellectual Movements,* rev. ed. (London, 1965) ; A. Blunt, *Art and Architecture in France, 1500 to 1700* (London, 1953). For discussions of printing, see Elizabeth L. Eisenstein, "The Advent of Printing and the Problem of the Renaissance," *Past and Present* 45 (1969) : 19–89, and R. Hirsch, *Printing, Selling, and Reading, 1450–1550* (Wiesbaden, 1967).

Translated texts are usefully collected in J. B. Ross and M. M. McLaughlin, eds., *The Portable Renaissance Reader* (New York, 1953) ; Lewis W. Spitz, ed., *The Northern Renaissance* (Englewood Cliffs, N.J., 1972), contains extracts from eleven authors with a brief general introduction; texts of Colet, Erasmus, and Lefèvre are to be found in John C. Olin, ed., *The Catholic Reformation: Savonarola to Ignatius Loyola: Reform in the Church 1495–1540* (New York, 1969). J. H. Lupton translated and edited Colet's *Exposition of St. Paul's Epistle to the Romans,* 2nd ed. (Ridgewood, N.J., 1965), and his *Exposition of St. Paul's First Epistle to the Corinthians,* 2nd ed. (Ridgewood, N.J., 1965). *On the Eve of the Reformation: "Letters of Obscure Men,"* trans. F. G. Stokes (London, 1909), appeared in a paperback edition (New York, 1964) with an introduction by Hajo Holborn. The many editions of *The Imitation of Christ* include a Penguin (London, 1952) translated by Leo Sherley-Price; *Utopia* forms vol. 4 of *The Complete Works of Sir Thomas More,* ed. E. Surtz and J. H. Hexter (New Haven, 1966) ; a convenient edition is that of the Everyman's Library (London, 1910), and the Yale edition appeared in paperback with introd. and notes by E. Surtz (New Haven, 1964). Foster Watson, ed., *Vives: On Education* (Cambridge, 1913), contains a translation of the *De Tradendis Disciplinis,* with a long introduction. Many of Erasmus's works have been translated into English. Outstanding recent editions are Margaret Mann Phillips, *The "Adages" of Erasmus: A Study with Translations* (Cambridge, 1964), and Craig R. Thompson, trans., *The Colloquies of Erasmus* (Chicago and London, 1965). The *Paraclesis* is translated, with other texts, in John C. Olin, ed., *Desiderius Erasmus: Christian Humanism and the Reformation: Selected Writings* (New York, 1965) ; the *Enchiridion* (though not the full text) is in Matthew Spinka, ed., *Advocates of Reform From Wyclif to Erasmus,* Library of Christian Classics, vol. 14 (London, 1953), and in a paperback edition translated and edited by Raymond Himelick (Bloomington, Ind., 1963). Erasmus's controversy with Luther has lately appeared as volume 17 of the Library of Christian Classics, edited by E. Gordon Rupp, A. N. Marlow *et al., Luther and Erasmus: Free Will and Salvation* (London and Philadelphia, 1969). For Erasmus's correspondence, see *Erasmus and Cambridge* (Toronto, 1963), containing the Cambridge letters of Erasmus translated by D. F. S. Thomson with a long introduction by H. C. Porter; and *The Epistles of Erasmus. From his earliest letters to his fifty-first year,* translated by F. M. Nichols (London, 1901–1918).

Luther as "Junker Jörg," a name he used when he was hiding in Wartburg. Woodcut ca. 1512 by Lucas Cranach. Cabinet des Estampes, Bibliothèque Royal de Belgique, Brussels.

4.

The Continental Reformation

JOHN M. HEADLEY

THE LAST CENTURIES of the Middle Ages witnessed a number of reform movements of which the Protestant Reformation was to be the most momentous. The continuing preoccupation with reform had as its object the revival of the Christian church, which in its papal government, its exercise of canon law, the administration of sacraments, and its vast landed wealth embraced and interpenetrated all of Western society. The church was at once a universal institution of salvation, a hierarchically organized empire, and an all-embracing cultural community. No other institution so deeply affected the lives of all inhabitants of the Christian commonwealth. Because the church was universal in its scope, giving more than a formal unity to Western society, its problems had a range and intensity that cut across the ill-defined and still barely perceptible national divisions. By challenging the most basic tenets of the church, the Reformation produced an upheaval that convulsed all of Christendom. The origin of this upheaval cannot be understood or explained as a response to particular abuses, but rather as a new apprehension of reality. A fundamentally religious movement, the Reformation raised the basic question of authority in the church, and thus called into question the whole system of scholastic theology, papal government, and monastic piety.

Immobilized by material concerns and preoccupied with power, the church, which had been so creative and flexible in the previous three centuries, seemed after 1300 to be unresponsive to a changed world. In three areas the church failed to provide answers to the new forces of the age: the impending dissolution of Christian community caused by the growing territorial states, the failure to meet the religious needs of an increasingly articulate laity, and a dangerous loss of focus in religious experience. These three issues, which pervaded the period, were finally resolved in the fundamental reinterpretation of authority that constituted the supranational movement called the Reformation.

The Ills of the Church

SOURCES OF DISSENT

In the opening decades of the fourteenth century, theoretical claims for the papal lordship of the world received their most extreme statement. From the quills of papal publicists emerged the vision of an all-encompassing state in ecclesiastical guise, admitting of no distinct secular jurisdiction and existing virtually in its head, the pope. Yet to modern eyes it appears as one of the crowning ironies of history that as the papal publicists and decretalists spun out their hierocratic theories, the church had been subjected to the terrible humiliation of Anagni (1303) and the period of "Babylonian Captivity" (1305–78) had begun. In these first years of the new century, the church became the object of a criticism whose extensiveness and severity surpassed anything that had been experienced heretofore, and served to delimit a new period. Among those who decried the way Holy Church had united the sword with the crook and cut itself loose from its spiritual moorings was Dante Alighieri, who in *On Monarchy* (1312–13), not content with affirming the secular jurisdiction of the empire, went on to posit a blessedness in this life distinct from the formerly unique blessedness of the next. The reassertion of the empire as the valid secular jurisdiction challenged the hierocratic theory, and the definition of a temporal blessedness presaged forces corrosive to the medieval order.

If Dante was merely suggestive, the critics of the early fourteenth century presented a perceptible threat to the church. The destructive significance of William of Ockham's thought for the papal view of society lay less in his political tracts than in his philosophic writings. Ockham's logic undermined the prevalent scholastic notion that "universals" were essences of things that possessed some form of metaphysical reality. He rejected the nice correspondence between mental processes and metaphysical reality, and dissociated the realm of knowledge from that of being. The universal was to Ockham not a superior corporate reality independent of all phenomenal existence but a mental sign involved in the act of understanding. The "nominalism" of Ockham and his successors exploded the whole hierocratic idea of political society as a church: since individual realities alone have true existence, the church can only be conceived in terms of the individual parts and members constituting it. In the light of such a view, the church became atomized, earthbound, its organization subject to contractual relationships and its individual members, now intrinsically important, opened up to a new percipience.

Ockham's form of nominalism had made possible a radically different view of the church. His political counterpart, Marsilius of Padua, proposed a secularly ordered society. *The Defender of the Peace* (1324) represented a frankly naturalistic appropriation of Aristotle's *Politics* and its application to the north Italian city-states. Marsilius cut through the venerable debate between empire and papacy by denying the latter any jurisdiction at all. According to his doctrine of popular sovereignty, only laws made by the body of citizens are effective and binding on all. Canon (church) law is invalidated, the church itself is defined as the whole of the faithful, which is also the body of citizenry, and the clergy is simply for teaching the faith and administering the sacraments. The church becomes a purely spiritual congregation of believers, and all coercive power is exercised by the secular authority. Political community exists neither for salvation nor to promote the life of virtue, but for security.

Within the Franciscan order, the third source of criticism and radical dissent, the proper spiritual function of the church, acknowledged by both Marsilius and Ockham, was to be dangerously exaggerated. St. Francis's injunction to his followers to observe poverty had created a rift in his order. The observants came to see themselves as a new church and to look upon those who did not pursue the ideal of poverty as representatives of the carnal church, a notion that hovered fitfully over the Roman Curia and could not help but prove inconvenient to ecclesiastical authority. In the bull *Cum inter nonnullos* of 1323, John XXII pronounced heretical the belief that Christ and his apostles had possessed nothing as individuals or in common. The General of the Franciscans, Michael of Cesena, found it advisable to flee, and together with Marsilius and Ockham obtained asylum from Lewis of Bavaria, emperor and principal secular opponent of Pope John. Well might Dante in his letter to the cardinals lament the fact that Rome had lost both her luminaries—empire and papacy. The polarization of authority at Avignon and Munich attested to the displacement which the medieval world had suffered and the criticism the church received in these years.

CENTRALIZATION OF THE CHURCH

The Avignon papacy and the subsequent difficulties of the church have become so inextricably associated with notions of decline and decay as to prejudice any assessment of the church in the Late Middle Ages. Striking as the gap was between the hierocratic claims for the papacy and the political realities of the new period, the position maintained by the papal publicists was far from irrelevant. In a legalistic–theological age when philosophic realism still predominated, thoughts and claims, titles and ideals had a peculiar reality of their own. Indeed, the hierocratic tradition was both a sort of ecclesiastical backdrop to the age and the theoretical context in which the church moved. It continued to flourish through the period of reform and schism and into the seventeenth century. Furthermore, the very ability of the papacy to free itself from its association with the city of Rome emphatically demonstrated the hierocratic argument for the jurisdictional omnipotence of the Vicar of Christ evinced in the legal dictum, "Wherever is the pope, there is Rome and the Roman church." Legalistically, therefore, Avignon represented a new exaltation of the papacy. Similarly with respect to administration, the papacy, once settled at Avignon, consciously developed its archives, internal organization, and administrative apparatus to a degree hitherto unknown in either secular or ecclesiastical spheres. The best measure of the progressive centralization of the church in this period is the ever-expanding and effective role of the popes in the bestowal of benefices. John XXII, a gifted administrator, virtually eliminated elections by cathedral chapters. John and his successors extended to its limit the right of reservation which permitted the Roman pontiff to confer a vacant benefice or one about to become vacant without consulting the local clergy. Probably at no other time in the history of the church would the elective principle be again so weak. Despite these advantages and strengths which the papacy enjoyed, the real question remained whether administrative ingenuity and legalistic legerdemain were sufficient for the church in an age of nominalism, national monarchies, and increasing lay literacy and piety.

RISE OF THE SECULAR MONARCHIES

The new secular monarchy threatened to curtail the aspirations and pretensions that the papacy entertained in the temporal sphere. The rudiments of the lay state evident in the France of Philip the Fair were shaped more by theories of Roman law than by Aristotle's *Politics*. The limitations of papal authority in dealing with secular rulers had already been manifested in the monarch's unilateral taxation of the French clergy, the humiliation of Anagni, and the suppression of the military order of the Templars. The pope might exert more authority over his own clergy and within the institutional framework of the church, but he needed to recognize a similar development within the jurisdiction of the secular ruler. Thus, after the tumultuous events from 1295 to 1314, both secular and spiritual monarchs moved toward an accommodation. The papacy was by no means in the pocket of the French ruler during the Babylonian Captivity. And in the matter of collation of benefices, where political power and ecclesiastical property were conjoined, the French king found it expedient to encourage John XXII to make extensive use of his powers of reservation. Already the church seemed to be drifting toward an age of princes and concordats. In the case of England, despite the parliamentary and episcopal resistance to papal provisions which emerged in response to the rather routine measures of the Statutes of Provisors (1351) and of Praemunire (1353), king and pope managed to carry on business over the heads of the local clergy.

STRUCTURE OF THE CHURCH

Unquestionably the papal concept of fullness of power (*plenitudo potestatis*) fared better within its own immediate jurisdiction—the ecclesiastical structure. Since the Gregorian reform in the eleventh century, papal sovereignty had come to express itself in terms of the pope's infinite capacity to legislate, his complete right to discipline or transfer any bishop, his ability to intervene directly at any point in the hierarchy and transfer to the Roman Curia the jurisdiction exercised by subordinates. In short, according to the words of the *Dictatus papae,* "he alone may establish new laws ... and is judged by none." Imposing and real as papal sovereignty was, it did not render the church a monolith. Tensions continued to exist between the pope on the one hand and the College of Cardinals, archbishops, or territorial episcopates on the other. Canon law itself was not univocal. In fact, a crucial text in the *Decretum,* the basic text of canon law, asserted that a pope could be judged by none unless he was guilty of heresy. In the hands of the early thirteenth-century canonist Huguccio and some later canonists, the list of crimes for which a pope could be punished was significantly extended. On the diocesan level, canon law was being explicated in a way that might provide a serious challenge to the existing constitution of the church in the West. In order to preserve the administrative continuity and authority of the corporation during an episcopal vacancy, some canonists argued that the corporation's authority was not concentrated in the head alone but existed also in all the members. Such a principle, adopted during the thirteenth century by the collection of semiautonomous corporations that made up the church, might have significant implications for the entire church, which was itself, obviously, a corporation. Yet to a world that saw all government as an analogue of God's role in the universe, and papal monarchy as thereby epitomizing the essential unity of the church under God, there was little need to worry about the further extension of this principle; barring some sort of crisis, the mass of corporations that constituted the church submitted to the centralizing influences of the papacy.

THE GREAT SCHISM

Nevertheless the crisis occurred. A year after the pope's restoration to Rome, the cardinals, following the death of Gregory XI in March 1378, elected Urban VI; then, quickly reacting to the new pope's harshness and violent temper, some repudiated him and elected Clement VII. Thus the very institution which was intended to affirm the unity of Christ's body had two heads. The Great Schism had begun. In the succeeding decades, the corporation theories of the canonists became the conciliar theory and presented the greatest single challenge to the constitution of the church. Ockham and Marsilius had earlier advocated the superiority of a general council to the pope. At the University of Paris there now emerged the conciliar thesis that supreme ecclesiastical authority resides in the universal church, which is represented by a general council. As neither of the rival popes nor their successors deigned to cede, and both the university and the College of Cardinals proved unable to end the schism, a council offered the only alternative.

Three problems stood before the council fathers assembled at Constance— schism, heresy, and reform. The first could be met more easily than the other two: Martin V was elected pope in 1417, and the rival popes were declared deposed. Concerning heresy, Wycliffe could be condemned and his bones later exhumed, Hus could be burned, but the Czech national reform movement was too deeply rooted; by the time the subsequent council at Basel had been compelled to come to terms with this movement, it had achieved the curious phenomenon of a Bohemian national church only tenuously related to Latin Catholicism. As for reform, which involved a review of papal taxation, provisions, and reservations, the council was of divided mind, proved maladroit, and allowed the issue to be handled through concordats, or separate arrangements between the pope and individual secular rulers. Although the great decrees of the council, *Sacrosancta* and *Frequens,* asserted the superior authority of council to pope and provided for regular meetings of councils, Constance had, by its very success in ending the schism, removed the emergency and with it the chief justification for the conciliar program.

CONCILIARISM AND CONCORDATS

In the ensuing struggle, however, the papacy was fighting for its existence; and it is a measure of the threat posed by conciliarism that succeeding popes, faced with the double challenge of this movement and the growing power of the secular ruler, chose to compromise with the latter in order to obtain support in crushing the former. It was an age not only of conciliarism, but also of princes—both secular and ecclesiastical—and of concordats. If church–state relations only became a subject for political theory at the end of the sixteenth century, it was in the course of the fifteenth that the conflict between state and church became explicit in the diplomatic negotiations involved in reaching concordats.

The policy of concordats had previously been used with good effect by the papacy at Constance in attaining separate agreements with secular rulers. When no general agreement could be reached, separate concordats had to be prepared for the Romanic nation (France, Spain, Italy), the German nation (Germany, Hungary, Poland, and the Scandinavian countries), and the English nation. The action acknowledged not simply the deep-seated divisions along "national" lines within the universal church but also the authority of the territorial rulers over the reduction of papal fiscality and reservations in their own lands. The emerging pattern culminated in the Vienna Concordat of 1448, which by defining relations between Rome and the German nation delivered a fatal blow to the council at Basel that had opposed the pope's authority.

THE TERRITORIAL CHURCH

Although the papal policy of concordats successfully subverted the conciliar movement, it served to educate the territorial princes in their exercise of ecclesiastical privileges and functions. In each instance the ruler's control over appointments to church positions was increased, as was evident in the indult granted to Savoy whereby Duke Amadeus, for renouncing his role at Basel as Felix V, the anti-pope, was granted the authority to approve of all candidates to abbacies, bishoprics, and archbishoprics in his duchy. If the papal grip upon the material life of the church was being relaxed, the papacy was quick to insist that these concessions marked only a renunciation of the exercise of certain rights, not the rights themselves.

To appreciate what was taking place during the century of concordats preceding the upheaval of the Reformation, one needs to consider briefly the operation of papal concessions on the territorial and local level. The relationship between pope and prince was much more one of collusion than of antagonism, and out of this collusion against the local bishop the territorial church was being shaped. In the Late Middle Ages the three Saxon bishoprics of Meissen, Merseburg, and Naumburg-Zeitz struggled with material distress. In 1399 the Margrave William I was able to obtain a papal bull placing Meissen under the immediate jurisdiction of the pope and thereby providing the basis for later direct negotiations between prince and pope above the heads of the local clergy. In subsequent decades the margrave steadily increased the number of cathedral canonries to which he could appoint. Recourse to any outside ecclesiastic was prohibited. When in 1476 Sixtus IV granted the privilege that all three bishops be drawn only from the territorial nobility or academic ranks, the Saxon princes were able to tighten their hold over Merseburg and Naumburg. Princes obtained such advantages not in opposition to the Curia but in league with it.

On the western edge of the empire in the Swiss Confederation, the case of Zurich illustrates a similar development. As with so many other late medieval city-states, the town council at Zurich had since the end of the fourteenth century sought to extend its authority over the life of the entire community. Its inroads upon the position of the church assumed multiple forms: the appointment of guardians to religious houses, the magistrates' right to nominate officials to enjoy the wealth of an ecclesiastical corporation (prebends), a regular tax upon ecclesiastical foundations both within and outside the walls of the town, the limiting of clerical immunity from civil justice and of arbitration by the Bishop of Constance, and the control of morality. However, in 1512, when the burgomasters petitioned Pope Julius II for the confirmation of some of these privileges, already exercised, he steadfastly refused. A privilege could be exercised by the secular power, but to make it a right would have undermined the constitution of the church. At issue was the control of the external church. The danger was rendered most acute by the phenomenon, widespread throughout the towns of southern Germany, of donations made by wealthy laymen and the *patronatsrecht* by which the town council stood as trustee, with the power to appoint clerics to these donations. Thus by 1500 significant segments of the lower clergy were more closely bound to the town council than to the local bishop.

In more conspicuous areas of the ecclesiastical hierarchy, the age witnessed the inroads of secular authority. In the Iberian kingdoms, the Catholic monarchs Ferdinand and Isabella steadily extended their capacity to appoint first to episcopal sees, then to all churches and cloisters in the lands confiscated from the Moors and later in the new world. With the introduction of the Spanish Inquisition, completely under royal control, a national church began to emerge. Across the Pyrenees, the French kingdom was the best example of a national solution to the major ecclesiastical issues of the period. Peculiar to the French scene was the ostensibly venerable doctrine, associated with emergent Gallicanism, that the French monarch has no superior in temporal matters. While harboring notions of a general council's supremacy, along with the most exalted interpretation of the king's role in the externals of the church, Gallicanism fed upon a very material interest in ecclesiastical benefices. A product of the Great Schism and of the general reaction to papal provisions, Gallicanism as it developed in the Parlement of Paris and in the University of Paris rapidly associated conciliarism with reform—reform of appointments to benefices. The national councils of 1398 and 1406 acted to withdraw the church in France from papal obedience and to reassert the right of election for major benefices and the right of the bishops for lower benefices. At least at the inception of Gallicanism, king, clergy, and Parlement moved together. But it was the Parlement that became the most able and vociferous champion of Gallican doctrine, presiding over the restored system of appointments to benefices. By the Pragmatic Sanction of Bourges in 1438, twenty-four decrees of the Council of Basel were written into the foundations of the Gallican church; besides reestablishing canonical elections and suppressing reservations, annates, and appeals to the Curia, the document asserted the conciliar theory of the superiority of a general council to the pope. The Pragmatic Sanction, the hallmark of Gallicanism, had its champions in the Parlement of Paris and the University, which benefited by the nomination of its graduates. But the preeminent role of the Parlement in the Gallican church was as little to the liking of the king as it was to that of the pope. After his victory at Marignano, Francis I hastened to reach a definitive settlement with Leo X. The resulting Concordat of Bologna (1516) abrogated the Pragmatic Sanction and introduced a new arrangement whereby the king obtained the right to nominate to virtually all major benefices and the pope confirmed the nominations. The Concordat of 1516 thus is a classic example of an agreement between two absolute rulers over the heads of the national clergy. The long but futile resistance of both Parlement and university attested to the decline of their position in the Gallican Church and the split between parlementary and royal Gallicanism. With a command over the French church and over patronage unsurpassed by any of his predecessors, the king was even less interested in programs of reform.

For the papacy, the abrogation of the Pragmatic Sanction meant the removal of the conciliar weapon from the arsenal of the French king and marked the culmination of the papal efforts to vitiate the conciliar program. The popes' struggle had begun with the concordats of Eugenius IV and had continued to Pius II's *Execrabilis* in 1460, which made it heretical for anyone but the pope to call a council. At every stage the issue of reform had been used by both conciliarists and papalists for their own ends, and actual reform had been the loser. In April 1517, with the papal policy of concordats apparently vindicated, Leo X brought the Fifth Lateran Council to a successful conclusion —a council replete with reforms that were not to be implemented. Rome was unchallenged as the center of international diplomacy and was about to enter upon a period of cultural leadership marked by the High Renaissance. The triumph of the papacy disguised the failure to recognize and react to much-needed reforms. Seen in the context of papal concessions to secular rulers, the growing gap between Christian ideal and Christian performance was leading to a dangerously explosive situation.

ECCLESIASTICAL ABUSES

The contemporary church suffered from abuses that are too well-known to need emphasis. Such practices as pluralism, nonresidence, commendations, the constant scrambling for benefices, accentuated by inflation and the new demands of court life, all bespoke monetary concern with ecclesiastical preferment to the detriment of pastoral care. As John Gerson, Chancellor of the University of Paris, observed, "Bishops today, and abbots and monks are the officials more of the fisc than of Christ." The perfunctory performance of religious ceremonies was only surpassed by the popular craving for an easy, tangible way to salvation. To study the abuses in the religious life of the period, however, brings us no closer to an understanding of the extremely complex process occurring within the late medieval perception of the world or of the forces that would effectively contribute to the upheaval of the later reformation. Behind the abuses and the frenetic character of the spiritual life of the period lay a profound moral and religious dilemma that convulsed Latin Christendom. This malaise, which hung as a pall over late medieval man, manifested itself in terms of a loss of relationship between the whole and its parts and a disjunction between internal and external experience.

THEOLOGICAL AND RELIGIOUS WEAKNESS

If theological developments do not offer us the precise causes for the specific religious character of the age, they at least reveal some of its salient features. In considering the contribution of regnant nominalism to the dissolution evident in every level of life, no judgment is being passed either on the Catholicity or the philosophic vitality of late medieval nominalism. Although Ockham was only censured and the nominalist tradition became a recognized and flourishing rival school in the theological faculties of the fourteenth century, nominalism still harbored elements promoting individualism and autonomy that might contribute to the dissolution of a corporate society. To the period's intense anxiety concerning salvation, cheap grace, and meritorious works, nominalism presented the terrible antinomy between an all-powerful God distinguished by will and man who possessed the religious initiative for his own salvation. For while a saving knowledge of God was recognized as a free gift on God's part, if a man made the very best use of his natural capacities in searching for God (*facere quod in se est*), God must then necessarily grant him grace. Such a doctrine would appear to provide theological sanction to a religious life that assumed the form of propitiating and winning God's favor by meritorious works. As the English theologian Thomas Bradwardine could attest, Pelagianism, the theological confidence in man's free will, was a major intellectual current of the period. Furthermore, the essential willfulness of God asserted by nominalism and the breakdown of the ultimate demonstrability of faith accented the need to cling to the authority of the church and its dogmas and ceremonies for their own sake.

A curious lack of focus pervaded late scholasticism. For while all would admit that scripture was the basic source of the knowledge of faith, the unity and primacy of scripture were becoming buried under commentary, exegesis, and scholastic method. Professional theologians treated scripture as an arsenal of arguments and propositions to meet the demands of philosophic inquiry and speculation. Whatever overriding authority or direct personal impact scripture might possess necessarily suffered from such practices. Amid a welter of authorities, the tradition of scriptural interpretation, whether at Paris or at Rome, had dangerously displaced the tradition of scripture.

Manifest everywhere in the religious life of the age is fragmentation and dissolution so extreme as to obscure or eradicate the original intention. One thinks of the monastery, which had long indicated its loss of a sense of community by replacing the single, common dormitory with individual cells, and by partitioning property among the members of the house; or, in the secular clergy, the multiplication of altarpriests commensurate with the proliferation of private altars; or, among the laity, the multiplication of saints' days, vows, pilgrimages. But the process of dissolution and loss of focus is best grasped in all its profundity by considering the development of the mass. For the early church, the eucharistic service had emphasized the participation of all in the corporate action of the liturgy and, through communion, the incorporation of all in Christ. During the course of the Middle Ages the church, to deal with the problem of the sheer numbers that had to be tended, erected a barrier between laity and clergy: the officiating priest came from behind the altar and turned his back to the congregation; the Frankish notion of the act as performed for, rather than with, the laity was introduced into the Roman text of the mass; later there came the choir screen and the removal of the cup from the laity, a mere convenience developed in the thirteenth century but officially sanctioned by the Council of Constance. Virtually cut off from the liturgical action, the laity found a new focus and meaning in the elevation of the host at the words of consecration, when they adored. Since specific beneficial effects were imputed to mere sight of the host, for many in the later Middle Ages attendance only at the elevation or in the Corpus Christi procession became the measure of piety. Similarly, the attribution of beneficial effects to the performance of the mass led to the multiplication of masses and the phenomenon of private and votive masses for individuals or groups. A new clergy of altarpriests emerged to meet the popular craving, deriving their income from endowments or mass stipends. The city of Strassburg alone had 120 mass foundations in 1521.

The worst feature of this development was that an inherently public action, encapsulating the whole experience of the worshiping Christian community, had become a private undertaking to produce material results. The architecture of the age betrayed this loss of focus and fragmentation. While the High Middle Ages had been a time of cathedrals, the Late Middle Ages was one of private chapels and family altars. The cathedral at Danzig was not unusual in having 48 altars, nor was the minster at Ulm, with over 60. And the great crowds of the laity attending low mass in the nave, removed as they were from the liturgical action, might each now withdraw into his own isolation to doze, or dream, or pursue private meditation or, for the increasing numbers of literate laymen, to read devotional literature in the vernacular. Little wonder that the age saw the greatest efflorescence of Western mysticism. Like the petrification of theology in the logic mills of the universities, the breakdown of the mass helped significantly to drive religious thought and expression to mystical ascents or underground.

Accompanying this atomization of public religious expression were evidences of anxiety and despair, frenzy and nihilism, which created a sort of spiritual schizophrenia in some of the religious types of the age. One could wear a hair shirt and waste oneself in penitential exercises and simultaneously commit outrageous acts. The most extravagant expressions of ceremonious piety could be linked with the most licentious indulgence. The dissociation of inner and outer actions suggested a more profound dissociation within the self. The frenetic character of religious life was magnified by the preoccupation with death. The Black Death and the recurrence of plagues throughout the entire period kept mortality and the defeat of all material gain before the individual mind. The Dance of Death, the Art of Dying, the Council of Florence's definition of the doctrine of purgatory, the practice of indulgences—all suffered life to be seen increasingly from the perspective of death.

Religious expression seemed hypnotized and imprisoned by traditional ceremonies and practices that had lost their content; only some sort of new beginning could release piety from this dead end. His mind bound by the external action and object, unable to address itself to the thing signified, the ordinary Christian multiplied his candles, his vows, his alms. Perhaps the most striking feature of this exaggerated form of piety was the remarkable vigor it betrayed even as late as the sixteenth century. Unless someone were to pick the stick up from the other end—unless there were some total transvaluation of values—this piety might continue to pullulate. Despite a few luminous figures like John Gerson and Nicholas of Cusa, the pastoral ministry seemed dangerously untended and a sense of peculiar deprivation, destitution, and neglect pervaded Holy Church. To more than one contemporary critic this feeling was conveyed by an image terrible in its implications: the church had become the widow of Christ.

SOURCES OF REFORM

The Late Middle Ages did not lack reformers, both catholic and heretic. The obverse of the ills of the church during these centuries was the positive strivings of intellectual and spiritual leaders whose movements sought some resolution to the problems of the period. To consider the intentions of these reformers is not to impute to them ideas that foreshadowed, or even influenced, the Protestant reformers. Although Luther would owe nothing to Wycliffe or Hus—except the warming assurance that he had not been alone in his opposition to the papacy —the intent and goals of these reformers warrant brief consideration in any attempt to understand the ills of the church and the nature of the remedies prescribed.[1] Four reforming movements claim attention: that of Wycliffe and Hus; conciliarism; the Brethren of the Common Life; and Erasmian humanism.

Wycliffism and Hussitism   Wycliffe's criticism of the contemporary church was moral, his reform moral. Through his doctrine of dominion, moral virtue became the criterion for reform. According to this idea, all men were direct tenants of God; thus all possessions and power were held righteously only as long as their tenants remained in a state of grace. Wycliffe's preeminent concern was fidelity to the example of Christ in the gospels.

The weakness of Wycliffism in England arose from the fact that after 1378 it was cut off from its intellectual base, Oxford, and, despite the scattered achieve-

---

[1] Despite the possibly misleading title Heiko A. Oberman's *Forerunners of the Reformation* (New York, 1966), esp. pp. 42–3, would not conflict with this position.

ments of the Lollards, driven underground. In Bohemia, however, it came upon a long- and well-established reform movement based at a great European university in a kingdom not easily accessible to Roman intervention. Here ideas of ecclesiastical disendowment, a purified pastorate, lay Biblicism, the appeal to the early church and the reverberations of Franciscan poverty and Marsilian secularism, all present in Wycliffe's thought, were welcomed and served to confirm and encourage similar strains in the preexisting Czech reform.

When Hus was appointed preacher to Bethlehem Chapel in Prague in 1402, he became the leader of the Czech populace supporting a deeply-rooted reform that emphasized the scriptures, clerical poverty, and more intense lay religious participation. Hus' greatest work is probably *On the Church,* completed in May 1413. He defines the church as the totality of the predestinate (elect) past, present, and future. He acknowledges the concept of the church militant, including both predestined and foreknown (reprobate), but only recognizes the former as true members of the mystical body of Christ. He weakens the Roman concept of office by asserting that a wicked priest holds his office validly, but not worthily. This idea, together with his emphasis upon the invisible and moral nature of the church as a spiritual entity, implicitly undermined the current canonistic concept of the church as a juridical corporation. At Constance, on the basis of Hus' authorship of *On the Church* and his leadership of an increasingly turbulent popular movement at Prague, Gerson and Cardinal D'Ailly prosecuted him as an outright Wycliffite, despite Hus' own disclaimers.

The Czech reform movement after Hus' death assumed a radical direction in the Taborite movement; an apocalyptic tone and a primitivist emphasis came to the fore. To the true pastor it meant virtual disendowment and to the clergy dependence upon freely-given alms. To the laity it meant reliance on the New Testament alone, communion in both kinds—the wine as well as the bread— infant communion, and avoidance of the Roman clergy. The ultimate ideal of Hussitism was the reduction of the world to the estate of the primitive church. The cup given to the laity, the symbol of the pan-Hussite movement, itself demonstrated this primitivism, by gaining support from its association with the church of the apostolic age.

The armies of Emperor Sigismund and Rome proved unable to master the Taborite menace. It was rather the Bohemian nobility itself, made up of both Catholic and moderate Hussite (Utraquist) members, that in 1434 destroyed the military power of the Taborite brotherhoods and with them the dominant role of the towns and urban middle groups. In the subsequent collaboration between the elected Czech king, Georg of Podiebrad, and the archbishop John Rokycana, the former moved for closer relations with Rome, while the archbishop sought to construct an autonomous structure for the Utraquists in a sort of Bohemian territorial church. Both accepted the Basel Compacts by which the Council had granted communion in both kinds, the free preaching of the Word of God, the punishment of mortal sins, and the curtailment of ecclesiastics acquiring property and ruling in secular matters. The Utraquist church remained a special but officially recognized ecclesiastical communion within the Roman church. While this ambiguous position seemed to imply, particularly in the light of the next century's events, a state of schism, the early fifteenth century allowed for a number of just such incongruous, innovative, and almost experimental arrangements. Here Hussitism in Eastern Europe compares with Gallicanism in Western Europe as only a slightly more extreme case of the formation of national churches. Both instances are marked by the desire to limit the papally-directed hierarchy over the territorial church, or even to replace it with a new complex combining the authority of the university and the legitimate political powers of the realm.

The Conciliar Movement   As a reform movement, the conciliar program also espoused local churches, but while the essence of Wycliffe–Hussite reform had been moral, that of conciliarism was legal and constitutional. Dietrich of Niem, an outspoken conciliarist, emphatically expresses this notion of reform as a legal and constitutional curtailment of papal authority. The power that belongs to the whole ecclesiastical body has, he argues, been usurped by the head. Hence, in drawing upon Marsilius' earlier conciliarism, Dietrich sees the first task as one of limiting the coercive and usurped power of the pope. Like other conciliar reformers, he appeals to the practices of the ancient church and thereby makes normative a pre-Avignonese, and even pre-Gregorian, church. For not only does Dietrich attack papal reservations, dispensations, and the bestowal of benefices; more specifically, he removes the supreme legislative authority within the church from the pope and vests it in councils.

The resounding failure of the councils, which opened the door to national churches, meant the end of neither conciliar theory nor the idea of a council, the strength of which lay in the desire for reform. In the years following Basel, the papacy held both council and conciliarism at arm's length. The age saw no lack of reform programs, but the will to implement them was absent. Conciliar criticism of papal usurpation was belied by the actual need for a firm hand at the top. The Renaissance papacy, for all its splendor and brilliance, was spiritually adrift. Absorbed in peninsular politics and torn by the private interests of its cardinals, the church universal was becoming a local Italian institution. The well-developed system of selling offices, whereby each held his post as a piece of property, dealt a fatal blow to any reorganization of the Curia. The ever-present and excellent plans for reform culminated at the Fifth Lateran Council, where the overriding conviction emerged that the church needed no new laws but only to enforce the old. If so, the council was to prove disappointing, for its good laws were vitiated by exemptions and the recognition of private interests. The opportunity to restore Christian community had been allowed to escape both council and pope.

The age called for "Reform in Head and Members." The Reform of the Head, the papal administration, which was legal and constitutional in character, failed. Nevertheless, the Reform of the Members, if removed from the levers of power, possessed the vitality for effecting a considerable intellectual and spiritual reorientation. The development of Italian humanism and its quickening influence upon Northern piety are treated elsewhere in this volume; but insofar as the *Devotio Moderna* and Erasmian humanism complete our present inquiry, a few observations may be made here.

The Brethren of the Common Life   Unlike Italian humanism the *Devotio Moderna* grew out of no encounter with the classical past nor any possible secularizing of Christianity. The reform espoused by its Dutch champions, the Brethren of the Common Life, focussed on the care of souls. Directing their efforts toward schoolboys, the Brethren began by concentrating upon the pastoral and not the specifically educational. Only in their capacity of tutoring the students for their lessons did they indirectly and gradually come in contact with humanist currents. In so far as they had a theology it was Biblical. More concerned with shaping an inner piety, the Brethren had by the end of the fifteenth century developed certain affinities for the moral philosophy of Antiquity and especially for that spiritual independence from all worldly attachments found in the Stoicism of Seneca. Although the movement's establishment of the Windesheim Congregation of Augustinian monks rooted the *Devotio Moderna* squarely within the institutional church, the lay orientation of the Brethren and the growing inwardizing and individualizing of religion had the implicit effect of making less valid the hierarchical institution of the church. Despite the difference in their origins the religious ideal of Italian humanism as evinced in Petrarch, Salutati, and Valla and that of the *Devotio Moderna* shared common areas of agreement. In both there was the attempt to withstand the petrification of Christianity and to form piety directly, practically, and personally. To both Desiderius Erasmus stood as heir.

Erasmian Humanism   It is highly revealing that the greatest man of the early sixteenth century was a scholar. Beyond his own very real talents, Erasmus's greatness was made possible by a unique combination of factors: the existence of a cosmopolitan community of readers and scholars, the growing demands of lay piety, enthusiasm for exploiting the intellectual resources of the past for the needs of the present, the advent of the printing press. In this context, the main endeavor and accomplishment of Erasmus's life was to bring to bear, before a literate, articulate public which he had been instrumental in creating, the central intellectual achievement of the Italian Renaissance upon the contemporary church, society, theology, and the self.

The character of Erasmian reform can be briefly glimpsed in the restoration of theology by good letters (*bonae literae*) and the *Philosophia Christi*. In turning to Lorenzo Valla at critical moments in his development, Erasmus had appropriated the profoundest element of Italian humanism—the application of a historically critical method to the literary documents of the past and, more specifically, of the early church. Erasmus now resumed the effort, suggested by Valla, to place theology before the bar of grammar and to direct humanistic theology toward biblical exegesis. Just as study of the texts of Cicero had brought humanists closer to the mind and purpose of that statesman, so might the study of the earliest Christian texts bring one closer to Paul and to Christ. The resort to the sources, the learning of Greek, the study of Jerome were but steps to the crowning achievement—the editing and publication of the New Testament. By clarifying the past, the present could be regenerated and learning could restore piety and civilization. Through purification of the text the true theology—the simplicity and clarity of Christ and his moral teaching—would be communicated to men.

The *Philosophia Christi,* the other side of the diptych, was a practical theology realizable in life. It upheld Christ as the single and universal norm for the ethical striving of all elements of society, regardless of rank. For, in striking contrast to monasticism, the redefinition of Christian piety bore the stamp of thorough engagement with the world. Erasmus wrote his *Enchiridion* for the correction of a wayward knight, and directed his biblical exegesis to pimps and prostitutes as well as artisans and peasants. In his colloquy *The Godly Feast,* only pious laymen come together to consider the meaning of a scriptural passage. But beside the lay emphasis of this ethic there also appeared a new intensity and profundity with which the ethical content of a text is spiritually imbued. The appeal to direct experience had been earlier evoked by late medieval mystics and even, within scholasticism, by the efforts of such thinkers as Duns Scotus, Bradwardine, and Ockham to remove secondary causality, the intermediaries, and relate God to man. What we learn, Erasmus now told his age, must not be simply stored in the memory but communicated to the emotions and to the very viscera of the mind (*in ipsa mentis viscera*) that we be transformed and made better by our learning. The new piety would manifest an affective, even visceral, response to the written and, soon, spoken word. This special sensitivity to the text was more broadly shared and expressed by leading figures of the Northern Renaissance: John Colet, lecturing after his return from Italy upon the First Epistle to the Corinthians, ignored the doctrinal content and sought to identify himself with the spirit and purpose of Paul; and Lefèvre d'Etaples, who in distinguishing a scriptural sense at once literal and prophetic that united the mind of the devout reader with the mind of Scripture's author, the Holy Spirit, allowed this same sensitivity to enter the new religious dimension of faith. Thus did the professional theologian's quest for apt arguments give way to the Christian humanist's passion for canons to live by. And thus did the moral vector within humanism join with its philological vector in directing its energies to the heart of a decaying church.

A review of the four major reform movements from 1378 to 1516 suggests a number of common characteristics. The moral criterion is uppermost as the measure and goal of reform. The ethical standard, less central to the legal–constitutional concerns of conciliarism, is most obvious in the case of Erasmus, who, confident in the educability of man, saw no conflict between sacred letters and good letters; Socrates, Plato, and Christ express a single moral teaching.

Beyond the moral criterion, the means of promoting reform had much in common; with the single exception of the *Devotio Moderna,* the reform movements looked to the secular authority for aid, drew arguments and inspiration from the Bible, and appealed to the early or primitive church. Finally, in varying degrees all these reforms sought to meet three pervasive needs of the *Respublica christiana* in this period: the reaffirmation, if not the redefinition, of community; the recognition of lay piety and religion; and the reintegration of the outer and inner self. Community, laicity, integrity—these three problems pervaded all the reforms of the age.

Unquestionably the most influential and significant of these reforms was Erasmian humanism, or the Northern Renaissance. While the rest had either proved abortive or became limited and localized, humanism in the early sixteenth century benefited enormously from the invention of printing, drew sustenance and support from a burgeoning literate and articulate public, and successfully met the current need of applying the aesthetic–individualist culture of the Italian Renaissance to the ethical, social, and religious problems of a North still feudally and ecclesiastically organized. The subtle, pervasive appeal of Erasmian humanism exerted its influence wherever men read and thought and talked, and would continue to be a force with which succeeding reforms would have to reckon.

Perhaps the most outstanding attribute of early sixteenth-century humanism was that it spoke meaningfully to an intelligent laity seeking more, rather than less, religion. For the generation coming into positions of responsibility in these years, the whole concept of *religio,* so redolent of the monastic, had to be expanded, and the tensions between the contemplative and the active life resolved, in favor of an asceticism which could be exercised in the world. The Christian Knight of Erasmus's *Enchiridion* directed himself to this problem and for many provided a resolution in the expression of an engaged piety. For both the London magistrate Thomas More and the Venetian aristocrat Gasparo Contarini, the conscious choice between the monastery and an asceticism exercised in the active life had early presented itself, and in each case the latter had been seized. And if neither More nor Contarini could entirely subscribe to Erasmus's tenet that monasticism was not piety, each strained toward a piety active in the world. The most tumultuous and definitive rejection of monasticism and all it signified was yet to come.

Luther and the Advent of the Protestant Reformation

LUTHER'S INSIGHT

On July 17, 1505, the doors of the Augustinian Eremites' cloister at Erfurt shut behind the young Martin Luther, enclosing him in a life, sanctified by over a millennium of saints and spiritual leaders, that intended to lead to man's right relationship with God. In the course of the next three years it would not be the enveloping walls of the monastery that troubled the ex-law student, now a devout monk, but rather the far more real confinement of experiencing oneself as walled in by the divine judgment and forever subject to the divine wrath. The decade ahead at Erfurt, and later at Wittenberg, would see the student of theology return ever again to those terrible words, "the righteousness of God," which so troubled his soul. In the depths of his spiritual anguish, and with a persistence that defied all the wise institutional solaces and strenuous efforts to fob him off, Luther attacked these words until they ultimately imparted to him a different and life-giving resonance. In this elemental intensity, he crystallized the religious needs and dilemma of an entire civilization and resolved the issue in a way that shattered Latin Christendom. In few other instances has the course of history suddenly narrowed to become identified with the quest of a single man.

Luther's quest was for a gracious God, and it proved significant for his reform that the traditional institutional answers not only failed to alleviate, but even accentuated, his frustration. The monastery itself evoked from Luther a scrupulous observance that served to heighten his sense of alienation. The sacrament of penance indicated to him how far he fell short of a true contrition based upon love rather than fear of God. Educated at the University of Erfurt in the Ockhamist theory, Luther was exposed to the *facere quod in se est,* which, in its apparently Pelagian confidence that man can prepare himself for the reception of grace, mocked Luther's efforts and drove him into deeper despair. Resources were not entirely lacking to Luther, confronted by the impossibility of the divine law and a just God who punishes and condemns at will; the German mystics gave momentary solace, and St. Augustine some reassurance, but it was his confessor John Staupitz who directed him to the wounds of Christ, to the Bible, and finally to work.

Had Luther been cut off from exegetical research and theological exposition, he could have never raised his religious problem, no matter how deeply experienced, to the level of universal reference for all members of Latin Christendom. The existential and the exegetical, the religious and the theological, fused in the thinking of the newly-promoted Doctor of Biblical Theology at the University of Wittenberg when in 1513 Luther began to lecture on the Psalms. Proceeding through the Psalms to Romans, then Galatians, Hebrews and again to Psalms, Luther's formal exposition of Scripture constituted the living source of his religious growth over the seven years that embraced the development of his reform. To attempt to chart chronologically Luther's spiritual odyssey during these years and to locate the moment of the supposed "Tower Experience," his insight into Romans 1:17, has only led to endless controversy among scholars. For Luther's thought was so complex, and moved on so many levels, that even the most profound perception would be long in communicating its structure and implications to other areas of his thinking.

Thus, while the traditional date of autumn 1514, assigned by scholars, still appears the most likely time for his insight, its effect upon his idea of scripture as overriding authority and the forensic character of justification did not attain maturity until the end of 1518, and his social and political thought was not fully elaborated until after 1522. As Luther himself warns, he did not learn his theology all at once but had to dig ever deeper for it.

Luther had continued to be troubled by the words *justitia dei* (the righteousness of God), for he perceived in them only God's wrath, Christ seated on the rainbow dispensing condemnation and punishment, the *iustitia activa* of retribution. To the task of lecturing upon Psalms Luther brought the traditional hermeneutics, which involved the application of four separate interpretations—the literal, the moral or tropological, the allegorical, and the anagogical. But Luther interpreted the literal in the prophetic sense of Lefèvre d'Etaples as that which agrees with the Holy Spirit. Christ thus becomes the point of reference for every passage of scripture. This Christocentric exegesis, laboriously developed over the months, he directed persistently to the exploitation of the tropological sense, which pertains to man, or, more properly, to the believer in Christ. The new weight given to the tropological sense makes it the exegetical means by which Luther could appropriate to himself and for his generation the spiritual import of Christ. Working within this hermeneutic he was creating by exercise, Luther came to perceive and realize *for himself* that the Righteousness of God means that righteousness by which He makes men righteous as do His strength, wisdom, and virtue refer to that by which we are made strong, wise, and holy. Of all the cycles of lectures during this period in which Luther might have found the nucleus for this central insight into the *iustitia passiva* of a merciful loving God, Psalm 71 (72):2 offers itself as the most probable. Under the pressure of later events, and in the course of subsequent lectures, the conviction would mature that through faith all which was Christ's is ours and our sins are no longer imputed to us. Nevertheless it is important to note that before he was drawn into the maelstrom of reforming action, Luther had posited the salient features of what would become Reformation theology: the totally alien nature of righteousness and the divine initiative in the religious relationship.

THE CONTEXT OF THE NINETY-FIVE THESES

The fateful year 1517 saw the young professor of biblical theology moving in a heavily charged atmosphere. At Rome in March, the Fifth Lateran Council ended its sessions with reform measures that rapidly proved abortive. Throughout the empire, a rising tide of anti-Romanism and anticlericalism found expression among the humanists, in the press, and in the lists of grievances (*Gravamina*) devised by successive diets. At the remote University of Wittenberg, Luther and his associates pressed a reform of the curriculum that displaced Aristotle and scholasticism with the Bible and St.

Augustine. The new theology manifested its self-conscious opposition to the old in Luther's *Disputation against Scholastic Theology* in early September: Aristotle the theologian was rejected. This advance in the Wittenberg professor's theological development communicated itself to the pastoral level with cataclysmic effect in less than a month.

Since 1343 the church had formally claimed to possess a treasury of merits acquired by Christ and the saints, from which indulgences could be granted to remit the temporal punishments for forgiven sins. Under popular pressure, indulgences had been extended in the course of the fifteenth century to include the remission of guilt itself and of sufferings in Purgatory. The granting of an indulgence was associated with a money payment but also technically required the contrition of the penitent. By uniting consciences with purses, the practice of indulgences provided the broad ground for drawing the exegetical and theological insight of Luther from the lecture hall to pastoral expression before an expectant and neglected Christendom. The specific instance arose from the efforts of Archbishop Albert of Magdeburg to pay for his recent acquisition of the Archbishopric of Mainz. The matter involved an outrageous example of pluralism, the financial needs of the pope for the rebuilding of St. Peter's, the excessive claims of the institutional church with regard to forgiveness, and the managerial talents of the banking house of Fugger—a holy business (*sacrum negotium*) indeed. Although Albert's instructions to his subcommissary were phrased to require contrition and confession, the Dominican John Tetzel and his pardoners, carried away with enthusiasm for the business, promised the purchaser of an indulgence full remission of all sins and all punishments. Banned from Electoral Saxony, where Frederick the Wise sought to preserve this traditional means of raising public sums for his own more pious ends, the indulgence sellers plied their wares in the neighboring territories of Mainz and Magdeburg. Not for the first time was Luther asked to express himself on the matter.

The resulting Ninety-Five Theses were less the product of an aroused reforming spirit than of an earnest pastor and inquiring theological professor seeking clarification on a current practice and its supporting doctrine. While the content of the Theses anticipated a new Theology of the Cross by viewing all of life under the sign of penitence, the idea of justification by faith was absent from them, papal authority and the existence of purgatory went unquestioned, and even indulgences, insofar as they canonically pertained to the remission of temporal punishments, were affirmed. Cognizant of the extremely sensitive nature of the issues involved, Luther, as was only appropriate, wrote to several bishops to apprise them of the indulgence preachers' inflated claims. On October 31, 1517, he wrote to Archbishop Albrecht and probably to his own ordinary, the bishop of Brandenburg, and began waiting for an answer. When nothing was forthcoming except evasive or implicitly menacing replies, Luther sent a few handwritten copies of his theses to his friends in the hope of eliciting some clarifying remarks. Copies multiplied; the one sent to Nuremberg circulated among Luther's delighted acquaintances and was translated into German before being sent on to Augsburg and Ingolstadt. Luther himself received from Nuremberg printed copies of the theses in German and Latin, and by early in the next year they had also been printed in Basel and in Leipzig. Circulating in the tense atmosphere of anti-Romanism and lay concern for religion, Luther's Theses, calling for a disputation or at least some written contributions to the problem, had within a few months aroused all Germany and, soon afterward, all Christendom.

In keeping with university practice, Luther appears to have posted the Theses.[2] After October 31, Luther grew by sporadic leaps into the role of the hero of faith; promoted by avid printers, supported by knights and humanists, first frustrated, then prosecuted, and increasingly incensed by an unresponsive church, Luther would move toward schism. But in 1517 and 1518 he was neither schismatic nor even reformer but simply inquiring professor and concerned pastor. Still more politically adroit than has often been assumed, this professed lover of the corner, this monk who deplored schism for its lack of charity, combined with his occasionally extravagant submissiveness a shrewd calculation that harbored a growing conviction. Part mover, part moved, he would become both reformer and schismatic as much by the hostility of an unhearing church and pressures within Germany as by the crystalizing force of the Word of God. For it is all the more alarming and revealing that the official leaders of the church were either so negligent or so preoccupied as to be unable to respond to an inquiry that carried with it explosive implications for Germany and for Christendom. The glaring failure of the bishops to respond with a pious earnestness matching that of their correspondent was ominous for any possible reform within the traditional church. They were dealing with a man who could neither be blandly diverted nor simply silenced by the imposition of authority. Luther would now bring the same persistence to bear in the arena of the universal church that he had directed toward his own problem over the past decade.

Nor did anyone come to debate the Theses. Indeed the front widened rapidly. Did the situation get away from Luther? Was he more led than leading? There was no historical precedent for the effect of mass media on the creation of a mass movement. The fateful interrelationship between an aroused anticlerical lay public, cultivated by humanist satire, and the new technique of printing created an uncontrollable situation which Luther may have dimly foreseen but from which he could now certainly benefit. Albrecht of Mainz had forwarded a copy of the Theses to Rome, and proceedings began against Luther. In order to define his position he wrote a "Sermon on Indulgences and Grace" for public consumption and, at the end of May, the *Explanations,*

---

[2] But cf. thesis of Erwin Iserloh set forth in his *Luther zwischen Reform und Reformation* (Münster, 1966), translated as *The Theses Were not Posted* (Boston, 1968), by Jared Wicks which, if it has engendered enormous controversy, has still cast considerable light upon the event.

in which, presenting his case to the pope with profuse humility, he suggested that only a general council could determine what was heretical. Shortly after Tetzel had received support from the Saxon Chapter of the Dominicans, the Chapter of the Augustinians at Heidelberg provided Luther with the opportunity to expatiate upon his Theses. Here he advanced his thought into the specific domain of grace, defined his "Theology of the Cross," and won the admiration of some of the younger theologians, including Martin Bucer and Johann Brenz.

THE DEVELOPMENT OF LUTHER'S POSITION

Several factors at this time fatally complicated the church's efforts to proceed against Luther. Complacence with the sheer imposition of its immense authority had the effect of blinding ecclesiastical officials to the religious import of the issue and thus alienating Luther all too quickly. A lack of theological clarity between rival schools of scholasticism made the lines between orthodoxy and heresy hard to determine and obscured the dangerous implications of Luther's position. Furthermore, it permitted lesser minds such as Tetzel and Prierias, the pope's official theological adviser, to fabricate at will binding doctrines out of personal opinions. Hardly less disturbing was the overinvolvement of the papacy in European politics, which distracted its attention from what was truly vital and led in the ensuing months to a series of compromises in which political interests were preferred to spiritual and religious ones. Finally, the most obvious stumbling block of all was the constitution of the empire, wherein real authority was exercised by a congeries of territorial princes and urban republics. Luther's prince, Frederick the Wise, a devout medieval catholic, harbored a sense of paternal responsibility toward all his subjects. He lovingly prized his new little university, which was now drawing students from all over Europe. Although he never renounced the traditional faith, he remained unconvinced that his outstanding theological professor had been proved wrong. Given the peculiar circumstances, it is not strange that the elector and Luther apparently never met. The relationship was to a degree regularized by the presence of Georg Spalatin, who was at once the chaplain and private secretary of Frederick and the close friend of Luther. Upon such a slight thread rested the future of the Saxon heretic and of reformation. Yet it sufficed.

By the summer of 1518, Luther's theology of grace and of the cross was beginning to manifest arresting implications for his understanding of the church—implications so singular and profound as not always to be evident to their author. For the initial question of salvation soon raised the related issues of the church's authority and structure. In his sermon on the excessive use of excommunication, Luther suggested a church whose definition was inward and spiritual.

Replying to Prierias, he asserted that the essence of the church existed in the immediate relations of the faithful to its invisible head, Christ. Summoned now before the imposing authority of Cardinal Cajetan at Augsburg, Luther found himself compelled to explicate further this spiritual definition of the church. Already Cajetan, having availed himself of some of the wayward monk's writings before the first encounter of October 12, was alarmed to note that Luther, in treating penance, required the certainty of faith on the part of the recipient of the sacrament that his sins were forgiven. To the cardinal this idea signified the foundation of an entirely new church by Luther. The meeting itself took an unexpected turn. By summoning Luther before the cardinal, Rome had hoped to compel him to recant, but when the Augustinian began to quibble, and then to argue that Christ was not the treasury of indulgences, he undercut the ecclesiastical basis for indulgences, accented the new Christocentric definition of the church and, worst of all, defied authority. The issues now began to emerge. For in the encounter with Cajetan, Luther had been driven to recognize that he had come to identify scripture as the sole supreme authority, opposing it to that of the pope. Little wonder that he found it expedient on the night of October 20 to flee Augsburg, and a month later made his appeal to a general council.

A prisoner of its own political interests, the papacy now weakened its process against Luther by attempting to cultivate his ruler. In the event of the Emperor Maximilian's death, Frederick the Wise could play a vital role in blocking the election of Charles of Habsburg. A situation which could have proved fatal to Luther dissolved into some diplomatic feelers that led to a détente: there followed a mutual agreement to refrain from further publishing on the controversy. The death of Maximilian on January 12, 1519, enhanced the role of the elector in the papal view of the international chessboard and compromised Rome's efforts to arrest Luther. The issue might have come to rest had it not been for the challenge presented by John Eck of Ingolstadt ostensibly to Luther's colleague Karlstadt but actually to Luther himself. The ambitious, flamboyant professor had contested Luther's statement that the Roman church's domination over all other churches dated from the fourth century. The sensitive question of ecclesiology was once again raised.

Did the papacy have a divine foundation? Responding to Eck's challenge, Luther immersed himself in a study of church history and of papal decretals and during the spring of 1519 prepared his famous Thirteenth Thesis for the forthcoming debate at Leipzig. The thesis, soon to be published as the tract *On the Power of the Pope*, asserted that the Roman supremacy derived only from papal decretals against which could be cited scripture, eleven hundred years of history and the Council of Nicaea. Neither to himself nor to Christendom was Luther rebel or schismatic, yet in this work the decisive rupture had occurred. The papacy was treated like the Turk or any other divinely ordained secular power that must be obeyed. It is hardly surprising that Luther, confiding in Spalatin, now began to identify the papacy with the Antichrist.

The Leipzig debate, held in early July of 1519, marks a turning point in the development of Luther's relation to the medieval church, for it was now that the consequences of his position came to be recognized both by himself and by Christendom at large. In the course of the debates Luther continually distinguished scripture from all other authorities and exalted it above the medley of authorities to which Eck appealed. Furthermore, he was trapped into admitting that councils could err, for the Council of Constance had condemned many articles of John Hus which were thoroughly Christian. Eck pressed home his tactical victory by identifying Luther with Hus. The Leipzig debate compelled Luther to recognize the magnitude of his difference with the institutional church and traditional authority. A reading of Hus's *On the Church,* a copy of which had been brought to him by a deputation of Bohemian supporters shortly after Leipzig, caused him to exclaim, "We are all Hussites . . . even Paul and Augustine."

FROM DEBATE TO REFORM

What had before Leipzig been considered an academic debate or a monks' squabble grew to convulse all of Germany. It was Luther's defiance of Rome, rather than the religious content of his theology, which popular feeling immediately grasped. Sixty years of abortive *gravamina,* the continuing cry for reform in both church and empire, and the widespread anticlericalism seemed to have found their spokesman in Martin Luther, before whose heroic figure the social and political walls partitioning late medieval Germany appeared to dissolve, at least momentarily, in a surge of national feeling against Rome. The most threatened social groups in the empire, the imperial knights and the peasantry, would recast Luther in their own respective images. For the moment, however, Luther welcomed the proffered contacts with humanists and printers. As early as October 1518, John Froben, Erasmus's printer at Basel, had published a collection of Luther's Latin writings, and in the course of 1520 both German and Latin editions followed from Strassburg and Basel. If Luther could not subscribe to all of Ulrich von Hutten's anti-Romanist program, a reading of the knight–humanist's edition of the *Donation of Constantine,* exposed by Lorenzo Valla as a forgery, further reinforced his movement away from Rome. Although Luther had early become disenchanted with Erasmus, he still could not afford to ignore him. At Wittenberg, Spalatin and the recently-arrived great-nephew of Reuchlin, Philip Melanchthon, provided him with channels to the humanist community. Melanchthon now helped to rework Luther's lectures on Galatians to humanist tastes for the Commentary that appeared in September 1519.

The year 1520 represented the *annus mirabilis* of Luther's productivity and witnessed his passage from theological inquirer to revolutionary reformer. Responding to the need to relate faith and works, Luther led off with the tract *On Good Works,* which presented to the ordinary layman a complete definition of a good Christian life: faith became the greatest of all works and the source of all good works. As a gift of God, faith is the foundation of one's life, not the mechanical acquisition of merit. *On the Papacy at Rome* raised the perilous question of ecclesiology once more: did the church require an external unity and a head other than Christ? Luther denied the need for both, and proceeded to define the church as a spiritual *Christenheit,* an assembly of all Christian believers as distinct from the physical assemblage of the Romanists as soul is distinct from body. The succeeding *Address to the German Nobility* carried this definition one step further to the decisive pronouncement on the priesthood of all believers: Luther rejected the idea of the clergy as a specially ordained spiritual estate and proclaimed for clerics and laity alike a single Christian estate; social and political distinctions derive from office and function, not from estate. Having demolished the traditional definitions of both priesthood and church, Luther called upon the secular authorities in Germany to intervene and effect a reform in church and society according to a specific program. With the *Babylonian Captivity,* appearing on October 6, Luther completed the ecclesiastical holocaust by attacking the basis of medieval catholicism, the sacramental system, and rejecting the sacrifice of the mass together with five sacraments. His reinterpretation put new emphasis upon the faith of the recipient of the sacrament, to the detriment of the priestly act. This year of enormous productivity ended in a return from the polemical to the pastoral; in *On Christian Liberty,* Luther expressed the nature of the new piety in terms of the joy and comfort of faith which allows man to approach his neighbor in love.

Luther's literary endeavors defined a reform unique in its doctrinal rather than moral emphasis. The seminal doctrine of justification by faith alone, arrived at by exalting scripture as an authoritative norm superseding all Christian traditions, held revolutionary implications for the church. In June 1520, Luther had drawn the issues: if scripture was to have its proper impact upon men, the pope could no longer function as pope. Further elaboration of his definition of the church would now lead to the rupture. The *Babylonian Captivity*'s treatment of the sacrament disturbed Luther's contemporaries more than any other of his writings and caused Erasmus to deem the breach irreparable. Understanding reform as a biblical correction of doctrine, Luther saw reformation not as the result of his own or any human agency but through the sole agency of God's Word. Just as faith must precede works, so must the correction of doctrine naturally lead to the improvement of lives and morals.

Luther's reinterpretation of authority was anything but abstract and irrelevant. It directly confronted the demands of laicity, integrity, and community. Concerning the first issue, Luther took the decisive step by redefining the church in terms of the priesthood of all believers, the Christian estate to which all might belong through faith. Faith could likewise heal the late medieval gap between the inner and outer self by allowing the inner man of faith to master the outer man and bring a new joy, certainty, and spontaneity to life. In regard to the restoration of Christian community, however, Luther's answer, while equally clear and direct, contained deep underlying ambiguities that militated toward later difficulties. The redefinition of the church itself represented a restoration of Christian community, if the reformer proved able to carry with him all of Christendom. On a more profound level, Luther turned late in 1519 to a major source of the basic malaise of the late medieval church—the loss of the eucharist's incorporative power as a result of its use in private and votive masses. In his *Sermon on the True Body of Christ and of the Brotherhoods,* he recaptured for a moment the sense of communion as an incorporation into the fellowship of saints. Although Luther never gave up the idea, it soon lost its central position in his eucharistic doctrine. The next year the sacrificial aspect of the mass diverted him, and he would be later drawn further away by the futile question of the Real Presence—in what way Christ is fully present in the eucharist. His achievement with respect to community, however, cannot be minimized; Luther reasserted the public nature of the liturgy. Nevertheless, the central doctrine of justification by faith rooted in the individual's relation to God and the increasing concern for the forgiveness of sins through the eucharist would tend to erode the sense of communion.

Early in 1520, the theological faculties at Louvain and Cologne had prepared detailed condemnations of Luther's works and forwarded them to Rome, whence came on June 15 the papal bull *Exsurge Domine,* condemning forty-one articles and urging him to recant. In reaction to the bull, Luther attempted through his writings, and particularly in the letter to Leo X which accompanied *On Christian Liberty,* to distinguish between the pope and the power structure of the church. But with the burning of Luther's books throughout the Netherlands, events pressed toward a final rupture. On December 10, at an announced university gathering to burn the books of canon law, scholastic works and writings of Eck and Emser, Luther, almost unnoticed, added the papal bull to the flames. He then returned to composing his defense of all the articles condemned by the bull.

The fate of Luther and of his reform was being decided not in Wittenberg but in Cologne and the western part of the empire. Charles of Habsburg had been crowned at Aachen on October 23, and among those in attendance upon the youthful emperor was Frederick the Wise. As the Elector of Saxony contemplated the rising tide of unrest throughout Germany, he had occasion to observe that unless Luther could be controverted by unambiguous scriptural passages, and not by the sole threat of ecclesiastical power, the most dreadful disturbances would befall Germany. While the elector was urging the emperor not to allow Luther to be condemned unheard, the papal nuncio, Aleander, sought to solve the present difficulty by the simple imposition of force. The struggle between these two personalities for the emperor's judgment would continue until January. Heir to centuries of curialism and overly confident in the sheer manifestation of power, the papal nuncio, like so many in high ecclesiastical places, viewed the problem in political terms. Aleander now had to watch an imperial invitation, couched in the most respectful language, being proffered to a man whom the new papal bull of January 3, 1521, had found heretical and commanded to recant within sixty days. That such an invitation was possible augured ill both for the emperor's relations to his estates and for the position of Rome in Germany.

THE AFTERMATH OF WORMS

Luther came to Worms, accompanied by an imperial herald; ignoring the shadow of Hus, the news of a mandate against his books, even the proffered protection of Hutten's knights, he approached the diet to argue before Caesar the exalted issues of God's righteousness and man's conscience bound to the authority of scripture. After the faint beginning there followed his second audience before the emperor on April 18 and his great witness. Subsequent efforts to dislodge Luther through debate on the nature and authority of the church proved futile; he could not even accept the decision of a council *per se* as binding. The rift was already tragically apparent but its extent remained to be disclosed by time. On the night of the twenty-fifth, Charles V announced his decision to proceed against the heretic, and on the next day Luther departed—soon to be whisked away according to the elector's arrangements to a place of safekeeping, the Wartburg. The other protagonist, the emperor, managed after a month's endeavor to have an edict banning Luther and his books accepted by a rump diet; and after providing for a regency government under his brother Ferdinand, he departed for Spain not to reappear in Germany for nine years.

Thus had the concept of *justitia dei*, working on the troubled conscience of a monk, led to a most fateful turn in Western history: the authority of fifteen hundred years had been challenged and rejected. In the course of the ensuing cataclysm, Luther would have occasion to explain that while he slept or drank good German beer the Word of God went forth and did its work. Denying his own agency, denying that the movement incited by God's Word represented either reform, reformation, or revolution, he viewed contemporary events in terms of a final resurgence of evangelical light before the world's end and the compelling force of God's announcement. Although the modern historian may balk at accepting the Word of God as an historical agent capable of influencing events, Luther's language nevertheless contains a fundamental truth: that once expressed, the religious content within his theological propositions advanced of its own accord—aided by printers, humanists, anticlericalism, and princely paternalism—to meet a profound religious hunger. The moral force of what is known as the Reformation lay in the exalted nature of the cause —*justitia dei;* a lesser theme would have been contemptible in the light of subsequent suffering. And the impact of Luther's witness at Worms, in the context of an aroused nation already beset by rebellious rumblings from knights and peasants, resides in the simplicity and trust that preserved him from partisan politics and from allowing the Word to be compromised.

THE SPREAD OF REBELLION

For the next ten months, Luther remained in hiding at the Wartburg. During this period he accomplished, among other works, the translation of the New Testament into German. The act was fundamental to his whole understanding of reform. But the forces released by the doctrine of Christian liberty swept past the secluded Luther. At Wittenberg a situation of liturgical uncertainty, resulting from unrest over reform and the still-fragmentary nature of Luther's ideas, was being exploited by popular agitation. Around November, the dean of the theological faculty, Andreas Karlstadt, lent his support to the inflammatory preaching of the Augustinian Gabriel Zwilling, who introduced the note of compulsion: Karlstadt proclaimed marriage of priests obligatory, urged communion in both kinds, and on Christmas Day celebrated an evangelical mass, without vestments and partly in the vernacular, without demanding confession before communion. The new year brought popular violence and the outbreak of iconoclasm. Confronted by the specter of evangelical liberty being imposed as a new sort of law, and aroused by the breaking of images, Luther hastened back to Wittenberg despite the warning of the elector that he would be unable to protect him from the pope or emperor. Before reentering the city, he made his position clear: the reform of the church was reserved to the secular authority, and was not up to individuals. Appearing in the pulpit from March 9 to 16, 1522, Luther, correctly cowled and tonsured, urged that Christian liberty did not permit attacking things not directly related to faith; religious reform could only proceed by the action of the Word and not by force. Luther's presence restored calm to the troubled town. Henceforth the overriding problem would be the redefinition of the church and, in effect, the creation of a new church.

The reform had begun to reveal its conservative aspect. Would it be able to moderate and divert the potential violence created by deep-seated social ills throughout Germany? Unfortunately many of Luther's earlier statements defining his position against Rome could easily be misconstrued in the context of long-existing social unrest. While his concept of Christian liberty should have been clear to an impartial reader, the popular mood in the period 1520–25 did not permit such a reading. Indeed, Luther could warn his prince in the same month as his return to Wittenberg that a great upheaval was impending, for the common man, misunderstanding the doctrine of Christian liberty, sought to apply it to social and political problems. As Luther had not publicly clarified his position with respect to the secular authority, a general anxiety existed as to the extent and limits of this revolution. During succeeding months, while addressing himself to the task of defining liturgy and church and translating the Pentateuch, Luther wrote his *Warning . . . to Guard against Rebellion* and *On Secular Authority*. Ironically, however, their impact was ambiguous, for although he posited a divine foundation to temporal rule, Luther warned rulers that the masses were no longer inarticulate and would not tolerate injustices. When the whirlwind burst with the attack of the Franconian Knights upon Trier, Luther bore little responsibility, for he had refused their proffered support. Although the Knights' Revolt was essentially a desperate attempt by a declining order to recover its former place in society, Lutheran ideas served as a catalyst. Such leading figures as Hutten and Hartmut von Kronberg saw Trier as a genuine effort to gain a foothold for the Word, and at the imperial diet in 1523 the campaign of the Swabian League against the Franconian nobles was considered not simply a punitive expedition against law-breakers but an effort to eradicate Luther's influence.

In the case of the Peasants' Rebellion of 1524–25 Luther's responsibility seems more evident, for he had appeared, in his warning to the princes, to sympathize with the peasants—only to turn on them later as mad dogs who had to be butchered that order might be preserved. Yet the apocalyptic terror of the radical prophet Thomas Muentzer threatened to subvert all order, and the integrity of Luther's reform, the Word of God, seemed to be in danger of extinction. Seeking to realize the Kingdom of God on earth by force, Muentzer urged a church of the elect that would root out the godless. He alone at a crucial moment disputed with Luther the orientation of the Reformation. Preservation of the reform's integrity meant the loss of wide segments of popular support throughout the empire. In both instances—the Knights' Revolt and the Peasants' Rebellion—the princes were the victors, and consolidated their territorial authority. After 1525, the Reformation in Germany was no longer a broad movement of the people but belonged increasingly to the princes.

INTERNAL DIVISIONS IN THE REFORM

Luther lumped Karlstadt and Muentzer together, and defined his own position over against the growing threat of what he considered Enthusiasm. He saw himself as pursuing a middle course between Rome and the burgeoning threat both to reform and to the princely order. Luther perceived in the Enthusiasts a new legalism, the reimposition of the law of Moses, and henceforth associated Rome and the "left wing of the Reformation" as cousins in doctrine, two wolves with their tails tied together.

The history of the radicals presents a number of bold footnotes to the thought of Luther. Where the Protestant reformers hesitated and drew limits, the radical reformers pressed on, fired by a combination of notions drawn from humanism and medieval popular religion. Derivative of the main current of the movement, these sectarian groups developed extreme and at times logical extensions of Reformation positions on authority, the church, lay religion, and ethical performance. Indeed, the vigorous discipleship of Christ exemplified by the pacific Swiss Anabaptists can be seen, apart from its literalism, as the fitting and logical outcome of the Reformation's effort to restructure lay religion: cut loose from all worldly attachments and even from the parish system, those who received the imperative call lived as pilgrims, evangelists, and martyrs. Without belonging to the Reformation itself, these varied groups of radicals served to define the limits and nature of the Reformation. Rather than seeking to become a sect, to build a utopia apart from society, or to usher in the millennium, the Reformation would accommodate itself to the secular authority and strive to reform the whole church. In respect to authority, it would shun any literal performance of New Testament ideals or realization of Old Testament models. Between Rome and the radicals the Reformation would be defined: in avoiding the creation of any spiritual elite, it sought to extend the realm of the religious in a new way to all of society.

THE BEGINNING OF PRACTICAL REFORM

Luther's controversy with the radicals provided a disturbed background to the shaping of the reform within Electoral Saxony. Once having returned to Wittenberg, he had to give institutional expression to his religious insight into scripture. Luther approached the problem of the church first from his doctrine of justification by faith, and only secondarily from his opposition to Rome. Before Worms he had persistently defined the church in terms of its essentially invisible nature, as characterized by faith. The idea of the church as the communion of believers, a fellowship of the people of God, accented the response of Christians in faith to the Word of God. Accused of having formulated an invisible church which, like Plato's republic, existed nowhere, Luther countered that Christ, the preached Word, makes the church visible to the believer. The Word of God as an objective reality alone sustains and nourishes the church and begets faith. Of the church's three signs—baptism, eucharist and evangel—the third is preeminent. This visible–invisible church, defined by and constituted of faith, yet with location and order, depended for its existence upon the free proclamation of the Word. That the Word could be ambiguous or promote differing interpretations was inconceivable to Luther—a fact which made his controversy with the radicals so distressing. Christian community and preached gospel constituted the distinctive elements in his view of the church. His confidence in the power of God's Word to create Christian community, his unwillingness to find in scripture any divinely-ordained ecclesiastical order, and his treatment of specific ceremonies and liturgical practices as indifferent matters promoted in Luther a passivity that endangered effective reform of the church.

The doctrine of the priesthood of all believers soon proved to be more effective as a critical than as a constructive principle. In May 1523, Luther tried to legitimize the congregational concept of the church by defending the right of a Christian group to judge all doctrines and to call, institute, and dismiss its own pastor. Luther's exhortation did not fall on barren soil, as evidenced by the Wendelstein community near Nuremberg eighteen months later, but peasant unrest and princely intervention were not to give such ventures enough time to mature. At Leisnig the effort foundered to establish a common chest of resources commandeered from mass foundations and supplemented by a levy on all parishioners. Similarly in the reorganization of the liturgy, Luther made some faltering steps that showed him in this respect to be less able and creative than his great enemy, Thomas Muentzer. *The Formula of the Mass* (1523) was remarkably conservative, for despite its amputation of the sacrificial element, it was a reformed Latin mass and not a German liturgy. Nevertheless, the last half of the treatise contains a demand for hymns in the vernacular and two important principles: that no mass is to be celebrated without communicants and that communication depends upon religious knowledge. Not until October 19, 1525, was mass celebrated at Wittenberg in German. The statement of the new liturgy published in the following year made explicit the earlier ambiguities of Luther's liturgical position and the reluctance of a reformer to impose new ceremonies and a new legalism. In *The German Mass* (1526), Luther treated the liturgy as something unnecessary to the mature Christian and adumbrated for the first and last time a sectarian view of the church that allowed a select disciplined group of earnest worshippers to exist within the larger church. It was his most extreme institutional expression of the congregational principle.

By 1525 the idea of the self-determining Christian congregation was in serious difficulty. Ignorance, impotence, and indifference on the parish level, the tumult of the Peasants' Revolt, and the growth of sects made necessary the intervention of the only remaining established authority, the prince. In his treatise *On Secular Authority* (1523), while granting that secular power is ordained by God, Luther directed his efforts to defining the limits of such authority in relation to that of the church. He was specifically concerned with the way Duke George in Meissen had prevented the sale and distribution of his recently-translated New Testament. Faced by direct interference with the dissemination of the Word, Luther urged that the secular authority must exercise no constraint in the religious domain. The task of the magistrate he defined as essentially negative: the maintenance of order and the punishing of all transgressions of the civil law. But he would soon suggest a more positive role for an evangelical prince whereby the ruler might promote the preached gospel and prevent the growth of false doctrines. Luther's confidence in the unaided Word of God allowed the traditional cult to be celebrated at the Castle Church in Wittenberg until Christmas, 1524, when he finally advocated the suppression of the mass, by force if necessary.

THE REFORM IN SAXONY

A vital distinction was maturing at this time in Luther's mind between the two ways that God rules the world—through a worldly and through a spiritual government (*Regiment*)—one distinguished by reason, law, and the sword, the other by the gospel and love. The Christian does not need the law, for he lives acccording to the gospel; in love for his neighbor he assumes multiple responsibilities in the world to secure peace and meet others' needs. The distinction grew out of his understanding of law and gospel, and in reaction to the papal jurisdiction that had made a law out of the gospel and a legal political order out of the church. Luther's emerging conception of the two distinct *Regimente* and their relations would prove decisive for his political thought and social ethic.

The prevailing ecclesiastical confusion and dislocation belied Luther's confidence in the efficacy of the unaided Word: the dissolution of monasteries proceeded haphazardly in a way that allowed the local nobility to appropriate church goods; pastors as well as flock remained in ignorance of the most elementary features of the Christian religion; the mass in Saxony had to be ended. Reform required both the collaboration of the secular arm and an understanding of its relations to the institutional church. Presented with such immense problems, Luther groped toward an answer that was partly forced upon him. The idea of a princely sponsored visitation, inquiring into the condition of religious bodies in electoral Saxony, originated not with him but with Duke John Frederick, the late elector's nephew, who had recently investigated unworthy priests in Thuringia. Princes had always enjoyed a multitude of rights within the church, and long before the Reformation the duke of Cleves spoke for most German princes when he claimed that in his own lands he was pope and master. Previous reforming princes had made visitations to monasteries, but these were considered as emergency measures and did not affect doctrine. The new visitations now to be undertaken in Saxony and in the territories of other evangelical princes would be more extensive and possess a theological intent which would make them channels for the ideas of reform.

Repeatedly asked to lend political support to reordering the church, the new elector John hesitated. A faltering effort was made early in 1526 to organize a church visitation composed of administrators and clergy. Luther moved further toward placing the dissemination of the gospel under the protection of the secular authority; he urged the elector to suppress the mass at Altenburg, where his friend Spalatin now preached, and argued that in order to avoid turmoil and sectarianism in any given place there should be only one form of preaching. In the meantime, the Diet of Speyer had concluded on a note that inadvertently allowed each prince, in effect, to proceed with reform in his own territory as he saw fit. This measure marked simultaneously the culmination of a long process and the historic point of origin of the territorial church orders.

In the subsequent secular intrusion, the Lutheran doctrine of magistracy provided the theological basis and the Speyer Recess lent legal support.

In his letters, Luther had directed the elector's attention to a situation becoming increasingly threatening and had urged him to intervene out of Christian love to restore order. Yet when the initial visitation articles appeared in the electoral *Instruction* of June 16, 1527, the imperious tone of secular authority, rather than that of Christian brotherhood, was sounded in the opening, "We have ordered." Far from performing a temporary function out of Christian love, the elector seemed to be assuming responsibility for the bishop's duties by virtue of his secular authority. The elector made himself responsible for the spiritual, as well as the physical, well-being of his subjects. Perhaps as a protest, but certainly as a formal statement of his own position on the matter, Luther provided a preface to the visitation articles of 1528. There he explained that only in times of distress may the elector name visitors, and that he does this not by right of his secular office but as a Christian brother out of love. It was a nice distinction, made necessary by the emergency but difficult to maintain.

EXTENSION OF THE LUTHERAN CHURCH ORDER

Only with the institution of consistories did the new princely territorial churches become established. The first instances of this occurred in Ernestine lands, where the need for judgments in marital cases gave the initial impetus. A commission called by the Elector John Frederick in 1538 presented its advice, and at the beginning of the following year a consistorium in Wittenberg began functioning. At first, four were planned, but after 1542 three sufficed for electoral Saxony; its members, two jurists and two theologians, were appointed by the elector, represented his will, and operated under his judgment and scrutiny to the least detail. The consistories assumed all responsibilities for the external organization and administration of the church; they controlled the training of the ministry, administered the properties and finances of churches, and exercised all jurisdictional authority, particularly concerning marriage laws and customs. Observing the Saxon experiment, other evangelical territories began to undertake similar church orders. If the degree of bureaucratic control varied according to locality, in no case did the congregation actively participate. Luther could acquiesce in the establishment of such church orders because he was most concerned with the inner, invisible character of the church. He was essentially satisfied with the way in which preaching and the administration of the sacraments were placed beyond the reach of the prince, who was himself subject to the Word of God. Furthermore, most of the evangelical princes manifested extraordinary conscientiousness about the well-being of their subjects, and for the better part of the century these rulers were not arbitrary but assumed their ecclesiastical tasks from a sense of duty. The prince took no important step without consulting his theologians, and although Luther himself occupied no formal position, he exerted great influence as an adviser. But as laws and institutions became fixed, the significance of great personalities waned. Only later, with the more aggressive prince and the obsequious court chaplain, would the Lutheran church order reveal its uglier aspect.

One may lament Luther's inability to effect a congregational basis for the church, but it would be wrong to associate the reformer with any particular ecclesiastical format. Reacting to the legalism and institutionalism of Rome, Luther refused to discover in scripture any divinely-ordained church order, and continued to think of the church not as an institution but as a group of believers. He remained consistent in his emphasis upon the essentially inner character of the church and in his willingness to accept any structure as long as it permitted the free working of the Word. When the church order for Hesse sought to implement some of Luther's congregational principles, he advised Landgrave Philip in January 1527 that the people were in their infancy and simply not ready for ecclesiastical self-government. Yet lay participation is by no means absent from Luther's reform. In the administration of the common chest, laymen were often named by the bishop or, in cities, elected by the community. Occasionally the community shared in church discipline. The most ambitious attempt to implement these practices was in the Hessian church order of 1539, inspired by Martin Bucer. Luther acclaimed the participation of elders there and upheld the Hessian case as an example for imitation. The institution of elders and lay participation were not unknown to the Lutheran church of the sixteenth century, but their role was consultative and an attempt to introduce the lay element in an organic way was to fail.

THE SPREAD OF LUTHERANISM

Luther always discountenanced a "Lutheran Church." He recognized only the Christian church and thought of reforming the entire church. In the first years of his reform, the dissemination of the Word of God, advanced by evangelical preachers and the printing press, seemed to carry all before it. While Luther's reform was losing popular support among the peasantry, the cities of northern Germany between 1525 and 1532 were being won over through the apparently spontaneous actions of the artisans and lower citizenry; in case after case they called in evangelical preachers on the parish level. The new doctrine served to articulate the opposition of the parish communities to the urban patriciate, town council, or cathedral chapter. In the north and the entire Baltic area, Luther's associate Bugenhagen and his pupils advanced reform. In the Scandinavian countries, reform was closely linked with the defining of royal authority and national identity. Nevertheless it had visible roots at Wittenberg, where, after a visit in 1524, the dethroned Christian II of Denmark had the New Testament translated into Danish, and where the future reformers of Denmark, Sweden, and Finland came to study. In Poland and Hungary, the sale of Lutheran books supplemented the humanism of a generation exposed to Italian universities, to Erasmus, and to the work of pastors who had begun to use the pulpit to promote ideas of reform. The role of printing in the spread of Luther's reform has been told too well to bear repeating. A massive effort of publication, from Froben's first edition of Luther's Latin works in October 1518 to the numerous translations of individual works by Luther made possible the penetration of the reformer's ideas into France, the Burgundian inheritance, England, and even the Iberian peninsula despite the efforts of the authorities.

Yet the mechanics of printing do not explain the rapid diffusion of Luther's works. To understand their avid reception requires an inquiry into already-existing currents of reform and raises the issue of the repeated refraction of Luther's ideas in varying degrees by a generation brought up on Erasmian humanism. Coming hard on the heels of this spiritual revival, Luther's movement was to a very real degree mistaken for it and derived initial support from it. At Nuremberg the city's secretary, Lazarus Spengler, could recommend the learned doctrine of Luther as an instruction conformable to reason and Christian laws. In the German pamphlet literature of reform, up to 1522 the mentality is thoroughly Erasmian with barely a trace of Luther: Evangelium is *lex Christi,* the simple law of Christ rather than the announcement of God's grace in Jesus Christ. In France the pastoral reform of Bishop Briçonnet and Lefèvre d'Etaples at Meaux innocently imbibed Lutheran devotional works only to be compelled by the Sorbonne and Parlement to disgorge them. Nor did the great controversy over the freedom of the will that broke out between the two giants, Luther and Erasmus, dispel the support given and the disguise cast over the German reformer by current humanism. Certainly to the end of the decade the Reformation in Denmark and Sweden, despite formal ties with Wittenberg, was characterized less by Luther's concept of the Word and of justification than by a biblical–legal Christianity derived from an evangelical humanism. In France, Louis de Berquin mixed Lutheran and Erasmian ideas until his execution by the Parlement of Paris in April 1529. Thus, while Luther's reform had obtained its initial reception and support from Erasmian humanism, it was only toward the end of the decade that the properly Lutheran elements in the broader Reformation movement began to crystallize. To the Erasmians of the thirties, however, Luther and Erasmus still belonged together, and it would fall to no less a figure than Luther's closest associate, Philip Melanchthon, to embody these powerful oppositions and attempt to reconcile them. Hopeless as the task might seem, ideas that appear to a later age as logically opposed were experienced by most people at the time as essentially indistinguishable.

Politics as well as press and pulpit advanced the Word. In July 1525 the newly-established secular duchy of East Prussia became the first to make Lutheranism the official religion, and from his position in the Polish senate its

Hohenzollern duke was able to advance the Lutheran faith in Poland. Nearer to Wittenberg, the evangelical princes, fearing a Catholic league was plotting to annihilate them, began to consider the possibilities of common defense. The most politically active among them, Philip of Hesse, conceived of a grand alliance that would include adherents to the reform in the Swiss cantons, German territories, Scandinavia, and Eastern Europe. The main impediment to such a Protestant alliance in 1529 was the increasingly acrimonious controversy between Wittenberg and Zurich over the nature of Christ's presence in the eucharist. Since 1523 Zwingli had espoused a symbolic and commemorative view of the sacrament, and in the following year he and Oecolampadius at Basel began to defend a purely spiritual consumption by the communicant. Not until 1526 did Luther join battle with the two Swiss theologians in defense of the corporeal presence of Christ in the sacrament. In the same year Bucer, from Strassburg, became the first to suggest a personal meeting between the two parties.

The controversy raged on. Neither Bucer nor Zwingli expected that a colloquy would achieve any religious settlement, but they sought a practical compromise that might form the basis for common political action. Luther, a declared opponent of religious wars, crusades, or political alliances as proper means of defending the faith, suspected the offer for what it was and refused. Only later, through the initiative of Philip, did the two parties convene at the landgrave's castle at Marburg in early October 1529. Zwingli appeared armed with a sword; Luther arrived as a confessor rather than a negotiator. An accord on the figurative meaning of the sacrament proved impossible; both the political intentions and the doctrinal position of the Swiss were entirely antithetical to Luther's mind. Furthermore, Melanchthon, ever desirous of keeping the reform movement within the traditional fold of Christendom, warned that any move in the direction of Zurich would prevent the German Protestants from reaching an agreement with Rome and the emperor. After proclaiming agreement on all matters except the one at issue, the meeting dissolved. The failure at Marburg meant more than the collapse of a comprehensive Protestant union; it signified the first rupture within the Reformation movement.

THE AUGSBURG CONFESSION

The emperor's return to Germany and his convocation of a diet to review dissident religious views and prepare the way for the expected ecumenical council prompted the Lutheran theologians to try to put their theological house in order. Because Luther was under the ban of the empire, the task fell to Melanchthon to present the evangelical position at the diet of Augsburg and to fuse the diverse statements of the Lutheran faith into an ordered confession. In many ways, he was superbly equipped for the role of evangelical spokesman and confessor, but the task was complicated by the fact that Melanchthon had two mentors: Luther and Erasmus. Both were invisibly present that summer of 1530 at Augsburg. Luther had come down to the Coburg castle and remained in intense correspondence with Melanchthon —advising, exhorting, and upbraiding him. Erasmus had refused an invitation, but his tactics and spirit were introduced by his partisans into the opening weeks of the diet. In his confession, Melanchthon wished to associate the evangelical church with the spirit of the ancient church and to emphasize points of agreement with Rome and deemphasize points of acute controversy: transubstantiation and *sola Scriptura* were not mentioned. Nevertheless, the finished product was thoroughly Lutheran and received Luther's firm approval. After its presentation on June 25 in the German language, the diet focused on negotiations concerning individual abuses. Melanchthon acted as though practices might be somehow separated from doctrine and strove desperately for an accord with the old church. Unwilling to dissolve the bond with Rome and with the emperor, he struggled manfully, much to the anxiety of Luther, to preserve the unity of Christian culture. In private communications with the cardinal–legate Campeggio, Melanchthon insisted that the evangelicals remained doctrinally in accord with Rome and obedient to the pontiff, even if a slight dissimilarity in rites seemed to resist concord. Still he stood firm on the essentials. The cup to the laity and marriage of priests might not present insurmountable problems, but the mass proved to be a stumbling block. On September 22, negotiations lapsed with the emperor's rejection of the Augsburg Confession, and in less than a month Charles ordered the reapplication of the Edict of Worms, the restoration of episcopal authority, and the restitution of ecclesiastical goods. The Melanchthonian effort at union had failed; the Lutheran desire to confess had been satisfied but the doctrinal front of Protestantism had broken into three groups: that of the Augustana, Zwingli's *Confessio Fidei,* and the Tetrapolitana—a joint confession from the cities of Strassburg, Constance, Memmingen, and Lindau.

PROTESTANTISM AS A POLITICAL FACTOR

The adherents to the new religious position, having earlier obtained a name —Protestants—and a confession, now moved rapidly toward political definition. For in the weeks following the collapse of negotiations at Augsburg, an attack by the emperor seemed impending and a defensive alliance among evangelical estates a necessity. Both Luther and Landgrave Philip were beginning to realize that the extent to which one ought to yield to the opponent was not a territorial problem but an all-German one. Luther counselled that no evangelical was to go to war for the emperor against his brother-in-belief. Although he continued to be unable to discover in scripture any justification for a Christian's resistance to properly constituted authority, when pressed by the jurists he conceded that, on legal and civil grounds, because the emperor had violated the constitution of the *Reich,* it was not unlawful to depart from the correct attitude of suffering obedience and defend oneself. The Schmalkaldic League of Protestant princes and cities which emerged during the winter of 1530–31 was to be plagued with many of these ambiguities concerning a defensive alliance against the emperor. While the exact proportion of influence between the princes and cities was not established until 1536, the basic outline of this Protestant alliance, under the alternating six-months' control of the Saxon elector and Land-grave Philip, was readily apparent. For fifteen years the Schmalkaldic League represented the greatest single political power in the empire.

The decade of the thirties saw strenuous and partly-successful efforts to achieve a rapprochement, or at least a conciliatory attitude. Bucer's at-tempts, evident at Augsburg, to achieve an agreement with Luther on Christ's presence in the Eucharist were finally rewarded in the Wittenberg Concord of 1536, which opened up south German cities to Lutheran pene-tration. From the new pontiff came diplomatic feelers for the convocation of a council, a prospect redolent of practical reform, which occasioned out-bursts of enthusiasm even in Protestant Augsburg and Ratisbon. Once more the Saxon elector called upon his theologians for advice, especially concern-ing the essentials that could not be negotiated. The hard line proposed by Luther in the Schmalkaldic Articles permitted no concessions on justifica-tion by faith, the abomination of the mass, the monastic life, and the Anti-christ of the papacy. Melanchthon, desirous of peace and general Christian unity, expressed his willingness to accept the pope and papal hierarchy as a product of human law, if the gospel might be freely disseminated. But while the theologians proposed, the princes disposed: the Saxon elector refused to attend a council convoked for the express purpose of considering heresies. Broadly popular as was the idea of a reforming council, the papal effort in the thirties to call a council encountered opposition from Francis I and Henry VIII as well as from organized Protestantism. The attempt failed.

The slowly-emerging rift between two irreconcilable religious camps, accentuated and given a new dimension by the politicization of the new religion, did not go unattended. The valiant effort of the humanists and humanistic theologians to reunite the already-crystallizing confessions stemmed from the theology of the aged Erasmus. The distinctive features of Erasmus's later theology were his reaffirmation of the church, a weak treat-ment of the sacraments, and his curious but enormously significant notion of a double righteousness which sought to grasp once more in an effective and convincing accord the divine initiative in man's salvation and his growth in faith through acts of love. The primary justification of God's gift of faith described by St. Paul now seemed to be linked with a secondary justification, found in James, that is a consequence of works. The Erasmian theology found its champions among men who had links with both camps: Bucer and Melanchthon for the Protestants; Gropper, Pflug, and Witzel for the old church. The importance of the Middle Group was enhanced by

the sensible tactics pursued and the effort to drive this movement of conciliation through political channels. The Erasmians promoted religious colloquies where the most divisive and contested matters were deferred to a later
time or to the next ecumenical council and the points of agreement were
emphasized in a mood of mutual accommodation. According to Erasmus,
the magistracy had the responsibility for initiating the reform of ecclesiastical life. In Jülich Duke John had been won over to a moderate reform which
he had entrusted to an Erasmian. In ducal Saxony the Chancellor Carlowitz
promoted an important religious colloquy at Leipzig in 1539 at which
representatives of Duke George and the old church sat down with representatives from Wittenberg and Hesse to try to reach an accord on the
basis of the first centuries of the church. Although a draft of such an accord
was advanced by Witzel and Bucer, it was ominously rejected on arrival
at Wittenberg.

Most fateful for the policies of the Middle Group was the support now
given by the emperor in the years 1539 to 1541. Time was running out for
his efforts to deal with the Lutheran menace. The impending convocation
of a general council, which Protestants would not attend, presented the
terrible danger that from their resistance to such a council's decisions, religious war would follow. Therefore Charles and, particularly, his chancellor
Granvelle earnestly joined their humanist theologians in the program of
religious colloquies, which moved from Frankfurt through Hagenau to
Worms, culminating in the Diet of Ratisbon in March 1541. The papacy
sought to prevent any independent religious accord sponsored by the emperor, but it could ill afford to be unrepresented at Ratisbon and sent Cardinal Contarini, the leading figure among liberal reformers in the Curia.
Politically supported, the Erasmians moved forward, promoting a conciliatory temper that for a moment seemed to dispel the ironclad clouds of
theological strife. Indeed, on the crucial question of justification an agreement satisfactory to both groups was reached and, though later rejected by
Rome and Wittenberg, the ephemeral achievement suggested the extent
to which the religion of justification by faith had penetrated all groups during the first decades of the century. It was rather the Eucharist, with its
theological complexity and its decisive implications for ecclesiastical polity,
that proved the stumbling block. The cardinal–legate held firm on transubstantiation. With the failure of the diet as a religious colloquy, Contarini
returned to an Italy that was passing rapidly from Catholic reform to
Counter-Reformation.

North as well as south of the Alps, events moved toward a military resolution of the religious issues. Caught between France and the Turk, the Habsburg brothers had been unable for two decades to concentrate upon the
Lutheran menace, which had only grown worse over the years. In successive
diets, the evangelical estates had adroitly used the Turkish presence to win
concessions and moritoria from Ferdinand. Even at Ratisbon French inter-

ference and news of mounting Turkish activity in Hungary had disturbed the diet. Having resumed war against the Valois, the emperor was not able to deal with the Lutherans until after the peace of Crépy in September 1544. A decisive settlement with heresy now seemed opportune. Furthermore, Philip of Hesse had compromised his vital role in the Schmalkaldic League: by committing bigamy, the landgrave had made himself subject to the criminal law of the empire, and since June 1541 had obligated himself to the emperor. In June 1546, Charles entered into separate alliances with the papacy and with the new Protestant ruler of Albertine Saxony, Duke Maurice, who, by aiding the emperor, saw an opportunity to acquire the electoral title for his line. At Eisleben early in 1546, Martin Luther died, his last months disturbed by news from Trent and by his sense of an impending holocaust within Germany. The Council of Trent had begun its sessions in the last days of 1545, and the emperor had intended to lead the defeated Protestants there for a settlement before the walls of doctrinal definition made reunion impossible. At the moment of triumph over Elector John Frederick of Saxony, Charles had the ground cut from beneath him by the pope's removal of the council to Bologna. The Protestants could never be induced to attend a council located in an Italian city and one moreover which, rather than addressing itself to specific reforms, had already promulgated decrees on the fundamentals of scripture and tradition, original sin, and justification. Stranded, the emperor proceeded to secure an independent religious settlement within the empire which would only increase the gulf between him and Rome and thus endanger the enforcement of the new arrangement.

The so-called "Interim" that emerged from the Augsburg diet of 1547–48 attempted to present a religious compromise that conceded clerical marriage and communion under both kinds to the Protestants but otherwise adhered to the old faith as defined by a medley of theologians including Protestants as well as Erasmians. It was intended to be binding upon Protestants and to regulate religion in the empire until a council could settle questions both doctrinal and practical. As a compromise it pleased no one, and immediately encountered opposition from Protestants. In Upper Germany, the next four years saw the collapse of the existing constitutions of twenty-eight cities, patrician regimes replacing a broader rule by the guilds, and often the more politically compliant Lutheranism replacing Zwinglianism; after an heroic resistance, Constance lost its freedom and proud Strassburg had to submit, compelling Martin Bucer to seek asylum in England. In Saxony Melanchthon, returning to a shattered university at Wittenberg, found it necessary to embark upon a program of accommodation that soon created a doctrinal rift and the seeds of future controversy within Lutheranism. For the cities of northern Germany were better situated to escape the full might of the triumphant emperor, and at Magdeburg Nicholas Amsdorf and Matthias Flacius Illyricus, among other stalwarts, promoted a tougher, more rigid Lutheranism. To stiffen resistance to the imperial Interim and to the army besieging the city, the pastors of Magdeburg published in 1550 a confession in which it was stated that when the superior magistrate threatens to subvert true religion, the subordinate magistracy (*untere Obrigkeit*) may justifiably organize resistance. Under the pressure of events, Protestantism's first justification of the right of resistance appeared in the Lutheran camp.

While the Elector Maurice of Saxony, as a demonstration of his loyalty to the emperor, prosecuted the siege of the doomed city, he joined a number of other princes in negotiating with France for the destruction of the emperor's position in Germany; in return for a heavy subsidy, Henry II was to be allowed to occupy Cambrai, Metz, Toul, and Verdun and be recognized as "vicar of the empire" and "Protector of the liberties of Germany and its captive Princes." For many a German prince the lengthening shadow of Habsburg monarchy in the empire induced considerable anxiety—anxiety that was hardly allayed by the captivity of Landgrave Philip and ex-Elector John Frederick. Charles appeared oblivious to the terrible danger that was developing during 1551 and 1552. His position was further weakened by a violent disagreement with his brother Ferdinand over the succession to the empire. Thus, when in the spring of 1552 the French seized Metz and Charles barely escaped capture by Maurice at Innsbruck, Ferdinand stepped forward to mediate. Unable to retake Metz that winter, Charles V began his personal withdrawal from German affairs and the devolution upon his brother which would lead to the final abdication. To King Ferdinand therefore fell the ugly task of settlement with heretics and rebels.

At the diet of Augsburg in 1555, Ferdinand's task was aided by the fact that he had been an apparent neutral. Because schism and the rupture of Christendom were still unthinkable, settlement became possible only on the basis of the dubious, yet necessary, belief that such an accord was provisional until the restoration of religious unity through a council. The Augsburg recess provided for the princes' care and control of religion according to the axiom, 'Where one ruler, there one religion'. Only the estates of the empire were permitted choice of confession between Catholicism and Lutheranism. In the free cities, parity was to be maintained between the two confessions—a parity which could only be destructive to the strong late medieval sense of urban community.

At the religious peace of Augsburg, emperor, pope, and their representatives were significantly absent from an agreement which by its continuance would mark the shattering of Christendom through the introduction of a second legally-recognized religion and the reduction of the empire to a league of territorial states. To Melanchthon, in Nuremberg at the time, the peace was an act of God whose results must be accepted with faithful endurance by the small gathering of true Christians until the world's end, which was imminent. At Geneva, where no such abrupt end to time was expected, and where in fact a mission of universal scope was gathering momentum, John Calvin saw in Augsburg a lamentable sundering of the two wings of Protestantism and increased difficulties for the direction of his reform in central and eastern Europe.

The Swiss-Rhenish Reform: The Problem of Church Discipline

Reformatio, or what Luther more frequently referred to as a restoration of the evangelical light, surpassed all previous ideas of reformation. The church had understood the term to connote personal, individual reform, and only after Gregory VII a reform of the lives of the clergy and perhaps of the church. Now, in the sixteenth century, a movement was rapidly developing from Wittenberg that had begun with doctrine and through its transformation had communicated a powerful impulse toward refashioning the church's very structure, as well as the lives of Christians. While it would later take Marxist communism over half a century to stumble to its feet, the present religious movement shook Europe from Seville to Reval within half a decade. The almost instantaneous response to Luther cannot be understood solely in terms of the man's genius for expression nor of the influence of printing. Rather, the fresh presentation of God's Word as the Christ *for us* struck a profound, responsive chord throughout a culture spiritually starved by late medieval theology and popular piety. Occurring within the still formal unity of the *respublica Christiana,* the Reformation was both extrinsically and intrinsically a single movement with several manifestations. To talk about a Swiss-Rhenish reform in Western Europe is not to suggest a movement distinct from the rest of the Protestant Reformation. Instead it represents a reform that shared an essentially common view of the Christian religion, reacted to basically similar problems, and yet manifested features considerably different from those of the Lutheran reform. Among these differences was the closer cooperation of civil and religious authorities in order to realize a Christian discipline. The two principal factors that distinguished the South German movement were the urban structure of reform and the more direct impact of humanism, particularly in its Erasmian expression.

THE URBAN CONTEXT OF REFORM

Whereas the context of Luther's reform had been preeminently territorial, princely, even monarchical, its western counterpart was distinctively urban, republican, and civic. Strassburg and the expanding Swiss city states of Bern, Basel, and Zurich shared the characteristic features of imperial cities, which were so numerous in the southwestern part of the empire. In the course of the Late Middle Ages a strong sense of the sacral community, which associated ever more closely the civic with the ecclesiastical community, pervaded these urban republics. In keeping with the belief that the city's government has been established to build up God's honor and to prevent major sins that might invite His wrath, the increasing aggrandizements and omnicompetence of the town council advanced especially at the expense of churches and religious groups. Despite its heavy responsibility before God for the total welfare of the community, the council did not intrude upon the independent realm of faith and doctrine. In its effective integration of the two authorities, spiritual and temporal, the German city began to manifest all the features of a *corpus Christianum* in miniature. Amplifying this notion, a concept derived from Roman law enjoyed an enormous currency at the time: the idea of *gemein nutz*, the common good or welfare (*publica utilitas*), expressed a total moral as well as political articulation of the community, interchangeable with the notion of the (*res publica*) state. Much would henceforth be done in the name of *gemein nutz*.

At first Luther's reform appeared to affirm the cities' heightened sense of the common good. For by declaring all Christians to be of one estate, Luther provided a new and deeper rationale for the city's existence and theologically legitimized the incorporation of ecclesiastical persons and institutions that soon followed. Nevertheless, the long-range effect of Luther's doctrines was to undermine the powerful sense of civil community, for by making decisive in one's relation to God the personal event of faith, rather than membership in the city and its cult, he essentially shattered the identification of the religious community with the civic community. Furthermore, Luther's unwillingness to grant the secular authority a properly Christian and positive role in the ordering of the community introduced an incoherence between the civil and the religious authority detrimental to *gemein nutz*. Thus, after his victory in 1547, Charles V preferred and promoted among Protestants the orthodox Lutherans in his reorganization of the South German towns. Beyond the emperor's reach, however, there had developed in the Swiss cantons at Zurich and under its influence a civic–religious reform that affirmed and built upon the integration of town council and pulpit.

Indeed, at the beginning of the sixteenth century the Swiss cantons possessed advantages that would permit them to pursue a role of European scope. Tucked away in the southwestern corner of the empire, the Confederates had by the peace of Basel in 1499 effectively won a *de facto* independence from the emperor. They were ideally located geographically to serve as a refuge for exiles from the Empire, France, and the Italian peninsula. Overpopulation had led to expansion and made war the major industry. Bern itself, instrumental in the destruction of Charles the Bold, was a major military power, and until the battle of Marignano (1515) the Swiss massed phalanx of pikes was the most formidable military unit in Europe. But it was as mercenaries, rather than as aggressors in their own interest, that the Swiss appeared on the international scene; their pikes were eagerly bought by the princes of Europe, and especially by the king of France. Coherence and order marked the political as well as military organization of the Swiss. In Bern, Basel, and Zurich, the civil community of guilds, by working through the great council, had displaced aristocratic members from the small council and affirmed a tight control over the clergy. Like Ulm and Nuremberg, each proceeded to expand into a city-state. The Florentine observer Niccolo Machiavelli could applaud what he considered to be the absence of an obstreperous nobility, the chief threat to any political order; in 1506 he expressed admiration for this well-armed and free people imbued with public spirit, and in 1513 he even feared that they might overrun Italy.

THE ROLE OF ERASMIAN HUMANISM

The role of humanism in shaping the Swiss-Rhenish reform can only be understood within the urban context; together, the new intellectual movement and the city environment were mutually supporting. A profound affinity existed between Erasmian humanism and these city-states. Erasmus himself was very much a city-dweller. His criticism of society and of the church derived from the urban environment, and his quest to bring all before the bar of Christian morality, reasonableness, and justice spoke to the needs of a lay public. In their heightened sense of public responsibility and communal pride, humanists and businessmen began to define a new sensibility exemplified by poor relief. For the town councillor intent upon securing a single common order buttressed by rigorous moral performance, Erasmus could supply the ideal of the Christian magistrate to whom is entrusted the moral direction of the community. For the busy layman whose religious feeling was frustrated by innumerable cere-monies and restrictions, Erasmus could provide a simpler, more convincing code of action. For a world whose religious performance was cluttered with saints' days and painted wooden images, and whose sense of piety was violated by clerical concubinage and luxury, Erasmus directed attention to Christ as Exemplar. Indeed the age demanded not less religion but more—changed in quality, differently organized, less clerical, more personally relevant. And one would be totally misconceiving both reform and Reformation to see secular control and lay witness as incompatible with Christian religion. For what is a city, Erasmus had remarked, but a great monastery?

ZWINGLI'S EARLY DEVELOPMENT

Ulrich Zwingli's advance to the role of reformer illustrates both his debt to humanism and the independence of the Swiss from the Wittenberg movement. Educated at Basel and Vienna, this son of a rural headman first seems to have meaningfully encountered the thought of Erasmus at the end of 1514, when during his pastorate at Glarus he found ample time to devote himself to hu-manistic and patristic studies. Already incensed with the practice of selling mercenaries, the young Zwingli eagerly appropriated Erasmus's ethical-political ideas and his Christocentric morality and spirituality. His understanding of Christ's doctrine or *philosophia* was ethically and intellectually shaped according to the humanistic educational ideal. Zwingli's pressing question was not, How do I find a gracious God? but rather, How may Christianity be restored in this present evil world? Yet in readings from Augustine and especially from Psalms and the Pauline epistles, he, like Luther, came to recognize that a Christian existence was not the product of a gradual enlightenment but occurred under the driving power of God's will. This new existential and theocentric quality of Zwingli's thought, which supplanted the Erasmian evolutionary and anthropocentric understanding of Christian faith, derived not from Luther but independently from his own pondering of scripture in the light of his narrow escape from the plague in 1519 and his new responsibilities at Zurich. The power of Christ came to replace the ideal of Christ, and God as object of thought gave way to God as living reality. Zwingli read Luther, but only to confirm a position already attained. It was Luther's bold stand at Leipzig, rather than his doctrine, that impressed Zwingli.

At the end of 1518, Zwingli had been summoned from Einsiedeln to fill the pulpit of the Great Minster at Zurich. The city had a population of five thousand, but its patriciate dominated the surrounding countryside of over ten times that many. Its economy had just completed a shift from weaving to trade. A new patriciate drawn from the artisan guilds had amalgamated with the remains of the older one, which lived on investments and frequently from a military entrepreneurship that enlisted the surplus rural male population as mercenaries. Linked by marriage ties and common interests, these two wings of the patriciate had by 1520 become one body, ruling in the Large Council, whose members were elected for life by the guilds, and in the Small Council, half of whose members were drawn from the Large Council, half named by the guilds and serving for a year. The successful reconstitution of the patriciate accounts for the relative ease and lack of social turmoil with which the reform would be introduced.

With scripture as his authority, Zwingli attacked the excessive ceremoniousness, irritating restrictions, and innumerable excrescences of a luxurious and arrogant church. Although the scriptural principle exerted its sovereignty over the reformer, the nature of reform in Zurich was from the outset practical and political. Particularly receptive were those crafts and trades that manifested technical innovation or economic change. During Lent 1522, the printer Froschauer with a group of citizens ate a sausage as a demonstration of evangelical freedom. Zwingli defended the act in what proved to be his first Reformation tract. On the peculiarly sensitive issue of clerical celibacy, another fissure emerged in the edifice of ecclesiastical discipline. Clerical concubinage had become so rampant that, in granting dispensations at the rate of four gulden for every illegitimate child, the bishop of Constance had come to expect from this source a yearly income of from 5,000 to 7,500 gulden. During his Einsiedeln ministry Zwingli himself had had relations with the daughter of an official; now he, along with several other priests, secretly proceeded to marry. After winning the city's clergy to the overriding supremacy of scripture and its proclamation, Zwingli published his *Archeteles*, in which he asserted this authority over against that of the bishop of Constance and the ecclesiastical hierarchy.

THE ROLE OF THE MAGISTRACY

The subsequent reform in Zurich, inspired by the pulpit and supported by significant segments of the population, nevertheless waited necessarily at every turn upon the confirmation and approval of the magistracy. At the first Zurich disputation (January 29, 1523), the council, not the bishop, summoned the territorial clergy and stood in judgment upon the proceedings. The magistracy's convocation of such a lay-ecclesiastical council already indicated that the civic community was considered a sufficient framework for the visible church. Here Zwingli, addressing the Christian assembly and appealing to scripture, denounced the sacrifice of the mass, the intercession of saints, ecclesiastical proscriptions, the monastic orders, celibacy, the misuse of the ban, and the spiritual jurisdiction of the church itself. As a consequence of this encounter between Zwingli and the Vicar-General of Constance, John Faber, the council sustained evangelical preaching and reform in keeping with what appeared to be the clear meaning of scripture. Proceeding therefore with the council's support, Zwingli and his associates directed their criticism toward the use of images and the mass in the liturgy.

These two issues necessitated the calling of a second disputation at the end of October, at which strenuous arguments were presented for the removal of images and the mass from the church service. The town council's determination not to act upon these demands for the moment proved decisive for reform in Zurich. By accepting its decision, Zwingli recognized the authority of the magistracy and its judgment on the timing of further changes; he affirmed a reform that was increasingly to be defined by a Christian magistracy. By not complying with the council's decision, Conrad Grebel and the radicals within the hitherto united reform movement in Zurich heralded a new church, the Anabaptist, which would exist independent of, and therefore persecuted by, the secular authority. The presence of old believers in the council and of strong elements within the Swiss Confederation hostile to the Zurich reform help to explain the caution, if not recalcitrance, of the magistracy at this juncture. Not until June of the following year were the images and recently-acquired organ removed from the Great Minster. The abolition of the mass had to wait until April 1525, when Zwingli, emboldened by the death of two conservative members of the magistracy, once again pressed the council to abrogate what was considered the crowning idolatry. The council acceded. In its place was introduced the stark simplicity of the evangelical service as a memorial. In the new austere surroundings there was only room for the Word. With the abolition of the mass, the Reformation had been established in Zurich.

The Christian community that emerged from this reform inevitably reflected the close association of the church with the magistracy. Zwingli had not created this relationship; rather, he had in his willingness to abide by the decisions of the town council affirmed a long tradition of increasing supervision of the city's religious life by the secular office. Yet, by using the superior authority of scripture to overthrow the clerical hierarchy and the whole notion of a separate institutionalized spiritual jurisdiction, he had carried that relationship to a new level of coherence. In Zurich Christian revival had been made possible by evangelical preaching, cautiously supported by the magistracy. Like Luther, Zwingli distinguished between the spiritual and the secular arm as well as between the visible and invisible church; unlike his Saxon counterpart, however, he effectively united the two powers in his emphasis upon the visible church and the realization of Christian community. Zwingli thought in terms of a Christian city with a Christian magistracy and Christian citizens; only a believing Christian could be a good magistrate and without that the church was, as it were, truncated and mutilated. Impelled by his humanist background, as well as by the traditions and events operative in Zurich, Zwingli's collaboration with the town council aimed at an integration of the two powers in a higher union dedicated to achieving a single moral-religious order. In 1525, the same year that the council began exiling and persecuting the Anabaptists, a marital court was established, whose powers were broadened in the following year to protect morals. Two laymen from each of the councils and two pastors constituted its membership. Organized to admonish the morally weak and punish the sinner, its machinery could be directed toward the political opponents of reform. Although the court was an instrument of the council, Zwingli's presence gave it a theocratic direction. It sought not clerical power but rather the realization of a sanctified community obedient to God's will and militantly committed to the evangel.

THE PROPAGATION OF THE GOSPEL

In his new office, conjoined with that of Zurich's leading pastor, Zwingli grew into the role of prophet. The contemporary church seemed to him to resemble that of the prophets more closely than it did the church of Christ and his apostles. In this mirror the magistracy assumed some of the qualities of the great reforming figures of Judaism, and Zwingli himself took on the features of the prophet-councillor, Ezekiel's Watchman. A generation earlier, the same analogue had gripped the Florentine prophet Savonarola. Both prophets were politically active in their quest for moral-religious renewal. Both identified *ecclesia* with *populus*, the Christian with the citizen, in the context of a Christian republic. This idea, reminiscent perhaps of Marsilius' thought and made intelligible by scripture, appealed to both prophets largely because of the structure and environment of the late medieval city-state. Zwingli's Zurich, like Savonarola's Florence, assumed the responsibility of extending a Christian renewal to Europe and to the world.

In promoting the Reformation in Swiss lands, humanist groups and Lutheran tracts competed with Zwingli. Humanist influences contributed to the reform of St. Gall and Schaffhausen, and at Basel the learned Oecolampadius advanced a spiritual interpretation of the eucharist in essential agreement with Zwingli's. In the central cantons and within the Confederation, the reform effected in Zurich encountered growing opposition and led to scattered clashes. Catholic opposition consolidated itself at the Baden disputation of 1526, where Oecolampadius had to contend with Eck, Faber, and Thomas Murner. The decision turned emphatically in favor of the nine catholic cantons and Zwingli, together with his writings, was proscribed. Baden signified a serious, if temporary, reverse; the consequent loss of Bern to the reform could not pass uncontested. In January 1528, therefore, a Bern disputation was convoked, to which Zwingli and his followers came in force. The outcome was a triumph for the reforming party. Bern was won to the Reformation and the mass was abolished there in the following month. Zwingli's success at the Bern disputation helped to strengthen the reform elsewhere. In 1529 at Basel the mass was abolished in a holocaust of iconoclasm and Erasmus moved to Freiburg. The problem of the Catholic cantons and of Zurich's expansion into contiguous, free bailiwicks still remained.

Beyond the Swiss Confederates, Zwingli's attention was drawn westward to France as a country open for conquest by the gospel. Bishop Briçonnet's circle of reforming spirits at Meaux had since 1519 aroused hopes in some observers for the cleansing of the church in France; the pastoral concerns of this group, their emphasis upon a preaching, evangelical in its scriptural focus, and Lefèvre d'Etaples' rendering of the New Testament into the vernacular in 1523 all suggested a movement still independent from, but in harmony with, the reforms occurring in the empire. Since 1519 Lefèvre's circle had been reading the Swiss reformer's writings. To Zurich came Francis Lambert of Avignon and later, among others, William Farel, urging Zwingli to carry the gospel into French lands. Thus, during 1524 the reformer came to recognize the need to present a formal statement of the faith in Latin to a French audience in order to advance the gospel.

The opportunity for promoting the gospel now demanded of Zwingli a withdrawal of his former hostile attitude to a France that had hired Zurich's sons for war. His subsequent *Commentary on True and False Religion,* which appeared in March 1525, was dedicated to the King of France. Francis I did not need Zwingli's advice as to his true interests and was even less drawn to Reformed dogmatics. Although he enjoyed projecting the image of the Renaissance patron-prince, the king did not share his sister Marguerite's interest in current religious literature nor her commitment to the Meaux circle. Certainly his settlement with the papacy in 1516, the Concordat of Bologna, granted him a grip upon the French church and an enormous fund of patronage, neither of which offered arguments for change. The only known reaction to the *Commentary* came from the recently-established machinery for censorship and ecclesiastical control: the Sorbonne supported by the Parlement of Paris. In their decision to condemn the work, the Paris divines were doubtlessly aided by its author's representation of them as a viperous group of illiterate and ignorant philosophers to be contrasted with the moral simplicity and godly cultivation of the Meaux reformers. Already the Sorbonne had begun to move against Meaux, and by the end of 1525 Briçonnet's group had dispersed, Lefèvre fleeing to Strassburg and Farel to the Pays de Vaud. Notwithstanding this disappointment, in the last year of his life Zwingli would return to France and her king with his *Exposition of the Faith*.

The political situation in the southwestern part of the empire and along the Rhine increasingly absorbed the reformer's attention. The menacing words of the Habsburgs and of the Catholic estates at the diet of Speyer, together with the Catholic cantons in the Confederation, compelled Zwingli to embark upon a policy of alliances. His distrust of the non-German speaking Charles, as well as the threat presented by the emperor to the liberty and religion of the cities, helped to make Zwingli an early and most articulate exponent of the struggle against an Hispanic Roman-Habsburg universalism. His conviction that the Christian citizen must be prepared to fight for the honor of God and the expansion of the faith now lent force to Zwingli's anti-Habsburg feelings. He envisaged a single confederated people east of the Rhine with its flanks resting on Strassburg in the north and Constance–Lindau in the southeast. In Philip of Hesse the armed prophet found one with whom he could share a community of religious-political ideas. His plans expanded to include Venice, Milan, and France within a single coalition, stretching from the North Sea to the Adriatic, that would support Protestantism, remove every foothold for the emperor on the Rhine, and defend Zurich amidst the Confederation. The failure at Marburg proved to be a serious setback, but in the same year a Christian Civic League had emerged, which included Constance, Bern, Zurich, St. Gall, Mulhausen in Alsace, and, in 1530, Strassburg. Zurich's first struggle with the Catholic cantons had ended indecisively. In pressing for a renewal of war, Zwingli encountered the latent resistance of those within Zurich who had never welcomed the reform. A general mandate of 1530 complained about the taverns being full during services and preachers being mocked. To face down the opposition to his war plans, Zwingli threatened to resign in 1529 and again in 1531. The application of economic sanctions against the Catholic cantons led to war at a time when the city was badly divided and abandoned by its allies. Zwingli himself sensed disaster on the evening that he marched off with the troops, helmeted and weaponed, to meet a brutal end on the field of Kappel.

For a few weeks following this event, the fate of the reform in Zurich remained dangerously in the balance. On December 9, 1531, the town council named Heinrich Bullinger, a disciple and confidant of Zwingli, as his successor. The council added the significant stipulation that the ministry should not interfere in worldly matters. Bullinger hesitated. Then, four days later, before the council, he accepted the post with the understanding that his preaching of the Word would receive no interference. From this simple agreement stemmed a working collaboration which, if undramatic, grew to become a pillar of Protestantism in sixteenth-century Europe.

THE ISSUE OF DISCIPLINE

Zwingli's brief decade of reforming activity had given a new direction and impetus to the Reformation, but his premature death left a number of questions unresolved and compelled a rethinking of the relationship between church and magistracy. Similarly, the question of relating law more directly to gospel, commandments to evangelical experience, in order to shape individual Christian performance in an urban context, still remained undefined. Overarching both these issues, and decisive for the character of Swiss-Rhenish reform, was the problem of realizing a Christian discipline that would leave its stamp on all citizens.

Concerning discipline, the case of Zurich and her marriage court is peculiarly significant. Just as this city created the first urban poor chest, so it created the first marriage court for the reform movement. The court that came into being on May 15, 1525, represented the culmination in the town council's gradual usurpation of the bishop of Constance's marriage court. The subsequent expansion of its role as a morals court empowered to inspect, admonish, and denounce made this body the most striking manifestation of Zwinglian "theocracy" and the first realization of political Puritanism. Its authority was derived from the Christian magistracy. Although punishment and executory power for its judgments originally did not belong to the court, still the special function of Zwingli and the omnicompetence of the magistracy allowed the morals court to function increasingly in an executive capacity. Nevertheless the town council prevented Zwingli from including the church ban in this system of moral discipline. In its operation and in the significant reinterpretation of marriage law, the court acquired an exemplary role in Swiss and upper Rhenish lands. But it was as a powerful educator of the people that the court left its decisive mark upon ethics. The register of the Argus-eyed court contains numerous examples of how a wayward person might by means of a single stern admonition be rendered "pious." The resulting legal Puritanism was at curious variance with the freedom of a Christian man. If the masses had first misunderstood the Reformation as liberation from all obligations, in the urban context of the Swiss-Rhenish reform, biblical humanism and the omnicompetence of the late medieval town council joined hands to raise the moral level by imposing a hard discipline.

The special features and operation of the Zurich marriage court had resulted from the virtual merging of the two authorities in that city. Yet this circumstance had also led to the disaster at Kappel. Other reformers, seeking to achieve a Christian discipline, struggled in their own contexts to win for the church a certain independence from the secular authority and the right to exercise the power of excommunication. Each town council, however, having relinquished one spiritual jurisdiction, was more than reluctant to surrender to a new one and jealously guarded its own exercise of the ban. The issues became clear at Basel after 1529, when Oecolampadius, as the new presiding minister, undertook to enforce church discipline freed from political influence. He attempted to establish a consistory of laymen and pastors empowered to ban persons of unseemly life and conduct from partaking of the eucharist. Nevertheless, the town council thwarted his efforts. Again at Ulm, where Oecolampadius collaborated with Martin Bucer in introducing the reform, the magistrates proved unwilling to allow such independence to the church. In Bucer, however, the vital issues of church discipline and Christian performance would attain an international significance.

BUCER AND THE EUROPEANIZATION OF REFORM

The geographical, economic, and political conditions of Strassburg allowed that city to develop a religious policy of European dimensions. Occupying the strategic bridgehead on the Rhine, Strassburg was an entrepôt for ideas as well as goods. The urban republic, if it did not ultimately stand to gain by the decline of the empire's constitutional order, nevertheless did not experience some of the ambiguities of other great imperial cities. The complex structure of council, assembly, and three permanent committees, fully defined by 1480, succeeded in integrating the old patriciate (*Constoffler*) and the more recent and powerful representatives of the twenty guilds into a single urban order. The traditions and physical location of the city, and the influence of Alsatian humanism, would promote in Strassburg's magistracy policies of moderation, tolerance, and stability.

The progress of the reform in Strassburg is typical of other cities in the period: first, the appearance of evangelical preachers; their establishment in individual churches; the positive response of separate guilds and a segment of the influential citizenry; the deliberate persuasion of the magistracy to remove the mass. Only in Nuremberg, where the town council seized the initiative in reform, did a significant variation occur in this general pattern. At Strassburg evangelical preaching began with Matthew Zell in 1521 and was enlarged in scope by Wolfgang Capito, Caspar Hedio, and Martin Bucer in 1523. A product of the famed humanist school at neighboring Schlettstadt, Bucer was an ex-Dominican who had been impressed by Luther at Heidelberg in 1518. Married and penniless, he appeared in Strassburg to seek the protection of the city as the son of a burgher. His furtive preaching soon drew crowds. Until the spring of 1524 the initiative for reform lay with this evangelical clergy, who broke from the rule of celibacy. The request of five parishes for evangelical preachers indicated broad, growing support, largely among the smaller trades, to which the council found it necessary to accede. Not without some violence did the property of the religious houses and monasteries come under the control of a council desirous of restoring order; at Christmas it required all clergy to assume the rights of citizens. The introduction of hymn singing into the church service and the removal of altars and images completed the first major stage of reform. In the next five years, however, the magistracy resisted the constant pressure of the reforming party to abolish the mass. The council envisaged its task as that of maintaining order. Unity of cult was still essential to the peace of the city, and any division might threaten that order and impair alliances with foreign powers. A persistent, articulate minority persuaded the council that the wrath of God might fall upon the whole community for its maintenance of an unscriptural practice. Thus, in the vote taken on February 20, 1529, the magistrates called for the abolition of the mass pending its vindication as a pious form of worship. Only relentless well-directed pressure had moved the magistracy toward that decisive measure, which marked the establishment of the reform in the city.

Once secure in the pastorate of St. Thomas, Bucer manifested those qualities of mind and spirit that would make him the reform's preeminent spokesman in the Rhineland as well as at Strassburg. In his first Reformation tract, *That no one Lives for Himself but for Others* (1523), he revealed that peculiar blend of Erasmus and Luther, whose works he had studied at Heidelberg. Developing Luther's exhortation, from *On Christian Liberty,* that a Christian must be useful to his neighbor, Bucer significantly shifted the emphasis from personal faith to individual performance and progress in Christian living. Guided by several passages from Erasmus' *Education of a Christian Prince,* he recommended to the magistrates the creation of a Christian city, conforming to the model discoverable in the totality of biblical legislation. The presence of radicals and Anabaptists stood as an accusation and made Bucer search for a means of discipline. He agreed with the essentials of Zwingli's identification of the church with the Christian civil community, but proved readier to assert the limits of magisterial authority and to summon it more positively to the task of sanctifying God's name and building up His Kingdom. At the same time, a clearer distinction between the two authorities seemed particularly necessary after Kappel.

Following his return from Ulm, Bucer and his fellow pastors worked with the magistracy to provide the city with a formal ecclesiastical order. The church wardens represented the early result; they constituted a lay committee of three members drawn from the magisterial class to preside over each of the seven parishes and observe the performance of the ministers. As an instrument of the council, they fell far short of achieving what Bucer understood by discipline. In letters of early 1532 he complains, "Nothing is more lamentable than the relaxation of church discipline. Without it what direction have we ?" And again, "There is virtually no church, no authority of the Word, no application of the sacraments." Writing to the ministers of Basel, he asserts the proper task of the reformers: it is not a question of founding a new church, but of purifying the old. Bucer goes on to define the church in terms of discipline: the church includes all Christians who, if they sin, accept correction from it. The disciplinary power is properly pastoral and is exercised by admonition rather than by excommunication. Nevertheless, he claims for the church the right of excommunicating the recalcitrant and expects the concurrence of the magistracy. As the months passed, Bucer became more pressing in his demands that the magistracy bring the Anabaptists under control. In fact, the reformers were in no position to attempt any definition of the church that might distinguish it from the magistracy. The final form of the ordinance that appeared in 1534 was almost expectably disappointing to the ministers: it provided neither for cooperation between the magistrates and the clergy nor for supervision and discipline of the entire Christian citizenry. What discipline existed was exercised by the magisterial church wardens and directed toward the clergy. All future efforts on the part of the pastors to wring from the magistracy a disciplinary board would meet with failure. The full measure of their frustration is evident in three vain appeals which the ministers made to the bishop of Strassburg residing at Zabern in 1537, calling for a reestablishment of the episcopal administration, providing that he accepted the German mass and marriage of the clergy. In 1546 Bucer proposed that some Christians be allowed to form cells for stricter discipline. The council refused.

Of all the major reformers, Bucer was perhaps the greatest churchman. What he failed to accomplish for Strassburg, he managed to realize in part elsewhere in Europe. To Bucer the church did not have a purely religious focus and spiritual nature as the locus of salvation. The Kingdom of God possessed a moral character and the gospel was a moral phenomenon with moral power. In his *Commentary on St. Matthew* (1527), he describes the law as a prescription for living and asserts that God has summoned us to the duty of fulfilling it. Departing from Luther in this integration of gospel and law, faith and works, Bucer exceeds him in claiming for the church a divinely established order, discoverable in the New Testament: through the offices of doctors, pastors, elders, and deacons, effective government will be provided the Christian community and the glory of Christ advanced. In one of his greatest works, *On True Pastoral Care* (1538), which bears traces of Erasmus's *Ecclesiastes*, Bucer argues that the Reformation is not merely a liberation from papal domination but the realization of Christian discipline. This task is not to be achieved by the secular authority; rather, the church itself exercises a continuing teaching and disciplining function—a government (*ein regiment*) by which the Christian may be helped to live in Christ. This discipline would require the exclusion from the church of all those who do not respond to admonition. The crucial function of the elder as overseer and governor Bucer identifies with the role of the apostolic bishop; they are one and the same. Elders were laymen, distinguished by their Christian life and knowledge, elected in part from the council. They were responsible for administering discipline and for the religious and moral supervision of church members. Bucer understood the exercise of church discipline to be nothing less than true pastoral care, which in itself required the collaboration of the four offices. This ideal achieved realization in his church order for Hesse, accepted at Ziegenhain in 1538. Although to some of his contemporaries Bucer's eucharistic doctrine was dangerously vague, inciting the despair and open hostility of Bullinger, the Strassburg reformer warned his age that Christianity did not exist in the external communion of sacraments and adherence to particular doctrines, but that the reign of God manifests itself in power—in spiritual and moral realities.

The second principal goal of Bucer's endeavor was the unity of the reform movement. Here he kept pace with the far-reaching policies of Philip of Hesse and of Strassburg's great *Stettmeister,* Jacob Sturm. The scope of his correspondence and activities reveals a European religious consciousness; he followed the progress of reform from country to country, city to city, ever the opponent of particularism and sectarianism, the champion of a unified reform movement. His most tangible success was the Wittenberg Concord. But his unstinting efforts to mediate between the Swiss and the Lutherans failed; differences over the eucharist persisted, and the Elector John Frederick steadfastly rejected any project for the admission of the Swiss into the Schmalkaldic League.

Concerning France, Bucer recognized the crucial position of the king for the advance of the reform, and he entertained a less severe and more credulous attitude toward Francis than toward Charles V. With the mission of Guillaume du Bellay in Germany in 1534, by which Francis sought to turn the German princes against the emperor, an opportunity for a religious rapprochement seemed to offer itself. The two representatives of moderate Lutheranism, Bucer and Melanchthon, submitted memoranda to the king as the basis for a religious colloquy. Bucer's statement agreed essentially with Melanchthon's in accepting, among other things, pontifical power and the authority of bishops, if properly reformed and controlled by scripture, thereby satisfying the church's need for government and discipline. As early as 1530, Bucer had considered eucharistic differences between the two Protestant groups to be the chief impediment to the full diffusion of the gospel in France. He now went beyond Melanchthon in attempting to present a united position to the French king on this most difficult issue. The Swiss Protestants proved unwilling to consider the advances of the royal agents, and events seemed to justify this suspicion. For the king, in response to the dissemination throughout France on October 18, 1534, of placards vilifying the mass in the most abusive language, undertook a savage persecution of the *luthéristes.* The king's new domestic policy toward reform cut across his foreign policy. From Zurich, Bullinger denounced the memoranda as encouraging the persecutions in France. Despite this failure, Bucer never surrendered his interest in the conquest of France by the gospel.

His *Commentary on St. Matthew* was translated into French, and preceded by a year the appearance of Calvin's *L'institution chrétienne*.

Bucer had only a year and a half to live when, refusing to subscribe to the emperor's Interim, he fled into exile. In England he wrote for Edward VI his *On the Kingdom of Christ,* one of the truly great works of Reformation literature, the consummate statement of a continental reformer to a backward kingdom undergoing ecclesiastical change. In the end, all Bucer's hopes and endeavors, his lifework, lay in ruins—except for the school at Strassburg that he had been instrumental in establishing. The permanence of his work suffered perhaps from its very universalism, as well as from the fastening of a harsh Lutheranism upon Strassburg after 1548. Nevertheless the themes of the Reformation which he had developed—the need for church discipline, the progressive nature of the Christian life, and the world mission of reform—would all attain fulfillment in the work of John Calvin. It would not be a simple case of direct influence, although influence of a sort was undeniable, but rather of Calvin's clarification of issues which were endemic to the urban Swiss-Rhenish reform and which by 1540 pressed for resolution.

CALVIN AND THE INSTITUTIONALIZATION OF REFORM

In January 1535 young John Calvin arrived in Basel, a fugitive from the persecutions raging in France. Until the fatal night of the placards, Renaissance and religious reform had in the French kingdom moved together with only occasional setbacks from the Sorbonne and Parlement; humanist, Platonic, and Lutheran ideas of reform mingled in an environment still largely scholastic. Calvin had been able to benefit from an intellectual milieu that still remained open. His formal training was in law, but humanist interests early attracted him and at Paris in 1533 he came under the influence of the remnants of Lefèvre's circle. His apparent involvement in an outspoken statement favoring reform, made by the rector of the University of Paris, necessitated his removal to Angoulême, where with a good library at his disposal he turned to the study of the Bible and the Fathers for four months, then pressed on to the court of Marguerite of Navarre at Nérac in order to meet Lefèvre, the father of French reform. Did that sudden conversion which he mentions in 1557 occur during this period of withdrawal? If so, it would have been a conversion to the evangel and fabrisian reform, not to Protestantism. His trip to Noyon, his birthplace, the following May to surrender his benefices signified a commitment to the evangel and not any deliberate rupture with the traditional church. As a Christian humanist and learned young scholar, he arrived in the capital of Northern humanism.

At Basel Calvin studied the theology of the Reformation for the first time, and it was of decisive importance that he should have turned to Luther rather than to Zwingli. Calvin's little manual, the *Institutes of the Chris-*

tian Religion (1536), was in its content and structure modeled on Luther's *Catechisms.* Once more the principles of the Reformation are set forth, but now with an emphasis upon advancing God's honor; the Word of God as the overriding authority, the criterion for truth and justice; faith as expressed more in exercise than in theological propositions. While Calvin's profound respect for Luther would never be shaken, he looked upon him not as an oracle but as a pathfinder and pioneer in whose footsteps one must press on. Calvin envisaged reformation as a progress, a movement from the fixed point represented by Luther. Claiming continuity with and legitimate development from Luther, Calvin began that creative appropriation which would give a new impetus and direction to a reformation-in-progress.

In 1536, after the publication of his little treatise, Calvin visited the court of Ferrara, benefited from a brief amnesty to clear up his affairs at home and then, finding the direct route to Strassburg blocked by war, sought to reach that city by way of Geneva. There Calvin found a population of approximately 10,000 emerging from a decade of revolution. An alliance of one civic faction with the Swiss cities of Bern and Freiburg had succeeded in expelling the prince-bishop and overthrowing the suzerainty of the House of Savoy. Political had led to religious rebellion in 1532 when William Farel appeared and began to preach. The support of Protestant Bern had been decisive in confirming the religious as well as political. innovations. In the spring of 1536 the environs of Geneva were no longer Catholic Savoyard but Protestant Bernese.

Preaching, iconoclasm, and tumult abounded in the autumn when Calvin appeared, but there was no reformation, no discernible church. With good reason the volatile Farel summoned, as if by the hand of God, the scholarly traveler to the solemn and terrible task of reform in Geneva. Reluctantly acceding to the vocation thrust upon him, the shy humanist assumed the modest post of Reader in Holy Scripture. But the need for an informed preaching and for ecclesiastical organization soon compelled him to undertake a larger role, in which his intellectual preeminence became apparent. Seeking to define the church at Geneva, he sought to realize a living community. To assure the progressive sanctification of its members, Calvin insisted the church must exercise a discipline and have the power to excommunicate. Through his *Articles, Confession of Faith,* and *Catechism,* Calvin provided the foundation for evangelical discipline and sound doctrine. The inhabitants of Geneva proved recalcitrant. When in 1538 the magistrates unilaterally adopted Bernese practices in the liturgy, Calvin, Farel, and Pierre Viret resisted and suffered expulsion. Essentially, the conflict had not been caused by the reformers' objections to the Bernese liturgy but by their desire to achieve some autonomy for the church.

Perplexed and humiliated, Calvin would have retired to the solace of study at Basel, had he not been persuaded by Bucer to come to Strassburg. The Alsatian capital and its eminent pastors proved a congenial environment that would transform Calvin into a confident and mature reformer. Entrusted with the pastorate of the French refugee community, Calvin developed a church discipline which with some dissimulation managed to comply with Strassburg ordinances of 1534. Although unable to excommunicate, he was able to apply, with greater effectiveness than his hosts, their recommendations for admitting to communion only those who had earlier presented themselves and been approved through examination. From Bucer he derived a belief in the divine institution of four ecclesiastical offices as prescribed in the New Testament. Calvin also shared with Bucer the common approach of humanists to the reform and a concern for sanctification, the progressive nature of the Christian life, and the realization of holiness. At the religious colloquies of 1540–41 he was introduced by Bucer to the larger world of ecclesiastical politics and to the universal mission of the Christian church. He became acquainted with Melanchthon and with the prince-ridden churches of Germany. His association with Bucer at the height of that ecclesiastical statesman's powers exerted a decisive and formative influence upon Calvin. Therefore the invitation to return to Geneva, where a shift in the balance of factions urged Calvin's restoration, appeared most unwelcome and for a year the well-acclimated Strassburg pastor resisted, hesitated, and allowed his responsibilities to detain him.

For Pierre Viret, as he reflected at Lausanne upon the faltering cause of reform in that winter preceding Calvin's return, the preeminent need appeared to be discipline. He expressed his anxiety and alarm in a letter to Bullinger. Ignorance and the impious neglect of religion, he said, had vitiated the good that might have been expected of the reform and the evangelical preaching. He continued:

We deplore this difficulty of the times, but meanwhile there is none among us who has the capacity to heal such evils. . . . We considered recalling to the church some sort of discipline which in similar circumstances has been destroyed. For necessity compels us to do this, but what kind of discipline, we are not sufficiently certain. We do not really know what ecclesiastical model we should set before ourselves. . . . Furthermore to restore the old discipline is not at all easy nor useful, partly because it is not without its own defects and may contain many things which, as they depart somewhat from the purity of the apostles, are not easily able to escape being dangerous to consciences and having the appearance and suspicion of papism. We desire discipline but only as long as it is able to be the simplest, purest and most apostolic. . . . We perceive and recognize the diseases but the more the evil cunningly thrives and gathers ever more strength, no one yet applies the healing hand, no one is engaged in seeking antidotes.[3]

---

[3] *Joannis Calvini opera quae supersunt omnia,* ed. G. Baum, E. Cunitz, and E. Reuss, 59 vols. (Brunswick and Berlin, 1863–97) XI, 20.

Calvin returned to Geneva neither as hero nor conqueror. But since he had been strenuously urged by the magistrates to bring order to a church upon which the welfare of the infant republic depended, Calvin was in a stronger position than other reformers to realize his goals. On his arrival in September 1541, he presented himself before the town council to explain that the church could not survive unless it had a government such as was prescribed by the Word of God and observed in the early church. There followed five weeks of negotiations that produced the *Ecclesiastical Ordinances*. The constitution of the Genevan church provided for the four offices of pastors, teachers, elders, and deacons; the impact of the Strassburg experience was plainly evident, but if the pattern originated with Bucer, the performance and achievement were thoroughly Calvin's. The preachers were incorporated as a body—the Venerable Company. The company examined new ministers and recommended them for approval by the city council and for election and calling by the congregation. Besides preaching and administering the sacraments, the minister enforced church discipline. Here he received significant aid from the elders, perhaps the most vital feature of the system. Although the twelve elders were drawn from the magistracy—two from the Small Council, four from the Council of Sixty, and six from the Large Council—they were intended to act as officers of the church in their supervision of the religious and moral life of the people. Together ministers and elders constituted the Consistory, the disciplinary body of the church. To facilitate the elder's work of reprimand and admonition, the city was divided into twelve districts. Hearings, exclusion from the Lord's Supper, and, finally, excommunication would make effective the authority of the Consistory, but on the crucial matter of excommunication the ordinances were deliberately ambiguous. For the magistracy saw the exercise of this power by a veritable spiritual police as a dangerous invasion of its jurisdiction. In 1541 the council refused to relinquish the power to excommunicate which remained the most contested issue until its final acquisition by the Consistory in 1555. The other offices, teacher and deacon, received briefer treatment. The creation of the former looked forward to the founding of a college, only to be realized in the Academy of Geneva in 1559; Calvin was unable to realize his plan for deacons of the church to serve as administrators of the hospital and of welfare. The deacons would continue to depend on the magistracy, as in Swiss cities, and only deacons of the foreign-speaking churches or of the *Bourse française* became ecclesiastical persons.

Discipline—or what Calvin and Bucer knew to be, and others soon recognized as being, the discipline of Christ—distinguished the church at Geneva and gave it that degree of autonomy which had heretofore remained unrealized. This discipline was not achieved all at once, nor, insofar as it pertained to the church, did it ever assume the form of physical force: one cannot speak of Geneva as a theocracy in the customary sense of the term but rather as a collaboration of church and city council to achieve a community under the Word of God. The issue of church discipline served to distinguish two groups in the government: the 'Calvinists' and the 'libertines.' Although the ascendancy of the latter party from 1548 to 1555 proved trying to Calvin, he was never without sufficient support in the government to maintain the church order. Beginning in 1550, however, the number of exiles, particularly from France, significantly increased, and in the subsequent twelve years approximately seven thousand religious refugees arrived in Geneva; of these only a fraction in the same period received citizenship, and none entered the Small Council. By contrast, the offices of the church were filled with refugees, the Company of Pastors and the later Academy being overwhelmingly French. Refugees dominated the printing industry and the professions of law and medicine. By 1555 the influence of the refugees had tipped the balance in favor of the Calvinist party, and in the same year the Consistory obtained the power of excommunication. Calvin's authority throughout these two periods remained moral and intellectual; although often a law consultant to the council, he never possessed any political power. But as a master of the written and spoken word, Calvin asserted his ascendancy over the minds of Geneva's inhabitants and over much of the world beyond. Similarly, the Consistory, despite the prying eyes of the elders, was a moral power and not a police force.

Calvin's catechism supplemented the system. Through it a new generation would be formed, drilled in Christian instruction, and would submit more readily to the discipline of Christ.

Mutual censure and exhortation, buttressed by the institutions of Calvin's reform, characterized the church of Geneva. That discipline which had been a major preoccupation of the Swiss-Rhenish reform had at last achieved an adequate realization in Geneva. Humanist moralism, civic responsibility, and the urban context had all prepared the way for the reception of the Reformation in these city-states and had helped to determine its final form. With a greater sensitivity to law and the performance of the law in a good life, the Swiss-Rhenish reform had expanded its central focus to include sanctification as well as justification. Was this the revenge of the moralists or the necessary adjustment of Luther's central insight to the pre-existing ground swell of biblical humanism? Under Calvin's influence, the Reformation concept of the calling was lent a new dynamic, effectively relating the inner experience of justification to the outer experience of honoring God. Through church discipline the community of Christians had been clearly defined. At Geneva had been realized a coherent church order that succeeded in reaffirming community, the greater participation of laity, and the meaningful relation of the inner and outer selves.

By 1555, the year of the Augsburg settlement, a revived and reorganized Protestantism in western Swiss lands had already embarked upon a universal mission. The discipline of Christ, realized at Geneva, would now serve as a model to the persecuted churches of France and to the world.

The Course of International Protestantism

The year 1541–42 was the decisive turning-point in the continental Reformation; the diet of Ratisbon, Calvin's return to Geneva, and the bull *Licet ab initio* would define confessional Europe and confessional strife for the next hundred years. Indeed, the failure of the Middle Group at Ratisbon —by signifying the collapse of the liberal wing within the Curia and hence of a mediating theology, evangelical and catholic within Christendom— heralded the emergence of a harder, more rigid Catholicism in conscious opposition to the nascent Protestantism. South of the Alps the papal bull of 1542, establishing the Roman Inquisition, fell heavily upon individuals and small groups of Antitrinitarians and Anabaptists; hitherto ill-defined within the rich matrix of Renaissance humanism, platonism, and evangelism that characterized Italian intellectual life, these religious zealots, now heretics, scurried for cover. Strassburg and the Swiss cities stood as asylums for these refugees, and among the first to flee were such commanding persons as Bernardino Ochino, General of the Capuchins, and the distinguished Augustinian Peter Martyr Vermigli. Bullinger's Zurich proved most attractive to these religious individualists, for its church appeared to be more independent from the secular authority than those at Bern and Basel and lacked the rigorous discipline recently established in Geneva. As the walls of ecclesiastical, as well as theological, definition began to go up in Europe, those who earlier might have served a mediating role as representatives of a broad undefined religious rebirth now had to conform, dissimulate, or flee, first to the Swiss-Rhenish cities and shortly afterwards to the periphery of Europe.

Calvin's awareness of a decisive rift in Christendom revealed itself that same year in new interpretations of the church's unity and the problem of schism. Calvin had previously experienced the church as universal and essentially indefectible, even if its present face was blighted. It was not for him a question of two churches—true and false—but of working within a context overlaid by lies and falseness to recall the church to the ancient model. In this task Calvin's own understanding of vocation was crucial. His conversion had been not a sudden break with the existing church but an abrupt recognition, and progressive discovery, of his vocation as reformer of that church. Unlike Luther, who as a priest rebelled against the inadequate witness of the contemporary church, Calvin, as a believing layman, assumed the role of reformer and pastor for the renewal of the entire catholic community; in his overwhelming sense of vocation he experienced the legitimization of his ministry. The reformer's understanding of his own vocation found its analogue in the Hebrew prophets, who, in stigmatizing the corruptions of Jerusalem, had not broken with the corrupt community. The impact of Ratisbon upon Calvin became apparent in his publications of 1543. His faith in the universal community of the church and its continuity from the apostles remained unshaken. But he now recognized a rupture as having occurred. He denied the accusation that the evangelicals had caused this rupture (*initium separationis*) and blamed the "papists," who had rejected the reforming party without having been rejected themselves.

THE LEADERSHIP OF CALVIN

The greatness of Calvin lay in his peculiar capacity to inspire and organize a movement of European scope. It is not simply that he found Protestantism faltering and uncertain and gave it a new direction and impetus; he provided the intellectual and institutional forms whereby the movement might effectively continue after his death, not dependent upon any particular leader. One is confronted with a double enigma: that of the shy retiring scholar become a person of European prominence and world historical dimensions; and the virtual effacement and anonymity of a powerful personality behind his work. This unique extension and incorporation of the self reveals itself in several ways: although he was the presiding minister within the Venerable Company of Pastors, his influence is rarely evident in the direction of the mission to France, which was accomplished in the name of the Company; and in his letter to Cardinal Sadoleto, he identifies himself so completely with the movement that he can attribute the following statement, so descriptive of his own achievement, to any member of his ministry:

As to the charge of forsaking the church, which they were wont to bring against me, there is nothing of which my conscience accuses me unless, indeed, he is to be considered a deserter, who, seeing the soldiers routed and scattered, and abandoning the ranks, raises the leader's standard, and recalls them to their posts. For thus, O Lord, were all my servants dispersed, so that they could not, by any possibility, hear the command, but had almost forgotten their leader, and their service, and their military oath. In order to bring them together when thus scattered, I raised not a foreign standard, but that noble banner of thine whom we must follow, if we would be classed among thy people.[4]

Calvin would be easier to succeed than Luther.

That special leadership which allowed for continuity after the passing of the leader cannot be understood either in terms of a Weberian 'routinization of charisma' or of an institutionalization of the self. One can point to the calmness and clarity of Calvin's mind and the mastery of direct, convincing expression to which his humanist training contributed. One can attribute to his legal education a temperament capable of accepting the creative role of a properly limited secular authority and of investing reform in immense organizational work and specific institutions: the Company, the Consistory, the Academy, and the disciplined church all possess a paradig-

---

[4] "Calvin's Reply to Sadoleto," in *A Reformation Debate,* ed. John C. Olin (New York, 1966), p. 84.

matic quality for a world religion. The crucial factor that distinguished Calvin and his reform, however, stemmed from his own perception of religion and response to scripture. While Luther's experience of religion, the discovery of a gracious God amidst the anguish of sin, was primarily personal both in its nature and its forms, Calvin's experience, if equally intensive and personal, allowed him to speak in less personal terms and with an outward focus. "By a sudden conversion," he wrote in 1557, "God subdued and brought my heart to docility." The image of a mastering hand making supple, ready, and intent a hitherto-hardened heart became Calvin's seal—the emblem of a life and of a total ethos. God's Word came not as solace to quiet the suffering soul but as a trumpet, calling to action in the service of His honor. This impelling sense of a sovereign Will, which he had experienced in more than one instance, Calvin would impart as the central theme and force in his theology and his work as a reformer. Calvin summoned men not to individual tasks, but to the Task, the vindication of God's honor and the restoration of His church in a corrupt world. As a continuing refrain there rings, "We are not our own ... we are God's." His inspired definition of the task would evoke the lives and energies of his own and succeeding generations to making visible in multifarious organized forms the advancement of God's kingdom on earth.

As citadel of the faithful and base for the reformation of the church, Geneva afforded great opportunities to a gifted leader. In urging his return from Strassburg in 1541, the ministers of Zurich pointed out to him the geographical advantage of the city, perched on the borders of France, Italy, and Germany, for the dissemination of the gospel in neighboring cities. As with the apostles, so with the reformers: the kingdom of Christ would best be expanded by winning over the metropolises. To Calvin, subject of the French king and religious exile, Geneva and the Genevans meant little and never engaged his affection. But the doctrine of the reform, and the ecclesiastical organization which it involved, meant everything. Though thoroughly French, the exile would later observe that we must prefer to our own country any region where God is purely worshipped. With the increasing persecutions in France, Geneva became the great asylum as well as model for the new reformed churches. To the jurist François Hotman, Geneva was the common fatherland of all the pious; to Ochino, a copy of the life eternal; to John Knox, the best school of Christ since the apostles. A place of refuge, increasingly a city of refugees, without hinterland or attachments to any territory, a place where Christ was preached in a multiplicity of languages, Geneva came to possess those cosmopolitan and supranational qualities which would enable it to promote a reform of universal scope. With the emergence of the Roman Antichrist, the church as an ordered polity had, according to Beza, been translated to Geneva, where it might worthily be recognized. From Geneva, as from an Archimedean point, the tyranny of Rome might at last be wrested from the face of the church.

THE MISSION TO FRANCE

Calvin's mission to France began to take shape at the moment of the young scholar's arrival in Basel. Though the first rendering of the *Institutes* was in Latin, Calvin announced in his dedicatory letter to his king that he had undertaken this labor especially for his French countrymen, of whom so many, he knew, thirsted for Christ. He intended the book for popular Christian instruction and, including as it did a *summa* of scripture's content, as an aid for the further study of the Bible. Through its clarity of exposition, elegance of style, and spontaneity, the first French edition of 1541 realized this aim. Successive French editions of the *Institutes* in 1545, 1551, and 1560, based on the definitive Latin of 1559, emphasized the point that the book, if intended for all, was particularly directed toward his fellow Frenchmen. Calvin himself marvelled at the reception his work enjoyed and, as each edition received its learned increment, what had once been a slender manual grew to a massive tome. Through its agency, preeminently, a generation of religious heroes was molded and a church established. It communicated to the faithful the awful sense of God's majesty and sovereign power and the call to the justified and regenerate to "represent Christ" in their lives and expand His kingdom. If the Reformation was to be saved, the summons to spiritual battle must be absolutely clear, imperative, without hesitancy or question.

In mounting this determined campaign of religious reform, Calvin was enormously aided by the press. During the 1520s and 1530s the presses of Antwerp, Strassburg, and Basel had poured forth the literature of religious propaganda that permeated the French kingdom. The printing industry in Geneva now experienced a growth that would make that city a center for European book production to the end of the century. Among those who participated in this remarkable development was no less a person than Robert Estienne, royal printer and renowned scholar, who in 1550 left the oppressive atmosphere created by the Sorbonne and Parlement of Paris to reside at Geneva. He would later print the definitive 1559 edition of the *Institutes* and, among other works, the *Commentary* of Bucer on the Gospels. Another person of international reputation was Laurent de Normandie, a counsellor-at-large for the Parlement of Paris and mayor of Calvin's Noyon. On account of his religious convictions, he had fled to Geneva in 1548. Ever since the edict of 1542, which forbade the printing, sale, and distribution of all heretical literature in France, Geneva had had to assume the major responsibility for providing neighboring lands with Bibles and religious literature. Laurent de Normandie had a network of contacts throughout Europe, and disposed of considerable sums for financing and distributing religious literature. In the critical period leading up to war, he acted as a sort of minister of Calvinist propaganda. A third person to enhance the intellectual atmosphere of Geneva was Theodore de Bèze (Beza), a humanist and member of the lower nobility who arrived in Geneva the same year as Laurent de Normandie. Although attached to the academy at Lausanne and serving there with Viret for the next decade, in 1559 he helped to reconstitute the educational system of Geneva and to found the Academy of Geneva. Beza—Calvin's representative on mission and heir apparent— was in large part responsible for making the Academy the center for theological instruction in the Reformed community.

The Venerable Company of Pastors represented the brains and driving force behind the evangelization of France, as well as the rest of Europe. Before the existence of the Academy, it trained candidates in theology and the languages. From 1555 until the outbreak of hostilities in 1562, this collective directorate supervised a vast missionary effort. Of the more than one hundred ministers it trained, accredited, and sent forth, eighty-eight went to France. These pastors were mostly recruited from France, many being subsidized by French congregations. As these new pastors would certainly be considered seditious, if discovered, and might well become martyrs, the Company exercised extreme caution and secrecy to protect both them and the Geneva council. They were mostly assigned to the cities: Poitiers, Dieppe, Orleans, Lyons, Paris.

After the Affair of the Placards, the French crown had turned increasingly to a policy of repression. News of edicts, persecutions, and martyrs incited Lausanne and Geneva to broaden their political base, both among the Swiss cantons and the princes of Germany, in order to bring greater pressure to bear upon the king of France but to no avail. With the accession of the very orthodox Henry II in 1547 and the establishment of a special prosecuting section in the Parlement of Paris, the 'Chambre Ardente,' persecution became more violent. Within the jurisdictions of the Parlement of Paris and of Toulouse the persecution of the faithful was particularly severe. The policy of repression only stimulated Geneva to greater efforts to win over France and her king.

After 1555 the nature of the reform in France changed with alarming rapidity. Until that time the faithful had gone without the regular administration of the sacraments, preaching, or a consistory. With the government's attention distracted by the war with Spain, the reformed church of Paris was formally established in September. Others followed. By 1559 these churches were sufficiently numerous to necessitate the calling of a national synod for the organization of the reformed church in France. The synod promulgated a confession of faith and an ecclesiastical discipline drawn up by Antoine de la Roche Chandieu, a pupil of Calvin, and inspired by the master. The Reformation in France began rapidly to assume the form of a pyramid of synods from individual local consistories to regional colloquies, from provincial synods to the national synod. By 1562 there were 2,150 churches embracing three million persons out of a population of less than twenty million. During this same period of seven years, the social makeup of the movement was transformed. Heretofore the greatest receptivity to the reform had been found among artisans and petty merchants, with some following among minor functionaries and a scattering of peasant support. Except for a few members of the lower nobility in the south, the reform had not yet received the support of the nobles. As Admiral de Coligny would later remark, "It is the little people of France who have preceded us into the kingdom of heaven." After peace had been made with Spain (1559), the existence of a Protestant nobility became evident. Jeanne d'Albret, daughter of Marguerite of Navarre, moved steadily into the orbit of the reform, bringing with her, it appeared, her inconstant husband Antoine de Bourbon, First Prince of the Blood. Although the Constable Anne de Montmorency, who vied with the Guises for the control of the king, remained Catholic, the Constable's nephews, the Châtillon brothers, turned to the reform—François d'Andelot in 1556, then Gaspard de Coligny in 1557, and later Odet, Cardinal de Châtillon, the first Protestant cardinal. When a Protestant service in the rue Saint Jacques was attacked on September 4, 1557, noblemen drew their swords to protect fellow believers.

If profound religious conviction accounted for the conversion of D'Andelot and Coligny, other factors also contributed to the wholesale defections from the old church by the nobility during the late fifties. Faced with fixed rents and rising prices, the nobility had been experiencing a dangerous economic crisis, and the two major means of recouping their losses were advancement at court or adventure in warfare. Nevertheless, with the bankruptcy of the Crown in 1557 and the hastening of both Valois and Habsburg to the peace table of Cateau-Cambrésis two years later, both channels were closed to an increasingly restless nobility. The monarchy might still have weathered the storm and perhaps even been successful in the policy of eradicating heresy upon which the king had just embarked. However, Henry II was accidentally killed in a tournament, leaving a wife and several sickly children exposed to the great rival factions at court; the predatory houses of Guise, Bourbon, and Montmorency now moved to subject the crown to dangerously centrifugal forces. At the same time the bankruptcy of the monarchy led many of its agents, officials, and lesser nobility to seek support as clients of great lords. During this same period, 1559 to 1562, the lesser lords extended their authority and protection over local conventicles of Huguenots. In this abrupt recrudescence of the "new feudalism," the retinues of an intransigently Catholic Guise or a Huguenot Bourbon could be suddenly swelled into armies. The propagation of the gospel proceeded in a charged atmosphere of economic crisis and general reaction to the royal centralization which contemporaries dated from Louis XI. As the lines of political adventure, economic distress, and religious conviction began to coalesce, Geneva was faced with a situation that threatened to develop beyond its control.

Calvin continued to observe a dutiful respect toward kingship. Nevertheless this respect fell short of awe, which, like sovereignty, Calvin reserved to the Lord God alone. Indeed, the student of Roman law applied to God all the terms that would later be used to define political sovereignty. In some of his less public works, Calvin expressed his distrust and even horror of hereditary monarchy, and portrayed the godlike king as a threat, an insult to the divine majesty. He preferred a republic with its political diversity and numerous levels of responsibility. Yet the opening lines of his letter to Francis I, dated August 23, 1535—precisely two months after the collapse of the Anabaptist kingdom at Münster—betray his genuine fear of sedition and anxiety that his own reform might be associated with the madness of that radical community of refugees, a fear that would evoke extraordinary caution in political matters from both him and Beza. In general, Calvin, like Luther, could only allow passive disobedience of a tyrant and the suffering of the consequences. Yet because authority is always to Calvin a mandate from God, the religious dimension invades magistracy and the character of office. Whoever overreaches his office and opposes himself to God is divested of his title. At his most unguarded, Calvin would say that religion compels us to resist or, as in the *Commentary on Daniel* (1561), that we ought to defy utterly a prince who has risen up against God. Calvin, however, did not define a right of resistance; he identified instead a locus of responsibility. At the end of all editions of the *Institutes* following 1541, he observed that subordinate governmental functionaries, such as the ephors against the Spartan kings or the tribunes against the Roman consuls, have the magisterial power and constituted rôle to withstand the willfulness of kings. In contemporary European monarchies he attributed this responsibility to the estates assembled, which in the case of France had met only twice in the century—in 1506 and quite abnormally in 1558. This idea of the inferior magistrate's competence had already been voiced in the resistance of Magdeburg in 1550, and Beza in both 1554 and 1560 reasserted this notion of a subordinate constituted authority prudently maintaining pure religion in the face of an oppressive overlord. Calvin soberly adjusted this current idea to his thinking in a way that would guard against any accusation of sedition.

In 1560 the Huguenots, as a minority faction faced with a protracted struggle, had to exert enormous care to win over, or at least not alienate, the uncommitted and to restrain their own nobility. Despite Beza's attendance at the French court and the court of Navarre, and in the following of the Huguenot leader Louis de Condé during the fateful years of 1560 and 1561 to 1563, the gap widened between Genevan theory and Huguenot practice. When Calvin was consulted on the conspiracy of Amboise, which sought to seize the young king Francis II and remove his apparent captors, the Guise brothers Duke Francis and the Cardinal of Lorraine, the Genevan reformer would not countenance such a desperate measure unless it had the support of Antoine de Bourbon, who, as First Prince of the Blood, he considered the appropriate inferior magistrate. The weak Antoine dissimulated, hedged, but never rose to the occasion, and the grip of the Guises tightened on the government. The death of Francis II caused their hold over the monarchy to relax momentarily and allowed Catherine de Medici to pursue her policy of mediation and moderation. Both Calvin and Beza placed their hopes in the sympathetic disposition of the Queen Mother and her sons, and looked to a reform that might be established by the royal government itself. As chief Calvinist spokesman Beza attended the colloquy called by the queen at Poissy in September 1561. But the effort on the part of this national council to achieve an accord between two increasingly intransigent religious camps broke upon that ever-sharp reef of discord—the doctrine of the eucharist. As early as March, Beza had reported to Calvin that civil war was impending. Yet along with the hovering fear of cataclysm there persisted the confidence that the truth would conquer. With the government condoning reformed services and the number of converts swelling, Beza could well hope that Huguenots might soon outnumber Catholics in France. Thus in November he urged the church at Lyons to be patient and hold its services in the suburbs in order to avoid tumult. The months of September 1561 to January 1562 saw the high tide of Calvinism. The Edict of Saint-Germain, or Edict of January, proclaimed a broad, if still imperfect, toleration; for the first time Calvinist worship in public was authorized, although banned from all walled towns. Beza and his fellow ministers, in explaining the edict to the reformed churches, expressed Calvin's policy for reform: inform the king and court on the true nature of the reform until they are convinced of its necessity; then promulgate it under royal protection.

Within six weeks of the Edict of January, the dreaded civil war burst upon France. The massacre of a Calvinist gathering at Vassy by the duke of Guise dashed any hope of peacefully winning France to the reform. Calvin had warned Coligny that if a single drop of blood was shed, rivers of blood would flow throughout Europe. In writing to the churches of the realm after Vassy, Beza sought to focus opposition upon the Guise camp: he exhorted them not to resist the king but his enemies, the disturbers of the kingdom. The Huguenot leaders would have difficulty maintaining the fiction of their loyalty to the Crown. Since November 1561, Catholicism in France had begun to rally, and, with the winning of Antoine de Bourbon to the side of the Guises, Catherine de Medici was compelled to abandon her policy of moderation and many of her links with the Huguenots. The Châtillons and, to Beza's dismay, Condé left the court to the Catholic chieftains who now took control.

None could have surmised in March 1562 that religious and civil wars would plague France for the next forty years, and that the pacification achieved by the Edict of Nantes in 1598 would be modeled on the earlier Edict of January. Although the triumph of Calvinism in France had always been unlikely, considering the Concordat of Bologna, the traditions of the Sorbonne and Parlement, and the temper of the majority, before the spring of 1562 there was nothing inevitable about the failure of Calvin's reform in his own land. At the outset of the struggle French Protestantism committed some bad political errors which were never to be rectified. When, in November 1561, the question arose, in the case of the Bishop of Troyes, whether in converting to the reform he could retain his titles and benefices, Calvin stood on principle and thereby erected a stumbling block in the path of moderate bishops passing over to the reform. Any other decision would have badly compromised the structure of his church; nevertheless, it closed the door to any possibility of a Gallicanism developing, like Anglicanism, in complete separation from Rome. Secondly, Condé's removal from Paris to Orleans in late March 1562 left the crown at the mercy of the Catholic Triumvirate. And again Condé erred when, in negotiating the peace after the first war in 1563, he provided for freedom of worship for the nobles in their chapels but, as Calvin bitterly observed, virtually ignored the artisanry, peasants, and lesser people of the realm. As a result of these initial political mistakes, Calvinism in France was condemned to the position of a minority religion.

The rapid politicization of French Protestantism cannot be directly attributed to Calvinist theology, nor can its greater resort to violence, when compared to Lutheranism, be explained by an inherent "activism." Again the context, quite different from that of the empire or Geneva, provides the main explanation for this violence and political involvement. The monarchy's policy of extermination, intensified over the decades, had compelled the reformed communities to seek the protection of a restless nobility and steeled them for a bitter defense of this faith. As early as the conspiracy of Amboise, the difference in attitude between Chandieu, caught up in the circumstances of the reform, and Calvin in Geneva began to emerge. Once war broke out, leadership shifted from the preachers to the nobles. The rapid mobilization of Huguenot forces and their concentration at Orleans indicates that the Calvinist conventicles and the structure of the reformed church provided the military cadres for the organization of an army. Calvin was shocked in 1562 to learn that the ministers of Lyons had participated significantly in bringing this center of finance into the Protestant camp. The ecclesiastical structure would continue to be drained for war funds. In the ensuing struggle, Geneva's city council cautiously sent financial assistance, religious literature, arms, gunpowder, and some volunteers to France. Nevertheless, the center of gravity had moved away from Geneva to the camp of Condé, whom Beza would serve as secretary and treasurer during the first war. The vital role played by religion, however, did not evaporate at the first shock of combat but persisted in a transmuted form. For henceforth religion alone would hold together the formidable parties, Huguenot and Catholic, welding the divergent interests of nobles, burghers, and peasants into a fighting force.

Periods of political upheaval and civil war usually create a milieu which demands a radical rethinking of the traditional order. The French wars of religion, so meaningless in themselves, have extraordinary significance in this respect. The dreadful experience of over forty years of bloodshed in the name of religion would compel a rethinking of the whole ideal of the *corpus Chris-*

tianum. Since A.D. 380, the Christian faith had been considered the basis of social order. Society was conceived as a unity ruled by two distinct, cooperating jurisdictions, the spiritual and the temporal power, so closely associated that any rift or dissent in one imparted itself to the other. Any dissent from the basic doctrines and practices of the church represented a poison, endangering the salvation of others, threatening society's foundation in Christian morality, and, as blasphemy before God, inviting His wrath upon the whole community. Calvin and the Inquisition agreed on this axiomatic principle and collaborated in the prosecution of the Antitrinitarian Michael Servetus, who ultimately suffered death by fire at the hands of the Genevan city council in 1553. Toleration in the sixteenth century was neither a virtue, a value, nor a principle; at best it was only an expedient. In the empire, which included a patchwork of semisovereign territorial states, the problem had not presented itself in its most acute form, for according to the Peace of Augsburg one might remove to a territory ruled by a prince of one's own faith. But in the French monarchy, with its unitive tradition and its principle of "Une foi, une loi, un roi," the Augsburg settlement was inapplicable. Because each camp thought of itself in terms of a totality admitting no dissent, the effect of the traditional notion of *corpus Christianum* was to heighten the violence and intolerance displayed by both sides. The experience of the French religious wars would demonstrate that religion, which had been the cement necessary for social order and political unity, could become in an age of profound doctrinal discord the source of conflict.

Nevertheless, from the outset there existed a middle group, at first ill-defined and uncertain but gradually better established and more comprehensive in its adherents as the wars dragged on. The obvious base for such a middle ground, at least until 1568, was the Queen Mother, who sought to preserve the crown by maintaining a precarious balance between the two rival camps of Navarre-Châtillon and Guise. The chief agent of a policy of moderation based on moral conviction and political insight was the humanist and jurist Michel de L'Hôpital, who became chancellor in May 1560. In addressing the Estates-General at Orleans following the death of Francis II, L'Hôpital urged the Erasmian virtue of compromise and the primacy of peace, order, and unity. The next year, supporting Catherine's idea of a national council, he sought to reach a religious accord between the two groups. The old ideal of a single religion within a single realm, though broadened, persisted. In the same year, there appeared an anonymous pamphlet called *Exhortation to the Princes and Lords of the King's Privy Council*, which for the first time entertained the arresting thought of the necessity for two churches within a single realm. The time had passed that one might cut off the offending member; amputation would mean death. Toleration became a temporary expedient. If the unity of the realm was to be preserved the links between the secular and the spiritual must be loosened. This apparent sacrifice of religious to political unity or, as the Guises were to express it, this preferring the repose of the kingdom to the salvation of one's soul, gave rise to the term *politique* for those who entertained this solution, hateful to Huguenots and Catholics alike. After the failure of religious conciliation at Poissy, L'Hôpital would move into the orbit of the *politiques* and, even after retiring from office in 1568, serve as a leading spokesman for this position. Religion was not an indifferent matter, but the real object of government was peace, order, and justice, rather than the maintenance of true religion. The Constable of France, Anne de Montmorency, shared the chancellor's ideas, and after his death in 1567 his sons, particularly Montmorency-Damville, the powerful governor of Languedoc, provided the nucleus for a party of moderates. It would nevertheless require two more decades of civil war before the majority of France would accept a *politique* solution.

The collapse of order and the impotence of the Valois made necessary a theory of government along *politique* lines, exalting the capacity of the monarch. In 1576 an Angevin jurist, Jean Bodin, trained in the tradition of Roman law, reacted to the public disorder with a definition of sovereignty and its role in a commonwealth. More than anything else, his concept established in European political thought the reality of the state. Sovereign power constitutes the state, and is definable essentially as the infinite capacity to make laws for all citizens and to accept none from them. This power is vested in the king, who is absolved from all positive law, *legibus solutus*. Such law is the prerogative of the ruler, to whom no resistance is permitted. This recognition of the creative capacity of legislation and its vesture in the monarch decisively defined and strengthened the secular political community. Unity of religion is highly desirable but not so much as to be allowed to promote civil war. The solution was that of a *politique*.

As well as provoking an absolutist theory of government, the breakdown of civil order afforded an opportunity for doctrines of resistance and constitutional ideas. By seeking to rid herself of Coligny's counsel in August 1572, Catherine inadvertently unleashed the St. Bartholomew's Massacre and thereby scrapped twelve years of effort toward civil toleration. No longer could the Huguenots see the young king as a possible Josias and entertain the fiction of evil counsellors usurping the throne. The abrupt loss of its leaders among the nobility not only had the effect of giving the movement's direction back to the pastors and townsmen, but also brought to the fore the appeal in Calvinist thought to the Estates and to the lesser magistrate to legitimize the right of resistance. In the works of Hotman, Beza, and Du Plessis-Mornay, a constitutionalist doctrine of the monarchy was expounded: kings are created by the people as the political community, to rule for its welfare; authorities exist independent of the king and are directly responsible to the people. They have the power to control the king and to defend the people's rights if the ruler lapses into tyranny. Mornay's *Defense of Liberty* (1579) was the most aggressive in its handling of resistance on religious grounds.

With the death of Henry III's only remaining brother in 1584, the prospect of a heretic king on the throne of France led to a curious reversal of roles: the

Huguenots now advocated strong monarchy and the Catholics succeeded to the constitutionalist doctrines of their opponents. The mortal threat to Catholicism in France made the last decade of struggle the bitterest. The intransigence of the Catholic League, the cooperation between Spain and the House of Guise, the abyss into which monarchy had fallen with the last Valois—all heightened the frantic violence of Catholic publicists. Only Henry of Navarre's acceptance of the religion of the majority of Frenchmen in 1593 permitted the imposition of a *politique* settlement upon France and the revival of the monarchy.

THE SPREAD OF CALVINISM

Common to Western European countries at mid-century was a deepening discord between their estates and the central government. The advance of the Genevan reform stood to benefit from these tensions in a way that allowed political and religious issues, common to adjacent countries, almost to stifle the awakening manifestations of a quasi-national life. Confessional and constitutional issues of France and the Netherlands ran parallel. After 1566 the two countries formed a single theater of war, whose rival combatants appealed for money, troops, and propaganda to Rome or Geneva, to Spain or England. Geneva's relations with the Netherlands were not as explicit as with France, yet the Dutch who later flocked to Geneva to study would substantiate Beza's boast that it was the nursery for the ministers of Holland, as well as those of France and England.

In the Netherlands the ground had been prepared earlier by Lutheranism and the violence of the Anabaptists. The first Calvinist ministers, coming from Strassburg, Emden, and 'Belgium', had the effect of encouraging violent revolutionary elements among the artisans and workers of the cities, particularly in the south. But such social unrest would have remained negligible had it not become linked with the far more important issue of the aristocratic reaction to Philip II's policies and the broadening sense of patriotism. Without the aristocracy's alienation from Habsburg rule, the religious issue might have gone unexploited. In contrast to the leading aristocrats, the lesser nobility proved particularly susceptible to the rhetoric of the new ministry. The outbreak of iconoclasm in cities linked with Calvinist agitation had the effect of alienating both the authorities and the majority of the population from the new religion. Nevertheless, the subsequent five years, marked by the rule of Alva, Philip's general, created an atmosphere of terror and exasperation upon which the movement could thrive. The seizure of the strategic port of Brill in 1572 by a violent Calvinist minority marked a fateful development in the Netherlandish revolt. For, at the critical moment, Alva found it necessary to turn his *tercios* southward to counter the threatened invasion by French troops. If the St. Bartholomew's Massacre abruptly ended Coligny's plans for uniting France against Spain, his diversion in the Netherlands had allowed the Calvinist revolt to consolidate itself in Holland and Zeeland behind the river system. Twenty years later, Philip ordered his great general Parma to relieve Paris, and for the second time a diversion compelled Spain decisively to lose her grip on the prosecution of the struggle in the Netherlands. The configuration of the rivers and the intransigence of a Calvinist minority began to define a new nation: the United Provinces. In effect, Calvinism captured a revolt. It was the achievement of a convinced, often fanatical, minority which by 1600 numbered only ten per cent of the population.

In addition to the constitutional tensions experienced by European countries, Geneva's alliance with Zurich significantly promoted the advance of the reform. Having begun to attenuate the notion of the Real Presence in his doctrine of the eucharist, Calvin the ecumenicist traveled to Zurich in 1549 to reach an accord with Bullinger. The resulting Zurich *Consensus* represented a definite modification of Calvin's doctrine in a Zwinglian direction. The accord strengthened enormously Calvin's Swiss base, but it inevitably impaired his relations with the Lutherans and led to a rupture. After 1546 Lutheranism had fallen apart in the struggle between the more flexible moderates represented by Melanchthon and the super-orthodox intransigents. Despite Calvinist penetration of the Melanchthonian camp, differences over the doctrine of the eucharist led the Genevan reformer into some nasty scuffles with Lutheran theologians. Increasingly disillusioned by Lutherans after the master's death, Calvin became convinced that the reform must find better bases outside of Germany. The *Consensus* held, preventing any real accord with the Lutheran wing, and continued to serve as the basis for the collaboration between Zurich and Geneva. Vital both to the definition of "Calvinism" and to its advance in Europe was the Second Helvetic Confession (1566), composed by Bullinger in 1561, accepted by his Protestant neighbors, and given to the Elector Frederick III of the Palatinate in 1565; together with the Heidelberg Catechism of 1563, it constituted the cornerstone of the Reformed Church. The two documents marked the Swiss reformer's penetration of the Palatinate, the establishment of reformed theology at its university, and the definition of a eucharistic doctrine that owed more to Zurich than to Geneva. Until the outbreak of the Thirty Years' War in 1618, Heidelberg and the Palatinate would provide a new center for Calvinism in Europe.

The cooperation of Bullinger with Calvin and his successor Beza gave the Reformed Church that form and direction which would allow it to stand up against a revived Catholicism. Awesome as are the dimensions of Calvin's vast surviving correspondence, they are nevertheless dwarfed by those of Bullinger's —almost three times as large and still to be critically assessed. The letters of both reformers, addressed to the churches, statesmen, and rulers of Europe, often possess the quality of encyclicals, counselling, exhorting, and instructing; they helped to create a movement of international scope. Both men served as the outstanding hosts and theological luminaries to the Marian exiles and as advisers to the Reformation in England. Bullinger preceded Calvin in the Netherlands, where the works of the Zurich theologian enjoyed in the forties an astonishing reception. In Italy the works of both Calvin and Bullinger, products of a city-state environment, came to displace those of Luther among the heretical literature in the vernacular. From Geneva the 1557 Italian edition of the *Institutes* spearheaded a flood of anti-Roman propaganda and evangelical theology that traveled clandestinely throughout the peninsula. A year before the first French version, the *Institutes* had been translated into Spanish and published at Ghent (1540). In distant Spain the ill-defined "Lutherans" of the earlier period crystallized as scattered groups of Calvinists in Valladolid and Seville (1559–60). Geneva's greater proximity made her influence more apparent in Spain. Nevertheless, even in France, the primary target of Calvin's reforming efforts, Bullinger had contacts and left his mark in the controversy on ecclesiastical polity in 1571.

In Eastern Europe the advance of Calvinism proved spectacular, but to a large extent ephemeral. The kingdom of Poland-Lithuania, stretching from the Baltic to the Carpathians and almost to the Black Sea, was ruled more by a democracy of the nobility than by its elected monarch. With its denial of any absolute authority over religion, Calvinism appealed to a landholding class asserting its independence. Reformed doctrine received wide acceptance among the nobles, who expected their subjects to adopt the new religion. One of the most powerful magnates, Nicholas Radziwill, brought vast estates and innumerable dependents over to Calvinism. Johannes à Lasco, disciple of Erasmus, minister first of the church at Emden and later of that of the refugees in London, returned home to try to fuse a single national Protestant church out of the groups of Lutherans, Bohemian Brethren, and Calvinists in Poland. By the time of his death in 1560, Poland was rapidly becoming an asylum for the Antitrinitarians, led by radical Italian reformers. The growing specter of Socinianism in Poland plagued the last months of Calvin's life and drove the existing Protestant groups to arrive at the Consensus of Sandomierz in 1570. But the divisions that vitiated relations between Lutherans and Calvinists in Germany communicated themselves to Poland and by 1595 the Lutherans had withdrawn from the agreement. The rapid recovery of Catholicism in Poland owed much to the inner divisions among Protestants and to the fact that the appeal of Calvinism was preeminently to the nobility. The Genevan model, derived from a Western urban context, had little meaning for a peasantry that was approaching the condition of serfdom. In Hungary and Transylvania, where Bullinger's counsel and sacramentarianism had early been evident, the same social conditions existed. Nevertheless the presence of the relatively tolerant Turk prevented the advance of the Counter-Reformation until the 1670s, and enabled Calvinism to persist as a major religion, particularly among the nobility.

Through the collaboration of the two foci of Swiss reform, a Calvinist Europe began to crystallize confessionally in the last years of Calvin's life: in 1559 the Gallican Confession, in 1560 the Scottish Confession, in 1561 the Belgic Confession, in 1562 the Hungarian Confession, in 1563 the Heidelberg Catechism. Protestantism looked to Geneva for discipline and ecclesiastical polity, to Zurich for sacramentarian doctrine. Beza, Calvin's undisputed successor, continued this cooperation. Under his presidency the characteristic features of Calvin's doctrine became more inflexible. This process of hardening was partly the work of the overly faithful and enthusiastic epigoni, partly a product of the siege mentality that settled upon Geneva after 1564, when she became an island in the surrounding Savoyard territories. First through Beza and later with the Heidelberg theologians, Calvin's idea of predestination came to assume an unnatural prominence. With respect to ecclesiastical polity, Beza waged a dangerous struggle with Jean Morély from 1562 until the National Synod of 1571 at La Rochelle. Morély sought to decentralize the church in France, and advanced a congregationalist polity in which laymen might assume a large role in virtually autonomous congregations. Compared to Calvin, who had been capable of suggesting a reformed episcopal order to the king of Poland, Beza appeared rigid in his presbyterianism.

The issue of ecclesiastical polity strained without disrupting the accord between Beza and Bullinger. Since the 1530s Zurich had claimed to detect a "papist" ring in Farel and Calvin's efforts to achieve a degree of independence for the church. The first clash between the rival polities had occurred with Bern's successful struggle against Lausanne in the fifties, whereby she imposed the Zwinglian order of a unitary Christian magistracy on the Pays de Vaud. One of the last acts of Bullinger's life was to appeal successfully to Beza in 1575 concerning Calvinist excesses in the exercise of excommunication in the Palatinate. One of the victims was a medical doctor, Thomas Erastus, who became the foremost exponent of a single, secularly-controlled jurisdiction in a Christian commonwealth. The continental rivalry between two different ecclesiastical polities, kept within bounds by Beza's collaboration with Bullinger, spread to England and would play a role in the civil war there in the following century.

The Reformation in Perspective

The Reformation grew out of the depths of a church that sacramentally and legally embraced all of society. If the progress of this movement was shaped by the social-political currents of the age, its point of origin is to be found in a question of authority raised by a troubled conscience and not in particular abuses. The late medieval church, through a process of excessive institutionalization, had sacrificed spirit to structure and had come to confuse authority with its own practices and judgments. Confusion over the actual tradition of the church was aggravated in the schools by the rending of scripture into a collection of arguments and propositions for philosophical inquiry. In each process scripture, the ultimate source of knowledge of the faith, had lost its unity and integrity. A jumble of competing images cluttered people's minds, as well as the naves of churches. Luther's insight had the effect of restoring to the center of Christian experience not simply the unity and authority of scripture but also the overriding fact of Christ as personal Savior. At Augsburg, Leipzig, and Worms, he exalted scripture above all other authorities, patristic, canonistic, and papal, defying a church grown overly confident in the exercise of its massive power.

To a religiously-starved generation Christ now appeared neither as a pious memory nor as a symbol in the mass but in the full and present reality of His person, communicated to the believer preeminently through the Bible—freshly and pungently translated and widely disseminated by the printing press. The direct encounter between Christ and the Christian who takes on the person of Christ was no longer a subject-object relationship, but one between persons in which Christ is always the same, a continuing reality. Here Luther and the Reformation struck a modern note and capitalized upon a strain in the experience of the Renaissance. What Catholic historians call "subjectivism," the profoundly spiritual event of personal appropriation, first emerged in the humanism of Petrarch, was shifted by Lorenzo Valla from classical texts to those of the early church, refocused by Erasmus on the example of Christ, and altered again by Luther to pertain to the gift of Christ. An essentially doctrinal reform, Christocentric and theocentric in character, it had an immense and immediate impact upon men thirsting for God in a society saturated with religion.

The reassertion of the divine initiative reoriented man from a straining for merits and external satisfaction to a new discovery of the self, its reception of the gift of faith, and the effective working of faith in man's calling and daily life. The reintegration of the outer and inner self in the concept of the calling would later attain its culmination in the Puritan who scrutinizes his inmost being and its performance for evidence of the Holy Spirit's operation in his life. Man attains a new complexity by appropriating the added dimension of direct moral and religious responsibility; he must be a monk, but a monk in the world. Life is no longer an artistic performance of the personality, as in the Renaissance, nor a flight into the imaginary world of the chivalric vision, but a duty, an obligation, a task. From the portraits of Lucas Cranach the Elder a new seriousness stares back at us.

Laicity, not to be confused with secularism, attained through the Reformation decisive expression in the realm of religion. The age wanted more religion and less clericalism. Sociologically, the Reformation was a movement of citizens whose claims upon the religious sphere Luther early articulated in his redefinition of the Christian estate, the doctrine of the priesthood of all believers, and again in the idea of the calling. Yet Luther was too reliant upon the territorial prince and remained fatefully unable to take full advantage of his own breakthrough. In an urban context, Zwingli the "democrat" and Calvin the jurist consciously sought to develop the motif of laicity. Through Calvin's ecclesiastical polity the lay element found effective expression.

Calvin's ecclesiology had the peculiar capacity of promoting at once a heightened laicism and a revived clericalism. If Protestantism was to survive after 1540, it had to be coherently institutionalized and submit to an up-to-date clericalism. Yet the presence of laymen as powerful elders in the consistories and the ability of the church to draw upon lay energies immeasurably strengthened Calvinist ecclesiastical polity. According to a pattern first evinced in the London church of Johannes à Lasco, "prophesying," as it was called, became common practice: in the French churches every Tuesday occurred a meeting of ministers, elders, and *designati*—a special category of laity—allowing the church effectively to penetrate more deeply into the community. They met for a reading and careful explication of the Bible, and to test the minister and his doctrine. In time the congregational challenge, originating in the French churches, became an instrument of lay control over ecclesiastical life.

The Reformation had sought to achieve a restoration of Christian community. On the most basic level—namely, individual witness and worship within local churches and congregations—the reformers succeeded in revitalizing the service through congregational hymn-singing, the use of the vernacular, and an improved preaching. The use of the vernaculars corrected a major ailment in the late medieval church. For, as Farel had early observed, if prayer and devotion had been meaningfully conducted in a language intelligible to the people, darkness would never have fallen upon the church. The ordinary layman became once more a participant. Yet the unity and more profound participation achieved in the eucharist through incorporation in Christ were fatefully displaced. The pruning and reduction of the mass had the effect of impoverishing a service already overly didactic and narrowly focused upon the pulpit.

With regard to the community of Christendom, the reformers failed to carry the whole of the church with them, thus perpetrating schism. Religious division decisively enhanced the opportunities of princes for controlling more effectively the already existing territorial churches. Nevertheless, the hallmark of the reformers' conservatism was their refusal to abandon the notion of the *corpus christianum:* collaboration between the spiritual and the secular authority was what constituted community. In the empire, Lutheranism both hastened and supplemented the advent of the territory as a moral-religious community for the upbringing of subjects under the patriarchal absolutism of the prince. In an age of political consolidation, no religion could withstand the control of the state. Nevertheless Calvinism, in alliance with estates, was the best equipped to limit this development. The divisions created within Christianity prepared the way for a decisively secular and territorial definition of community.

Reformation had led to schism. At what point did this schism occur? Did it arise inevitably from the clash of two fundamentally different doctrinal positions? Or was it essentially a product of historical circumstances, a terrible misunderstanding aggravated by personal styles and the accidental limitations of institutions? Certainly there existed several conditions which seriously impaired communication between established authority and reforming dissent: the deafness of the church in 1517, the animosity existing between rival religious orders, the escalating violence of Luther's polemic, the current belief that nothing about a heretic could possibly possess any veracity or goodness, and the structure of *corpus christianum* which allowed for no dissent on fundamental matters. If extrinsic, these factors undeniably promoted a rupture by driving Luther to a more strident definition of the issue. Was justification by faith alone that issue? Luther's discovery was new to him but, except for the intensity with which it was held, familiar to the medieval church and the Augustinian tradition. The continuing respect for Augustine and fascination with the Pauline epistles helped to create, together with Erasmus's later writings, a religion of justification by faith that blurred ecclesiastical and confessional boundaries. At Ratisbon in 1541, it was not the doctrine of justification upon which an agreement faltered. Rather, it was that of the eucharist—the chief source of division and confessionalism. Yet the initial differences over the eucharist and the papacy that emerged in Luther's tracts of 1519–1520 were but expressions of a deeper rift. On ultimate authority in the church Luther differed from Rome after 1518. Scripture—self-evident, self-communicating, self-interpreting as Christ, the Word of God—became the critical norm for judging the entire life of the church, its creature. This critical principle of scripture directly conflicted with the Catholic view of scripture, which made the church its interpreter. For Luther, the Word of God was the agent of man's justification and opposed the sacramental and juridical structure of the contemporary church.

The Reformation had been advanced as much by humanistic preparation as by the support of secular princes. Erasmian humanism, incorporating a biblical Christianity, represented the most powerful intellectual current of the age. More than any other development, it provided that broad ground of reform upon which the Protestant Reformation could build. Yet as Erasmus, the advocate of evangelical peace and Christian community, recognized, Luther's violence would disrupt both Christendom and the whole humanist program of reform. The very strength of northern humanism proved to be its weakness: its subtle, pervasive influence over several generations defied adequate institutional expression. On the other hand, the Reformation rapidly succeeded in institutionalizing itself. The collapse of the splendid ideal of a reformed Christendom, united and reconciled to moral and practical reform, which had been advanced by the moderates in the thirties, left two irreconcilable camps and divided the humanists. Motivated by respect for the traditional order, the majority remained with the old church. Only over the next century would the residuum of humanism, aided by the impact of religious wars, erode the confessionally hard magnitudes and, by seeking to define a neutral ground, point to a secularly ordered society.

The Reformation confronted the most fundamental problem of church history: the relationship of the church to the world, or God's redeeming purpose, howsoever instituted, for unredeemed mankind. By shattering the traditional unity of Christendom, the Reformation appears from the perspective of the present to have affirmed a process of secularization originating in the early fourteenth century. Although it contributed greatly, if inadvertently, to this end, the charge of secularization applies more properly to other contemporary forces, such as the emerging state and humanism. Calvin and Luther reacted against the "modernism" of Renaissance philosophical influences as well as against the contemporary church, for they believed that both subverted the primacy and centrality of Christ. Considered in terms of its intentions and initial impact, the Reformation represents a momentous readjustment of church to world—the last major effort in Western history to adjust the mantle of religion to cover all aspects of life. In the eleventh century, Gregory VII had met the problem by exalting the role of the clergy and extending the bounds of its jurisdiction to bring the world within its control. Luther consciously undid this process, snapping the juridical links in both theology and ecclesiology and replacing them with moral and religious ones. Among the greatest achievements of the Reformation was its attention to church order in an effort to reincorporate a New Testament sense of fellowship and restore vitality to individual congregations; nevertheless, the dominant influence of the individual evangelical experience had in time the effect of rendering secondary other currents and motifs, including ecclesiastical polity. Through the primacy of justification by faith, and its corollary in the doctrine of the calling, the evangelized person rather than the institutional church became the bearer of Christian witness in the world.

Selected Bibliography

Of the numerous general studies on the Reformation, this essay is particularly indebted to Emile G. Léonard, *La Réformation,* vol. 1 of *Histoire générale du Protestantisme* (Paris, 1961), and Erwin Iserloh, *Die protestantische Reformation,* that constitutes half of *Reformation, Katholische Reform und Gegenreformation,* Handbuch der Kirchengeschichte, edited by Hubert Jedin, vol. 4 (Freiburg, im Br., 1967). The first written by a Protestant, the second by a Catholic, both are ecumenical in approach and arresting in conceptualization. Neither, however, does justice to the Reformation in France.

On late medieval ecclesiastical polity and conciliarism, the following are outstanding: Michael Wilks, *The Problem of Sovereignty in the Later Middle Ages,* (Cambridge, 1963) ; Brian Tierney, *The Foundations of the Conciliar Theory* (Cambridge, 1955) ; and Hubert Jedin, *A History of the*

Council of Trent, vol. 1, translated by Dom Ernest Graf (London, 1957). Useful for the emergence of church-state relations is W. Bertram, *Der neuzeitliche Staatsgedanke und die Konkordate des ausgehenden Mittelalters* (Rome, 1942). Though often poorly documented, Imbart de la Tour's *Les origines de la Réforme,* vol. 2 (Melun, 1946), is still valuable for the condition of the church in France. Important for understanding the relations between ecclesiastical structure and urban polity is Alfred Schultze, "Stadtgemeinde und Kirche im Mittelalter," *Festgabe für R. Sohm* (Munich and Leipzig, 1914). On late medieval scholasticism, one should consult the articles of Heiko A. Oberman and his *Harvest of Medieval Theology* (Cambridge, Mass., 1963); on the tone of piety and spiritual life there are the sensitive studies of J. Huizinga, *The Waning of the Middle Ages* (London, 1924), and Lucien Febvre, *Au coeur religieux du XVIe siécle* (Paris, 1937), the latter including insightful essays on the general age and spirit of reform; on the pastorate and liturgy, Josef Jungmann's *Pastoral Liturgy* (New York, 1962) and *The Mass of the Roman Rite* (New York, 1961), and Gregory Dix's *The Shape of the Liturgy* (London, 1945) are outstanding.

On Hus, Matthew Spinka's *John Hus' Concept of the Church* (Princeton, 1966) is a sane product of recent Czech scholarship; Howard Kaminsky ably presents the radical development following Hus in *A History of the Hussite Revolution* (Berkeley, 1967). For the Northern Renaissance and reform three works warrant special mention: Paul Mestwerdt, *Die Anfänge des Erasmus* (Leipzig, 1917); Myron Gilmore, "Fides et Eruditio: Erasmus and the Study of History" in *Teachers of History: Essays in Honor of Lawrence Bradford Packard* (Ithaca, 1954); and P. Albert Duhamel, "The Oxford Lectures of John Colet," *Journal of the History of Ideas* 14 (1953): 493–510.

For Luther, the basic source is his own works and correspondence in the authoritative Weimar edition (1883–), parts of which are being redone as the edition attains completion. The Muhlenburg and Concordia presses (Philadelphia and St. Louis) are jointly in the process of publishing most of Luther's writings. Of the innumerable works on Luther himself, particular notice should be given to Karl Holl, *Luther,* vol. 1 of *Gesammelte Aufsätze zur Kirchengeschichte* (Tübingen, 1923), which effectively brought Luther scholarship into the twentieth century. Outside of the vast literature by German scholars, the works of three notable writers in English have contributed greatly to the field: F. Edward Cranz's *An Essay on the Development of Luther's Thought on Justice, Law, and Society* (Cambridge, Mass., 1959); Wilhelm Pauck's *The Heritage of the Reformation* (Boston, 1950), which also includes some important articles on Bucer and Calvin, his "The Ministry in the Time of the Continental Reformation," pp. 110–47 in *The Ministry in Historical Perspective,* edited by H. Richard Niebuhr and Daniel D. Williams (New York, 1956), and his edition of *Luther: Lectures on Romans,* Library of Christian Classics, vol. 15 (Philadelphia, 1961); and

Ernest G. Rupp's sensitive and perceptive *The Righteousness of God* (London, 1953) and more popular and biographical *Luther's Progress to the Diet of Worms* (London, 1957). The best of modern Catholic research on Luther and the Reformation in Germany is represented by Joseph Lortz, *Die Reformation in Deutschland* (Freiburg, 1962), and by Lortz's student Erwin Iserloh, *op. cit.* On the eucharistic question, Yngve Brilioth, *Eucharistic Faith and Practice, Evangelical and Catholic* (London, 1953), and Herman Sasse, *This is My Body* (Minneapolis, 1959) can be consulted with profit. On Luther and Erasmus, C. R. Thompson's introduction to his edition of the *Inquisitio de fide* (New Haven, 1950) is magisterial. Excellent on the question of toleration and political thought for the entire age in Europe is Joseph Lecler, *Histoire de la tolérance au siécle de la Réforme* ([Paris], 1955), available in English (*Toleration and the Reformation,* translated by T. L. Westow, [New York, 1960], 2 vols.). Concerning Luther's ecclesiastical polity, Emil Sehling's *Geschichte der protestantische Kirchenverfassung* (Berlin, 1914) significantly takes issue with Rudolf Sohm's thesis that no legal order properly belongs in Luther's concept of the church. On humanist influences in the thirties, R. Stupperich's *Der Humanismus und die Wiedervereinigung der Konfessionen* (Leipzig, 1936) is important. Heinrich Lutz, *Christianitas Afflicta* (Göttingen, 1964) is a superb study of Europe and the empire in the decisive years of Charles V's collapse in Germany.

The cities in the age of the Reformation have received a good deal of attention since Hans Baron's pioneering articles: "Religion and Politics in the German Imperial Cities during the Reformation," *English Historical Review* 52 (1937): 405–27, 614–33, and "Calvinist Republicanism and its Historical Roots," *Church History* 8 (1939): 30–42. The most outstanding work in formulating the problem and the issues is Berndt Moeller, *Reichsstadt und Reformation* (Gütersloh, 1962). Less synoptic but more specific are Gerald Strauss, *Nuremberg in the Sixteenth Century* (New York, 1966); Miriam Usher Chrisman, *Strasbourg and the Reform* (New Haven, 1967); E. William Monter, *Calvin's Geneva* (New York, 1967); and Robert C. Walton, *Zwingli's Theocracy* (Toronto, 1967), which focuses on Zwingli's idea of Christian community as evinced in Zurich. From the social point of view, in conflict with Walton and recent German research, is Norman Birnbaum, "The Zwinglian Reformation in Zurich," *Past and Present* 15 (April, 1959): 27–47. On Zwingli's career, Oskar Farner, *Huldrych Zwingli* (Zürich, 1943–60) emphasizes the political. On his early development Arthur Rich, *Die Anfänge der Theologie Huldrych Zwinglis* (Zürich, 1949) is definitive. Walther Koehler, one of the greatest Zwingli scholars, wrote an important study of the marriage court and its significant aftermath, *Zürcher Ehegericht und Genfer Konsistorium* (Leipzig, 1932–42). For his theology, a balanced Catholic approach is that of J. V. Pollet in the *Dictionnaire de théologie catholique;* the same author's *Huldrych Zwingli et la Réforme en Suisse* (Paris, 1963) is incisive. On Bucer, Pollet's *Martin Bucer: Etudes sur la correspondence* (Paris, 1958, 1962) presents penetrating studies of individual documents and correspondence. Bucer's writings are in the process of being edited and published. Particularly important for his concept of the church is volume seven of the *Opera omnia, Martin Bucers Deutsche Schriften,* edited by R. Stupperich (Gütersloh, 1964). On Calvin, the standard biography and general study of his theology is François Wendel, *Calvin— Origins and Development of his Religious Thought,* trans. Philip Mairet (New York, 1950). Alexander Ganoczy, *Le Jeune Calvin* (Wiesbaden, 1966) is an extremely important contribution to Calvin's development to 1536 and is particularly suggestive on such problems as vocation, schism, conversion, and reform. For the relation between Calvin and Luther, Brian A. Gerrish, "John Calvin on Luther," in *Interpreters of Luther,* edited by Jaroslav Pelikan (Philadelphia, 1968) is useful. Articles appearing in *Zwingliana* constitute an important secondary source for the Swiss reform.

On the diffusion of Calvinism, besides the writings and correspondence of Calvin himself, *op. cit,* the correspondence of Beza, in the process of being published, is most valuable especially for its rich annotation: *Correspondence de Théodore de Bèze,* edited by Henri Meylan, Alain Dufour *et al.* (Geneva, 1960–), 6 volumes to date. The John T. McNeill–Ford Lewis Battles edition of the *Institutes* for The Library of Christian Classics (Philadelphia, 1960) represents the definitive rendering of this work in English. The numerous works of Lucien Romier on the period 1550–62 emphasize the political nature of the religious wars: *Les origines politiques des guerres de religion* (Paris, 1913–14). More sensitive to the religious aspects are the absolutely essential studies of Robert M. Kingdon, *Geneva and the Coming of the Wars of Religion in France 1555–63* (Geneva, 1956), and the *Consolidation of the French Protestant Movement* (Geneva, 1967). Paul F. Geisendorf, *Théodore de Bèze* (Paris, 1949) is an important supplement. For Calvin's political thought, Hans Baron, *Calvins Staatsanschauung und das konfessionelle Zeitalter* (Berlin, 1924) cannot be overlooked. Articles of decisive importance for the general problem are Alain Dufour, "Le mythe de Genève au temps de Calvin," *Schweizerische Zeitschrift für Geschichte* 9 (1959): 489–518; H. G. Koenigsberger, "The Organization of Revolutionary Parties in France and the Netherlands during the Sixteenth Century," *Journal of Modern History* 27 (1955): 335–51; and G. N. Clark, "The Birth of the Dutch Republic", *Proceedings of the British Academy* 32 (1946): 189–219. General treatments of Calvinist Europe and late sixteenth century Lutheranism can be found in E. G. Léonard's second volume, *L'Etablissement* (Paris, 1961), Ernst Walter Zeeden's *Das Zeitalter der Gegenreformation* (Freiburg, 1967), and T. M. Parker's incisive article "Protestantism and Confessional Strife" in the *New Cambridge Modern History,* vol. 3 (Cambridge, 1968), pp. 72–125. On the rival Swiss ecclesiastical polities, Helmut Kressner, *Schweizer Ursprünge des anglikanischen Staatskirchentums* (Gütersloh, 1953) ably presents the issues.

The Submission of the Clergy Act (approved in 1532–33) forbade Convocation to legislate except with the consent of the crown and permitted the crown to appoint a committee to review canons passed by Convocation. Sixty-six bishops signed the document in 1533. ADD. Mss 38, 656, folio 3. Copyright The British Museum.

5.

The English Reformation

ARTHUR J. SLAVIN

THE FOLLOWING ACCOUNT of the English Reformation makes use of what might be called the method of political analysis. This procedure has the advantage of dispensing with the appearance of inevitability and predetermination that so often inform histories which locate the roots of all reform in the failure of "tradition" to meet new challenges. It also subordinates stress on "conditions in society" which favor the rise of "movements," allowing the inertia of tradition and social dynamics a place in the story of how men by their conscious acts changed religious life and institutions when the opportunity arose to do so. We thus achieve a double perspective on the Reformation and can see in it an effort to resurrect a fondly-imagined "golden age of Christian life" as well as a revolution. For the Reformation did become a conscious effort to restore the past, while it was producing changes in society which transformed political organization, altered the control of property, wrenched old social structures off their foundations, and began the creation of a new myth of social order and justice.

The Secular Power of the Church

The Church in England was part of the mystical body of Christ and of the communion of the faithful. It was also a powerful and rich landlord. It had shared in the profits of agricultural expansion which accompanied population growth in Europe between about 1050 and the mid-fourteenth century. As virgin land came under the plow, the classic outlines of lordship developed. With it there came constant shifts in the value of land, money, and labor and in the social obligations which rested on land. Hence the ties which bound the faithful to the church in worship were reinforced by contacts of an entirely secular nature. During the era of expansion before the Black Death, the church built new parish units and widened the scope of its services in older settlements, paying the bills out of the profits of agriculture. It obliged lay lords and powerful secular interests by distributing gifts, leases, and offices. Prosperity facilitated the harmonizing of interests of the lay and clerical elites and allowed the church to be fully integrated into the social order of an agrarian society with a minimum of conflict.

The acute dislocation of the labor force which resulted from the Black Death (1347–1350) and subsequent plague epidemics which raged well into the 1500s ended this happy situation. The economy contracted. Land newly brought into production fell out of use. Famine and disease took a terrible toll, while panic and apocalyptic speculation grew. Labor became increasingly scarce. Where workers could be found, they demanded higher wages, personal freedom, and release from the bondage which had been fundamental to the society in which the church had expanded its wealth and power. Cultivation of the demesne by unfree peasants had served as the backbone of institutional life and paid the bills for clerical education. Abbots and bishops knew how futile it was to separate the wealth of the church from the cure of souls. Authority and religious discipline rested on land.

To cope with increased labor costs and shrinking demands for food as the population declined in the period 1350–1450, landlords often relinquished direct management of estates by leasing their demesnes to farmers.[1] The church thus underwent an involuntary conversion from seigneurial lordship to the collection of rents. Individuals and corporations also solved problems of labor-intensive cultivation by abandoning grain farming for sheep-raising or other enterprises which required little labor. But cutting the wage bill also meant dissolving traditional social relationships, obligations rooted in tenures which bound peasants to the will and interests of their lords. Feudal relations gave way to the more fluid ties which characterize wage contracts at every level in systems of agrarian capitalism. Hence the choices necessary to adjust to population change and accompanying shifts in the economy were painful. Should one obligate men to services once freely given but now deemed odious? Or ride out the storm by yielding control of the peasant and surrendering the rights inherent in the direct exploitation of the land?

That this was no abstract dilemma can be proved by looking closely at the records of a great church lordship, that of the Archbishop of Canterbury. After about 1350 there is no evidence in his manorial records of men rendering homage and allegiance.[2] In his courts, once-dependent men insist he recognize their simple freedom and newly-won titles of social distinction. All the evidence points to a gradual transfer to laymen of powers and initiatives formerly in clerical hands. By the middle of the fifteenth century, the gentry[3] of the counties had come to dominate relationships in which they had once been subordinate. These changes were accompanied by a growing abrasiveness in lay-clerical contacts and proved to be one of the deep roots of anticlerical feeling in the century before the Reformation. Farmers rankled at paying old dues. There were rent strikes among peasants. Skirmishes broke out because of the customary exercise of church jurisdiction over laymen in special ecclesiastical courts. Tenants evicted from church lands came to look on the local clergy as oppressors. Priests, formerly held in great esteem, were no longer so regarded as traditional values and hospitality were sold at a discount. Worse yet, some clerics beset with bad neighbors used whatever force lay at hand to discipline them, often confusing attacks prompted by strong passions with sacrilege. It was a time when merely putting a man on notice in church courts meant wrongful persecution as well as rightful prosecution.

The operation of the church courts was thus a particular grievance, the more so as the secular interests of the church seemed to threaten men's property as well as their souls. A system of courts Christian, which had arisen, side by side with the ordinary secular courts, supervised the affairs of the clergy, protected the clergy in relations with laymen, and exercised jurisdiction over laymen in matters of religion, morals, and certain other areas reserved from the secular courts. To look at their areas of jurisdiction is to grasp the courts' potential for provoking conflict. They judged worldly behavior as well as crimes against doctrine and ritual. Men might find themselves charged with riotous conduct in church, failure to pay tithes and other "spiritual dues," sexual misconduct, or heresy. They might also be indicted for matters of matrimony or wills. The law administered in the ecclesiastical courts was Rome's canon law rather than the common law of the realm. And the penalties imposed, which ranged from minor penances to total excommunication, tended to destroy men's credit and reputation. In the case of relapsed heretics, secular authority was invoked to carry out the death sentence which courts Christian could not execute.

The jurisdiction of these courts infringed heavily on the lives of laymen. The two issues which excited the most resentment were doubtless tithes and heresy. The celebrated murder of Richard Hunne in 1514 by agents of the Bishop of London arose out of a petty dispute about property in which a priest claimed as a mortuary duty the winding sheet in which Hunne's infant son had been wrapped. The London merchant refused to pay, and a long series of suits and countersuits eventually led to his imprisonment in Lollard's Tower, where he was found hanged. The jury refused to find a verdict of suicide, instead indicting several clerks of the London diocesan administration for willful murder. Before the furor abated, the Bishop of London feared to leave his house because of anticlerical hatred, and the king himself had to intervene to keep the offending clerks from being tried on the murder charges.

The case of Hunne illustrates in microcosm how fear and resentment of the church courts fed anticlericalism. Surviving records make it apparent that men resented the incomprehensible Latin procedures, excessive and oppressive fees, the vexatious suits, and the constant threat to property rights posed by the courts' power to prove wills. The outcome of Hunne's case, which began as a dispute about an indirect tax, was a posthumous sentence of notorious heresy and the public burning of the exhumed body of a man whose cause seemed just in the eyes of most ordinary Londoners.

When the London annalist Charles Wriothesley[4] noted in his *Chronicle* that "Hunne was made a heretic" because he had challenged clerical pretensions, he implicitly contrasted the widely differing powers of Hunne's dead body and those of the quick Bishop of London, Fitzjames.[5] The equation of resistance to a tax on death with heresy greatly escalated anticlerical sentiment. It also highlighted the fact that little dissent from the lower ranks of society was tolerated in early Tudor society. The crown and the church agreed that plebeians if given scope for their complaints, might upset the order of things. Men in power acted as though the willful use of force might itself reinvigorate authority weakened by unseemly secular ambitions.

The Failures of the Clergy

If the courts Christian stoked the furnaces of lay discontent with the fuel of excessive zeal, the great vested property interests of the church added readily combustible material. The visible sins of the hierarchy and the daily contacts of the parishioner with his often too-worldly priest were fundamental causes of alienation. In order to fully understand the causes and course of the Reformation in England after 1529, we must therefore look at the prelates and the parochial clergy. In the habits of great ecclesiastics we can see the stuff of which agitation for reform was made—especially in Wolsey, the gaudiest animal in the ark of the Church. And in humble, poverty-ridden parish priests we will encounter the failure of the church in its daily contacts with the faithful.

The *secular clergy* was responsible for pastoral care, under the headship of seventeen bishops and the archbishops of Canterbury and York. Ranged below these princes were lesser elites of clerical administrators of- the law and finances, diplomats, choirmasters, and cathedral canons, as well as many well-educated clerics employed in the king's government and supported by church endowments. Their incomes varied greatly, from the few pounds of a young aspiring administrator to the many thousands of the rich and powerful bishops of London, Winchester, Lincoln, and York.

Above them all, from 1515 to 1529, loomed the colossal figure of Wolsey, the "Great Cardinal" and chief minister of Henry VIII. This careerist's rise to power came on the heels of his demonstration of competence as a war minister during the Anglo-French campaigns of 1513–1514. Gaining early notice as an Oxford don and in the service of the well-connected marquess of Dorset, Thomas Grey,[6] Wolsey had risen rapidly in the service of Henry VIII. By 1515 he had achieved a degree of power in both church and state which no earlier prelate had exceeded and few, if any, had equalled. Perhaps only Becket, who had been both chancellor of England and archbishop of Canterbury, and the great Henry Beaufort—chancellor, cardinal, and legate *a latere*—approached the influence amassed by this son of an Ipswich butcher. By 1519 a Venetian observer could note that "this cardinal is the man who rules both the king and the entire kingdom." Himself a Renaissance prince in pomp and authority, Wolsey lived for glory. He showed the king how the wealth and power of the church could enhance the dignity of the monarchy, chiefly by using his combined authorities to assert English influence in the sphere of international affairs. For a time Wolsey became the arbiter of Europe.

To his power he added the trappings of unequalled wealth and patronage. A stern disciplinarian in the exercise of episcopal and secular authority, Wolsey enhanced the prestige of the king, often at the expense of the aristocrats who surrounded both king and cardinal. After obtaining the cardinalate from Rome in 1515, he added to his ordinary powers of papal legate *natus,* which inhered in every metropolitan bishopric, a special status as legate *a latere* for life. This position involved massive powers, including that of general reformation of ills in the church in England. Wolsey showed himself not at all reluctant to use these powers, often to the dismay of other bishops and of William Warham, Archbishop of Canterbury, who found himself subordinated to his junior archbishop of York. While Wolsey's contributions to English spiritual life may have been minor, he was always a staunch champion of clerical privilege and maintained the power and dignity of the church when it was most unpopular—in the aftermath of the Hunne case, for example—and in other circumstances when lesser men might have drawn back. Yet he also showed himself unsympathetic to Parliament and to the legislative assembly (Convocation) of the provinces of York and Canterbury. In his personal life he was far from blameless. Rich beyond comparison, he built lavishly, provoked the king's jealousy by the scale of his projects at Whitehall and Hampton Court, sired a bastard son on whom he showered church preferments with a net worth of nearly three thousand pounds per annum, accumulated a number of bishoprics (Bath and Wells, Durham, and Winchester) in addition to York, and farmed the incomes of Salisbury, Worcester, and Llandaff, whose nonresident Italian bishops drew only fixed stipends from their sees. He also converted the courts Christian to courts legatine, using them to coerce his fellow bishops, usurp their patronage, intimidate local officials, and directly control both the filling of benefices and the profits of probate jurisdiction.

Wolsey also exercised vast powers over the monasteries, disciplining some and dissolving about two dozen others on the grounds of irregularities. The funds liberated by their suppression between 1525 and 1528 he applied to the erection of Cardinal's College, Oxford, and the grammar school of St. Mary's, Ipswich. To both he drew humanists and reformers, a fact which we must note to appreciate how fully Wolsey embodied both the flagrant abuses of his time and its best hopes for change. It was not for nothing that Thomas More dedicated his *Utopia* to the cardinal in 1516, nor in vain that Thomas Cromwell, who was to inherit his power in the 1530s, learned in Wolsey's employ both how to manipulate the levers of power and what was amiss in church and commonwealth. During his ministry Wolsey formed palace elites of sycophants. On the other hand, he planned to found thirteen new bishoprics to help administer the needs of the faithful, rescued the youthful Hugh Latimer from a heresy-hunting bishop, and schemed to reform the monasteries. But his attention to reform was diverted by politics, vanity, and the supreme self-interest which marked his career.

Others in the hierarchy were no match for Wolsey in either wealth, pomp, or power. But some were great men, like Foxe of Winchester,[7] an important crown servant under Henry VII and Henry VIII, and Wolsey's early patron. Warham[8] was an ambitious careerist of no particular distinction who enjoyed Canterbury as a reward for political services. Bishops like Fitzjames of London and Tunstal[9] of Durham were learned and humanistically-oriented men who in other times might have served the church as reform leaders. But they and others were caught between the religious aspirations of their order and the king's ambitious expansion of royal power and influence at home and in Europe. Pressed into services they either coveted or learned to find congenial, they deprived the dioceses of England of a vigorous resident episcopal leadership. Under their aegis, hundreds of middle-rank careerists swarmed over the body of the church, picking off benefices and adding income to income to support themselves in the style they deemed suitable to administrators whose attention skittered between the tasks of religion and those of the king. From Wolsey to the archdeacons charged with power over diocesan subdivisions, this pattern of careerism weakened respect for the church among the faithful and sharply isolated the interests of both parishioner and parish priest from those of the elite corps of lawyers, theologians, and accountants who grew rich in God's service.

The conduct of the parochial clergy charged with the cure of souls was not such as to relieve the strain caused by the habits of the great churchmen and their dependents. At the parish level the church was also failing to adequately distinguish secular from religious business. And it was within the parish, the fundamental unit of church government and religious life, that clerical failings were most evident to ordinary people, and thus a continual source of outrage and resentment. The character of the English parish clergy on the eve of the Reformation can shed considerable light on the violent anticlerical outbursts of the 1520s and the programs of reform which shaped the Reformation in the 1530s.

The challenge to the parish priest who wished faithfully to discharge his duties was formidable. He had to preach the Faith; teach the Creed, the Ten Commandments, and the Lord's Prayer; give instructions in the seven deadly sins; and catechize the young in the rudiments of the sacraments which constituted the channels of grace. He was thus charged with the immediate supervision of the whole economy of salvation by which the Christian was brought to God. To fulfill these obligations and the countless small social acts which bound him to his neighbors and his flock, he was provided with an endowment both spiritual and material. He had manuals of devotion and collections of sermons he might mine for his parochial work. These might help him convey to rude and unlettered men the mysteries of grace and God's redeeming mercy—themes prominent in the wall paintings of parish churches, where we find mute testimony to the burden of priestly life. He also had the tithe, or tax in kind, of one-tenth of all that was produced by the laity of the parish, especially the great tithe of grain which was the main economic support of parochial incumbents.

But this rough balance sheet of burdens and endowments begs the important questions: how adequately were the priests trained for their tasks, and how faithfully did they discharge them? For if the odor of sanctity did not cling to every priest, men did not demand saintliness from him as much as they did neighborliness and the orderly provision of guidance. In the parish priest common people found their chief link with the church, a link which was continuous, intense, and likely to breed disillusion and dissent, should it prove weak. If the clerks men encountered on the parish level were often unsuitable, slothful, incompetent, and immoral, how much was this due to indiscriminate ordination and irresponsible exercise of patronage, both lay and ecclesiastical, and how much to such economic factors as the grinding clerical poverty which drove some priests to avarice, pluralism, neglect of duties, and despair? To what extent were parish priests in direct economic and social competition with their flocks? And to what degree were their problems created from above by capricious enforcement of law in courts Christian and defective administration? Was the failure of the church inexplicable, or merely unavoidable in a society where fallible men were endowed with power and privilege?

Recent studies of individual dioceses provide provisional answers to some of these questions. Together with the more intimate approach long favored by historians who have mined the literary sources of complaint and advocacy of reform, the statistical approach made possible by studies of the parish clergy in Lincoln, London, Canterbury, Durham, Bath and Wells, Hereford, Norwich, and York, may serve to clarify the part the parish priest played in the alienation of the church in England from the international church.

The charges of reformers are noteworthy for their unanimity. William Tyndale,[10] a clever and persuasive advocate of reform, wrote many sharp attacks on clerical ways, especially in his *Practice of Prelates*. The book, part of a series of exchanges between the Lutheran apologist and Sir Thomas More, criticizes the way in which the sins of the hierarchy set the pattern for the lower clergy and describes how parish priests ran hungrily after benefices in plurality, neglected preaching, financially exploited the faithful, led gross and corrupt personal lives, and too often sought outside employment that conflicted with parochial needs. While More quarrelled bitterly with Tyndale in matters of doctrine and disputed his remedies for such ills as he acknowledged, it is noteworthy that in *Utopia* and his less famous works priests are most laudable when they are few in number. More feared the contempt in which parishioners held both learned but unworthy priests and their often crude and unlearned colleagues. Other English humanists and reformers shared this fear. William Melton,[11] chancellor of York diocese, a friend of John Colet,[12] and the owner of a fashionable humanist library, published a sermon addressed to newly-ordained priests in 1509 or 1510. In it he argued that a renewed sense of pastoral zeal was needed to defend the clergy against sloth and sin. But priests who were innocent of studies lacked the basic tools of learning which, in Melton's view, alone could save a priest from idleness and sin. And Melton considered far too many ordinands ignorant and unsuitable for their parochial tasks.

Colet, in his *Sermon preached to the Convocation of the Clergy of Canterbury* in 1512, made a wholesale indictment of his audience on the grounds of their failure to sever themselves from worldly riches and thus better to serve the poor in Christ. He specifically charged the mass of the clergy with indiscriminate heresy-hunting; ignorance of scripture; greed in the pursuit of benefices in plurality; commercial competition with parishioners; moral laxity, especially in sins of incontinence; and a host of shortcomings in the daily administration of the sacraments of the church. He also protested the exploitative application of canon law in courts Christian, warning the prelates that such practices led to misplaced zeal among priests and alienated laymen from God's Word. While basically conservative Catholic humanists addressed themselves to particular abuses, aggressive Protestants like Tyndale and mere radical anticlericals of no religious persuasion often magnified the ignorance, negligence, lack of discipline, and avarice of the clergy. But they agreed more than they quarrelled over the grave faults of the parish clergy.

The facts available in obscure records allow us to go beyond the literature of complaint and reform to assay the scale of abuses. This information suggests that the problem had its sources in ordination itself. By the early sixteenth century many newly-examined and ordained priests fraudulently evaded requirements governing their admission to the priesthood. After satisfying examiners as to their age, education, and moral suitability, ordinands had to show that they had title to a living, that is, a guaranteed source of maintenance capable of sustaining them until they found regular employment as priests. Bishops who ordained men without adequate titles were commanded by canon law to support them. But diocesan records indicate that many ordinands were not even examined on this point, and that among those who were, titles were alleged to exist in religious houses which did not actually deliver the promised income. Much evidence suggests that incalculable numbers of clergy connived with such houses, perhaps in order to escape beggary, or secure in the knowledge that if they could overcome the obstacles to ordination they could find safe and undemanding employment in a private household chapel. Many such men sought ordination in a diocese other than that of their residence, where local men might testify to their character and learning. Thus examinations for entry into the priesthood appear to have been lax. The letter of the law was being observed rather than its spirit, and the clergy's ranks were thereby inflated with large numbers of men lacking true vocations and thus likely to bring scandal on the order of priests as a whole.

York diocese achieved the reputation of being such an ordination center. In 1510–1511, 265 men were ordained priests, while 544 took orders as deacons or subdeacons, apparently in the hope that they too could eventually become priests. It is clear that there was no useful employment for such numbers in the diocese, especially when we compare these figures with those from Lincoln. In the whole period 1495–1520, only 2,609 men took final vows as priests in that diocese, where about one-fifth of all parochial cures, or offices, in England were located. York, with far fewer parishes to fill, was ordaining more priests annually. Data from other areas reveal similar patterns.

Many of the priests so inducted into holy orders could not expect to find regular employment. The problem was aggravated by the practice of *appropriations*, whereby a private person or a corporation—monasteries were the worst offenders—became the permanent patron of a parish church. Patronage carried with it the right to name the new priest when a vacancy occurred by death or translation; it also included the right to take the rectorial tithe, that is, the tithe of hay and corn intended for the sustenance of the parish priest. This act of appropriation necessitated the endowment of a vicarage in place of the rectory, and the provision of both an income and a man—the vicar—to do the work of the absentee rector. But many wealthy houses and some cathedral chapters of clergy either did not endow vicarages or did so inadequately. From the funds skimmed off in this way only small stipends or salaries remained, and these clearly inadequate livings did not attract well-educated and zealous clergy to the parish cure of souls. Moreover, in many cases where the appropriation was personal rather than corporate, the absentee rector might be a pluralist serving the king or some agent of ecclesiastical government. Parish livings had thus become items of commerce in the later Middle Ages. More and more rectories were reduced to vicarages; and in the 1400s vicarages themselves were declining in numbers and endowments, while the number of mere salaried cures filled by stipendiary priests and chaplains climbed rapidly. In Lincoln diocese about 1500 there no longer existed any real relationship between titles to livings, ordinations, the number of actual parish benefices to be filled, and the ability of a parish to support the incumbent named to a church living. Half of the total number of parish churches had been appropriated. The king held 123 of them, while great monasteries like Ramsey, Peterborough, Croyland, and Osney held over 200 livings. Thus patronage became concentrated beyond the control of the bishop charged with overseeing the cure of souls in a diocese, and while some priests accumulated benefices others entered the church with no hope of rising to one. The prospect of a sort of clerical vagabondage grew as unbeneficed clergy swelled the ranks of clerical life.

The consequences of such practices were dire. Kings, bishops, abbots, and lay aristocrats used the parish endowments to pay their servants. Benefices were given to nonresident clergy, while absenteeism rose and the holders of parochial positions were increasingly deputies, whether true vicars or mere salaried clergy doing the work without enjoying the fruits of the benefice. The effect of this situation on morale and clerical discipline can hardly be exaggerated, as it meant the creation of a ladder-like progression of clerical elites and proletarians of the church. Nonresidence was greatest in the richest benefices and among the best-educated clergy. Influential priests with powerful patrons gained lucrative posts in which they did no service, procuring easily the licenses which exempted them from the obligation of actually living in their parishes and performing pastoral duties. In one diocese there was little nonresidence in livings worth only four or five pounds, but in those worth more than fifteen pounds, 22 per cent of all priests were reported as absentees. Among the nonresidents in Lincoln diocese, thirty-five of every hundred were university graduates; however, graduates constituted less than 15 percent of the whole number of parish priests. Thus the men best suited by education to an active, preaching parish ministry were the least likely to so serve. This correlation between income and education is vital to understanding how clerical careerism sapped the vitality of the church.

This siphoning-off of income and skilled men from the cure of souls is vitally relevant to questions we have raised about the adequacy of their deputies and other clerks at the parish level, where the potential for alienation was greatest. As curates with titles but no benefices were forced into posts stripped of tithes, the parish faithful were increasingly conscious of the fact that they were often forced to pay in tithe their ultimate egg but could expect little service in return. In the great survey of church endowments undertaken by Henry VIII's government in 1535 (the *Valor Ecclesiasticus*), 87 percent of all parishes were worth less than £20 per annum; 77 percent less than £15; 60 percent less than £10; and one in every ten worth less than £5. This information lends urgency to the opinion of the reformer and Henrician Bishop Hugh Latimer,[13] who thought £10 the line which distinguished poverty from mild affluence for a priest. A lesser income prevented a priest from acting in a neighborly way, buying books, or playing a fruitful role in the life of his community. Latimer saw a causal relationship between the decrease in parish endowments and the prevalence of clerical ignorance and immorality. Edward Lee,[14] archbishop of York during the crucial decade 1535–1544, also noted the relationship between clerical poverty, ignorance among the clergy, and lay alienation from the church. Speaking of his own diocese, he said:

Many benefices be so exile [of income] ... that no learned man will take them, and we be fain therefore to take such as are presented, so they be of honest conversation and can competently understand what they read, and minister the sacraments. And in all my diocese I do not know secular priests that can preach, any number necessary for such a diocese, truly not twelve, and they that have the best benefices be not here resident. ...

The worldly careerism and secular pursuits of some churchmen thus implied the decline in standards of clerical education and moral suitability at the parish level. This was the case at a time when the English clergy as a whole were apparently better-educated than ever before in their history. There had been in the 1400s an expansion of facilities for clerical education in the universities, and the revolution of printing had markedly increased the availability of texts and other aids to the cure of souls. Men who had attended one of the colleges at Oxford or Cambridge were more conspicuous among ordinands; graduates with advanced degrees in law and theology were on the increase in clerical ranks. Such men were certainly adequately educated for their priestly functions, but we have seen that the likelihood of their performing parochial duties decreased in direct proportion to their learning. This meant that priests who perhaps had little more than a year of university training, or, at best a grammar school education, filled the majority of parish livings. There are no statistics which would allow us to speak confidently, for ordination records seldom include educational histories, except in the all-too-rare cases of candidates rejected because of ignorance. But there is reason to believe that some clerks were only slightly better educated than the folk they served, that many knew little Latin besides the canon of the Mass, and that large numbers regarded scripture and the writings of the Church Fathers as closed books. In a world rapidly moving toward the concept of a preaching ministry, this educational poverty caused more discontent among the faithful than it might earlier have done.

More vital still was the fact that unlearned priests, already depressed economically, were more likely to entertain themselves in ways incompatible with their profession. Our evidence supports the charge that many parish priests lived immorally. Complaints about moral failures and a lack of sociability were rife. And popular awareness of such abuses, promoted by shrewd propagandists, made them important as a source of alienation out of proportion to their actual incidence. Ordinary men and women knew that Wolsey had illegitimate children and that he lavished gifts on his son. In a visitation to a Welsh diocese in 1504, eighty priests were cited for incontinence and ordered to give up their mistresses. The cardinal himself was worried enough about incontinence to publish ordinances in 1518 forbidding priests to keep "housekeepers" of an age likely to cause scandal. Concubinage was not rare. At Stratton Audley, the faithful cited their minister as a whoremaster. And in a large number of parishes in Lincoln diocese parishioners complained about clerical immorality.

Even more often noted in complaints by parishioners were offenses by clerks against the fabric of the church and the social and economic life of the parish. Tithe disputes were notorious causes of grievance. In one Leicestershire parish a priest claimed a man's son as a tithe-due because the father had ten sons! Complaints about the use of alms-box funds were frequent. Villagers often cited priests for taking their last cow or other domestic animal in payment of "spiritual dues." At Quadring the pastor was a farmer "in and out of season," which probably meant that he sold tithe grain at prices which undermined the local market. A parson at Fleckely wore his hair too long and was oddly clothed. At Surfleet the priest was a sheep-thief, while the vicar at Wooten lodged his flock in the church aisle and kept his horses in the confessional. The most frequent complaint was that the priest did not maintain the parish church, with the result that men and women at worship felt the scourge of cold winter rains and wind. In Lincoln diocese these were common complaints.[15]

Yet the evidence does not support a wholesale indictment of the clergy. Indeed, a balanced view of abuses related to absenteeism, morals, and learning must make us wary of uncritical modern generalizations or contemporary polemicists' wholesale condemnations of the clergy. In cases of indiscipline, the church showed real diligence in detection, care in conviction, and zeal in finding appropriate penalties. Nonetheless, allowing for crude magnifications, by 1529 resentment had exceeded the bounds of mere anticlericalism. People recognized that poverty-stricken and often unlearned parish priests were not only their ministers but also their social and economic competitors. Celibacy was an economic as well as a psychological burden in an agrarian society. Poverty bred loneliness and ennui, as well as anxiety. Every resultant crime of adultery was a threat to village social solidarity and to the integrity of the family relationship. Every dispute over chickens and eggs might make the difference between subsistence and hunger for priests and laymen alike, especially among the depressed clerical proletariat, who suffered in proportion to the glory and opulence of clerical elitists who waxed fat in government service. The rural parson lived like his neighbors while he was being victimized by the careerism and parasitism which disfigured the church and made the lower clergy an easy target for scorn. The failure of the church at the parish level derived from a basic structural weakness which sapped its strength.

Whatever the reasons for this failure, the roots of alienation ran deep; and men believed the judgment of God to fall heavily on such derelictions. Christians tithed. They had to answer a common call to death, judgment, heaven, or hell. But some were better served, and hence better prepared than others for the Day of Judgment. Some men died without the *vade mecum*. Others noticed in their priests scant resemblance to Christ, who had proclaimed that he was the image of all future bishops and priests. Where, they asked, was His poverty, His chastity, and His obedience? The situation of the church in society seemed incompatible with the fulfillment of its mission. An age of revolutionary criticism was at hand.

Nowhere was this more apparent than among the *regular clergy* of monks and nuns. In 1536 there were about 11,000 monks and 1,600 nuns in England and Wales. These figures represent a decline from those of the turn of the century, indicating that the cloistered life excited less zeal than it had earlier, especially since the population as a whole had been increasing since about 1480. Erasmus attributed this decline to the growth of the idea that in a properly-ordered Christian community no walls against the world are necessary. The world itself was a monastery in which men and women could realize a Christian life. Moreover, life within monastic communities was often luxurious and incompatible with the rule professed by their inhabitants. In the great houses especially, the religious were surrounded by lay servants, administrators, corrodents who had purchased the right to monastic hospitality, and numerous "abbey-lubbers" drawn by the magnetic power of great wealth. Polemicists like Simon Fish[16] wrote savage indictments of the regular clergy, often grossly exaggerating their numbers and their wealth. But ordinary men found in his *Supplication of the Beggars* the color of truth. His facts and figures were devoured with gusto by the London and provincial public. When Fish castigated monks and their dependents as parasites on the commonwealth, few men could have known what the survey of 1536 revealed: that the 825 houses of religion in England and Wales had a combined annual income of about £136,000.

Many people must have had first-hand evidence of the corruption of monastic life and thus been prepared to receive not only hostile attacks like that of Fish but also the damning reports of the crown commissioners who surveyed the monasteries in 1535–1536. Earlier reports by visiting bishops and other authorities had indicated that religious communities were equally undistinguished in sin and sanctity. Where evil of a grand nature was absent, there was baleful evidence of venial sin: ownership of private property was widespread, fashionable dress was worn, monks kept groaning banquet-boards where plain fare was the rule, abbots had fine apartments inhabited by good-looking women. On London's better streets monks could be seen garbed in silk robes with gold ornamentation, their boots decorated with satin rosettes, their fingers with jewels.

Many men in rural England knew that monastic accounts disguised peculation, and that abbots and priors often gave favorable leases to friends and relatives. Some even alienated permanently properties which were by law the inalienable endowment of the church. In some houses the brethren were argumentative and disobedient to their superiors; in others rapacious and sometimes cruel superiors lost the respect of subordinates and thus the capacity to rule them effectively. Morale was understandably low in such places, and morality perhaps still lower. Since young men and women took vows before fully recognizing their own sexuality—a point Erasmus raised in criticism of pledging novices who were little more than infants—cloistered communities sometimes served to satisfy needs alien to that spiritual asceticism which denies the flesh to feed the spirit. Life under the rule too often seemed a pleasant and premature retirement from social obligations and the burdens of making a living.

The monastic clergy were, in this regard, as bound by the prevailing patterns of early Tudor society as were the parish clergy. Discipline could hardly thrive where selfish laymen lived on monastic incomes and used religious houses as places to fob off ugly or sinful daughters. The letters of Henry VIII's great minister Thomas Cromwell often describe aristocrats and local gentry building political factions in the religious houses under their patronage, pitting a group of monks against the abbot or prior and the rest of the community. Cromwell also portrays patrons sponsoring among the monks drinking bouts, fixed monastic elections, dances, hunts and gambling sessions, and other activities repugnant to the rules of religion but not to the life of gentility which so many monks and nuns refused to abandon upon entering the cloister. Far from being retreats from the world, houses of religion were often playgrounds of aristocratic ambition and taste.

Religious corporations also showed themselves to laymen in the role of secular landlords. All too often they seemed oppressive, whether as appropriators of tithes, rack-renting landlords, arbitrary enclosers of common land, or usurers. Thomas More listed among the worst criminals of his time "certain abbots, holy men no doubt," who evicted peasants from farmland in order to graze their large flocks of sheep. Less than 3 per cent of the total monastic endowment of the religious orders seems to have been spent on charitable works and hospitality. The English communities provided no parallels to the famous German and Italian teaching, nursing, and missionary orders. Only the small congregations of Observant Franciscans, Carthusians, and Bridgettines were distinguished for their piety. Nor did the monasteries and nunneries of the early 1500s excel in the maintenance of schools. All in all, laymen saw only a small return to society for a large share of the landed wealth of England and a great measure of its political power.

Not surprisingly, therefore, when Henry VIII turned his wrath toward Rome and all its works, neither the secular clergy nor the regulars found many defenders. They had mislaid the capacity for both self-government and internal reform.

The Sources of Religious Revolution

It is against this background that we must understand both Henry VIII's revolt from Rome and the confluence of movements of protest which shaped the English Reformation. Long before the English king found grievances in Clement VII's refusal to grant him a divorce from Catherine of Aragon, ordinary Englishmen had shaped movements of resistance to clerical abuses and found in popular indignation the potential for revolt. The accident of a royal change of heart and mind thus freed popular anticlericalism from the constraints which had bound it; as Henry VIII slowly abandoned his assent to Rome's power in England, he gave scope to the native desire for reform. The king's own rebellion was the occasion of the Reformation in England, but not its cause.

Church and crown in England had long feared the alliance of social radicalism and religious dissent. Ever since John Wycliffe's[17] attacks on the temporal dominion of the church found popular support among the heretics called Lollards in the late fourteenth and early fifteenth centuries, the kings of England had demonstrated their orthodoxy by suppressing popular dissent from church teachings, especially when such opinions raised questions about the legitimacy of royal power. This had happened in two revolts led by Lollard gentlemen, against Henry V in 1415 and against the regency government of Henry VI in 1431. After the suppression of those threats the Lollard movement had gone underground. It thrived among rural wage laborers and small-scale artisans, especially in the counties around London and in East Anglia. It drew its strength not from Wycliffe's abstract and obscure doctrines but from homespun versions of the faith rooted in lay resentment of clerical authority, privilege, and abuses.

English popular dissent before the 1520s—when Lutheran ideas imported from Europe and English humanist criticism sharpened its focus—was characterized by an array of anticlerical and antisacramental beliefs. Radical condemnation of the church hierarchy and of Roman power in English affairs was typical. Hostility to the Mass was common. Celibacy and its social consequences were railed against. The superstitious consecration of saints' relics and other physical objects, pilgrimages, and prayers for the dead were, in the popular imagination, excuses for the exploitation of laymen. The Lollards also denounced clergy who served as ministers in royal government, coupling this with a pacifism deeply disturbing to a government engaged in ceaseless campaigns against the French in Europe. Many dissenters held up to scorn a religion which made preaching of the gospel subordinate to the administration of the sacraments. And, perhaps most vital for the future, the rank-and-file of Lollardy believed passionately that scriptures in English were indispensable to the reform of popular religion.

Repeated efforts to extirpate Lollards and their views failed. In the early sixteenth century, Lollard cells plagued bishops in several dioceses. Official records from York show their prevalence in the North. During the Hunne uproar, Fitzjames conducted a vigorous persecution of London heretics, including in his sweeping investigations Colet, the Dean of St. Paul's. It was well known that Lollards flocked to his sermons. In 1521 the bishop of London summoned 350 accused Lollards to his church courts. Six of them he executed as relapsed heretics, while fifty were forced to abjure their errors. In Kent, Essex, Lincoln, and the West Midlands, Lollard activity was widespread. And in London itself, colorful lay preachers like "Old Father" John Hacker evangelized the artisan classes under the government's nose.

The London Lollards showed a keen appreciation of the encouragement their ideas might derive from Luther's revolt in Germany. Given the general mobility of rural and town society, it is not surprising that England's earliest Protestants were in touch with the leaders of the older domestic dissent. By 1526 a notable company of English Lutherans flourished, among them William Tyndale, Robert Barnes,[18] Hugh Latimer, and Thomas Bilney.[19] Friar Barnes engaged in the retail dissemination in Tyndale's *New Testament* in 1527; we know from contemporary records that he arranged to sell it to groups of Lollards, who up to that time had zealously circulated English fragments of what was known as the *Lollard Bible*. The well-informed London Lutheran Richard Hilles once told Bullinger that a man executed at Smithfield for Lutheran heresies was, in fact, "nought but a follower of our Wyccliffe".

Nor were less sympathetic contemporaries blind to this mingling of old Lollard and new Lutheran. English followers of Erasmus—More, Tunstal, and Fisher—were fearful that the popular forms of heresy would make an open hearing for humanist reform impossible. They recognized that native dissent was in some ways closely related to their own movement to purge abuses in the church and give primary emphasis to the preaching of the Word of God. Like their own movement, Lollardy was insistently anticlerical and hostile to ceremonies and ecclesiastical lordship. But they looked with deep suspicion on the Lollard toleration of lay preaching and the active role Lollards assigned to the congregation in determining the views of their pastor. This looked dangerously like Luther's priesthood of all believers. It frightened the English bishops and humanists, who were so often clerical elitists. Their misgivings made them draw back somewhat from championing the bible in English. Among older English humanists it became a commonplace that Lollardy sparked the flames of Lutheranism.

A block was thus placed in the road which might have led to a union of Lollards, Lutherans, and Erasmians. Men like More preferred satire and elliptical criticism to frontal attacks of the Lollard sort. They couched their protests in elegant Latin or Greek. To the attack on abuse they contributed more logic than passion. They also lent it what the Lollards and Lutherans never could: status within the elites which governed church and commonwealth, access to the press, and positions in the universities and government. Their stress on educational reform and the slow conversion of Christian hearts to the imitation of Christ was thus more acceptable than Lollard ideas, which were popular in their inspiration and heavily burdened by the history of sedition in the 1400s. Humanists often sought the same changes favored by Lollards and Lutherans. But they championed reform from above, with emphasis on gradual cultural transformation. To those in power, this blueprint looked safe because it was slow and depended on the help of the hierarchy so despised by the radicals. Early English humanism thus partook of that species of reform which hopes the violence of the radicals will insure a hearing for the moderates who were playing for time. After the German Peasants' Rebellion of 1524–1525, however, England's first-generation humanists and their church patrons were driven by their fear of the sectarian excesses of German radicalism to active persecution of Lollardy and Lutheranism. And Henry VIII, as yet not moved to see the gospel light by his passion for Anne Boleyn,[20] was more orthodox than the pope.

Thus on the very eve of the divorce and England's separation from Rome, there was little reason for advocates of reformation to be hopeful. In the circumstances, optimism was a fool's luxury. Yet hope was necessary for the faithful. Everywhere men hostile to the established church looked for the miracle of grace that would transform Christ's church. Little could they know that when it came it would be wrapped in the wrath of Henry VIII, an anger which denied time to the men of More's generation and gave scope to the radicals.

As the opposing intellectual and social forces of reform and reaction tilted in unequal combat, Henry VIII's wish to divorce Queen Catherine and marry Anne Boleyn tipped the balance in favor of reform. As early as 1522 or 1523, the king had had doubts about the validity of his marriage to the Spanish woman who had originally come to England betrothed to his brother Arthur, the Prince of Wales. That marriage ended in Arthur's death. Henry's took place only after Pope Julius II suspended canon law forbidding marriage between a man and his brother's widow. Henry's scruple arose from the fact that Catherine had provided him no male heir. The marriage must be cursed. Two texts from Leviticus seemed to forbid it. Henry came to view the succession of miscarriages and still-births of male children as a proof of God's judgment on the marriage. By 1527, Catherine was past further childbearing, and the needs of the dynasty as well as the growing estrangement of Henry VIII and Charles V, the Habsburg emperor and

King of Spain, made a sonless Queen who supported Spanish policy less than welcome at court. Anne Boleyn's refusal to become the king's mistress further weakened the Queen's position. The scruple of conscience thus grew into a certainty.

The desire for a sentence of divorce sanctioned by the pope was entrusted to Wolsey's diplomatic skills. Amity between Henry and Clement VII was rooted in the king's orthodoxy—he had been styled Defender of the Faith in 1521 for his vigorous attack on Luther's heterodox notions about the seven sacraments. Henry trusted in a putative papal wish to accommodate a loyal son of the church. But the sack of Rome by Charles V's victorious imperial forces in 1527 made Clement's position delicate. The pope was a Medici, and his diplomacy tended to center on the creation of a French alliance to counter Habsburg power. To Clement VII, English problems were peripheral. Perhaps this best explains the two years of tedious negotiations which finally resulted in the appointment of Wolsey and Cardinal Campeggio, a powerful curial official, to a special legatine court with authority to hear the case in England. What English lawyers arguing their king's case did not know, however, was that Campeggio had been secretly instructed by Clement to solve the problem by some course less scandalous than a public trial of the Spanish king's aunt.[21]

Campeggio tried to convince the proud and stubborn Catherine to enter a nunnery. By so doing she could avoid the confrontation and provide the pope with the grounds for annulling the marriage. She refused. When the king's attorneys based their case on the argument that even the pope had no power to dispense what God had forbidden, because Arthur had carnally known Catherine, the Queen swore she came to Henry VIII's bed a virgin. She appeared in the legatine court at Blackfriar's in London only to refuse to recognize the jurisdiction of the court and to appeal directly to the pope. The trial, which had opened amid high hopes on a summer's day in 1529, ended in farce, with Campeggio announcing that his court was Roman and would keep a Roman term. The August holiday necessitated adjournment on July 31st, until autumn.

The trial scheduled to reconvene in October never took place. In response to Catherine's appeal, Clement VII issued letters prohibiting further hearings on the matter in England and summoning Henry VIII to appear in his own court in Rome. Henry raged at this suggestion and publicly announced he would not repeat the humiliation of the medieval Emperor Henry at Cannossa. He blamed Wolsey for the embarrassing failure of English policy. Thus the first consequence of Clement's and Campeggio's action was to cast Wolsey from power, the victim of an aristocratic coup well larded with popular anticlerical outbursts.

Few could have anticipated its less immediate consequences. The church as it had existed for centuries in England came to an end. A revolution in ecclesiastical polity ensued, and in its wake came a revolution in religious life. Roman power was banished from England. The monasteries were pulled down and their wealth confiscated. The forces of anticlericalism and reform, which for decades had needed the king, were now necessary to him in his campaign to coerce Rome to do his will in the divorce. When first Clement VII and then Paul III refused to satisfy this stubborn and petulant king, Henry became the leader of the one true political and social revolution England was to experience between the Norman Conquest and that of industrialization in the nineteenth century. Within a decade, Europe's staunchest papal ally became a Protestant commonwealth.

Parliament was the agency of transformation, and its instruments of revolution were statutes. Behind each legislative act lay a barrage of propaganda managed by the great minister and political genius Thomas Cromwell, who had learned his craft so well as Wolsey's factotum. Under his aegis, the Church of England took form in a flood of oaths, injunctions, formularies of a revised faith, and vernacular bibles. There were also created out of the unleashed energy of popular enthusiasm the rudiments of a Protestant culture, the birth of which can be studied in the plays, woodcuts, sermons, ballads, and pageants of the 1530s. The monarchy had taken over the management of the forces of anticlericalism and reform and shaped them to its own needs.

The Creation of the English Church

The major thrust of the Reformation in England was directed against those aspects of the church which had for years met with the most vehement objections: abuse of its temporal dominion; the burden it laid on society by absorbing wealth and power and returning little; Roman jurisdiction, which was a barrier to the social, economic, and political integration of English life. Reformers of widely varying beliefs agreed that the church must yield to the claims of the commonwealth. Finally, there was the religious upsurge, the pietistic feeling informing Lollardy, Lutheranism, and Erasmianism alike. Its adherents argued that radical change was necessary for the sake of Christian life. More and Fisher had advocated reform without revolution or the destruction of Roman power, but humanists of the second generation joined Lollards and Lutherans in disbelieving in the capacity of internal reform to accomplish what they wanted: the sanctification of lay life as a vocation and a simple, biblical, evangelical religion. The king, his minister Thomas Cromwell, and the politicians and thinkers around them recognized that reformation on such a scale would require the consent of all the communities of the realm. And it became clear that such consent could only be given by parliament, the community of communities, embodying as it did the will of the king, the lay aristocracy, the clergy itself, and the burgesses of the chief towns of the kingdom.

The Parliament which assembled in November 1529 is famous as the Reformation Parliament. When it was convoked, people anticipated that it would deal with reform in church and commonwealth, but few of the members summoned could have expected their work to extend over seven sessions between 1529 and 1536. And even fewer could have anticipated the outlines of the legislation in which the major tenets of the Henrician revolution were formulated. This Parliament would do far more than cast down Wolsey, provide Henry with his long-sought divorce, reform social ills, and enrich the royal treasury with monastic spoils. It would also spell out three tenets which together created a new base for Christian monarchy in England: the king was sole overlord of the English church; the church in England owed Rome no tutelage; the king had a divinely-appointed mission in the cure of souls. The government maintained that right order in a Christian monarchy depended on adherence to these propositions, and in their realization every substantive measure of reform had its place.

In the first three years of its legislative history the Reformation Parliament clipped the wings of churchmen and circumscribed the independence of the church. Emboldened by the sight of Wolsey humbly submitting to a common law indictment in king's bench,[22] Parliament enacted statutes which reduced death dues and scaled testamentary fees to the means of the public. Priests were forbidden to engage in commerce. Men in minor orders lost the protection of benefit of clergy[23] in cases of murder, arson, burglary, and highway robbery. This gave common law courts power over clerics once exercised exclusively by the courts Christian. An act of 1530 reformed abuses of nonresidence and pluralities.

In the same year the crown won a significant test of strength over the clergy. Writs of *praemunire*[24] were served on seven bishops and eight other divines, charging them with having aided Wolsey in the illegal exercise of papal jurisdiction in England. Specifically, they were accused of making illegal payments to the cardinal in return for acts of grace deriving from his legatine commission. Early in 1531 the charge was extended to apply to the whole of the clergy. Badly frightened by the fate of the cardinal—he had been stripped of his wealth and titles and banished to die in disgrace—the clergy in their convocation[25] of York and Canterbury pleaded guilty to the charges collectively and compromised the crime by offering to pay a fine of £118,840 to the king. Their submissiveness merely opened the way to a new demand, that Henry VIII be acknowledged "Protector and Supreme Head" of the church in England. In serious disarray, the clergy yielded, provided the clause "so far as the law of Christ allowed" be added to the declaration. But their saving clause could not hide their defeat.

This legislation by Parliament and concession by convocation prepared the way for the king's absolute headship over the church in England. But Parliament had not yet dealt directly with papal power. And it had not addressed itself to the role of the monarchy in the cure of souls and the reform of religious life. England was still in communion with Rome. Thomas

More had used his office as lord chancellor, presiding in the House of Lords, to keep within the bounds of schism and tradition early thrusts at reform. The rise of Thomas Cromwell to power in the king's council in 1531–1532, however, led to More's defeat and the complete surrender of the church's legislative independence. When that happened, magisterial reformation on the Lutheran model beckoned. Mere anticlericalism gave way to revolution.

Thomas Cromwell was the presiding genius of the revolution which took place between 1532 and 1540. His training and beliefs were shaped by various employments, chief among them his service with Cardinal Wolsey. But this son of a Putney blacksmith had had earlier experiences that prepared him for the attack on Roman power which constituted the first phase of the revolution (1532–1535) and also for the religious and doctrinal reform of the period 1535–1540, which Froude[26] dubbed "the heroic age of the English Reformation." His early life is wholly obscure. He seems to have spent some time in Italy, perhaps as a soldier of fortune for a few years, certainly as a commercial agent. He had also taken a hand in managing the commercial interests of his father-in-law, especially the cloth trade with the Low Countries. Early in the 1520s he studied common law in the Inns of Court[27] and gave a very well-received series of "readings" in the course of gaining a solid reputation in London. To the knowledge of military affairs he gained in Italy, his experiences in Florence had added an understanding of banking. Joining expertise and finance, the law, and commerce to his sharp wit and humanistic learning, he began an apprenticeship in statecraft in Wolsey's employ about 1520. By 1523 he had distinguished himself as a member of Parliament opposed to the policy of war with France favored by his mentor.

During the years of Wolsey's greatest power, before the divorce, Cromwell established himself as the cardinal's indispensable man. He handled political matters, dealt with difficult members of the nobility, managed the dissolution of monasteries whose wealth contributed to Wolsey's educational building program, and in countless other ways learned how power was exercised in the monarchy and in the administration of the church. During this time he had easy access to the king and court. Thus, while it is not easy to say precisely when he gained the confidence of the king, there is no need to believe the unlikely story of Cardinal Pole[28] that in the course of an interview in the garden of Westminster Palace shortly after Wolsey's death (1530) the Machiavellian Cromwell advised the king to appropriate the wealth of the church and thus make himself the richest king in Christendom. There is evidence of a number of interviews between Cromwell and the king well before that time. For years Cromwell had established in the minds of Henry VIII and many others confidence in his capacities for many kinds of business. When the Reformation Parliament met in 1529, Cromwell was a burgess for Orford.

More believable is John Foxe's[29] statement that Cromwell's rise to power in Henry VIII's council derived from his support of the radical anticlerical document called the *Supplication of the Commons Against the Ordinaries.* Between 1529 and 1532 a struggle for power in the council was waged between the moderates of More's persuasion and the more radical reform-minded men who gravitated toward Cromwell. During this time More managed to limit attacks on the church to the reform of clerical abuses. But late in 1531 and early in 1532 there circulated in the council several drafts of the *Supplication,* which had first been presented in 1529. Each of the four surviving drafts are in Cromwell's writing or bear his corrections. Its revival in 1532 may well have been his doing, and suggests that the struggle over policy had reached a critical stage, in which More lost mastery. For the *Supplication,* which was allowed to gather dust in 1529, became the focal point for the campaign which ended Roman jurisdiction in England in 1532–1535. It achieved this prominence by skilfully fusing the unsatisfied anticlerical feelings of the Commons and the needs of the king. The *Supplication* combined two themes: the right of the king to terminate the legislative independence of the church, and the lay desire to escape the burdens imposed by the courts Christian. It also revived the popular anticlerical themes of nepotism, pluralism, and the execrable vices of the clergy in general. What had seemed an extremist attack from outside the orbit of government in 1529 had become the policy of a faction of the council in 1532. It thus signalled a renewal of violent criticism of the church and a shift in royal policy.

The bishops made a vigorous reply in Stephen Gardiner's[30] *Answer of the Ordinaries,* which so angered the king that he invited the Commons to join with him in an attack on the church. Henry made it his goal to force the clergy into utter submission to him as their supreme head. This became the main legislative business of Parliament and convocation in the spring of 1532, and after much debate and royal threats of *praemunire* against every clergyman who maintained the independence of the church in legislation and its courts, convocation gave in to Henry's demands. The Submission of the Clergy, on May 15, 1532, marked the defeat of More's policy of maintaining the independence of the church. He resigned from office and was replaced by Cromwell's staunch ally Thomas Audley,[31] the Speaker of the Commons who had first presented the *Supplication* two months earlier.

The king may well have been satisfied with this victory. But he was now to discover that he could not drop the church from the heights of its eminence and bid it stop halfway down. Parliament pressed the attack on clerical independence and Roman authority and influence, under Cromwell's guidance and with the king's support. Several statutes spelled out fully the implications of the Submission and the king's headship of the church. Cromwell drafted most of them; they reflect his political creed. The 1532 act of Annates withheld from Rome papal taxes on new episcopal appointments and forbade Roman consecration of English bishops. It also declared that no papal interdict or excommunication could keep the faithful in England from the benefits of the sacraments. Early in 1533 the Act in Restraint of Appeals abolished appeals from the sentences of English courts to Rome. In its preamble, the claim was made that England was a society independent of any other secular authority, a sovereign state composed of diverse lay and clerical groups bound in allegiance to the king and subject to the jurisdiction of laws made by common consent of the community of the realm in Parliament. Under the provisions of this statute the new Archbishop of Canterbury, Thomas Cranmer, provided Henry VIII with his divorce from Queen Catherine.

In 1533–1534 the revolutionary thrust of statutes clarified the political situation by making less ambiguous the implications of the royal supremacy. A second act of Annates utterly suspended all payments from England to Rome. It provided for episcopal elections by royal license. A Dispensations Act established that laws regulating pluralism and other matters pertaining to beneficed clergy would be enforced by the Archbishop of Canterbury. Another statute stipulated that convocation could legislate in the future only upon the receipt of a royal license. Statute was also used to clarify the succession to the throne. Anne Boleyn, whom Henry married in 1533, became his only lawful wife, and her daughter Elizabeth was made the king's sole heir. Princess Mary, Catherine of Aragon's one surviving child, was declared a bastard. This Act of Succession warned all who would defame Anne or her children that such utterances were treasonable. The act also enjoined on the clergy and office-holders an oath upholding the provisions of the Succession. Thomas More and John Fisher, Bishop of Rochester,[32] refused to take the oath, later provided in the Act of Supremacy, on the grounds that the Succession Act had not included an oath and that the oath furnished by the Act of Supremacy exceeded the intention to guarantee the integrity of the dynasty by requiring all jurors to acknowledge royal supremacy, specifically and in a form that allowed no admission of papal power in England. For their defiance, More and Fisher were executed in 1535. Papal sympathies became treasonable in the first basic expansion of the treason law since 1352. More and Fisher were thus the first men to bear witness to their faith in a time when "Papist" had become synonym for political criminal. Not only had papal power in England been extinguished by a flurry of statutes; windows had been opened onto the souls of men. And this scrutiny would lay up troubles for the commonwealth of the future.

The legislative revolution undertaken between 1532 and 1535 also involved a wholesale attack on church property beyond the level of annates and direct papal taxation. The Act of First Fruits and Tenths annexed to the crown the income of all benefices in an amount equal to the first year's value. A tax which in papal hands applied only to bishops' incomes now fell on all clergy. This was the first of Cromwell's confiscatory measures to enhance the financial position of the crown. It led directly to the establishment of the first of several new revenue courts to handle the profits of such confiscations. The act also prepared the way for the great survey of clerical wealth, the *Valor Ecclesiasticus*, in which the value of every nunnery, monastery, and secular benefice was calculated and summarized for the use of the crown.

The dissolution of the monasteries was doubtless one result of the *Valor*. It is impossible to determine when Cromwell and the king decided to suppress these bastions of Roman sentiment or whether fiscal motives dominated their thoughts. What we do know for certain is that schemes for suppression of the houses of religion circulated among Cromwell's agents and propagandists as early as 1534. Cromwell had had experience in such matters under Wolsey, and his own closest adherents included known opponents of monastic religion, both younger English humanists and secular-minded anticlerical radicals. The minister's Lutheran supporters urged the policy as well. By 1535 there were in existence numerous state papers discussing the possible suppression of the monasteries and how their endowments might be employed to finance expanded social services and enhance the position of the monarchy.

In the cold autumn of 1535 Cromwell appointed a number of visitors to survey the monasteries and report on their vices and virtues. Their reports, the *comperta* or complaints, became the pretext for the bill to suppress religious houses with annual incomes of less than two hundred pounds. Debate on the bill revealed few defenders of the religious orders. The crown maintained that the less wealthy houses by and large had insufficient inhabitants to maintain the rule and perform divine services. They were also guilty of the worst irregularities. These arguments indicate that the government had other purposes than mere fiscal expediency in setting the upper limit for dissolution at two hundred pounds. Clauses providing for the transfer of religious from suppressed houses to standing houses also make it unlikely that a cynical policy of general suppression had been decided on in 1536. Of the 304 houses covered by the act of 1536, 67 were exempted for various causes. Hundreds of clergy chose to become secular priests rather than remain in the cloister, but licenses to transfer to standing monasteries were freely given. And Cromwell had also worked hard on a series of injunctions designed to reform religious life in existing houses. Dom David Knowles, the greatest living historian of English monasticism, likens Cromwell's orders to a call back to the spirit of the Hildebrandine reforms. Furthermore, even during the course of suppressions in 1536, Henry VIII was founding a Benedictine house for fourteen monks and an abbot from the dissolved Augustinian house at Bisham; he also refounded a nunnery at Stixwold, Lincolnshire, at the time. It is hard to understand these acts as consonant with a deliberate, phased policy of suppression.

Ironically, the movement toward general suppression may have been prompted by a popular rising in the North of England called the Pilgrimage of Grace. The dissolution of the lesser houses throughout the kingdom had been met by local acts of resistance. Housewives in Exeter tried to prevent the closing of St. Nicholas' Priory, a place famous for its charity and hospitality. In York and Lincoln, local bands drove away crown agents overseeing the "surrender" of several houses. These incidents have led some historians to talk of the large-scale rising in the North as inspired by Catholics resentful of the dissolution and of religious changes in general. This explanation, however, does scant justice to the Pilgrimage. The reaction of the North did not fundamentally arise out of religious conservatism. The unrest was social and economic in nature, and widespread in York, Lincoln, and the border areas touching Scotland. Peasants suffered from the effects of sharply rising rents and declining real wages. The gentry feared popular revolt, and often joined in peasant uprisings in order to protect their local interests. The great feudal magnates—the Percys, the Nevilles, and the Dacres—resented crown policies which pointed to the suppression of the last great liberties and territorial franchises of the baronial families. They tended to see the drive against church privilege as part of a larger movement to accomplish the political unification of the North which loomed so large in Cromwell's political schemes. They feared the loss of offices and leases of church lands which might result from crown management of confiscated properties. To this mixture of ills and fears, plague and harvest failure added further pressure. Thus, while some Pilgrims railed against Cromwell and Cranmer's novel policies in religion, and some abbots played a major and ill-fated role in the rebellion, the movement was at heart a massive protest rooted in the problem of poverty and the crown's drive against the great baronial families of the North.

The government won a complete victory over the Pilgrims, after a period of great danger late in 1536 and early in 1537. This victory became the point of departure for a ruthless administration of justice against the rebels and the extension of the campaign to suppress both baronial liberties and the monastic houses which had supplied leadership to the rebels. It provided ammunition in the new campaign for a general dissolution of monasteries, and gave impetus to Cromwell's determination to force religious houses to make "voluntary surrenders" of their sites and endowments. Before the second Act of Dissolution passed Parliament in 1539, nearly 200 houses had made such voluntary surrenders. By 1540 all of the 825 religious houses in England had ceased to be.

Before discussing the religious changes which occurred during the period of the dissolution and until the death of Cromwell in 1540, it will be useful to sketch the results of the social revolution which put an end to monastic houses in England. The dispossessed religious did not come off badly. Every monk and nun was pensioned from grants payable by the Court of Augmentations, created to handle the flow of monastic revenues. Pensions were given in proportion to the wealth and status of houses and officers. Many monks became beneficed secular clergy under "faculties," or licenses. Nuns were harder hit, of course, since they could not continue in clerical employment. Friars were denied pensions, on the grounds of the mendicant nature of their orders, but they were often qualified by training as preachers, and in the new dispensation of religion most of them found parochial work.

Nor did either the lay dependents of religious houses or the better-placed gentry and aristocrats who had exploited monastic wealth lose in the process which transferred that wealth to the crown. The evidence from local records is that servants were not reduced to pauperism; the new occupants of monastic sites needed domestics just as had the monks. There is even less evidence to suggest that a new "upstart" aristocracy resulted from the dispersal of monastic property. Cromwell had intended a permanent augmentation of the crown's revenue through the policy of confiscation. But after his death, and especially after 1542, when Henry VIII abandoned the pacific policy of the 1530s and renewed war in France and Scotland, the crown was impoverished and forced to sell or lease much of the former monastic land. The men best situated to exploit the crown's misfortune were those who had already enjoyed the management of monastic estates and offices: the principal local landowners and monastic patrons; courtiers and London politicians; and the officials of the new Court of Augmentations. Such men knew good land from bad. Few strangers infringed on their monopoly of the best grants.

The net social effect of the dissolution was thus to accelerate already-begun shifts in the distribution of wealth and power in the counties and to further strengthen the local landed gentry and government servants, on whom the monarchy was already dependent for support. The great political dynasties of the future could trace their ancestry to gentry servants of the crown fortunate to be in the right place at the right time.

There were further consequences of the dissolution that had great significance politically and culturally. Abbots and priors vanished forever from the House of Lords, leaving the lay peers a clear majority over the spiritual ones. Six new bishoprics were founded with the profits of dissolved houses: at Bristol, Gloucester, Oxford, Peterborough, Chester, and Westminster. This helped redress an imbalance of dioceses which had occurred in the earlier Middle Ages, concentrating them in the southeastern parts of the country. The new foundations looked toward the needs of the northern and western areas which had grown in population and wealth in the fifteenth century. Some monastic wealth also went to endow expanded cathedral chapters and grammar schools. At the universities, Wolsey's college was completed and converted to a royal foundation with the proceeds of the dissolution, and the Regius Professorships in law, medicine, theology, and Greek were founded on such funds. On the negative side, we must list permanent harm to scholarship and the arts. Great libraries were broken up and never restored. The antiquarian Leland did rescue some 250 monastic books for Henry VIII's library, but the loss was tremendous. And in architecture and the plastic or decorative arts, we can still appreciate the loss when we look at the lovely but fractured arches and gateways which were once the marvel of the mason's craft and at the works of artists forever lost to posterity.

The suppression of the regular clergy cannot be fully understood apart from the general movement of reform in religion which Cromwell began in 1535. If the anticlerical legislation of 1529–1532 promised to control abuses in the church, if the antipapal campaigns of 1532–1535 established the Church of England as a political reality, only the effort to redefine popular religion undertaken by Cromwell in 1535 shows clearly how much progress was made in the 1530s toward realizing the three tenets of Henricianism. And only a study of the religious revolution left incomplete at Cromwell's death in 1540 can help us to understand the struggles of reformers in the period which ended with the Elizabethan settlement of religion in 1570.

The transformation of religion as it manifested itself to the faithful took place in three distinct areas: doctrine and ritual, including liturgical materials; church discipline and supervision of the clergy in their exercise of pastoral care; and the availability of the Bible in English. In each area Cromwell played a crucial role, cooperating with Thomas Cranmer, the Archbishop of Canterbury. Together they shaped the elements of a popular religious culture which continued to influence the English people for centuries. In their work they had the support of young humanists and reformers born in the sixteenth century and more open to radical change than the first-generation advocates of reform, who had looked to More, Fisher, and Erasmus for leadership. Under the aegis of Cromwell and Cranmer, there gathered a remarkable community of men who blended humanist and Protestant ideas in a synthesis distinguished by its rejection of both Romanism and the most advanced sectarian practices of the Continent. In the 1530s these men fashioned the *via media*—the middle way—of the Church of England.

Cromwell had early in his career exhibited an openminded attitude to new ideas about politics, social institutions, education, and religious reform. He had befriended and patronized a number of young scholars of various shades of opinion, among them the Lutherans Miles Coverdale,[33] Sir Francis Bigod,[34] and William Tyndale. His circle also included Erasmians like Richard Taverner,[35] Richard Morison[36] and Thomas Starkey,[37] as well as a variety of anticlericals and social reformers, among them the legal theorist Christopher St. German[38] and the economic pamphleteers Clement Armstrong[39] and William Marshall.[40] Friar Robert Barnes, Hugh Latimer, William Jerome, and Thomas Garrett[41] were more radical in their advocacy of reformation, and it is significant that they too were in Cromwell's entourage; all of them suffered martyrs' deaths because of their advanced religious ideas. In Cromwell's employ, these men wrote on a wide variety of subjects, especially ecclesiastical polity, matters of doctrine, iconoclasm, clerical education, monastic wealth, popular devotion, and the need for vernacular scriptures.

They also had the support of Cranmer, a donnish man who emerged from obscurity on the strength of his suggestion that Henry VIII gather support for the divorce from the universities of Europe. For many years before 1529, the future archbishop had frequented Protestant discussions in Cambridge. The ubiquitous Friar Barnes led him toward Lutheran views, a shift of opinion sharply reinforced by Cranmer's travels in Germany, where he met and married the niece of Osiander, the celebrated Lutheran divine. While still a tutor in a Cambridge college, Cranmer taught his students to exalt scripture above other authorities. He also developed a reputation for that loyalty, modesty, clarity of style, and sound scholarship which endeared him to his king and promoted his friendship with Cromwell. Both men wished to insure that royal supremacy meant a remaking of religious life in England. They recognized that the way had been prepared in the 1520s and early 1530s by an unprecedented flood of religious works in the Lutheran and radical humanist traditions. And they seized the opportunity of the king's attack on Roman jurisdiction, making certain that more than monasteries and clerical power over laymen would be affected.

Between 1536 and 1547 several new formularies of the faith appeared in England. The most important of these, the *Bishop's Book* (1537) and the *King's Book* (1543), followed on the heels of sets of articles of religion, the *Ten Articles* (1536) and the *Six Articles*. In each case the earlier sets of articles and books were more advanced in their religious opinions than those which followed. The works of 1536–1537 bore a marked resemblance to the classic formulations of German Protestantism, the *Augsburg Confession* (1530) and Melanchthon's *Apology* (1531). A combination of domestic and diplomatic political forces worked to promote retreat from the bold positions of the earliest formularies. But even the *King's Book* and the *Six Articles* preserved many doctrinal features which marked a decisive break with Roman Catholic belief.

The *Ten Articles,* ambiguous on many points, enjoined belief in only three sacraments: baptism, penance, and communion. The others were left in limbo, to be partially restored in 1539. They did not prescribe a belief in transubstantiation or the value of prayer for the souls of the faithful in purgatory. And on the central Lutheran doctrine of justification by faith, they adhered to Melanchthon's very delicately shaded views, which allowed men to minimize the place of good works in the economy of salvation. While the *Bishop's Book* compromised in some ways the advanced views of 1536, there was no retreat on the sacrament of the altar. It upheld the 1536 distinction between "true sacraments," those based on a scriptural sign and a promise of grace, and those traditional rites—ordination, marriage, confirmation, and extreme unction—not so supported in the Bible. The Lutheran exposition of justification also remained intact. Although the 1537 book did not have the king's official support, he allowed it to be given to bishops and by them to priests as a guide to the cure of souls.

We also know that the king engaged Cranmer in lively debate on many points of doctrine. Henry VIII disliked ideas which hinted at the brotherhood of man, the sufficiency of faith in salvation, and predestination. He reacted to them with vigorous assertions of his own beliefs, in which free will and faith formed by good works were central. Henry's theological leanings were a source of great danger to Cranmer especially after 1540, when Cromwell's execution on charges of treason and dissemination of heresy deprived Cranmer of his friend's political intelligence and power in the king's council. But the archbishop maintained his ground, rejecting any royal views which would serve to emphasize the mass, relics, pilgrimages, shrines, and all other abuses of religion which had helped to promulgate mechanical views of salvation and condemned machines which amazed pilgrims by their ability to perform contrived miracles. Over the years, Henry VIII accepted many of his archbishop's ideas: among them that oral confession had no sanction in divine law; that some sacraments were scriptural in origin and others were not; that confirmation, for example, was but a "Jewish ceremony"; that chrism (holy oil) provided no special grace to the anointed. Even the 1537 formulary ignored the mass, omitted any mention of the indelible character conferred on priests at ordination, allowed no distinction between simple priests and bishops, and in general undermined belief in the special status of priests in society. Cranmer's doctrine emphasized preaching as the central function of the ministry, downgrading the administration of sacraments and, by extension, the powerful hold priests had over laymen. In the supposedly reactionary *King's Book* of 1543, Henry gave his blessing to positions embodying all of Cranmer's views on these points. In 1540 he had required conservatives to prove from scripture that holy orders conferred a special grace on the recipient. Failing that, he wished to know why priests should not be regarded merely as convenient overseers of congregational life.

Thus it was with the king's knowledge and support that Cromwell and Cranmer—and then Cranmer alone—moved English doctrine and worship services in the direction of Protestantism before 1547. Long before the religious settlement accomplished by Queen Elizabeth, with the aid of former exiles whose opinions had taken form in Europe during the Catholic rule of Mary Tudor (1553–1558), the crown in England had embraced doctrines at odds with tradition. The king supported doctrinal radicalism in ways which aided his own pervasive anticlerical campaign, especially in the attack on holy orders and the priestly dispensation of grace through sacramental channels. While he continued to burn men who denied the real presence of Christ in the Eucharist, Henry VIII gave his consent to doctrines which had little in common with his 1521 opinions defending the seven sacraments against Luther's attacks.

To effect doctrinal changes at the parish level, Henry had named Cromwell, a layman, his vice-gerent and vicar-general in spiritual affairs. Cromwell used his power over the clergy not merely to suppress monks or punish unruly secular priests, but to reform them as a whole. The instruments of reform and the enforcement of discipline among the clergy were two sets of *Injunctions,* issued by Cromwell in the king's name in 1536 and 1538, which stressed the nature of elementary Christian belief and education. All priests were enjoined to teach the young the Creed, Paternoster, and Ten Commandments in the vernacular. The priest was told that he must share his responsibility in such matters with parents and the lay teachers and masters of pupils and craft apprentices. This injunction was only one aspect of a radical insistence on lay responsibility for religious reform, a motif that gives weight to the thesis that Cromwell understood the need to secularize teaching if a stable commonwealth free of clerical oppression was to take shape. The *Injunctions* increased the powers of the parish priest in at least one respect, however: he was given the authority to withhold the sacraments from any person unfit to receive them by virtue of ignorance of the faith. Disciplinary exclusion from the sacraments had always been practiced in the church, but there had never before been such emphasis on lay learning and understanding of the faith.

Not unnaturally, therefore, we find in the injunctions great stress on training a better-educated clergy to encourage lay learning through good preaching. Both sets of orders provided that clerics with wealthy livings had to contribute to the support of grammar school pupils and university scholars. Cromwell coupled such schemes with tax-relief legislation, which allowed for a remission of Parliamentary taxes (the tenth) to colleges, provided that such funds were used to endow public lectures to advance Christian worship and understanding of the faith. Nonresidence also became subject to disciplinary measures. Nonresidents were ordered to distribute fixed shares of their incomes to paupers and to give 20 per cent of such incomes toward the physical repair of churches. In this way Cromwell hoped to make less attractive the sort of careerism which drained parish monies from the maintenance of the church and its poorer members.

The injunctions also dealt directly with a major source of conflict between parish priests and their flocks: the abuse of shrines, images, miracle-working statues, and icons. Characteristic was the milking of funds from parishioners to support cults attached to miraculous relics and images. Cromwell ordered that objects subject to such abuse be pulled down. To enforce this order and instruct Christians how such abuses obscured the promise of redemption made by Christ, he licensed preachers to preach quarterly sermons on Biblical religion, requiring them totally to eschew scholastic commentaries. He ordered priests to lecture on the vanity of past practices, in addition to the special lectures appointed by him. Priests who did not do so, or who absented themselves from their cures without license, were subject to very heavy fines.

To help ensure that the new Biblical religion reached all of the faithful, Cromwell ordered that parish registers of baptisms, marriages, and deaths be kept from 1538. This also served to relieve people from oppressive practices in courts Christian. People living in small villages and lacking reliable records of family affiliation often contracted marriages within the degree of affinity forbidden under canon law. Priests sometimes contributed to the problem by inventing affinities where none existed, or by ingeniously interpreting the law to promote their own financial interests in litigation and the profits of justice. The maintenance of records admissible in common law courts, in conjunction with the order that priests be fined for neglecting to make the required entries in the registers, was a step in the direction of safeguarding lay interests. It was also a watershed in government record-keeping, marking the age when adequate statistical material on population first became available in England.

It cannot escape our notice that Cromwell's injunctions were addressed directly to the root causes of discontent with parochial life. In matters of discipline, education, preaching, church maintenance, clerical oppression, community order and nonresidence, they attacked at the parish level the chief roots of alienation. Thus began the process of purging anomalies and abuses and bringing parochial religion into closer consonance with the doctrinal and ritual norms of Christian life. Lay life and informed devotion were thus made more compatible, since any change which served to reduce anticlerical agitation was beneficial to the parochial community.

Significant though these achievements in matters of doctrine and discipline were, by far the most important accomplishment of Cromwell and Cranmer was the provision of the English Bible. Nothing was more vital to the creation of a Protestant England than the preaching of the Word, buttressed by vernacular scriptures. The evangelical view of the ministry which characterized the various books and articles of the period rested on the assumption of authorized translations of scripture. Nor is this conjecture. The 1538 injunctions clearly assumed that such translations were then in preparation and would become available to parish priests without long delays. The rough drafts of these orders commanded that a Bible in English be chained in public view in every parish church, for "every man that will look and read thereon," with the admonition that God's words were the "spiritual food of man's soul."

The Bible Cromwell had in mind was the work of Miles Coverdale, a pupil of Barnes. Cromwell had first encountered Coverdale in 1527, in circles frequented by London Lutherans. He had discussed with the zealous young radical the problem of rendering scripture in an English form free of the taint of Lutheran polemic which attached to Tyndale's forbidden versions. Coverdale was a graceful writer, familiar with Luther and also with Tyndale's efforts. The future minister and the scholar thus joined an issue in anticipation of the events of the 1530s which gave them the power to implement their schemes. Yet for several years no progress was made. In the early 1530s Cromwell had focused his efforts on the exiled Tyndale, who had fled to the continent to escape the king's wrath over his criticisms of the divorce proceedings. Coverdale had followed Tyndale and other early English Protestants into exile. Bereft of the best men, Cromwell had given his support to Erasmian paraphrases of scripture and had sponsored English primers of the faith. In 1535, apparently thinking the time ripe for an English Bible, he brought Coverdale back from exile under the mantle of his protection as vice-gerent in spiritual affairs, and asked him to make an authorized English version of the Bible he had published in 1535 at Zurich.

Late in 1536 an English printer in Cromwell's service, James Nicholson, printed Coverdale's new edition, and in 1537 two revisions of the text appeared. Cranmer had likewise been busy in this field, and in 1537 there also appeared a translation by one "Thomas Matthew," the pseudonym of John Rogers,[42] an advanced Lutheran whose views were unacceptable to Henry VIII. Cromwell licensed the sale of this version as well, despite its frank avowal of Tyndale's text. This was a dangerous admission, since the king had continued his vendetta against Tyndale and had secured his capture and execution in 1535.

This confused situation did not begin to approximate Cromwell's intention, which was to produce a version bearing the stamp of the king's approval. Thus, in 1538 he sent a circular letter to all of the bishops in England and Wales, ordering them to fix a date for the installation in every church of the new Bible he was then actively engaged in creating. Under Coverdale's supervision, Cromwell had arranged for English printers among his clients to go to Paris and oversee the printing of a new version. From June until December, 1538, the work went forward without delay. Then the French Inquisitor-General and the censors of the Sorbonne stopped the printing, alleging that the Bible would endanger the faith in France. Cromwell, suspecting that conservative elements in the English hierarchy had triggered the French action, replied by pointing out that not enough Frenchmen knew English to make his project a threat to orthodoxy in France. He also assured the Frenchmen that all copies of the Bible would be sent to England. His protests were to no avail.

Cromwell managed to circumvent the suppression of the project. We are not certain how he managed this, but we do know that part of the Paris printing arrived in London, perhaps smuggled in wine vats. Technical evidence indicates that some pages of the Great Bible of 1539 were printed on French presses, while the balance was supplied by London printers in Cromwell's employ. Cranmer supplied the preface which has led some scholars to dub the work "the Cranmer Bible." Holbein was enlisted to do a woodcut, in which the king is shown receiving the Bible from Cromwell and Cranmer and giving it to the people. Cromwell managed the mundane details of setting the price, revising it downward within a year to facilitate the most widespread private purchase, and finally authorizing a very cheap paper issue priced to the pockets of men of modest means.

The English Bible of 1539, the first wholly authorized English vernacular

Bible, owed its existence to the planning, financing, political and diplomatic machinations, and zeal of the great reformation minister Thomas Cromwell. Along with many primers and liturgical works jointly sponsored by him and Cranmer, the Bible was testimony to his purposeful pursuit of a unified religious policy, the object of which was to raise men up from clerical domination to the freedom of a reformed commonwealth. His last remarks on that subject took the form of a Parliamentary speech in April 1540, a scant two months before his arrest for heresy and treason. In it he told his audience of his wish to see in England a Biblical religion flourish free from sectarian brawls and the crushing weight of persecution by churchmen. His earnestness in this view lends the color of truth to the charges against him in 1540: that he had allowed the dissemination of heretical views and books in England that had given comfort to heretics.

During the years of his power (1532–1540), as we have seen, Cromwell used his office to link popular currents of dissent, Erasmian motifs of reform, and Lutheran doctrine. He had made policy what had before been pious exhortation, and had promulgated that policy with a campaign of propaganda and political pressure unprecedented in English history. His efforts had in fact sculpted the outlines of Anglicanism, a church eschewing Romanism and radical Protestant sectarianism; comprehensive in its willingness to embrace individuals of divergent opinions in the arms of a tolerantly ambiguous doctrine; grounded in scripture, conserving what was useful in traditional practices and rejecting what seemed abusive; and alert to the distinction between things truly necessary for salvation and accretions of the centuries which were "things indifferent" to right religion. Thus vestments were kept while idols were swept away in the iconoclast movement of 1538. Thus, also, the way was cleared for the triumph of Protestantism under Edward VI and Elizabeth I, after the brief period of the Henrician reaction (1540–1547) and the reign of Mary Tudor (1553–1558). The process of change begun in the 1530s proved irreversible. Once Englishmen came to know the lovely cadences of Coverdale and the liturgies of Cranmer, once they had heard the gospel stories in their own mother tongue, and had read for themselves Paul's letters, it made little difference that Cromwell was executed, that the "hero" of the English Reformation's "heroic age," as John Foxe called him, was so poorly paid by his king.

During the reaction which set in from 1540 to 1547, Cranmer fought resolutely to preserve the gains of the 1530s. During the peak of the campaign to limit his influence, when he too was charged with heresy in 1543, the archbishop was fashioning an English breviary, missal, and other liturgical works. In 1545, Cromwell's old friend and printer Richard Grafton[43] published an English litany for the dead in which prayers addressed to saints were wholly absent. In the same year, Parliament passed an act suppressing chantries, chapels in which "mass" priests lived on endowments given in the belief that prayers could free the souls of the faithful departed but lingering in purgatory. Grafton also printed that year a new version of the primer sponsored by Cromwell in 1539 and dedicated to him by Bishop Hilsey.[44] Thus, even the years of the supposed "reaction" to the advanced reforming zeal of the 1530s witnessed the consolidation of earlier achievements. There was no counterrevolution. The education of the Prince of Wales, Edward, was entrusted to men of a markedly Protestant or radical humanist persuasion. In 1546 an alarmed imperial ambassador, Van der Delft, reported that Henry VIII was talking about the abolition of the mass! The same year he also noted that the only men fit to govern after Henry's death—it was then clear the king was in decline and would die while Prince Edward was still a boy—were of the "advanced party."

Indeed, the king's death in 1547 brought about the triumph of men we might well call "Cromwellians," the political and religious heirs of the partnership which had joined the dead vicar-general and the still quick archbishop. And this fact made possible the renewal of the revolution which had been slowed but not halted in 1540.

The Consolidation of Protestantism

The transfer of power from Henry VIII to his son Edward VI in 1547 marked the advance of Protestantism in England as well. The king's uncle and regent, Sir Edward Seymour, Duke of Somerset and Protector,[45] and the men who exercised power with him in the king's council, took up vigorously the work of Cromwell and Cranmer and pressed it further than they had dared or been able to do before 1540. To a marked extent the Edwardian Reformation was a continuation of the Henrician. The pressures, religious and social, which had moved reform in directions which even the willful Tudor king had been unable to anticipate or fully to control, were still at work in English society. The gentry and the merchant oligarchs possessed the ultimate resources of power, based on their wealth and expressed in their domination of the Commons. And they had since the 1520s, slowly and in ways not yet fully explored by historians, became irreversibly Protestant.

This is most evident in some of the earliest developments of Edward VI's reign. On July 31, 1547, new injunctions were issued to the clergy in the king's name. These proclamations have been variously hailed as radical Protestant innovations and as the first steps in the process of purging anomalies and abuses in the practice of religion. But the most recent historian of Edward's early kingship has pointed out that these instruments revived Cromwell's attack on the roots of alienation among laymen.[46] He has emphasized that the orders of 1547 were neither new nor more Protestant than those of 1536–1538. Like the earlier injunctions, those of 1547 addressed the practice of religion rather than doctrine. They reiterated changes made in the 1530s regarding images, the support of clerical education, popular instruction, vernacular scripture, the reform of nonresidence, and the importance of maintaining churches in good repair. More important than the fact that they were derivative, however, is that their pervading temper reflected the Protestant leanings of influential men in the country and at court. They thus implied a new impetus that would lead toward yet more substantial innovations, even in doctrine.

Within a year of their proclamation, commissioners sent throughout the country to enforce the orders had reported to the council about the temper of the nation. These men, presiding over the process of inquiry and execution of orders, had been named by Cranmer in league with the council. The men who dominated the commissions were for the most part staunch Protestants. Many of them—Sir John Mason,[47] Richard Cox,[48] Richard Morison and John Hales[49]—were relics of the ministry of Cromwell. Much to their surprise, they found Protestant values firmly rooted in most dioceses, even those ruled by Bishops Bonner[50] (London) and Gardiner (Winchester), the two men who most vehemently resisted the new orders and the firm establishment of a reformed commonwealth in England. The recalcitrant bishops were sent to the Fleet Prison, and uncooperative cathedral staffs were reconstructed to be more favorable to innovation.

The government quickly took advantage of the momentum gained by these attacks along lines already planned. Between 1547 and 1553, first under Somerset's leadership and then under that of the Duke of Northumberland,[51] the Protestant revolution was consolidated through a new series of acts of Parliament and several new liturgical works by Cranmer. The court and the circles surrounding the boy king were characterized by a willingness to pursue plans Cranmer had drawn up nearly alone in the period 1540–1547. And Parliament was to show itself a willing agency of reform once more. Since 1540 there had been added to the Lutheran currents of reform prevalent in England's ruling elites the powerful leaven of Calvin's influence and ideas. By 1547 the success of Calvin's experiments in Geneva had brought him unrivalled authority in the Protestant world. Englishmen had studied with him, and had absorbed the special brand of Biblical theology, with its central insistence on God's terrible predestination, which he added to Luther's insistence on justification by faith. Calvin elaborated the idea that God had known since Creation that some men would be eternally damned and others saved. With perfect foresight of the merits of men, yet in utter disregard for them, God made a choice which demonstrated his absolute sovereignty and incomparable power. Calvin emphasized that men could not grasp fully the problem of reconciling God's crushing omnipotence and man's free will. And he derived from this dilemma the proposition that the Christian must live with anxiety and uncertainty, but that subjectivism and individual license, which had so troubled Henry VIII and his council, could be resolved in the framework of a godly ministry working in a reformed commonwealth.

This is not to suggest that the Edwardian reforms were Calvinist in character. In fact, Cranmer's reworking of doctrine was a mixture of his own "Anglican" theology and borrowings, mainly from Luther. But Calvin was held in high esteem by Somerset and had also sent advice to Edward VI. Several of the king's teachers and court officials were in regular touch with the Geneva theocrat, and a number of influential English and foreign divines working for reform in Edwardian England had accepted Calvin's doctrines and his sense of disciplined work. Others looked to Zwingli's successors at Zurich. The massive propaganda campaign launched against the Mass in 1547–1549 was decidedly Swiss rather than German in its sources. And when Englishmen were faced with the reversal of their reformation under Mary Tudor (1553–1558), many exiles expressed more interest in Calvin's holy commonwealth than they did in the lukewarm institutionalized Protestantism which had by then replaced Luther's early heroic acts of defiance. The two decades which spanned the reigns of Edward and Mary, and the first ten years of Elizabeth I's, finally ended the age of the English Reformation. And during those years it was still at issue whether the church in England would exhibit a Roman, Lutheran, or Calvinist character, or would combine elements of the three in a unique English blend.

During the first Edwardian stage of this struggle, the most salient advances encountered opposition. Little clamor was raised when Parliament revived Henry VIII's scheme to dissolve chantries and add their wealth to the government's coffers and to those of gentry, courtiers, and officials, who vied for good farmland once dedicated to prayers for the faithful departed. But there was considerable doubt as to the wisdom of a wholesale revision of the doctrine of the Eucharist. Early in 1547, Parliament passed a statute allowing communion in both kinds to laymen. But another clause in the same act provided stiff penalties for those who in any way reviled the sacrament of the altar or doubted Christ's real presence in the Mass. Trimming was necessary to placate dissident elements, and an act that provided for the appointment of bishops by letters patent issued by the crown was quickly repealed in favor of election by the cathedral chapter acting under a royal license. This tinkering with the endowment of the church and its hierarchy was of less interest to laymen, however, than the repeal of the repressive parts of Henry VIII's 1539 Act to Abolish Diversity of Opinion, better known as the Six Articles.

The prevalence of religious disputes, however, underlined the wisdom of Cranmer's position that a minimal clarification of doctrine was essential for the maintenance of public order. After two years of frantic religious argument and unrest, as well as hectic propaganda on the sacraments and church government, Edward's council introduced in Parliament the first Edwardian Act of Uniformity, intended to resolve ambiguities stemming from the existence of conflicting versions of English prayer books. The act provided that after Whitsunday 1549 the only legal form of worship was that set forth in Cranmer's First Prayer Book. Together with the English Bible, Cranmer's Litany (1544), and the Cromwellian primers, the Prayer Book of 1549 and its revision in 1552 became the cornerstones of English Protestantism. For many years reformers had differed among themselves about the Mass. Radicals and moderates agreed on communion in both kinds, and concurred in denying that the Mass was a re-enactment of Christ's crucifixion. What they did not agree on was the nature of Christ's presence in the wafer and wine of the communion. Nor could they agree easily on such issues as the vestments proper to priests, or whether a plain table should replace the old consecrated altar, redolent of saints' relics and superstitious practices. It was the genius of the Acts of Uniformity and the lovely English cadences of Cranmer's Prayer Book that they resolved these questions in a suitably ambiguous way. Fusing Latin and other liturgies, Cranmer found English phrases which suggested both the abolition of the doctrine of transubstantiation and its retention. Even so conservative a man as Gardiner found the new formulary acceptable. But rebels in the southwest rejected it in 1549 and waged a small war against being compelled to use the Prayer Book.

After the civil wars hastened Somerset's downfall, Cranmer and Northumberland collaborated in a number of schemes which pushed Protestantism toward new doctrinal formulations. Working closely with radicals like Nicholas Ridley,[52] who had already substituted a plain communion table for the altar in his cathedral church of Rochester, and the Strassburg exile Martin Bucer,[53] the archbishop proceeded to introduce radical innovations. The council ordered all bishops to emulate Ridley in the matter of the table. In 1552 a new Act of Uniformity established a revised prayer book as the sole authorized form of English worship. Cranmer's second *Book of Common Prayer* omitted the idea of sacrifice from the celebration of the Mass. Instead, the crucial emphasis was shifted to Christ's "Do this in remembrance of me," with the result that the ceremony now seemed more memorial than alive. The words spoken by the priest stressed thanksgiving and commemoration. Traditional vestments were banished. When some very radical enthusiasts (Bishop Hooper[54] of Gloucester and John Knox,[55] Calvin's disciple) noted that kneeling was still enjoined, as if in adoration —a remnant of tradition—Cranmer refused new alterations. But by now the archbishop was not as advanced as were some of the king's lay councillors. By conciliar order, the famous Black Rubric was added to the Prayer Book, specifically denying that kneeling implied any adoration of the bread and wine, or the real presence of Christ's natural body in the sacrament of the altar.

These truly radical innovations in worship rested on a striking development in the tenor of the theology which was coming to represent established opinion. While not yet unambiguously "Swiss", it was no longer Henrician, and we have seen the extent to which even Cranmer had yielded to a momentum outstripping his own ideas. This disturbing development was accompanied by a spate of new legislation. One act abolished all positive laws forbidding clerical marriage. This was the logical consequence of the Cromwellian idea that the ministry was a convenience in the administration of religion and not a special caste operating under divine sanction. And only a month before Edward's death on June 12, 1553, Cranmer had the satisfaction of seeing his Forty-Two Articles of Religion embodied in statute with the royal assent. These propositions were the decisive formulation of a Protestant faith for Englishmen. They accepted Calvinist teachings on predestination, condemned the sacrificial concept of the Mass, the doctrine of purgatory, saints' images, Anabaptist ideas, and other practices condemned as superfluous and superstitious in the Cromwellian injunctions of 1536–1538. The Elizabethan religious settlements of 1563 and 1570 were in fact little more than revisions of Cranmer's forty-two propositions. As the Thirty-Nine Articles they are still the basic formulary of the faith in England, buttressed by the Elizabethan adaptations of his great Prayer Book.

Edward VI's reign had been plagued by rebellions and the machinations of bands of politicians bent on the self-interested misgovernment of the commonwealth. Somerset was overthrown by Northumberland, who tried to prevent Mary Tudor from coming to the throne. But the political actions of desperate men ought not to divert our gaze from the lasting achievements —whether of innovation or consolidation—which linked this brief reign to the longer period of initial reform led by Cromwell and Cranmer under Henry VIII's aegis. The Protestants and humanists who had gathered their powers and risked their lives together with courageous ministers had built sturdily. Neither Northumberland's efforts to put Jane Grey on the throne nor Mary Tudor's brief and sterile reign could root out what they had planted. Englishmen had become Protestant, and they stood in 1553 for both the legitimacy of the Tudor dynasty and the faith which had been hammered out in the two decades of crisis which saw More's fall and execution, Cromwell's alleged treason, Henry VIII's faltering grasp on power, and the sordid political manipulations of Edward's reign. The efforts of the "Commonwealth men" and the radical religious reformers, who found in England a refuge from persecution in Europe, insured that there would be continuity after 1553 when they contested with their Catholic Queen for the soul of the nation. While most ordinary people were sluggish and indifferent to changes which little affected their small worlds of farm village, or county town, the political elites of England were by 1553 often willing to defend the Protestant religion, and nourished it with the blood of martyrs.

This resolution generated the problems which characterized Mary's feeble efforts at a Catholic Counter Reformation in England. The particular form of that reaction chosen by Mary was a simple scheme to replace the Church of England with a renewed communion with Rome. Cardinal Pole, the Queen's cousin, was urging on her an immediate submission to the Pope. Only a small minority of English Catholics supported this policy. Yet in successive Parliaments in 1553–1554, legislation turned the clock back to 1547, by repealing all of the Edwardian doctrinal changes, and then to 1529, by repealing the vast body of Cromwell's legislation affecting the constitution of the church in England. The landed classes would not, however, allow the restitution of church lands. Mary, Pole, and Julius III had to accept an agreement by which these lands were allowed to remain in lay hands as the price of tacit consent to the religious reaction then underway. Rebellions against this reaction and Mary's marriage to Philip II of Spain failed. Resistance to persecution and to religious intolerance began increasingly to be expressed in the Commons, where the articulate Englishmen of the politically powerful classes exhibited much of the sturdy independence usually considered the hallmark of the Elizabethan Parliaments. Protestants organized propaganda campaigns against the reaction. Some— Latimer, Ridley and Cranmer, for example—died at the stake, martyrs for their faith, confident in the assurance Cranmer gave them: that they would with their bodies light a fire not easily put out!

It is easy to argue that the Marian reaction failed because of Mary's death without Catholic heirs. But it is more to the point to say that her sister Elizabeth was of a different mold. Elizabeth's accession in 1558 raised the hope that a settlement reflecting purely English motifs might be fashioned. The new queen had had a humanist and Protestant education. Calvinist radicals cast her in the role of a Protestant Deborah, seeing in Henry VIII's daughter the leader of a faction rather than the uniter of the nation. She proved unwilling to play that role, and her reasons bear close scrutiny, for they reflect her own understanding of the English experience of Reformation. Her family history—she was Anne Boleyn's daughter—helped her to understand that she could not find a solution to the permanent crisis in both politics and religion by herself embracing the views of the most zealous of her subjects. The roll of failures who had fallen on that stony path was familiar to her: More, Cromwell, Somerset, Northumberland, Mary. The new queen realized that the royal supremacy was potentially both a blessing and a curse: a blessing if it could be exercised to harmonize the interests of most of her subjects; a curse if its use fomented treason, caused sedition to be uttered in the countryside, and put good men out of hope that they would enjoy peace, prosperity, and freedom from persecution.

The Pilgrimage of Grace, The Prayer Book Rebellion in 1549, Kett's Rebellion in the same year, the many risings of gentry in various parts of England under Mary in 1554–1556, and the upheaval in the north during her own reign (1569) all served to remind Elizabeth that Englishmen lived in a state of constant fear of foreign intervention in their domestic affairs and uncertainty as to how the supremacy would be exercised at home. Gentlemen in their counties and oligarchs in their towns were capable of generating opposition to a government bent on exercising massive and incompletely defined powers in ways unacceptable to the governed. This made of the supremacy and the crown's control over religion a breeding-ground for dissent and opposition. Parliament had still not matured as a forum where opposition could be focused and legitimized, and sedition often seemed the best redress of grievance to the inhabitants of Kent, Warwick, Devon, and Leicester, places scattered about the kingdom as idly as pearls on Elizabeth's gowns. The acceptance or rejection by local leaders of society of reform and the changes it wrought was one of the governing issues of Tudor politics in the age of the Reformation. Somerset had forgotten that and paid dearly for his forgetfulness. Where tacit or active commitment to the motifs of reform was lacking, governors could either face the evil prospect of rebellion or suffer conduct that did not coincide with their expectations.

Though fully armed with the powers of sovereignty and the legitimacy of statute, Tudor sovereigns—and this Elizabeth knew best of all—could not exercise a monopoly of violence against their subjects. What had been accomplished by consent in the Parliaments of the 1530s and 1540s could not be maintained by coercion in the 1550s or 1560s. Mary tried and failed. Elizabeth preferred to avoid the risk by returning to the demonstrably acceptable settlement of the articles of religion and the prayerbooks and injunctions shaped by Cromwell, Cranmer, and the Edwardian religious reformers. She would go neither back to Rome nor forward to Geneva, for she knew that the success of the Reformation depended on the consent of the parliamentary classes. Elizabeth knew it was better to allow some measure of revolt within the limits of government, as her father had demonstrated in giving scope to radical anticlericalism, than to force her people to a contest in which their goods and souls were the prize. Royal power daily impinged on the lives of Englishmen. If grievances were many and unrelieved, only a resort to force would resolve the crisis. But this was the forfeit of government. The other way was to adjust the relationship between the crown and the community both in theory and practice. Her subjects wanted to know what the queen would do with the throne. How would she deal with those inward men of radical temper discontent with the halfway house of the English church, suspended, as it were, between popery and the Puritan ideology of Calvin's disciples in England? How would she abate the fury of factions bent on realizing a paradise for their sect in England? Many seemed to cherish less the commonwealth than the particular well-being of sectarians who shared the love of a policy aimed at the abolition of episcopacy and the erection of congregational power over the choice of ministers and the practice of religion. Would the royal authority be used to balance the conflicting demands of sectarians, or to throw England from the safety of her ambiguous and tolerant religious settlement into the chaos of enthusiasm, whether that of Counter-Reformation Jesuit partisans or zealots who wanted to purge the church root and branch?

These questions had first been raised in the controversy which cast Cromwell from power in 1540, when he appeared to push reform forward faster than the king or council were willing to follow. They haunted Edwardian ministers and councillors. Mary tried to end them by a cynical settlement that united religious reaction with the economic self-interest of the classes which had reaped the spoils of the successive redistributions of church lands. But beneath the apathy of many flowed the commitment of powerful men to the reformed Protestant commonwealth. Elizabeth and her most influential advisors opted for a policy of gaining the consent of the many and coercing the few. They refused to make private beliefs a matter for government inquiry. Elizabeth's government did demand external conformity to the acts of Parliament of 1563 and 1570 which, defeating the hopes of the radical Puritans, rested the Reformation in England solidly on what Cromwell and Cranmer had achieved between 1532 and 1553. Protestantism in matters of piety had led the way toward Protestantism in worship and doctrine. An intentionally ambiguous revival of the Edwardian formularies opened the way for an Elizabethan church and nation at once comprehensive and tolerant. Where Henry VIII had hanged papists and Sacramentarians from the same tree because he reprobated their ideas, Elizabeth would reluctantly condemn Puritans and papists only when overt acts of sedition and treason gave voice to their thoughts. She would bind the formidable governing classes to her interest by continuing the policy of "buttering the rook's nest," or distributing fat bounties of church goods to laymen. Above all she would identify her government with the comfortable Protestantism fashioned by men who had blended Luther, Erasmus, Calvin, and some parts of English genius while she was still a girl.

An Appendix of Tables

I / ORDINATIONS IN FIVE DIOCESES, 1495–1520

Diocese	Average number of ordained priests inclusive of religious at one ordination	Number of parishes as a fraction of the number of parishes in the Lincoln diocese	Estimated average number ordained at one ordination if diocese were same size as Lincoln
Lincoln	30	—	30
Exeter	13	$\frac{1}{3}$	39
Hereford	7	$\frac{1}{7}$	49
Bath & Wells	10	$\frac{1}{4}$	40
Ely	8	$\frac{1}{16}$	128

II / TITLES AND BENEFICES GIVEN BY RELIGIOUS HOUSES, 1514–1521

House	Order	Number of titles given, 1514–20/1	Number of presentations* made of those to whom titles given 1514–20/1	Number of presentations made of those with other titles, 1514–20/1
Bardney	Benedictine	9	1	2
Crowland	Benedictine	2	0	6
Godstow	Benedictine	1	0	7
Ramsey	Benedictine	1	0	6
Garendon	Cistercian	44	0	0
Heynings	Cistercian	11	0	0
Louth Park	Cistercian	2	0	1
Chicksands	Gilbertine	1	0	4
Nocton	Augustinian	16	0	1
Osney	Augustinian	16	0	4
Ulverscroft	Augustinian	18	0	2
Northampton	Augustinian	17	0	0
St. James Croxton	Premonstra- tensian	1	0	0
Axholme	Carthusian	1	0	0
Total		140	1	33

* The "presentation" of a living was the actual "gift" or bestowal of a church with cure of souls on a priest.

III / DURATION OF ABSENTEEISM, 1489–1526

Archdeaconry	First visitation Date	Number of absentee parishes	Second visitation Date	Non-resident	Resident	Unknown
Lincoln	1500	51	1519	14	20	17
Huntingdon	1507	19	1518	8	5	6
Leicester	1489	4	1518–26	2	2	
	1498	12	1518–26	5	7	
	1509/10	14	1518–26	7	7	
	1518	52	1526	20	19	13
Total		152		56	60	36

IV / DISTRIBUTION OF INCOME

| | Gross income | | Net income | |
	Rectors	Vicars	Rectors	Vicars
Up to £4. 19s. 11d.	41	44	20	14
£5–£9. 19s. 11d.	279	336	63	26
£10–£14. 19s. 11d.	297	119	46	17
£15–£19. 19s. 11d.	87	25	24	5
Over £20.	129	21	21	4

V / CLERICAL OFFENSES IN LINCOLN DIOCESE, 1500–1521

		1,359 parishes visited 1500–1510	*1,006 parishes visited in general episcopal visitation* 1514–1521*	*Projected occurrences if all 1,700 parishes reported same incidence† 1500–1510*	*1514–1521*
			Beneficed clergy		
Moral offenses	Incontinence	8	126	10	213
	Irregular clothes and hair	2	0	3	0
	Unacceptable behavior	0	7	0	12
	Farming or sheep-running	0	3	0	5
Pastoral offenses	Irregular services	2	17	3	29
	Sacraments wrongly administered	5	12	6	20
	Failure to preach or visit sick	1	7	1	12
	Failure to perform duties due to age	0	5	0	8
Offenses against church fabric	Church or chapel decay	—	88	—	850
	Vicarage or rectory decay	—	23	—	223
	Cemetery decay	—	44	—	425
	Vestments, books, vessels decayed	—	29	—	283

V / CLERICAL OFFENSES IN LINCOLN DIOCESE. 1500–1521 (Continued)

		Unbeneficed clergy			
Moral offenses	Incontinence	10	12	12	20
	Irregular clothes and hair	0	2	0	3
	Unacceptable behavior	0	17	0	29
Pastoral offenses	Irregular services	1	8	1	14
	Sleeping outside parish	2	5	3	9
	Failure to preach or visit sick	0	1	0	2
	Ignorance	0	1	0	2
	Unspecified inadequacy	0	2	0	3

* These figures represent several visitations to each parish.

† These figures represent the projected total of abuses if all parishes in the diocese were visited and the rate of incidence of abuses remained stable.

Notes

1. The term "farmer" here refers not to a person directly engaged in agricultural labor, but to a man who leases a substantial property on which he employs others as agricultural laborers.

2. The terms "homage" and "allegiance" signify the obligation of direct personal loyalty which was a condition of the "tenure" of a parcel of land.

3. "Gentry" were those gentlemen "farmers" whose social status was clearly above that of dependent peasants and small farmers (yeomen, husbandmen) but less elevated than that of the titled nobility or lay aristocrats.

4. Charles Wriothesley (1508?–1562), herald and chronicler, was the son of Sir Thomas Wriothesley, Garter king-of-arms, and the first cousin of Sir Thomas Wriothesley, Earl of Southampton and Lord Chancellor of England. His *Chronicle* continues that of Richard Arnold and is especially valuable for the reign of Henry VIII.

5. Richard Fitzjames (d. 1522) had a distinguished Oxford academic career, was chaplain to Edward IV, and had been bishop of Rochester (1497–1504) and Chichester (1504–1506) before his advancement to London. At Oxford he introduced reforms in Merton College.

6. Thomas, first marquess of Dorset (1451–1501), a prominent partisan of Edward IV, made a successful transition into the Tudor era by virtue of his support of Henry VII, when the young Earl of Richmond took arms against Richard III.

7. Richard Foxe or Fox (1448?–1528) was a bishop, statesman, and founder of Corpus Christi College, Oxford. He held the bishoprics of Bath and Wells and of Durham before his translation to Winchester. He was a famous chancellor of Cambridge University, a great diplomat, and administrator, and benefactor of grammar schools and Oxford colleges. In his old age he retired from politics, devoting himself to educational reform and translating St. Benedict's "Rule" for women.

8. William Warham (1450–1532) was a canon lawyer and church careerist who rose through political work and diplomatic activity. He is famous chiefly for his protests against reform.

9. Cuthbert Tunstal, Tunstall, or Tonstall (1474–1559) was Master of the Rolls, a lawyer, diplomat, and humanist, a celebrated mathematician, one of the leading administrative stalwarts under Henry VIII, and a man conformable to the Reformation before 1547. Under Edward VI he opposed further religious changes and spent some time in prison. Restored to office and influence under Mary, he refused the Elizabethan oath of supremacy and was deprived of the see of Durham.

10. William Tyndale, educated at Oxford and Cambridge, was an early English biblicist and Lutheran who became involved in disputes with the clergy. Much of his early continental work (1524–1530) had the approval of Henry VIII, but in 1530 Tyndale wrote against the divorce. In 1535, after several years of narrow escapes from royal agents, he was taken at Vilvorde by imperial officers. Despite Cromwell's intercession, he was martyred in 1536.

11. William de Melton was of the same generation as Foxe and Warham. He had a distinguished academic career before his appointment at York in 1496. He died in 1528.

12. John Colet (1467?–1519) Dean of St. Paul's, London, and founder of the famous school there. He was a pluralist and nonresident rector during his studies in Europe, but after his return gave himself to educational reform work in the circle of London humanists about Erasmus and More. He openly criticized the clergy and the king's wars in France, and patronized reformers.

13. Hugh Latimer (1485–1555), the Henrician Bishop of Worcester, early achieved a reputation for heterodox opinions. In 1525, Wolsey protected the Cambridge Lutheran against his irate ordinary, West of Ely. Latimer rose to power in the 1530s, but resigned over his refusal to accept the Six Articles in 1539. On Edward VI's accession he achieved prominence as a court preacher. His sermons are justly famous, as is his martyrdom at Oxford in 1555 during the Marian Reaction.

14. Edward Lee (1482?–1544) was another of the remarkable Henrician "conservatives," whose early career was distinguished by diplomatic service and government patronage. His known hostility to reform—even Erasmian reform—makes his commentary all the more cogent.

15. See Tables 1–5, which bear on all the main points of this analysis.

16. Simon Fish, a noted lay theologian and pamphleteer, is one of the more obscure polemicists, biographically speaking. He was educated in the common law, and was apparently well known about London. In the 1520s he twice fell afoul of Wolsey and fled to Holland. Charged with heresy at Warham, he died in 1531 before his views became fully acceptable in government circles.

17. John Wycliffe was a religious reformer and Oxford theologian prominent in university circles and in the entourage of Edward III's son, John of Gaunt, Duke of Lancaster, between 1361 and his death in 1384. He was repeatedly tried on heresy charges (1377–1381) and forbidden to teach.

18. Well-known as a Protestant divine and martyr, Robert Barnes (1495–1540) was of the Austin Friars, Cambridge. In 1523–1526 he was repeatedly in trouble with authorities on account of his Lutheran opinions. He escaped to Holland in 1528 from a Cambridge prison, and did not return to England until 1531, when he came under Cromwell's protection. He flourished in the 1530s until his patron's fall, but in 1540 was burnt for heresy.

19. "Little" Thomas Bilney (d. 1531), another Cambridge Lutheran in trouble throughout the late 1520s, was finally executed, despite a recantation of errors made in 1529.

20. Anne Boleyn, the second queen of Henry VIII (1507–1536) and daughter of Sir Thomas Boleyn, educated at the French court, was a shrewd, capable politician in her own right. She was the mother of Elizabeth I.

21. Catherine of Aragon (1485–1536), daughter of Ferdinand and Isabella, was the aunt of the Habsburg Emperor Charles V. His mother was Catherine's sister, Juana.

22. One of the central common law courts located at Westminster, then a western London suburb. Its chief business was criminal law, in which the crown was the party of prosecution.

23. A translation of *beneficium clericale,* the privilege claimed by the medieval church to try and punish in ecclesiastical courts clergymen accused of crimes in temporal courts.

24. The legal writ of *praemunire facias* ("that you cause to warn") was issued by chancery, under the authority of 14th-century statutes, charging an offense of one of the following kinds: procuring translations, processes, excommunications, bulls, or other actions or benefits from the pope, against the king, his crown, or the realm.

25. A "convocation" was a meeting of the clergy in a single province (York or Canterbury), in which representatives met under the authority of canon law before the Reformation and of ordinary statute thereafter. Hence, also, the term used to designate the legislative assemblies of the provincial churches. That of Canterbury met simultaneously with the Reformation Parliament.

26. James Anthony Froude (1818–1894), historian and man of letters, is chiefly

famous for his great twelve-volume *A History of England from the Fall of Cardinal Wolsey to the Death of Elizabeth* (1856–1870), in which his strong Protestant sympathies show constantly.

27. The Inns of Court were originally residences or hostels for students engaged in studies of the common law, but in the course of time became institutions for the study and admission to practice of law in London. Cromwell was a member of Gray's Inn in 1524.

28. Reginald Pole (1500–1558), the Marian archbishop of Canterbury and Henry VIII's cousin, after years of study abroad with royal support broke publicly with his kingly relative, defended Rome against England, and received the red hat in December 1536. Thereafter, he had a varied career as a Catholic reformer and agent.

29. John Foxe (1516–1587), the great English martyrologist, resigned his Oxford fellowship in 1545 because he could not accept university statutes in religious matters. He first drafted his *Acts and Monuments* or *Book of Martyrs* while in exile during Mary's reign.

30. Stephen Gardiner or "Wily Winchester" (1483?–1555), a humanistically educated civil and canon lawyer, had a distinguished career in both church and state. Once Wolsey's secretary, he served Henry VIII as secretary of state. In 1531 he became Bishop of Winchester. From 1540 to 1551 he was Chancellor of Cambridge, and upon Mary's accession in 1553 became Chancellor of England.

31. Later Baron Audley of Walden (1488–1544), Sir Thomas had a steady rise in legal and administrative offices, first with Wolsey's patronage. From 1533 to 1544 he was Lord Chancellor of England.

32. John Fisher (1459–1535) had enjoyed a distinguished career as a reformer of education at Cambridge, where he founded or helped found several colleges. He was spiritual advisor to Henry VIII's mother, Margaret Beaufort, and secured Rochester in 1504. An early supporter of Erasmus and opponent of Luther, his writings in the 1520s foreshadowed his defiance of the king on the divorce and succession crises. He was executed for treason, for refusing to acknowledge Henry VIII's supreme headship of the church.

33. Miles Coverdale (1488–1568) was early associated with Latimer, Cromwell, and Barnes. His development as a divine ended with his adoption of Puritan views in the 1560s.

34. Francis Bigod (1508–1537) was another of Wolsey's men who later moved in Cromwell's entourage. A leading "reformer" in Yorkshire, he was also active in the Pilgrimage and was hanged for treason in 1537.

35. A religious reformer and prolific author, Richard Taverner (1505?–1575) was educated at Cardinal's College, Oxford, under Wolsey's aegis. Later a Cromwellian, he was a biblical translator, a Member of Parliament, sheriff of Oxfordshire, and a licensed lay preacher under Edward VI. He was perhaps best known as a translator of Erasmus.

36. Primarily known as a diplomat, Richard Morison (d. 1556) was in Cromwell's employ in the 1530s. He went into exile at Strasburg in 1553, where he later died.

37. The greatest of the Cromwellian humanist defenders of the early Reformation, Thomas Starkey (1499?–1538) had been Pole's secretary in Italy before joining Cromwell's circle in 1533. His best known work, *The Dialogue Between Cardinal Pole and Master Lupset,* was not published until 1876. His *Exhortation to Unity and Obedience* (1535?), printed under royal license, made an explicit defense of the *via media* in religion.

38. A legal writer and controversialist, Christopher St. German (1460?–1540) was educated at Oxford, and became a barrister of Inner Temple. The two books of his 1523 Latin treatise *Doctor and Student* were translated into English in 1530 and 1531. His work is vital for the legal ideas behind English Reformation political thought.

39. Clement Armstrong or Urmeston (floruit 1525–1535) had a career in the royal service, chiefly in connection with the Revels office and the decor of pageants and tournaments. His reputation as a thinker about social and economic reform rests on several pamphlets attributed to him.

40. William Marshall (floruit 1535) was a reformer, printer, and translator, enthusiastically Protestant, who took an active role in the formulation of legislation about the relief of poverty. He was especially staunch in his iconoclasm.

41. Both William Jerome and Thomas Garrett are historically obscure. Apart from state papers mentioning them and Foxe's references to their religious views, they are almost unknown.

42. Priest and martyr (1500?–1555), this John Rogers was on friendly terms with Tyndale and had lived in Wittenberg as a Lutheran pastor. He enjoyed several good benefices between 1537 and 1554, when Mary's government imprisoned him for heresy, on which charge he was executed a year later.

43. Richard Grafton (d. 1572?) was also a chronicler. He and Edward Whitechurche were the printers of the Great Bible and had the monopoly patent for primers and service books. In 1541 he got in trouble over some ballads defending Cromwell, the late Earl of Essex, but Grafton survived to print the Prayer Book.

44. John Hildesleigh or Hilsey (d. 1538) succeeded Fisher at Rochester in 1535. He was a Dominican monk sympathetic to reform who enjoyed Cromwell's patronage. Active in the exposure of relics and miraculous statues, he also compiled the *Manuall of Prayers* or *Prymer in Englysche* (1539) dedicated by him to Cromwell.

45. Edward Seymour (1506?–1552) was a well-established courtier before his sister Jane became Henry VIII's third queen. The birth of her son, the future Edward VI, in 1537, cost Queen Jane her life but assured the success of her family. Her eldest brother, Sir Edward, had a sound military career in the 1530s and 1540s, complemented by high state office, an earldom (Hertford) in 1537, and the dukedom which marked his political coup in 1547.

46. See W. K. Jordan, *Edward VI: The Young King* (Cambridge, Mass.: Harvard University Press, 1968), pp. 325–347.

47. Statesman, scholar, diplomat, and courtier (1503–1566), John Mason also held many high secretarial offices, was repeatedly a Member of Parliament, and made the adjustments necessary to find favor under Queen Mary.

48. The Bishop of Ely (1500–1581), this Richard Cox was one of Cranmer's Cambridge friends who found much favor in the 1530s. A Marian exile from 1554 to 1558, he was an ardent critic of John Knox and the more radical Calvinists after 1558.

49. John Hales (d. 1571), writer, clerk of the hanaper in chancery, Member of Parliament, Enclosure Commissioner (1548), and Protestant propagandist, was part of the Wolsey–Cromwell coterie of civil servants who provided continuity of administrative experience throughout the early phases of the Reformation.

50. Educated at Pembroke College, Oxford, Bonner (1500?–1569) became a prominent civil and canon lawyer. He was Chaplain to Wolsey, took an active role in Henry's divorce suit, and found favor with Cromwell in the late 1530s. He received the bishopric of London in 1539. During Edward VI's regime he spent most of his time in prison for nonconformity, and was again deprived and imprisoned in 1559. He died in the Marshalsea ten years later.

51. Sir John Dudley (1502?–1553) was eldest son of the early Tudor administrator Edmund Dudley and father of Sir Robert, Earl of Leicester, the Elizabethan favorite. A successful soldier and court official, he was Great Admiral of England, Earl of Warwick and, after his coup against Somerset, the most powerful man in England. He was made a duke in 1551, toppled Somerset in 1552, this time fatally, and in 1553 plotted to replace Mary in the succession with his daughter-in-law, Lady Jane Grey.

52. Nicholas Ridley (1500?–1555), successively bishop of Rochester and London, came from an ancient gentry family of the North. One of Cranmer's chaplains, he had an academic career, was personal chaplain to Henry VIII (1541), and after 1547 was reckoned part of the radical reformation group in Edward's government. Declared a heretic in 1554, he died at the stake with Cranmer and Latimer.

53. Martin Bucer or Butzer (1491–1551) became a Protestant after 1518 and owed his conversion directly to his correspondence with Luther. After 1523 he settled at Strassburg, where he led the Reformation until 1549. By 1529–1530 he had adopted Zwingli's views on the Eucharist. Forced from Strassburg by the Imperial Interim of 1548, he found refuge in England, where he became Regius Professor of Divinity.

54. John Hooper (d. 1555) was another of the martyrs of 1555. Bishop of Gloucester and then Worcester, this former Cistercian monk was in exile from England after Cromwell's fall. He was much influenced by Swiss reformers, and on his return to England in 1549 served as Somerset's chaplain and a leader of the advanced reformers. He was a noted homilist and expounder of the Bible.

55. John Knox (1507–1572), the great Scottish Calvinist reformer, met Calvin while in exile in 1554 and took up very advanced positions, which he propagated among English-speaking refugees in their church at Frankfurt-am-Main. He was a prolific polemicist and historian.

Selected Bibliography

In recent years several good surveys of the Reformation in England have appeared. The best of them is A. G. Dickens, *The English Reformation* (London, 1964), which fully develops the view that the Elizabethan and Stuart history of papists and Puritans must be separated from Reformation history. The most important Catholic account is Philip Hughes, *The Reformation in England* (London, 1951–1954), 3 vols. Two briefer books repay close attention: Joel Hurstfield, ed. *The Reformation Crisis* (London, 1965), a collection of essays by leading scholars; and T. M. Parker, *The English Reformation to 1558* (London, 1950). Among older works, perhaps the most valuable are G. Constant's two volumes, both translated from the original French by R. E. Scantlebury (vol. 1) and E. I. Watkin (vol. 2) : *The English Schism: Henry VIII* (London, 1934) and *Introduction of the Reformation into England: Edward VI* (London, 1942).

The student wishing to read original sources will find them listed in often bewildering array in several bibliographies, the best of which are Conyers Read, *Bibliography of British History: The Tudor Period,* rev. ed. (Oxford, 1959), and Mortimer Levine, *Tudor England, 1485–1603* (London, 1968). There are, however, several good collections edited for student use: A. G. Dickens and D. Carr, eds., *The English Reformation to the Accession of Elizabeth* (London, 1967) ; A. J. Slavin, ed., *Humanism, Reform and Reformation* (New York, 1969), and also Slavin, ed., *Thomas Cromwell on Church and Commonwealth: Selected Letters, 1523–1540* (New York, 1969). The many volumes of the Parker Society Publications make readily accessible the writings of the great English reformers, including the letters and treatises of Cranmer, Coverdale, Hooper, Latimer, and Tyndale. The major Reformation works of Fisher and More are available in The Early English Text Society publications, where one can also find the polemical writings of Simon Fish, John Bale, and Henry Brinkelow. Two monumental works of John Strype are useful for documents: *Annals of the Reformation,* 4 vols. (Oxford, 1824) and *Ecclesiastical Memorials,* 7 vols. (Oxford, 1816). The same is true of G. Burnet, *History of the Reformation of the Church of England,* in the 7-vol. Oxford edition (1865).

On the condition of the church in society before the Reformation, the student will find especially helpful the following: H. Maynard Smith, *Pre-*

Reformation England (London, 1938); Peter Heath, *The English Parish Clergy on the Eve of the Reformation* (London, 1969); M. Bowker, *The Secular Clergy in the Diocese of Lincoln, 1495–1520* (London, 1968); I. Churchill, *Canterbury Administration,* 2 vols. (London, 1933); R. F. S. Du Boulay, *The Lordship of Canterbury* (London, 1968); O. Marti, *Economic Causes of the English Reformation* (New York, 1929); A. Savin, *English Monasteries on the Eve of the Dissolution* (Oxford, 1909); and Dom David Knowles' magisterial *The Religious Orders in England,* 3 vols. (Cambridge, 1950–1959). The secular side of the social and economic history of early Tudor England can best be studied in Peter Ramsey, *Tudor Economic Problems* (London, 1963), and R. H. Tawney, *The Agrarian Problem in the Sixteenth Century* (London, 1912), supplemented by J. Thirsk's *Tudor Enclosures* (London, 1959) and *The Agrarian History of England and Wales, 1500–1640* (Cambridge, 1967). Also basic is Eric Kerridge, *The Agricultural Revolution* (London, 1967), and C. Hill, *The Economic Problems of the Church* (Oxford, 1956), which shows how persistent in Elizabethan and Stuart England were the problems of church finance and the concomitant social and economic involvements of the clergy. The *Economic History Review* is indispensable for all questions relating to the demesne, price and population trends, changes in tenure and peasant life, the wealth of the church, and the economic side of lay-clerical relations.

On Lollards, early English Protestantism, and Humanism, the bibliography is vast, topically and biographically. The following selection from that literature will, however, serve most of the beginning student's needs: A. G. Dickens, *Lollards and Protestants in the Diocese of York, 1509–1558* (Oxford, 1958); J. A. F. Thomson, *The Later Lollards, 1414–1520* (London, 1965); *Lollardy and the Reformation in England,* 4 vols. (London, 1908–1913), by J. Gairdner, is marred by his distaste for heresy; W. H. Summers, *The Lollards of the Chiltern Hills* (London, 1906); and M. Aston, "Lollardy and the Reformation: Survival or Revival," *History* 49 (1964): 149–174. On humanism and especially English Erasmianism, see J. K. McConica, *English Humanists and Reformation Politics* (Oxford, 1965); H. A. Enno van Gelder, *The Two Reformations of the Sixteenth Century* (The Hague, 1961); H. C. Porter, *Reformation and Reaction in Tudor Cambridge* (Cambridge, 1958); E. W. Hunt, *Dean Colet and his Theology* (London, 1956); A. B. Ferguson, *The Articulate Citizen and the English Renaissance* (Durham, 1965); R. P. Adams, *The Better Part of Valor: More, Erasmus, Colet and Vives on Humanism, War and Peace, 1496–1535* (Seattle, 1962); J. Hexter, *More's Utopia: the Biography of an Idea* (Princeton, 1952); F. Caspari, *Humanism and the Social Order in Tudor England* (Chicago, 1954); K. Charlton, *Education in Renaissance England* (London, 1965); F. Seebohm, *The Oxford Reformers* (London, 1938); Joan Simon, *Education and Society in Tudor England* (Cambridge, 1966); and W. G. Zeeveld, *Foundations of Tudor Policy* (Cambridge, Mass., 1948). The best recent general work on the origins of Protestantism is W. A. Clebsch, *England's Earliest Protestants, 1520–1535* (New Haven, 1964). Among the best older studies are: M. Maclure, *The Paul's Cross Sermons, 1534–1642* (Toronto, 1958); L. B. Smith, *Tudor Prelates and Politics* (Princeton, 1953); E. Routley, *English Religious Dissent* (Cambridge, 1960); and two books by E. G. Rupp, *Six Makers of the English Reformation* (New York, 1957) and *Studies in the Making of the English Protestant Tradition* (Cambridge, 1947).

On particular aspects of the fashioning of a Protestant commonwealth in England, certain topical and biographical studies are basic. Among biographies, the following are especially good: A. G. Dickens, *Thomas Cromwell and the English Reformation* (London, 1959); A. G. Chester, *Hugh Latimer* (Philadelphia, 1954); C. Hopf, *Martin Bucer* (Oxford, 1946); J. F. Mozley, *William Tyndale* (London, 1937); A. F. Pollard, *Thomas Cranmer* (London, 1926); John Foxe's *Book of Martyrs,* or *The Acts and Monuments of John Foxe,* edited by G. T. Townsend and S. R. Cattley, 8 vols. (London, 1837–1841); J. Ridley, *Nicholas Ridley* (London, 1957) and his *Thomas Cranmer* (Oxford, 1962). Studies of opponents of the Reformation often shed considerable light on the movement for reform. This is especially true of W. Schenk, *Reginald Pole* (London, 1950); C. Sturge, *Cuthbert Tunstal* (London, 1938); J. A. Muller, *Stephen Gardiner* (London, 1926), and R. W. Chambers, *Thomas More* (London, 1935). Also enlightening are studies of major political figures, especially A. F. Pollard's *Wolsey* (New York, 1929) and *Henry VIII* (London, 1970), as well as W. K. Jordan's *The Reign of Edward VI: The Young King* (Cambridge, Mass., 1968).

The following studies of aspects of the Reformation are also fundamental: C. Butterworth, *The English Primers* (Philadelphia, 1953); E. T. Davies, *Episcopacy and the Royal Supremacy* (Oxford, 1950); A. G. Dickens, *The Marian Reaction in the Diocese of York* (London, 1957); C. W. Dugmore, *The Mass and the English Reformers* (London, 1958); C. H. Garrett, *The Marian Exiles* (Cambridge, 1938); H. Gee, *The Elizabethan Clergy and the Settlement of Religion* (Oxford, 1898); W. Haller, *The Rise of Puritanism* (New York, 1938); P. Hughes, *Rome and the Counter-Reformation in England* (London, 1942); M. Knappen, *Tudor Puritanism* (Chicago, 1939); E. C. Messenger, *The Reformation, The Mass and The Priesthood,* 2 vols. (London, 1936–1937); J. E. Oxley, *The Reformation in Essex to the Death of Mary* (Manchester, 1965); J. H. Primus, *The Vestments Controversy* (Kampen, 1960); W. H. Frere and F. Proctor, *A New History of the Book of Common Prayer* (London, 1902); N. S. Tjernagel, *Henry VIII and the Lutherans* (St. Louis, 1965); and W. T. Whitley, *The English Bible under the Tudor Sovereigns* (London, 1937).

Lastly, the Reformation cannot be studied apart from its political context. Some biographies already cited are useful in this regard, but several general studies and a few monographs are also necessary. Among them the surveys of J. S. Brewer, *The Reign of Henry VIII,* 2 vols. (London, 1884), which ends with Wolsey's fall, and J. D. Mackie, *The Earlier Tudors, 1485–1558* (Oxford, 1952), are basic. So also, in a different sense, are S. T. Bindoff, *Ket's Rebellion* (London, 1949) ; M. H. Dodds and R. Dodds, *The Pilgrimage of Grace,* 2 vols. (Cambridge, 1915) ; M. Levine, *The Early Elizabethan Succession Question* (Stanford, 1966) ; D. M. Loades, *Two Tudor Conspiracies* (Cambridge, 1965) ; A. Ogle, *The Tragedy of the Lollards Tower* (Oxford, 1949) ; and G. R. Elton, *The Tudor Revolution in Government* (Cambridge, 1953).

A sixteenth-century engraving of the Council of Trent. Copyright British Museum.

6.

The Catholic Reformation

JOHN C. OLIN

THE SIXTEENTH CENTURY was marked from its opening years by a
lively awareness of the need for reform in Christian life and Christian
society and by the phenomenon of personal conversion and more extended
spiritual renewal. The times unquestionably quickened and challenged man's
religious consciousness. A changing social and economic environment, the
geographical expansion of the European world, the intellectual alertness and
cultural creativity we associate with the Renaissance suggest some of the factors then at work. It would have been odd indeed if the most basic and pervasive feature of Europe's civilization, its Christianity, had not undergone
change, or if individual Christians had not responded to their changing times.

We know, of course, that they did, and that the entire church in the early
sixteenth century underwent a tremendous crisis and upheaval. The latter
event in all its complexity is known as the Reformation, and we are accustomed
to focusing our attention on the experience and actions of the Protestant
reformers who broke with the established church and preached to differing
degrees new doctrines and practices. These changes and reforms were not, however, the only religious stirrings of the age. In this essay we shall look briefly
at efforts toward renewal and reform which sought to realize their goals
within the framework of the Catholic Church's teaching and authority.
This movement, almost as varied and certainly as far-reaching as early Protestantism, we shall call the Catholic Reformation.

Catholic reform in all its manifestations, potential and actual, was profoundly influenced by the crisis and subsequent schism that developed after 1517. It did not suddenly arise then, but it was given new urgency, as well as a new setting and a new dimension, by the problems that Protestantism posed. What had been, and probably would have remained, a matter of renewal and reform within the confines of religious and ecclesiastical tradition became also a defense of that tradition and a struggle to maintain and restore it. A very complex pattern of Catholic activity unfolded under the shock of religious revolt and disruption. It cannot satisfactorily be labeled the Counter Reformation, for the term is too narrow and misleading. There was indeed a reaction to Protestantism, but this factor, as important as it is, neither subsumes every facet of Catholic life in the sixteenth century nor adequately explains the source and character of the Catholic revival.

Our initial task, then, is to break through the conventional stereotype of Protestant Reformation and Catholic Counter Reformation to view Catholic reform in a more comprehensive and objective way. This will entail consideration of the reaction to schism and the advance of Protestantism, but this subject can neither serve as a point of departure nor be allowed to usurp the stage. The survival of Catholicism and its continued growth suggest another perspective, as do the lives and devotion of so many of the most important Catholic figures of this time. Indeed, if the real significance of the Catholic Reformation must be found in its saints, as has recently been remarked, then emphasis on schism, controversy, and the more secular reflexes of ecclesiastical man may be slightly misplaced. At any rate, we must try to give every aspect of the story its due.

This essay will be positive in approach, and more concerned with describing currents of reform in the Catholic Church than in detailing repressive and combative measures against Protestantism or highlighting inadequacies and failures. The latter approach, which tends to view sixteenth-century Catholicism from the vantage-point of the Protestant revolt, has been fairly standard in most Reformation manuals and texts.[1] We shall depart from this tradition in the hope of redressing the balance and examining more fully the nature of the Catholic revival.

This account will span the years approximately from 1495 to 1565—that is, from the time of Savonarola to the adjournment of the Council of Trent. It will deal with a number of important individuals, but the common cause they served will not be obscured from sight. They represented a coherent and effective movement, and supply the key to an understanding of the church's survival in this age of crisis.

---

[1] For example, Preserved Smith, *The Age of the Reformation* (New York, 1920), chapter 8, and G. R. Elton, *Reformation Europe, 1517–1559* (New York, 1966), chapter 7.

Early Proponents of Reform

The church at the close of the Middle Ages was, both institutionally and spiritually, in a state of depression and decline. "Almost everywhere," observes Ludwig Pastor in his *History of the Popes,* "ecclesiastical life was full of abuses and evils, and the prestige of the Papacy was seriously shaken." A widespread dereliction of duty and gross secularization degraded and corrupted religious life. These ills were manifested in a number of ways: unworthy men held office in the church; venality, skullduggery, and politics dominated the papal court; bishops failed to reside in their dioceses and seriously care for their flocks; priests were often ignorant and untrained; monastic discipline was lax and the behavior of the monks and friars too frequently coarse, arrogant, and offensive. At the level of popular practice and devotion the results were baleful. Superstition was rife, morality at low ebb, and the gospel message itself deformed and unclear. "It looked," Erasmus wrote in 1519 in a kind of ultimate judgment, "as if, with things ever headed for the worse, the spark of Christian piety, whence an extinct charity could be rekindled, would at last be totally put out." There were many instances of real sanctity and dedication during this time, but in general Catholic life in the late Middle Ages was grievously depressed and in urgent need of vigorous reform. Indeed, the demand for reform had long been commonplace. However, the cry for "reformation in head and in members," as it was called, went largely unheeded, and as time wore on zealous men everywhere grieved for "the ruin of the church." It was this situation which provided the occasion, though not the source or total context, for reform and renewal in the sixteenth century.

At the threshold of this century stood the charismatic figure of the great Florentine preacher Girolamo Savonarola. Calling for repentance and reform, he prophesied the imminent judgment of God on a sinful world. Savonarola was a fervent and learned Dominican friar, born in Ferrara in 1452 and prior of the monastery of San Marco in Florence in the last fateful years of his life, 1491–1498. His career and prophetic message are intimately bound up with political events in the Italy of his day—the invasion by Charles VIII of France in 1494, the fall of the Medici from control in Florence, the diplomatic role of the great Renaissance city—and he rose meteorlike in the 1490s to a dominance few others had ever attained in Florence. His sermons were the instrument of his influence and power. They are relevant to the political scene, but they also have a deeper purpose and significance and reveal first and foremost the religious reformer whose consuming aim, enlivened by a Renaissance spirit, was the revival of Christian faith and Christian life. Savonarola lashed out at the sins of priests and prelates and finally at the notorious Borgia Pope Alexander VI; he saw the avenging "sword of the Lord" about to strike, called men back to the straighter path, and prophesied the eventual renovation of the church. Savonarola's dominance in the tumultuous city on the Arno lasted only a few years. Under pressure by the pope and his own enemies at home, he soon fell from power and was brought to trial and the scaffold in the spring of 1498. The impact of his message, however, by no means disappeared. Michelangelo's great image of Christ in judgment in the altarpiece of the Sistine Chapel evokes Savonarola's memory, and his voice ringing through the Duomo echoed down the crucial years that followed. "Had his voice been listened to," writes his biographer Roberto Ridolfi, "perhaps beyond the Alps Luther would not have arisen, or his influence would have been less; and Reform, of which every Christian heart felt the need, would then have been born in the very bosom of the Church of Rome."

If we may view Savonarola as an "ancestral voice" prophesying judgment and renewal, the figure of his contemporary Francisco Ximenes de Cisneros, the Cardinal of Spain, affords an example of a different kind of Catholic reform at the turn of the sixteenth century. From 1495 until his death in late 1517 this remarkable man, an austere Franciscan, held the primatial see of Toledo and was unquestionably the most important personage in the court of Ferdinand and Isabella. He was primarily an administrator and statesman in the later years of his very long life (he was born in 1436), but such responsibilities in no way undermined his religious zeal. In fact, they account for the effectiveness of his efforts to restore the discipline and enhance the quality of the Spanish church. In his synods of Alcalá (1497) and Talavera (1498), Ximenes enjoined his priests to high standards in their own lives and to their duties to preach the gospel and conscientiously care for the souls entrusted to them. The emphasis on the pastoral mission—the care of souls—at the heart of his church reform was influenced by humanism, which was beginning to pervade all of Europe in his day. He founded the University of Alcalá in the early sixteenth century for the education of a clergy who would constitute, in the words of Marcel Bataillon, "the cadres of a Church more worthy of Christ." Alcalá was from the start the center of humanism in Spain, and there Ximenes gathered an array of distinguished scholars. He tried to lure the famous Erasmus to Castile. The greatest achievement of the Alcalá humanists was the Complutensian Polyglot Bible. "We present this work," wrote Ximenes in his dedication to Pope Leo X, "so that the hitherto dormant study of Holy Scripture may begin to revive."

The scriptural revival underway in Europe in the early decades of the sixteenth century was the soul of the movement called Christian humanism. Its scholarly precursor was the humanism of Renaissance Italy, but its thrust and intensity derived chiefly from the need for spiritual renewal in a Christendom disordered and depressed. "The world is weighed down," is an expression we frequently find in Erasmus; it "thirsts for the Gospel truth." This need, however, was more an activating or catalyzing force than a formative influence. The deeper roots of the scriptural revival and of Christian humanist reform lie in the heritage of Christianity and in those spiritual currents of the late Middle Ages, like the *Devotio Moderna*, that sought a more direct and more personal religious experience. A return to the "sources" of the Christian faith—to the model of Christ and the primitive church, to Holy Scripture and the early Fathers—thus became the means for renewing and reforming Christian life.

Ximenes' Complutensian Bible, though undoubtedly a landmark, was neither the first beacon nor the most important. As early as 1496 the English scholar and future dean of St. Paul's, John Colet, having returned from several years of study on the continent, began lecturing on the Epistles of St. Paul at Oxford in a new and stimulating way. He adapted the grammatical and historical method of the Italian humanists to scriptural exegesis, and sought to give greater meaning and relevance to the sacred text. It would appear that, under the influence of the Florentine Platonists and of Savonarola, Colet had come back to England a humanist reformer. His Oxford lectures stirred wide attention, and were directed toward both a reform in theological study and a more general religious revival. A famous sermon Colet delivered some years later in 1512, at a convocation of the clergy of Canterbury province, offers striking evidence of his continuing devotion to reform. Taking as his text St. Paul's injunction in Romans XII not to conform to the world but to be reformed with a new mind, he pleaded with the prelates to forsake worldly and secular ways and to live by the laws that must govern Christ's church. "Return to the God of love and peace, return to Christ . . . return to the true priestly life," he adjured them, and asked pardon for his importunity as "a man sorrowing for the ruin of the Church." One hears an echo of Savonarola.

Colet had a distinguished career as a priest, educator, and preacher until his death in 1519, but his pioneer work at Oxford as a scriptural scholar and exegete in the humanist tradition was perhaps his chief contribution; it is especially noteworthy because of his influence on Erasmus. The great Dutch humanist first visited England in 1499 on the eve of his own career, and Colet, whom he met at Oxford and with whom he began a long and close friendship, helped set the course of his life's work. With Erasmus we encounter the greatest exemplar of the movement to reform Christian learning and Christian life through a return to the sources of Europe's faith. His active career, extending from the first publication of his *Adages* in 1500 to his death in 1536, is truly a monument of labor and dedication, and the merit of his work as well as his enormous output won him a stature and influence rivaled by few others in European history. Erasmus was essentially a scholar, though the wit and grace of his style, as well as his erudition and moral purpose, made him the most widely-read author of his day. New editions of his books issued constantly from the presses of Europe—Froben in Basel, Badius in Paris, Martins in Antwerp, Schürer in Strassburg—and reached the educated and influential everywhere.

Erasmus, though the outstanding intellectual personage of his time, was not alone in his scholarly and reformist endeavors. The work of the great French humanist Jacques Lefèvre d'Etaples, for example, paralleled his own. The latter's scholarly edition of the Psalms with five variant Latin texts appeared in 1509, his edition of St. Paul's epistles in 1512, his important commentaries on the gospels in 1522, and his French translation of the New Testament in 1523. Lefèvre prefaced these works with introductions of the greatest importance for promoting and directing the course of the scriptural revival. He was also actively engaged from 1521 to 1525 in the administration and reform of a diocese in France—the bishopric of Meaux, then headed by his lifelong friend and patron Guillaume Briçonnet. Lefèvre's efforts were compromised and made suspect by the rise of Protestantism in the 1520s, and the Meaux circle that centered around him was dispersed in 1525, but, like Erasmus, Colet, and Ximenes, he must properly be acknowledged as belonging to a movement aimed at Catholic renewal.

One can indeed ask of this movement whether its thrust was authentically Catholic. Did it not pose a danger to the established church? Did it not in fact pave the way for Protestantism and schism? Historians have given a variety of answers to these questions, which arise in the first place because of the divisions in Christendom that came after 1517. Similarly, the Protestant-Catholic polarization that so rapidly occurred in the midst of the religious crisis influenced the attitudes and judgments men expressed. For example, Erasmus from his own time until quite recently has been viewed by many as "laying the egg Luther hatched," and Lefèvre has been seen as a kind of proto- or crypto-Protestant. However, the several reformers we have discussed indubitably considered themselves Catholic and their activities as being within the orbit of the existing Catholic Church. They strove to reform that church and its members, not to defy it, work outside it, or create another church in its place. Erasmus, replying to Luther's attack, wrote in his *Hyperaspistes* (1526), "I have never defected from the Catholic Church . . . I will bear with this Church until I see a better one, and it must bear with me until I become better." If at times the methods or criticisms of the humanists raised the hackles of some of the professional theologians at Paris or Louvain—the scholastic theologians, as they are labeled, or the *modern* theologians, as Erasmus called them—or the ire of certain monks, that neither excluded them from the church nor negated their Catholic faith. The church, after all, did revere scripture as the revealed Word of God, "the very storehouse of faith," to quote Thomas More, himself both a humanist and a Catholic. The scriptural emphasis and exegesis of the Christian humanists is now being more accurately appraised as fully orthodox, in keeping with the patristic tradition, and geared to effecting the renewal of theology and the reform of religious life within the existing structure.[2]

But the peaceful and progressive realization of such a reformation was not to be. On almost the day of Ximenes' death, Luther advanced to the center of the stage, and the great controversy stemming from his Ninety-five

---

[2] See, for example, Louis Bouyer, "Erasmus in Relation to the Medieval Biblical Tradition," in *The Cambridge History of the Bible,* vol. 2, edited by G. W. Lampe (Cambridge, 1969), 492–505.

Theses began. We need not elaborate here on the crisis that now ensued. Suffice it to say that the church was rent, the authority of the pope overthrown in many lands, and important aspects of the doctrine and practice of centuries disputed or denied. However one appraises the role of Luther or analyzes the causes of his revolt, it is clear that the historical Catholic Church was newly and most gravely challenged, and that its very life was cast into the balance. A very complex pattern of Catholic activity now developed. There was obviously a response to the Protestant challenge: Catholic doctrine was to be defended, heresy condemned, the revolt checked and suppressed, the church maintained and restored. This movement we are accustomed to calling the Counter Reformation, a term originating with the German historian Ranke nearly a century and a half ago. But the preexisting concern for renewal and reform *within* the Catholic Church also continued. Yet clearly the scene had radically changed after 1517.

Reform of abuses and shortcomings in the church became all the more urgent as men witnessed the "tragedy" that had occurred. "God permits this persecution to afflict His Church," declared Pope Adrian VI in 1522, "because of the sins of men, especially of the priests and prelates of the Church." And he pledged himself to "expend every effort to reform first this Curia [the papal court], whence perhaps all this evil has come. . . ." However, certain features of the earlier Catholic reform became either suspect, inappropriate, or more difficult to sustain as religious controversy widened and positions became more rigid and extreme. For example, Erasmus' sharp criticism of the monks and the pious and somewhat mystical *évangélisme* of Lefèvre seemed all the more dangerous and subversive to their opponents under the conditions that now prevailed. Erasmus himself said that, if he had foreseen what was coming, he would not have written certain things or he would have written them in a different way. Ongoing currents of reform nevertheless survived, and signs of positive spiritual revival, quite independent of the crisis and the schism, persisted and multiplied in the Catholic fold. One of the chief evidences of this revival is the formation of many new religious orders in the period after 1517—including the Theatines, the Capuchins, and the Jesuits, to name but three of the most important. And these new orders did not merely serve as signs of a religious awakening within Catholicism; they became instruments for the accomplishment of further reform.

The Nature of Catholic Reform

Catholic spirituality at this time was highly individualistic and activist, in contrast to the more communal and contemplative spirituality of the Middle Ages. The stress was on the individual's interior religious experience—on private prayer and meditation, self-discipline, personal sanctification and spiritual growth—rather than community devotions and formal liturgical piety. The heightened "personalization" of the religious impulse had an exterior side as well, expressing itself—overflowing, so to speak—in a more intense active life. This took numerous forms: a literature prescribing religious *exercises* (the term is most interesting), a deep concern with conduct and with moral or ethical questions, emphasis on the virtue of charity, the desire to be of service to others, the renewal of the pastoral ministry, missionary zeal and endeavor. "Love ought to manifest itself in deeds rather than in words," St. Ignatius Loyola wrote in his *Spiritual Exercises*, and this principle, appearing in a famous book of exercises for "the conquest of self and the regulation of one's life," expresses as well as any other single statement the nature and thrust of the new spirituality. Indeed Ignatius' whole life— his conversion, his labors and apostolate, his *Spiritual Exercises*, his injunction to seek God in all things—exemplifies in almost classic form this spirituality which in the course of the sixteenth century was to enliven and renew the Catholic Church.

This new spirituality was prefigured by currents in the fifteenth century such as the *Devotio Moderna* in northern Europe and the devout humanism of so many Italian scholars, and Erasmus reveals its most salient features. In his *Enchiridion* or *Handbook of the Christian Soldier,* written in 1501, he expresses a personal inward piety, completely Christocentric, which must manifest itself not in outward ceremonial or legalistic observance but in charity and the moral life. This attitude was drawn from Holy Scripture, but it was also formed by the moralistic tendencies of the *Devotio Moderna* and by the spiritualizing influence of Renaissance Platonism. It remained throughout Erasmus' life the very core of his religious thought.

A similar spirituality can be seen at work in the lay religious societies, or confraternities, which existed in Italy in the early sixteenth century, notably in the Genoese and Roman Oratories of Divine Love. The Genoese Oratory was founded in 1497 by a prominent layman, Ettore Vernazza, inspired by a remarkable woman then in charge of a hospital in Genoa, the very practical-minded mystic known as St. Catherine of Genoa. The Oratory was a predominantly lay association whose members sought to cultivate their spiritual lives through the faithful practice of religious devotions and works of charity and benevolence, specifically assistance to one another in times of need and the care of the sick. "Our fraternity," their charter begins, "is not instituted for any other purpose than to root and implant in our hearts divine love, that is to say, charity." Sometime prior to 1517 another Oratory, patterned after the Genoese society, was established in Rome—an event which historians have often singled out as marking the beginning of effective Catholic reform because of the number of prominent reformers who were associated with it. These include Gaetano da Thiene, a devout priest and curial official, later canonized; Gian Pietro Carafa, Bishop of

Chieti and papal diplomat who subsequently reigned as Pope Paul IV; and several other notable figures whose names will become familiar in the pages that follow. Even Guillaume Briçonnet, Bishop of Meaux and Lefèvre's patron, who was on embassy in Rome in the years 1516 to 1518, is said to have come under its influence.

St. Catherine of Genoa's doctrine of divine love or charity, which bears a resemblance to the religious philosophy of Marsilio Ficino and the Platonic Academy, inspired the establishment of the Genoese and Roman Oratories, which in turn gave rise to significant reform efforts. One of the first and most fruitful of these was a new religious order known as the Theatines, the pioneer of several new orders of priests actively engaged in pastoral and charitable work. The Theatines, founded in 1524 by da Thiene and Carafa and two other members of the Roman Oratory, represent a more structured and permanent expression of the Oratory's ideal. Theatine priests lived in communities under a rule but also undertook an active apostolate. The term Theatine, derived from Carafa's bishopric of Chieti or Theate, soon became synonymous in Italy with an austere and reformed priesthood.

After the devastating sack of Rome by mutinous imperial troops in May, 1527, the Theatines—then numbering fourteen members with Carafa their first superior—took refuge in Venice, where they continued their work and had close ties with the eminent Venetian noble and humanist, Gasparo Contarini, and the reforming bishop in neighboring Verona, Gian Matteo Giberti. The names of both Contarini and Giberti have traditionally been associated with the earlier Roman Oratory, but they will henceforth be linked more firmly with that of Carafa in the general movement of Catholic reform. In Venice, Carafa became deeply concerned at the laxity and disorder of the Venetian church and at the spread of heresy in the maritime republic. His concerns, which he expressed in an appeal to Pope Clement VII in 1532 to take energetic measures to reform and strengthen the church, reveal all too well the problems then confronting the Catholic reformers. They were dealing not only with the correction of abuses and the renewal of pastoral activity and religious life in the church, but also with the rising tide of heresy and revolt. These separate problems, though interrelated in the reformers' minds, evoked their specific remedies and counter-measures. The Theatines during these years remained a small but influential order. They set new standards for the priestly life and vocation in Italy, and signaled a badly-needed revitalization of the church's pastoral mission.

The Capuchin order appeared in Italy at the same time as the Theatines. Quite different in inspiration and background, they originated in 1525 with the decision of a young Franciscan Observant, Matteo da Bascio, to leave his friary in the Marches of Ancona to lead a solitary life in more strict and faithful accordance with the Rule of St. Francis of Assisi. He was soon joined by other Franciscan Observants. The Capuchins, named after their square hood or *cappuccio,* were not the first to attempt to return to the primitive simplicity and poverty of St. Francis, but they were the most successful, and their emergence at this time is a striking manifestation of the forces making for religious revival in the sixteenth century. Confined to Italy until 1574, their growth was phenomenal: they numbered some seven hundred members by 1536, when definitive constitutions were drawn up and Pope Paul III confirmed the order, and membership continued to expand rapidly. Grouped chiefly in small hermitages, they followed a strict life of penance and prayer, though also devoting themselves to the work of preaching the gospel and caring for the poor and the sick. Their evangelical inspiration is particularly noteworthy, and can be related to the broad movement of scriptural revival. Their constitutions stress that they "must always bear the holy Gospel in the interior of their hearts.... read and study the Holy Scripture...." and preach from the gospels, "so that being evangelical preachers, they may fashion an evangelical people."

The early expansion of the Capuchin movement was attended by certain difficulties, particularly the hostility of the Observant authorities who saw it as a rebellion in their own ranks and a standing criticism. The apostasy of the Capuchin superior Bernardino Ochino and his flight to Calvin's Geneva in 1542 was another severe trial which almost led to the order's destruction. The significance of Ochino's flight extended beyond the Capuchin movement. Dramatizing the thrust and danger of Protestantism in Italy, it coincided with the establishment of a restructured and more effective inquisition at Rome under Carafa's direction in 1542.[3] Ochino, then under suspicion of heresy, had been summoned before it. At this same time there occurred the death of Cardinal Gasparo Contarini, who had headed the more liberal reform party at the papal court and represented a more conciliatory attitude toward Protestantism. The coincidence of these three events in 1542 has frequently been viewed as a major turning-point in the Catholic Reformation—the point at which spirits cleaved and a far more repressive and intransigent attitude began to dominate the Catholic movement. The inquisition took over, and the fiery Carafa replaced the more moderate Contarini. The defection of Ochino in a sense triggered this transition. One must guard, however, against too simplistic an analysis of these events or too exaggerated an estimate of their significance. Each one, of course, is important, but the gradual evolution of Catholic attitudes during these years and other circumstances affecting the course of Catholic reform loom even larger on the historical stage.

[3] This was the so-called Roman Inquisition, established by Pope Paul III to check the spread of Protestantism. It was confined almost exclusively to Italy. It should not be confused with the more notorious Spanish Inquisition, dating from 1478 and operating largely under royal auspices in Spain and her dependencies. There was also the earlier medieval Inquisition, whose procedures had been organized and centralized under Gregory IX in the thirteenth century. Paul III's tribunal was intended to reactivate the latter.

The work and influence of Gian Matteo Giberti, the bishop of Verona, is a case in point. Born in Palermo in 1495, Giberti first came to Rome in 1513 to become a secretary to Cardinal Giulio de'Medici. When that prelate was elected Pope Clement VII in late 1523, Giberti served as his most trusted minister and adviser. He was a friend of Carafa and a staunch supporter of the early Theatines. After the sack of Rome in 1527, he withdrew to the see of Verona, where he had previously been appointed bishop, and resided there until his death in 1543. His diocesan reforms and his role as a conscientious and enlightened bishop are his chief contributions to the reform movement. Giberti truly cared for his flock; saw that worthy men served as priests and that they preached the gospel and instructed the young; established a society for the relief of the poor; and patronized learning. By his own life, as contemporaries were quick to observe, he set the best example. Both his example and his reforms had wide influence. His diocesan regulations, the *Constitutiones Gibertinae* (1542), served as a pattern for many of the reform decrees of the Council of Trent. In weighing the significance of Giberti, it must be stressed that the restoration of the bishop's office and responsibility was one of the most pressing needs of the church at this time. Many of its ills stemmed from the fact that bishops were neglecting their pastoral duties. This problem was one of the main preoccupations of the Catholic reformers, and progress in this sphere—the selection of good men for the episcopal office, residence in their sees, devotion to their tasks and duties—is an important measure of Catholic revival. Here Giberti led the way, a model for episcopal reform.

The ideal of the good bishop, however, predated Giberti's work in Verona; several years before, his friend and colleague Gasparo Contarini had written a short treatise on the office and duties of the bishop. This essay, entitled *De officio episcopi* (1516), was composed for a friend who had just been appointed to the see of Bergamo. It was Contarini's first important writing, and may be said to have inaugurated his active career. It is also evidence that his zeal for reform anteceded the Lutheran controversy and his own later service as cardinal and counselor at the court of Pope Paul III. Contarini is one of the most impressive figures in the story of the Catholic Reformation. Born in 1483 to one of the oldest Venetian families, he studied from 1501 to 1509 at the University of Padua, where he received a thorough grounding in the classics and in philosophy and theology. One of his teachers was the noted Renaissance Aristotelian Pietro Pomponazzi, with whom he later took issue on the philosophical question of the immortality of the soul. He wrote a treatise in 1517 refuting Pomponazzi. Contarini himself was a Thomist—a follower of the school of St. Thomas Aquinas—and a humanist, a combination by no means unusual at this time. After leaving Padua, he continued to cultivate his studies in the company of several very close friends. Their thoughts turned more and more to questions of religion and to the sad plight of the church. Around 1511 two of these friends, Tommaso

Giustiniani and Vincenzo Quirini, entered the Camaldolese order and tried to persuade Contarini to join them in the contemplative monastic life. This coincided with a personal religious crisis not unlike that which Martin Luther was shortly to undergo in his monastery at Wittenberg. Contarini stood firm against the pleas of Giustiniani and Quirini and decided to follow a lay vocation, convinced that active service in the world was not only fully consonant with the highest Christian ideals but necessary for the welfare of Christian society.

It was against this background that Contarini wrote his treatise on the duties of the bishop in 1516 and began his own career in the public service of his native Venice, serving as ambassador to the court of Emperor Charles V from 1521 to 1525 and later to the papal court. He wrote an important political treatise on the government of the Venetian republic, extolling its well-ordered and successful constitution, which Professor Felix Gilbert speculates may have been a reply to More's *Utopia*. In the 1530s Contarini was a prominent member of what we may call the Venetian reform circle, a group which included the Theatine leader Carafa; the abbot of the Benedictine monastery of San Giorgio Maggiore, Gregorio Cortese; the young English noble and scholar at Padua, Reginald Pole; and Giberti in Verona. In May, 1535 Contarini, still a layman, was quite unexpectedly made a cardinal and called to Rome by the recently-elected Pope Paul III. The other members of the Venetian circle were soon to follow.

Papal Sponsorship of Reform

It is at this point in 1535, when Paul III summoned Contarini to Rome, that the Counter Reformation in one sense of the word may be said to have begun. Under the aegis of Paul III the Catholic Church now began to put its house in order, in full recognition of the religious crisis that was underway, and the disparate efforts of Catholic reformers began to coalesce. This movement was directed toward reform, and was also in its new character and shape generated by the very serious challenges that had come. Hence there is some justification for calling it a counter reformation. This is a departure from the traditional meaning of the term but, given the inadequacy of the old concept of Counter Reformation, it may well be a more suitable application of the time-honored phrase. The summoning of Contarini by the Pope can be seen as the inauguration of this development because it represents the conjunction of papal initiative and leadership with reform. Both men were truly outstanding, and their union in a common cause, despite setbacks and difficulties, heralded a new day for the Catholic Church.

Paul III, the former Cardinal Alessandro Farnese and dean of the College of Cardinals, was elected Pope in late 1534 and his pontificate, the longest of the century, extended until late 1549. He was a wily, intelligent, experienced Renaissance prelate in whom the old habits of the papal prince contended with the demands of these troubled and perilous times, but these demands were heard and a serious response was made. From the start he sought to convene the General Council of the Church that so many desired, and he finally assembled it at Trent in December, 1545. From the start he grappled with the stubborn problems of curial reform, though less than effectively. "He talked but he didn't act," judged the Augustinian Prior-General Girolamo Seripando. It was he who commissioned Michelangelo to paint the gigantic altarpiece of the Sistine Chapel, the Last Judgment. This tremendous work, begun in 1536 and completed in 1541, embodies the vision of a world in judgment and may be said to epitomize this era of crisis and to express profoundly its anguish and its faith. Paul III established the Jesuits in 1539–40 and dispatched them on their first missions. He reorganized the Roman Inquisition in 1542 and broadened its jurisdiction to deal more effectively with the spread of heresy in Italy. Above all, he brought many of the most able and dedicated Catholic reformers to Rome and thereby infused new life and leadership into the papal administration.

Of these reformers Contarini was the first and the greatest, and from 1535 until his death in 1542 he served as one of the Pope's closest and most trusted advisers. Two events involving him are especially notable during this period. One is the convocation in Rome, under Contarini's direction, of a committee to examine the causes of disorder in the church and to draft a comprehensive reform program. The other is his participation in a conference with the Protestants at Ratisbon in 1541 in an attempt to resolve the schism in Germany.

In 1536 Paul III convened a reform committee in Rome at Contarini's suggestion. Its members were Carafa, Cortese, and Pole from Venice; Giberti from Verona; the renowned humanist scholar and prelate Jacopo Sadoleto, then resident in his bishopric at Carpentras; another noted scholar and papal diplomat, Jerome Aleander; Bishop Federigo Fregoso of Gubbio; and the papal theologian Tommaso Badia. It sat for several months, and in March, 1537, Contarini formally presented its famous report, the *Consilium de emendanda ecclesia,* to the pope. One of the most important documents of the Catholic Reformation, the report attacked curial practices which had permitted—indeed, produced—corruption and mismanagement in the church, and called for the correction of many specific "abuses" so that the church's pastoral ministry could be properly discharged. Better men must be selected for the episcopacy and for the priesthood, bishops and priests must reside in their churches and care for the faithful, lax religious orders must be abolished, Rome itself must be made an example rather than a scandal to those who view it. It particularly assailed the venality and simony involved in papal appointments and benefice-holding, attributing these evils to an exaggerated concept of papal authority. "From this source as from a Trojan horse," the report declared, "so many abuses and grave diseases have rushed in upon the Church of God that we now see her afflicted almost to the despair of salvation." It emphasized throughout the command of Christ: "Freely you have received, freely give." In conclusion, it appealed to Paul for action:

We hope that you have been chosen to restore in our hearts and in our works the name of Christ now forgotten by the nations and by us clerics, to heal the ills, to lead back the sheep of Christ into one fold, to turn away from us the wrath of God and that vengeance we deserve, already prepared and looming over our heads.

Catholic reformers at this time had a lively awareness of the responsibility of the papacy and of clerics in general for the disaster that had occurred, and they saw prompt and radical reform as the necessary road to reunion and survival. Michelangelo's great figure of Christ in judgment was no mere aesthetic conceit. The pope did not respond with energy and dispatch to the recommendations of the *Consilium,* though its automatic enactment, given the deep-seated evils that prevailed, was not a simple procedure. The report nevertheless provided an authoritative analysis and program, raised the banner of reform at Rome, and helped prepare the way for eventual remedy. The church under the pope was beginning to show signs of movement.

The Ratisbon conference in which Contarini participated was held in conjunction with a meeting of the imperial Diet in the spring of 1541. It was the climax of an effort by Emperor Charles V to bring about a reconciliation between Lutherans and Catholics in Germany through conferences of theologians from both sides. Paul III sent Contarini to direct the Catholic delegation. The high point of the colloquy was the agreement reached on the basic doctrinal question of justification, the very issue that Luther had originally raised and that was so central to his theology and to all of early Protestantism. Luther had insisted that men were saved not by their works but by faith in a merciful God who gratuitously imputes justice to the sinner. The Catholic response in general, like Erasmus's argument in his *De libero arbitrio* (1524), sought to preserve man's freedom and responsibility in the justification process. At Ratisbon, Contarini and the other theologians agreed to a compromise formulation called double justification which held that any *inherent* justice man himself attained had to be supplemented by a divinely *imputed* justice if he was to be saved. Contarini in particular is credited with the achievement of this mutually acceptable theological concept. His own earlier spiritual crisis in the years after he had left the University of Padua undoubtedly enabled him to understand more fully the Lutheran insistence on man's dependence on divine grace. The promise of this achievement, however, was not fulfilled. Agreement on other important theological questions—the doctrine of the Eucharist, for one— was not attained, and the colloquy as a result failed. Nor was the notion of double justification eventually sustained either by Wittenberg or by Rome. Carafa and Sadoleto, for example, had misgivings about it from the start, though the pope himself took a neutral position. The fathers at Trent after long debate rejected the concept of double justification, which was then supported by the Augustinian Seripando, and in their decree of January, 1547, laid down a different theology for the Catholic world.

Another of Contarini's contributions should be mentioned. It was with his support that Ignatius Loyola and his companions, who by early 1538 had come to Rome, won favor at the papal court and approval for their new order, the Company of Jesus. This brings us to a decisive development in the story of the Catholic Reformation, one that must be approached not through Contarini or Paul III, however important their roles, but through the experience and activity of a Spanish saint.

Loyola and the Jesuits

Ignatius Loyola is perhaps the most important figure in our story. As Don Iñigo Lopez de Loyola, he was born in 1491 to a noble Basque family in the province of Guipuzcoa in the kingdom of Castile. In his youth Ignatius served as a page at the royal court and then as a soldier under the banner of the Spanish kings. He was gravely wounded in the spring of 1521 in the siege of Pamplona at the time of the French invasion of Navarre. The event was a turning point in his life. During his long convalescence at the family castle, Ignatius underwent a religious conversion. Reading of Christ and the saints in the only books available to him, Ludolph of Saxony's *Life of Christ* and Jacopo de Voragine's collection of saints' lives, he resolved to serve a higher Lord than Charles V and to do heroic deeds in imitation of the saints. This determination initially found expression in the desire to go to Jerusalem, and in early 1522 he set out on his pilgrim's way. His journey took him to the shrine of Our Lady at Montserrat in Catalonia and then to the nearby town of Manresa, where he remained for several months. At Manresa Ignatius experienced a maturing or deepening of his religious commitment. He describes it in his autobiography as an illumination, and it would seem to represent a new insight into his purpose and vocation and a profounder understanding of the nature of service in the kingdom of Christ. The chivalry of the knight now gave new form and vigor to the *Devotio Moderna*'s highest ideal, the following of Christ. It is a development prefigured to some extent in Erasmus's *Handbook of the Christian Soldier,* and it was very likely influenced or even impelled by Ignatius's discovery at Manresa of Thomas à Kempis' great book, *The Imitation of Christ.*

Ignatius set off for the Holy Land, but he soon returned to Spain "inclined to study so as to be able to help souls," as he expressed it. Thus began a long and eventful process of education that lasted from 1524 to 1535 and took him to Ximenes' foundation at Alcalá, to the University of Salamanca, and finally in 1528 to the University of Paris. The Paris years mark a most important phase: Ignatius' zeal continued unabated; his doctrine, which found expression in the principles and meditations of the *Spiritual Exercises,* developed; and from the college of Sainte-Barbe, the school he attended in Paris, he gathered about him the remarkable group of companions with whom he was eventually to form the Company of Jesus. In August, 1534, when their studies for the Master of Arts drew to an end, Ignatius and six of his friends, including the young Francis Xavier of Navarre, the brilliant Diego Laynez, and the newly-ordained Pierre Favre, vowed to go to Jerusalem and labor for the conversion of the Turks. Given events in Europe at the time and the prevailing hostility to the Turks, as well as the threat they posed to Christian Europe, it is a most surprising resolve. The pacifist Erasmus, who had often expressed himself on the need to win the Turks to Christ, would certainly have approved, had word of the intention of the graduates of Sainte-Barbe reached him in retirement at Freiburg. At any rate, the resolve casts considerable light on the outlook and spirituality of Ignatius and his friends. They appear quite oblivious to the internal problems then convulsing Christendom.

The group had agreed that if it proved impossible to reach the East they would go to Rome and offer their services in the meantime to the pope. And so it was that in early 1538, after a long delay in Venice, they converged on the Rome of Paul III and immediately came to the attention of the papal court. Contarini especially was impressed by their fervor and by the ideas and religious exercises of Loyola. The pope welcomed and aided them, and employed them from the start, urging them to find their Jerusalem in Italy. It may well have been his suggestion that they organize more formally as a religious order. The group discussed this at length among themselves (they were now ten in number), and in the summer of 1539 drew up a statement of purpose and organization for papal approval. Paul gave preliminary approval immediately and more formal approbation in September, 1540, in the bull *Regimini militantis ecclesiae,* a delay having been caused by the hesitations of some conservative cardinals at the new departure the order represented. Meanwhile, new members joined their ranks, and they began to disperse on assignments from the Pope. Laynez and Favre went to Parma for pastoral work, Paschase Broet to Siena, and Xavier and Alfonso Rodriguez to Portugal at the request of King John III, who wanted missionaries for

India. Ignatius alone of the original band stayed on in Rome to direct the fast-growing society. Thus the Jesuits came into being—the most significant of all the chapters in the Catholic Reformation.

By the time of Ignatius' death in Rome in July, 1556, over a thousand Jesuits were studying and working in all parts of the world, the earliest and largest community being at Coimbra in Portugal. (Ignatius' letters to the Coimbra Jesuits are among his most important writings.) They engaged in a host of religious and scholarly activities, for from the start the Jesuits laid great stress on education and sought God not in the cloistered contemplative life—that was the old monasticism they had rejected—but in all things. An intensely active spirituality, as well as a highly personal one, characterized the movement. It seems to have been based on the Erasmian dictum that monasticism in itself is not piety—*Monachatus non est pietas*—but rather that a religious life consists of an interior conversion to Christ and active service in His name.[4] Hence they called themselves the Company of Jesus, pledged "to work for the advancement of souls in Christian life and doctrine," and undertook to do this wherever the need arose and the Pope, Loyola, or their successors directed. They were missionaries (Francis Xavier) and theologians (Diego Laynez), they founded schools and colleges (Jerome Nadal), they strengthened and defended the Catholic cause in divided Germany (Peter Canisius). There was an unusually large number and wide variety of outstanding individuals in the early society, many of whom have been recognized as saints—Ignatius himself, Francis Xavier, Pierre Favre, Peter Canisius and Francis Borgia only begin the list.

It is hardly necessary to point out that the Jesuits were not founded to combat Protestantism. It is a misrepresentation to picture them as shock troops mustered by a hard-pressed Church to give battle to the heretic. Their militancy is that of "spiritual combat," a metaphor of ancient Christian origin employed, for example, by Erasmus in his *Handbook of the Christian Soldier*. Their devotion to the church, however, made the Jesuits its staunch defenders. With Ignatius they believed that the church was the mystical "spouse of Christ," and they saw it as the measure of spiritual authenticity and Christian truth. Such a concept is basic to the spirituality and theology of Ignatius and the early Jesuits, and in this sense Ignatius is the great Counter-Luther, just as the early Jesuits appear as Counter-Protestants. However, it was never their intention, their task, or even their achievement simply to defend the Catholic cause against Protestantism. The entire movement, from its inception in the experience of a Spanish

---

[4] This fundamental aspect of Ignatian spirituality, which can be summed up in the term "contemplation in action," deserves special emphasis in a consideration of the historical significance of the new order and its activities. Jean Danielou, "The Ignatian Vision of the Universe and of Man," *Cross Currents* 4 (Fall, 1954): 357–66, affords a very useful and penetrating explication.

knight, had a different focus and a deeper and more positive religious purpose.

The Council of Trent

By the 1540s Erasmus' statement that "the sum of our religion is peace and concord" was far from descriptive of the historical scene, and barely had meaning any longer as a viable Christian ideal. Under these circumstances the long-delayed General Council of the Church assembled in December, 1545, in the city of Trent, an imperial city just beyond the Brenner Pass on the road to Italy. Trent, though by no means the conclusion of the Catholic Reformation, was the point when the Catholic Church as an institution took collective action against the ills and perils that beset it. Hubert Jedin has called the council "the Church's answer to the Protestant Reformation." It was indeed the most comprehensive and authoritative response to the crisis that had engulfed the Catholic Church. In his bull of convocation of 1542, Paul III, recalling his earlier attempts to convene a council, stressed the dissensions and dangers that existed and exhorted all bishops and princes to attend. The reply was far from unanimous, but the assembly opened, and the long-awaited General Council began its work.

Its course itself was checkered and prolonged. The council lasted for eighteen years, until December, 1563, though there were lengthy interruptions between sessions. It actually met only in 1545–47, 1551–52, and 1562–63, and consisted of twenty-five formal sessions and innumerable general congregations and committee meetings of bishops and theologians. Representation was always rather limited: some 30 fathers, mostly Italian, attended sided over by a series of papal legates, many of them very distinguished the opening; some 250 approved and signed the final decrees. It was pre-Hosius, Giovanni Morone. The Protestants, with one minor exception in men—Reginald Pole, Marcello Cervini, Girolamo Seripando, Stanislaus 1552, refused to attend, viewing it as a council of Antichrist because of its papal sponsorship and direction. Nor was there any real French representation until the final period, at which time the Cardinal of Lorraine heading the French delegation played a leading role. Ignatius Loyola did not attend, though several Jesuits—notably Laynez—were important participants. The council was plagued by politics from beginning to end, the fortunes of Habsburg–Valois rivalry frequently determining its continuation and course. Nevertheless, it met and grappled with a good many of the most pressing questions of doctrine and reform, and produced a large body of legislation, promulgated by Pope Pius IV in 1564 as its canons and decrees.

Theoretically, the Council had three main goals: 1) to effect needed reformation in the church, 2) to clarify and define disputed doctrine and condemn heresy, and 3) to restore the peace and unity of the church. These aims were closely related and can be viewed, as they are in Cardinal Reginald Pole's keynote address to the second session in January, 1546, as an attempt to remedy the ills and afflictions of the church and to rebuild it. "We the shepherds," he told the assembled fathers, "should hold ourselves responsible for all the evils now burdening the flock of Christ," and urged them in his remarkable plea for contrition to lead the church to a genuine renewal and to peace. The council, however, made little headway toward the goal of unity and peace. Religious division between Protestant and Catholic in Europe was now too deep-seated and entrenched to permit resolution in such a tribunal. Political as well as doctrinal factors account for this, but most important were the rival conceptions of the church that now prevailed. Whatever authority the council claimed was rejected by the Protestants who refused to cooperate with it, and this opposition stemmed from very divergent views of the nature of the church and of authority within it. The council was thus confined, in jurisdiction as well as representation, to the Catholic world, and functioned not as an instrument of reconciliation or reunion but as a body legislating and defining for those who remained in the Catholic fold. It undertook this task from the start, agreeing after some initial argument to take up questions of doctrine and problems of reform simultaneously.

One of the earliest and most important of its doctrinal discussions was the long debate on justification. A detailed decree on this fundamental issue was finally accepted unanimously by the council at its sixth session in January, 1547. It declared that man is justified and saved only through God's grace freely bestowed on those who are baptized and have faith, but it insisted that man participated in the process through a disposition for grace and a voluntary reception of it. Justification, it declared, is also "the sanctification and renewal of the inward man," and it stressed the need for good works and observance of God's commandments if man is to grow in sanctity and gain eternal life. The Lutheran tenet of justification by faith alone, as well as the notion of double justification which Contarini had championed at Ratisbon, were rejected, but the primacy of divine grace merited for man by Christ's redemptive act was acknowledged from beginning to end. The decree is completely scriptural in its argument and presentation, and is not a scholastic formulation. This may in general be said of all the Tridentine decrees. Appended to the decree was a list of thirty-three short canons condemning specific "errors" concerning justification. It is frequently declared that this decree and its canons—or, more broadly, the Tridentine pronouncements as a whole—shut the door on compromise and conciliation with the Protestants. By this time, however, that door was no longer ajar, and it can hardly be surprising that the Catholic Church, in

view of the widespread doctrinal controversies raised by the Protestants, examined these theological issues and clarified its thought and faith. Not to
have done so in these circumstances would have been to disavow that *mag-
isterium,* or teaching authority, it claimed to exercise.

The council also framed canons and decrees on such matters as the seven
sacraments, the Mass, the existence of purgatory, and the invocation of the
saints. The decree on the Mass, the central act of Catholic worship, was approved at the twenty-second session in September, 1562, and ranks after the
justification decree as the most important theological definition of the council. In opposition to the Protestants who had rejected the Mass as an
"abomination" and "idolatry," the council affirmed and explained its sacrificial character. It defined the Mass as a commemoration of the sacrifice of
Christ on Calvary, but also as a reenactment, or rendering present, of that
unique sacrificial act. Another major issue vigorously raised by the Protestants, the primacy and authority of the pope in the church, was not formally
discussed at the council, though it was affirmed *de facto* throughout the
conciliar proceedings. The omission is nevertheless interesting. The Protestant attitude found no partisans among the fathers or theologians at Trent,
but the question of papal power was too sensitive and controversial, im-
pinging as it did on issues involving episcopal and conciliar authority, for
the council to reach agreement on a detailed statement. The bypassing of
the question is thus understandable, though paradoxical in view of the enhanced role of the pope in the post-Tridentine Church. Stronger papal
leadership emerged not so much from the council itself, and certainly not
from any of its declarations, as from the needs and demands of the times.

In the area of reform, the council tackled four basic problems: the training of priests, the duty of preaching the gospel, the jurisdiction of bishops, and
the obligation of residence for bishops and pastors. All four directly concerned the Church's pastoral mission, that supreme task—*salus animarum
suprema lex*—by which its effectiveness must be judged. These problems
were raised and discussed in the council's early months, and were the subject of several reform decrees in 1546–47. It was not, however, until the
final period of the council that detailed and adequate legislation was
approved, and this came only after a very serious deadlock and crisis in the
council over the nature of the bishop's obligation to reside in his diocese had
been resolved. The council was split in 1562–63 between those, led by the
Archbishop of Granada and later the Cardinal of Lorraine, who held that
the obligation of residence was a divine law, and those, led by Cardinal
Simonetta and several Italian bishops, who saw a threat to the papacy and
curial tradition in this line of reasoning. Behind the bitter and prolonged
argument lay the conviction on the one hand that the divine law, or *ius
divinum,* principle was essential if meaningful reform was to be achieved in
the church, and the fear on the other hand that such a principle overex-

tended the autonomy of the bishop and jeopardized the authority of the pope. The issue tended to divide the Spanish and French fathers from the Italian, and the more radical reformers from the more conservative. It threatened to break up the council. The acute *contretemps* that developed in an atmosphere of mutual suspicion and distrust was finally dissolved, largely through the diplomacy of the presiding papal legate, Cardinal Giovanni Morone, who late in 1563 won the support of both factions for a compromise program. Jedin calls Morone the savior of the council; he was unquestionably the man primarily responsible for Tridentine reform. After a standstill of ten months, the council moved again, and in its three concluding sessions, approved a number of important reform decrees.

These decrees are the chief contribution of the Council of Trent to Catholic reform. They focus mainly, though not exclusively, on the role and responsibility of the bishop. The divine law sanction for episcopal residence was dropped, but the obligation of the bishop to reside in his see was vigorously affirmed. The bishop's powers were considerably strengthened and enlarged. He was given greater authority over clergy and members of religious orders in his diocese with respect to exemptions and papal dispensations, as well as in matters of priestly conduct and pastoral care. He was to conduct a visitation of his diocese every two years and hold a diocesan synod every year. Provincial synods were to be convened every three years. Accumulation of benefices, which had been one of the worst abuses in the church, was forbidden. In short, the administrative responsibility of the bishop was substantially restored at the same time that his obligations were more clearly defined and his primary role as pastor and teacher of his flock strongly emphasized. This was the core of Tridentine reform, though the council's program was by no means limited to reform of the episcopacy. Its effects were intended to reach far beyond that office. In this regard, one reform deserves special mention: each bishop was enjoined to establish a college or seminary for the training of future priests for his diocese, remedying one of the most serious deficiencies of the late medieval church. This innovation was directly inspired by Cardinal Pole's similar reform at the London synod in 1556 after he had returned to England as papal legate during the reign of Mary Tudor. The examples of Giberti in Verona and of the numerous Jesuit colleges springing up throughout Europe were also influential. This was one of the most famous and far-reaching of Trent's decrees, and Jedin declares it no exaggeration to say that, if the council had done nothing else for the renewal of the church, it would have done a great deal.

Judgment of the council's work is not a simple matter. The pressures that affected it, as well as the possibilities open to it, have to be realistically appraised. And it must be judged in terms of the survival and renewal of the Catholic faith in these difficult times. Neither the schism itself nor its continuation can properly be attributed to it. Whether the council might have played a more conciliatory or ecumenical role does not seem under the circumstances a very practical question.

What then can we say of this General Council? It clarified and defined many doctrines then in dispute, it legislated basic reforms, it rallied and strengthened the church for the severe crisis it faced in the sixteenth century. The council did not work a revolution in the ecclesiastical order, but it did affirm what it conceived to be the truths of faith on a number of important points, and took steps against some of the most salient abuses and defects in the church. In this sense the council may be said to have restructured, or at least reoriented, the Catholic Church for the days ahead. If it was, doctrinally speaking, "the Church's answer to the Protestant Reformation," it was also the institutionalization of a significant program of ecclesiastical reform. This latter achievement should not be underestimated. The difficulties confronting the council, both endemic and external, were formidable. Nevertheless, it accomplished much, and under its sign a resurgent church, still *mater et magistra* for a large portion of mankind, pursued its historic mission.

In order to take effect, of course, the conciliar decisions had to be implemented and enforced. In 1564 Pope Pius IV promptly approved and published the Tridentine decrees, circulated them to all Catholic bishops, and established a committee of eight cardinals—later known as the Congregation of the Council—to oversee their interpretation and enactment. The same year, pursuant to the council's instructions, he proclaimed the Tridentine Profession of Faith, and issued a revised Index of Forbidden Books which modified the excessive severity and rigidity of the index Paul IV had published in 1559. His successor, Pius V, also completing work projected by the council, published a standard Roman catechism in 1566, a uniform breviary in 1568, and a uniform missal in 1570. The papal court was infused with new vigor and efficiency. The turning point had been the pontificate of Paul III, but in the period that now ensued the forceful leadership of Pius V, Gregory XIII, and Sixtus V, ruling from 1566 until 1590, firmly established the papacy as the chief agent of Catholic reform. A new atmosphere prevailed in Rome: the worst ills of curial practice were corrected; a major reorganization of the papal government took place in 1588 with Sixtus V's creation of a large number of committees or congregations of cardinals to handle administrative affairs; the system of resident papal nuncios and apostolic visitors was greatly expanded, chiefly to enforce the Tridentine decrees. The post-Tridentine era was characterized by the strengthening of the church's institutional life and its centralization under Roman auspices and direction. The Council of Trent laid the foundations, but it was the understanding and effort of those who followed that gave it effect in the ongoing life of the Catholic Church.

Perspectives on the Catholic Reformation

Certain basic lineaments stand out in the Catholic reform movement, from the days of Savonarola and Ximenes to the close of the Council of Trent. The first and most obvious was the widespread awareness of the need for reform and the serious efforts made to achieve it. This movement was in the beginning scattered and disparate, a matter of individual initiative and endeavor rather than a coordinated program affecting the church as a whole. Ximenes is the major example of an ecclesiastical or institutional reformer prior to 1517. Erasmus and the Christian humanists, however widespread and deep their influence, worked in a private capacity, so to speak, and sought essentially personal reorientation and renewal, though they did envision a broader reform of Christian life and society. With the pontificate of Paul III, Catholic reform became more concerted and official, and reached out to encompass the entire church. The arrival of Contarini in Rome in 1535 ushered in the new era. New blood was infused into the papal administration, the early Jesuits were organized and began their extensive activities, and the General Council was finally convened at Trent. Despite its diversity, the movement had an inner unity and coherence and followed an identifiable and continuous course.

Of what did this inner unity and coherence consist? It was manifested in the first place in the desire for religious reform so emphatically expressed in the works of the individuals we have discussed; from Savonarola, Colet, and Ximenes to Giberti, Loyola, and Pius V, it is a dominant theme, an integrating principle. Of course, Luther, Zwingli, and Calvin can also be included under such a rubric, and indeed must be in any comprehensive perspective on sixteenth-century reform. Our focus, however, is on Catholic reform, and by definition limited to reformers who remained in the existing Catholic church and sought to achieve renewal within the framework of its structure and tradition. Aside from this we may ask what features distinguish the Catholic reformers and link them in a common endeavor. As we see it, two characteristics run like a double rhythm through the Catholic Reformation: the preoccupation of the Catholic reformers with individual or personal reformation, and their concern for the restoration and renewal of the Church's pastoral mission. In short, Catholic reform had a marked personal and pastoral orientation.

The Catholic reformers focused on the individual Christian and his spiritual and moral life. They sought essentially a *reformatio in membris* rather than dogmatic or structural change. The members of Christ's church must lead better Christian lives and be instructed and guided along that path. This is the burden of Savonarola's prophetic preaching, the goal of Erasmus and the Christian humanists, the objective of Ignatius Loyola and his *Spir-*

itual Exercises. The Theatines, Capuchins, and Jesuits emphasized this in terms of the greater commitment and sanctification of their members. The reforms of Ximenes in Spain, Giberti in Verona, and the Council of Trent for the universal church had this as an underlying purpose in their concern for the instruction and spiritual advancement of the faithful. "Men must be changed by religion, not religion by men," declared Egidio of Viterbo at the Fifth Lateran Council in 1512—a dictum that sums up, in Pastor's judgment, the true spirit of Catholic reform. Even the doctrinal decrees of Trent, such as the very important one on justification, may be said to reflect this emphasis on the moral life of the Christian.

Such a focus presupposes concern for the reform of the institutional church as well, for if men are to be changed by religion, then religion itself must be correctly represented and faithfully imparted. Thus the church's pastoral mission—the work of teaching, guiding, and sanctifying its members—must be given primacy and rendered effective. Hence the stress on training priests, selecting good men as bishops and insisting that they reside in their dioceses, instructing the young and preaching the gospel, restoring discipline in the church, and rooting out venality and unworthiness in the service of Christ and the salvation of souls. The Bark of Peter was not to be scuttled or rebuilt, but to be steered back to its original course with its crew at their posts and responsive to their tasks. The state of the clergy loomed large in Catholic reform. If their ignorance, corruption, or neglect had been responsible for the troubles that befell the church, as nearly everyone affirmed, then their reform required urgent attention and was the foundation and root of all renewal. This involved personal reform, that of the priests and bishops who are the instruments of the church's mission, and its purpose and consequence were a matter of the personal reform of the faithful entrusted to their care. The immediate objective, however, was institutional and pastoral. The church itself was to be restored so that its true apostolate might be realized.

Obviously, personal reform and renewal of the church's pastoral mission are complementary goals, but they also contained in some instances an element of tension and divergence. Certainly Erasmus' approach was different than Giberti's, just as in the latter half of the century the great Jesuit apostle Peter Canisius operated in a different way than the vigorous Archbishop of Milan Charles Borromeo. The difference was perhaps largely functional, but beyond the office or the role of the individual reformer lay dissimilarities in attitude and temperament and priorities. The contrast between Contarini and Carafa—one the man of dialogue with the Protestants, the other of the inquisition—has often been underscored to bear this out, though here it was more a matter of dealing with Protestantism than of reform itself. Both were, after all, the principal authors of the *Consilium de emendanda ecclesia.* Diversity nevertheless was bound to exist in so broad a movement, and it is attributable, in part at least, to the distinction, even the tension, between the reform of the Christian and the reform of the church. In such diversity lies much of the drama of the Catholic Reformation, though the movement as a whole strove for a common end: the revival of religion, that is, the reform of the individual Christian in a church renewed and rededicated to its spiritual tasks.

Selected Bibliography

There is no adequate history of the Catholic Reformation. The best introduction to the movement is H. O. Evennett, *The Spirit of the Counter-Reformation*, edited by John Bossy (Cambridge, 1968. Notre Dame, 1970). It is limited in scope, but enlightening and indicative of the kind of inquiry and analysis that should be pursued in this field. Wilhelm Schenk's *Reginald Pole, Cardinal of England* (London, 1950) can also serve as an introduction. It focuses on Italian reform. The German scholar Hubert Jedin is perhaps the foremost historian working in this area, and his works are indispensable for the serious student. The most notable is his *History of the Council of Trent*, 2 vols., translated by Dom Ernest Graf (St. Louis, 1957–61), a work still in progress. Volume 1 covers the background of Trent and a wide range of reform developments. Volume 2 is confined to the first period of Trent, the 1545–47 sessions. Jedin's *Crisis and Closure of the Council of Trent*, translated by N. D. Smith (London, 1967) is a brief account of the final period. He also wrote the entry on Trent in *The New Catholic Encyclopedia* 14: 271–78. John C. Olin, *The Catholic Reformation: Savonarola to Ignatius Loyola* (New York, 1969) contains key documents for the 1495–1540 period and has extensive bibliographical references. Pierre Janelle, *The Catholic Reformation* (Milwaukee, 1949) has the status of a standard survey, but it is rather discursive and now out-of-date. The recent paperback by A. G. Dickens, *The Counter-Reformation* (London and New York, 1969) is a broad and quite conventional sketch.

The inquiring student is well advised to turn to more detailed or specialized works, with Evennett perhaps as an introductory guide. A few such works, in English and relatively accessible, can be mentioned here. Outstanding, and a veritable mine of relevant information, is Ludwig Pastor's monumental *The History of the Popes from the Close of the Middle Ages*, 40 vols., translated by F. I. Antrobus, R. F. Kerr *et al.* (St. Louis, 1891–1953). On the humanist background there is Charles Trinkaus, *In Our Image and Likeness*, 2 vols. (Chicago, 1970), and on scriptural humanism Werner Schwarz, *Principles and Problems of Biblical Translation* (Cambridge, 1955). Books and essays on Erasmus are legion. Margaret Mann Phillips, *Erasmus and the Northern Renaissance* (London, 1949) is a good introduction. For a sample of his own writings on reform, see *Christian Humanism and the Reformation: Selected Writings of Erasmus,* edited by John C. Olin (New York, 1965). Other Catholic humanist reformers are treated in John W. O'Malley, *Giles of Viterbo on Church and Reform* (Leiden, 1968); Richard M. Douglas, *Jacopo Sadoleto* (Cambridge, 1959); and Dermot Fenlon, *Heresy and Obedience in Tridentine Italy: Cardinal Pole and the Counter Reformation* (Cambridge, 1972). There is unfortunately no full study of Contarini, but the following can be highly recommended: Felix Gilbert, "Religion and Politics in the Thought of Gasparo Contarini," in *Action and Conviction in Early Modern Europe,* edited by Theodore K. Rabb and Jerrold E. Seigel (Princeton, 1969), pp. 90–116; Peter Matheson, *Cardinal Contarini at Regensburg* (Oxford, 1972); and James Bruce Ross, "Gasparo Contarini and His Friends," *Studies in the Renaissance* 17 (1970): 192–232, and "The Emergence of Gasparo Contarini: A Bibliographical Essay," *Church History* 41 (March, 1972): 1–24.

On Ignatius Loyola and the Jesuits there is considerable material. James Brodrick, *The Origin of the Jesuits* (New York, 1960) and *The Progress of the Jesuits (1556–79)* (New York, 1947) are good introductions. Paul Dudon, *St. Ignatius of Loyola,* translated by William J. Young (Milwaukee, 1949), is probably the best biography. On his thought and spirituality, see Hugo Rahner, *The Spirituality of St. Ignatius Loyola,* translated by F. J. Smith (Westminster, Md., 1953), and *Ignatius the Theologian,* translated by Michael Barry (New York, 1968). For an analysis of the Erasmus-Ignatius relationship, see John C. Olin, "Erasmus and St. Ignatius Loyola," *Luther, Erasmus and the Reformation: A Catholic-Protestant Reappraisal,* edited by John C. Olin, James D. Smart, and Robert E. McNally (New York, 1969), pp. 114–133. Evennett's *The Spirit of the Counter-Reformation* is focused in large part on Ignatius and the Jesuits. For the new religious orders in general, see Evennett's chapter "The New Orders," in *The New Cambridge Modern History, II: The Reformation,* edited by G. R. Elton (Cambridge, 1958), pp. 275–300.

With regard to the Council of Trent, Jedin is the surest guide. In addition to the works already mentioned, there is his *Papal Legate at the Council of Trent: Cardinal Seripando* (St. Louis, 1947). There is also H. O. Evennett's early work, *The Cardinal of Lorraine and the Council of Trent* (Cambridge, 1930). The decrees of the Council are available in H. J. Schroeder, *Canons and Decrees of the Council of Trent* (St. Louis, 1941). Several articles may also be cited: Stephan Kuttner, "The Reform of the Church and the Council of Trent," *The Jurist* 22 (April, 1962): 123–42; Robert E. McNally, "The Council of Trent and the German Protestants," *Theological Studies* 25 (March, 1964): 1–22; and Giuseppe Alberigo, "The Council of Trent: New Views on the Occasion of Its Fourth Centenary," *Concilium* 7 (September, 1965): 38–48.

In conclusion, two very different and stimulating appraisals of Catholic reform can be cited: Robert E. McNally, *The Unreformed Church* (New York, 1965), and John Bossy, "The Counter-Reformation and the People of Catholic Europe," *Past and Present* 47 (May, 1970) : 51–70. Lastly there are two comprehensive bibliographical articles on the subject and the period for those who would pursue further study: John W. O'Malley, "Recent Studies in Church History, 1300–1600," *The Catholic Historical Review* 55 (October, 1969) : 394–437; and Eric Cochrane, "New Light on Post-Tridentine Italy: A Note on Recent Counter-Reformation Scholarship," *The Catholic Historical Review* 56 (July, 1970) : 291–319.

Detail from Portuguese Carracks *attributed to C. Anthoniszoon, ca. 1521. National Maritime Museum, London.*

7.

The Expansion of Europe

RICHARD B. REED

Cease man of Troy, and cease thou Sage of Greece,
to boast the Navigations great ye made;
Let the high Fame of Alexander cease,
And Traian's Banners in the East display'd:
For to a Man recorded in this Peece
Neptune his Trident yielded, Mars his Blade.
  Cease All, whose Actions ancient Bards exprest:
  A brighter Valour rises in the West.

The Lusiad, I, iii.[1]

L UIS DE CAMÕES' EPIC POEM, the supreme literary expression of
the age of geographical discovery, celebrates the overseas accomplishments of Vasco da Gama and his contemporaries. But while the grandeur of
Camões' sixteenth-century verse is an eloquent testimonial to Portuguese
oceanic supremacy, it is not at all clear whether he, or any other Renaissance
observer, fully understood the significance of Europe's overseas adventure.
Was it recognized that the expansion of the fifteenth and sixteenth centuries was more than a series of spectacular discoveries, explorations, and
conquests—that the "brighter Valour" of Portugal was the initial phase of
a revolution in western man's comprehension of his world? Or that the
Renaissance search for knowledge, whether in the leaves of a Greek manu-

---

[1] Luis de Camões, *The Lusiad,* translated by Richard Fanshawe, edited with an
introduction by Jeremiah D. M. Ford (Cambridge, Mass., 1940), p. 30.

script or on the deck of a three-masted caravel, joined the scholar and the adventurer in a common endeavor? While it is apparent to the modern critic that Europe's early overseas expansion inaugurated a half-millennium of change, there is no certainty that Renaissance man attributed importance to this undertaking beyond its immediate geographical consequences and the obvious political and economic alterations that it provoked. The Renaissance and Reformation was a period of considerable turmoil and crisis, and while the discovery of new lands, new oceans, and new peoples aroused excitement and stimulated curiosity, Europe was preoccupied with itself. Events beyond its borders were of secondary importance.

The Pre-Expansion European World View

At the beginning of the fifteenth century, the prevailing concept of the world was still a blend of classical geographic theory, medieval fancy, and fact. Basically defined by Ptolemy and Strabo, it owed something to Marco Polo and John de Mandeville. It was a restricted view that conformed to the humanist preoccupation with Greek and Roman scholarship, but recognized, to some extent, the worth of more contemporary observations. Medieval geography had suffered a static subservience to theology, but the discovery of the classics in the thirteenth and early fourteenth centuries had introduced early Renaissance scholars to a wealth of information—and misinformation—that revitalized the discipline and terminated its thousand-year decline. This was a mixed blessing, however, for the deference paid to classical theorists tended to inhibit the development of a more dynamic and realistic world-view reflecting contemporary knowledge. In the fourteenth century, the writings of Hecateus, Eratosthenes, Plato, and Aristotle, in addition to Ptolemy, were consulted for information about the world— a world little changed, in theory at least, from that known to the Greek and Roman savants.

The discovery of classical geography did prove to be a vast improvement over the medieval concept of the inhabited world. The Ptolemaic system superseded the old biblically-inspired T-O maps that depicted the three continents divided by a stylized Mediterranean Sea, bisected by the Nile and the Don and surrounded by a circular ocean; the flat-earth theory, which had gained some credence, was put to rest. The Greeks were the geographers of the ancient world; they made the first fairly accurate measurements of the globe, conceived the ideas of continents and zones, devised the principles of longitude and latitude, and produced the first recognizable maps based upon positive geographic data. Their accomplishments, however, should not obscure the fact that they were occasionally wrong, and that the revival and acceptance of their geographic literature in the early Renaissance had a negative as well as a positive effect.

While the classics were the theoretical cornerstone of fourteenth-century geographic thought, other sources furnished information of equal, if not greater, importance. The thirteenth and fourteenth centuries had produced the first European travel accounts of Asia and Africa—accounts that included descriptions of places and peoples entirely unknown to the ancients. The writings of such travelers and ambassadors as John of Plano Carpini, William of Rubruck, Odoric of Pordenone, Andrew of Perugia, and, above all, Marco Polo described in detail the mysterious Mongol empire and the farthest reaches of Asia, while Ibn Battuta and Ibn Fathima had described parts of Africa with which even the most enlightened Greek was unfamiliar. Rumors of islands in the Atlantic appeared occasionally, and it was vaguely known that Portuguese and Italian mariners had sailed west, possibly in search of a passage to India, as early as the thirteenth century. The influence of the travel narratives was occasional and confined primarily to details; except for Marco Polo's *Travels,* they had little real impact upon the early Renaissance view of the world. The voluminous compendia of such scholars as Dominicus Bandius, Pierre d'Ailly, and Aeneas Silvius exhibited an almost complete dependence upon the classics, and a deeper acquaintance with Pomponius Mela and Solinus than with Marco Polo, Ibn Battuta, or even Roger Bacon.

The medieval fascination with the unknown gave rise to a talent for invention, and the early Renaissance mind retained a persistent belief in mythical and fanciful places and things. Nor did the age of discovery immediately dispel medieval mythology. After almost a century of Portuguese voyaging, the celebrated *Nuremberg Chronicle* was published the same year that Columbus returned from his first expedition, reproducing a number of woodcuts of grotesque creatures much more appropriate to Solinus and Mandeville than to Renaissance sophistication. The Ocean Sea was thought to be full of unidentified beasts which, when they were not tormenting terrified sailors, could be found attacking the myriad mythical islands that dotted the mysterious Atlantic. From Plato's Atlantis to the rocks of St. Brandon, Antillia, and Brazil, the sea was the refuge of every lost race that had ever inhabited the earth, and the search for these illusive promontories and civilizations lasted far beyond the period of Renaissance expansion.

On the eve of the period of discoveries Europe had only an uncertain awareness of what lay south of the Mediterranean, east of the Black Sea, and west of the Atlantic littoral. The general location of India and the Spice Islands was a matter of record, and there was some acquaintance with the northern periphery of Africa and the Levant, but Asia, and China in particular, remained an enigmatic but vaguely recognizable landmass to the east. It was essentially a revised Ptolemaic world-island, characterized by an enclosed Indian Ocean and the great southern continent *Terra Incognita,* with a few undefined islands to the north and to the west. The voyages of the Scandinavians had made no impression on the consciousness of medieval Europe, the celebrated *Vinland Map* notwithstanding, and the Atlantic

Ocean was a barrier of incredible mystery. But it was not an entirely static world, and there were men who were stimulated by the challenge of the unknown, men who found the classics provocative rather than definitive, men who were the heirs of Marco Polo rather than Pliny or Strabo.

The most immediate and obvious consequence of Europe's overseas expansion in the fifteenth and sixteenth centuries was an enormous increase in knowledge of the physical proportions of the world. In the two centuries that separated the Portuguese conquest of Ceuta in 1415 from the first permanent English settlement in North America in 1607, the prevailing concept of the globe was drastically altered. Ptolemy was superseded by Copernicus, Ortelius, and Mercator, while Marco Polo gave way to Vasco da Gama, González de Mendoza, and Sir Francis Drake. The "diversities" and "marvels" that John de Mandeville had conjured out of the medieval imagination were replaced with vivid accounts of previously unknown pagan empires, strange sources of apparently unlimited wealth, and natural wonders beyond belief. In the three decades between 1492 and 1522, not only was a "New World" discovered, but a great empire was conquered, the sources of eastern luxuries were revealed, and an ocean of incredible proportions was navigated. Discovery followed discovery, and it is little wonder that old traditions often refused to die when confronted by such revelations —fancy was sometimes more credible than fact.

The expansion of the known world would have provided diversion and satisfied the curiosity of only a few had it not coincided with one of the most significant developments in the history of Western civilization—the invention of printing. The ability to reproduce words by means of movable type was not new to the craftsmen of the east in the fifteenth century, but it was a discovery that revolutionized European learning and communications within a few decades. The medieval manuscript was often a work of great beauty, and our appreciation of the past is heavily dependent upon the tedious labors of calligraphers, but it was expensive, took a long time to produce, and had a limited circulation—in short, it was no match for the printed page, which could be reproduced cheaply, rapidly, and in great quantity. The printing press helped to make Renaissance expansion a geographical revolution, and one or two printings of Columbus' *Epistola* reached more people in more countries in less than a year than all the manuscript copies of Marco Polo's *Travels* did in a century.

From the letters and pamphlets announcing the news of the Spanish and Portuguese voyages to the great collections of Hakluyt, De Bry, and Hulsius, a permanent record exists of Europe's overseas expansion. It is a dynamic literature that reflects the spirit of the age. Its purpose was to educate and stimulate, as well as to entertain, and in the sixteenth-century travel book Renaissance man found much of the knowledge and inspiration that eventually changed his world. In words and illustrations of the histories, chronicles, letters, and news-sheets published in a half-dozen languages from Rome to

London and Antwerp, one experiences most fully the wonder that this expansion aroused in early modern Europe.

The Politics of Expansion

The expansion of Europe was but one manifestation of a continual and complex process of change that transformed a conglomeration of feudal principalities into the dominant world force of the past five centuries. The transition from the Middle Ages to the Renaissance provided the political, economic, religious, scientific, and sociocultural incentives that made the age of geographical discovery and exploration possible, and insured that Europe, and not Asia, Africa, or even America, would ultimately lead the rest of the world into the modern era. If expansion was at least partly classical and medieval in formulation, it was decidedly Renaissance in execution, and in the eventual emergence of the "Europa triumphant" so dear to the artists and engravers of the seventeenth and eighteenth centuries, it achieved an allegorical symbolism that represented the Renaissance ideal to perfection.

The expansion of Europe was an intensely nationalistic phenomenon. It was an aspect of the trend, most evident in the late fifteenth and early sixteenth centuries, toward the establishment of strong centralized authority in the "new monarchies," as they have been called, and the emergence of the nation-state. A policy of overseas expansion required a degree of internal stability and national consciousness that only a powerful central govern- -ment could command. Portugal achieved this position long before her eventual competitors, and under the leadership of the dynamic house of Avis became a consolidated kingdom comparatively free from feudal divisions before the end of the fifteenth century. While Spain was still divided into a number of conflicting political jurisdictions, England and France were preoccupied with their own and each other's affairs, and the Dutch were still an appendage of the Empire, the Portuguese combined the advantages of their natural geographic situation with their political and economic stability to initiate the age of discovery. Spain in the sixteenth century, and England, France, and the Netherlands in the seventeenth century, became active colonial powers only after each had matured into strong national entities, independent of feudal political and economic restrictions.

The emergence of the nation-state as a colonizing power had an enormous influence upon the traditional political and military rivalries of Western Europe. Economic benefits derived from overseas colonial possessions or the development of a lucrative commercial empire transformed the Iberian kingdoms, and eventually their northern competitors, into the great powers of Europe, and made the Atlantic eclipse the Mediterranean as the hub of international seafaring. The superiority of the Italian city-states slowly declined as Lisbon and Seville—and later Antwerp, London, and Amsterdam —became the commercial centers of the new expansion.

The importance of the nation-state in Renaissance expansion is particularly apparent when the Italian city-states are considered. Venice and Genoa, cities that had contributed so many of the medieval travelers and early Renaissance geographers and mapmakers, did not participate directly in Europe's overseas expansion. Yet Italian names dominated the rolls of the early voyagers. Prince Henry employed Venetians and Florentines in his naval establishment, while Columbus, Vespucci, Verrazano, the Cabots, and many others sailed for Spain, France, and England. Italian cartography was the best in Europe until the second half of the sixteenth century, and a high proportion of the books and pamphlets that chronicled new discoveries emanated from the presses of Vicenza, Venice, Rome, and Florence. Italian bankers and merchants were also very active in the commercial life of the principal Iberian cities. A divided Italy was instrumental in making Renaissance expansion possible, but it could not take full advantage of its own endowments. Germans, too, figured prominently in the expansion of the sixteenth century, as the names of Federmann, Staden, Welser, and Fugger attest. But Germany, like Italy, was not united, and the emergence of these two nations as colonial powers had to wait until their respective consolidations in the nineteenth century.

While every nationality in Western Europe was represented in Renaissance expansion, it was by no means an international venture. On the contrary, it was very much an expression of that nationalistic fervor that characterized political developments in the fifteenth and sixteenth centuries. It was primarily a state enterprise, often financed privately but controlled and protected by the governments of the concerned powers. There was no cooperation between nations, and even after the upheaval of the Protestant Reformation, when political loyalties and alignments were conditioned by religious sympathies, there were no colonial alliances that provided for mutual Protestant or Catholic overseas policies. The English were made well aware of this when the traditional Anglo-Dutch alliance against the Habsburgs did not prevent Dutch raiders from massacring the English settlement at Amboyna in 1623. That we have a *New England,* and that there once was a *Nueva España,* a *Nova Francia,* and a *Nieuw Amsterdam* is a clue to the character of Renaissance expansion—it is extremely unlikely that anyone ever considered *Nova Europa* as a placename.

To some extent, political power in Western Europe followed the development of economic power as it was reflected in an expanding colonialism. Portugal's limited resources prevented her from becoming a really important political and military force, but Spain, the key to Habsburg ambitions and the possessor of the fabled wealth of the Indies, was the basis for the empires of Charles V and Philip II that dominated Europe in the sixteenth century. Spanish power was not entirely founded on the gold and silver of

Mexico and Peru, but the arrival of the New World treasure fleets assured the Habsburg monarchs that the armies of the Counter Reformation would survive yet another season of battle. When the flow of bullion was disrupted, as it occasionally was, the royal treasury suffered temporary but disconcerting insolvency.

As the excesses of Habsburg imperial ambitions, combined with economic disaster, conspired to diminish Spanish power in the first half of the seventeenth century, the northern countries began to invest in their own overseas enterprises, and the balance of power shifted from Iberia to France, England, and, to a lesser extent, the Netherlands. By the end of the reign of Elizabeth I, the Tudors had provided England with more than a century of strong, almost autocratic government that not even the Stuarts could destroy, and a merchant class had evolved that was prepared to invest heavily in the development of a commercial empire in both the east and the west. France survived the religious wars of the sixteenth century, and when the Bourbons finally consolidated their authority, Frenchmen seized the opportunity to invade the waters of southeast Asia and the forests of the St. Lawrence valley. The Dutch, throughout their long struggle with Spain, had been steadily developing an extensive maritime establishment, and long before the Peace of Westphalia had taken over much of the European carrying-trade and supplanted the Portuguese as the primary commercial agents of the East Indies. The Anglo-Dutch wars of the seventeenth century, and the "hundred years' war" between England and France in the eighteenth and early nineteenth centuries were as much colonial as they were European conflicts, reflecting the same determination to reserve the colony for the benefit of the mother-country that motivated Iberian exclusiveness in the Renaissance.

While Renaissance expansion was primarily an Iberian undertaking, it reflected the prevailing differences between Portuguese and Spanish continental aspirations. Portugal, realizing its inherent physical limitations, never attempted to develop an extensive territorial empire to bolster dynastic ambitions in Europe itself. Instead, Almeida, Albuquerque, and their successors concentrated on the establishment of a commercial superiority in the east that would undercut the monopoly the Italian city-states and the Arab traders had so long enjoyed. It was a geographically extensive but peripheral empire, heavily dependent upon the cooperation of native authorities. It was a maritime empire based upon the effective control of a few strategic enclaves, and trade, not political domination, was the key to its success. When that trade was challenged, and the fragile vulnerability of the Portuguese position was exposed, the empire went into a fairly rapid decline.

The *feitoria*, or trading-post, was the instrument through which the Portuguese established their presence along the coasts of Africa, India, Persia, and in the islands of the East Indies. São Jorge da Mina, on the Gold

Coast, was the *entrepôt* for the extensive trade in gold and slaves that the Portuguese conducted in Africa, but its prosperity continued only so long as interlopers were kept out and commodities from the interior found their way to its docks. Ormuz, Goa, Diu, and Calicut served essentially the same purpose in Persia and India, as did Malacca, Macao, and many other ports farther east. The spices, silks, ivories, jades, and other exotic products that flooded into Lisbon gave Portugal a brief period of economic glory, but it was a tenuous enterprise whose profits were more often than not siphoned off by Italian and Flemish entrepreneurs or consumed in the perpetual struggle to preserve the bureaucratic structure and provide the security that made it possible. When the Portuguese throne fell to Philip II in 1580, it provided the excuse the English and Dutch needed to appropriate much of an empire that the Portuguese were unable to defend and the Spanish had little inclination to protect.

Spain, on the other hand, was destined from the first decade of the sixteenth century to become a continental power. Ferdinand of Aragon was one of the most ambitious monarchs in Spanish history, and although he did not live to see the fulfillment of his imperial designs, he bequeathed a dynastic mélange to his successors that assured Spain an important voice in European affairs for a long time to come. His interests were in France and Italy, and he had little time for Columbus' New World, but his grandson, the Emperor Charles V (Charles I of Spain), inherited the full legacy of Ferdinand's diplomatic maneuvering—half of Europe and the greater part of the new-found Indies. Charles' interests were also European, and he devoted his energies not only to consolidating his enormous legitimate continental inheritance, but also to conquering vast portions of Italy, fighting the French and the Ottoman Turks, and repelling the spread of Protestant heresy in his imperial dominions. He was never really interested in his overseas possessions—the material wealth of the Indies contributed little to Charles' military ambitions—and there is little evidence that he ever thought of them in the same imperial terms he applied to his European domains. The colonies enhanced the power-image of the Habsburg dynasty, but they were never integrated into the universal monarchy that the emperor had seemed destined to establish.

Philip II was much less bound to the continent, his inheritance did not include the imperial crown, and his power was much more dependent upon a maritime supremacy than Charles' had been, but his problems also derived from Europe and from the Turk and, in spite of the great wealth he received from the New World, he too never grasped the idea of an oceanic community. Philip's obsession with his crusade against the Protestant Reformation, and his struggles with the Dutch and the English in the North and the Turks in the Mediterranean, restricted his view; he conceived of the Indies almost exclusively as a source of wealth to support Spanish ambitions in Europe. Santo Domingo and Cuzco were just too remote for a king whose travels barely extended beyond London, Milan, and Brussels. But it should be noted that Charles V established a printing press in Mexico less than two decades after the conquest, and that before the end of the sixteenth century books and pamphlets were being printed in Peru. The importance of the press as an instrument of administration and government and as an aid to the propagation of Christian doctrine was recognized by the Habsburg rulers at an early date, and a press controlled by both church and state was a significant factor in colonial development.

The rest of Europe, in particular those nations that were anti-Habsburg for religious and political reasons, looked upon the influx of American gold as the source of Spanish power. It was a convenient explanation, simplistic and obvious, often exaggerated for propaganda purposes. Richard Hakluyt, the most prolific propagandist for the establishment of an Elizabethan overseas empire, argued in his *Discourse of Western Planting* (1584) that "if you touche him [the Spaniard] in the Indies, you touche the apple of his eye, for take away his treasure which is *nervus belli*, and which he hath almoste oute of his west Indies, his olde bandes of souldiers will soone be dissolved, his purposes defeated, his power and strengthe diminished, his pride abated, and his tyranie utterly suppressed."[2] Hakluyt's enthusiasm for an English colonial venture tended to blind him to the substantial revenues that Philip II derived from his continental possessions; it was pure wishful thinking on the Englishman's part to surmise that "weare yt not that he [Philip] doth possesse suche a masse of treasure oute of the Indies, the frenche kinge of onely one kingdom with his onely people of ffraunce were able to drive him oute of all his domynions that he hath in the worlde."[3]

The Spanish overseas empire in the sixteenth century was administered on the same basic assumption as was its European counterpart—that effective political and territorial control was essential to profitable economic exploitation. The Spanish possessed Mexico and Peru in much the same way they controlled Sicily or the Piedmont. Unlike the Portuguese, they did not seek to establish a trading empire, although a lively transoceanic commerce did evolve in both the Atlantic and the Pacific. The Spanish were more concerned with developing their colonies as distinct political entities and extracting from them those products and services most valuable to Spain itself. The *conquistadores* were rarely interested in settlement; their ambitions usually involved becoming as wealthy as possible, and returning to Europe where that wealth would be a passport to political and economic power. Few gentlemen, or potential gentlemen, would have considered making Mexico or the Philippines their permanent residences, and of those who survived the perils of conquest, the majority retired to Spain and died in Estramadura or Castile.

[2] Richard Hakluyt, "Discourse of Western Planting," in *The Original Writings & Correspondence of the Two Richard Hakluyts*, 2 vols. (London, 1935), 2:249.
[3] *Ibid,* page 251.

All of the Renaissance imperial powers looked to overseas colonies as a place of exile for the undesirable elements of European society. If restive forces at home could be transported to faraway places, it was believed, the political and religious strife that characterized sixteenth-century Europe would be lessened considerably. Hakluyt and Coligny both proposed overseas colonies as a perfect solution to the problem of accommodating dissident groups, and saw in the comparative internal calm of the Iberian powers a confirmation of their observations. Spain and Portugal were both spared much of the turmoil that the Protestant Reformation visited on the North, but how much this was due to the deportation of heretics and criminals to the colonies is difficult to say. Heresy was pursued as diligently in the Indies as it was in Spain, and the *auto-da-fé* aroused as much terror in Mexico as in Seville. Strong and autocratic governments with almost absolute control over both church and state, and the absence of any effective representative legislature (the *Cortes* in both countries was virtually powerless), in addition to the specter of the Inquisition, made protest or rebellion very risky. There was undoubtedly some advantage gained from deporting restless elements, but to say, as one historian recently has, that "the internal history of Spain would surely have been radically different had the like of Cortés and Pizarro remained in Iberia,"[4] is surely an overstatement. Many dynamic individuals served the Habsburgs in Europe, and there is no reason to assume that Cortés or any other *conquistador* could not have contributed as much to continental policy as did Don Juan of Austria, the Duke of Alba, or the great Gonzalo de Córdoba.

If there was such a thing as an "imperial policy" or a "colonial idea" in the sixteenth century, it was predicated on the principles of the monopoly system —the notion that overseas possessions exist solely for the benefit of the colonizing power, and that they are subject to total control by the mother country. From Seville, Madrid, Valladolid, or Salamanca—wherever the Spanish court happened to be—a steady stream of *ordenaciones* and *reglas* were promulgated by the *Casa de Contratación* and the *Consejo de las Indias,* which regulated virtually every aspect of colonial life. There was no question of parity or equality; the modern imperial concept that overseas territories are an integral part of the mother country, or members of a "commonwealth" of colonial states, would have been totally alien to the Renaissance observer. Colonies were appendages, of distinctly secondary importance in the political and economic hierarchy. This idea lasted well beyond the period of the Renaissance, and was refined by the English and French into the classic mercantilism of the seventeenth and eighteenth centuries.

Renaissance Europe's image of the rest of the world was based primarily on the mineral wealth of America, the luxury goods of Asia, and the human resources of Africa—commodities that had obvious and immediate value in

---

[4] G. V. Scammell, "The New Worlds and Europe in the Sixteenth Century," *The Historical Journal* XII (1969) : 407.

the political and economic patterns of Western Europe. There was little realization, in the first half of the sixteenth century at least, that India and the Moluccas had more to offer than spices, or that the Spanish Indies could provide more than the coveted gold and silver from the mines of Mexico and Peru. But as the century progressed and it became increasingly important to consolidate existing conquests, a new breed of *conquistadores* began to investigate other benefits that might be derived from the colonial dominions. Garcia da Orta and Cristoval Acosta studied and described the many exotic but unfamiliar medicinal plants of the East, while Benzoni, Monardes, and José de Acosta provided an introduction to the natural marvels of the New World. It took time, however, for these products to be fully appreciated in Europe, and in the Portuguese Indies, in particular, the traditional spices, silks, and ivories continued to dominate commercial exchange until well into the seventeenth century. Eastern luxuries were familiar to Europe through several centuries of occasional contact and trade, and their impact in the Renaissance was less novelty than availability and increased knowledge of their origins.

The natural resources of the Americas, aside from mineral wealth, were new and different, but with few exceptions they were of little importance in the sixteenth century. Columbus had observed the natives of the islands smoking tobacco, and by the middle of the century it had become a significant factor in the Spanish trans-Atlantic trade, but the agricultural products of the New World, which would eventually have such enormous effects upon the dietary habits of the world—potatoes, maize, pumpkin, tomatoes, new varieties of beans, peppers, and many other commodities, in addition to quinine and cocaine—were curiosities or, at best, luxuries only the very wealthy could afford. In the seventeenth and eighteenth centuries, as the cultivation of these products increased in the colonies and in Europe and they spread in popularity, they assumed an importance that dwarfed the gold of Mexico and the silver of Peru.

The economic consequences of Iberian expansion were felt throughout Western Europe. The influx of new materials, particularly American bullion, encouraged the development of new commercial techniques, new industries, and new politico-economic rivalries. The growing dependence in the fifteenth and sixteenth centuries on an expanding money economy, and the increasingly international character of European trade, were accelerated by the discovery and exploitation of non-European sources of wealth. Spain, more than any other nation, was directly affected by the metallic increase of the sixteenth century, and her economy alternately benefited and suffered from her overseas treasure-stores. While Renaissance economic theories were far from precise, and governments tended to manipulate coinage and mercantile policies, it is evident that the importation of vast quantities of precious metals contributed to an exaggerated inflation that virtually destroyed the Spanish economy in the second half of the sixteenth century.

Habsburg economic policies assumed that the maintenance of Spanish power was dependent, to a large degree, upon the retention of as much bullion as possible within the empire itself. But Spain's dependence upon the rest of Europe for many of its material goods, the price rise, increasing administrative costs, and the enormous military expenditures necessary to keep the empire together made it impossible for it effectively to pursue a narrow mercantilist policy. Consequently, Seville often served as a mere transferral point between the New World and the bankers of Antwerp and other northern cities. The gold and silver remained in Spain just long enough to inflate the economy, and then passed on to other parts which were in turn affected by the inflationary tendencies of the new wealth. By the middle of the sixteenth century, Antwerp, the commercial and financial entrepôt of the north, was one of the most expensive cities in Western Europe in which to live and conduct business. England and France, as well as the Italian city-states, felt the effects of Spanish bullion, and were confronted with economic problems similar to those of their Iberian neighbors. Much of what has been described as "the crisis of the seventeenth century"—the economic dislocations occasioned by the lengthy transition from a feudal to a capitalistic society—can be traced to the influence of the new wealth derived from Europe's overseas expansion in the Renaissance.

The Role of Religion in Expansion

Renaissance secularism, so evident in the political and economic patterns of overseas expansion, does not tell the complete story of Europe's external interests. The Christian church, as a political and intellectual unifying force, had lost some of its appeal by the end of the fifteenth century, but the crusading spirit was still a powerful incentive, particularly to the Portuguese and Spanish, and religious motives played an important role in the early Iberian conquests. Centuries of struggle with the Moslems had given the Spanish, and to a lesser extent the Portuguese, a sense of destiny that was not fulfilled by the ultimate expulsion of Moorish political influence from the peninsula. The impetus to carry the crusade to the lands of the "heathen" themselves and to convert them to Christianity—or at least undermine their economic supremacy —gave early Renaissance expansion a decidedly religious character. In many respects hypocritical and excessively orthodox, it provided a convenient excuse to expand that otherwise might have been lacking. Whether God deserves priority in the familiar triad of God, glory, and gold is, of course, problematical.

The crusading idea was, in its medieval context, confined primarily to Portuguese expansion in Africa and the East. Gomes Eannes de Azurara, in his *Chronica do descobrimento e conquista de Guiné*, one of the major sources for the history of the Henrician voyages, lists several reasons for the Infante's interest in Africa, not the least of which was "his great desire to make increase in the faith of our Lord Jesus Christ and to bring him all the souls that should be saved," and his equally serious determination to locate any Christian prince who might aid in the war against the infidel.[5] The holy war was deliberately not extended to the non-Arabic natives of the Guinea coast, and in the middle of the fifteenth century, the Venetian traveler Alvise da Cadamosto wrote that the Portuguese prince was concerned about the possibility of alienating the sub-Saharan Africans whom he hoped by "mixing with Christians, . . . may without difficulty be converted to our faith," since they knew the Moslem religion only by hearsay.[6]

The legend of Prester John pursued the Portuguese to India and beyond, and the chronicles of the period are full of references to the search for the illusive Christian king of the East. Pero da Covilhã, in the last decade of the fifteenth century, penetrated Abyssinia, where he thought he had found the fabulous Christian kingdom, but his discovery, if it was known in Portugal at all, did not deter Vasco da Gama and his successors from continuing the search well into the sixteenth century. The failure of the Nestorian and St. Thomas Christians to conform to the rites and tenets of the Roman Church disturbed and perplexed their European contacts, but their very existence confirmed the long-held belief that isolated Christian communities existed throughout Africa and Asia, and stimulated the evangelical impulses of lay and ecclesiastical authorities in Lisbon and Rome.

As the Portuguese expanded their trading empire, their missionaries—particularly the members of the newly-founded Society of Jesus—made every effort to convert non-Christians to the Catholic faith. They established themselves in India and in the islands of Southeast Asia, and in the second half of the sixteenth century made furtive contacts with the vast Chinese empire and with Japan. The Chinese were extremely hostile to foreign intrusion, and did not prove susceptible to the initial Christian proselytizing efforts, but the Japanese were different, and in 1594 the great Francis Xavier enthusiastically reported that "this land of Japan is very fit for our holy faith greatly to increase therein; and if we knew how to speak the language, I have no doubt whatsoever that we would make many Christians."[7] The Jesuit saint exhibited the optimism that characterized his profession, but his moderate success left little doubt among his superiors that the East was a promising place for the further expansion of the Christian religion. His successors, though often martyred, retained his zeal, and the history of early European influence in

[5] Gomes Eannes de Azurara, *The Chronicle of the Discovery and Conquest of Guinea*, 2 vols. trans. and ed. by Charles R. Beazley and Edgar Prestage, (London, 1896), 1:29.

[6] Alvise da Cadamosto, *The Voyages of Cadamosto*, trans. and ed. by G. R. Crone (London, 1937), pp. 18–19.

[7] Francis Xavier, S.J., to the Jesuits at Goa, November 5, 1549. Quoted in Charles R. Boxer, *The Christian Century in Japan 1549–1650*, Appendix 1 (Berkeley, 1951), p. 402.

Asia is almost as much religious contact as it is economic and political. Indeed, one of the most persistent complaints voiced by Portuguese colonial administrators was the excessive fervor of the missionaries and their interference in secular matters.

The crusade in America differed from its African and Asian counterparts in that it involved no conflict over established political and economic sovereignties such as those in the Levant or the Indian Ocean. The natives of the Indies were considered by most Europeans ideal subjects for conversion rather than enemies of the true church. The motives that impelled Columbus and his followers have been debated endlessly, but there is no question that the admiral himself and most of the early *conquistadores* were men of intense religious convictions, and that while practical economic considerations were of primary importance, the desire to convert played a highly important secondary role. Columbus described the natives of his newly-discovered islands as "a people to be delivered and to be converted to our holy faith rather by love than by force"[8]; Cortés asked his Spanish sovereigns if it was not their absolute duty to see that "these people [the Mexicans] are introduced into and instructed in the holy Catholic faith," and predicted that if "the devotion, trust and hope which they now have in their idols [was] turned so as to repose with the divine power of the true God . . . they would work many miracles."[9] This was more than just lip-service to the church. In spite of the excesses perpetrated in the name of religion, there was a genuine conviction that Christians had an obligation, whether through "love" or "force," to make the benefits of the church available to the peoples they encountered. Hundreds of thousands of New World natives were baptized—usually after a most perfunctory catechism—and the establishment of Jesuit, Franciscan, and Dominican missions from Paraguay to California reflected a continuing concern for the spiritual as well as physical welfare of the newly-converted "Christians." The Spanish were uniformly revolted by what they considered the barbaric aspects of the native religions, but while condemning human sacrifice and cannibalism, so devout a Christian as Bernal Díaz del Castillo could casually write that he and his companions used the fat of a "stout" Indian to soothe their battle-inflicted wounds. The double standard that often prevailed in political and economic dealings occasionally characterized religious encounters as well.

The Protestant Reformation added a new dimension to Europe's overseas expansion in the sixteenth century, and had almost as massive an influence on colonial development as it had on Europe itself. Prior to the schism, there had been little European opposition to Spanish and Portu-

---

[8] *The Voyages of Christopher Columbus,* translated and edited by Cecil Jane (London, 1930), p. 148.

[9] *Hernando Cortés: Five Letters, 1519–1526,* translated by J. Bayard Morris (New York, 1962), p. 24.

guese conversion efforts, and the northern monarchies often applauded the great number of souls the Iberians were saving for the Catholic Church. But after Protestantism had become established in Germany, the Low Countries, England, and, to a lesser extent, France, and religion and politics had become inseparably intertwined, one of the standard Protestant arguments in favor of overseas expansion was the need to counteract the spread of Catholicism in colonial areas. The Counter Reformation and the popular identification of Spain as the secular arm of a militant papacy provided the English, French, and Dutch with a cogent spiritual rationale to reinforce practical commercial motives for aggressive imperial policies. Richard Eden had urged the English in the 1550s to colonize North America, and for "goddes cause" to "doo for owr partes as the Spaniards have doone for theyrs,"[10] while Hakluyt, in a more prophetic vein than he might have intended, wrote in 1584, that by establishing a plantation in North America, England could "provide a safe and a sure place to receave people from all partes of the worlde that are forced to flee for the truthe of gods worde."[11]

It was a Spanish missionary, ironically, who provided Protestant Europe with its most devastating anti-Habsburg propaganda. Bartolomé de las Casas, the legendary "Apostle of the Indies," had become the conscience of sixteenth-century Spanish imperialism in the New World. At a time when the American Indians were viewed by many as fit only for slavery or extermination, he recognized them as human beings and devoted the greater part of his career to assisting them in their efforts to survive the excesses of the conquest. His famous "tracts" were published in nine parts under the collective title *Brevissima Relación de la Destruyción de las Indias* in 1552 and 1553, and while his estimates obviously, but probably sincerely, exaggerated native mortality, his descriptions of Spanish brutality have conditioned impressions of the conquest to this day. His powerful indictment of Spain provided English and Dutch Protestants, and French Protestants and Catholics alike, with proof of Habsburg tyranny; portions of the tracts, translated and adapted as publishers saw fit, and embellished with gruesome illustrations, were issued as part of the anti-Spanish literature that circulated so freely in Europe in the last two decades of the sixteenth century.

The treatment of natives, particularly those of the New World, provided the Christian church with the only consequential debate that resulted from early European expansion. Although medievalism still influenced theology, the humanistic tradition and the secularism of the Renaissance had given the church an unprecedented resiliency. The discovery of new lands and new peoples did not pose the challenge to established doctrine it might have

---

[10] Richard Eden, *The Decades of the newe worlde or west India* (London, 1555), sig. ci (verso).

[11] Richard Hakluyt, "Discourse of Western Planting," p. 318.

in an earlier age. While Columbus was convinced that he had located the Terrestrial Paradise in the highlands of Venezuela, few theologians accepted his view. Though new discoveries occasionally undermined biblical authority, the church adapted, modified, and assimilated them into an acceptable theological position. No fundamental Christian doctrines were altered by Renaissance imperialism. Copernicus and Calvin had a much deeper effect on the physical and spiritual composition of the sixteenth-century church than did Columbus or Magellan.

However, the discovery of large non-Christian populations, some with advanced and complete civilizations, did provoke uncertainty regarding the relationship between Christian and native societies. The Portuguese had no qualms about enslaving their Moslem enemies or the black Africans they encountered on the Guinea coast, but they acknowledged the power and accomplishments of the more highly-developed cultures of the East, and preferred to work and trade within the confines of a mutual, albeit somewhat grudging, respect. Europeans were often highly critical of the Eastern nations they sought to penetrate—Cristovão Viera thought the Cantonese "full of much cowardice," and "presumptuous, arrogant, [and] cruel"— but at the same time recognized that a successful commercial venture in India, China, Japan, or the Spice Islands depended heavily upon the goodwill of the local authorities. Tomé Pires, a minor Portuguese official in Malacca, who saw this as clearly as any of his contemporaries, urged the Lisbon government to "win the confidence of the [native] merchants and navigators," and advised that the newly-established *feitoria* should be "provided with excellent officials, expert traders, lovers of peace, not arrogant, quick-tempered, undisciplined, dissolute, but sober and elderly." As an added inducement he predicted that "whoever is lord of Malacca has his hand on the throat of Venice."[12]

The New World posed an altogether different problem, one which emphasized the prevailing dissimilarities in attitudes and methods between the two Iberian colonial schemes. In Spanish America conquest preceded commerce, and few attempts were made to establish a cooperative trading empire. While the architectural accomplishments of the Incas and Aztecs provoked initial wonderment, Renaissance man found little to admire or respect in native cultures. The Spanish and the other Europeans who managed to visit the Indies were unimpressed and often revolted by the primitive and unrefined societies they encountered. The Mexican and Peruvian civilizations were not distinctly inferior to those of the Chinese or the Hindus of India, yet Pedro de Gante, in 1558, could describe the New World natives as resembling animals without the power of reasoning, and others questioned their ability not only to learn and rationalize, but to achieve any form of

---

[12] Tomé Pires, *The Suma Oriental of Tomé Pires*, translated and edited by Armando Cortesão (London, 1944), 2:285–287.

social and political organization. The tendency in Europe was to regard the natives as children or inferior beings, capable of very limited intellectual understanding and fit primarily to serve their European masters. The Spanish crown, recognizing its obligation to the aborigines of the Indies, established a commission to study the problem, and in 1512 the celebrated *Leyes de Burgos* defined the position of the Indians and, in effect, put them under the protection of the state.

While the Laws of Burgos provided the framework for a coherent Spanish Indian policy, they did not answer the theoretical questions that the existence of the natives continued to pose. Throughout the sixteenth and seventeenth centuries, and even to the end of the colonial period, debate persisted concerning who the American aborigines were, how they had escaped biblical recognition, and what their position should be in an expanding international society. Efforts were made to identify them as the lost tribes of Israel and the descendents of the sunken continent of Atlantis—classical and medieval mythology was the basis of much Renaissance anthropology—and both Plato and Aristotle, as well as a host of lesser authorities, were invoked to justify a distinction between civilized man and the barbarian. Semantics often clouded the picture. Theologians and legal writers of the sixteenth century spent as much time arguing relative degrees of heathenism and barbarism as they did finding solutions to the problems of coexistence. While there was rarely any question about the humanity of African and Asiatic peoples, it was necessary for the pope in 1537 to explicitly recognize the aborigines of the New World as "true men," even if there remained uncertainty about their origins.

It was difficult for sophisticated Europeans to view these people objectively, and the writings of the period tend either to idealize or denigrate them, depending upon the predilections of the observer. Partisans of the natives were quick to extol their virtues—Las Casas described them as "simple people without evil and without guile"—and nurtured the "noble savage" concept that persisted until the nineteenth century. The idea of a life uncomplicated by the religious, political, and economic conflicts of Renaissance civilization appealed to a number of people, and attempts were even made in Europe to recreate the idyllic existence the American Indian seemed to enjoy. To some, simplicity and purity were synonymous, and the lack of European amenities was not a sign of bestiality. Las Casas and his followers argued that the Indians were fully rational beings, capable of intelligent actions and not hostile to the Christian church, and as such were not deserving of enslavement or extermination.

The detractors of the natives looked upon them as hardly better than animals, incapable of reasoning or adapting to European norms, fit only to serve their European masters. They were revolted by the Indians' personal habits and contemptuous of their refusal, or inability, to comply with the practices of Christian tradition. They quoted Aristotle on the propriety of slavery and the natural division of men into masters and slaves. Even the arguments of so great a jurist as Francisco de Vitoria, one of the most profound pro-Indian writers of the period, failed to temper such expressions of contempt for the native cultures. The introduction of African slaves into the Spanish Indies compounded the problem and forced an unnatural comparison that usually worked to the Indians' disadvantage. The Africans were physically stronger than the Indians, and adapted much better to the demands of servitude in the Americas. The Indians could not survive the rigors of enforced labor on plantations or in the mines, and large numbers quickly succumbed to the ravages of European diseases and European civilization.

While the Renaissance expansionists generally maintained an attitude of total superiority toward other peoples, they eventually began to exhibit curiosity about the societies they encountered. A rudimentary anthropology— primarily based upon direct observation—began to manifest itself in the second half of the century, and appreciation of some aspects of African, Asian, and American cultures grew. Awareness increased that the non-European world had something to offer besides gold, spices, and slaves, and that benefits might be derived from the study of the native societies and even from the preservation of artifacts. Indian and Chinese treasures, as well as those of the advanced American societies, were collected and exhibited in Europe, and for every Aztec and Mayan codex that was burned by an overzealous priest, others were saved and studied for evidence about a rapidly vanishing way of life. Chronicles of conquest were usually prefaced by a description of the conquered, and writers such as Barros, Benzoni, and Acosta devoted entire sections of their histories to descriptions of the native peoples of Asia and America and their environments. Such accounts were not always objective, but their authors could hardly have been expected to abandon all of their preconceived ideas and European prejudices.

Influences of Expansion on European Consciousness

Renaissance curiosity was responsible for much of the motivation behind overseas expansion, but there is little evidence that it deeply influenced the overall intellectual and cultural development of fifteenth- and sixteenth-century European civilization. Painters and sculptors had little interest in immortalizing the overseas discoveries on canvas or in stone. While Dürer rejoiced over an exhibition of Aztec treasure, his work was not influenced by its "subtle ingenuity." Leonardo da Vinci, the complete "Renaissance man," interested in virtually everything, has left nothing to show that he ever contemplated the accomplishments of his Iberian contemporaries; and Titian, so closely identified with the Habsburg court, recorded none of his imperial patrons' overseas glories. It was an egotistical age, and both Charles V and Philip II, like most other Renaissance rulers, believed that art should be reserved for the master, not the servant; thus it was Charles rather than Cortés who sat for the Venetian. The wealthy patron, upon whom most Renaissance artisans depended, dictated subject matter, and the princes of church and state were much more interested in the immortality of their own visages than they were in people and events thousands of miles away. For Europeans, the battles of Pavia and Lepanto were much more compelling events than the conquest of a pagan Indian and his remote Mexican empire. On the other hand, Europeans did not hesitate to impose their own art-forms on the cultures they subjugated. The Portuguese destroyed Hindu temples in India and built Christian churches in their places, and the Spanish erected European cities atop the ruins of magnificent native temples and palaces in the New World. Appreciation of non-European art did not prevent the wholesale destruction of that art as a corollary to the establishment of European hegemony.

Renaissance art was heavily symbolic, and navigational instruments or globes occasionally appeared in such paintings as Holbein's "The Ambassadors" and the famous "Armada" portrait of Elizabeth I of England, in which the queen's right hand is resting on a stylized globe, protectively and prophetically covering North America! Symbolic quadrants, ships, and maps were only incidental, however, and artistic representations of the new discoveries had to be found in the printed books and elaborate atlases that presented a visual record of Renaissance expansion. From the Columbus letter to the multi-volume collections of travel narratives produced at the end of the sixteenth century, pictures played an increasingly important role in the dissemination of geographical knowledge. Initially they were fairly simple woodcuts, but as the century progressed and the art of engraving became more sophisticated, these illustrations developed into quite accurate representations of the phenomena that had impressed the European conquerors. There was a natural tendency to "Europeanize" the subject matter, and the earliest illustrations bore slight resemblance to actuality. In the Bergmann de Olpe edition (1493) of the Columbus letter, the illustrations of the islands appear to belong to the Old World, not the New, and the medieval castles and villages of "Isabella and Fernandus" resembled Palos and Seville more than they did the rude settlements Columbus had established a few months before.

The men who cut the blocks and drew the pictures for these books almost always worked from written descriptions of things they could hardly imagine, and if the Brazilian Indians were variously depicted as totally nude, wearing feathers, or clothed in flowing Renaissance robes, it was a reflection of the sixteenth-century imagination, not a deliberate distortion.

Asia and Africa had had a place in the European consciousness much longer than had the Americas, and the earliest illustrations of those areas were considerably more accurate; nevertheless, the medieval imagination did not die easily, and Mandevillean distortions continued to appear in them throughout the sixteenth century. Illustrations of the East were much less common than were those of the New World, and except for a few elaborate title-pages, there were few illustrated books on Asia before the middle of the century. Many manuscripts contained elaborate illustrations, but the great printed histories and chronicles of João de Barros, Fernão Lopes de Castanheda, Damião de Goes, and Antonio Galvão, to mention a few, appeared without pictures.

Imaginative literature, like pictorial art, offers little evidence of influence from overseas expansion. *Os Lusiadas* more properly belongs in the category of historical chronicle, despite its poetic format, as does Ercilla's *La Araucana,* the epic of the conquest of Chile. Sir Thomas More set his Utopia in the New World, and exhibited familiarity with Vespucci's voyages and the early literature of American discovery, and the *Tamerlane* of Christopher Marlowe has obvious origins; but in an age that produced Shakespeare, Spenser, Cervantes, and Erasmus, there is a paucity of imaginative literature concerned with non-European affairs. The conquests of Mexico and Peru, the epic circumnavigation by Magellan and his crew, and Drake's exploits all failed to inspire the century's most talented writers. Europe was very much concerned with itself, and the literary themes of the day were heavily influenced by preoccupation with the past, or the present disguised as the past. Political and religious considerations, arising from the necessity to please a critical audience whose concerns were principally European, dictated the emphasis in Renaissance literature. In addition, the wealth of geographic information available in the chronicles, histories, and collections of voyages made it unnecessary for a playwright or a poet to cover the same ground. Camões, the most important exception to this generalization, had been in India and knew of what he wrote firsthand. Few Renaissance writers had ventured far beyond their own homelands, and even fewer had the great Portuguese poet's familiarity with his subject.

The Renaissance mind found it difficult, if not impossible, to comprehend the enormous changes that were occurring as a result of overseas expansion; the limited world of western European society, even with its occasional upheavals, must have seemed comforting and secure to many in the face of an ever-enlarging globe. The humanists felt little affinity with explorers, and for them the classics were a refuge and a source of enlightenment that contemporary events could not provide. Alexander Barclay, in his English adaptation of Sebastian Brant's *Das Narrenchrift,* typified the humanist ideal when he wrote:

> *Ye people that labour the worlde to mesure*
> *Therby to knowe the regyons of the same*
> *Knowe firste your self, that knowledge is moste sure*
> *For certaynly it is rebuke and shame*

For man to labour onely for a name
To knowe the compasse of all the worlde wyde
Nat knowynge hym selfe nor howe he sholde hym gyde.[13]

The majority of the scholars of Western Europe appear to have heeded Barclay's advice, for while their curiosity was piqued by the new discoveries, they rarely considered them germane to the search for a meaningful relationship between God and man, or, for that matter, between man and the physical world. When scholars could no longer ignore the new information gained from exploration they tried to place it in the familiar context of established learning —as footnotes to the truths propounded by traditional authorities. Medieval cosmography received a new lease on life, and the writings of Pomponius Mela, Solinus, Sacrobosco, and a host of others were studied and restudied for clues to the meaning of the new data. These classical works were printed in dozens of editions throughout the sixteenth century, but *de situ orbis* included little detailed information concerning the New World or the further reaches of Africa or Asia, and Ptolemy's *Geographia*, reprinted many times before 1550, almost always contained the old maps as well as the new.

Not all men of learning were content to interpret new discoveries as a part of the undefinable or the past. Though not yet part of the curriculum, geography began to receive some attention from intellectuals in the universities; men such as Sir Thomas Smith at Cambridge, Henricus Glareanus at Basel, and Marineo Siculo at Salamanca all took an interest in the new expansion that occasionally transcended the mere academic. Richard Eden, the first exponent of an English overseas empire, acknowledged his debt to Smith's teachings, and both Glareanus and Marineo produced geographies that incorporated much of the new information available in Europe. Their observations, though hardly profound, were substantially more accurate and informative than the medieval works so long in vogue.

Science in the century of Vesalius and Copernicus was still in its formative stages—often ill-defined and little-studied, circumscribed by superstition and excessive orthodoxy. The overseas discoveries were a unique opportunity to increase knowledge of botanical, zoological, and geological phenomena on an unprecedented scale but, aside from a few amateur observations, scientific understanding of the natural world barely advanced in the sixteenth century. The unfamiliar flora and fauna provoked some curious speculation, but this curiosity was customarily expressed in medieval terms. A few studies were made by men with an inadequate background for true scientific inquiry. The scientific discovery of the non-European world did not occur in the Renaissance but in the eighteenth and nineteenth centuries, when great botanical and zoological expeditions traversed the globe in search of those phenomena the sixteenth century had largely ignored.

Increased experience was the major benefit to the science of navigation dur-

[13] Sebastian Brant, *This present Boke named the Shyp of Folys* (London, 1509), f. cxl.

ing the period of discovery and exploration. Fifteenth- and sixteenth-century sailors adapted old techniques to new situations—the astrolabe and the compass were both medieval inventions, and ship design owed much to Arabic innovations in the Red Sea and the Mediterranean. The caravels, naus, and galleons that bore the burden of Renaissance navigation evolved from the need for faster, more seaworthy vessels capable of withstanding the hazards of increased oceanic traffic; they were practical solutions to a problem that had been anticipated centuries earlier. Scandinavians had crossed the North Atlantic in vessels far less seaworthy than Columbus' three ships, and the Arab lateen-rigged traders had dominated the Indian Ocean long before Vasco da Gama reached its shores. But the experience the Renaissance sailor acquired in the fifteenth and sixteenth centuries made modern imperialism possible. A far-flung colonial empire could be only as secure as the men and ships that held it together, and the Renaissance sailor's life and fortune depended upon his ability to navigate in every conceivable situation.

Unfamiliar coastlines and the vagaries of uncharted waters made the cartographer a valued companion of the navigator, and his maps and charts often possessed exceptional utility and beauty. The earliest navigators had been forced to rely upon their own skills and instincts, and the few sailing aids they happened to possess, but as more information became available, sea-charts and atlases made sailing easier and safer. The medieval *portolano,* a European sea-chart, was adapted to the coastal waters of America, Africa, and Asia; trading routes were surveyed and marked; and sheet maps and atlases traced the progress of Europe's expanding global interests. Cartography became both an art and a science in the Renaissance. Maps, both in manuscript and in printed form, were the prime means by which Europe learned just how much had been accomplished in the discovery of the world. The challenges posed by an unprecedented accumulation of geographic information were well met by the cartographers of sixteenth-century Europe, and in the magnificent productions of such draftsmen as Jacopo Gastaldi, Gerard Mercator, Abraham Ortelius, Gerard de Jode, Pieter Goos, and the Blaeu family, mapmaking achieved an artistic excellence that linked overseas expansion and the craftsmanship that characterized Renaissance civilization.

The Effects of Expansion

When Pierre Radisson, during his wanderings in French Canada in the seventeenth century, exclaimed that "we weare Cesars, [there] being nobody to contradict us," he was providing an apt commentary on Renaissance Europe's concept of its own overseas expansion. Just as the legions of Rome had conquered much of western Europe, so did western Europe conquer, or at least establish its presence, contradicted or not, throughout much of the rest of the world in the fifteenth and sixteenth centuries. It was a multi-faceted experience, derived from the changing ideas of an increasingly sophisticated and complex society, at once European, but charged with that spirit of Renaissance individualism that made each discovery the unique phenomenon that it was. Renaissance expansion evoked the best and the worst from men of varying backgrounds—social, political, economic, and religious. To each it meant something different, but to all it was an opportunity for Caesar to march again, not just for the glory of one empire, but for the benefit of all of western Europe.

For the *conquistador*, participation in Europe's overseas adventure held the promise of quick fame and fortune. The tales of discovery and conquest that reached the Old World stimulated men to try for glory in the "Indies," both East and West; to have sailed abroad gave a man a distinction the "stay-at-home" could not achieve. It was a risky business to embark for strange lands, however, and few actually attained their goal. For every success there were thousands who died in the quest or retired in poverty and obscurity. But for many the opportunity to escape the restrictions of established social patterns and the trials of religio-political conflict made the effort worthwhile. Productive land was becoming scarce in Europe, and the prospect of vast territories offering unlimited land-owning opportunities appealed to the propertyless soldier-of-fortune and the dispossessed peasant alike. At a time when changing economic conditions were forcing more and more people from rural areas to increasingly crowded urban centers, some European statesmen viewed overseas colonies as a solution to the problem of real or imagined overpopulation. It has been estimated that in 1500 the population density of Europe was approximately twenty-six persons per square mile, and that for each individual there was available about twenty-four acres of land. The opening of the "great frontier," as one prominent historian has termed the discovery of the non-European world, potentially reduced density to less than five persons per square mile, and increased the amount of land per person to 148 acres.[14] Such a bonanza, though only dimly perceived by most contemporaries, had a profound impact on those who considered demographic questions. All the propagandists for empire encouraged emigration and stressed the benefits of life away from the cities of Europe, which even in the sixteenth century was beginning to be plagued by urban problems. Emigration during the Renaissance was slight, and confined primarily to those who sought the El Dorado of instant wealth rather than the settled atmosphere of the plantation; from the seventeenth century on, and particularly after the dramatic population

---

[14] Walter Prescott Webb, "The Great Frontier," in *The Expansion of Europe: Motives, Methods, and Meanings*, edited by De Lamar Jensen (Boston, 1967), p. 101.

increases of the eighteenth and nineteenth centuries, millions of Europeans took advantage of the frontier to establish themselves permanently in all parts of the world.

The conquest of parts of Africa, and Asia, and America by Europeans was often cruel and brutal—De Bry's graphic engravings make that all too clear—but there were moments of nobility that cannot be denied. The heroic figure of Cortés contrasts sharply with that of the illiterate and degenerate Pizarro, but both were engaged in essentially the same pursuit—to achieve personal grandeur and to prove the inherent superiority of European civilization as it was reflected in the glory of Spain and the Christian church (which many considered one and the same). A certain naiveté gave a medieval touch to the entire enterprise. Marco Polo's descriptions of the fabled East inspired a host of imitators eager to see the twelve thousand bridges of Kinsai or the golden palaces of Cipangu; and Ponce de León, Coronado, Frobisher, and many others were convinced that their expeditions would reveal the truth of medieval legends to the skeptics of the sixteenth century. As sophisticated a man as Sir Walter Raleigh believed in Mandevillean monsters; John Dee, an enigmatic Elizabethan man of science and the occult, friend of both Mercator and Ortelius, did not hesitate to adapt twelfth-century tales to support his queen's claims to North America. The Renaissance explorer often saw what he wanted to see, and when he deluded himself into believing that Hindus were Christians, like Da Gama, or that Pamlico Sound was the Pacific Ocean, like Verrazano, he was interpreting reality in the light of traditional expectations —blending Renaissance curiosity and the medieval sense of order.

To the statesmen, politicians, and merchants of Europe, overseas expansion was synonymous with national prestige and wealth. Power, it came to be believed, was at least partly derived from lucrative colonial possessions or the establishment of profitable commercial empires. But empires, in the modern sense, did not exist in the Renaissance; while Charles V was an emperor, his dominion was Europe, and his title came from Germany, not the Indies. Cortés, in his second letter to his king, advised Charles that he was emperor of Mexico just as he was of Germany, but Charles' vision rarely extended beyond Europe and the Moslem world. There was no threat to European civilization from beyond the seas, and the problems of expansion were insignificant compared with those of administering a vast continental empire. The Turks and the Protestant Reformation were of much more immediate concern.

The monopoly system dominated colonial economic policies. Even when it was obviously detrimental, as in the Anglo-Spanish peace negotiations of 1603 and 1604, for the Habsburg to deny access to the Indies to English merchants, national jealousies inhibited diplomatic realities. As Philip III's ambassador explained, the Iberians had procured their colonial possessions "with great charge and loss of men," and it was therefore only proper that they should have exclusive rights in those areas. It was impossible to separate political power from territorial acquisition and commercial privilege in the sixteenth century. As long as total political and economic control was profitable, there was no point in altering the existing arrangement, and even after overseas expansion became more of a liability than an asset, as in the case of sixteenth-century Portugal, there was a genuine reluctance to forego the prestige that it entailed. Philip II assumed the Portuguese throne in 1580 for historical and strategic reasons, but he was certainly not unaware of the enormous influence that an amalgamation of the two Iberian empires might produce; while nothing was done to prevent the consolidation, the rest of Europe was extremely apprehensive. Predictions of a world monarchy based upon the wealth of both Indies were widespread.

It is extremely unlikely that any of the Spanish Habsburgs ever contemplated universal hegemony. However, the Catholic Church, true to its heritage, had worldwide ambitions, and saw in the expansion of Renaissance Europe an opportunity to extend its influence. The Protestant Reformation accelerated this desire, and in an era of *cuius regio eius religio,* church and state combined to proselytize the rest of the world. Missionaries often searched for souls in areas that the soldier or merchant had yet to visit, and while their influence was occasionally debilitating, it did impart a sense of civility to overseas expansion that ameliorated its more violent and brutal aspects. Martyrdom was a common occurrence, from the Philippines to Paraguay, but it did not obscure the church's mission; on the contrary, it seemed to stimulate evangelical zeal. In spite of their mistakes, and they made many, the priests and missionaries of Renaissance expansion were almost as important as the mariners and adventurers, and were certainly as hardy and dedicated a group as the age produced.

Much of the religion imparted in overseas areas was superficial and, from the point of view of the newly-converted, accepted more out of expediency than faith. In many parts of the world, particularly the Spanish and Portuguese possessions, Christianity was adapted to local traditions, producing a hybrid Catholicism that persists to this day. Where the Europeans encountered strong established religions, such as Hinduism in India and Buddhism in Japan, they had little initial success in wholesale conversion, but where deity was attributed to temporal authorities, who usually proved extremely vulnerable to European persuasions, there was less resistance to the imposition of Christian doctrine. Both Montezuma and Atahualpa were invested with divine powers by their respective peoples, and their elimination left the Aztecs and Incas without the visible leadership that their political and religious establishment demanded. The Christian church took advantage of the opportunities offered by conquest, and in time established itself as the most durable influence of the Renaissance on subject peoples. Its traditional resistance to change gave it permanence and continuity that has endured centuries of political, economic, and social modifications.

Europe's overseas expansion in the fifteenth and sixteenth centuries grew out of the changing world of the Renaissance: the growth of nationalism, an expanding money economy, refinements in technology, and an inherent curiosity all combined to provide incentives for a broadening geographical awareness. But without the ability to publicize his achievements, Renaissance man might have accomplished little more than had his medieval predecessors. The printed word made it possible for all of western Europe to share the knowledge that a few explorers had uncovered. While the immediate intellectual impact of the discoveries was apparently minimal, the great number of printed works relating to the new expansion indicates a level of interest that would have been impossible before the time of Gutenberg. The church, the state, and the merchant would have been hard-pressed to maintain the momentum of overseas expansion without the tremendous advantages of the printing press, and in the literature of this ambitious undertaking Renaissance Europe left a remarkable legacy.

The Renaissance was the age of geographical discovery, and in no similar period of history has so much been learned on so vast a scale. With only a fraction of the technical skills available to the modern explorer, and without the apparatus of unlimited governmental support, the Renaissance adventurer encompassed the globe and tripled the size of the known world. He demolished centuries of myth and misconception, and provided both church and state with new dimensions and unlimited opportunities for growth and exploitation. He altered existing commercial and economic patterns, and introduced Europe to a vast array of new goods that eventually changed the lives of millions. The balance of power was sharply transformed, and nationalism, based partially upon overseas rivalries, was given an impetus that lasted far beyond the sixteenth century. Governments in time became dependent upon colonial development, and more than one fell in the eighteenth and nineteenth centuries because of imperial mistakes. An international community, barely foreseen in the Renaissance, evolved from the exploits of the sixteenth-century expansionists, and European politics became the concern not only of Europe, but of the rest of the world as well.

Selected Bibliography

The literature of Renaissance expansion is enormous, but bibliographies of the subject are rare, and those that do exist are far from complete. For the student the best guides are Wilcomb E. Washburn, *The Age of Discovery* (Washington, 1966), a pamphlet from the Service Center for Teachers of History, and Charles E. Nowell, "The Expansion of Europe," pp. 404–426 in *The American Historical Association's Guide to Historical Literature* (New York, 1963), and the sections of the same publication devoted to the various national histories.

Edward G. Cox's *A Reference Guide to the Literature of Travel,* 3 vols. (Seattle, 1935–1949), is useful for source materials but is cumbersome and rather difficult to use. The bibliographies appended to the works of Lach, Boxer, Parry, and others mentioned below are specialized, but do contain valuable references of a general nature. Some of the best bibliographical aids available are the catalogues of bookdealers, particularly those of Maggs Brothers of London, which could almost serve as bibliographies in their own right.

Every student of Europe's overseas expansion must be indebted to the Hakluyt Society. Since 1846 this organization has been engaged in publishing in English "original narratives of important voyages, travels, expeditions, and other geographical records," covering medieval to modern times. The French, Dutch, Portuguese, and Spanish have all been fairly diligent about printing their national records of overseas expansion, but none can match the Hakluyt Society for the breadth and scope of its interests or the quality of its work. The most convenient one-volume collection of source materials, derived in large part from Hakluyt Society publications, is J. H. Parry, ed., *The European Reconnaissance: Selected Documents* (New York, 1968).

The popularity of the age of discovery has provided the historian with a multitude of general histories, most of which are not particularly distinguished. J. H. Parry's *The Age of Reconnaissance* (London and Cleveland, 1963) is the best work available on all aspects of the subject, and Boies Penrose's *Travel and Discovery in the Renaissance* (Cambridge, Mass., 1952) has become a sort of classic of its kind. It contains the best survey of Renaissance geographical literature in print, derived in part from the author's own remarkable collection of original source materials. Charles E. Nowell's *The Great Discoveries and the First Colonial Empires* (Ithaca, 1954), is brief but useful as an introduction, as is Parry's *Europe and a Wider World, 1415–1715* (London, 1949). *The Expansion of Europe: Motives, Methods, and Meanings,* edited by De Lamar Jensen (Boston, 1967) includes a number of interpretive essays and selections from larger works, including salient parts of the O'Gorman, Washburn, and Batillon arguments about the "discovery" or "invention" of America. Robert G. Albion has edited *Exploration and Discovery* (New York and London, 1965), which contains excerpts from Penrose, Parry, Nowell, and others. Very recently two studies have been published that attempt to assess the influence of Renaissance expansion on Europe: G. V. Scammell's "The New Worlds and Europe in the Sixteenth Century," in *The Historical Journal,* XII (1969), pp. 389–412, is provocative and informative, even if some of his conclusions are open to question; and J. H. Elliott's *The Old World and the New, 1492–1650* (Cambridge, 1970) provides an excellent survey of America in European thought.

For Portuguese expansion, the standard history in English has long been Edgar Prestage's *The Portuguese Pioneers* (London, 1933), but it has now been superseded by Charles R. Boxer's *The Portuguese Seaborne Empire: 1415–1825* (New York and London, 1969). The same author's *Four Centuries of Portuguese Expansion, 1415–1825: A Succinct Survey* (Johannesburg, 1961) and *Race Relations in the Portuguese Colonial Empire, 1415–1825* (Oxford, 1963) are briefer introductions to the same subject. Francis M. Rogers' *The Quest for Eastern Christians* (Minneapolis, 1962) is an excellent study of the role of religion in motivating discovery, particularly with regard to the Portuguese interest in Asia. Donald F. Lach's monumental *Asia in the Making of Europe* (Chicago, 1965–), in 3 volumes so far, is an exhaustive study of Asia's influence on Europe throughout the Renaissance. All of these works contain extensive bibliographies of both source materials and secondary works in many languages.

Spanish expansion, particularly in the Americas, has long fascinated professional and amateur historians on both sides of the Atlantic. Columbus alone has been the subject of thousands of books, articles, pamphlets, and monographs in every conceivable language. Samuel Eliot Morison's *Admiral of the Ocean Sea* (Boston, 1942), in its 2-volume edition, is the standard biography, although it is primarily a study of the great discoverer as a navigator. J. H. Parry has provided the best single-volume study of Spanish expansion in his *The Spanish Seaborne Empire* (London and New York, 1966). It, like the Boxer volume on Portuguese expansion, replaces an older work, *The Spanish Conquistadores* (London, 1934), by F. A. Kirkpatrick. Both the Boxer and Parry books are part of the series entitled "The History of Human Society," edited by J. H. Plumb, while Prestage and Kirkpatrick were part of "The Pioneer Histories." Edward G. Bourne's *Spain in America, 1450–1580* (New York, 1904) is old, but still one of the best surveys of the Spanish conquest in English, while Clarence Haring's *The Spanish Empire in America* (New York, 1947), remains the standard administrative history of Spain in the New World. It may be supplemented with J. H. Parry's *The Spanish Theory of Empire in the Sixteenth Century* (Cambridge, 1940).

While Columbus has been the subject of most of the biographical writings on Spanish expansion, Vespucci has had his share of partisans, including Germán Arciniegas, whose *Amerigo and the New World* (New York, 1955) presents the case for the Florentine, as does Edmundo O'Gorman's controversial *The Invention of America* (Bloomington, 1961). Cortés and Pizarro were immortalized by William Hickling Prescott in his classic nineteenth-century histories of the conquests of Mexico and Peru—works that, in spite of their age, are still informative and highly readable. Cortés' letters and the narrative of Bernal Diaz del Castillo are available in translation in several editions. Adequate biographies are available in English of Balboa, Magellan, Coronado, Alvarado, and most of the *conquistadores*. Lewis Hanke has devoted years to Las Casas, and his *Bartolomé de las Casas: An Interpretation of his Life and Writings* (The Hague, 1951) is as good a biography as can be found. Hanke has also published separate works on Las Casas as an historian and a scholar, and has synthesized his researches in *The First Social Experiments in America* (Cambridge, Mass., 1935) and *The Spanish Struggle for*

Justice in the Conquest of America (Philadelphia, 1949). The economic and commercial consequences of Spanish expansion may be studied in Clarence Haring's *Trade and Navigation Between Spain and the Indies in the Time of the Hapsburgs* (Cambridge, Mass., 1918), and in Earl J. Hamilton's *American Treasure and the Price Revolution in Spain, 1501–1650* (Cambridge, Mass., 1934).

Dutch expansion has been admirably studied by Charles R. Boxer in his *The Dutch Seaborne Empire, 1600–1800* (London and New York, 1965), and in George Masselman's *The Cradle of Colonialism* (New Haven and London, 1963). Both volumes have good bibliographies. Boxer's *The Dutch in Brazil, 1624–1654* (Oxford, 1957) and his *Jan Compagnie in Japan, 1600–1850* (The Hague, 1950), are somewhat beyond the scope of this essay, but both are very readable and contain background material valuable for the earlier period. The most important sixteenth-century source for Dutch interest in the East is Jan Huyghen van Linschoten's *Itinerario,* which was published in translation by the Hakluyt Society in 1885.

The French, like the English, have not yet had their "Seaborne" volume published in "The History of Human Society" series, but both have been promised. When completed, these five volumes will provide a comprehensive and factual account of pre-nineteenth-century European expansion that should stand for years to come. Francis Parkman did for France in the New World what Prescott did for Spain, and his *Pioneers of France in the New World,* in many editions, is still as authoritative as it was when first published in 1865. Cartier and Champlain have both had their biographers, and the *Works* of the latter have been edited by H. P. Biggar in seven volumes (Toronto, 1922–1936). Samuel Eliot Morison's latest work, *The European Discovery of America: The Northern Voyages* (New York, 1971), is full of fascinating details about not only French voyages to North America, but those of the Norse, Portuguese, and English as well. It is vintage Morison, and the Admiral's unique style is evident on every page. The illustrations, maps, and chapter notes provide an extraordinary mine of information.

English and American historians have more than made up for Tudor tardiness in joining the Renaissance expansionists. The Cabots have been scrutinized by James A. Williamson in his *The Voyages of the Cabots and the English Discovery of North America* (London, 1929) and *The Cabot Voyages and Bristol Discovery under Henry VII,* a 1962 publication of the Hakluyt Society. David B. Quinn is an indefatigable student of early English overseas interest, and his *The New Found Land: The English Contribution to the Discovery of North America* (Providence, 1965) is a brief but important summation of one historian's research into northern voyaging. E. G. R. Taylor's *Tudor Geography, 1485–1583* (London, 1930) and her *Late Tudor and Early Stuart Geography, 1583–1650* (London, 1934) provide an excellent survey of English geographic thought and practice in the Renaissance.

The Elizabethans have received the most attention from historians of English overseas activity, and James A. Williamson's *The Age of Drake* (London, 1938) is the standard modern survey of the period. A. L. Rowse has studied *The Elizabethans and America* (London, 1959) and *The Expansion of Elizabethan England* (London, 1955), but neither work is on a par with his definitive biography of *Sir Richard Grenville of the Revenge* (London, 1937). Julian Corbett's *Drake and the Tudor Navy*, 2 vols. (London, 1917) and his *The Successors of Drake* (London, 1900), are both outdated, but may be perused with profit. Vilhjalmur Stefansson's *The Three Voyages of Martin Frobisher*, 2 vols. (London, 1938), is a fine study, incorporating most of the known source materials. Williamson's *Hawkins of Plymouth* (London, 1949), and George B. Parks' *Richard Hakluyt and the English Voyages* (New York, 1928) are both masterful biographies, written by recognized authorities.

The cartography of Renaissance expansion has been explored in Lloyd A. Brown's *The Story of Maps* (Boston, 1949), in the various works of the late R. A. Skelton, in Leo Bagrow's *History of Cartography*, rev. ed. (London, 1964), and in R. V. Tooley's *Maps and Mapmakers* (London, 1952). A. E. Nordenskiöld's *Facsimile-Atlas to the Early History of Cartography* (Stockholm, 1889) and *Periplus: An Essay on the Early History of Charts and Sailing Directions* (Stockholm, 1897) are extremely important, not only for their fine illustrations, but also for their contributions to an understanding of Renaissance cartography. *The World Encompassed* (Baltimore, 1952), a beautiful catalogue to an exhibition of maps, atlases, and globes held at the Baltimore Museum of Art, contains fine reproductions of many Renaissance cartographic items. The recent *Landmarks of Mapmaking* (Amsterdam and Brussels, 1968) is an excellent example of modern techniques employed in the reproduction of fifteenth- and sixteenth-century maps, and the text is informative and precise. For sheer sumptuousness and visual delight no recent publication can compare to the magnificent *Portugaliae Monumenta Cartographica*, 6 vols. edited by Armando Cortesão and A. C. Teixeira da Mota (Coimbra, 1960–1963). The scholarly periodical *Imago Mundi* (1935–) is devoted entirely to cartography, and contains articles by leading authorities as well as an extensive annual bibliography of published writings in the field.

Lawrence C. Wroth's *The Way of a Ship: An Essay on the Literature of Navigational Science* (Portland, Me., 1937), presents the subject in easy-to-understand terms, somewhat more successfully than does E. G. R. Taylor in her *The Haven-Finding Art: A History of Navigation from Odysseus to Captain Cook* (London, 1956). Both Parry and Morison have included chapters on ship-design, rigging, and the techniques of oceanic navigation in their works, and Carlo M. Cipolla has analyzed *Guns, Sails, and Empires: Technological Innovation and the Early Phases of European Expansion, 1400–1700* (New York, 1965).

One of the most fascinating aspects of Renaissance expansion is the literature that evolved from Europe's overseas experience. To study it, of course, requires a facility in languages that few people possess, and the efforts of such groups as the Hakluyt Society make life much easier for the Anglo-American specialist. There is no comprehensive survey of this literature, except possibly the chapter on "The Geographical Literature of the Renaissance" in Boies Penrose's previously mentioned *Travel and Discovery*. Geoffroy Atkinson has studied French works in his admirable *La Littérature Géographique Française de la Renaissance*, 2 vols. (Paris, 1927–1936), and P. B. Baginsky has provided a bibliography of *German Works Relating to America, 1493–1800* (New York, 1942), based upon the extensive holdings of the New York Public Library. The nineteenth-century bibliographies of Henry Harrisse and José Toribio Medina are still indispensible tools, as are the catalogues of the great collections in the John Carter Brown Library, the Henry E. Huntington Library (Church Collection), and the British Museum, among others. John Parker ably surveys English geographical literature of the Renaissance in his *Books to Build an Empire* (Amsterdam, 1965), as does Franklin T. McCann, on a somewhat more limited scale, in *English Discovery of America to 1585* (New York, 1952). An unusual work, distinguished not only by its scholarly bibliographic detail but also by the fact that it was compiled by the last King of Portugal, is the superb *Early Portuguese Books, 1489–1600, in the Library of H. M. the King of Portugal*, 3 vols. (London, 1929–1936). Manoel II was a bibliophile as well as a monarch, and the Royal Library contained copies of the monuments of Portuguese literature, including most of the great chronicles of early Portuguese expansion. They are fully described in this great catalogue.

The Ambassadors *by Hans Holbein the Younger, 1533. Courtesy of the National Gallery of Art, London.*

8.

Power Politics and Diplomacy: 1500—1650

DE LAMAR JENSEN

THE CENTURY-AND-A-HALF from the High Renaissance to the end of the Thirty Years' War was a period of great change and innovation in the purposes and conduct of European affairs. During this formative period in the evolution of the nation-state, a European system of international relations developed out of the earlier experiences of Italian diplomacy. Of course, diplomacy was not an exclusively Italian invention. It was practiced by everyone possessing political authority. But during the fifteenth century the conduct of foreign relations by means of continuous diplomacy became well-established in the Italian city-states. This system of institutionalized power relations—with many modifications and adaptations added in the sixteenth century—spread throughout Europe in the period 1500–1650, and from there throughout the world.

International relations in this period were characterized by many remnants of medieval thought and practice, reflecting in particular the ideal of a European Christian community. But they also operated by principles of power and sovereignty which have a distinctively modern flavor. Power politics, defined here as expedient and "realistic" political relations between independent sovereign states, played a significant role during this period in the gradual creation of an international state system. But the political arrangement which resulted from this century-and-a-half of upheaval and readjustment was not just a crude conglomeration of greedy giants intent on devouring one another. Arnold Toynbee's recent representation of the post-Westphalian era as a time of "anarchy by treaty" contains an element of truth, but fails to ac-

327

knowledge the continuing endeavor of statesmen and diplomats to pursue national goals and interests within a larger framework of law and justice.

In this essay I intend to demonstrate that international relations, both theoretical and practical, developed rapidly during this period, and that the ingredients of that development grew out of medieval concepts of community as well as Italian city-state politics. Furthermore, I hope to show that the conflicting interests of the new and powerful national monarchies dictated the development and expansion of their diplomatic machinery, and promoted the application of realistic rules to the conduct of international relations. These rules did not always coincide with current practice, but they did correspond sufficiently with general needs to provide a primitive framework of international law acknowledging both the autonomy and the community of nation-states.

Renaissance Politics: Power and Community

The medieval practice of foreign relations, with its ad hoc embassies of personal *nuncii* and *legati* representing their principals in all manner of negotiations, was based on the idea of a *Corpus Christianium,* a Christian commonwealth or family of states unified in ideal by the concept of divine law and in practice by the religious jurisdiction of the Roman pontiff. A degree of symbolic community was also represented by the Holy Roman Emperor. The unity of this *Respublica Christiana* was greater in theory than in practice, but the intellectual reality of a Christian community was deeply imbedded in the European consciousness. It was not just a pious dream on the part of a few churchmen. There were many unifying features in the ecclesiastical organization of the medieval church: its establishment of rules for the conduct of wars, for example; its Europeanwide system of ecclesiastical jurisdiction; and its network of courts, procedures and law. The canon lawyers and papal *legati* lent further credibility to the concept of Christendom, as did many other institutions, occupations and practices. The Latin language was a common medium of communication for lawyers, scholars, and statesmen, just as it was for clerics. But the strongest bonds of community were intellectual and psychological. The concept of Christendom as an organic entity possessing common traditions, both cultural and religious, was accepted by all European Christians in the Middle Ages. And although not everyone agreed with Dante's argument that the Holy Roman Emperor possesses a *potestas jurisdictionis* in the Christian church-state, they did believe that emperor and pope represented in complementary fashion the community of Christendom.

In the Renaissance the ideal of unity remained in vogue, and was even expanded by some to include Muscovite Russia and wild Lithuania. Thomas More insisted to his death that Christendom was indivisible, and Erasmus believed, as had medieval churchmen, that all Christians were "members of one body," the body of Christ. To Montaigne, late in the sixteenth century, Christendom was still as meaningful an entity as it had been to Aquinas. Even after the Reformation the concept of Christian community persisted among Protestants as well as Catholics. Richard Hooker's interpretation of Christian unity, expounded in his *Laws of Ecclesiastical Polity* (1594), illustrates the persistence of this medieval theme in the Renaissance and Reformation. Even hardnosed politicians and grasping monarchs paid lip service to the ideal of unity. Ferdinand and Isabel never hesitated to remind Henry VII of his duties as a Christian prince, and Henry acknowledged that the common peace of Christendom had always been his chief desire. In 1512 Pope Julius II placed Venice under interdict because the republic refused to join in a holy Christian alliance—but then the papacy usually expected more gestures toward unity from princes and politicians than they supplied. On the other hand, Emperor Charles V harangued the pope no less frequently about his obligations to Christendom. In 1523 Charles tried to persuade his former mentor, Pope Adrian VI, to abandon his neutrality and join in a military alliance for "the peace of Christendom." "It is the duty of the Pope and of the Emperor to be always united" argued the emperor, "and to watch that no wrong be done in the Christian Republic, the Pope wielding the spiritual and the Emperor the temporal weapon."[1] In this statement, the concept of a single society with both spiritual and temporal functions persists.

Nevertheless, there was occurring in the late fifteenth and early sixteenth centuries a widening gap between the theory of Christian commonwealth and the actual practice of realpolitik among its separate parts. Sixteenth-century writers continued to talk of "the common welfare of Christendom," "Christian brotherhood," "joint and common consent," and "reducing Christ's people into one perfect unity"; some affirmed that "the common law of Christendom" prevailed throughout Europe. Yet, in spite of such high assertions, European politics were conducted on a more mundane level. The second half of the fifteenth century had been a fertile season for the growth of secular states, accompanied by the development of a new attitude toward politics. Closer and more frequent contacts among these states, and the increasing complexity of their interests, made it difficult for the new nation-states to act the part of brothers. The Cardinal of Sion remarked in 1518 that the fundamental and long-standing differences between France and England were so great as to render friendship between the two monarchies impossible.

In Italy the difficulty of maintaining a Christian community was particularly acute. The deterioration of political morality in Renaissance Italy, amply

---

[1] *Calendar of State Papers, Spanish: Henry VIII* (London, 1866), 2:522. Adrian countered with the accusation that Charles preferred to indulge his own private quarrels and lust for power than to unite with the other Christian princes against the Turkish threat.

attested to by every Italian writer from Bruni to Varchi, is not only a reflection of the widening gap between theory and practice, but also an outgrowth of a new conception of power that had come to prevail in the relations of the larger Italian city-states. Less impressed than most European rulers by the pretensions of the Holy Roman Emperor, and no longer intimidated by the pope, the successful princes of Quattrocento Italy paid little attention to scholarly professions of Christian unity. What they did take seriously was the strength of an enemy's army, the cost of hiring a successful *condottiere*, and the political value of information sent by an ambassador. Such princes as Lodovico Sforza of Milan and his crafty father-in-law Ercole d'Este, duke of Ferrara; Federigo Gonzaga of Mantua; the Malatestas of Rimini; and the Neopolitan magnate, Ferrante of Aragon recognized few moral sanctions in their conduct of political affairs. They ruled by power and diplomacy and within their principalities came closer to being absolute rulers than any king of France or Spain.

It seems strange, therefore, that sixteenth-century readers should have been so shocked by Machiavelli's frank observations on power politics. Contemporaries surely recognized the baldness of interstate relations. Perhaps their outrage was due to the customary separation of theory and practice in these matters. Whatever the reason, Machiavelli's readers—at least those north of the Alps—seem to have been scandalized more by his political writings than by the scandalous activities of the princes themselves. Machiavelli observed carefully the workings of interstate relations, and noted the value and uses of power. As early as November 1502, in a dispatch from Imola, Machiavelli commented that alliances between rulers were maintained only by force of arms, an observation which he repeated many times later. Force, Machiavelli believed, is useful to keep the nobility in check and to achieve power. Machiavelli did not necessarily equate power with force, however. He defined power as the possession of authority, whether by a prince, a parliament, or a people. Machiavelli would have accepted Bertrand Russell's definition of power as "the production of intended effects," or, more accurately, the immediate potential to produce intended results. Power can be acquired by various means, among them inheritance, election, purchase, deceit, or force. It may also come to one by good fortune. Legitimate power—that is, power obtained lawfully—is more lasting and dependable, and therefore more desirable for the good of the state. But armed force may legitimately be used in the acquisition of power, if it is used to liberate rather than enslave; to win honor instead of wealth. He might have said, with Hannah Arendt, "Power needs no justification, being inherent in the very existence of political communities; what it does need is legitimacy."

Machiavelli's application of the concept of "legitimate power" to the interpretation of foreign relations resulted in a view of international politics that is both pragmatic and idealistic. The interests of the state, whether political, economic, or religious, become the touchstone of policy. Alliances should be entered only when they promise concrete gains. But when collaborative efforts between states seem profitable, alliances should be made with a weaker state rather than with a stronger one. Neutrality, too, should be avoided if one party in a war is stronger than the other. Above all, a state should aspire to self-sufficiency so it need not depend on outside aid.

Machiavelli's grasp of the intricacies of power politics in Renaissance Italy is impressive, though his political judgment frequently left much to be desired. Yet all of his ideas were filtered through a point of view narrowed by its exclusive focus on Italian experience and institutions, and blinded by the afterglow of ancient Rome. Machiavelli never really understood his own times, outside the limited world of the petty Italian states. He did not see the connection between power and community in European affairs, and did not comprehend the relations of sovereign yet interdependent states. His quick and transient mind never grasped the meaning of the political and administrative metamorphosis taking place in Europe beyond the Alps. His understanding of the developing nation-states was limited to such shallow observations as, "They [the French] are full of avarice, pride, cruelty, and treachery, . . . for they have always been of one sort and have under all conditions and with everybody shown the same habits."[2] He was obsessed by the Italian experience —understandably so, since beyond the Alps lived barbarians! Politically he was entirely oriented toward the city-state rather than the national or territorial monarchy. Machiavelli's idealistic vision of an Italy unmolested by foreign intervention did not call for the impossible transformation of the peninsula into an organic nation, but it did anticipate the equally impossible phenomenon of a patriotic and virile prince holding back the voracious giants beyond the Alps while the fragmented and staunchly individualistic city-states resumed daily life *a la Roma classica*. Machiavelli understood the power relations of Italian diplomacy but not the broader implications of international statesmanship. Yet it was these very Italian diplomatic institutions, and the Machiavellian conception of independent power politics, that were adopted into European practice and theory, resulting in the evolution of modern international relations.

Machiavelli's compatriot, Francesco Guicciardini, shared the view that political relations are a function of power. Neither man paid much attention to the claims, theoretical or practical, of the *Respublica Christiana*. For them, politics involved the interests of individual states rather than universal obligations. They had too often seen the pope on horseback protecting his own petty states against other petty princes or foreign invaders to recognize him as a symbol of universal unity. Nevertheless, Guicciardini did allow for the tactical advantage of Christian alliances against the Turks. He parted company with Machiavelli in his more pessimistic outlook on the future of Italian relations with the European states. Guicciardini knew the European monarchs better than Machiavelli did, and had less faith in the controllability of *fortuna*. His outlook is summarized in the maxim, "Pray to God that you are always on

[2] Niccolò Machiavelli, *Discorsi,* 3: chapter 43.

the winning side, for you will get credit even for things in which you had no part. If, on the contrary, you are a loser, you will be blamed for an infinite number of things, of which you are entirely innocent."[3]

But Guicciardini's vision was also limited in regard to the real nature of the developing territorial states. Monarchism was a phenomenon only partially understood by Renaissance Italians. Don Pedro de Ayala's report to the Catholic kings that the king of Scotland moved about the country with his court living at the expense of the noble hosts, for "the greatest favour the king can do to his subjects is to go to their houses and live at their expense," would have been difficult for Italian patricians to comprehend. The art of kingship was assiduously cultivated by Renaissance monarchs, for it created a mystical identity between ruler and subject that allowed maximum sovereignty with minimal oppression. To the majority of Frenchmen, monarchy represented an increase in political and economic stability over the aristocracy-dominated Middle Ages, as well as a greater degree of individual freedom. A Provençal peasant certainly preferred the distant and relatively uniform justice of the king to the immediate and capricious rule of the local count. Claude de Seyssel assured everyone in his *La grand monarchie de France* (1519) that, of all types of government, "monarchy is the best as long as it has a good prince who possesses the intelligence, experience, and the desire to govern well and justly."[4] And, of course, France had that kind of prince in Francis I.

Sixteenth-century governments functioned on several "levels" of jurisdictional rights and authority: monarchical, seigneurial, bureaucratic, ecclesiastical, and what we have come to call representative. Francisco de Vitoria, the renowned Dominican jurist at the University of Salamanca, emphatically denied the imperial claim to universality, describing the sovereign territorial state as a "perfect community, . . . one which is complete in itself, that is, which is not a part of another community, but has its own laws and its own council and its own magistrates, such as the Kingdom of Castile and Aragon . . . "[5] Ayala defined the state in the Ciceronian sense as "an assemblage of individuals compacted into a society by identity of law and community of interest,"[6] ruled by a prince who is sole sovereign.

Thus we see the medieval Christian commonwealth being transformed into early modern nation-states by ideas of power and interest originating on both sides of the Alps. But in the early transitional era of the sixteenth century this growing national consciousness strengthened the kings' power without fully defining the limits of that power. Thus the overlapping jurisdictions of various

---

[3] Francesco Guicciardini, *Ricordi,* Series C, No. 176.

[4] Claude de Seyssel, *La monarchie de France et deux autres fragments politiques* (Paris, 1961), p. 103.

[5] Francisco de Vitoria, *De Indis et de iure belli relectiones* (1526), Classics of International Law (Washington, D. C.., 1917), 7:169.

[6] Balthazar Ayala, *De iure et officiis bellicis et disciplina militari libri tres* (1582), in Classics of International Law (Washington, D.C., 1912), 2:15, p. 15.

corporate and random bodies—from noble peers and ecclesiastical courts, to merchant guilds and municipal *fueros*—obscured the lines of authority and complicated the play of politics. It was in an effort to assert their authority, usually against that of the great magnates, that monarchs developed the administrative and coercive machinery to extend and consolidate royal power. The resulting "absolute monarchy" was not always absolute in practice, but it did give birth to a respect, bordering on worship, for the person of the king, "His Sacred Majesty." It also considerably increased the authority of the crown. The king of France stands above the law, confessed Charles de Guillart, president of the Parlement de Paris, in 1527, and cannot be constrained by statute or ordinance. Royal power, according to the testament of Isabel the Catholic, "is a power which is essentially above human or positive law and thus carries with it the power to make laws, to accord exemption from all or part of them, and to revise them."[7] The Henrician Act in Restraint of Appeals declared royal power to be "plenary, whole, and entire," with "preeminence, authority, prerogative, and jurisdiction to render and yield justice and final determination to all manner of folk residents or subjects within this his realm."[8]

But power is not a finite or static quantity. An increase in its exercise by one body does not necessarily imply a concomitant loss of power elsewhere. The total volume of power certainly increased in the sixteenth century, accounting for the otherwise confusing phenomenon of nobles, bourgeoisie, merchants, and lawyers all expanding their prerogatives and dominion while the power of the king also increased. This dynamic theory of power also helps explain the seemingly contradictory simultaneous growth of parliaments and absolute monarchy. All these elements of the Renaissance state played key roles in shaping the diplomatic history of early modern Europe. With heightened power and modern technical instruments, both military and bureaucratic, the new nation-states developed a feeling of community: not yet full-blown nationalism, but a growing sense of mutual interest identified not with the broader Christian commonwealth but with the purposes and undertakings of the national monarch. For in the person of the king were embodied the corpo-

---

[7] José Antonio Maravall, "The Origins of the Modern State," *Cahiers d'Histoire Mondiale* 6 (1961): 801. But Spanish jurists were quick to remind monarchs that administrative authority, even absolute monarchy, does not imply ownership. "Only the administration of the kingdom is entrusted to the king, not the ownership of things," wrote the jurist Palacio Rubios. And Ayala echoed, "For however much kings may be styled lords of all, this is to be interpreted as referring to sovereignty and power and not to ownership and possession, which are matters affecting private parties." *De iure et officiis*, p. 81.

[8] *English Historical Documents*, vol. 5: 1485–1558, edited by C. H. Williams (New York, 1967), p. 738. Thirty years later, Sir Thomas Smith declared, "the prince is the life, the head and the authority of all things that be done in the realm of England." *De republica anglorum*, 62–3, in *The Tudor Constitution: Documents and Commentary*, edited by G. R. Elton (Cambridge, 1965), p. 14.

rate interests of his people. This community of interests was in turn institutionalized in a growing bureaucracy and a sprawling network of interlinking
civil and religious services.

Emergence of the Great-Power Aggregates

Whatever its nature and structure, the modern nation was largely a by-product
of interstate and international struggles, both military and diplomatic. The
preservation of national security and integrity in turn became the principal
functions of the sovereign ruler. Diplomacy, of course, operated on many levels,
but the official conduct of relations among territorial powers was the prerogative of heads of state. By the sixteenth century the functional association of
diplomacy and sovereignty was the rule.

Permanent diplomacy—that is, formal and more or less continuous ambassadorial representation at foreign courts—had become widespread in Renaissance Italy after the Peace of Lodi in 1454. Resident ambassadors located at
vital listening posts throughout the peninsula provided valuable information
about the shifts of political winds, the movements of armies, and actions of
potential friends and foes. By 1500, the system involved most of the Italian
states and in some instances linked these states with the larger European
powers. Venice was particularly active in the sixteenth century, with resident
observers holding the rank of ambassador in every major Italian city and at
the courts of Spain, France, the empire, England, and intermittently at Constantinople. The Venetian Senate was deeply involved in European diplomacy, as was the Council of Ten. The Ten, in its desire to be informed about
everything and everybody, conducted its own systematic and sometimes subversive diplomacy with a network of agents, spies and counter-spies. These
agents sometimes worked within the official system, frequently functioned
separately, and occasionally worked against it. In Venice, diplomacy was considered an art. Venetian ambassadors seemed to possess outstanding talent for
observation and exposition. A popular Venetian maxim suggested that the
secret of their success was their great love of public affairs.

During the latter half of the fifteenth century, however, it was Milan, not
Venice, that operated the most extensive and best-organized diplomatic network in Italy. The Milanese machinery had been created half a century
earlier by Gian Galeazzo Visconti, and was expanded by his first Sforza successor. For many years Francesco Sforza's position in Milan, and in Italy as a
whole, was precarious enough to demand an active participation in diplomacy
beyond the Alps as well as throughout the peninsula. He established the first
resident embassy in Paris and reactivated several listening posts that had been
abandoned by his predecessors. At the same time he accelerated the conduct
of secret diplomacy through special agents and spies at many foreign courts.

With the French invasion of Italy in 1494, diplomatic contacts were greatly increased, and the European monarchs—especially Ferdinand of Aragon— soon saw the uses and advantages of Italian-style diplomacy. Ferdinand employed ambassadors and agents at several foreign courts, especially those with whom he maintained or hoped to establish military alliances. Parsimonious, dilatory, deceitful and distrustful, Ferdinand nevertheless laid the foundation for a professional diplomatic service soon to become the envy of Europe. The objective of Ferdinand's diplomacy was the isolation and defeat of France, the populous and rich rival to the north that had all the military and geographic advantages over Aragon and possessed several times its economic resources. After the marital consolidation of Aragon and Castile, Ferdinand could count on well-disciplined Castilian soldiers and the devoted expertise of the Castilian *letrados* to bolster his foreign policy. The three principal links in Ferdinand's anti-French chain were England, with whom he negotiated a marriage alliance in 1489 (the Treaty of Medina del Campo, by which Catherine of Aragon was betrothed to Arthur, Prince of Wales) and maintained continuous diplomatic relations after 1495; Emperor Maximilian, who agreed to seal the alliance with a double Austrian-Aragonese wedding that was soon to link most of Europe in one polyglot empire; and Venice, with whom Ferdinand entered a Holy League in 1495 (along with the pope, Maximilian, and Henry VII) against the French king, who had invaded Naples six months earlier.

The French invasion suddenly sucked all of transalpine Europe into the vortex of Italian politics, converting Italy into the political cockpit of Europe and the focal point of international diplomacy and war. The Italian wars thus became the catalyst not only for international upheaval but eventually for the evolution of a European states system. In the early years of the Italian wars, other monarchs began adopting the principles and practices of Italian diplomacy, beginning with the establishment of permanent embassies in Rome, then in other Italian states, and finally in the larger European capitals. The primary function of these diplomatic agents, like their Italian predecessors, was to establish and maintain alliances and to acquire information which might be useful to their governments in formulating policy.

The need for information, negotiation, and representation was especially great during these years of instability and chaos. The first twenty years of the Italian wars saw the emergence of a recognizable power structure, with Spain and England allied against France, and the emperor, pope, and Venetian republic joining them whenever they were not fighting among themselves. The ascension of Francis I to the French throne in 1515, and his immediate reinvasion of Italy, further crystallized the relations of these power aggregates. It may be premature to talk of this relationship as a European states system, as Fueter did in his classical work of half a century ago, but a pattern of involvement and commitment, largely national in conception and European in scope, did emerge from the apparent chaos.

The growth of great-power aggregates, accelerated by the rivalry over Italy and the development of diplomatic machinery on a Europeanwide scale, brought to the fore a number of intellectual problems requiring fresh interpretation. Warring princes still glibly spoke of peace and the common welfare as they feverishly prepared to attack their nearest neighbors. Intellectual recognition of the new power structure came very slowly. Diplomats and ambassadors tended to view international diplomacy in less idealistic terms than did the theologians and jurists.

One of the most difficult issues in the expansion of European diplomacy, crucial to the evolution of international law, was diplomatic immunity and exterritoriality. If an ambassador represents a sovereign independent power at a foreign court which is also sovereign and autonomous, what are his legal rights and obligations? Does he carry his own national laws with him or is he subject to those of his host? How would his legal status differ if he represented not a sovereign state but a sister nation within a family of nations?

There were no simple answers to these questions; they were solved differently by different governments, and the solutions changed considerably in the course of the century. In general the trend was away from allowing a diplomat to move from one part of Christendom to another enjoying the protection of universal law, and toward the notion of exterritoriality. This concept recognizes the diversity and autonomy of national laws and the right of an ambassador to carry his own law with him, unless he violates divine law (which was accepted as universal) or endangers the safety and sovereignty of his host nation. The sixteenth-century ambassador came to expect almost total immunity from the civil laws of the host state. Immunity, however reluctantly granted or frequently violated, was deemed by governments a necessary concession in exchange for the same privilege for their own ambassadors. The practitioners of diplomacy were coming to understand *quid pro quo* as a valuable operating principle. It took the theorists a little longer. In a treatise on ambassadorial immunity, *De immunitate legatorum* (1541), the humanist Etienne Dolet recognized precedents in Roman law for the idea that a representative carries his own law with him as did Conrad Brunus seven years later in *De legationibus*. It was not until the early seventeenth century, however, that Grotius spoke plainly of ambassadors being granted *extra territorium*.

The European powers wasted very little time waiting for these issues to be resolved before acting. With the election in 1519 of King Charles of Castile-Aragon as Holy Roman Emperor, the varied interests of Austria, Burgundy, and Spain were consolidated in dynastic opposition to France, and a new phase in international diplomacy began. The Habsburg-Valois rivalry now became the focus of international politics.

Henrician England was committed by marriage and interest to the Habsburg alliance, even though the diplomatic finesse of Henry VIII's powerful minister, Cardinal Wolsey, was aimed at making a friend of France and Henry's marital escapades eventually led to a rupture with Rome. Venice worked with the emperor whenever the French threat was imminent; when it was not, all the diplomatic skill of the Spanish bureaucracy was required to retain Venetian support. The papacy was almost continually allied with the emperor until 1527, when Pope Clement VII was persuaded to change sides. The result was disastrous for the papacy. It has been suggested that Henry and Clement were trying to maintain a balance of power in Europe, but it seems more likely that the English king sought not to balance the Habsburg-Valois scales, but to overbalance it in favor of his own side. From Henry's (and Wolsey's) point of view, a French alliance now offered more opportunity for Tudor aggrandizement than did the imperial tie. Wolsey hoped, by shifting England's diplomatic weight from Habsburg to Valois, to offset the political stalemate and promote an Anglo-French-papal victory in northern Italy. His miscalculation led directly to his humiliation and downfall. Pope Clement's motive was the liberation of the papacy from the emperor's domination. But with the imperial sack of Rome in 1527, his plan backfired completely.

Charles V's diversified polyglot empire now cut directly across the national interests of several states and thoroughly confused the interests of others, making David Jayne Hill's remark about the motivation of the Italian wars, that "neither national interest, nor public morality, nor religious zeal had any place in them," applicable to the entire Habsburg-Valois rivalry. Dynastic security and expansion became the obsession of power politics.

Still the concept of Christendom was not entirely dead, nor was the idea of a community of Christian interests. The Protestant Reformation, which divided Europe into fanatical sects, at the same time revived discussion of the "Christian community." Many Protestants after 1521 echoed the opinion of King Ferdinand that God was punishing the princes of Christendom for their neglect of the church, which was in need of thorough reformation. Luther loudly refuted the imperial charge that he was disrupting the unity of Christendom, declaring that he was strengthening it against the persuasions and condemnations of the "pope's church." Half a century later, Richard Hooker could write that all Christians should abide "the rule of one only Law, to stand in no less force than the law of nature's doth."[9]

Nevertheless, the Reformation did obscure the lines of Christian allegiance and complicate international diplomacy. Charles V was not the ruler of "the whole monarchy of Christendom." The Lutheran princes and those associated in the Schmalkaldic League contradicted the emperor's policies on almost every count. As early as 1531, the Schmalkaldic princes joined with the Catholic duke of Bavaria to attract both England and France into a

---

[9] Richard Hooker, *Laws of Ecclesiastical Polity,* Book 8 (Houk edition), as cited in Franklin L. Baumer, "The Church of England and the Common Corps of Christendom," *Journal of Modern History* 16 (1944): 8.

broad coalition against the emperor. Francis I encouraged such talk and sent his own ambassador, Guillaume de Bellay, to keep negotiations open. In 1538, Henry VIII sent Christopher Mundt to discuss with Melanchthon the possibilities for Anglo-German collaboration. Within six weeks, a delegation from Saxony, Lüneburg, and Hesse arrived in London to begin protracted negotiations for a military alliance against the emperor, for "the glory of Christ and the discipline of religion."

Henry VIII's own foreign policy after the break with Rome was, of necessity, predicated on new principles. "The king's great matter" and its politico-ecclesiastical consequences forced Henry to concern himself more than ever before with national survival. Any lull in the Habsburg-Valois wars might easily give rise to a joint operation against England. Thus the king's diplomacy was geared to promoting chronic war on the continent, a feat he found he could not accomplish without entering the fray himself, bankrupting the nation, or both.

The Habsburg-Valois duel and the spread of Protestantism aggravated another important facet of international relations and further underlined the dichotomous nature of sixteenth-century diplomacy. For centuries the Ottoman Turks had played the role of *bête noir* to Latin Christendom. The constant threat of heathen invasion tended to consolidate Christian opinion, at least on that one issue, and gave rise to recurring talk about a united crusade even though the crusading spirit in Europe was all but extinct by the sixteenth century. The idea of Christian solidarity against the infidel threat, and the related concept of *Respublica Christiana*, persisted much longer than most writers recognize. A transition occurred in people's allegiance from Christendom to Europe, from a religious to a secular entity, but it did not entirely abolish the use of religious terminology and concepts in writings concerning the Turks and the theory of international relations. Two years before his death, Henry VII begged the pope to use his authority to bring peace to Christendom, and recommended that he call a crusade of all Christian princes against the infidels. Henry VIII made several comparable requests. Charles V was very anxious to gain Europe-wide Christian support for a Turkish crusade, partly because his own territories lay directly in the path of Suleiman's advance. Philip II frequently echoed his father's concern. The battle of Lepanto is testimony to the partial success of these pleas for Christian cooperation.

Similar sentiments were voiced by jurists and political writers. Alberico Gentili included the Turks in the general *societas gentium,* but posited the reality of a narrower commonwealth of Christian nations engaged in "almost natural" war against the infidel. "With the Saracens," he wrote, "we have an irreconcilable war"[10]—irreconcilable not because of religious differ-

---

[10] Alberico Gentili, *De iure belli libri tres* (1612), Classics of International Law (Washington, D.C., 1933), 16:56.

ences, but because of the constant threat to Christian life and property. European theorists, statesmen, scholars, and churchmen all wrote in favor of unity against the Turks, but few acted—another instance of the growing chasm between the theory and practice of Christian unity.

The realities of power politics dictated expedients incompatible with the obligation of continuous hostility toward the Turks. Venice negotiated with the Porte whenever it seemed necessary to insure against overextended resources. Even Spain, joining Venice and the papacy in the League of Lepanto in 1571, was careful not to offend the Sultan needlessly. And Elizabeth of England openly sought Turkish aid against the threat of the Armada in the 1580s. France's flouting of the Christian cause was earlier and more brazen. Francis I's defeat at Pavia (1525) first prompted him to make serious overtures to Suleiman the Magnificent, the "Sultan of sultans, sovereign of sovereigns, Distributor of crowns to the monarchs of the globe, the Shadow of God on Earth." Suleiman replied favorably, initiating a long and fruitful friendship between France and the Ottoman Empire. In 1536, a formal treaty was drawn up in which the sultan agreed to attack the emperor in the east while Khaireddin Barbarossa, the grand-admiral of the Turkish fleet, harassed the coastal towns of Italy and Spain. The Franco-Turkish alliance, which weathered many vicissitudes in the next few years, remained a useful tool in French diplomacy throughout the century, and was attended by unique commercial advantages.

The emergence of the great-power aggregates in the sixteenth century— especially France, England, and the Austrian-Spanish Burgundian block— accelerated the spread of permanent diplomacy and complicated the problem of relations with non-Christian states. At the same time, it intensified rivalries among European states, and prompted western monarchs to improve the machinery of administration and foreign policy.

State-Building in the Western Monarchies

The gradual development of centralizing institutions and administrative bureaucracies, coinciding with the rapid growth of royal authoritarianism, is one of the salient features of sixteenth-century politics, especially in the territorial monarchies. Foreign affairs received increasing attention as international rivalries grew in intensity. The institutionalization of foreign policy lagged behind other areas of statecraft because monarchs were loath to accept less than total control. Whenever foreign policy-making threatened to become a function of the bureaucracy, or of public institutions such as the expanded chancery in fifteenth-century England, the king reclaimed it as his own prerogative. Nevertheless, institutionalization continued.

The principal organ of government, after the king, was the royal council, usually selected from among the great nobles. But the sixteenth-century creation of smaller, more manageable cabinets of the monarch's most trusted advisors marked an important stage in the development of efficient government bureaucracies. Claude de Seyssel wrote at length of the integrated balance of the French monarchy, deriving from the efficient councils which advised and counseled the king. Under Francis I, central government took on a new shape. Francis was in some ways a medieval monarch, ruling by personal will through various household offices from *grand-maître d'hôtel* to *valets de chambre*. His court was a magnificent assemblage of the royal household, officers of the crown, councilors, and princes of the blood. Yet, Francis did not entirely neglect the more important organs of government. The grand council which he had inherited from his predecessors was too large and heterogeneous a body to serve the needs of an organized state. In its place, he selected five or six trusted advisors to meet with him as a sort of royal cabinet, known as the *Conseil des Affaires*, to transact the major business of governing France and dealing with foreign states. Another step toward the development of a coherent governmental organization was the creation of a central department of finance, administered under the newly-created *Trésor de l'Epargne*. This bureaucracy provided the French crown with adequate revenue to meet the growing expenses of government and conduct an aggressive foreign policy.

Governing the distinct and individualistic kingdoms of Spain, each of which had its own institutions and laws, was a supremely difficult task. The essential machinery of Spanish monarchial rule was a system of councils created by the Catholic Kings. The largest of these bodies was the aristocratic *Consejo de Estado,* which advised the king on matters of state and foreign policy and, with the addition of a few military experts, was also the Council of War. However, the great magnates in the Council of State, vying for position and influence, cancelled out much of the real power the council might have exercised. Both Charles V and Philip II found that the smaller, hand-picked Council of Castile was a more efficient organ of administration. Other specialized councils handled the affairs of Aragon, Italy, Flanders, the Indies and Portugal, finances, the inquisition, and military orders.

In England, the power of the monarch was potentially great. "If the lion but knew his own strength," noted Sir Thomas More, "it were hard for anyone to hold him." The gradual realization and institutionalization of that power by the Tudors made England a significant force in European affairs. Henry VIII was largely responsible for creating a manageable Privy Council that could function as both an advisory body to the crown and an executive arm of the king. But only under Elizabeth was its full potential realized. The Elizabethan Privy Council dealt with the full range of administrative, advisory, and judicial business, including the discussion of foreign affairs. It also drafted bills and pronouncements to be presented to Parliament and steered them through the treacherous shoals of parliamentary debate. When bills became law, the councilors supervised their enforcement. Like their French and Spanish counterparts, they were responsible individually and collectively only to the monarch.

The growing volume and complexity of diplomatic correspondence was largely responsible for the growth of an office which had, by the end of the sixteenth century, attained paramount importance in the machinery of government and, especially, in the operation of foreign affairs. This was the secretariat of state, whose development has not yet received the attention it deserves from historians. Originally a clerk who recorded the king's correspondence and carried out other simple tasks, the secretary gradually came to occupy an increasingly responsible position, first as liaison between king and council, and later as a special council member. Soon the secretary came to be responsible for most of the diplomatic correspondence with ambassadors in the field and other diplomatic agents. He drafted letters and governmental instructions, and his signature was attached to the document below the king's. He also received, read, deciphered, and translated all communications to the king, and presented them to him in summary or in full, as the king wished. With his intimate knowledge of the diplomatic service, including its personnel, his advice was frequently sought on a variety of subjects. It was not, of course, his prerogative to make policy, but there is abundant evidence that he influenced it through his close association with the crown. The office did not develop into a full-fledged ministry in the sixteenth century, but in the capable hands of men like Pérez, Villeroy, and Sir Francis Walsingham, it was a very close approximation.

Drawn usually from the middle or lower classes, secretaries were chosen for native ability rather than influence or wealth. In a time when patronage and clientage prevailed on every level of government and society, it was refreshing to have unembellished merit thus rewarded. Of course, the office did not remain free from venality and spoils. Rewards, gratuities, and outright bribes were not unknown to secretaries, and the office could become an important stepping-stone into the landed aristocracy itself, as in the case of Lord Burghley. In the seventeenth century, the secretariat went through several metamorphoses, of a different kind in each country, and emerged hardly recognizable. But for a brief period, primarily during the second half of the sixteenth century, it was an important organ of foreign affairs—and precursor of the foreign office—in all of the new monarchies.

The secretarial office under Philip II of Spain possessed some characteristics of a true secretariat of state, but in other ways it continued to resemble that of a private clerk. During the first twenty years of his reign, Philip's principal secretaries were the Aragonese functionary Gonzalo Pérez, who had served the emperor for many years, and his ambitious son Antonio. The latter, an unscrupulous and disreputable courtier, was also a skilled politician and able administrator, who rose to great prominence through a combination of ability and royal favor. But royal patronage was a capricious tool. Antonio Pérez lost favor with the king when his nefarious role in the murder of a rival was uncovered. He was removed from office, placed under arrest, and subsequently transferred to Aragon, where he became a major factor in the Aragonese rebellion of 1591. After the fall of Antonio Pérez, the position of secretary went to his rival, Mateo Vázquez, a mediocre Corsican cleric who shared secretarial responsibilities with three other men: Juan de Idiáquez, a capable and devoted Basque functionary who handled most of the foreign correspondence; Cristobal de Moura, secretary for Portuguese affairs; and the count of Chinchón, secretary and treasurer-general for Aragon and Italy. While this group was close to the king, Philip's relationship to it was always personal rather than institutional. These men were secretaries, not ministers, and since the king did much of the paperwork himself, their responsibilities were undefined and overlapping. Before Cardinal Granville died in 1585, a committee composed of the secretaries and Granville, and known as the *Junta de Noche,* met in the royal chamber to study dispatches from ambassadors and various governors and viceroys. The king was, of course, under no obligation to follow their advice.

The French secretaries of state, like their Spanish counterparts, played many roles in royal government, from the king's private clerks to advisors and administrators of foreign affairs. From the accession of Henry II until the end of the century, responsibilities were divided, geographically rather than functionally, among four secretaries. For this purpose France was divided into four quarters, with one secretary in charge of the domestic matters and correspondence of each, as well as foreign affairs with countries adjacent to that section of France. The actual distribution of assignments varied during the half-century, but domestic and foreign affairs were almost always combined.

The English office of principal secretary of state was created by Thomas Cromwell. During the middle years of the century the office grew, as it did in France and Spain, from royal scribe to confidant and advisor to the crown, finally taking over some of the functions of the chancellor. The secretary of state corresponded with ambassadors, and was privy to the most confidential matters of state. Indeed, the whole problem of national security—both the preservation of domestic law and order and the defense of the kingdom against foreign powers—became the direct responsibility of the principal secretary during Elizabeth's reign. In 1592 Robert Beale, clerk of the Privy Council and brother-in-law to Sir Francis Walsingham, wrote to Sir Edward Wotton (who expected to become principal secretary) that, "It is a Secretarie's dutie before hande to consider of the Estate of the Realme and all ye rest of the Princes' Estates w[i]th whom ther have bine and are anie doinges, . . . Wherefore, if occasion serve, no opportunitie is to be omitted to compounde all discontents w[i]th neighbors abroad, so as the same may be with the honnor of God and benefitt of the Realme, and to procure as much friendship as may be."[11] A short time later, Dr. John Herbert summarized the duties of the secretary under Elizabeth as follows:

First, to inform myself of all treaties with foreign princes ...

To be acquainted with the particular actions and negotiations of ambassadors to her Majesty and from her;

To inform myself of the power and form of proceeding at the Council of the Marches in Wales and the Council in the North, and to understand the manner of the warden's government;

To be informed of the state of Ireland....

The charge of the Low Country Wars....

To oversee the order of the Council book and the Muster book of the realm;

To have the custody of letters from foreign princes to the Queen and the answers made to them;

To have care to the intelligence abroad.[12]

Sir William Cecil was principal secretary from 1558 to 1572, and lent the office a distinction and authority that it retained throughout the reign. When Cecil was made Lord Burghley and lord treasurer, Sir Francis Walsingham became principal secretary, a post he vigorously magnified until his death eighteen years later. During Walsingham's tenure, Tudor England faced its greatest threat from abroad and its most serious challenge from within. Much of Elizabeth's success in foreign affairs and in the maintenance of relative tranquility at home were due to Walsingham's constant vigilance. Under Walsingham the office took on the flavor and functions of an espionage bureau as the secretary's agents and spies were dispatched into all parts of Europe. In the crucial 1580s, Walsingham's secret service was particularly active and effective. Sir Robert Cecil, Lord Burghley's son, who occupied the office from 1596 to 1612, summarized this aspect of the secretary's duties as the "liberty to negotiate at discretion at home and abroad, with friends and enemies in all matters of search and intelligence."

The role of the nobility in foreign affairs and diplomacy merits special attention. In the power structure of the Renaissance state, nobles still occupied a special position. Although some of the nobles' power had been appropriated by the king, and the royal bureaucracy was made up of middle-class functionaries, aristocrats did not withdraw from politics. Many of them found new prestige and wealth within the monarchial structure. Their position and influence was altered, but not noticeably reduced, as the king

---

[11] [Robert Beale], "A Treatise of the Office of a Councellor and Principall Secretarie" (1592), reprinted in the appendix to Conyers Read, *Mr. Secretary Walsingham and the Policy of Queen Elizabeth* (Oxford, 1925; Hamden, 1967) 1:432.

[12] Prothero, *Selected Documents,* p. 166, in Read, *Mr. Secretary Walsingham,* 1:269–70.

gradually assumed the new role of sovereign. Some titled magnates became "kings' men" and applied themselves to the implementation of foreign policy and diplomacy. Furthermore, through the quirks of dynastic marriages and inheritance, monarchies tended either to devour one another or, as in the case of Charles V's empire, to become large agglomerations of states, titularly ruled by a single sovereign but in fact still dominated by the nobility.

In the sixteenth century, monarchic authority was most frequently directed toward promoting the dynastic ambitions or maintaining the status quo of the ruling house. Dynasticism's chief diplomatic tool, political marriage, was an important instrument of state-building and a cornerstone of sixteenth-century power politics. Like the Protestant Reformation, international marriage contracts tended to complicate diplomacy more than simplify it. Decisions and commitments became hopelessly entangled and unrecognizably intertwined in dynastic considerations.

All of the ruling houses engaged in marriage politics, but none played the game more intently or successfully than did the Habsburgs, whose application of the motto *Bella gerant alii, tu felix Austria nube* ("Leave the waging of wars to others but you happy Austria marry") brought them to the threshold of European domination. Marriage diplomacy won them control of the Burgundian Netherlands, Luxembourg, Franche-Comté, Castile (and the vast New World territories), Aragon (including Valencia and Catalonia and the Mediterranean possessions of Sardinia, the Balearic Islands, Sicily and Naples), Austria, Styria, Carinthia, Carniola, Hungary, Bohemia, Moravia, and Lusatia. With them came the crown of the Holy Roman Empire, although this was less a result of dynastic diplomacy than of plain financial bribery.

It was not necessary actually to marry in order to play the game of marriage diplomacy, as Queen Elizabeth understood. For the first twenty-five years of her reign, the English queen used her virginity to great advantage in the power struggle with ambitious neighbors, encouraging each successive suitor just enough to keep him interested yet not so much that the others would give up the quest. Until the mid-1580s Elizabeth achieved astounding diplomatic success by dangling before the princes of Europe the hope of a promising marriage alliance, and becoming coyly noncommital when it came to deciding among them.

Nevertheless, marriage diplomacy was a capricious tool, complicated and dangerously unpredictable. Sometimes it worked; sometimes it did not. Catherine de Médicis, queen dowager of France, possessed almost unlimited resources for its successful employment—four sons and three eligible daughters—and tried desperately to perpetuate the dynasty and increase the power and influence of her family through favorable marriages. But fortune did not smile on her as it had on the Habsburgs. All of her schemes ended in failure. When her son, Henry III, was assassinated in 1589, the Valois dynasty ended.

Diplomacy and Dogmatism: Civil Upheaval and the Growth of Absolutism

More predictable than marriage diplomacy, but hardly less complicated, was the mounting impact of religious ideology and civil upheaval upon international relations and upon the further growth of monarchial absolutism. The bitter rivalry between militant Protestants and revitalized Catholics could not be contained within the bounds of doctrinal discussion. Religious dogmatism—compounded by social and economic upheaval, personal rivalries, and dynastic ambition—seriously strained the institutions of international intercourse during the second half of the sixteenth century. That they survived, and even expanded, was due more to the recognized need for diplomatic relations than to the planning of governments.

The Peace of Cateau-Cambésis, ending the Habsburg-Valois wars in 1559, marked a major turning point in the international affairs of the period. By the terms of this treaty, the French crown abandoned all claim to Italy, where Spanish preeminence was now recognized; England gave up its continental bases; and Franco-Spanish friendship was sealed by a contract of marriage between Philip II and the French princess Elizabeth of Valois. The peace was a watershed because it marked the beginning of a new power system in Western Europe. France was no longer the disturber of the peace. Its rapid political deterioration during the reigns of the last three Valois kings made it a target rather than a source of aggression. Civil war and religious fanaticism further neutralized French diplomatic prominence. The long partnership between England and Spain, which had been almost continuous since the treaty of Medina del Campo, was now dissolved. Freed from the burden of Austrian and imperial responsibility, Spain emerged as the major power of Europe.

Philip's attitude toward the civil disorders in France was one of cautious concern. As long as France refrained from molesting the Spanish Netherlands (Philip's inheritance from his father, Charles V), and the French king could battle the Huguenots on more than equal grounds, Philip had no great apprehension about his northern neighbor. When Huguenot forces threatened the vital Lowlands, however, the Catholic king felt forced to intervene.

Closely connected with affairs in France was the complicated situation in Scotland. Here too, civil upheaval, pitting the Catholic monarchy of Mary Stuart against the determined opposition of the thundering Scot, John Knox, and his Calvinist cohorts, attracted Philip's closest attention. In the revolution that followed, eventually driving Mary from her throne, Philip was faced with a major dilemma. He had no sympathy for the Scottish Reformation, but to assist Mary would be to play directly into the hands of France and the House of Guise, Mary's ambitious relatives on the continent. His policy, therefore, was to remain aloof, supplying sympathy, encouragement, and occasional money to the Scottish Catholics, but avoiding any action that would involve him in a hopeless cause.

Philip's relations with England were equally difficult. Half a century of partnership should not be dissolved overnight. His first diplomatic move was a proposal of marriage to the new English monarch, Elizabeth, half-sister to his former wife, Mary Tudor. But the cautious and astute queen shrewdly rejected his offer. She wished to avoid closing the door on an avenue of diplomacy that offered such rich possibilities. During the first thirty years of Philip's reign, relations with Elizabeth fluctuated with the shifting patterns of international affairs. Hostilities might have broken out a number of times, had not both rulers been determined to preserve the peace in spite of growing public agitation. While Philip delayed and vacillated, Elizabeth flirted with Habsburg, Valois, and Scottish Protestants alike, growing stronger as the stakes mounted higher. When war finally came in the late 1580s, Philip discovered he had vacillated too long.

The key to Spanish foreign policy, and to European politics after 1567, was France and the Netherlands. Philip could not permit his rich Burgundian territory to slip from him. Therefore, the attitude toward, and participation of, the various European states in the revolt of the Netherlands determined Spanish attitude and policy toward those states. France would probably not have interfered in the Netherlands revolt had it not been for the revolutionary ideas springing from Calvinist sources and the rapid growth of the Huguenots in France. The government of Catherine de Médicis tried desperately to steer a middle course between the Spanish Scylla and the Protestant Charybdis, but it was doomed from the beginning. Not only were French diplomatic relations with Spain threatened by the eager Protestant pamphleteers and impetuous nobles, but the very foundations of the Valois monarchy were challenged.

Notwithstanding John Calvin's frequent exhortations to civil submissiveness ("for magistrates were ordained of God and rule the world by his will"),[13] he made one clear exception to the rule of absolute obedience: "That it not seduce us from obedience to Him to whose will the desires of all kings ought to be subject."[14] Magistrates, wrote Calvin, "are not to rule for their own interest, but for the public good; nor are they endowed with unbridled power, but what is restricted to the well-being of their subjects; in short, they are responsible to God and to men in the exercise of their power." Rulers must be obeyed unless they exceed the limits of their office, in which case "we ought rather utterly to defy than to obey them," wrote Calvin in his thirteenth commentary on Daniel.

[13] John Calvin, *Commentaries on the Epistle to the Romans,* chapter 13, commenting on Paul's "Let every soul be subject unto the higher powers," etc. In the *Institutes,* 4: chapter 25, Calvin wrote: "We owe these sentiments of affection and reverence to all our rulers, whatever their characters may be."

[14] Calvin, *Commentaries,* chapter 32.

Other Calvinist writers, particularly in France, so enlarged the definition of the limit on royal power that they have been credited with inaugurating a Protestant revolutionary tradition. In particular, Pierre Viret, Calvin's friend and associate from Lausanne; Theodore Beza, Calvinist apostle to the French; and François Hotman, the Huguenot jurist, hammered relentlessly at the bastions of unlimited monarchy, giving substance and meaning to political resistance to a tyrannical and ungodly ruler. Some of the Huguenot writers went even further than the biblical-medieval contract theory of limitation and resistance, elaborating in some detail a more modern constitutionalism. In the *Francogallia,* Hotman held that the "supreme administration" of the kingdom rested in the Estates General, as the direct representative of the people. He even challenged the prerogative of the king in council to conduct the affairs of state, claiming that only those ministers appointed by the estates and representing the kingdom were authorized to officiate in public matters, and that the secretaries were empowered only to conduct the king's personal affairs. Similar theories on constitutional limitations upon royal absolutism were propounded in Beza's *Du droit des magistrates* (1574), in the pseudonymous *Reveil-Matin des François* (1574), and in Innocent Gentillet's *Discourse sur les moyens de bien gouverner et maintenir en bonne paix un Royaume . . . contre Nicolas Machiavel* (1576). Gentillet especially blamed the perfidious government of Catherine de Médicis for introducing Machiavellian principles of power into France. The political thought of these Protestant revolutionaries is best summarized in Du Plessis Mornay's *Vindiciae contra tyrannos* (1579), which denies the primacy of political power to the monarch and declares the constitutional authority of the people's representatives—Estates General and magisterial nobles—to resist a tyrannical ruler.

These writings did not, of course, create the religious wars of sixteenth-century France. But they did help justify the actions of those who defied the government or took up arms against their rivals. The perceptive imperial ambassador in France, Ogier Ghislain de Busbecq, noted in June 1575 that "the respect for the Majesty of the King has been weakened in a strange manner and that the minds of men are wild, having shaken off their respect for the name of king just as [beasts] shake off a strong yoke."[15] Power, privilege, and poverty all contributed to the disorders of France and the Netherlands, as did religion and confessional divergence.

The civil wars in France seriously weakened the government's ability to negotiate on a par with neighboring states. Loss of prestige as the bloodletting dragged on, financial chaos, the diversion of military strength, and the personal weakness of the crown all weighed heavily on French diplomacy. Yet France continued to maintain a viable diplomatic service, and in spite

---

[15] *Letters of Ogier Ghislain de Busbecq to the Holy Roman Emperor Maximilian II,* edited by R. E. Jones and B. C. Weber (New York, 1961), p. 108.

of internal defeat and disruption achieved a remarkable degree of diplomatic success. Much of the credit for this must go to the energy and skill of a nucleus of French ambassadors, who refused to lose heart when everything went wrong, and to the dogged persistence of the queen-mother, Catherine de Médicis.

The least successful aspect of French foreign policy was its relations with the neighboring Netherlands and with its own alienated Huguenot minority. In order to reduce Spanish apprehension and the danger of intervention, Catherine de Médicis tried to remain aloof from the Dutch revolt. The confessional sympathies of the Huguenots, however, coupled with the unpredictable behavior of her temperamental sons (who hated one another as much as they did their enemies), soon led to impossible complications between the States General and France. The duke of Anjou campaigned recklessly in the Netherlands in defiance of his brother the king, and, although he came near to winning a throne for himself, reaped only resentment and disgrace for France. As for the Huguenots—and a growing number of *politique* followers of Montmorency-Damville—they had to be treated as a rival state. Henry of Navarre, the Huguenot leader, negotiated independently with the English, Dutch, and Rhineland states.

Catherine looked to Spain for help against the Protestant threat and leaned toward England for support against the equally dangerous Catholic League, whose alliance of French towns with Guise-Lorraine nobles threatened to capture the crown after 1584. League theory was as strongly *monarchomach* (monarch-hating) as Huguenot writings had been, and more deeply rooted in medieval law and concepts of religious community. The *Respublica Christiana* was not dead after all! But by the mid-1580s League theory had gone far beyond those foundations, and was advocating open rebellion and even tyrannicide. Louis d'Orléans argued for an unequivocally Catholic succession to the French throne against the Huguenot king of Navarre (who became heir apparent following the death of Anjou in 1584). Jean Boucher called for a rising of the masses against the tyrannical Henry III.

But the tide of the times favored neither the constitutionalist views of the Huguenots nor the radical resistance theories of the Catholic League. The trend was toward absolutism—more royal authority and fuller power to exercise it. As the religious wars wore on in France, people grew weary. Except for the die-hards on either side, they became less concerned about social and political abuses and more preoccupied with order. The civil upheavals had cut deeply into the fabric of French society. Ideological and confessional strife produced a new conservatism. Constitutional and religious arguments about the nature of rule now seemed less important than ending disorder and maintaining a stable regime. Religious dogmatism and extremism helped pave the way to political absolutism.

During the later years of the religious wars a new party arose, dedicated to ending civil strife and establishing a respected government in France. The so-called *politiques* were the intellectual offspring of men like Chancellor Michel de l'Hôpital, who believed that the primary concern of the state was the maintenance of order, rather than the establishment of "true religion." The intellectual roots of the *politiques* were various. Their chief legal theorist was Jean Bodin, who advocated a strong and centralized monarchical government. He defined sovereignty as a condition of superiority to civil law. "It is the distinguishing mark of the sovereign," Bodin wrote in his *Six Livres de la République* (1576), "that he cannot in any way be subject to the commands of another. . . . that is why it is laid down in the civil law that the prince is above the law." Furthermore, "If the prince is not bound by the laws of his predecessors, still less can he be bound by his own laws." In other words, he acts simply from his own free will. "It is clear," Bodin concluded, "that the principal mark of sovereign majesty and absolute power is the right to impose laws generally on all subjects regardless of their consent."[16] This line of argument was echoed by many *politique* pamphleteers of the 1580s and 1590s, and by the dedicated apologists for the new Bourbon king, Henry IV. The doctrines of absolutism and divine right acquired further refinement and preeminence from the late sixteenth- and early seventeenth-century legists, who made a place for them in the broader framework of legal thought.

The heat generated by French religious war and polemical pamphleteering was not confined to France alone. As the ideological line became more sharply defined and the simplicity of dogma replaced the subtleties of reason, international politics too began to polarize. There was less room for negotiation and compromise, and more propensity for exaggeration and extremism. Political loyalties were coming to coincide with religious confessions as English, Dutch, and German Protestants lined up against Spanish, papal, and imperial Catholics. Split by religious dissent, Europe became a battleground of conflicting ideologies and competing confessions. Spanish theologians and jurists were especially anxious to argue their case in terms of restoring Christendom. To the Catholic king, Christian unity and Spanish hegemony were synonymous. Divided Christianity, which paid lip service to a united Europe whenever the Turks were at the walls, found less in common when the Saracens no longer threatened. Community gave way to contention and conflict.

The Spanish conviction, born in the *reconquista* and nourished by a half-century of crusading against heretics and heathens, that Spain carried the burden and responsibility of Christianity on her shoulders, and that the evil intentions of certain caluminous individuals were responsible for the mounting disorder and rebellion in Europe, gave birth to commensurate Spanish

---

[16] Jean Bodin, *Six Books of the Commonwealth,* translated by M. J. Tooley (Oxford, n.d.), 1: chapter VIII, pp. 28, 32.

actions. Philip II hoped to restore universal order in Europe, but found the financial and logistical problems of a multi-front war to be almost insurmountable. Diplomacy was a practical and much less expensive alternative.

It is a mistake to believe that diplomacy was abandoned in the age of religious wars. Garrett Mattingly's observation that "the religious wars nearly wrecked the diplomatic institutions" is understandable, but not really true. The system functioned remarkably well, in spite of remarks like that of Carlo Pasquale that permanent diplomacy was a "miserable product of this miserable time." The resident ambassadors were targets of endless criticism and suspicion, but the institution of permanent diplomacy was too valuable to be abandoned. The same volatile international situation that strained diplomatic machinery also made its continued use imperative. Diplomacy was expanded in many directions during the late sixteenth century, although its purposes were sometimes diverted from their primary course and its methods adapted to unworthy ends. Philip II pursued his policies aggressively throughout Europe, spearheaded by such enterprising ambassadors as Diego Guzmán de Silva in England, Bernardino de Mendoza in England and France, Francés de Alava in France, Guillén de San Clemente in Austria, and the count of Olivares in Rome.

Spanish ambassadors in England took great liberties with diplomatic immunity, and soon found themselves under fire from both queen and council for their overzealous activities. De Spés was imprisoned in 1571 for espionage, and a few years later Mendoza was expelled for his role in a plot against the life of the queen. When he was reassigned to Paris, he became as much Philip's agent to the French Catholic League as his resident ambassador to France. English ambassadors in Spain and France engaged in the same kind of activities and got into the same kind of troubles. Sir Nicholas Throckmorton, Elizabeth's resident in France, openly aided the Huguenot cause and found himself ostracized from the French court and placed under arrest. The doughty John Man clashed head-on with church and king in Spain, and was eventually withdrawn from that country to save his own head.

Man may have been removed for other reasons as well. Resident diplomacy did not really suit Elizabeth's temperament or her pocketbook. She was glad to revoke Man's commission, and may even have planned the affair to facilitate the termination of his embassy, for she chafed at having a permanent agent abroad, especially in Spain, whom she could not directly control. She preferred to exercise tighter direction of affairs through special agents and envoys extraordinary. Diplomatic relations with Spain were not severed with Man's removal in 1568 but were thereafter carried out through ad hoc diplomacy, satisfying both Elizabeth's personality and her parsimony.

During the years just prior to the Armada, Elizabethan diplomacy was at its most active. In 1580, Elizabeth broke the French Levant monopoly and established diplomatic relations with the sultan. At the same time negotiations for an active alliance with France were under way, and English diplomatic courtship of the Dutch moved into high gear. In 1585, after learning of the formation of the French Catholic League and its resolute action against Henry of Navarre, Elizabeth sent Thomas Bodley to Brunswick, Hamburg, and Copenhagen to promote a Protestant front against the renewed Catholic threat from Spain and the League in France. At the same time, she communicated with Duke Casimir of the Palatinate and other German princes on behalf of the alliance. "You will justly deem that it behooves all of us who profess the Gospel," she wrote to Casimir, "to confer together how we may apply a remedy to the common evil; and since we are well assured of your extreme piety toward the Christian Commonwealth . . . we have made choice of you to be the confident [sic] of our thoughts."[17] Frederick of Denmark responded favorably to the proposal of a Protestant front, but some of the German princes were less enthusiastic. The elector of Saxony, in fact, wrote to Frederick explaining that after consideration of the political and economic risks of flouting the emperor "to enter into a foreign confederacy," he thought it best not to participate in the project. In the meantime, Spain too tried to organize a "Christian League," composed of Catholic states willing to cooperate against "heresy and rebellion." But Philip found the resistance of France and others who desired a union of Christian nations, though not at the expense of their own sovereignty, too stiff to overcome. The seeds were sown, however, and twenty-five years later such an alliance system, pitting Protestant Europe against Catholic Europe, came into being.

The Law of Nations

The dogmatic exuberance with which relations were conducted during the religious wars should not be allowed to obscure the simultaneous growth of the importance of law to the conduct of international diplomacy. Civil lawyers and jurists were called on increasingly to advise and give judgment on ambassadorial and sovereign rights, neutral rights, and maritime law.

In Elizabethan England, the debates and decisions of jurists were particularly pertinent to the development of international law. The Italian jurist Alberico Gentili, who fled to England in 1580 and subsequently became Regius Professor of civil law at Oxford, was the most respected authority on the rights and obligations of diplomatic legation. Gentili was consulted— along with that other expatriated lawyer and diplomat, Jean Hotman of France—in the *cause célèbre* of Bernardino de Mendoza, the Spanish ambassador who was guilty of involvement in the Throckmorton plot to overthrow the queen. Both advised the queen and council that nothing more

---

[17] *CSP/For., Eliz.* 19:447. Also see pp. 433 and 636–639.

drastic than expulsion was warranted, since Mendoza's diplomatic immunity protected him from the usual dictates of civil law by making him subject to the higher law of nations.

From Gentili's considerations of this and other cases involving diplomatic legation came a small book, *De legationibus* (1585), dedicated to the poet-diplomat Sir Philip Sidney, in which he developed the view that continuous diplomacy is an asset to international understanding, and that the resident ambassador should be treated as the honored representative of his nation instead of being distrusted, mistreated, and misunderstood, as was usual in the sixteenth century. The ambassador, in turn, should earn this respect through faithful attention to his work. Gentili believed in the legitimacy and value of diplomatic legation, and consequently in the inviolability of the ambassador's person and property. Inviolability had long been granted to ad hoc diplomatic missions, but the growth of resident embassies had introduced complicating factors. A resident ambassador was more able and likely to spy on the host government or plot with dissident subjects than was a temporary emissary. Gentili too was suspicious of resident embassies, but placed very high value on ambassadorial performance and behavior. Once accredited by his sovereign and admitted by his host, the ambassador should obtain broad rights of immunity and inviolability as the personal representative of his state. On this assumption, Gentili argued—not always clearly, and with the embellishment of a mass of Biblical and classical citations—that the law of nations granted the ambassador unique legal status. But the issue was not quite so simple. If a serious offense, such as treason, was committed by an ambassador, he should be punished by the law. But which law? And by whom? Gentili maintained that he should be judged by the law of nations and by his own government's tribunals. In other words, he advocated the principle of extradition. Gentili concluded, after treating in some detail the extent and limits of the ambassador's legal immunity, that except for major violations of the law of nations the ambassador, his residence, and his suite were all inviolable and untouchable.

But the time was not yet ripe for the full application of diplomatic immunity based on the legal recognition of territorial sovereignty. As long as there persisted a residual opinion that an ambassador represented the brotherhood of Christendom as well as the sovereignty of his own state, any violation on his part of the civil or criminal law of his host was usually considered a violation of the *ius gentium,* and appropriate (or, frequently, inappropriate) action was taken. Moderation in the treatment of foreign diplomats resulted more from the threat of retaliation than from the application of universally-accepted rules. Immunities for princes, although implied in the rights of legation, were even less uniformly applied. The classic example is the case of Mary Queen of Scots, who was admitted, then detained, imprisoned and tried, and finally beheaded in England while still claiming the sovereignty of Scotland, with its accompanying prerogatives and immunities.

Legal opinion and monarchial fiat in matters of maritime law also affected the long-range development of European diplomacy. The issue of *mare liberum* versus *mare clausum* was important in sixteenth-century relations, and was made especially acute by the Anglo-Spanish naval rivalry and the growing importance of England's overseas trade. Drake's devastations of Spanish shipping in 1578–80 brought immediate protests from the Spanish ambassador, Mendoza, who demanded the restoration of property stolen by the English pirate. Elizabeth's reply, "that the Spaniards by their hard dealing against the English, to whom they had prohibited Commerce contrary to the Law of Nations, had drawne these michiefs upon themselves," skirted the issue of free versus closed seas. But she met it head-on in her subsequent declaration: "Other Princes may trade in these countries, and without breach of the Law of Nations, transport colonies thither, where the Spaniards inhabite not, for as much as prescription without possession is little worth; and may also freely navigate that vast ocean, *seeing the use of the Sea and Ayre is common to all.*"[18] Her argument was drawn directly from Roman law. It articulated the assumption upon which the Elizabethan Admiralty subsequently operated: that the seas are free for any and all nations to navigate and use without restriction by other powers.

This declaration of *mare liberum* had many diplomatic implications and consequences. In the first place, it implied the freedom of the seas for exploitation as well as for transit, denying the right of any nation to "fence off" a portion of the ocean, even those areas close to its shore, for its exclusive use. When the king of Denmark claimed exclusive fishing rights in the waters of the North Sea, Elizabeth protested strongly and sent a commission to negotiate the issue, instructing them to declare "that the Law of Nations alloweth of fishing in the sea everywhere; as also of using Ports and Coasts of Princes in Amitie." By the same law she protested the Danish claim to dominion of the sea between Norway and Iceland by right of ownership of the land on both sides. This declaration was later to plague English jurists hard-pressed to justify English jurisdiction in the English Channel and the Irish Sea. John Selden wrote in 1635 that Elizabeth's pronouncement was a special pleading relevant to the Danes only, for "Propertie of Sea, in some small distance from the Coast, maie yield some Oversight and Jurisdiction . . . as is well seen in our Seas of England, and Ireland, and in the Adriaticke Sea of the Venetians, where We in ours, and they in theirs, have Propertie of Command." Selden

---

[18] William Camden, *The Historie of the Most Renowned and Victorious Princesse Elizabeth, . . .* (London, 1630) 2:116. Cf. Thomas A. Walker, *A History of the Law of Nations* (Cambridge, 1899) 1:160–162; and Edward P. Cheyney, "International Law under Queen Elizabeth," *English Historical Review* 20 (1905): 659–660.

did admit, however, that "neither Wee in ours, nor they in theirs, offer to forbid Fishing, much lesse Passage to Ships of Merchandize; the which, by Law of Nations cannot be forbidden ordinarilie."[19] Whenever it did not undermine English interests, the Danish claim was also asserted by the English. Gentili, in the High Court of Admiralty, arguing from the *corpus iuris civilis*, even declared that England's natural jurisdiction extended one hundred miles out from the shores.

The second principle of international maritime law advocated by Elizabethan jurists was the right to seizure and confiscation. Letters of marque and reprisal, granted by governments to legitimize piracy, were common in the sixteenth century, even though the maxim "no peace beyond the line" implied their superfluity. Little justification was required for the seizure of ships of recognized enemies of the state. The case of neutrals was different. The issue, still unresolved in World Wars I and II, of whether neutral ships make neutral goods or belligerent goods make belligerent ships, was crucial in the Armada war of 1588–1604. Drake was instructed in February 1589 to seize war materials from any neutral ships bound for Spain. Four months later, he and Sir John Norris captured almost an entire Hanse fleet bearing supplies, munitions, and victuals to Spain. The Privy Council's public justification was based on Roman prize law, as applied by the High Court of Admiralty to the confiscation of contraband goods, and on the monarch's previous warning against supplying material to England's enemies. A formal protest from the Hanse merchants was answered by the council with a long list of precedents dating back to Henry VIII and with the injunction that "the right of neutrality must be used in such a way that none in our alliance are injured."[20] Lord Burghley followed this proclamation with one of his own, declaring, "Her Majesty thynketh and knoweth it by the rules of law as well of nature as of men, and especially by the law civil, that whenever any doth directly help her enemy with succours of any victell, armor, or any kynd of munition to enable his shippes to maintain themselves, she may lawfully interrupt the same; and this agreeth with the law of God, the law of nature, the law of nations, and hath been in all tymes practised."[21]

With somewhat more success, a Danish embassy protested similar English treatment of their merchant ships. A list of licit and illicit articles was drawn up by the Privy Council for the guidance of English naval commanders. But the English practice of seizing the cargo of neutral ships—especially those of

---

[19] Percy E. Corbett, *Law in Diplomacy* (Princeton, 1959), pp. 12–13. Cf. Gentili, *Hispanicae advocationis libri dvo* (1661), Classics of International Law (New York, 1921) 1: chapter 8.

[20] British Museum, Cotton Mss., Nero, B.III, f. 290. *Acts of the Privy Council,* new series, edited by J. P. Dasent (London, 1899), 18: 29–33: Several cases are illustrated in Cheyney, "International Law," pp. 664–671.

[21] Cheyney, "International Law," p. 664. Cf. Philip C. Jessup and Francis Deák, *Neutrality* (New York, 1935), pp. 57–59.

her allies, Denmark, France, the Netherlands, and the Hanse—proliferated, as did the protests of the injured parties and the legal justification by Elizabeth, the Privy Council, and the High Court of the Admiralty. In 1590, a proclamation was issued to the Dutch (who were also at war with Spain, but had not discontinued trade), ordering them, "upon pain of confiscation," to cease carrying to Spain, "or other places and ports neighboring or adjacent to Spain," such provisions as "munitions of war, powder, artillery, arms, sails, cables, anchors, cordage, masts, peas [the tip of an anchor], or other provisions for land war, or apparel or furniture for ships."[22]

There resulted from these diplomatic controversies a series of ad hoc negotiations and an accumulation of government opinions defining the legitimacy of seizure and confiscation of contraband goods. This was a law of nations interpreted one way by belligerents and quite another by neutrals. But, since the rights of neutrals had not yet received the attention from lawyers that the rights of war had, the advantage usually belonged to the ships with the biggest guns. Each case was heard separately in Admiralty Court, but the decision was usually the same: the law of nations, like the civil law or the medieval *libri feudorum*, was interpreted to fit the prince or territorial state who invoked it. Corbett's conclusion seems justified: "The English had to rely upon a law of nations which, according to them, permitted a belligerent, independently of special agreement, to seize anything calculated to strengthen his foes. It is quite clear, too, that they intended to do the calculating. For reasons of policy they might make concessions, especially where harshness might drive a neutral over to the enemy. . . . They might limit seizures to listed goods. But *they* made the lists. Their law of nations was one over whose content they exercised firm control."[23]

In 1597, when the Polish ambassador formally complained to Elizabeth of the English depredations against neutral shipping by which she set herself up as "intolerably superior to other princes and cut off others' intercourse with Spain simply because she had a quarrel with the Spanish king," Elizabeth sprang to her feet and reprimanded the startled legate in lusty but lucid Latin. After effectively cutting him down to size, she answered, "Since you have so often in your oration quoted the law of nations you ought to know that when war has broken out between kings it is allowed to one party to intercept the aid or succors sent to the other, and to provide that no injury thence arise to himself. We declare that this is in conformity to the law of nature and of nations!"[24]

---

[22] R. G. Marsden, *Documents Relating to Law and Custom of the Sea*, Publications of the Navy Record Society, vols. 49 and 50 (London, 1916), 1:262–63, cited in Jessup and Deák, *Neutrality*, p. 57. See also Grotius's *De jure praedae commentarius* (1604), Classics of International Law (Oxford, 1950), 22: 165, 231, 240, and 262.

[23] Corbett, *Law in Diplomacy*, pp. 17–18.

[24] British Museum, Lansdowne Mss, 94, f. 50. Camden, *Annales, rerum anglicarum. . .* 2: 139. Reported in Cheyney, "International Law," 666–668.

But Elizabeth's practical diplomacy required no higher justification than did Henry IV's *droit d'audaine* (the right exercised by the French crown to confiscate the goods and personal property of deceased English merchants in France). It merely illustrates the point that community succumbed to sovereignty sooner in the realm of power politics than in the realm of ideas. And even in the latter, idealism sometimes gave way to practicality, *ius gentium* accommodated to *ius inter gentes,* and private and common interests were subordinated to national interests. Gentili, the strongest defender of freedom of the seas and of trade, found it quite easy to justify English confiscation of Hanseatic and Danish vessels—even when they carried such innocuous products as wheat, rye, and meal—and to condemn Dutch appeals to the law of nations and freedom of commerce when they trafficked with eager Spanish buyers. "The law of trade is just," conceded Gentili. "But that of maintaining one's safety is more so. The former is the law of nations, the latter of nature. The former concerns private citizens, the latter kingdoms. Let trade therefore give way to kingdom, man to nature, money to life."[25]

From this conception of nature and *ius gentium* grew Gentili's view of what we today call international law—the law governing reciprocal relations among states. Gentili did not clearly define or fully understand all its ramifications, but did conceive and describe the concept of law applicable to all nations. In the process Gentili widened the concept of community from the ideal of narrowly Christian confederation to the notion of *humanum,* or *gens humana,* embracing all mankind—even the Turks. His *societas humana,* however, is not an international organization as such, but a legal community in which the same rights and obligations are recognized and accorded in matters of political and economic intercourse among nations. Still, Gentili had difficulty, as did all of his contemporaries, distinguishing between the law that is simply common to mankind and the law that governs relations between states.

The clearest enunciation of this law of nations is from the prolific pen of the Spanish Jesuit, Francisco Suárez, professor of philosophy and theology at the University of Coimbra. Suárez recognized, perhaps more clearly than any of his Catholic contemporaries, that "the medieval empire has fulfilled its function and is no longer tenable, especially since Christendom has been broken up and every kingdom claims autonomy." He regarded tenable and functional, however, a larger international society of individual states functioning not by a *ius gentium* common to all states, but by a law between nations, "a law which all peoples and nations ought to observe between themselves."[26] In his *De legibus ac Deo legislatore* (1612), Suárez expresses a more modern notion of international community based on the necessary association of sovereign states, and on the law of nations as a dynamic and developing system of

---

[25] Gentili, *De iure belli libri tres,* p. 101.
[26] Luigi Sturzo, *Church and State* (Notre Dame, 1962) 1: 249. Thomas J. Lawrence, *The Society of Nations* (New York, 1919), p. 28.

law growing out of this association. This conception of international law grew out of Suárez's belief that "the human race, into howsoever many different peoples and kingdoms it may be divided, always preserves a certain unity, not only as a species, but also a moral and political unity.... Therefore ... although a given sovereign state, commonwealth, or kingdom may constitute a perfect community in itself, consisting of its own members, nevertheless, each one of these states is also, in a certain sense, and viewed in relation to the human race, a member of the universal society."[27] Some system of law is necessary for these sovereign communities to maintain their association, and such laws should be introduced through the reasoned adherence of the various states. "For just as in one state or province law is introduced by custom," he reasons, "so among the human race as a whole it was possible for laws to be introduced by the habitual conduct of nations." Still wedded to medieval notions of natural and divine law, Suárez took a giant step away from the exclusively Christian community toward the difficult concept of sovereign state with universal community.

Hugo Grotius, the widely-acclaimed master of early modern international relations theory, was strongly influenced by both Gentili and Suárez, though he was reluctant to acknowledge that debt. The great Dutch writer and diplomat of the early seventeenth century conceived of a society of nations in which sovereignty is possessed by each state without annulling the laws of the society which are common to all nations (*communia popularius jura*). In other words, to Grotius, as to Suárez, the law of nations is "the law which is between nations."

We can see developing, then, the gradual elaboration of a new concept of international relations and law, based on the larger community of diversity among sovereign nation-states, each with its own national laws within the framework of a common body of laws governing the relationship among them. The Thirty Years' War, which began almost a decade before the publication of Grotius's *De iure belli ac pacis*, was the primary testing-ground for this new conception of balance between sovereignty and natural law.

Power and Diplomacy in the Thirty Years' War

The first two decades of the seventeenth century were a time of political retrenchment and growing absolutism in much of Europe. The radical and constitutional ideas swirling out of the civil disorders in France and the Netherlands were temporarily ignored or repressed by a society dedicated to peace and recovery. The doctrines of the militant Huguenots and the iconoclasm of

---

[27] Francisco Suárez, *De legibus, ac Deo legislatore* (1612), Classics of International Law (Oxford, 1944), 20: 348–49.

the Dutch rebels, as well as the extreme dogmatism of the French Catholic League, gave way to a social and political conservatism based on the de-emphasis of religion and the affirmation of political power. The revolutionary movements and civil disorders in France, the Netherlands, Scotland, England, and even Spain had left a scar of fear throughout Europe and a deep, though temporary, longing for stability and order. The victory of the *politiques* in France opened the way for a secularized political absolutism there and represented the trend toward conservative authoritarianism throughout Europe.

But the movement toward absolutism did not go unchallenged. Authoritarian enforcement of law and order led to further dissatisfaction and discord. Coupled with latent religious dissension, growing social frustration (among the aristocracy as well as the lower classes) and devastating economic calamities, this discontent erupted before mid-century in a holocaust of riots, rebellions, and civil war.

In the meantime, Europe basked in the calm of a precarious peace sandwiched between the wars of 1588–1598 and 1618–1648. But, as in most periods of truce, the time was spent by the great powers in jockeying for position and advantage as tension mounted and crisis followed crisis. In 1609–1610, the disputed Jülich-Cleves succession nearly upset the equilibrium and brought Europe to the brink of war. Three years later, crisis occurred in the marquisate of Montferrat, followed in Venice, then in the Valtelline, and finally in Bohemia. The play of diplomacy was intense.

Spain, riding the crest of its previously-won military power and prestige, reached the apogee of its diplomatic skill in the years just prior to the Thirty Years' War, during the reign of the pious but indifferent Philip III. Why the Spanish diplomatic machinery functioned so well, given the combination of apathy and avarice that prevailed in Madrid, is still something of a mystery. But it may be accounted for in part by the well-honed ambassadorial system that had evolved during the previous century, and the unusual skill of the resident ambassadors serving Spain in the courts of Europe. Alfonso de la Cueva, marquis of Bedmar, was the eager Spanish representative in Venice; Baltazar Zuñiga served the king at the imperial court of his Austrian cousins; Diego Sarmiento de Acuña, count of Gondomar, spearheaded Spanish policy in England. These three were by no means the only dedicated diplomats in Philip's service. Almost every post was occupied by a devoted representative who promoted Spanish interests assiduously. Through the discriminating use of money and the cultivation of friends at court and elsewhere, the Spanish ambassadors were able to supply the government with reliable and pertinent information, and at the same time to represent it vigorously abroad. Occasionally, as in the case of Bedmar in Venice, they even independently instigated and carried out actions they believed to be in the best interest of Spain. Gondomar was so successful in his two English missions that James I scarcely initiated any foreign or domestic policy without seeking first the advice of the Spanish ambassador.

In the meantime, war clouds were gathering over much of Europe, and especially over the strife-ridden Holy Roman Empire. Although Philip III's Austrian cousins, Rudolf II and Matthias I, reigned over more of Europe's surface than any other Christian prince save the king of Spain, they did not *rule* the fragmented German, Czech, Hungarian, and other states of their imperial patrimony. Real power was in the ambitious hands of local rulers —the Wettins in Saxony, the Wittelsbach in Bavaria and the Palatinate, the Hohenzollern in Brandenburg—and of the barons of over three hundred other rival states. The religious peace of Augsburg, furthermore, had created a false façade of religious agreement over a situation of growing resentment and confusion. Tensions rose over the "Ecclesiastical Reservation" and were heightened by the exclusion of Calvinism from the empire. Soon the Rhineland, upper and lower Palatinate, Nassau, Hesse, Anhalt, and even Brandenburg were seedbeds of seething Calvinist activity.

The volatile situation was made worse by the polarization of Germany into rival and aggressive politico-religious alliance systems. The Protestant Union was formed under the leadership of Frederick, Count Palatine of the Rhine, and of Christian of Anhalt. It was composed of Protestant (mostly Calvinist) rulers of western Germany and dedicated to resisting the Catholic policies of the emperor. A rival Catholic League was created by Maximilian of Bavaria. Under the aegis of the French king, Henry IV, and through the active Dutch diplomacy of Francis Aertsens and Cornelis van der Myles, the German Protestants were merged into an international network directed against the House of Habsburg. According to Sully's questionable testimony, France, England, the United Netherlands, Sweden, and Denmark were all to be part of Henry IV's "Great Design." There is no doubt, however, that Henry hoped to promote a grand alliance against the Habsburgs to counter the dynastic entente of Spain and Austria. His assassination in 1610 deprived the alliance of its only capable leader.

Even after the eventual outbreak of war, diplomacy determined the course of events almost as decisively as did the clash of arms. Negotiations in 1624–1625 between England, the Netherlands, and Denmark resulted in Danish intervention. Four years later, Gustavus Adolphus of Sweden entered the arena, partly due to the enticements of Richelieu's diplomacy. Following the 1635 Peace of Prague, Richelieu augmented French diplomacy with armies to wrench the scepter of power from Habsburg hands. He strengthened the Rhine frontier, and extended the French presence northward to the Baltic and south into Italy through a series of treaties with the Netherlands, Sweden, Savoy, and Saxe-Weimar. Four years later, he added an alliance with Catalonia, and in 1641 brought Portugal into the successful system after the duke of Braganza had assumed the throne and severed his allegiance to Spain.

Not until after mid-century was Europe restored to peace, and even then it was a peace based upon full recognition of the absence of a Europeanwide ideological community or a body of acceptable universal law. All bonds of unity had apparently dissolved. The medieval concept of *Respublica Christiana* had been destroyed, and Europe as a political entity seemed a mere fantasy. The treaty of Westphalia declared simply that the representatives of the Roman Emperor and the king of France, through the mediation of Venice, "and with the consent of the Electors of the Sacred Roman Empire, the other Princes and States," agreed upon terms of peace "to the Glory of God and the Benefit of the Christian World."

Sovereign nations ruled by absolute monarchs were the hallmark of European society after Westphalia. Relations between those sovereign states were unembarrassedly conducted on principles of power and necessity. This had long been true, but the self-deception of a Christian commonwealth had now disappeared from scholarly parlance. The primacy of territorial states was embodied in the treaty's recognition of the sovereignty of the German states and their legal right to negotiate and form alliances with foreign powers. Machiavelli might have smiled. He had known 150 years earlier that states are responsible only to themselves, and that force and necessity are the only sanctions of order. But was he correct? Was there not more to international relations than force and deceit? Europeans had learned much about the realities of power politics since Machiavelli's time. And one of these lessons was that it was usually advantageous to treat other nations with respect, according to the laws and customs of the time, if one desired the same kind of treatment of one's own nation and its representatives.

Superficially, Cardinal Richelieu seemed to vindicate the Florentine's cynical observations. Like Machiavelli, Richelieu was a shrewd and observant politician—although, unlike him, he was an experienced and successful administrator. His comments in the *Testament politique* (1688) originated within the power structure, and his realism was the realism of experience—and of success. Furthermore, he spoke of the nation-state and of its relation with other sovereign nation-states.

Richelieu immediately and repeatedly emphasized, in regard to the conduct of international affairs, the necessity of continuous and active negotiation by every means at the monarch's disposal and in every court, near and far. "Common sense teaches us that it is necessary to watch our neighbors closely, because their proximity gives them the chance to be bothersome. . . . But those to whom God has given more intelligence, learning from doctors that with the most serious diseases the manifestations are more visible at the extremities, omit nothing which can fortify them thoroughly against any eventualities." Once begun, negotiations should never be interrupted. "It is necessary to pursue what one has undertaken with an endless program of action so ordered that one never ceases to act intelligently and resourcefully, becoming neither indifferent, vacillating, nor irresolute."[28]

But even in a system of autonomous states, some order, whether self-imposed or external, must be recognized. The forsaking of the *Respublica Christiana* did not mean the abandonment of all standards and ideals to the caprice of

---

[28] *The Political Testament of Cardinal Richelieu,* translated by Henry Bertram Hill (Madison, 1965), pp. 96, 99.

naked power. A new community of interests might be distinguishable in the overall political equilibrium of diverse and autonomous powers. For independence also implies interdependence, and interdependence requires at least a minimum of justice and truth. As Grotius wrote in his *De iure belli ac pacis* "If no community can subsist without observing some standard of right, . . . with greater reason the human race, or a number of peoples, cannot dispense with it." The same Sir Henry Wooton who made the famous quip that an ambassador was a person sent to "lie abroad for the good of his country" advised seriously that a diplomat should always speak the truth, for "you shall never be believed [if you lie]; and by this means your truth will secure yourself."[29] Even Richelieu conceded, "Kings should be very careful with regard to the treaties they conclude, but having concluded them they should observe them religiously." "I well know," he continued emphatically, "that many statesmen advise to the contrary, but without considering here what the Christian religion offers in answer to such advice, I maintain that the loss of honor is worse than the loss of life itself. A great prince should sooner put in jeopardy both his own interests and even those of the state than break his word, which he can never violate without losing his reputation and by consequence the greatest instrument of sovereigns."[30]

This appeal to integrity, by one of the more notorious practitioners of power politics, should not be taken lightly. It is not the starry-eyed delusion of a dreamer. Richelieu knew from experience that though honest dealing in diplomatic affairs did not always guarantee reciprocal treatment, deceitful action would certainly insure it. His half-disguised affirmation of the principle of *quid pro quo* has become the hallmark of modern diplomacy. The recognition of retaliatory sanctions gradually secured the acceptance of the broader secular idea of an international community composed of autonomous but increasingly interdependent states. This broadened understanding of the nature and purposes of power politics was the result of a century-and-a-half of turbulent but developing diplomacy.

Selected Bibliography

For a general look at European diplomacy and international relations during the period covered by this essay David Jayne Hill, *A History of Diplomacy in the International Development of Europe,* vol. 2 (London, 1906; New York, 1967), and Gaston Zeller, *Les temps modernes, Ie partie,* vol. 2

---

[29] Logan Pearsall Smith, *The Life and Letters of Sir Henry Wooton* (Oxford, 1907, 1966) 1: 109–110.

[30] *Political Testament,* pp. 101–102. Richelieu's regard for law, and his rejection of Machiavellian principles, is emphasized by Fritz Dickmann in "Rechtsgedanke und Machtpolitik bei Richelieu," *Historische Zeitschrift* 196 (1963): 265–319.

of *Histoire des relations internationales,* edited by Pierre Renouvin (Paris, 1953), are both helpful and suggestive. Zeller's "Les relations internationales au temps de la Renaissance" and "Les relations internationales au temps des guerres de religion," which appeared serially in the *Revue des Cours et Conférences* from 1935 to 1938, are also very perceptive examinations of early modern diplomatic history. More current is Henri Lapeyre, *Les monarchies européennes du XVIe siècle: Les relations internationales* (Paris, 1967) in the "Nouvelle Clio" series. This handy volume contains an extensive bibliography of both manuscript and printed sources. Léon van der Essen, *La diplomatie* (Brussels, 1953), although relatively unknown in this country, is a reliable guide to the machinery and operation of early modern diplomacy, but it does not compare with Garrett Mattingly's *Renaissance Diplomacy* (Boston, 1955) for breadth of coverage, literary excellence, and scholarly penetration. Charles H. Carter's "The Ambassadors of Early Modern Europe," in *From the Renaissance to the Counter Reformation: Essays in Honor of Garrett Mattingly,* edited by C. H. Carter (New York, 1965), pp. 205–229, is a perceptive addition to Sir John Neale's earlier "The Diplomatic Envoy," *History* 13 (1928) : 204–218. A useful guide to some of the primary sources is Carter's *The Western European Powers, 1500–1700* (Ithaca, 1971).

In addition to the standard works of Carlyle, Dunning, Genet, Gierke, and McIlwain on late medieval and early modern conceptions of community and sovereignty, see J. N. Figgis, "Respublica Christiana," *Transactions of the Royal Historical Society,* 3rd ser., 5 (1911) : 63–88; Michael Wilks, *The Problem of Sovereignty in the Later Middle Ages* (Cambridge, 1963); Pierre Mesnard, *L'Essor de la philosophie politique au XVIe siècle* (Paris, 1936); and Franklin Le Van Baumer's discussions of this subject in "The Church of England and the Common Corps of Christendom," *Journal of Modern History* 16 (1944) : 1–21; "The Conception of Christendom in Renaissance England," *Journal of the History of Ideas* 6 (1945) : 131–156; and "England, the Turk, and the Common Corps of Christendom," *American Historical Review* 50 (1944) : 26–48.

The literature on Machiavelli is so vast and polemic the reader would do well to ignore most of it and turn directly to the primary sources. A convenient English edition of Machiavelli is *The Chief Works and Others,* 3 vols., edited by Allan Gilbert (Durham, 1965). Many of Guicciardini's major writings are now also available in English. See in particular his *Maxims and Reflections of a Renaissance Statesman,* edited by Nicolai Rubinstein (New York, 1965); *Selected Writings,* edited by Cecil Grayson (New York, 1965); *History of Italy and History of Florence,* edited and abridged by John R. Hale (New York, 1964); and *The History of Italy,* translated by Sidney Alexander (New York, 1969). For an evaluation of Machiavelli as a diplomat, see E. D. Theseider, *Niccolò Machiavelli, diplomatico* (Como, 1945), and Edouard-Felix Guyon, "Machiavel, agent diplomatique," *Revue d'His-*

toire Diplomatique 81 (1967) : 97–124. Discussion of other aspects of Italian political thought and diplomatic action are less readily available, but Bruno Brunello, *Machiavelli e il pensiero politico del Rinascimento* (Bologna, 1964) is a useful introduction to the political thought of the period.

I disagree with José Antonio Maravall's opinion that the Italian city-states "provided neither an institutional nor any other basis for the mon-archical political organizations" (see "The Origins of the Modern State," *Journal of World History* 6 (1961) : 790). In the area of diplomatic organi-zation and procedure, the European dependence upon Italy was overwhelm-ing. Abundant evidence of this can be found in the documents of the time and is demonstrated in such modern works as Armand Baschet's *La Diplo-matie venitienne* (Paris, 1862), which reprints many documents from the Venetian archives; Willy Andreas' *Staatkunst und Diplomatie de Venezianer* (Leipzig, 1943) ; René de Maulde-la-Clavière's comprehensive classic, *La diplomatie au temps de Machiavel*, 3 vols. (Paris, 1892–1893). Particularly provocative for the theory and practice of Venetian diplomacy is Felix Gil-bert's "Venetian Diplomacy before Pavia: From Reality to Myth," in *The Diversity of History: Essays in Honor of Sir Herbert Butterfield*, edited by J. H. Elliott and H. G. Koenigsberger (Ithaca, 1970), pp. 79–116. See also Vincent Ilardi's careful analysis of earlier Franco-Milanese-Italian diplo-macy in "The Italian League, Francesco Sforza, and Charles VII," *Studies in the Renaissance* 6 (1959) : 129–166. Nevertheless, Maravall's article, and his earlier *Carlos V y el pensamiento político del Renacimiento* (Madrid, 1960), are insightful and suggestive essays on the role of Spanish political thought and the development of the nation-state. Further studies include Maravall's *Pensamiento política, internacional y religiosa de Fernando el Católico* (Zaragoza, 1956) ; José M. Doussinague's *La política interna-cional de Fernando el Católico* (Madrid, 1944) ; and Richard Konetzke's "Die Aussenpolitik König Ferdinands des Katholischen von Spanien," *His-torische Zeitschrift* 175 (1953) : 463–482. On the unique position of Charles V in Europe see H. G. Koenigsberger, "The Empire of Charles V in Eu-rope," *The New Cambridge Modern History*, vol. 2 (Cambridge, 1958), pp. 301–333, reprinted in Koenigsberger, *The Habsburgs and Europe, 1516–1660* (Ithaca, 1971), pp. 1–62.

For the Italian wars and the expansion of European diplomacy, see in particular J. R. Hale, "International Relations in the West: Diplomacy and War," *The New Cambridge Modern History*, vol. 1 (Cambridge, 1957), pp. 259–291; Garrett Mattingly, "International Diplomacy and Law," *The New Cambridge Modern History*, vol. 3 (Cambridge, 1968), pp. 149–170; Willy Andreas, "Italien und die Anfänge der neuzeitliche Diplomatie," *Histor-ische Zeitschrift* 167 (1942) : 259–284, 476–496; Charles Kohler, *Les Suisses dan les guerres d'Italie de 1506 à 1512* (Geneva, 1896) ; Baron de Terrateig, *Política en Italie del Rey Católico*, 2 vols. (Madrid, 1963) ; and "La embajada de España en Roma en los comienzos del reinado de Carlos

V, 1516–1519," *Anales del Centro de Cultura Valenciana* 19 (1958) : 119–210. Garrett Mattingly brilliantly describes the activities of two of the key ambassadors of this period in "A Humanist Ambassador," *Journal of Modern History* 4 (1932) : 175–185, which discusses the imperial agent in England, Eustace Chapuys, and "The Reputation of Doctor de Puebla," in *English Historical Review* 55 (1940) : 27–46. Otto Krauske's *Die Entwicklung der ständigen Diplomatie* (Leipzig, 1885) is old but contains much useful information. For the broader development of international relations at this time, the classic is Eduard Fueter, *Geschicte des europäischen Staatensystems von 1492 bis 1559* (Munich, 1919). Jean Zeller, *La diplomatie française vers le milieu du XVIe siècle* (Paris, 1881; Geneva, 1969), deals effectively with a later period of the Habsburg-Valois rivalry, as does E. Harris Harbison, *Rival Ambassadors at the Court of Queen Mary* (Princeton, 1940).

The impact of the Turks on European diplomacy has not been studied much after Dorothy Vaughn's *Europe and the Turk: A Pattern of Alliances, 1300–1800* (Liverpool, 1954), although Fernand Braudel provides some brilliant insights into the general effects of Ottoman penetration in the second volume of his *La Méditerranée et le monde méditerranéen à l'époque de Philippe II,* 2nd ed. (Paris, 1966). Further background can be gleaned from Robert Schwoebel, *The Shadow of the Crescent: the Renaissance Image of the Turk* (New York, 1967) ; Paul Coles, *The Ottoman Impact on Europe* (London and New York, 1968), a very handy guide; W. E. D. Allen, *Problems of Turkish Power in the Sixteenth Century* (London, 1963) ; and V. J. Parry, "The Ottoman Empire, 1520–1566," in *The New Cambridge Modern History,* vol. 2 (Cambridge, 1958), pp. 510–533. On Sultan Suleiman, see R. B. Merriman, *Suleiman the Magnificent* (Cambridge, 1944). Some of the diplomatic implications are assessed by J. Sánchez Montes in *Franceses, Protestantes, Turcos: los Españoles ante la política internacional de Carlos V* (Madrid, 1951) ; and Luciano Serrano, *La Liga de Lepanto entre España, Venecia y la Santa Sede,* 2 vols. (Madrid, 1918–1920) treats one important diplomatic phase of the European-Turkish conflict in the next generation.

The role of the secretaries of state in sixteenth-century state-building and foreign affairs has received spotty attention from scholars. The only biography of Secretary Villeroy is Joseph Nouaillac's unreliable *Villeroy, secretaire d'état et ministre de Charles IX, Henri III et Henri IV* (Paris, 1908), but N. M. Sutherland, *The French Secretaries of State in the Age of Catherine de Medici* (London, 1962), provides some corrective. Edmund Dickerman's *Bellièvre and Villeroy: Power in France under Henry III and Henry IV* (Providence, 1971) is a stimulating look at these functionaries at work, as are Raymond F. Kierstead's *Pomponne de Bellièvre: A Study of the King's Men in the Age of Henry IV* (Evanston, 1968), and David Buisseret's *Sully and the Growth of Centralized Government in France, 1598–1610* (London, 1968). For the next reign see Orest A. Ranum, *Richelieu and the*

Councillors of Louis XIII: A Study of the Secretaries of State and Super-intendents of Finance in the Ministry of Richelieu, 1635–1642 (Oxford, 1963). Angel González Palencia, *Gonzalo Pérez, secretario de Felipe Segundo,* 2 vols. (Madrid, 1946); Gregorio Marañón, *Antonio Pérez,* 6th ed., 2 vols. (Madrid, 1958); Fidel Pérez-Mínguez, *Don Juan de Idiáquez, embajador y consejero de Felipe II* (San Sebastian, 1934); Gregorio Marañón, *El Conde-Duque de Olivares,* 4th ed. (Madrid, 1959); and J. H. Elliott, "The Statecraft of Olivares," in *The Diversity of History* (Ithaca, 1970), pp. 117–147, offer some provocative thoughts on administrative structure and personnel in Spain. Compare also J. Vicens Vives, "Estructura administrativa estatal en los siglos XVI y XVII," in *Rapports du XIe Congrès International des Sciences Historiques,* vol. 4 (Stockholm, 1960), pp. 1–24, and J. A. Maravall, *Teoría española del Estado en el siglo XVII* (Madrid, 1944). Florence M. G. Evans's *The Principal Secretary of State: A Survey of the Office from 1558 to 1680* (Manchester, 1923) elaborates on the secretary's role in English government. For studies of individual secretaries see F. G. Emmison, *Tudor Secretary: Sir William Petre at Court and Home* (London, 1961); Mary Dewar, *Sir Thomas Smith: A Tudor Intellectual in Office* (London, 1964); Conyers Read, *Mr. Secretary Walsingham and the Policy of Queen Elizabeth,* 3 vols. (Oxford, 1925; Hamden, 1967); *Mr. Secretary Cecil and Queen Elizabeth* (London and New York, 1955); *Lord Burghley and Queen Elizabeth* (London and New York, 1960); and P. M. Handover, *The Second Cecil: The Rise to Power, 1563–1604, of Sir Robert Cecil, later first Earl of Salisbury* (London, 1959). Michael B. Pulman's *The Elizabethan Privy Council in the Fifteen-Seventies* (Berkeley, 1971) answers many questions about the activities of the council during one vital decade of the century.

The first years of the civil wars in France are painstakingly chronicled in J. W. Thompson, *The Wars of Religion in France, 1559–1576* (New York, 1909, 1958) and subjected to careful analysis in Lucien Romier's trilogy: *Les origines politiques des guerres de religion,* 2 vols. (Paris, 1913–14); *La royaume de Catherine de Médicis: la France à la veille des guerres de religion,* 2 vols. (Paris, 1922); *Catholiques et Huguenots à la court de Charles IX* (Paris, 1924); and in Nancy Roelker's excellent biography of Henry IV's mother, *Queen of Navarre: Jeanne d'Albret, 1528–1572* (Cambridge, 1968). The complex later phase, from 1576–1598, has yet to be adequately analyzed, although some good monographs and articles have been written on certain aspects of it. See, for example, H. G. Koenigsberger, "The Organization of Revolutionary Parties in France and the Netherlands during the Sixteenth Century," *Journal of Modern History* 27 (1955): 335–351; Henri Drouot, *Mayenne et la Bourgogne, 1587–1596,* 2 vols. (Paris, 1937); and Corrado Vivanti, *Lotta politica e pace religosa in Francia fra Cinque e Seicento* (Turin, 1963), which analyzes the struggle for religious reconciliation at the beginning of Henry IV's reign. Myriam Yardeni's *La conscience nationale en France pendant les guerres de religion* (Paris, 1971) is a thought-provoking examination of the impact of civil war on the development of national feeling in sixteenth-century France. The best general study of the wars is Georges Livet, *Les guerres de religion* (Paris, 1962), in the "Que Sais-Je?" series. J. H. Elliott's *Divided Europe, 1559–1598* (London and New York, 1969) is a masterful synthesis of the whole period.

Constitutionalism and resistance theory in France can be studied in William F. Church, *Constitutional Thought in Sixteenth-Century France* (New York, 1941, 1969); Robert M. Kingdon, "The First Expression of Theodore Beza's Political Ideas," *Archiv für Reformationsgeschichte* 46 (1955): 88–99; A. A. van Schelven, "Beza's *De Jure Magistratuum in Subditos,*" *Archiv für Reformationsgeschichte* 45 (1954): 62–81; Robert D. Linder, "Pierre Viret and the Sixteenth-Century French Protestant Revolutionary Tradition," *Journal of Modern History* 38 (1966): 125–137; C. Edward Rathé, "Innocent Gentillet and the First 'Anti-Machiavel'," *Bibliothèque d'Humanisme et Renaissance* 27 (1965): 186–225; and Julian H. Franklin, "Constitutionalism in the Sixteenth Century: the Protestant Monarchomachs," *Political Theory and Social Change,* edited by David Spitz (New York, 1967), pp. 117–132. Franklin's abridged English edition of Hotman's, Beza's, and Mornay's treatises, in *Constitutionalism and Resistance in the Sixteenth Century* (New York, 1969), is a useful source. Rathé has republished Gentillet's 1576 edition of the *Anti-Machiavel,* with extensive commentary and notes (Geneva, 1968). Vittorio de Caprariis, *Propaganda e pensiero politico in Francia durante le guerre di religione, 1559–1572* (Naples, 1959), examines the relationship between religious propaganda and political thought in the early years of the wars. An old but still suggestive study is Georges Weill, *Les théories sur le pouvoir royal en France pendant les guerres de religion* (Paris, 1891). J. H. M. Salmon traces the later impact of these ideas in *The French Religious Wars in English Thought* (New York, 1959).

The French diplomatic service of the latter sixteenth century has not received the attention it deserves. My forthcoming *French Diplomacy in the Age of Catherine de Medicis and Henry IV* is intended to fill some of the many gaps in our knowledge of this subject. For the present, we have only a few very dated biographies of a handful of French ambassadors, such as Edouard Frémy's *Un ambassadeur liberal sous Charles IX et Henri III* (Paris, 1880), on Arnaud du Ferrier; Guy de Bremond d'Ars' *Jean de Vivonne, sa vie et ses ambassades* (Paris, 1884); Gustave Hubault's brief *Ambassade de Michel de Castelnau en Angleterre* (Saint-Cloud, 1856); and Alfred Richard's *Charles de Danzay, ambassadeur de France en Danemark* (Poitiers, 1910)—along with Frémy's uneven *Essai sur les diplomates du temps de la Ligue* (Paris, 1873) and Edouard Rott's detailed *Histoire de la representation diplomatique de la France auprès des cantons suisses,* 10 vols. (Paris, 1900–1935). The latest and most substantial study of the peace negotiations and treaty ending the Franco-Spanish war is Arthur E.

Imhof's *Der Friede von Vervins 1598* (Aarau, 1966). Many good collections of diplomatic correspondence have been published—mostly during the nineteenth century—but the greatest untapped sources of documents are the rich manuscript collections of the Bibliothèque Nationale and other archives of France and neighboring countries.

Literature on the Spanish diplomatic system in the time of Philip II is scarcely more adequate than that on the French. For general statements on policy and practice, see Gabriel Maura Gamazo, *La política internacional de Felipe II* (Madrid, 1922) and, more recently, Miguel Ruíz Morales, "La diplomacia en tiempo de Felipe II," in *El Escorial, 1563–1963,* vol. 1 (Madrid, 1963), pp. 303–338. Manuel Fernández Alvarez, *Tres embajadores de Felipe II en Inglaterra* (Madrid, 1951) is a sound but neglected monograph. Erika Spivakovsky's *Son of the Alhambra: Diego Hurtado de Mendoza, 1504–1575* (Austin, 1970) illustrates the role of one important Spanish diplomat and author. See also De Lamar Jensen, *Diplomacy and Dogmatism: Bernardino de Mendoza and the French Catholic League* (Cambridge, 1964), and "Franco-Spanish Diplomacy and the Armada," in *From the Renaissance to the Counter Reformation: Essays in Honor of Garrett Mattingly,* edited by Charles H. Carter (New York, 1965), pp. 205–229. For the early seventeenth century cf. Carter's excellent *The Secret Diplomacy of the Habsburgs, 1598–1624* (New York, 1964); "Gondomar, Ambassador to James I," *The Historical Journal* 7 (1964): 189–208; and "The Informational Base of Spanish Policy," *Journal of World History* 8 (1964): 149–159.

Some feeling for Elizabethan and early Stuart diplomacy may be acquired from Conyers Read's works, previously cited, and from Amos C. Miller's *Sir Henry Killigrew, Elizabethan Soldier and Diplomat* (Leicester, 1963); Lawrence Stone's *Sir Horatio Palavicino* (Oxford, 1956); F. J. Levy's brief but instructive "A Semi-Professional Diplomat: Guido Cavalcanti and the Marriage Negotiations of 1571," *Bulletin of the Institute of Historical Research,* 35 (1962): 211–220; R. B. Wernham's more general *Before the Armada: The Growth of English Foreign Policy, 1485–1588* (London and New York, 1966); and J. B. Black's dated *Elizabeth and Henry IV* (Oxford, 1914). Anglo-French relations in the subsequent decade have been lucidly reviewed in Maurice Lee, Jr., *James I and Henri IV: An Essay in English Foreign Policy, 1603–1610* (Urbana, 1970). See in addition Albert J. Loomie, "Sir Robert Cecil and the Spanish Embassy," *Bulletin of the Institute of Historical Research* 42 (1969): 30–57; Frederick Shriver, "Orthodoxy and Diplomacy: James I and the Vorstius Affair," *English Historical Review* 85 (1970): 449–474; Maurice Lee, Jr., "The Jacobean Diplomatic Service," *American Historical Review* 72 (1967): 1264–1282; and Michael J. Brown, *Itinerant Ambassador: The Life of Sir Thomas Roe* (Lexington, 1970).

Summaries of the Mendoza case may be found in Ernest Nys, *Les origines de la diplomatie et le droit d'ambassade jusqu'a Grotius* (Brussels, 1884), and

Henri Nezard, "Albericus Gentillis," in *Les Fondateurs du droit interna-tional,* edited by Antoine Pillet (Paris, 1904), pp. 37–93. The best biography of Gentili is Gesina H. J. van der Molen, *Alberico Gentili and the Develop-ment of International Law,* 2nd ed. (Leyden, 1968). All of Ernest Nys' works, although old and sometimes repetitive, are indispensable to the study of early diplomatic theory and international law. Other worthwhile studies are Thomas A. Walker, *A History of the Law of Nations,* vol. 1 (Cambridge, 1899): E. R. Adair, *The Exterritoriality of Ambassadors in the Sixteenth and Seventeenth Centuries* (New York, 1929); and Heinrich Rommen, *La teoria del Estado y de la comunidad internacional en Francisco Suárez* (Madrid, 1951).

In the absence of a general diplomatic history of the Thirty Years' War, the following studies illuminate some aspects of it: Alexandre van der Essen, *Le Cardinal-Infant et la politique européenne de l'Espagne, 1609–1634,* vol. 1 (Louvain, 1944); Bohdan Chudoba, *Spain and the Empire, 1519–1643* (Chicago, 1952); Dieter Albrecht, *Die auswärtige Politik Maximil-ians von Bayern, 1618–1635* (Göttingen, 1962); Romolo Quazza, *Politica europea nella questione Valtallinica* (Venice, 1921); A. Leman, *Richelieu et Olivares* (Lille, 1938); and Fritz Dickmann's monumental *Der West-fälische Frieden* (Münster, 1965) on the peace negotiations and treaty. For discussions of Richelieu's controversial political testament, see Roland Mousnier, "Le testament politique de Richelieu," *Revue Historique* 201 (1949): 55–71; Erich Hassinger, "Das politische Testament Richelieus," *Historische Zeitschrift* 173 (1952): 485–503; and Rémy Pithou, "A propos du testament politique de Richelieu," *Schweizerische Zeitschrift für Gesch-ichte* 6 (1956): 177–214.

The Contributors

RICHARD L. DEMOLEN earned his Ph.D. in history from the University of Michigan in 1969. He is the editor of *ERASMUS OF ROTTERDAM: A Quincentennial Symposium*, Richard Mulcaster's *POSITIONS (1581)*, *Erasmus, Printing and the Renaissance*, and *One Thousand Years: Western Europe in the Middle Ages*. Since 1970 he has devoted full time to research at the Folger Shakespeare Library.

MARGARET E. ASTON took her D.Phil. from Oxford University in 1962. For the past ten years, she has been engaged in independent research as a fellow of St. Anne's College, Oxford, Newnham College, Cambridge, the Folger Shakespeare Library, and the Henry E. Huntington Library. Her major works are *Thomas Arundel: A Study of Church Life in the Reign of Richard II* and *The Fifteenth Century: the Prospect of Europe*.

JOHN M. HEADLEY earned his Ph.D. from Yale in 1960. He has taught at the University of Massachusetts, the University of British Columbia, and, since 1964, at the University of North Carolina, where he is professor of history. Professor Headley has published *Luther's View of Church History* and *Responsio ad Lutherum*. In 1973 he received a Guggenheim Fellowship.

DE LAMAR JENSEN is chairman and professor of history at Brigham Young University. He was awarded a Ph.D. from Columbia University in 1957. Professor Jensen's major books are *Machiavelli: Cynic, Patriot, or Political*

Scientist, Diplomacy and Dogmatism: Bernardino de Mendoza and the French Catholic League, and *The Expansion of Europe: Motives, Methods, and Meanings.* He was a Rockefeller Foundation fellow in 1964.

LAURO MARTINES completed his Ph.D. at Harvard University in 1960. Prior to his appointment to U.C.L.A. in 1966, he taught at Reed College. Professor Martines has been awarded fellowships or grants-in-aid by the American Council of Learned Societies, the John Simon Guggenheim Memorial Foundation, the Ford Foundation, the National Endowment for the Humanities, and the American Philosophical Society. His two principal studies are *The Social World of the Florentine Humanists* and *Lawyers and State-craft in Renaissance Florence.*

JOHN C. OLIN, professor of history at Fordham University, received his Ph.D. from Columbia University in 1960. He has published the following major works: *Christian Humanism and the Reformation: Selected Writings of Erasmus, Calvin and Sadoleto: A Reformation Debate, The Catholic Reformation: Savonarola to Ignatius Loyola, The Autobiography of Ignatius Loyola,* and *Luther, Erasmus and the Reformation.*

RICHARD B. REED of Bowdoin College is a graduate of Bucknell University, the College of William and Mary and the University of Wisconsin, where he earned his Ph.D. in history in 1970. Following a Fulbright fellowship in Brazil, Dr. Reed served as the curator of the Bernardo Mendel Collection at the Lilly Library, Indiana University, from 1962 to 1967. He is a frequent contributor to *The Hispanic American Historical Review, The William and Mary Quarterly,* and *The Newsletter of the Society for the History of Discoveries.*

ARTHUR J. SLAVIN, professor of history at the University of California, Irvine, received a Ph.D. from the University of North Carolina in 1961. He has published *Politics and Profit: A Study of Sir Ralph Sadler, The New Monarchies and Representative Assemblies, Henry VIII and the English Reformation, Thomas Cromwell on Church and Commonwealth: Selected Letters, 1523–1540, Humansim, Reform and Reformation in England, Tudor Men and Institutions,* and *The Precarious Balance.*

Index

Abelard, Peter, 28
absolutism, growth of, 345–51, 357–58
Admiralty, High Court of, 354–55
Adrian VI, Pope, 273, 329
Africa, Portuguese expansion in,
    306–7, 308
Agricola, Rudolph, 73, 76, 77, 108
Albert, Archbishop of Magdeburg, 150
Alberti, Leon Battista, 39, 52, 55, 57, 60
Alcala, University of, 98, 99, 114, 270,
    282
Aleander, Jerome, 156–57, 279
Alexander VI, Pope, 269
Alfonso de la Cueva, 358
Alfonso of Aragon, 30, 42
ambassador
    legal status of, 352
    permanent, 33
Ambrose, 98
    edition by Erasmus of, 107
Anabaptists, 160, 176–177, 182, 190,
    196, 201
Anagni, humiliation of, 132, 134
Angelico, Fra, 7, 53
Anglicanism, 16, 17, 22, 245
Annates, act of, 234, 235
antipredestination, Arminius' doctrine
    of, 22
antischolasticism, 118–20
Antitrinitarians, 190, 203
architecture, in Italian Renaissance,
    10, 55
Arendt, Hannah, 330
Aretino, Pietro, 50
Ariosto, Ludovico, 12, 49
Aristotle, 8, 28, 40, 44, 62, 91, 96, 99,
    149, 296, 311
Aristotelianism, Renaissance, 8–9, 37
Armstrong, Clement, 239, 260
art
    influence of overseas expansion on,
        312–14
    quality of Renaissance, 13–14
    support by Italian cities, 5
art, Italian Renaissance, 50–55
    characteristics, 50–1, 52
    effect of Italian Wars on, 35

influence of patrons on, 53
innovations in, 10, 50, 52, 53, 58, 67
mathematics applied to, 58
personal individuality in, 67
relation to science, 57, 68
Ascham, Roger, 81
Asia, European expansion in, 307–8
Athanasius, Saint, 91
    editions by Erasmus of, 107
Audley, Thomas, 234, 259
Augmentations, Court of, 237, 238
Augsburg, Diet of, 171
Augsburg, Peace of, 199
Augsburg Confession, 166–67, 240
Augustine, Saint, 80, 89, 102, 103,
    108, 148, 150
    edition by Erasmus of, 107
Azurara, Gomes Eannes de, 306

Babylonian Captivity, 16, 132, 134, 155
Bacon, Roger, 75, 120
Badia, Tommaso, 279
balance of power, first instance of, 3
Bancroft, Richard, 22
Barnabites, 22
Barnes, Robert, 228, 239, 240, 243, 258
Baro, Peter, 22
Bartolus, 60
Barzizza, Gasparino, 39, 76
Bascio, Matteo da, 275
Basel, Council of, 114, 136, 137, 138
Basil, Saint, 91, 98
    edition by Erasmus of, 107
Bataillon, Marcel, 270
Beaufort, Henry, 217
Beccaria, Antonio, 91
Belges, Jean Lemaire de, 121
Belgic Confession, 203
Bellay, Joachim du, 121
Bembo, Pietro, 49, 91
benefices, 134, 138–39, 198
    misuse of, 220, 222
Berquin, Louis de, 165
Bessarion, Cardinal, 74, 76
Beza, Theodore, 192, 193–94, 196, 197,
    198, 200, 204, 347

371